D1134658

Refo500 Academic Studies

Edited by
Herman J. Selderhuis

In co-operation with
Christopher B. Brown (Boston), Günter Frank (Bretten),
Barbara Mahlmann-Bauer (Bern), Tarald Rasmussen (Oslo),
Violet Soen (Leuven), Zsombor Tóth (Budapest),
Günther Wassilowsky (Frankfurt), Siegrid Westphal (Osnabrück).

Volume 72

Anna Vind / Herman J. Selderhuis (eds.)

'Church' at the Time of the Reformation

Invisible Community, Visible Parish, Confession,
Building …?

Vandenhoeck & Ruprecht

Bibliographic information published by the Deutsche Nationalbibliothek:
The Deutsche Nationalbibliothek lists this publication in the Deutsche Nationalbibliografie; detailed bibliographic data available online: https://dnb.de.

Cover design: SchwabScantechnik, Göttingen
Typesetting: le-tex publishing services, Leipzig
Printed and bound: Hubert & Co. BuchPartner, Göttingen
Printed in the EU

Vandenhoeck & Ruprecht Verlage | www.vandenhoeck-ruprecht-verlage.com

ISSN 2198-3089
ISBN 978-3-525-57099-9

Contents

Church and Ecclesiology

Church and Unity

Foreword

The Reformation was launched not the least due to discussions of the church. Whereas Erasmus tried to argue for an irenic concept of church within the papal institution, Luther's criticism of the papacy gave rise to his thinking about the church as a creature of the word, creatura verbi. With roots in Augustine Zwingli pondered upon the relation between visible and invisible church, whereas Calvin focused upon the church-institution as the mother of all saints, piorum omnium mater. The concept of church eminently mirrored the theological diversities in the age of Reformation, and it lay under the establishment of the many different 16th century church institutions.

The present volume aims at a clarification and a discussion of the church in the 16th century: What did the reformers think about the essence and origin of the holy, apostolic and Catholic church? What was seen as the aim of it, its assignment? Can human beings see the true church or not? Does it have one existence in this world and another in the world to come? The concept of church is indissolubly connected to the theological concepts of sin, faith, justification, sanctification, and salvation, and the study of it also involves reflections such as those of the nature and scope of the sacraments, the role of the clergy, the aim of the church-buildings, the significance of the inventory and the reflections upon the constituent parts of the mass/church service. Finally and not the least it is important to investigate the role of the church in the societies of the 16th century, such as the impact of the ruling power upon them, their significance for education and social cohesion, and the cultural significance of migrating believers, on the run within and beyond the borders of Europe. Together with the theological, philosophical and art historical questions, these issues are considered in order to create a picture of the church at the time of the Reformation.

The book is the result of the sixth annual RefoRC conference, which was held in Copenhagen in May 26–28 in 2016.

Anna Vind and Herman Selderhuis

List of Abbreviations

ADB — Allgemeine Deutsche Biographie, Historische Kommission bei der Königlichen Akademie der Wissenschaften (ed.), 56 vols., München, reprint, Berlin: Duncker & Humblot, 1981.

ARG — Archiv für Reformationsgeschichte, Gütersloh: Gütersloher Verlagshaus, 1903ff.

Benzing — Josef Benzing/Helmut Claus, Lutherbibliographie: Verzeichnis der gedruckten Schriften Martin Luthers bis zu dessen Tod, 2nd ed., 2 vols., Baden-Baden: Koerner, 1989–1994.

BOL — Martin Bucer, Martini Buceri Opera Latina, Leiden: Brill.

BSLK — Die Bekenntnisschriften der Evangelisch-Lutherischen Kirche. Vollständige Neuedition, Irene Dingel (ed.), Göttingen: Vandenhoeck & Ruprecht, 2014.

CA — Confessio Augustana.

CB — Confessio Belgica.

CCSL — Corpus Christianorum. Series Latina, Turnhout: Brepols, 1953ff.

CG — Confessio Gallicana.

CO — JEAN CALVIN (1863–1900), Ioannis Calvini Opera quae supersunt omnia, Corpus Reformatorum vol. 29–87, Guilielmus Baum/August E. Cunitz/Eduard W.E. Reuss (ed.), 59 vol., Brunswick: C.A. Schwetschke.

COR — JEAN CALVIN, Ioannis Calvini Opera Omnia: Denuo Recognita et Adnotatione Critica Instructa Notisque Illustrata, Geneva: Droz.

CR — Corpus Reformatorum, Karl Gottlieb Bretschneider e.a. (ed.), 1834ff.

CSEL — Corpus Scriptorum Ecclesiasticorum Latinorum, 1864ff.

Denzinger — HEINRICH DENZINGER (2014), Kompendium der Glaubensbekenntnisse und kirchlichen Lehrentscheidungen. [Enchiridion symbolorum definitionum et declarationum de rebus fidei et morum], Peter Hünermann (ed.), 44th ed., Freiburg im Breisgau: Verlag Herder.

Herminjard — AIMÉ-LOUIS HERMINJARD (1866–1897), Correspondance des réformateurs dans les pays de langue française, recueillie et publiée avec d'autres lettres relatives à la Réforme et des notes historiques et biographiques, Genève: H. Georg/Paris: M. Levy frères, G. Fischbacher.

LThK^3 — Lexikon für Theologie und Kirche, 3th ed., Konrad Baumgartner/Horst Bürkle/Klaus Ganzer/Walter Kasper/Karl Kertelge/Wilhelm Korff/Peter Walter (ed.), Freiburg im Breisgau: Verlag Herder, 2006.

LW — MARTIN LUTHER (1900–1986), Luther's Works, J.J. Pelikan/H.C. Oswarld/H.T. Lehmann (ed .), 55 vols., Philadelphia: Fortress Press.

MBW — Philipp Melanchthon, Melanchthons Briefwechsel, Kritische und kommentierte Gesamtausgabe, Heinz Scheible (ed.), Stuttgart: Frommann-Holzboog.

MySal	Mysterium Salutis. Grundriss heilsgeschichtlicher Dogmatik, 5 vols., Johannes Feiner/Magnus Lohrer e.a. (ed.), Zurich: Einsiedeln/Koln: Benziger, 1963–1981.
OS	JEAN CALVIN (1926–1936), Joannis Calvini Opera selecta, P. Barth/G. Niesel (ed.), Munich: Chr. Kaiser Verlag.
PG	Patrologia Cursus Completus, Series Graeca, J.P. Migne (ed.), Paris: 1857–1912.
PL	Patrologia Cursus Completus, Series Latina, J.P. Migne (ed.), Paris: 1862–1865.
SC	RÜCKERT, HANNS e.a. (ed.) (1936–2000), Supplementa Calviniana, 1–11.2, Neukirchen-Vluyn: Neukirchener Verlag.
VD16	Verzeichnis der im deutschen Sprachbereich erschienenen Drucke des 16. Jahrhunderts, www.vd16.de.
WA	MARTIN LUTHER (1983–2009), D. Martin Luther's Werke. Kritische Gesamtausgabe (Weimarer Ausgabe), Schriften /Werke, 56 vols., Weimar: Böhlau,.
WABr	MARTIN LUTHER (1983–2009), D. Martin Luther's Werke. Kritische Gesamtausgabe (Weimarer Ausgabe), Briefwechsel, 12 vols., Weimar: Böhlau.
WADB	MARTIN LUTHER (1906–1961), D. Martin Luther's Werke. Kritische Gesamtausgabe (Weimarer Ausgabe). Die Deutsche Bibel, 12 vols., Weimar: Böhlau.
WATR	MARTIN LUTHER (1912–1921), D. Martin Luther's Werke. Kritische Gesamtausgabe (Weimarer Ausgabe). Tischreden, 6 vols, Weimar: Böhlau, 1912–1921.
ZW	HULDREICH ZWINGLI (1905ff), Huldreich Zwinglis sämtliche Werke, Corpus Reformatorum vol. 88–101, Emil Egli e.a. (ed.), 13 vols., Brunswick: C.A. Schwetschke.

'Church' at the Time of the Reformation

Peter Walter †

Die 'konservative' Ekklesiologie des Erasmus von Rotterdam

Erasmus hat kein Buch geschrieben, das den Begriff Ekklesiologie in seinem Titel trägt. Aber das haben die Theologen der alten Kirche und des Mittelalters allesamt auch nicht. Das erste Buch mit einem solchen Titel stammt von dem als Dichter zu Recht berühmten Angelus Silesius (1624–1677), der es unter seinem bürgerlichen Namen veröffentlichte, und datiert auf das Jahr 1677.[1] Die Sentenzen des Petrus Lombardus, das bis ins 16. Jahrhundert maßgebliche theologische Schulbuch, enthält keine eigene Abteilung über die Kirche, ebenso wenig die *Summa Theologiæ* des Thomas von Aquin, die jenes in dieser Funktion ablöste. Ein maßgebliches ekklesiologisches Werk ist die *Summa contra Ecclesiae et primatus apostoli Petri aduersarios* des Dominikaners Juan de Torquemada (1388–1468), die erstmals 1489 in Rom und auf Kosten von Papst Innozenz VIII. (1484–1492) posthum gedruckt wurde (vgl. Turrecremata: 1489; Prügl: 2006). Torquemada, der auf dem Basler Konzil die päpstlichen Rechte verteidigte und dafür 1439 zum Kardinal erhoben wurde, liefert hier das Vorbild einer papalen Ekklesiologie. Kein Wunder, dass das Werk in der Schlussphase des Trienter Konzils, als die Päpste ihre Stellung innerkirchlich zu konsolidieren suchten, eine Neuauflage erlebte (Turrecremata: 1561). Der *Tractatus de Ecclesia* seines Ordensbruders Johannes von Ragusa (1390/95–1443), der auf dem Basler Konzil eine konziliaristische Auffassung vertrat und als Kardinal des schismatischen Papstes Felix V. starb, also ekklesiologisch eine Gegenposition zu Torquemada einnahm, wurde dagegen erstmals 1983 gedruckt (Stojković: 1983; vgl. Laudage: 2006). Ekklesiologie, das wird allein schon an dieser Gegenüberstellung deutlich, hat viel mit kirchenrechtlichen Fragen zu tun. Als solche war sie eine Domäne der Kanonistik, die im Mittelalter nicht an der theologischen, sondern an einer eigenen Fakultät betrieben wurde. Solche Fragen standen nicht im Vordergrund der Interessen des Erasmus, aber er hatte dazu, wie noch zu zeigen ist, durchaus eine Meinung, die er aber nie systematisch entfaltete.[2]

---

1 Vgl. Scheffler: 1677. Bei diesem Werk handelt es sich jedoch um keine Ekklesiologie im heutigen Sinn, d. h. um einen systematischen Traktat über die Kirche, sondern vielmehr um eine Sammlung von 39 „Tractätlein" zu ekklesiologischen Themen, mit denen der Konvertit seine Glaubensbrüder stärken und protestantische Angriffe abwehren möchte.

2 Grundlegend für das Folgende ist Pabel: 1995. Hier ist die gesamte bis dahin erschienene Literatur zum Thema verarbeitet, die deshalb nicht nochmals aufgelistet werden muss.

1. Die Offenheit der ekklesiologischen Diskussion zu Beginn des 16. Jahrhunderts

Das zu Beginn des 16. Jahrhunderts erschienene und vielfach nachgedruckte Theologische Wörterbuch des Johannes Altenstaig (um 1480–nach 1525) bietet zwar bereits ein Lemma 'Ecclesia',[3] eine umfassende Ekklesiologie sucht man allerdings auch dort vergeblich. Ein kurzer Blick darauf zeigt, was man sich zur Abfassungszeit unter Kirche vorstellte. Da Altenstaig nicht eigenständig formuliert, sondern ganze Passagen aus den Werken anderer übernimmt, steht er auch für eine gewisse Kontinuität zur theologischen Tradition. Im vorliegenden Fall ist es der konziliaristische Theologe und Kardinal Pierre d'Ailly (um 1351–1420) (vgl. Miethke: 2006), den er abschreibt.[4] Der Oberbegriff der Darstellung ist der der *ecclesia militans*. Dieser steht zum einen für die *ecclesia universalis* und zum anderen für die *ecclesia particularis*. Erstere ist die einzige Kirche, außerhalb derer es kein Heil gibt, und von der als dem Leib Christi Paulus in Kol 1:24 spricht. Letztere wird für eine Vielzahl von Kirchen gebraucht (vgl. Röm 16:16). Die *ecclesia universalis* kann sowohl synchron ("pro congregatione omnium fidelium actu existentium") als auch diachron ("pro congregatione omnium fidelium a tempore Christi vel Apostolorum vsque nunc succedentium") verstanden werden. Sie unterscheidet sich von der Synagoge. Sie ist auch gemeint, wenn Augustinus sagt, er würde dem Evangelium nicht glauben, wenn ihn die Autorität der Kirche nicht dazu triebe. Also habe die Kirche eine größere Autorität als das Evangelium, da der Evangelist nur ein Teil von ihr sei. Bisweilen wird der Begriff noch allgemeiner verstanden im Sinne aller Glaubenden (!) vom Beginn der Welt bis zu deren Vollendung ("pro congregatione omnium fidelium a principio mundi vsque ad consummationem seculi"), und so umfasse er nicht nur die Kirche Christi, sondern auch die Synagoge und diejenigen, die unter dem Naturgesetz stehen. Als Beispiele für diesen Sprachgebrauch werden Augustinus und Gregor der Große zitiert. Auch im Sinne der *ecclesia particularis* kann *ecclesia* unterschiedliche Bedeutungen haben. Nach derjenigen, die eine Versammlung von Männern und Frauen meint, wofür es neben 1 Petr 5:13 zahlreiche weitere biblische Beispiele gebe, stellt Altenstaig im Gefolge von Pierre d'Ailly fest, dass der Begriff Kirche *auch* gebraucht werde, um den Klerus zu bezeichnen, wofür es aber keine biblischen Beispiele gebe. Die Kleriker würden sich den Begriff aneig-

---

3 Vgl. Altenstaig: 1517, fol. LXXII^v–LXXIII^r. Der leichteren Erreichbarkeit halber wird im Folgenden die Neubearbeitung durch den Jesuiten Johannes Tytz herangezogen, die sich bei diesem Stichwort nicht von der Erstausgabe unterscheidet: Altenstaig: 1619, 271–273. Zu Altenstaig vgl. Bäumer: 2006.

4 Für das Folgende vgl. Altenstaig: 1619, 273. Die wörtlichen Zitate sind dieser Seite entnommen. Vgl. De Aylliaco: 1500, fol. Di^v.

nen, indem sie sich 'ecclesiastici' nennten.[5] Das Kirchenrecht nenne sogar einzelne Klerikerkollegien Kirche. Zusammenfassend wird festgestellt: Die Universalkirche umfasst alle gläubigen Menschen, die aktuell oder habituell implizit oder explizit glauben oder andeutungsweise (*aenigmatice*) alle katholischen Wahrheiten verstehen. Die klare Erkenntnis der letzteren ist den Heiligen in der *ecclesia triumphans* vorbehalten (vgl. Altenstaig: 1619, 272).

Daneben gibt es ein weiteres Stichwort: „Ecclesia Petri". Wiederum im Anschluss an Pierre d'Ailly unterscheidet Altenstaig hier die Personalgemeinde, welcher der Apostel vorstand, von der *ecclesia particularis*, in der er seinen Sitz eingenommen hat, sozusagen die Territorialgemeinde Rom.[6] *Ecclesia Romana*[7] kann nun wiederum verschiedenes bedeuten: manchmal den Papst und die Kardinäle, wobei Wert darauf gelegt wird, dass letztere keine in der Bibel begründete Institution bilden; manchmal alle Kardinäle, manchmal alle Gläubigen, die den der römischen Kirche verkündeten apostolischen Glauben bekennen; manchmal alle Kleriker, manchmal alle Gläubigen der Diözese Rom. So kann auch die Universalkirche als römische Kirche bezeichnet werden und alle Gläubigen als Römer. Dass dabei die Ostkirchen nicht in den Blick kommen, sei nur am Rande bemerkt. Von der römischen Kirche wird nun mit Berufung auf das „Decretum Gratiani" behauptet, dass sie im Glauben nicht irren könne.[8] Dies wird dann mit Bezug auf Pierre d'Ailly weiter ausgeführt und biblisch begründet. Am Ende legt Altenstaig mit nicht näher spezifizierter Berufung auf den Konziliaristen Jean Gerson (1363–1429) dar, dass die Kirche Petri immer im Glauben verharren werde, sei es in allen, sei es in einigen Gläubigen, obwohl die Kirche in Bezug auf Tatsachen irren könne, jedoch nicht in Bezug auf den Glauben.[9] Wenn man die hier kurz entfaltete Ekklesiologie als damaligen „Mainstream" betrachtet, immerhin ist sie in einem weitverbreiteten und immer wieder nachgedruckten Wörterbuch enthalten, erscheint das, was Erasmus zu ekklesiologischen Themen zu sagen hat, keineswegs als ungewöhnlich.[10]

---

5 "Alio modo sumitur [sc Ecclesia] specialiter pro tota congregatione clericorum, & sic nunquam accipitur in textu scripturae diuinae. Sed clerici nomen ecclesiae appropriauerunt ad seipsos, vocantes se Ecclesiasticos" (Altenstaig: 1619, 273; vgl. De Aylliaco: 1500, fol. Di^r).

6 Vgl. Altenstaig: 1619, 273f. Die von Altenstaig zitierten Passsagen finden sich bei Petrus de Aylliaco (1500, fol. Dij^r, Diiij^r, Diij^v).

7 Zu den vielfältigen Deutungen dieses Terminus vgl. Tierney: 1955, 36–46; 279f (Reg. s.v. Roman Church).

8 Vgl. Altenstaig: 1619, 274 mit Bezug auf Decreti Gratiani secunda pars, C. 24; q. 1; c. 23; 33; in: Corpus: 1879–1881, Bd. 1, 974; 978f. Einschlägig erscheint hier allerdings nur die erstgenannte Stelle.

9 "Et ita Petri ecclesia semper in fide perseuerabit in omnibus, vel in aliquibus, etc. quamuis ecclesia in his quae facti sunt, sed non quae fidei errare potest, vt in multis locis habet Gers[on]" (Altenstaig: 1619, 274). Zu Gerson vgl. Bauer: 2006.

10 Weder Altenstaigs Wörterbuch noch die Werke des Pierre d'Ailly befanden sich in der Bibliothek

2. Die Sicht des Erasmus

Erasmus war auf unspektakuläre Weise Glied der Kirche, dreißig Jahre gehörte er dem Orden der Augustinerchorherren an, Priester blieb er, auch nachdem er vom Papst von den Gelübden entbunden worden war. Über die Art und Weise, wie er sein Priesteramt ausgeübt hat, ist wenig bekannt.[11] Von seinem englischen Freund, dem Dekan der St.-Pauls-Kathedrale in London John Colet (1467–1519) (vgl. Walter: 2006), einem geschätzten Prediger, berichtet Erasmus, dass dieser nur an Sonn- und Feiertagen sowie gelegentlich zelebriert habe. Zum einen habe er die Zeit zum Studium und für seine kirchlichen Aufgaben gebraucht, zum andern habe er dadurch der Routine vorbeugen wollen. Er habe allerdings den damals in England bereits üblichen Brauch der täglichen Zelebration nicht verurteilt.[12] Daraus kann man, muss man aber nicht schließen, dass Erasmus es ebenso gehalten habe. Erasmus und Colet mussten nicht täglich zelebrieren, denn sie waren nicht wie viele einfache Priester ihrer Zeit darauf angewiesen, ihren Lebensunterhalt mittels Messstipendien zu bestreiten. Colet hatte eine auskömmliche Pfründe, Erasmus die Unterstützung zahlreicher Gönner. Als ihm einer davon, Erzbischof William Warham von Canterbury (um 1456–1532), in Kent eine Pfarrei verleihen wollte, wehrte er zunächst ab, da er aus Unkenntnis der Landessprache zur Seelsorge nicht fähig sei. Nachdem der Erzbischof mit der Begründung, Erasmus sei nicht der Prediger einer kleinen Landpfarrei, sondern durch seine Schriften der Lehrer aller Pastoren, nicht von seinem Vorhaben abließ, kümmerte Erasmus sich wenigstens um einen eifrigen Vikar (Marc'hadour: 1995, 124; vgl. auch Knighton: 1987). Dass Papst Paul III. (1534–1549) Erasmus zum Kardinal kreieren wollte, weiß man nur aus zahlreichen Äußerungen des Erasmus. Ob es sich dabei um mehr als Vermutungen des möglicherweise zu ehrenden handelt, muss offenbleiben. Die Briefedition von Allen, die jeweils auch römisches Archivmaterial zitiert, bietet dafür keine Belege. Lediglich die Verleihung der Propstei St. Lebuinus in Deventer,

---

des Erasmus, soweit diese sich rekonstruieren lässt. Das sagt allerdings nichts aus über eine mögliche Verwendung. Auf eine „flüchtig[e]“ Erwähnung Pierre d'Aillys (Erasmus, Hyperaspistes I: in: Erasmus: 1703–1706, Bd. 10, 1278D–F) verweist Dolfen: 1936, 92. Ein weiterer, sachlich nicht zutreffender Bezug findet sich in: Erasmus, De conscribendis epistolis: in: Erasmus: 1703–1706, Bd. 1, 429D.

11 Daran ändert nichts auch der im Titel mehr Informationen verheißende Artikel von Marc'hadour: 1995, 121. Präzisere Nachweise zur Gottesdienstteilnahme und den Zelebrationsgewohnheiten des Erasmus bei Halkin: 1984, bes. 690; 701.

12 Vgl. das Lebensbild, das Erasmus posthum von ihm zeichnete: Erasmus: 1906–1958, Bd. 4, 528; 491–498 (Nr. 1211). Zur zeitgenössischen eucharistischen Frömmigkeit in England vgl. Marc'hadour: 1995, 139f.

die die materielle Basis für den Kardinalat bilden sollte, ist durch ein Breve Pauls III. bezeugt.[13]

2.1 Kirche als Konsensgemeinschaft

So selbstverständlich Erasmus zur Kirche gehörte, so „normal" ist das Bild, das er von dieser hat. Es ist ganz geprägt von biblischen und patristischen Vorstellungen. Kirche ist für Erasmus ganz allgemein eine 'Konsensgemeinschaft':[14] "totius populi Christiani consensu[s]".[15] In dem im März 1524, ein halbes Jahr vor *De libero arbitrio*, veröffentlichten Colloquium *Inquisitio de fide*, in dem Erasmus auf der Basis des Symbolum Apostolicum eine Einigung der streitenden kirchlichen Parteien erreichen möchte, bekennt der Lutheraner Barbatius durchaus im Sinne des Erasmus:

> Ich glaube die Heilige Kirche, die der Leib Christi ist, das heißt eine gewisse Versammlung aller auf dem ganzen Erdenrund, die im Glauben an das Evangelium übereinstimmen, die den einen Gott, den Vater, verehren, die ihr ganzes Vertrauen auf dessen Sohn richten, die sich durch dessen Geist leiten lassen.[16]

Auf Nachfrage seines Gesprächspartners Aulus begründet Barbatius, warum er nicht gesagt hat, er glaube *an* die Kirche. Er beruft sich dafür auf die Auslegung des Apostolicums durch Rufinus von Aquileia (um 345–411/2), nach dem man allein an Gott glauben könne, und unterstützt dies mit dem Hinweis, dass die Kirche aus Menschen bestehe, "die getäuscht werden könnten und täuschten".[17] Als die Sorbonne Erasmus deswegen zensuriert, ist es ihm ein leichtes, für seine Position eine Wolke von patristischen und mittelalterlichen Zeugen aufzurufen.[18] Ausge-

---

13 Einen Überblick über die Aussagen des Erasmus bietet Erasmus: 1906–1958, Bd. 12, 65, Reg. s.v. Cardinalate. Vgl. auch Devonshire Jones: 1987, 55.

14 Für das Folgende stütze ich mich auf die umfassende Aufarbeitung dieser Thematik durch Becht: 2000, 140.

15 Erasmus an Willibald Pirckheimer, 19.10.1527 (in: Erasmus: 1906–1958, Bd. 7, 216; 59f, Nr. 1893); vgl. Erasmus an Willibald Pirckheimer, 30.07.1526 (in: Erasmus: 1906–1958, Bd. 6, 372; 26f, Nr. 1729).

16 "Credo Sanctam Ecclesiam, quae est Corpus Christi, hoc est, congregatio quaedam omnium per vniversum orbem, qui consentiunt in fide Euangelica, qui colunt vnum Deum Patrem, qui totam suam fiduciam collocant in eius Filio, qui eodem huius Spiritu aguntur" (Erasmus, Inquisitio de fide; in: Erasmus: 1960ff, Bd. 1.3, 371; 256–259).

17 "[Homines] qui falli possunt et fallere" (Erasmus: 1960ff, Bd. 1.3, 372; 265). Es tut nichts zur Sache, dass Erasmus den Kommentar Rufins fälschlicherweise Cyprian von Karthago zuschreibt (vgl. dazu Bakhuizen van den Brink: 1977, 287).

18 Vgl. Massaut: 1968. Die konziliaristisch orientierte Sorbonne steht dabei in der Tradition des Basler Konzils, auf dem die Väter nach dem Zeugnis Torquemadas ins Glaubensbekenntnis vor der

rechnet der im Auftrag des Tridentinums veröffentlichte *Catechismus Romanus* wird Erasmus Recht geben (vgl. Catechismus Romanus, pars I, caput 10, 22 in: Catechismus Romanus: 1989, 118).

Kirche wird an der zitierten Stelle von Erasmus gut biblisch als 'Leib Christi'[19] bezeichnet. Theologisch interpretiert er diesen als weltumfassende Gemeinschaft derer, die in dem Glauben übereinstimmen, der im Evangelium gründet, das heißt im Glauben an den dreieinen Gott. Um diese trinitarische Basis der Kirche festzustellen, muss man kein großer Theologe sein. Aber im gesamten Lemma bei Altenstaig ist weder von Gott, dem Vater, noch vom Heiligen Geist die Rede, die Kirche wird christologisch enggeführt. Darauf trifft der Vorwurf der Geistvergessenheit, den die orthodoxe Theologie der westlichen macht, voll zu (vgl. Freitag: 1995).

Dass dieser Glaube an den dreieinen Gott nicht nur eine synchrone, sondern auch eine diachrone Gemeinschaft hervorbringt, zeigt Erasmus unmittelbar im Anschluss daran, wenn er 'communio sanctorum' erklärt als "eine gewisse Gemeinschaft aller Güter unter allen Gottesfürchtigen vom Beginn bis zum Ende der Welt"[20] und dies mit dem Austausch unter den Gliedern desselben Leibes erläutert. Zu den bereits genannten Kriterien der dafür notwendigen Übereinstimmung (Bekenntnis zum einen Gott, Evangelium, Glauben und Hoffnung) zählt er hier auch "die Teilhabe am selben Geist und an denselben Sakramenten."[21] Vergleicht man damit den siebten Artikel der sechs Jahre später vorgelegten Confessio Augustana, kann man unschwer eine Übereinstimmung feststellen: "Est autem Ecclesia congregatio sanctorum, in qua Evangelium recte docetur et recte administrantur Sacramenta. Et ad veram unitatem Ecclesiae satis est consentire de doctrina Evangelii et administratione Sacramentorum" (CA, Art. VII; in: Bekenntnisschriften: 2014, 103). Man könnte sagen, dass die Ausdrucksweise des Erasmus biblischer und weniger dogmatisch ist als die des evangelischen Bekenntnisses. Er spricht von

---

Nennung der Kirche 'in' eingefügt und die Knie gebeugt haben, wie sonst nur beim Bekenntnis der Inkarnation in der Mitte des Credo (vgl. Lubac: 1975, 136.

19 Zur Kirche als Leib Christi bei Erasmus vgl. Hentze: 1974, 47–49. Für biblisch-theologische und theologiegeschichtliche Erstinformationen zum Thema insgesamt vgl. Söding/Jorissen: 2006.

20 „[Q]uaedam communio bonorum omnium inter omnes pios, qui fuerunt ab initio mundi vsque ad finem" (Erasmus, Inquisitio de fide; in: Erasmus: 1960ff, Bd. 1.3, 372; 274f). Erasmus trifft hier sehr präzise den ursprünglichen Sinn von „communio sanctorum", womit nicht die Gemeinschaft heiliger Personen, sondern die Anteilhabe an heiligen Dingen bezeichnet wurde. Vgl. Kelly: 1972, 381–390.

21 „Vt nihil aliud sit Ecclesia, quam vnius Dei, vnius Euangelii, vnius fidei, vnius spei professio, eiusdem spiritus, eorundem sacramentorum participatio" (Erasmus, Inquisitio de fide; in: Erasmus: 1960ff, Bd. 1.3, 372; 272ff).

"fides evangelica", jenes von "doctrina evangelii", er von "participatio", jenes von "administratio sacramentorum".[22]

'Konsens' ist für Erasmus untrügliches Wahrheitskriterium. Das gilt zunächst für die übereinstimmende Verkündigung und das einträchtige Zusammenleben der ersten Verkünder des christlichen Glaubens. Michael Becht hat dies in seiner gründlichen Analyse der Paraphrasen zum Neuen Testament und der Psalmenkommentare des Erasmus gezeigt. Für ihn ist das Konsensverständnis des Erasmus, der natürlich die die in der Antike ausgeprägte Auffassung vom "consensus omnium" als Wahrheitskriterium kennt, durch und durch biblisch grundgelegt (vgl. Becht: 2000, 142–150, bes. 150). Außerdem zeigt er, dass Erasmus zutiefst vom "Zusammenhang von Natur, Ordnung und der Eintracht alles Lebenden" überzeugt ist (Becht: 2000, 152; 150–154), und kommt zu dem Schluss:

> Das entschiedene Eintreten für Verständigung und Eintracht und die tiefe Abneigung und Furcht des Humanisten vor Chaos und Tumult wurzeln nicht einfach in der Friedensliebe des Irenikers, sondern diese gründet wiederum in der tiefen Überzeugung, daß Aufruhr dem gottgewollten und im Schöpfungsakt gestalteten *ordo* diametral entgegensteht.[23]

Kirchliche Lehrentscheidungen bedürfen, wie Erasmus am Beispiel des sog. Apostelkonzils zeigt, des Konsenses, der für ihn ein von Gottes Geist getragenes und ermöglichtes Geschehen ist. Das Ineinander des Wirkens des göttlichen Geistes und der an der Entscheidung beteiligten Menschen, das die Apostelgeschichte auf die parataktische Formulierung bringt: "visum est spiritui sancto et nobis" (Apg 15:28), interpretiert Erasmus in seiner Paraphrase durch Hinzufügen einiger weniger Worte: "*Visum est enim Spiritui Sancto et* huius instinctu *nobis* consentientibus"[24] als ein voll und ganz von Gottes Geist geleitetes konsensuelles Geschehen. Auch diese Formulierung spricht für ein hoch entwickeltes theologisches Gespür. Erasmus stellt den Heiligen Geist und die kirchlichen Entscheidungsträger nicht einfach nebeneinander, sondern betont den absoluten Vorrang des göttlichen Geistes. Die kirchlichen Führer werden von diesem, durch seine Eingebung ("instinctus"), zur Zustimmung bewegt.

---

22 Zwar begegnen sowohl die von Erasmus wie die von der Confessio Augustana verwendeten Worte im Neuen Testament, aber die von Erasmus gebrauchten erscheinen genuiner: Der Glaube an das Evangelium fasst Jesu Einladung an die Menschen zusammen (vgl. Mk 1:15), Gemeinschaft mit Christus und untereinander durch Teilhabe an den eucharistischen Gaben ist eine paulinische Kernaussage (vgl. 1 Kor 10:16).

23 Becht: 2000, 153. Erasmus paraphrasiert Eph 6 :1: „Nec enim consensus ac tranquillitas esse potest, ubi confusus fuerit ordo." Erasmus, Paraphrasis in Epistolam Pauli Apostoli ad Ephesios, 6,1: Clericus, Opera, Bd. 8, 988A.

24 Erasmus, Paraphrasis in Acta Apostolorum, 15,8 ; in : Erasmus: 1703–1706, Bd. 7, 728F. Kursiv der ursprüngliche Text.

Auch die im Verlauf der Kirchengeschichte abgehaltenen Konzilien stellen für Erasmus Konsensereignisse dar, ihre Glaubensentscheidungen geben den Gläubigen Halt. Dies ist für Erasmus freilich kein einliniger Vorgang, wie ihn die neuscholastische Theologie nach dem Schema von Befehl und Gehorsam gedeutet hat, nach der die Gläubigen fraglos zu glauben haben, was ihnen das kirchliche Lehramt zu glauben vorlegt. Für Erasmus erlangen Konzilsentscheidungen erst ihre definitive Bedeutung durch den syn- und diachronen Konsens des christlichen Volkes, durch denjenigen Prozess, der in der heutigen Theologie, Rezeption genannt wird (vgl. Beinert: 2006). Da das zu seinen Lebzeiten abgehaltene 5. Laterankonzil (1512–1517) diesen Konsens nicht fand, stellte es in seinen Augen "gar kein Konzil dar".[25] Im ersten Teil seines *Hyperaspistes*, seiner Antwort auf Luthers *De servo arbitrio*, betont Erasmus, dass er in manchen Gebräuchen die Kirche zwar für reformbedürftig, ihre Entscheidungen jedoch für von Gott kommende Aussagen halte. Dies gelte vor allem dann, wenn sie von allgemeinen Konzilien getroffen und durch den Konsens des christlichen Volkes gebilligt worden seien, auch wenn er sie mit seinem kleinen Geist mit menschlichen Argumenten nicht zu ergründen verstehe.[26]

Deutlich wird dies in seiner Einstellung zu theologischen Kontroversen, wie etwa in der Auseinandersetzung mit den oberdeutschen Reformatoren über das rechte Verständnis der Eucharistie und mit Luther über den freien Willen (vgl. Becht: 2000, 140; 158f). Auch die Lehre von der Jungfräulichkeit Mariens wurde durch den großen Konsens der Völker ("magno consensu gentium") gebilligt (Becht: 2000, 159; 162–164). Solchen durch den kirchlichen Konsens gestützten Lehren kommt nach und mit den Aussagen der Heiligen Schrift die höchste Autorität zu. Ja, der kirchliche Konsens begründet "auch solche Lehren theologisch ausreichend [...], die sich nicht auf das Zeugnis der Schrift berufen können" (Becht: 2000, 161). Dementsprechend wehrt Erasmus sich "gegen den reformatorischen Anspruch, die seiner Ansicht nach legitime Weiterentwicklung der kirchlichen Lehre als mit dem Offenbarungszeugnis der Bibel unvereinbar darzustellen und das Ideal einer Rückkehr zur frühen Kirche zu postulieren" (Becht: 2000, 161). Die Bemühungen der Reformatoren, die Kirche aus der Heiligen Schrift allein zu reformieren, kommen ihm, wie er in seiner "Epistola contra Pseudevangelicos" schreibt, so vor, als wolle man einen Erwachsenen wieder in die Wiege legen. Letztlich diene ihnen die Beru-

---

25 Becht: 2000, 154 mit Anm. 822 (Lit.). Zum Thema Konzil und Konsens vgl Becht: 2000, 154–157. Vgl. jetzt auch die umfassende Aufarbeitung des Themas durch Sieben (2011).

26 "[...] fateor me semper optasse repurgari Ecclesiam, a quibusdam moribus, nec me per omnia assentiri omnibus dogmatibus Scholasticorum, caeterum Ecclesiae Catholicae decreta, praesertim ea quae generalibus Synodis prodita sunt, et Christiani populi consensu comprobata, tantum apud me ponderis habent, ut etiamsi meum ingeniolum humanibus rationibus non assequatur quod praescribit, tamen velut oraculum a Deo profectum sim amplexurus" (Erasmus, Hyperaspistes I: Clericus; in: Erasmus: 1703–1706, Bd. 10, 1262 A/B).

fung auf die „niemandem bekannte Kirche" dazu, dass jeder nur tue, was er wolle.[27] "Man solle nicht zu altkirchlichen Riten zurückkehren, sondern zu jener Heiligkeit, die die Alte Kirche in so beeindruckender Weise gelebt habe" (Becht: 2000, 161). Becht fasst treffend zusammen:

> Es ist der dauerhafte Konsens des christlichen Volkes, der in seinen [sc des Erasmus] Augen dogmatisch zählt und dessen Urteil er sich beugt. Sowohl die radikale, die Kirche in ihren Fundamenten erschütternde Kritik lehnt er ab, als auch einen blinden Gehorsam, der hinter allem Ketzerei vermutet und auf jegliche Kritik verzichtet. Der *consensus ecclesiae* erscheint Erasmus als tragfähiger dogmatischer Grund kirchlichen Lehrens, auch wenn er zwischen Schrift und kirchlichem Zeugnis durchaus zu differenzieren weiß und die beiden Autoritäten nicht vermischen möchte. Die von reformatorischer Seite wiederholt erhobene Forderung, den kirchlichen Lehr- und Sittenkanon auf den Umfang der Heiligen Schrift zu begrenzen, lehnt der Humanist als Mißachtung der theologisch wichtigen Tradition ab (Becht: 2000, 165–166).

2.2 Der Umfang des Konsenses

Freilich hat Erasmus den Umfang der vom Konsens der Kirche gedeckten Lehre und Bräuche nicht festgelegt. Auf jeden Fall möchte er den Kreis nicht zu weit zu ziehen. Wer zu viel definieren möchte, schafft nur neue Ketzer.[28] Ihm genügen die Heilige Schrift und das Apostolische Glaubensbekenntnis als Basis der kirchlichen Lehre. In den Hauptfragen des Glaubens und den zentralen kirchlichen Riten ('principalia') soll nach ihm Übereinstimmung bestehen,[29] ansonsten darf es durchaus eine gewisse Vielfalt geben (vgl. Becht: 2000, 166–170).

In seinem letzten Vermittlungsversuch, dem 1533 unter dem Titel *De sarcienda ecclesiae concordia* veröffentlichten Kommentar zu Ps 83(84) präzisiert Erasmus seinen Vorschlag:

> In der Zwischenzeit soll das Buhlen um die Gunst [des Volkes] und das halsstarrige Eifern um Überlegenheit aufgegeben werden, aufhören sollen Begünstigungen samt persönlichen Hassbekundungen, es schweige das taubmachende Geschrei des wahnsinnigen Zankes, so dass schließlich jene friedfertige Wahrheit aufleuchtet. Es komme hinzu jenes Anpassungsvermögen [*synkatabasis*], damit jede Seite sich ein wenig der anderen annähert, ohne das keine Eintracht bestehen kann. Aber man komme sich so weit entgegen,

---

27 Erasmus, Epistola contra Pseudevangelicos; in: Erasmus: 1960ff, Bd. 9.1, 304; 623–625; 338; 249f.

28 Diese Überzeugung bringt Erasmus 1524 in einem Brief an den Erzbischof von Canterbury William Warham auf die Formel: "quo plus est dogmatum, hoc vberior est haeresium materia" (Erasmus: 1906–1958, Bd. 4, 466, 49 [Nr. 1451]). Zum Zusammenhang von „dogma" und „haeresis" bei Erasmus vgl. Chomarat: 1981, 1129–1139.

29 Vgl. Erasmus, Supputationes errorum in censuris Natalis Bedae; in: Erasmus: 1960ff, Bd. 9.5, 310, 162: Die römische Kirche soll in Fragen der liturgischen Gebräuche großzügig sein, "modo consensus sit in iis quae sunt principalia".

dass die unbeweglichen Dinge [*ta akineta*] nicht bewegt werden, und soweit soll die Schwachheit der Menschen ertragen werden, dass sie allmählich zu Vollkommenerem eingeladen werden. Jenes aber muss allen tief eingeprägt sein, dass es weder gefahrlos noch zur Förderung der Eintracht nützlich ist, blindlings von den Dingen abzulassen, die durch die Autorität der Vorfahren überliefert und durch lange Übung und Konsens der Jahrhunderte bestätigt sind. Und es darf auch nichts gänzlich verändert werden, wenn dies nicht entweder eine Notwendigkeit erzwingt oder ein erkennbarer Nutzen dazu einlädt.[30]

Was die Rechtfertigungslehre angeht, möchte Erasmus den Streit über den freien Willen den Theologen überlassen. Ansonsten schlägt er folgende Verständigungs-formel vor:

Es genügt, dass wir in der Zwischenzeit darin übereinkommen, dass der Mensch aus eigenen Kräften nichts vermag, und er, wenn er in irgendeiner Angelegenheit etwas vermag, es ganz der Gnade dessen schulde, durch dessen Geschenk wir sind, was wir sind, damit wir in allem unsere Schwäche erkennen und das Erbarmen Gottes rühmen. [...] Wir wollen zugestehen, dass wir durch den Glauben gerechtfertigt werden, d. h. dass die Herzen der Gläubigen gereinigt werden, wenn wir nur bekennen, Werke der Liebe seien notwendig, um das Heil zu erreichen. Denn auch der wahre Glaube kann nicht müßig sein, da er Quelle und Pflanzstatt aller guten Werke ist.[31]

Im Einzelnen spricht Erasmus dann und in dieser Reihenfolge die Themen an, bei denen er einen reformierten Status quo beibehalten möchte:
– Heiligenverehrung: "Der Aberglaube, welcher, wie ich gestehe, bei der Anrufung und Verehrung der Heiligen in sehr großem Umfang herrscht, ist zu verurteilen; das fromme und einfache Empfinden ist bisweilen zu ertragen, auch wenn es mit irgendeinem Irrtum verbunden sein mag" (Erasmus: 1960ff, Bd. 5.3, 305, 668–670). Auch wenn er durch Idolatrie hervorgerufenen Ikonoklasmus verstehen kann, lehnt er ihn als "maßlos" ("immodicum") ab (Vgl. Erasmus: 1960ff, Bd. 5.3, 305, 672f). (Der Basler Bildersturm von 1529 hat ihn veranlasst, die ihm liebgewordene Stadt Richtung Freiburg zu verlassen.) Darstellungen der Heiligen und ihres Lebens möchte er als katechetische Hilfen nicht missen. Bilder und Plastiken seien "tacita poesis", die mehr auf die Affekte wirke als Reden.[32] Die Verehrung der Bilder gelte den Dargestellten, nicht dem Medium. Erasmus zieht zur Erklärung den Vergleich mit einer Frischvermählten heran, die das

---

30 Erasmus, De sarcienda ecclesiae concordia; in: Erasmus: 1960ff, Bd. 5.3, 304, 617–624. Für eine nähere Interpretation dieser Passage vgl. Walter: 2015a, 118–124.

31 Erasmus, De sarcienda ecclesiae concordia; in: Erasmus: 1960ff, Bd. 5.3, 304, 626–630; 633–636 (Übersetzung: Michael Hauber).

32 Vgl. Erasmus: 1960ff, Bd. 5.3, 305f, 676–678. Die Bezeichnung der bildenden Kunst als "tacita poesis" stammt von Plutarch, De gloria Atheniensium 3, 346F, der diese auf den Dichter Simonides zurückführt (vgl. Sprigath: 2004, 243).

Zeichen der Liebe küsst, das ihr abwesender Gatte ihr hinterlassen hat.[33] Die beste Heiligenverehrung bestehe freilich darin, deren Leben nachzuahmen (Vgl. Erasmus: 1960ff, Bd. 5.3, 306, 712f).

– Beichte: Auch wenn "die heutige sakramentale Beichte" nicht "von Christus selbst gestiftet wurde", soll man "sie wie eine heilsame und aufgrund von großem Nutzen empfehlenswerte und durch die Erfahrung vieler Jahrhunderte erprobte Sache bewahren" (Erasmus: 1960ff, Bd. 5.3, 306, 714–717). Ihr Nutzen hängt von dem ehrlichen Bekenntnis der Todsünden – andere unterliegen nicht der Beichtpflicht – und von einem erfahrenen und gebildeten Beichtvater ab. Erasmus ist wie auch andere Theologen der Ansicht, dass man nicht dazu verpflichtet ist, jedwedem Priester seine Todsünden zu beichten, sondern dass man sich den Beichtvater aussuchen darf.[34] Eine in der Erasmus-Literatur wenig bekannte Tatsache ist, dass Erasmus bis ans Ende seines Lebens gebeichtet hat.[35]

– Messe: Erasmus zählt die einzelnen Bestandteile des Messritus auf und fragt, was daran nicht fromm und verehrungswürdig sei. Ausufernde Gesänge und Gebete solle man abkürzen oder streichen. Die Eucharistie solle wie in der Sixtinischen Kapelle nur an einem einzigen Altar gefeiert, Privatmessen während des Hauptgottesdienstes also untersagt werden. Ebenso solle die Zahl der Votivmessen reduziert werden (vgl. Erasmus: 1960ff, Bd. 5.3, 307, 747–308, 788). Aber letztlich geht es dabei um Dinge, die man ertragen oder korrigieren könne (vgl. Erasmus: 1960ff, Bd. 5.3, 307, 789). Hatte er sich bislang mit der Messpraxis beschäftigt, kommt Erasmus nun auf theologische Streitpunkte zu sprechen. Die Opferterminologie sei durch die "veteres sacri doctores", gemeint sind wohl die Kirchenväter, eingeführt. Christus sterbe nicht noch einmal, sondern das einzige Opfer werde durch mystische Riten gleichsam erneuert, indem wir dieser unerschöpflichen Quelle neue Gnade "entlocken" ("elicimus") (vgl. Erasmus: 1960ff, Bd. 5.3, 309, 794–797). "Da schließlich jede Bitte, jeder Lobgesang und Danksagung zurecht 'Opfer' genannt wird, passt diese Bezeichnung ganz besonders zur Messe, die all das noch geheiligter enthält" Erasmus: 1960ff, Bd. 5.3, 309, 799–801). Was die Kommunion innerhalb der Messe angeht, schreibt Erasmus deren Ausfallen der mangelnden Nachfrage der Laien zu (vgl. Erasmus: 1960ff, Bd. 5.3, 309, 801–808). Da Christus in den eucharistischen Gaben gegenwärtig

---

33 Vgl. Erasmus: 1960ff, Bd. 5.3, 306, 700–702. Erasmus überträgt dies auch auf die Reliquienverehrung (vgl. Erasmus: 1960ff, Bd. 5.3, 306, 704f).

34 Vgl. Erasmus: 1960ff, Bd. 5.3, 306, 717–307, 746. Zur Wahl des Beichtvaters Erasmus: 1960ff, Bd. 5.3, 307, 735–738. Die Position des Erasmus entspricht derjenigen Hadrians von Utrecht, des späteren Papstes Hadrian VI. (1522/23), der seinerseits auf den Franziskaner Richardus de Mediavilla (gest. 1307/8) rekurriert. Für diese und weitere Vertreter vgl. Walter: 2015b, 185f.

35 So bezeugt es der langjährige Freiburger Beichtvater des Erasmus Ioannes Brisgoicus nach dessen Tod (vgl. Hartmann: 1958, 10, 3–5 (Nr. 2045a). Halkin (1984) nennt dieses Zeugnis nicht.

ist, darf er auch verehrt werden. Da die Eucharistie aber zur Speise eingesetzt ist, kritisiert Erasmus die Verehrung derselben außerhalb der Messe in Prozessionen usw. Dies sei kein alter Brauch, sondern man habe dem Verlangen der Menge mehr als genug nachgegeben (vgl. Erasmus: 1960ff, Bd. 5.3, 309, 817–821). Den Glauben an die Realpräsenz verbürgt die Überlieferung der katholischen Kirche, die Art und Weise der Gegenwart Christi möge ein Konzil entscheiden. Der Streit darüber entehre die Eucharistie (vgl. Erasmus: 1960ff, Bd. 5.3, 310, 841–850).

– Kirchengebote: Von den kirchlichen Festtagen sollen außer den Sonntagen nur diejenigen mit einer biblischen Grundlage beibehalten werden (vgl. Erasmus: 1960ff, Bd. 5.3, 310, 851–856). Feste der Bruderschaften sollten zusammen mit denselben von den Behörden verboten werden (vgl. Erasmus: 1960ff, Bd. 5.3, 310, 859–861). Das Fastengebot und andere bischöfliche Vorschriften sollen nur von denen eingehalten werden, die davon einen geistlichen Nutzen haben (vgl. Erasmus: 1960ff, Bd. 5.3, 310, 862–872).

Am Ende wiederholt Erasmus nochmals seinen Aufruf, aufeinander zuzugehen, bis das erwünschte Konzil entschieden hat:

> Wenn ein geregeltes Aufeinanderzugehen den Höhepunkt der Auseinandersetzungen abmildert, wird es geschehen, dass die Medizin der Synode glücklicher auf die Eintracht hinwirkt. Auf ähnliche Weise nämlich bereiten die Ärzte, bevor sie eine kräftige Arznei verabreichen, die Körper durch leichte und angenehme Getränke, die sie Sirup nennen, vor (Erasmus: 1960ff, Bd. 5.3, 311, 884–888).

Es fällt auf, dass zwei Streitpunkte, die immer mehr zu konfessionsspezifischen Unterscheidungsmerkmalen wurden, hier bei Erasmus gar nicht vorkommen: Laienkelch und Priesterehe.

2.3 Die Träger des Konsenses: die Rolle der Universalkonzilien und des Papstes

Wenn Erasmus vom "consensus populi Christiani" spricht, meint er damit freilich keine demokratisch verfasste Kirche, in der jeder ein Mitspracherecht hätte. Auch wenn Erasmus, wie er in der *Paraclesis*, einer der Vorreden zu seiner Edition des Neuen Testamentes, schreibt, seine bibelphilologischen Arbeiten unternommen hat, damit die Bibel in alle möglichen Sprachen übersetzt wird, auch ins Arabische und Türkische, und von allen Menschen gekannt und vom Bauer beim Pflügen, vom Weber bei seiner Arbeit und vom Wanderer unterwegs meditiert werden kann (vgl. Erasmus, Paraclesis ad lectorem pium; in: Erasmus: 1964, 142, 18–23), sind es doch vor allem die Gebildeten, um deren Konsens es geht (vgl. Becht: 2000, 131–138).

Im Idealfall gehören auch diejenigen dazu, die eine kirchenleitende Funktion innehaben, Papst und Bischöfe. Dass Erasmus gerade diesen gegenüber mit Kritik nicht spart, ist bekannt. Seine Kritik freilich zielt vor allem auf eine Verbesserung des

Bildungsstandes der Verantwortlichen. Durch seine Veröffentlichungen versucht er seinen Teil dazu beizutragen.

Für die Ekklesiologie des Erasmus spannend ist auch, wie er sich in der zu seiner Zeit virulenten Frage nach der obersten Leitungsgewalt in der Kirche positioniert hat, die heute unter den beiden Begriffen 'Konziliarismus' und 'Papalismus' diskutiert wird. Diese markieren idealtypisch zwei Extrempositionen, wie sie in Kanonistik und Theologie des 15. und frühen 16. Jahrhunderts, selten in Reinform, vertreten wurden. 'Konziliarismus' meint in seiner Extremform, dass die oberste Entscheidungs- und Leitungsgewalt in der Kirche allein dem Konzil zusteht, das diese repräsentiert, in gemäßigter Form, dass das Konzil, wie in Konstanz geschehen, in Notfällen ein Schisma beenden kann (vgl. Smolinsky: 2006). 'Papalismus' bezeichnet die monarchische Oberhoheit des Papstes über die Kirche, die absolut gedacht oder durch aristokratisch-oligarchische Momente, wie etwa die Beteiligung des Kardinalskollegiums, abgefedert werden kann. Brian Gogan zählt in seiner Arbeit über "ekklesiologische Themen in den Schriften des Thomas Morus" mit den beiden Extremen insgesamt sechs Positionen auf, wobei man die letztlich auf Ockham zurückgehende, dass die Kirche im Notfall in einer einzigen Person "überleben" könne, auf sich beruhen lassen kann (vgl. Gogan: 1982, 342–344; Zusammenfassung bei Fabisch: 2008, 228f). Die Position des Erasmus entspricht am ehesten derjenigen, die Gogan "konstitutionalistisch" bzw. "pluralistisch" nennt und die an der Universität Paris von dem einflussreichen schottischen Theologen John Mair (um 1466–1555) vertreten wurde (vgl. Slotemaker/Witt: 2015). Nach ihr sind Episkopat, Papsttum und die Kirche als ganze jeweils von Gott gestiftet und besitzen jeweils eine eigene göttliche Autorität (vgl. Gogan: 1982, 344). Bei Erasmus brauchte es eine Weile, bis sich diese Position herausgebildet hat.

In der *Ratio verae theologiae*, seiner theologischen 'Methodenlehre', die er 1518 in einer erweiterten Neuausgabe herausbrachte, nimmt er verschiedentlich auf das Papstamt Bezug. Hier teilt er das christliche Volk in drei konzentrische Kreise ein, die um Christus als einzigen Mittelpunkt gelagert sind, dem alle nacheifern sollen (vgl. Erasmus, Ratio verae theologiae [1518]: Erasmus: 1968, 202, 1–32). Dabei handelt es sich, wenn man es genau nimmt, nicht um ebene Kreise, sondern innerhalb dieser Kreise gibt es jeweils eine Steigerung, sodass man insgesamt eher von einer Halbkugel mit übereinander gelagerten Kreisen auszugehen hat. Den obersten Kreis bilden die Stellvertreter Christi, die Priester, Äbte, Bischöfe, Kardinäle und Päpste. Erasmus reserviert den Titel des Stellvertreters Christi also nicht für den Papst, sondern dehnt ihn auf alle aus, die gegenüber denjenigen, die sich im zweiten und dritten Kreis befinden, eine geistliche Aufgabe erfüllen. Damit trifft er durchaus den ursprünglichen Sinn des Begriffs 'vicarius Christi'.[36]

---

36 Zur Entwicklung des Ausdrucks hin zum exklusiven Papsttitel vgl. Maccarone: 1953.

Den zweiten Kreis bilden die weltlichen Fürsten, den dritten das Volk. Die innere Rangordnung innerhalb der Kreise wird deutlich, wenn Erasmus etwa die Aufgabe der Priester beschreibt: Wenn sie das Messopfer darbringen,[37] predigen, beten und Fürbitte halten, wenn sie sich durch Studium für ihre Aufgabe rüsten, dann sind sie Christus näher als wenn sie sich den Sitten der Fürsten und des Volkes annähern, um diese zu bessern. Bei den Päpsten zählt er eine ganze Reihe von Tätigkeiten auf, bei denen sie nicht sozusagen auf der Höhe ihrer Aufgaben sind. Dass dazu die Pfründenvergabe, die Verteidigung des Kirchenstaates und der Krieg gegen die Türken gehören, wird nicht verwundern. Aber dass Erasmus dazu auch die Gewährung von Ablässen rechnet, durch die die Päpste die Trägen oder die der Verzweiflung Nahen aufrichten, erstaunt doch.[38] Diese Aussagen münden in die rhetorische Frage, ob die Päpste, selbst wenn sie es noch so sehr wollten, ihre Gesetze, die sie zum allgemeinen Wohl der Menschen erlassen, so formulieren könnten, dass sie in allem den Anordnungen Christi entsprechen. Er beantwortet die Frage, indem er die Päpste als schwache Menschen charakterisiert, die sich um schwache Menschen in unterschiedlichen Situationen kümmern. Da könne es gar nicht anders sein, als dass ihre Vorschriften hinter denen Christi zurückblieben. Dennoch überragten diese auch das, was an den Gesetzen der weltlichen Fürsten am göttlichsten sei (vgl. Erasmus, Ratio verae theologiae [1518]; in: Erasmus: 1968, 203, 20–33).

In einer Einfügung aus dem Jahre 1520 nennt er bei den Beispielen für kirchliche Auffassungen, die der wahren Frömmigkeit eher schaden, ohne den Begriff zu gebrauchen, den Papalismus:

> Es gibt nämlich Leute, die den gesamten Leib der Kirche allein auf den Papst einengen, dem allein sie jegliche Irrtumsfähigkeit absprechen, sooft er über Sitten und Glauben Aussagen macht. Die ganze Welt, die in einer abweichenden Meinung übereinstimmt, müsse allein seinen Sätzen glauben und sei, wenn sie dies nicht tue, als schismatisch zu erachten (Erasmus, Ratio verae theologiae [1520]; in: Erasmus: 1968, 206, 19–24).

Nach einem Seitenhieb auf die Leute, die dem Papst eine solche Autorität nur zuschrieben, wenn es ihnen selber zugutekomme, fragt Erasmus: "Wird durch solche Auffassungen nicht der Tyrannei ein riesiges Fenster geöffnet, falls eine

---

37 "sacerdotes sacrifiis litant deo" (Erasmus, Ratio verae theologiae [1518]: Erasmus: 1968, 202, 22f). Hier wie auch sonst gebraucht Erasmus Opferterminologie, um eine, wenn auch nicht die alleinige, Aufgabe der Priester zu umschreiben. Als er an Ostern 1534 aus Krankheitsgründen privat zelebriert, beschreibt er dies: "Ipso die Paschae sacrificaui in cubiculo" (Erasmus: 1906–1958, Bd. 10, 375, 9f [Nr. 2922]). Zur von Erasmus nicht in Frage gestellten Auffassung der Eucharistie als Opfer, die freilich bei ihm nicht im Vordergrund der Eucharistietheologie steht, vgl. Bosshard: 1978, 13f, 29f.

38 Vgl. Erasmus, Ratio verae theologiae (1518); in: Erasmus: 1968, 203, 10–20. Zur Position des Erasmus, der den Ablass nicht grundsätzlich in Frage stellte, aber die Auswüchse scharf kritisierte, vgl. Halkin: 1983.

so große Macht einem pflichtvergessenen und unheilstiftenden Menschen zuteil-wird?"[39] 1522 fügt Erasmus eine Einschränkung ein:

> Wir missgönnen der Majestät des Papstes nichts. Möge er doch wirklich besitzen, was jene ihm zuschreiben, und möge er nicht strauchlen können in dem, was zur Frömmigkeit gehört. Möge er doch wirklich die Seelen aus den Qualen des Fegfeuers befreien können.[40]

Die letzte Bemerkung zielt darauf, dass die theologische Streitfrage, ob der Papst für Seelen im Fegfeuer mehr tun könne, als für sie zu bitten, d. h. ob er sie effektiv daraus befreien könne, erst durch Papst Leo X. (1513–1521) in einer an Kardinal Cajetan gerichteten Dekretale vom 9. November 1518 bejahend entschieden wurde.[41] Wer meint, Erasmus habe dadurch den Papalisten ein Zugeständnis machen wollen, sieht sich durch den Nachsatz eines Besseren belehrt:

> Wir haben nichts dagegen, dass die zu jeglicher Ausschweifung neigenden Sitten des Volkes durch solche Schranken in Zaum gehalten werden, wenn die evangelische Aufrichtigkeit erlaubt, andere zu zwingen und die Gewissen anderer zu fesseln, und wir die platonische Fiktion ["mendacium"] zulassen, nach der der Weise das Volk zu dessen eigenem Wohl täuscht.[42]

Da die Sorbonne die Dekretale Leos X. nicht akzeptierte, konnte Erasmus es sich leisten, in seiner Antwort auf deren Zensuren noch im Jahre 1532 zu bezweifeln, ob die Vollmacht des Papstes bis ins Fegefeuer reiche.[43]

In einer weiteren aus dem Jahre 1520 stammenden Einfügung zur 'Ratio verae theologiae' kritisiert Erasmus die kirchlichen Führer, aus der Bibel nur die Aussagen hören zu wollen, die von ihren Vollmachten sprechen, nicht jedoch diejenigen, die

---

39 Erasmus: 1968, 206, 29–31. Vgl. auch Responsio ad annotationes Eduardi Lei (1520); in: Erasmus: 1960ff, Bd. 9.4, 334f, wo Erasmus die Auffassung einiger Theologen, dass der Papst etwas gegen das Zeugnis der Schrift entscheiden könne, in Frage stellt. Darin, einem einzelnen Menschen solche Vollmacht zu geben, sieht er eine große Gefahr ("ingens periculum").

40 "Utinam habeat vere, quod illi tribuunt, nec labi possit in his, quae sunt pietatis. Utinam vere possit animas eximere e purgatorii suppliciis" (Erasmus, Ratio verae theologiae [1520]; in: Erasmus: 1968, 206, 37–207, 2. Die Formulierung mit "utinam" besagt keineswegs, dass Erasmus die Autorität des Papstes hier geschickt in Zweifel ziehe (So McSorley: 1974, 45). Wenn dies der Fall wäre, hätte Erasmus nicht den Konjunktiv Präsens wählen dürfen, der einen erfüllbaren Wunsch für die Gegenwart ausdrückt, sondern hätte den Konjunktiv Imperfekt einsetzen müssen, der einen irrealen Wunsch bezeichnet (vgl. Linnenkugel: 1957, 211).

41 Vgl. die entscheidenden Abschnitte: DH 1447f. Der Adressat hat diesen Text selber im Auftrag des Papstes verfasst (vgl. Walter: 2017, 649).

42 Erasmus, Ratio verae theologiae (1520); in: Erasmus: 1968, 207, 2–7. Die Hg. verweisen auf Plato rep. III 389b, V 459c. Zum Thema vgl. auch Marc'hadour: 1995, 132f.

43 Erasmus begründet seine Zweifel damit, dass diese Lehre von keinem Konzil ausgesprochen worden sei. Vgl. Halkin: 1983, 151. Zur Position der Sorbonne vgl. Walter: 2017, 649.

sie kritisieren. Dabei kommt er zweimal auf den Papst zu sprechen. Dieser werde "vicarius Christi" genannt. Also solle er an das Beispiel Christi, dessen Tod, denken und demjenigen in der Haltung ("affectus") nachfolgen, dem er als Stellvertreter und im Titel nachfolgt (vgl. Erasmus, Ratio verae theologie [1520]; in: Erasmus: 1968, 286, 17–19). Am Ende dieses Abschnittes spricht er den Papst direkt an, der sich darin gefalle, das auf sich zu beziehen, was Christus zu Petrus gesagt habe: Weide meine Schafe (Joh 21:17). Er möge aber auch bedenken, dass Jesus dreimal von jenem die höchste Liebe zu ihm gefordert habe.

> Du stehst den anderen Bischöfen vor. Deshalb wird dir aufgetragen, auch an Liebe her-auszuragen, dir wird aufgetragen, entsprechend dem Beispiel des obersten Hirten die Unversehrtheit aller durch die Hingabe deines Lebens zu schützen. Du freust dich, dass du auf Erden den Platz einnimmst, der Christus am nächsten ist. Bedenke aber, dass es deine Aufgabe ist, ihm auch an Heiligkeit des Lebens nahezukommen (Erasmus, Ratio verae theologiae [1520]; in: Erasmus: 1968, 286, 32–287, 7; Zitat: 287, 2–7).

Erasmus bezweifelt in diesen Aussagen keineswegs die Autorität des Papstes, auch nicht, wenn er in anderen Zusammenhängen eine historische Entwicklung der päpstlichen Prärogativen und deren kirchlicher Anerkennung konstatiert (vgl. Gebhardt: 1966, 267–269). Die Christologie dient ihm als Beispiel dafür, dass es Zeiten gab, in denen eine Glaubenswahrheit, die Gottheit Christi, noch nicht explizit formuliert wurde, obwohl jener immer Gott war (vgl. Erasmus, Apologia ad Stunicae conclusiones, De primatu pontificis, 3 [1524]; in: Erasmus: 1960ff, Bd. 9.8, 270, 293f). Seine Zweifel an der päpstlichen Vollmacht hätten sich, so Erasmus in der Antwort an seinen spanischen Kritiker Stunica 1524, nicht darauf bezogen, dass diese dem Papst übertragen, sondern darauf, ob diese öffentlich in Anspruch genommen und anerkannt worden sei.[44] Harry McSorley (1974, 43 Anm. 34; 45 Anm. 43) vermutet, dass Erasmus die Formulierung von der "potestas tradita" der am 6. Juli 1439 verabschiedeten Unionsbulle "Laetentur caeli" des Konzils von Florenz (1439–1445) verdankt, in der es in Bezug auf den Papst heißt:

> Ebenso bestimmen wir, dass der heilige Apostolische Stuhl und der Römische Bischof den Primat über den gesamten Erdkreis innehat und der Römische Bischof selbst der Nachfolger des seligen Apostelfürsten Petrus und der wahre Stellvertreter Christi, das Haupt der ganzen Kirche und der Vater und Lehrer aller Christen ist; und ihm ist von unserem Herrn Jesus Christus im seligen Petrus die *volle Gewalt* übertragen worden, die gesamte Kirche zu weiden, zu leiten und zu lenken, wie es auch in den Akten der ökumenischen Konzilien und in den heiligen Kanones festgehalten wird.[45]

---

44 "Sed fingat mihi dubitasse; si quid dubitatum est, dubitatum est de potestate agnita vel exerta, non de tradita". (Erasmus, Apologia ad Stunicae conclusiones, De primatu pontificis, 3 [1524]; in: Erasmus: 1960ff, Bd. 9.8, 272, 345f).

45 "Item diffinimus, sanctam Apostolicam Sedem, et Romanum Pontificem, in universum orbem tenere primatum, et ipsum Pontificem Romanum successorem esse beati Petri principis Apostolorum et

Diese Formulierung ist Erasmus wohl durch die im März 1521 erschienene Schrift Kardinal Cajetans über die Einsetzung des päpstlichen Primats durch Christus in Petrus bekannt geworden. Cajetan zitiert hier ganz am Ende, gleichsam als Zusammenfassung einer langen Reihe von Belegstellen aus Kirchenvätern und mittelalterlichen Theologen, diesen Passus (vgl. Caietanus: 1925, 99; 11–21). Er hat das freilich auch schon zehn Jahre zuvor in seiner Schrift "De comparatione auctoritatis et concilii" getan, dabei allerdings den einschränkenden Nebensatz ("wie es [...] festgehalten wird") weggelassen, mittels dessen die Konziliaristen die Aussage in ihrem Sinne interpretierten.[46]

In der Replik auf Martin Luthers *De servo arbitrio* sagt Erasmus, dass die Kontroverse über die Frage, ob der Papst der Hirte der Universalkirche sei, durch ein kirchliches Dekret entschieden worden sei. Welches das sei, gibt er nicht an, wahrscheinlich meint er die zitierte Aussage des Concilium Florentinum. Für nach wie vor offen hält er jedoch die unter den Scholastikern diskutierte Frage, ob die Autorität des Papstes gewichtiger sei als die des Generalkonzils.[47] Zeitgleich mit dem *Hyperaspistes* veröffentlicht Erasmus im Februar 1526 in einer Neuauflage seiner *Colloquia familiaria* das Kolloquium "Fischessen", in dem er die "auctoritas" des Universalkonzils mit der der Evangelien gleichsetzt oder nur kurz unterhalb ansiedelt. Erlasse eines solchen Konzils sind für ihn ein "coeleste oraculum". Der Papst als Mensch dagegen könne einem Irrtum über Personen und Sachen unterliegen.[48] Wenn Erasmus hier die Entscheidungen der Universalkonzilien den Evangelien, d. h. der darin enthaltenen Lehre Jesu, an die Seite stellt, vertritt er eine Position, wie sie vor allem im ersten Jahrtausend gang und gäbe war, als man die ersten Konzilien als inspiriert betrachtete und sie hinsichtlich ihrer Offenbarungsqualität der Bibel an die Seite stellte (vgl. Congar: 1965, 152–169). Im Hoch- und Spätmittelalter wird die Sicht differenzierter. Erasmus schließt sich der zu seiner Zeit am meisten verbreiteten Position an, "daß dem legitimen Generalkonzil bei der autoritativen Entscheidung von Fragen der Glaubens- und Sittenlehre die der Kirche verheißende

---

verum Christi vicarium, totiusque Ecclesiae caput et omnium Christianorum patrem ac doctorem exsistere; et ipsi in beato Petro pascendi, regendi ac gubernandi universalem Ecclesiam a Domino nostro Iesu Christo *plenam potestatem* traditam esse, quemadmodum etiam in gestis oecumenicorum Conciliorum et in sacris canonibus continetur" (DH 1307; Hervorhebung P.W).

46 Vgl. Caietanus: 1936, 18. Vgl. dazu Sieben: 1990, 520f. Der einschränkende Sinn entspricht durchaus der Intention des Florentinums (vgl. Sieben: 1990, 515 Anm. 9).

47 "Dubitatum est a Veteribus, an Romanus Pontifex esset universalis Ecclesiae Pastor, & licuit donec accederet Ecclesiae decretum: et adhuc controversum est inter Scholasticos, an Romani Pontificis auctoritas sit gravior auctoritate Synodi generalis" (Erasmus, Hyperaspistes I: Clericus; in: Erasmus: 1703–1706, Bd. 10, 1305B).

48 "Nam et in Pontificem vt hominem cadit ignorantia personae factiue. Caeterum, quod ex autoritate Concilii vniversalis proficiscitur, coeleste oraculum est et pondus habet par Euangeliis aut certe proximum" (Erasmus, Ichthyophagia [1526]; in: Erasmus: 1960ff, Bd. 1.3, 508, 461–464).

Irrtumslosigkeit zugeschrieben werden muß."[49] Was es mit dem Papst als Amtsträger auf sich hat, wird daraus jedoch nicht klar. Die Unterscheidung zwischen der Irrtumsfähigkeit der einzelnen Personen, sei es der Papst oder seien es die Bischöfe, und deren Irrtumslosigkeit bei der Wahrnehmung ihrer Aufgaben ist eine traditionelle. Altensteig, der sich dafür auf Gerson beruft, hat sie vertreten.[50] Erasmus scheint hier die Unfehlbarkeit des Universalkonzils der Fehlbarkeit des Papstes als Person gegenüberzustellen. Es handelt sich jedenfalls um keine ganz klare Aussage.

Georg Gebhardt zieht in seiner noch immer grundlegenden Arbeit über die Stellung des Erasmus zur römischen Kirche aus der zuletzt genannten Unterscheidung des Erasmus den Schluss, dass dieser die oberste Lehrgewalt dem Universalkonzil, die oberste Hirtengewalt hingegen dem Papst zuschreibe (vgl. Gebhardt: 1966, 270). Erasmus scheint die Aufgabe des Papstes vor allem in der "Vermeidung eines Schismas" zu sehen (Gebhardt: 1966, 271). In Fragen der kirchlichen Lehre und Disziplin hingegen baut er, wie er immer wieder deutlich macht, auf ein künftiges Konzil (vgl. Anm. 9).[51] Dass dieses Konzil, das neun Jahre nach dem Tod des Erasmus endlich in Trient zusammentrat, seine Hoffnungen nicht mehr erfüllen konnte, hat viele Gründe, über die hier nicht mehr zu handeln ist.

3. Schluss

Erasmus hat, wie ich zu zeigen versucht habe, keine originelle Ekklesiologie vertreten, sondern lässt sich ohne weiteres in die breite Skala der 'Ekklesiologien' seiner Zeit einordnen. Bei allem Idealismus, wie er jeden Pädagogen auszeichnet, war Erasmus auch Realist, was die Einschätzung der menschlichen Schwächen, auch seiner eigenen, angeht. So schreibt er an Luther:

> Von der katholischen Kirche bin ich niemals abgewichen. Danach, deiner Kirche anzugehören, stand mir niemals der Sinn. Obwohl ich ein unter vielen Hinsichten sehr unglücklicher Mensch bin, so halte ich mich gewiss in diesem Punkt für glücklich, dass ich mich von eurem Bündnis standhaft ferngehalten habe. Ich weiß, dass es in der Kirche, die ihr die papistische nennt, vieles gibt, was mir missfällt; aber solches finde ich auch in deiner Kirche. Man erträgt aber die Übel leichter, an die man sich gewöhnt hat. Ich ertrage also diese Kirche, bis ich sie gebessert sehe, und auch sie ist gezwungen mich zu ertragen, bis ich ein Besserer geworden bin. Es ist nicht der unglücklichste Kurs, zwischen zwei gegenteiligen Übeln hindurch zu segeln.[52]

---

49 Schüssler: 1977, 285. Zu dieser Position vgl. Schüssler: 1977, 285f. Die beiden anderen Positionen sind: die Unfehlbarkeit des Papstes (Schüssler: 1977, 287f) und diejenige der Gesamtkirche (Schüssler: 1977, 288f).

50 Vgl. o. bei Anm. 9.

51 Vgl. etwa die oben zit. Stellen aus De sarcienda ecclesiae concordia. Vgl. dazu auch Sieben: 2011, 69.

52 "Ab Ecclesia Catholica nunquam defeci. Tuae Ecclesiae adeo nunquam fuit animus dare nomen, ut

Bibliografie

Quellen

IOANNES ALTENSTAIG (1517), Vocabularius Theologie complectens vocabulorum descriptiones, diffinitiones & significatus ad theologiam utilium: et alia quibus prudens et diligens lector multa abstrusa et obscura theologorum dicta et dissolvere et rationum et argumentorum difficiles nodos [...] intelligere poterit, Hagenau.

IOANNES ALTENSTAIG (1619), Lexicon Theologicum [...] magna ex parte ad mentem D. Thomae [...] accommodatum auctum et in meliorem ordinem redactum studio et labore R. D. Ioannis Tytz [...], Köln, reprint: Hildesheim/New York, 1974.

AMERBACHKORRESPONDENZ (1958), Die Amerbachkorrespondenz, Alfred Hartmann (ed.), Bd. 5, Basel: Verlag der Universitätsbibliothek.

PETRUS DE AYLLIACO (1500), Questio Vesperiarum, in: Questiones Magistri Petri de Aylliaco Cardinalis Cameracensis super libros sententiarum. Vna cum laudibus theologie et quibusdam alijs questionibus de potestate ecclesie in suis vesperijs disputatis, [Lyon]; https://archive.org/details/ita-bnc-in2-00001350-001 [29.04.2016].

BEKENNTNISSCHRIFTEN (2014), Die Bekenntnisschriften der Evangelisch-Lutherischen Kirche. Vollständige Neuedition, Irene Dingel (ed.), Göttingen: Vandenhoeck & Ruprecht.

THOMAS DE VIO CAIETANUS (1925), De divina institutione pontificatus romani pontificis (1521), Friedrich Lauchert (ed.), CCath 10, Münster in Westfalen.

THOMAS DE VIO CAIETANUS (1936), De comparatione auctoritatis papae et concilii cum apologia eiusdem tractatus, M. Vincentius/Jacobus Pollet (ed.), Rom.

CATECHISMUS ROMANUS (1989), Catechismus Romanus seu Catechismus ex decreto Concilii Tridentini ad parochos Pii Quinti Pont[ificis] Max[imi] iussu editus, Petrus Rodríguez (ed.), Città del Vaticano/Pamplona: Libreria Editrice Vaticana.

CORPUS (1879–1881), Corpus Iuris Canonici, Aemilius Friedberg (ed.), 2 vols., Leipzig: Bernhardus Tauchnitz; reprint: Graz: Akademische Druck, 1959.

DESIDERIUS ERASMUS (1703–1706), Desiderii Erasmi Roterodami Opera omnia emendatiora et auctiora, Ioannes Clericus (ed.), 10 vols., Leiden: Petrus van der Aa; reprint: Hildesheim: Olms, 1961f.

DESIDERIUS ERASMUS (1906–1958), Opus epistolarum Des[iderii] Erasmi Roterodami denuo recognitum et auctum, P. S. Allen/H. M. Allen/H. W. Garrod (ed.), 12 vols., Oxford: Oxford University Press.

---

homo plurimis alioqui nominibus infelicissimus, hoc certe nomine videar mihi felix, quod constanter a vestro foedere abstinuerim. Scio in hac Ecclesia, quam vos Papisticam vocatis, esse multos qui mihi displicent: sed tales video & in tua Ecclesia. Levius autem feruntur mala quibus assueveris. Fero igitur hanc Ecclesiam donec videro meliorem: & eadem me ferre cogitur, donec ipse fiam melior. Nec infeliciter navigat, qui inter duo diversa mala medium cursum tenet" (Erasmus, Hyperaspistes I: Clericus; in: Erasmus: 1703–1706, Bd. 10, 1257f).

DESIDERIUS ERASMUS (1960ff), Opera Omnia Desiderii Erasmi. Recognita et Adnotatione Critica Instructa Notisque Illustrata (Amsterdam Edition), J. Trapman e.a. (ed.), 54 vols., Leiden/Boston: Brill.

DESIDERIUS ERASMUS (1964), Desiderius Erasmus Roterodamus. Ausgewählte Werke, Holborn, Hajo/Holborn Annemarie (ed.),2nd ed., München: Beck.

JOHANNES SCHEFFLER (1677), Ecclesiologia oder Kirche-Beschreibung, Neisse/Glatz: Wagner und Rueß, http://diglib.hab.de/drucke/xb-4f-229-1/start.htm [12.04.2016].

JOHANNES STOJKOVIĆ DE RAGUSIO (1983), Tractatus de Ecclesia, Franjo Šanjek (ed.), Zagreb.

IOANNES DE TURRECREMATA (1489), Summa contra Ecclesiae et primatus apostoli Petri aduersarios, Rom: Eucharius Silber.

IOANNES DE TURRECREMATA (1561), Summa de Ecclesia, Venedig: Jean Trechsel.

Forschungsliteratur

BAKHUIZEN VAN DEN BRINK, J.N. (1977), Erasmus, Explanatio Symboli Apostolorum. Introduction, in: Desiderius Erasmus, Opera Omnia Desiderii Erasmi. Recognita et Adnotatione Critica Instructa Notisque Illustrata (Amsterdam Edition), Leiden/Boston: Brill, vol. 5.1, 179–200.

BAUER, MARTIN (2006), Art. Johannes Charlier Gerson, LThK[3] 5, 909f.

BÄUMER, REMIGIUS (2006), Art. Altenstaig, LThK[3] 1, 449f.

BECHT, MICHAEL (2000), Pium consensum tueri. Studien zum Begriff „consensus" im Werk von Erasmus von Rotterdam, Philipp Melanchthon und Johannes Calvin, RGST 144, Münster/Westfalen: Aschendorff.

BEINERT, WOLFGANG (2006), Art. Rezeption I–III, LThK[3] 8, 1147–1149.

BOSSHARD, STEFAN NIKLAUS (1978), Zwingli – Erasmus – Cajetan. Die Eucharistie als Zeichen der Einheit, VIEG 89, Wiesbaden: Steiner.

CHOMARAT, JACQUES (1981), Grammaire et rhétorique chez Erasme, Paris: Belles Lettres.

CONGAR, YVES (1965), Die Tradition und die Traditionen, vol. 1, Mainz: Matthias-Grünewald.

DEVONSHIRE JONES, ROSEMARY (1987), Art. Paul III, ContEras 3, 53–56.

DOLFEN, CHRISTIAN (1936), Die Stellung des Erasmus von Rotterdam zur scholastischen Methode, Osnabrück: Meinders & Elstermann.

FABISCH, PETER (2008), Julius exclusus e coelis. Motive und Tendenzen gallikanischer und bibelhumanistischer Papstkritik im Umfeld des Erasmus, RGST 152, Münster: Aschendorff.

FREITAG, JOSEF (1995), Geist-Vergessen – Geist-Erinnern. Vladimir Losskys Pneumatologie als Herausforderung westlicher Theologie, Studien zur systematischen und spirituellen Theologie 15, Würzburg: Echter.

GEBHARDT, GEORG (1966), Die Stellung des Erasmus von Rotterdam zur römischen Kirche, Marburg an der Lahn: Oekumenischer Verlag.

Gogan, Brian (1982), The Common Corps of Christendom. Ecclesiological Themes in the Writings of Sir Thomas More, SHCT 26, Leiden: Brill.

Halkin, Léon-E. (1983), La place des indulgences dans la pensée religieuse d'Érasme, BSHPF 129, 143–154.

Halkin, Léon-E. (1984), La piété d'Erasme, RHE 79, 671–708.

Hentze, Willi (1974), Kirche und kirchliche Einheit bei Erasmus von Rotterdam, KKTS 34, Paderborn: Verlag Bonifacius-Druckerei.

Kelly, John N.D. (1972), Altkirchliche Glaubensbekenntnisse. Geschichte und Theologie, Göttingen: Vandenhoeck & Ruprecht.

Knighton, C.S. (1987), Art. Warham, ContEras 3, 427–431.

Laudage, Johannes (2006), Art. Johannes Stojković v. Ragusa, LThK³ 5, 960.

Linnenkugel, Albert (1957), Lateinische Grammatik, Paderborn: Schöningh.

Lubac, Henri de (1975), Credo. Gestalt und Lebendigkeit unseres Glaubensbekenntnisses, Theologia Romanica 6, Einsiedeln: Johannes Verlag.

Maccarone, Michele (1953), Vicarius Christi. Storia del titolo papale, Lateranum NS 18, 1–4, Roma: Facultas Theologica Pontificii Athenaei Lateranensis.

Marc'hadour, Germain (1995), Erasmus as Priest: Holy Orders in His Vision and Practice, in: Hilmar M. Pabel (ed.), Erasmus' Vision of the Church, Sixteenth Century Essays & Studies 18, Kirksville: Sixteenth Century Journal Publishers, 115–149.

Massaut, Jean-Pierre (1968), Érasme, la Sorbonne et la nature de l'Église, in: Colloquium Erasmianum. Actes du Colloque International réuni à Mons du 26 au 29 octobre 1967 à l'occasion du cinquième centenaire de la naissance d'Érasme, Mons: Centre universitaire de l'État, 89–116.

McSorley, Harry J. (1974), Erasmus and the Primacy of the Roman Pontiff: Between Conciliarism and Papalism, ARG 65, 37–54.

Miethke, Jürgen (2006), Art. Peter v. Ailly, LThK³ 8, 101–103.

Pabel, Hilmar M. (1995), The Peaceful People of Christ. The Irenic Ecclesiology of Erasmus of Rotterdam, in: Hilmar M. Pabel (ed.), Erasmus' Vision of the Church, Sixteenth Century Essays & Studies 18, Kirksville: Sixteenth Century Journal Publishers, 57–93.

Prügl, Thomas (2006), Art. Johannes de Torquemada, LThK³ 5, 973f.

Schüssler, Hermann (1977), Der Primat der Heiligen Schrift als theologisches und kanonistisches Problem im Spätmittelalter, VIEG 86, Wiesbaden: Franz Steiner Verlag.

Sieben, Hermann-Josef (1990), Vom Florentinum zum Ersten Vatikanum. Zur Ökumenizität des Konzils von Florenz und zur Rezeption seiner Primatslehre, ThPh 65, 513–548.

Sieben, Hermann-Josef (2011), Velut oraculum a deo profectum. Erasmus von Rotterdam über das ökumenische Konzil, ThPh 86, 38–72.

Slotemaker, John T./Witt, Jeffrey C. (ed.) (2015), A Companion to the Theology of John Mair, Brill's Companions to the Christian Tradition 60, Leiden/Boston: Brill.

Smolinsky, Heribert (2006), Art. Konziliarismus, LThK³ 6, 349–351.

Söding, Thomas/Jorissen, Hans (2006), Art. Leib Christi, LThK³ 6, 769–773.

Sprigath, Gabriele K. (2004), Das Dictum des Simonides: der Vergleich von Dichtung und Malerei, Poetica 36, 243–280.

Tierney, Brian (1955), Foundations of the Conciliar Theory. The Contribution of the Medieval Canonists from Gration to the Great Schism, Cambridge Studies in Medieval Life and Thought NS 4, Cambridge: Cambridge University Press; reprint: 1968.

Walter, Peter (2006), Art. Colet, LThK³ 2, 1255.

Walter, Peter (2015a), Humanismus, Toleranz und individuelle Religionsfreiheit. Erasmus und sein Umkreis (2007), in: Günther Wassilowsky/Peter Walter (ed.), Syngrammata. Gesammelte Schriften zu Humanismus und Katholischer Reform, RGST Suppl. 6, Münster: Aschendorff Verlag, 113–134.

Walter, Peter (2015b), Eucharistie und Sündenvergebung. Eine historische Rückbesinnung aus aktuellem Anlass, in: Catholica 69, 182–196.

Walter, Peter (2017) Unbelehrbar? Die Reaktion der katholischen Kontroverstheologie auf Luthers Ablasskritik, in: Andreas Rehberg (ed.), Ablasskampagnen des Spätmittelalters. Luthers Thesen von 1517 im Kontext, Bibliothek des Deutschen Historischen Instituts in Rom 132, Berlin/Boston: De Gruyter, 629–654.

Dorothea Wendebourg

Martin Luther's Ecclesiology

One might say I have been assigned the wrong topic. For the Church did not stand at the center of Martin Luther's interest. Neither was ecclesiology the main object of his theological passion, nor were his reflection and activity focused on the reform of the Church, the much discussed *reformatio ecclesiae*. The centre was rather justification, the gift of salvation through the gospel of Jesus Christ appropriated by faith alone. It was only from this angle that the Church came into the picture. Luther asked what the right understanding of justification meant for the definition, the shape, and the life of the Church. However, from this angle the Church did come into the picture – and in that sense my topic is not so wrong after all. For in Luther's eyes it went without saying that without the Church there is no justification, no salvation, and no Christian faith. Only through the Church can a human being hear the gospel. And when he or she trusts the gospel he or she becomes a member of the Church. Thus the same Luther for whom the Church never came first, but always second, wrote emphatically: "*Ecclesia* shall be my fortress, my palace, my chamber" (WA 44, 713,1). Outside of the Church "there is no truth, no Christ, no salvation" (WA 10.1.1, 140,17).

1. The Sources

The theological background I have just outlined explains how Luther dealt with the Church in his writings. There is a host of statements about this subject from his pen, but very few of his works are explicitly ecclesiological. In most cases he dealt with the Church in the context of other issues or discussed practical questions which were important for the establishment of an evangelical ecclesial body. Besides, the concerns prevalent in his statements on the Church vary according to the state of the theological debates and the historical situations. Thus he never laid down a systematic ecclesiology. However, the basic lines which governed whatever he said and wrote about the Church remained the same since the evangelical doctrine of justification had found its final shape. Thus while the lack of a comprehensive and systematic ecclesiological treatise makes it necessary to look for statements on the Church in all kinds of works written by him in the course of his life, it is also possible to do so because of their theological coherence.

In his early years Luther mentioned the Church but rarely and marginally. He went into the subject more broadly only when he criticized the church of his time which he did less for individual grievances than for severe spiritual defects. After Rome's conflict with the Saxon monk had begun (1518) his criticism, embedded in a comprehensive negative judgement on the state of the church of his time which in Luther's eyes lived in a 'Babylonian Captivity', was directed sharply against the church's authorities, first of all the Papacy. This led to his first ecclesiological treatise *Vom Papsttum zu Rom wider den hochberühmten Romanisten zu Leipzig* (1520) (WA 6, 285–324). As soon as it became necessary to reform the territories where the Reformation had taken hold according to evangelical insights, Luther complemented his critical arguments with constructive writings on various questions of the institutional structure of the Church which included implicit or explicit ecclesiological statements. The first of these writings was *Daß eine christliche Versammlung oder Gemeine Macht und Recht habe, alle Lehre zu urteilen* from 1523 (WA 11, 408–416); then followed treatises on the reform of worship in the middle of the 1520s (particularly WA 12, 35–37; 205–220; 19, 73–113) and the Wittenberg liturgy of ordination in 1535 (WA 38, 423–433, commented upon in WA 41, 457,33–459,11; 762,18–763,18), finally the *Exempel einen rechten christlichen Bischof zu weihen* (WA 53, 231–260), written 1542 in the context of the endeavour to create a genuine evangelical episcopacy. In his later years Luther also produced several treatises which were largely dedicated to the theological understanding of the Church, called forth not least by the ever more evident reality of two antagonistic church bodies side by side. Of particular weight were *Von der Winkelmesse und Pfaffenweihe* (1533) (WA 38, 195–256), his most important ecclesiological work *Von den Konziliis und Kirchen* (1539) (WA 50, 509–653), and *Wider Hans Worst* (1541) (WA 51, 469–572).

2. The Church as *communio abscondita*

There is one *cantus firmus* which runs through all of Luther's statements about the Church from his early period right to the end. It is the declaration that the church is the communion of those who hear the Gospel and believe in it. This declaration is nothing short of a definition as the Smalcaldic Articles say: "Thank God, a seven-year-old child knows what the Church is, namely the holy believers and 'sheep who listen to the voice of their shepherd'. For thus pray the children: I believe one holy Christian Church" (WA 50, 250,1–7; cf. WA 50, 624,14–18).

This definition means: The church in its essence is communion – the 'gathering' (WA 7, 219,3; WA 26, 506,31; WA 50, 624,17), the "band of Christ-believing human beings" (WA 10.1.1, 140,14f; cf. WA 50, 624,17f), "Christendom" (WA 26, 506,35; 507,7; WA 30.1, 250,9–12), the "Christian, holy people" (WA 50, 624,29; 625,21) or "people of God" (WA 40.3, 505,1), the "communion of the saints" (WA 30.1, 189,28f) or "*communio sanctorum*" (WA 7, 712,39), as Luther wrote in ever new variations. Throughout his translation of the New Testament Luther consequently rendered the Greek word εκκλησία by 'Gemeine' (communion), which is at times to be understood in the sense of 'local congregation' and in other instances means the whole of Christendom. In other words, the Church is first of all the totality of the persons who belong to it, not an institution. It is not bound to a certain place or a single church but lives "in all the world" (WA 26, 506,31), as in Wittenberg so also "under the pope, the Turks, the Persians, the Tartars, and all over" (WA 26, 506,38f).

However, the definition quoted before shows that the Church is a particular communion, the communion of those who believe in Christ (WA 50, 624,29; cf. WA 6, 300,35f). It is such not by its own strength but thanks to the power of the Holy Spirit. The Spirit "calls, gathers, illuminates, sanctifies Christendom and keeps it in the true, one faith" as we read in the *Small Catechism* (WA 30.1, 368,1–3). In other words, the spirit makes the communion of believers the One, Holy, Catholic, and Apostolic Church. From the fact that the Spirit brings forth the Church by creating the communion of believers follows a fundamental consequence: The One, Holy, Catholic, and Apostolic Church is not an entity evident to anybody, but a hidden reality: "*Abscondita est ecclesia, latent sancti*" ("the Church is hidden, the saints are concealed", WA 18, 652,23). This does not mean that the Church is not an empirical reality in space and time (cf. WA 7, 683,8–26) – in order to avoid this widespread misunderstanding Luther prefers the wording "hidden Church" (*ecclesia abscondita*) to the traditional Augustinian formula "invisible Church" (*ecclesia invisiblis*). As a communion of physical, visible, and audible human beings the Church is indeed visible and audible. But its essence, that which makes the Church the Church, is not accessible to human senses – it is 'hidden'. This is true because as the communion of believers it is manifest only to God, since only he can see into the heart of human beings (WA 17.2, 501,32–35; cf. WA 21, 332,37–333,2) and diagnose who is a believer and thereby part of the church (WA 6, 298,2f; WA 17.2, 510,37f).

Yet the hiddenness of the church has still another dimension. It has to do with that particular trait of salvation history Luther calls God's acting *sub contrario* ("under the contrary"). The church is hidden insofar here on earth it is miserable, powerless, foolish, and scandalous, often exposed to derision and persecution – its real life thus being hidden *sub contrario* like that of its crucified Lord until it shall be manifest splendidly in heaven (WA 4, 450,39–451,27; cf. WA 5, 285,35f; WA 42,187,14–16). What is more, it is also hidden under sin, which sticks to the Church while it is in this world, since as the communion of the faithful it is the communion of the justified who on earth are at the same time still sinners – *simul iusti et confessores*. Thus the Church hides its spiritual reality by its own failure, abuses, scandals, divisions, under which only the eyes of faith are able nevertheless to identify the Church of Jesus Christ (WADB 7, 418,9–13; 418,36–420,4; cf. WA 7, 710,1f). This sin can seize the doctrine, the form, and the life of the Church to such a degree and set them in such opposition to its essence that what comes to the fore is a false Church. In that case the Antichrist is at work about whom the Bible not accidentally says that he is active within the Church of Christ – I shall come back to this point.

3. The Church as *communio externa*

All these statements about the Church's hiddenness imply that the visible reality under which it is hidden has something to do with the Church itself, since otherwise it would be impossible to say that it is hidden precisely here and that what is hidden here is precisely the Church. Thus the Church has also a visible side, it is also the "bodily, external" church (WA 1, 639,3; WA 6, 297,2). It presents itself as an identifiable number of human beings whose unity has an institutional shape, who profess one common faith and do certain things together. In other words, the church has several external marks (*notae*) by which it can be seen, heard, and experienced: "First, this Christian, holy people can be recognized thereby that it has the Word of God […]. Secondly, it is to be recognized by the holy sacrament of Baptism". Thirdly, "by the holy sacrament of the Lords Supper"; forthly, "by the keys"; fifthly, "by [the fact] that it ordains ministers or has ministries"; sixthly, by "prayer, praise of God, and public thanksgiving"; seventhly, "by the sacred cross which it has to suffer in order to become like Christ its head" (WA 50, 628,29–642,4).

The number of the Church's marks which Luther puts together varies: at times it is larger, at times smaller (cf. WA 51, 479,4–487,2). They are, however, not all of the same weight. For not all of them are equally unequivocal in the sense that they allow to say with certainty that wherever they are, there is the Christian Church. This is so only in the case of one essential feature which is yet another, the third implication of the definition in the Smalcaldic Articles cited above: The Church is wherever the Word of God, more precisely, wherever the Gospel can be heard. In saying this, it is vital for the function of the Word as mark of the Church that 'to be heard' means real, sensuous audibility, external "sound and words" (WA 56, 426,1), proclaimed by human mouths: "We speak about the external word, preached orally by human beings as you and me. For such a thing Christ has left behind as outward sign by which one should recognize his Church or Christian holy people in the world" (WA 50, 629,16–20; cf. WA 11, 408,8–10). What is true of the gospel proclaimed orally is also valid for the other sensual forms of the Word of God, the sacraments. Thus it can be said as a summary: "The marks by which one can recognize externally where in the world is the Church are baptism, sacrament [i.e. the Lord´s supper], and the Gospel" (WA 6, 301,3f). In the precise, unequivocal sense only these are *notae ecclesiae*. For where the Gospel is preached, where baptism takes place and the Lords's Supper is held it cannot be otherwise: Human beings come to have faith or are being kept in faith; communion of the faithful comes into existence or continues to exist: "God's Word cannot be without God's people" (WA 50, 629,34f). Thus God himself has promised (Isa 55:11): "My Word shall not come back empty" (WA 11, 408,13; WA 50, 629,31). Hence it follows:

> Wherever you hear such a Word or see it preached, believed, confessed, and obeyed, do not doubt that there must certainly be a true *Ecclesia sancta Catholica*, a Christian holy people, even if there are but very few. For God's Word does not go forth void (WA 50, 629,28–31).

In short, the Word of God in its different forms is the unequivocal external mark of the Church because it creates the Church, and it creates the Church because it creates faith and thus also the communion of the faithful.

The affirmation that God's Word creates the Church does not compete with the statement that the Church is the work of the Holy Spirit. Rather the Spirit achieves his hidden work of creating and preserving the communion of the faithful only in such a way that human beings "hear the voice of the shepherd", that they come to faith in the external, audible Gospel: "I have been brought here by the Holy Spirit and incorporated into the Church through having heard God's Word and still hearing it" (WA 30.1, 190,9–11). Conversely it is true that "wherever Christ is not preached there is no Holy Spirit who creates, calls, and gathers the Christian Church" (WA 30.1, 189,1f). More than anything else Luther urged upon his hearers and readers this dependency of the Church on the Word of God: "Through the Gospel alone [the Church] is conceived, shaped, raised, born, educated, nourished, dressed, adorned, strengthened, armed, and preserved" (WA 7, 721,10–12). The Church is "*creatura Euangelii*" (WA 2, 430,6f). It is such not in the sense as if it has been created once by the Word of God and since then continues thanks to a strength that is now its own intrinsic life, but it remains dependent on being incessantly filled with life by God through the Gospel: "*tota vita et substania Ecclesiae est in verbo dei*" (WA 7, 721,12f). Which means nothing else but that the Church in its essence is the communion of believers who become and remain believers through the very Word in which they believe.

The first place of the Gospel cannot be outstripped. This holds true although it is the Church that proclaims the Gospel and human beings come to faith only under the condition that the Church does so. Luther can emphasize this aspect under which the Church precedes faith with strong words. Thus he calls the Christian communion "the mother who begets and bears each Christian through the Word of God" (WA 30.1, 188,24f). But he outlines the Church's role very precisely: First of all its motherly function is restricted to passing on the – external – Word in oral proclamation and distribution of the sacraments. To 'reveal' this Word to the hearers in such a way that their hearts are kindled and they become and remain faithful and members of the communion of the faithful is the work of God the Holy

Spirit himself (WA 30.1, 188,25–27). Secondly, the Church, also when passing on the Word of God, is subject to it both regarding its being and regarding the norm of its actions: It *is able* to pass on God's Word because, being *creatura verbi*, it owes its very existence to it; although being mother of the faithful, in relation to the Word it is "not mother", but "daughter", "born from the Word" (WA 42, 334,12; cf. WA 6, 560,33–561,2). And the Church can only *pass on* God's Word, without additions of its own making or alterations, obedient to the revelation of Christ which has preceded it (WA 38, 239,1–7). The yardstick of the Church's obedience is the testimony of the Holy Scriptures. Thus the obedient passing on of the Gospel by the Church is carried out in the faithful explication of the Scriptures and in the distribution of the sacraments according to the Scriptures (WA 51, 481,7; WA 50, 630,22f; 631,7f).

4. The distinctions within the *communio externa*

The audible and the visible Word as the external means and marks of the Church are the pivot by which the external, visible dimension and the hidden dimension of the Church are connected. What corresponds to the external means in the first instance is the communion which uses them equally externally, the communion of the hearers, the baptised, the communicants. But this 'bodily', visible church is not a second church besides the hidden one. After all, the members of the hidden church, the believers, having become and remaining such only through the Word of God, are themselves part of the external communion of the hearers, baptized, and communicants. Thus external and hidden Church are two dimensions of the same thing (cf. WA 1, 639,2–4). At the same time they differ from each other: in the external church there are distinctions which do not exist in the hidden one, the distinction between believers and non-believers, the distinction between ministers and the other Christians, and the distinction between true and false church.

4.1 Corpus permixtum

Concerning the first distinction, not all members of the external church are part of the communion of believers. Both dimensions are not coextensive. For not all who hear the Gospel and receive the sacraments thereby become or are believers. Among them there are also human beings who are not touched internally by these external means. Yet both are part of the external church. Where exactly the dividing line runs between them is known to God alone who knows the human heart (WA 21, 332,31–39). The Christian for his part will consider every member of the external church also as part of the communion of believers since his "yardstick" is love, which means he assumes the best about everybody (WA 18, 651,34–652,4).

4.2 *Ministerium*

Among the members of the external church there are holders of ministry vis-à-vis the other Christians. In the communion of believers, however, there is no such distinction, here all are equal, namely "truly of Christian estate" (WA 6, 407,13f); i.e., they all equally have immediate communion with God, which means they all are priests since a stance of such immediacy with God is a characteristic feature of priesthood (WA 41, 153,30f). This is a position they do not have in their own right. Rather the Christians are priests because they participate in Christ's own priesthood (WA 12, 179,15–21; WA 41, 207,20f; WA 45,6 83,20f). Indeed all of them do – "all Christian men are priests, all women priestesses, whether they are old or young, lord or servant, mistress or maid, learned or lay" (WA 6, 370,25–27). The basis of this common priestly estate of the Christians is baptism, their priestly ordination (WA 6, 408,11f). The oil used for this act is the Holy Spirit who through the external sacramental means "anoints" the hearts, i.e. creates the respective persons' faith in Christ which is the consummation of their priesthood (WA 17.2, 11–17). Thus this new spiritual estate can be considered as the priesthood of all believers and of all baptised, two terms which designate the two dimensions of the same reality. However, the priests receive their new estate not only for themselves. In it is included an obligation (WA 11, 412,5–13) which regards other people: the priestly task to help others to get into the same relation with God or to preserve it (WA 45, 540,17–19). This obligation is fulfilled through the distribution of the means by which God creates faith as well as through intercessory prayer. Thus to the same priestly estate corresponds the same priestly power: Those who are "all equally priests" also all have "the same power regarding the Word and every sacrament" (WA 6, 566,27f; cf. WA 8, 273,12f; WA 10.3, 395,3–9), namely the same power to teach, "to preach and proclaim the Word, to baptize, to consecrate or hold the Lord's Supper, to administer the keys, to intercede for others, to sacrifice, and to judge all doctrine and spirits" (WA 12, 180,2–4). Sent by Christ himself, the Christian where he or she acts as priest stands vis-à-vis their fellow human beings in Christ's own name and with his authority (WA 49, 139,3–7; WA 10.3, 394,32).

Insofar as the priestly activities consist in the distribution of the external means of grace they take place within the external church. This, however, happens in a certain order which generates a differentiation between the priests. Therefore Luther, as much as he underlines the commonness of the priesthood of the Christians and as extensively as he defines the powers entailed in this priesthood, often adds a qualifying clause "Although we are all equally priests, nevertheless we cannot all […] preach" (WA 7, 28,34f). Or: All Christians are truly of a spiritual estate, there is no difference between them – "except only regarding the ministry" (WA 6, 407,14f). Under the aspect of ministry it must be said: "It needs to be entrusted to one only, and one alone has to preach, baptize, absolve, and distribute the Lord's Supper, the others have to be content with this and consent" (WA 50, 633,8–10). The restriction in using the powers of the priesthood of all believers and the difference between the priests stated in these quotations have solely one reason: The proclamation of the Gospel is not only a private matter "between brother and brother", but it is also a public affair directed at the whole congregation and realized in the name of the whole congregation. Such public proclamation in word and Sacrament has to be done by individual Christians entrusted with this special ministry:

> It is necessary to have bishops, pastors, or preachers who publicly and exclusively give, distribute, and exercise the four pieces or sacred things named above [sc. preaching, baptism, Lord's Supper, absolution] for the sake and in the name of the congregations and moreover because of Christ's institution, as St. Paul says in Eph. 4: *Dedit dona hominibus.* He has instituted some as apostles, prophets, evangelists, teachers, governors etc. (WA 50, 632,36–633,5).

As this citation shows, Luther presents two seemingly contradictory reasons for the tie of public proclamation to holders of a special ministry: the priesthood of all believers resp. baptized and the institution by Christ. Thus he says on the one hand: it is "because of and in the name of the Church" (cf. also WA 49, 600,12f) that individual Christians entrusted with this task have to perform the public proclamation of the Word of God, precisely because all Christians possess the power for proclaiming. For this very reason there must be "one person [...] who speaks and does the talking because of the command and permission of the others" (WA 49, 600,13f; cf. WA 38, 227,20ff; 247,10–31; WA 50, 633,4–6; WA 54, 251,31–34). Otherwise there would be a scandalous 'chaos' in the church (WA 12, 189,23; cf. WA 50, 633,6–8). Or some individuals would arrogate the proclamation in the church to themselves although they do not own more power than their fellow-Christians (WA 12, 189,17–23). Then both would be damaged: God's Word would not come across any more as the Word spoken – to all – by God but as the word of human individuals, and the priesthood of all baptized resp. believers would cease to be common to all. Only when the public proclamation, oral as well as sacramental, is entrusted to individual Christians by the entire communion, for which and to which they are to speak, can this damage be avoided. Therefore the church is not free to undertake such entrusting or not: it "must have bishops, pastors, or preachers" (WA 50, 633,1).

At this point Luther's other argument for the ministry of public proclamation comes into play which does not base the ministry on the commonness of the priesthood but on the explicit will of Christ: "Moreover", one must have such ministers "because of Christ's institution" (WA 50, 633,3; cf. WA 6, 441,24f). It is important to note that Luther does not speak of the institution of the ministry in the same sense as he speaks of the institution of the oral proclamation of the Gospel or of the Sacraments, namely as a commandment of Christ which can be quoted as such from the Gospels. When he speaks about the founding act of the Church's ministry he rather points to the Christian congregation after Easter (WA 50, 633,4f [see above]; 634,11f). Nevertheless, by having a ministry the Church is obedient to an institution by Christ: to his commandment to propagate the Gospel. For what is done through the ministry, public proclamation, is a necessary implication of that very same commandment. Therefore "apostles, evangelists, prophets who do God's Word and work must always be, however they want to be named or can be named" (WA 50, 634,13–15; cf. WA 11, 411,22–24). To have such ministers, the Church has to entrust the ministry of public proclamation to individual holders of the common priesthood by way of ordination, which is the calling (*vocatio*) exclusively to fulfill this task, but not the conferment of a special spiritual quality which would distinguish them from the rest of the communion (WA 38, 228,27–29).

The primary place of the ministry is the congregation assembled around one pulpit, one baptismal font, and one table. Its primary holder is the pastor of such a congregation whom Luther because of the identity of his task with the original episcopacy programmatically called 'bishop' (e.g. WA 6, 440,21f; WA 12, 205,3f). Nevertheless Luther was not a Congregationalist who advocated the complete independence of the individual congregation. He rather maintained that the essential oneness of the Church across the borders of the local congregations should find expression also in the visible church. Thus he provided for regular visitations of the congregations. He also strove for the establishment of an evangelical diocesan episcopacy whereby this office after having degenerated into a mainly political function was to become genuinely spiritual again. However, the Wittenberg Reformation was able to establish such an episcopal office only on the regional level, the so-called office of superintendent. On the level of the former dioceses the installation of bishops was possible only outside of the Holy Roman Empire – in the case of Prussia where Luther was involved himself (cf. WA 12, 232–244; WA 18, 408–411); in the Holy Roman Empire where bishops were also, if not primarily imperial princes the political conditions did not allow such a step. Luther's personal efforts in this matter which culminated in two installations of bishops performed by himself (1542 Naumburg, 1544 Merseburg) show how much an independent ordering of the evangelical churches beyond the congregational level mattered to him. What came into being instead, the church government of the princes (Landesherrliches Kirchenregiment), he viewed with undisguised mistrust (cf. WABr 10, 436).

As regards the worldwide oneness of the Church, Luther rarely addressed the question whether, and if so, how it should be expressed in the external church. Where he did he favoured a conciliar form: the bishops, all vested with equal authority, should lead the Church together, as was the case with the apostles and in the beginning with the bishops in the Ancient Church (WA 50, 217,5–17). Above them there is only the one Head who does not himself belong to the external church, Jesus Christ (WA 50, 217,7; WA 51, 494,10f). Thus the claim of the pope to be the visible head of the Church is rejected. He owns no superiority according to divine right whatsoever; to declare that he does is an expression of anti-Christian presumption (WA 50, 217,23–218,18). Yet Luther also rejects a superiority of the pope over the church according to human law (WA 50, 215,14–216,15). For papal superiority would be respected by its subjects only on the binding basis of a divine commandment – which does not exist; based on human law it would only lead to competition and new divisions (WA 50, 216,23–28). Consequently such a more modest argument for the position of the pope would "not help Christianity at all" either (WA 50, 216,22f). What can help the Christian Church is not the exercise of ecclesial power, but only a regime of spiritual concordance in which "we all live under one head Christ and the bishops, all equal according to their office, hold eagerly together in unanimous doctrine, faith, sacraments, prayers, and works of love etc." (WA 50, 217,7–12).

4.3 *Ecclesia vera et falsa*

Finally there is yet a third difference within the external church which does not exist in the hidden church, the difference between "true" and the "false church" (*ecclesia vera et falsa*) already mentioned. It is rooted in the fact that the means of grace are handed on by human beings. Human beings, however, even Christian ones, are not immune to error and sin. Thus preaching and distribution of the sacraments are performed by ministers who are sinners, at times even unbelieving. This is a situation familiar to Christianity from ancient times which Luther countered with the classical anti-Donatist argument: The effectiveness of the means of grace does not depend on the dignity of the person who passes them on (e.g. WA 38, 241,6–23). Yet there is a perversion which is worse and affects the church's life on a deeper level: It so happens that the Gospel is proclaimed and taught and the sacraments are distributed in a way which is not in accordance with Holy Scripture. In fact, the perversity can reach such a degree that the opposition to the Gospel is not restricted to individual cases but becomes customary and systemic and takes on even the form of official ecclesial doctrine and practice. In that case one must conclude: Here is a 'false church'. Such ecclesial opposition to the Gospel in Luther's eyes was due not only the human beings involved. It was a demoniac perversion triggered by none other than the antagonist of Jesus Christ announced in the New Testament, the Anti-Christ (WA 26, 147,27f; WA 38, 232,15–17; WA 51, 505,11f). All the more urgent it is for Christians to have a criterion which allows to diagnose where the Church is, the Church which he has to hold on to and in which he truly receives the means of grace. The criterion is the mark whereby the Church can be recognized: the proclamation of the Gospel in Word and Sacraments. In short: The marks of the Church are by definition the marks of the true church (WA 43, 388,7–9; WA 51, 479,1ff).

For Luther the church in opposition to the Gospel was realized particularly in the papal church: This is "not the true church" (WA 43, 386,21), but the "false" church (WA 42, 193,4), indeed, the church of the Antichrist (WA 26, 28f; WA 50, 217,23–31), which contradicts the Gospel in more than one fundamental dimension: in its doctrine (WA 51, 493,8–16), in its use of the sacraments (WA 6, 501,35f; 527,25f; 543,12f; WA 39.2, 160,13f) and in the claims of the hierarchy and especially the papacy (WA 51, 494,24–26). Therefore the papal church cannot claim to be truly Church (WA 43, 157,9f). Rather the evangelical congregations show that they are true Church since they have turned to the right proclamation of the Gospel and administration of the sacraments and have done away with the perversions in this field thereby (WA 43, 387,21–24; cf. WATR 4, 179,9–11).

However, what is true and false church cannot simply be distributed among two ecclesial institutions. This becomes clear precisely in Luther's judgements on the papal church. On the one hand he characterized it as the church of the Antichrist and wrote about it: "We do not concede to them that they are the Church, indeed, they are not the Church" (WA 50, 249,24f). Yet on the other had he wrote: "Although the city of Rome is worse than Sodom and Gomorrha, in it remain baptism, the Lords Supper, the proclamation and text of the Gospel, Holy Scripture, offices, the name of Christ, the name of God" (WA 40.1, 69,23–26; cf. WA 38, 221,18–31). And "Where these things have remained there certainly have remained the Church and several saints" (WA 40.1, 69,31f). Moreover, Luther freely admitted that he and the other Reformers, as well as the evangelical congregations themselves, owed all those goods to the church under the pope: "I want to praise you [sc. the papal hierarchy] even more highly and confess that we have received everything from the church under you (not from you)" (WA 51, 501,23–25; cf. WA 26, 147,13–15). If both kinds of statements are equally correct that means that the true church is entwined with the false one; the "holy Church is the holy place of the abomination" (WA 38, 221,18), the Antichrist is a phenomenon within the Church (WA 51, 505,10–12; cf. WA 26,1 47,29–35) and with his perversion of the Gospel deprives Christians of salvation (WA 51, 505,16–506,1). If the Church in which the Antichrist sits nevertheless remains the Church and if within it the Gospel and the sacraments continue to be passed on and Christians continue to exist, then it is Christ himself who takes care of that: Christ "has needed all his might to preserve" the means of grace, and "he needed all his might to preserve the Christian' hearts so that they have not lost nor forgotten their baptism, Gospel, etc. in spite of so much scandalous ado" (WA 38, 222,1–6). Christ carries all this through against the doings of his adversaries who thanks to their baptism are and remain "in the Church", but who are not any more in the spiritual sense "of the Church or the Church's members" (WA 51, 505,10;13).

Although Luther developed these thoughts in his altercation with the papacy, the interwovenness of true and false church, the battle between Christ and Antichrist was not, in his eyes, restricted to this institution. He saw the Antichrist was at work also in the groups of the Radical Reformation (WA 50, 646,27–647,5). And he warned the evangelical congregations not to become the field of the Antichrist themselves. The true Church, after having barely survived under the official government of the false church, was now embodied in an institution in which the official doctrine and practice corresponded to the criteria of true proclamation of the Gospel and right administration of the Sacraments, i.e. the evangelical churches. Yet the followers of the Reformation must not "presume" and flatter themselves that the Antichrist was "far from us" (WA 50, 468,10–469,5; cf. WA 43, 428,42). The battle between true and false church, between Christ and the Antichrist is not an occasional happening. Rather it accompanies Christendom from its beginnings until the Last Judgement. Thus it forces the faithful to constant vigilance and incessant prayer (WA 50, 468,10–469,1).

However fierce the battle, there can be no doubt who will finally end up victorious: the true church, which carries "the victory until doomsday" (WA 51, 291,20f; cf. WA 5, 493,12f). In itself weak (WA 51, 291,1–5), the Church owes this perspective to Christ alone, the "victor over the world" (WABr 5, 412,38). He "remains with his Church until the consummation of the world" (WA 18, 649,31–650,1). He does so by preserving Word and Sacrament and through them the communion of the believers. Thus he keeps the Church in unity although its members find themselves across the world and in different institutional churches (WA 26, 506,38f). Thus he keeps the Church inerrant in the truth (WA 51, 515,30), though its doctrine often enough is not pure (WA 42, 423,30f). And thus he keeps it in unbroken spiritual continuity (WA 50, 593,7– WA 14, 628,16–19). *He* does so, whereas the church's own outward, institutional continuity, e.g. the succession of its representatives, far from keeping the continuity of the Gospel (WA 43, 387,14–19), again and again ran counter to it (WA 43, 157,9;14). Thus Christ several times had to make new beginnings with the Church and preserve its continuity through external breaks – which he might have to do again (WA 42, 332,35–37; 333,30–34). Until at his second coming its hiddenness will end and the Church, free from sin, frailty, and suppression, will in its very essence be manifest (WA 30.1, 191).

5. Conclusion

Martin Luther's ecclesiological thought was fundamental for all Reformers, Magisterial and Radical. Yet they did not always uphold his resolute commitment to understand the Church through the lens of the doctrine of justification, nor the way in which he differentiated between the church's spiritual and external dimensions and connected them at the same time. The so-called spiritualists and Radical Reformers left Luther's ecclesiology behind in favour of a more spiritual vision of the Church.

The principal theologian of the Reformed Reformation, Jean Calvin, gave more independent weight to its external, institutional side, as did Philip Melanchthon later in his life. Yet all the Reformers had one fundamental ecclesiological insight in common which they owed to the very experience of the Reformation: No ecclesial structure is able to guarantee that the Church remains faithful to the Gospel and thus remains the – One, Holy, Catholic, and Apostolic – Church. Rather the visible Church may turn into a false church against which the faithful cannot but resist. The positive side of this lesson was the Reformers' firm conviction that even under such circumstances Christ finds ways to keep up the proclamation of the Gospel and to preserve communions of the faithful, the true Church, against and within the anti-evangelical framework. Resistance in the name of the Gospel then aims at embodying the true Church again institutionally. Thus by breaking with the existing institution, such resistance paradoxically serves the Oneness of the Church, and by breaking with tradition it serves its Apostolic continuity, since both its oneness and continuity are basically those of the gospel itself. What was the experience of the 16th century, in today's ecumenical world has become the ecclesiological legacy of that part of Christendom which has gone through the Reformation: a particular awareness of the dependency of the Church on the Gospel, the call for watchfulness to remain true to the Gospel in proclamation, practice, and structures, and the consciousness of how quickly and easily the Church may fail in this respect, even to the point of making necessary once again ruptures with existing institutions. Part and parcel of this legacy is the confidence that it is Christ himself who carries the Church through until the end.

Jon Balserak

"The church that cannot err."

Early Reformed Thinking on the Church

It is a commonplace that the Reformed church is Augustinian. Yet though axiomatic, this might still be scrutinized. Ulrich Zwingli's use of Augustine in relation to the doctrine of the church is particularly open to scrutiny, as we shall see. A range of topics have occupied Zwingli scholarship, but this chapter will focus principally on his use of Augustine within his polemics; that is, his work of reforming the church in Zurich and the region. Given Zwingli's significance to the beginning of the Reformed church, our focus below will be upon him[1] and Zurich[2] though our purview will expand near the end of the essay.

1. The Reforming of the Church in Zurich

"The church that cannot err" (Zwingli: 1524, Bii). The phrase belongs to Zwingli, as we will discover. In fact, in 1523 it was something of a refrain for him, repeated on a number of occasions. He employs it particularly in debate, though it does eventually make its way into a more systematic work such as his *Commentarius de vera et falsa religione* (1525, 174; see 176–194 for his whole treatment of the church)

Zwingli had arrived in Zurich and been made Leutpriestertum (or, people's priest) in 1519. By that time, he had already been preaching elsewhere. He had been parish priest in Glarus and Einsiedeln. With his arrival in the city, he eschewed the standard lectionary of biblical readings, choosing rather to preach *lectio continua* – an indication of the biblical and reform-oriented direction in which he was headed. By this time he had already come to oppose pilgrimages and indulgences. Nor were these the only issues on his mind. On 9 March 1522, the well-known sausage eating incident in Froschauer's house took place, which demonstrated the direction of Zwingli's thinking as regards the idea of Christian freedom. The incident, which was dealt with relatively leniently by the city council, prompted concerns in other quarters. Additionally, in the summer of 1522, he petitioned the bishop of Constance concerning clerical celibacy. His claim was that the denial of marriage was driving

---

1 While working on this chapter, I did not have access to *Sämtliche Werke* (1905–1959), so accessed old copies of relevant writings of Zwingli via e-rara.

2 Recent histories, see Thomas Lau (2012) and Gordon (2002).

priests into illicit acts and thus that it would be better if they could marry. This request was made more provocative when it was learned that Zwingli had himself actually married, Anna Reinhart (in 1522).[3]

By 1523, he had been in Zurich for four years. Two disputations would be held in Zurich that year. Zwingli's developing program had eventually won sufficient support of those on the city council that they called for a public disputation in order to, in effect, demonstrate the orthodoxy of what he and others like Jud were doing. It was scheduled for 23 Jan 1523. Zwingli prepared sixty-seven articles[4] which were to be the agenda for discussion. These articles read as ad hoc assertions quite specific (in many cases) to their specific historical context. They feature criticisms of the Roman church, specifically the mass, the pope, intercession of the saints, etc. These provide some sense of his thoughts on the contemporary church.

During this year of 1523, Zwingli wrote his treatise "An Essay on the Canon of the Mass" (*De Canone Missae Huldrychi Zuinglii Epichiresis*) in late August. There were many at the time who felt that they could not use the whole text of the standard mass book. Leo Jud had, in fact, in 1523 introduced a modified baptismal service in German. Accordingly, Zwingli wrote this to help them and to answer the criticisms that had been levelled against for doing this. November of 1523 saw an increase in acts of iconoclasm in the city, prompted, most people seemed to think, by the inflammatory preaching of Zwingli, Jud, Ludwig Hatzer, Johannes Stumpf and others. While much could be said about these events, they are indicative of the progress Zwingli and his colleagues were making.

This progress continued such that on April 11, 1525 Zwingli, Leo Jud, Kaspar Megander, Heinrich Engelhard, and Oswald Myconius petition the Zurich city council to abolish the mass. And not long after that, on Maundy Thursday in fact, they had the first Reformed celebration of the Lord's Supper. They had already been accused of heresy and now were potentially guilty of schism.

2. The Church in Christian Thought

Charges of heresy and schism immediately carry us back into history. These are to Christian theology what the accusation of adultery is to marriage. They indicate the belief that a fundamental breakdown may be taking place.

Most of the standard creeds state that the church is "one, holy, catholic, and apostolic" (Schaff: 1990, 1:28). Important here were texts like 1 Timothy 3:15 that

---

3 For an excellent new biography of Zwingli, see Opitz (2015). The best English biography of Zwingli is Potter (1976).

4 In Zwingli's *Auslegen und Gründe der Schlussreden* (1523) published on 14 July, he filled out extensively the meaning of these sixty-seven articles.

declares "the church is the pillar and ground of the truth." Moreover, Jesus' apparent declaration that he would build his church on Peter, the rock, (Matt 16:18) would seem to confirm the church's authority and permanence (though there was debate about the identity of the rock to which Jesus referred). The Church of Rome claimed these texts were speaking of her. Others made similar claims. Accordingly, the Roman Church found herself continually having to defend herself from false teachers and schismatics, who set out rival versions of Christianity, which they insisted were the only true form of the faith (Ehrman: 2003).

Early responses to the problem of false teachers were numerous. In the second century, Irenaeus of Lyon spoke to the church's handling of divergence from her truth in his *Adversus Haereticorum* in which he urged on the community of true Christians the importance of the *regula fidei*.(1857, II.27.2; II.41.4, etc) The Christian community holds fast to this rule against heretics and false prophets. It is known and adhered to only by those churches that were in a direct succession from the apostles. This, Irenaeus argued, is at once utterly reliable and denied by the heretic.

Tertullian also addressed the issue in his *De Praescriptione Haereticorum* and also employed the notion of the *regula fidei* when treating it (Tertullian: 1893, 12.5). Being particularly attuned to the fact that heretics pretend to be Christians but in reality accept only their own opinions, Tertullian proposed treating heretics by means of the prescriptions that were a part of Roman law according to which a plaintiff's case could be thrown out of court. His tactic was to refuse to give a heretic the platform he desires to articulate his views.

In the fourth century, Vincent of Lerins produced another response to these problems. Witnessing the debates between Pelagius and Augustine, Vincent was prompted by these debates to produce his *Commonitories*, which he wrote under the pseudonym Peregrinus. In this work, he contended the church should distinguish orthodox teaching from innovation, by regarding the Catholic faith as consisting only of "what has been believed everywhere, always, and by all" (*quod ubique, quod semper, quod ab omnibus creditum est*) (Vincent: 1915, II.3).

Augustine also addressed these concerns. His approach to false teachers was more diffuse and cannot be identified by reference to just one writing, but was nonetheless extremely significant. One important aspect of his approach related to his views on predestination and the doctrine of the church. For Augustine, God's secret predestination was apologetically helpful. Through the doctrine of predestination, Augustine could acknowledge that not all the elect were in the Roman Church at present. This concession could be made by him without requiring him to give up belief in the singular authority of the Roman Catholic Church. It could be the case that some of the elect were, at present, outside of the Roman fellowship, but even though that was true, Augustine could still insist (in, for instance, *de Baptismo*) that the Roman Church was the only place in which salvation was to be found. "[I]t is the church that gives birth to all" (Augustine: 1841, 1.15–23 cited by Pelikan: 1971, 303). The Roman Catholic Church was, as he said time and time again, the church that was established through the performing of miracles through which God testified that this was *his* church. Augustine's famous words about how he would not have been moved to believe the gospel had it not been for the testimony to it by the Catholic Church offers more evidence as to the character of Augustine's ecclesiology.

Of these, Vincent's approach is arguably the most conservative. Pursuing, as it did, a kind of via media between (what he perceived to be) the excesses of Pelagianism and Augustinianism (and especially that of Augustinianism, since the condemnation of Pelagius would have drastically reduced his impact upon subsequent Christian theology), Vincent's approach sought to shut-out doctrinal novelty. Yet though sophisticated, Vincent's solution still left unanswered questions. How does the church apply the Vincentian Canon? By papal decision? By council? Who decides what has been believed by everyone, all the time, everywhere? In other words, how ought one to understand the idea of authority?

Key to this question of authority is the issue of sources. While Vincent may appear prima facie to handle the problem of novelty by means of an extra-biblical tradition which was to serve as a separate source and complement the biblical record, a closer reading suggests the opposite. Here I agree with Heiko Oberman's assertion that Vincent did not want "the interpretation of the Church, ... to become a second tradition or source apart from Holy Scripture" (Oberman: 1986, 280). Rather, following the Vincentian canon would likely ensure that no second source was created. For him tradition would seem to have simply represented the living interpretation of the source of the sacred scriptures.

In this regard, the solutions offered by Irenaeus, Tertullian, and Augustine were perhaps more straightforward. They placed authority in the Roman fellowship which embraced the *regula fidei*, and while they clearly possessed profound reverence for the sacred scriptures, they also acknowledged, with varying degrees of clarity, tradition as a separate source of authority. Understanding of the content of this tradition was placed solely in the hands of the Roman Catholic Church.

3. Defending the Church in the Middle Ages

While thinking on the church continued into the Middle Ages, the authority of the patristic authors meant that their methods for handling false teachers would have an enormous influence on this period. As the church met with various false teachers, these heretics would sometimes embrace ancient heresies, like Docetism, Donatism, Arianism, Novatianism, Montanism, Sabellianism, or Marcionism. Others concentrated "on the institutions and practices of catholic Christianity rather

than on its dogma", but did nonetheless "diverge from the church in some fundamental doctrinal ways" (Pelikan: 1978, 3:236). The premier example Pelikan points
to in order to illustrate his point is that of the Cathari.

Heresy was rarely simple to define and prosecute. Nor did it help that the church
frequently suffered from its own internal moral, institutional, and doctrinal problems. There were problems like those about which Peter Damian complained in
his *Liber Gomorrhianus* (PL 145: 159–90), which attacked the problem of clerical
homosexuality in the eleventh century. The huge problems into which the institutional church fell with the Avignon papacy may also be mentioned here – problems
which had undoubted ramifications on subsequent centuries.

Additionally, the church did not always find the work of interpreting her own
tradition easy or even (at times) possible. This is perfectly illustrated by Peter
Abelard's *Sic et Non* (1976–1977), in which the Frenchman demonstrates and
attempts to develop rules for handling apparent disagreements between patristic
authors. Naturally, the difficulty the church faced in this analysis (of these patristic
authorities) only added to the complexity of her efforts to condemn heretics and
censure schismatics.

Prompted by such internal issues, some theologians began asking. "What is the
church of God, and where is it, and why is it? (PL 192:1294 cited by Pelikan: 1978,
236), as Hugh of Amiens, the twelfth century French Benedictine queried. Joined
with such questions was a concern for the unity of the Christian church. Being
attacked from without and troubled from within, the Christian church became
more reflective. This reflection would continue well into the Early Modern era and
in some senses has never stopped. Accordingly Dietrich of Nieheim, the fifteenth-
century historian of the western schism, asked precisely the same questions raised
by Hugh, querying also why it was necessary to work for the union of the universal
church if in fact that church has always been undivided and unified.

At the commencement of the fourteenth century, Pope Boniface VIII confidently
mentioning the creedal declaration of the church as one, holy, catholic and apostolic
in *Unam Sanctam* (1881, 1245). An explanation of the meaning of those four
identifiers was not produced by Boniface. He, head of the church, spoke with the
authority ascribed to him (he believed) by Christ in Matthew 16. It was, I might
suggest, a statement out of line with the uncertainty that was about to visit the
church over the next several hundred years.

The fourteenth century would also witness the aforementioned Avignon Papacy
and the start of the Italian Renaissance. Both would have a profound impact on
thinking on the church. Part of the fruit of the Renaissance was the rediscovery of
ancient writings, among which those of Aurelius Augustine shined as of profound
significance. Indeed, this is apparent in the father of the Renaissance, Petrarch,
whose love of Augustine is well-known. This rejuvenation of Augustinianism can
also be seen in the theology of individuals like Gregory of Rimini and Thomas

Bradwardine. The latter's treatise *De causa Dei* (2013), appearing roughly forty years after *Unam Sanctam*, would contribute to a vigorous retrieval of Augustine's thought and influence figures like John Wyclif who, in turn, would influence Jan Hus.

This retrieval of Augustine was, at least in some quarters, a vigorous and thoroughgoing rejuvenation of his thought, with impressive adaptations made to suit the late-medieval context. One place this can be seen is in the doctrine of the church. The *de ecclesia* locus had received no special attention from major thirteenth century figures like Peter Lombard in his *Sentences* or Thomas Aquinas' *Summa Theologica* (which does not contain a set of questions on the subject).[5] Yet, by the fourteenth century this would change.

Jan Hus would, in his *De Ecclesia*, engage in some quite-impressive adapting of Augustinian themes which he applied to the church. The church, he insisted, consists of the "totality of all who have been predestined" (1956, 1.B). Likewise Hus, following John Wyclif (1894, 5:408–409), insisted that the church being referred to in Matthew 16, where Jesus declared that he would build his church on Peter, was not the Roman Catholic Church (nor was the rock referred to in the text actually Peter). It was, rather, "the gathering of the predestined" (1956, 7.B-C).

For Hus and Wyclif (and as we shall see, Zwingli) to talk confidently *in this context* about the gathering of the predestined carried considerable weight because of Augustine's authority. Yet to some it was not a welcome re-assertion of an authoritative church father, because of the polemical usage to which they put this Augustinian emphasis. Some within the Roman Church found their usage of predestination profoundly worrying. So, when Hus declared that the only church deserving of obedience was the church which contained the predestined and morally upright and not the Roman Catholic church, he was, Jean Gerson insisted, destroying "all certainty about the church and with it all ability to function in the church" (1960–1973, 2:164, Epistle 35). Even some of the Hussites agreed that such a distinction, based as it was on defining the church exclusively as the company of the predestined, was ultimately unworkable.

So, did men like Gerson simply oppose the theology of Augustine? That is of course a possibility. But irrespective of the answer given to that question, Gerson's concerns raise a larger problem related to the use being made of Augustine.

---

5 For Aquinas on the church, see Sabra (1987).

4. Reformed Thinking on the Church: A New Augustinianism

Returning now to Zwingli, we will investigate his appropriation of predestination in his polemics against the Roman Catholic Church. Of the disputations in which Zwingli was involved, we will first take up two that occurred between 1523 and 1524, leading up to his petitioning (along with Jud, Myconius, et al.) of the Zurich city council in the spring of 1525 to abolish the mass.

Zwingli took part in a disputation with the Roman Catholic authorities in Zurich which opened on 29 January 1523. By the end of 1522 the circumstances were too troubling to continue without some resolution on a number of affairs. Zwingli had been denounced as a heretic. Zurich was accused because of their tolerating of his provocative sermons. The disputation called to settle these matters was not to be an academic debate. The bishop and representatives of the diocese were to put the opposing case but also to listen, advise and mediate. From Constance Johannes Fabri, the vicar-general of the diocese was sent. But no doctors of the church were present and the debate was held in the vernacular. The second disputation we will examine was Zwingli's written argument with Jerome Emser. In response to Zwingli's *Epichiresis* on the Canon of the Mass (1523) Jerome Emser wrote *Canonis Missae contra Huldricum Zuinglium Defensio* in 1524. Zwingli responded to that with *Adversus Hieronymum Emserum canonis missae adsertorem Huldrychi Zuinglii antibolon*, which contains five sections, one of which is on the church.

In the first disputation, Zwingli came up against unprepared disputants. Their remit was non-aggressive. The people were to decide the winner. At one point, one of the representatives of the diocese urged Zwingli to submit to the authority of the church, as the councils and papal decisions have been invested with divine authority. "The church", Zwingli was told, "cannot err" (1901, 83–84). To this, Zwingli – after complaining about the errors which indisputably had been produced by pope and council, declared: "But when he declares the Church has decreed such and such, and she cannot err, I ask what is meant by 'Church?'" (1901, 85).

Here is a nice reiteration of the question asked by Hugh of Amiens, Dietrich of Nieheim, and (implicitly) by Pope Boniface VIII and, after a certain fashion, by Irenaeus, Tertullian, Vincent, and Augustine in an earlier age. Now all of them – but particular for our purposes, Augustine – would have surely answered this within a polemic context by clarifying that the Roman Catholic Church was what we mean by 'Church'. Zwingli, however, took a very different tact.

Continuing, he queried whether what was meant was "the pope at Rome, with his tyrannical power and the pomp of cardinals and bishops?" (Zwingli: 1901, 85). He asserted that this church "has often gone wrong and erred, as everyone knows" (1901, 85). He then countered: "there is another Church which the popes do not wish to recognize", adding a moment later that "[t]hat Church cannot err" (1901, 85). And Zwingli said precisely the same thing in his response to Emser's defence in their written disputation. "There is, therefore, another kind of church" (*Est igitur alterum Ecclesiae Genus*) (1524, n.p.).

What becomes clear as one examines these Zwinglian utterances, is that he is identifying the gathering of the predestined as the church that cannot err. In other words, in both these disputes with representatives of Roman Catholicism, Zwingli used Augustine's emphasis on predestination towards the end of seeking to acknowledge the authority of the church of Jesus Christ but to find it *outside* of the Roman fellowship.

That Zwingli had in mind the elect alone when he was speaking about the church becomes apparent when we see that Zwingli, at one point, complained that some insist that such a church can no more exist than can Plato's Republic (1524, n.p.).[6] Moreover he spoke in other places, such as in his *Auslegen und Gründe der Schlussreden* (1523) and *Fidei Ratio* (1530) of the church as consisting only of the predestined. It is a common theme in his ecclesiology.

As he proceeded, Zwingli plainly identified himself and his fellow believers (that is, the fledgling Reformed church) as that church; the church that cannot err; *his* church that would enjoy a Reformed celebration of the Lord's Supper on April 13, 1525. What he explicitly said about the true church – this other church that the Popes do not want to recognize – is worth paying attention to as well. In both disputations, he identified it with Paul's words in Ephesians 5:25–27, where Paul says that Christ gave himself for the church so that he might sanctify her, presenting her to himself without spot or wrinkle. He explained his views on it further by saying that this church:

> is no other than all right Christians, collected in the name of the Holy Spirit and by the will of God, which have placed a firm belief and unhesitating hope in God, her spouse. ... That Church cannot err. Cause: she does nothing according to her own will or what she thinks fit, but seeks only what the spirit of God demands, calls for and decrees. (1901, 85).

Thus, Zwingli has followed a Hussite path (though surely not self-consciously[7]) in his appropriating of this Augustinian notion of predestination in relation to the church and argued, in effect, that he and his co-religionists owed honor and obedience to *this* church and *not* to the Roman Church.

His approach is severely scrutinized in a later dispute in which Zwingli was involved. He faced a more-theologically-astute interlocutor than either Johannes Fabri or Jerome Emser when he came up against Johan Eck, who produced *Repulsio*

---

6 This Plato's Republic criticism was first raised by Thomas Murner, as is noted by Schreiner (2011, 177).

7 Zwingli's indebtedness to Augustine is well-attested (see for instance, Stephens: 1986, 17–21). His indebtedness to Hus and Wyclif, though often proposed, is extremely doubtful (see Potter: 1976, 63).

Articulorvm Zvvinglii C[a]es. Maiestati oblatorum in 1530 to refute Zwingli's *Fidei Ratio*. As Susan Schreiner summarizes, Eck was essentially asking Zwingli, "How could a person identify a church that consists of inward faith and is known to God alone?" (2011, 180). Indeed, Eck was hugely critical of Zwingli's manner of speaking about the church, in particular his assertion that the church is the gathered elect. "It is", Eck said, "a damnable error to teach that the church consists only of the predestined" (1530, 36r). Eck mocked Zwingli for contending that the church is known to God alone but also that it is somehow also known "to the Zwingli saintlings (*sanctulis*)" (1530, 37v). And when Zwingli acknowledged that there are other meanings of the word "church" – which he did do (e.g. 1524, n.p.),[8] including the idea that it can refer universally to everyone who has professed faith in Christ – Eck lambasted him for his duplicity. Eck also challenged Zwingli that if he were willing to concede the legitimacy of this designation for the word "church," then he should at once acknowledge that this sense of the word is "really the proper one" (1530, 38r), and so he should stop insisting on speaking about the church as consisting only of the elect.

The force of Eck's complaints highlights the difference between Augustine's use of predestination and Zwingli's use of it. Augustine acknowledged the existence of members of the elect who were presently outside of the Roman Church, but that was all he did; all he needed to do. He did not need to say anything about them or, more importantly, to identify them. He only needed to explain that they had a real existence; that there were currently members of the elect who were outside of the Roman Church, but who would eventually come into it (since it "gives birth to all" (Augustine: 1841, 1.15–23)). Zwingli, however, attempted to do precisely the opposite. He attempted to identify the elect who were outside of the Roman Catholic Church, and say that they actually constituted the true church. In point of fact, some Reformed theologians would turn Augustine's argument completely on its head by arguing that there were members of the elect within the Roman Catholic Church who would eventually come out of it and into the Reformed fellowship.

This difference raises some interesting questions. It broaches the concern voiced by Joachim Westphal that heretics like Zwingli and the Zwinglians lacked

---

8 There is a discussion in Locher (2004, 57) about whether, or not, Zwingli identifies three senses of the word, "church" There Locher argues that while Rohls (1987, 205), Stephens (1986, 263) and Locher himself (1979, 218) all contend that Zwingli does set out three senses – one, the church universal "including even unbelievers and hypocrites," two, the "community of the saints according to the *apostolicum*," and three, the "single parish" – the vast majority of the time, Zwingli discusses only two senses. He can alternate between which two, but he usually discusses only two. Whether Locher is correct (and I would argue that he is), it is clear to any who read Zwingli's *Fidei Ratio* that he discusses three senses there, which Eck attacks mercilessly (1530, 36r–40r). For an important attempt to work out different phases in Zwingli's understanding of the church, see Alfred Farner (1930, 3–6).

sufficiently-deep knowledge of Augustine (1555, 7r as cited by Visser: 2011, 84).[9] It also raises the already-mentioned concern articulated by Jean Gerson against Hus, namely, that by speaking about the church in the way he did, Zwingli was destroying "all certainty about the church and with it all ability to function in the church" (1960–1973, 2:164, Epistle 35). Indeed, the similarities between Hus and Zwingli here are undeniable.

But perhaps most significantly, the difference reveals something about the character of early Reformed thinking on the church. Zwingli saw himself and his colleagues as chosen by God and faithful to God's word. Part of that faithfulness seems to have issued precisely from the fact that they were a *different church* from the (corrupt) Church of Rome. Here I acknowledge what Locher argues (2004, 57), namely, that Zwingli can (albeit rarely) treat the Roman Church simply as one of the congregations that make up the earthly church – but contend that the vast majority of his polemic work functions on the idea that the Roman Church is effectively a false church. A second part of that faithfulness seems to have been found in a kind of perfectionism which Zwingli associated with the true church. In his polemic against Roman, he lambasts the Roman Church as having "often gone wrong and erred, as everyone knows" (1901, 85). He furthermore contends of the true church (which Rome did not wish to recognize) that he and his colleagues do not err; they "[do] nothing according to her own will or what she thinks fit, but seeks only what the spirit of God demands, calls for and decrees", as he declared (1901, 86). These linked sentiments are at the heart of Zwingli's thinking on the church. Third, by narrowing the church so much, Zwingli and his co-religionists would seem to run the risk of contradicting various scriptural passages that speak of the church in this present life as a mixed body (which is, incidentally, another Augustinian emphasis). The church, insisted Eck, is not flawless in this life, and yet Zwingli has the audacity to "set up a church without spot or wrinkle made up of his saintlings" (1530, 37r). Zwingli, of course, conceded the point Eck was pressing on him, yet the drift of his thought ran along different lines – it was fundamentally polemic in character.

And the same three points are also applicable, to a greater or lesser degree, to many of those who followed Zwingli within Reformed thought. Similar emphases can be seen in the *First Helvetic Confession* of 1536 (written by Heinrich Bullinger, Jud, Myconius and others) and Leo Jud's *Catechismus* of 1539, the locus on the church produced by Peter Martyr Vermigli, John Calvin's *Institutio Christianae Religionis* (1559), Wolfgang Musculus's *Loci Communes* (1560), and Bullinger's *Decades* and

---

9 Here I am not questioning specifically which writings of Augustine Zwingli may have read (on which see Backus: 1996, 2: 627–660) but rather how deep his understanding of Augustine and the patristic era was.

his *Second Helvetic Confession* (1566). Even if we move geographically further afield, the *Heidelberg Catechism* (1563) conveys something of these emphases as well.

5. Concluding Reflections

Zwingli's identifying of the "church that cannot err" with the number of the pre-destined, while predicated on an Augustinian understanding of the church, would appear to diverge in ways from the North African's ecclesiology. A more thorough analysis of this issue would need to be taken up before a definitive judgment on it can be made. This short chapter has only been able to highlight the subject and raise questions about it. It should, of course, be acknowledged that Augustine and Zwingli worked within profoundly different polemical circumstances. The extent to which this explains any apparent differences between them is difficult, at this point, to comment on.

Bibliography

Sources

Peter Abelard (1976–1977), Sic et Non, Blanche Boyer/Richard McKeon (ed.), Chicago: University of Chicago.

Aurelius Augustine (1865), De Baptismo contra Donatistas, libri VII, in: PL 43:107–143.

Bradwardine, Thomas (2013), Thomas Bradwardine: De causa Dei contra Pelagium et de virtute causarum, Anna Lukács (ed.), Göttingen: Vandenhoeck & Ruprecht.

Heinrich Bullinger (1552), Sermonum Decades quinque, Zurich: C. Froschauer.

John Calvin (1559), Institutio christianae religionis, in libros quatuor nunc primum digesta, certisque distincta capitibus, ad aptissimam methodum: aucta etiam tam ... opus novum haberi possit, Geneva: Robertus Stephanus.

Peter Damian (1853), Liber Gomorrhianus, in: PL 145: 159–190.

Dietrich of Nieheim (1697), De modis uniendiae reformandi ecclesiam/De difficultate refor-mationis in concilia universali, Hermann von der Hardt (ed.), in: Concilium, 1,68–142.

Johannes Eck (1530), Repulsio Articulorvm Zvvinglii C[a]es, Maiestati oblatorum Augsburg: s.n.

Jerome Emser (1524), Canonis Missae contra Huldricum Zuinglium Defensio, Leipzig: s.n.

Jean Gerson (1960–1973), Oeuvres completes, Palémon Glorieux (ed.), 10 vols., Paris: Desclée.

Jan Hus (1956), Magistri Johannis Hus Tractatus de Ecclesia, Cambridge: University of Cambridge.

Hugh of Amiens (1855), Contra hereticos sui temporis sive de Ecclesia et eius ministris, in:

PL 192:1141–1352.

IRENAEUS (1857), Adversus Haereticorum, Cantabrigiae: Typis academicis.

JUD LEO (1539), Brevissima christianae religionis formula … utilitatem excusa, Zurich: C. Froschauer.

WOLFGANG MUSCULUS (1564), Loci Communes, Basel: Joannem hervagium.

PHILIP SCHAFF (1990) Creeds of Christendom; with a history and critical notes Grand Rapids: Baker.

POPE BONIFACE VIII (1881), The bull Unam Sanctam (November 1302), in: Corpus Iuris Canonici, II. Leipzig: Bernhard Tauchnitz, col. 1245–1246.

TERTULLIAN (1893), De Praescriptione Haereticorum ad martyras, Oxford: Clarendon press.

PETER MARTYR VERMIGLI (1580), Loci Communes, Robert Masson (ed.), Zurich: C. Froschauer.

VINCENT OF LIRENS (1915), Commonitorium, Cambridge: Cambridge University Press.

JOACHIM WESTPHAL (1555), Collectanae sententiarum divi Aurelii Augustini Episcopi Hipponensis de Coena Domini …, Regenersburg: Joannis Carbo.

JOHN WYCLIF (1883–1914), Wycliffe's Latin Works, 35 vols., London: The Wycliffe Society.

ULRICH ZWINGLI (1523), Canone Missae Huldrychi Zuinglii Epichiresis, Zurich: C. Froschouer.

ULRICH ZWINGLI (1523), Auslegen und Gründe der Schlussreden, Zurich: C. Froschauer.

ULRICH ZWINGLI (1523), De Canone Missae Huldrychi Zuinglii Epichiresis, Zurich: C. Froschauer.

ULRICH ZWINGLI (1524), Adversus Hieronymum Emserum canonis missae adsertorem Huldrychi Zuinglii antibolon, Zurich: C. Froschouer.

ULRICH ZWINGLI (1525), Commentarius de vera et falsa religione, Zurich: C. Froschouer.

ULRICH ZWINGLI (1530), Ad Carolum Romanorum imperatorem Germaniae comitia Augustae celebrantem fidei Huldrychi Zvinglij Ratio…, Zurich: C. Froschouer.

ULRICH ZWINGLI (1901), Selected works of Huldreich Zwingli (1484–1531). The Reformer of German Switzerland, series 2, v. 1, Philadelphia: University of Pennsylvania Press.

ULRICH ZWINGLI (1905–1959), Sämtliche Werke, Emil Egli/Georg Finsler/Walther Köhler (ed.), Berlin: Schwetschke.

Secondary literature

BACKUS, IRENA (1996), Ulrich Zwingli, Martin Bucer, and the Church Fathers, in: Irena Backus (ed.), The Reception of the Church Fathers in the West:From the Carolingians to the Maurists, 2 vols, Leiden: Brill, 2:627–660.

EHRMAN, BART (2003), The Battles for Scripture and the Faiths We Never Knew, Oxford: Oxford University Press.

FARNER, ALFRED (1930), Die Lehre von Kirche und Stadt bei Zwingli, Tubingen: J. C. B. Mohr.

GORDON, BRUCE (2002), The Swiss Reformation, Manchester: Manchester University Press.

HAUSER, M. (1994), Prophet und Bischof: Huldrych Zwinglis Amtsverständnis im Rahmen der Zürcher Reformation, Freiburg (Schweiz): Universitätsverlag.

LAU, THOMAS (2012), Kleine Geschichte Zürichs, Regensburg: Pustet.

LEY, ROGER (1948). Kirchenzucht bei Zwingli, Zurich: Zwingli-Verlag.

LOCHER, GOTTFRIED WILHELM (1979), Die Zwinglische Reformation im Rahmen der europäischen Kirchengeschichte, Göttingen: Vandenhoeck & Ruprecht.

LOCHER, GOTTFRIED WILHELM (2004a), Sign of the Advent. A Study in Protestant Ecclesiology, Fribourg: Academic Press.

LOCHER, GOTTFRIED WILHELM (2004b), Sign of the advent: From the Ecclesia Invisibilis to the Visible Spiritual Community, in: Internationale kirchliche Zeitschrift: neue Folge der Revue internationale de théologie 94, 156–187.

OBERMAN, HEIKO (1986), The Dawn of the Reformation, Edinburgh. T&T Clark.

OPITZ, PETER (2015), Ulrich Zwingli: Prophet, Ketzer, Pionier des Protestantismus, Zurich: TVZ.

PELIKAN, JAROSLAV (1971–1989), The Christian Tradition, 5 vols, Chicago: University of Chicago Press.

POTTER, G.R. (1976), Zwingli, Cambridge: Cambridge University Press.

ROHLS, J. (1987), Theologie reformierter Bekenntnisschriften: von Zürich bis Barmen, Göttingen: Vandenhoeck & Ruprecht.

SABRA, GEORGE (1987), Thomas Aquinas' Vision of the Church, Mainz: Matthias-Grünewald-Verlag.

SCHREINER, SUSAN (2011), Are You Alone Wise? The Search for Certainty in the Early Modern Era, Oxford: Oxford University Press.

STEPHENS, PETER (1986), The Theology of Huldrych Zwingli, Oxford: Clarendon Press.

VISSER, ARNOUD S.Q. (2011), Reading Augustine in the Reformation. The Flexibility of Intellectual Authority in Europe, 1500–1620, Oxford: Oxford University Press.

Charlotte Methuen

Ordering the Reformation Church in England and Scotland[*]

Introduction

> It is evident unto all men, diligently readinge holye scripture, and
> auncient aucthours, that from the Apostles tyme, there hathe bene
> these orders of Ministers in Christes church, Bisshoppes, Priestes,
> and Deacons.[1]

Thomas Cranmer's words in the preface to the 1550 English ordinal asserted a historical certainty to the three-fold order of ministry which was far from evident to many of his fellow reformers. Reading the same sources by the early 1540s, as Cranmer presumably knew, Calvin had come to argue for not a three-fold, but a four-fold order of ministry: doctors, or teachers; pastors, or preachers; elders and deacons (*Institutes* 4.3.1–9). Luther's view of orders was much more fluid: having argued in 1520 that ordination was not a sacrament, he became increasingly convinced of the need for an ordered and authorised ministry, but was less concerned about what form that ministry should take. It is clear, however, that Lutherans did not assert the threefold ministry as scripturally and historically self-evident, and this must have been clear also to Cranmer, who had after all spend some time in Nürnberg in the early 1530s.

Ten years after Cranmer drafted the English ordinal, as the Reformation was introduced in Scotland in 1560, the Book of Discipline envisioned a system of locally elected superintendents who were to replace bishops in overseeing the Scottish dioceses. By 1572, in the Second Book of Discipline, these superintendents, the responsibility for whose appointments was proving too tempting for nobility and monarch to leave to local elections, had in turn been replaced by presbyteries. Fifty years later, civil war raged in England and Scotland (and Wales and Ireland) caused

* I am grateful to Refo500 for the invitation to speak at the conference in Copenhagen in 2016. A condensed version of this article has appeared in the meantime: Charlotte Methuen, "Episcopacy in the Reformation," *Scottish Episcopal Institute Journal* 2 (2018), 35–51 (online at: https://www.scot-land.anglican.org/wp-content/uploads/2018-24.pdf).

1 1550 Ordinal, Preface, online at http://justus.anglican.org/resources/bcp/1549/Deacons_1549.htm (accessed 6 January 2020).

in large part by conflicts centred on precisely this question of church order: was church order in England and in Scotland – by now two countries under one crown – to be episcopal or presbyterian? The result, which finally took shape in the 1660s in England and the 1690s in Scotland, was that Scotland's church (and monarch) would be presbyterian whilst England's church (under the supreme governorship of the same monarch) would be episcopal. Ecumenists are still grappling with the consequences of these historical developments. This paper, then, explores the question of church from the perspective of church order. What do the conflicts over episcopacy, the arguments for and against retaining and rejecting episcopacy in England and in Scotland, the pleas for synodical, presbyterian government, reveal about the practical challenges of reforming a national church? What understandings of the church do they reveal? And in particular, what do they tell us about how the church was conceived in relationships to political power? A key question emerges: who had authority in the churches of the Reformation?

Methodologically, I am going to offer a number of comparisons. I begin with quite a detailed consideration of the reforms undertaken in the English church under and by Henry VIII, exploring them in the context of what was happening at a similar period in Saxony and other territories in the Holy Roman Empire which introduced the Reformation. In a second step, I then trace the situation of the bishops in England in the Reformation of Edward VI (1547–1553), the Restoration of Mary I (1553–1558) and the Protestant Settlement of Elizabeth I (1558–1603). The third, much shorter, section turns to Scotland, exploring what the context in which Reform was introduced there, and assessing the underlying assumptions of the long-drawn-out process of replacing episcopacy with a presbyterian church order, which took the Scottish and English churches through the rejection of episcopal order in the commonwealth, its restoration in both church and Kirk in 1660 and finally to the Scottish presbyterian settlement after the 1688 Revolution. The point of offering this long and comparative perspective is double: first to highlight the different challenges that accompanied the Reformation of a national rather than a smaller territorial church, but also to consider how the relationship between temporal and spiritual powers in the late middle ages shaped what structures proved feasible at the introduction of the Reformation. A third interest relates to my own involvement in ecumenical dialogues which for Anglicans so often hinge on "the historic episcopate, locally adapted in the methods of its administration to the varying needs of the nations and peoples called of God into the unity of his Church." Can a better historical understanding of how and why episcopacy was and was not retained during the Reformation help us to overcome ecumenical difficulties around ministry?

1. Henry VIII and the Bishops

In approaching this question, it is instructive to consider the very different ecclesiastical and political contexts of the late-medieval Holy Roman Empire in comparison with those of first England and then Scotland. Reformation church order was not *creatio ex nihilo*, but built on – or in reaction to – the structures of the medieval church. In the German lands, the birthplace of the Reformation, these were distinctive. Here, as nowhere else in the Western Church, bishops were prince-bishops:[2] although their spiritual jurisdictions extended over the territories of other princes, they also exercised civic jurisdiction which placed them not only on a par with their secular counterparts, but often in direct competition with them. Although nominally subject to imperial and papal power, most of the German bishops were elected by cathedral chapters which were firmly in the hands of noble families who took it in turns to nominate a candidate for office, usually a younger son from their own ranks (Methuen: 2017, vol. 1, 521–538). In England, in contrast, although elections of bishops were conducted by cathedral chapters this process was largely a formality. Kenneth Carleton observes that "the usual procedure was for the king to indicate his choice to the chapter by means of a *congé d'élire*, who would proceed with the election; the bishop-elect would then be commended to the pope" (Carleton: 2001, 7). As in the German lands, the sees of English bishops included temporal estates which the bishops held on the same basis as lay lords (Carleton: 2001, 8), and English bishops were, as Felicity Heal puts it, "spiritual noblemen" (Heal: 1980, 20), but an English bishop owed a strong allegiance to the king, who had either recommended him for office or actively agreed to his appointment (Carleton: 2001, 7–8). English bishops were integrated into the national structures of governance – they sat in the House of Lords, for instance – and this made them part of national system headed by the king. This becomes particularly significant at the Reformation: the German princes and city councils who moved to introduce the Reformation into their territories in a situation in which they had – often for a long time – been seeking to wrest power from the local bishop. In England, when the king moved to assert his authority over the church and deny that of the Pope, and claimed the right, amongst others, to appoint bishops directly and without reference to the papacy or any other foreign power, he was, as Carleton recognises "abrogating to himself a jurisdiction which for many years had *de facto* been exercised by the crown; the claim was for the *de jure* right to exercise that appointing power" (Carleton: 2001, 7). Here too the contrast to the German situation is apparent. The Duke of Jülich and Berg, for instance, had

---

2 German bishops were listed under *principi* in the Vatican filing system, whilst English (and presumably also Scottish) bishops were listed under *vescovi* (Brandt: 1988, 1).

in the late fifteenth century sought to strengthen his authority over the church in his territory, rejecting the authority of the Archbishop of Cologne as a "foreign power" and introducing the office of "*Landesdechant*" (Territorial Dean) appointed by the Duke himself (Flüchter: 2006, 96). Here the (arch-)bishop was the foreign power, while in the English context that role would be reserved for the pope: the bishops, although they needed, in Henry's eyes, to be brought under his authority, were integrated into a political system which had mechanisms by which this could be done.

There are good reasons, therefore, to see the continuation of the episcopal structure in the English church as related to the national scale of its reformation, and I shall be arguing in this paper that this was indeed a key factor. It is important also, however, that, as Heal points out, "the structure of the church over which [the bishops] presided was relatively well integrated into the English commonwealth" (Heal: 1980, 19).[3] This proved significant in the Reformation, for if what was wanted was a reformed church to serve the whole of England, then structures were needed that extended across the country, linking parishes into a united hierarchy; this was what the medieval system of parishes, dioceses and provinces offered. However, the transition was not seamless, and there are indications that the place of bishops in the church created by Henry VIII's break from Rome was not assured. Considering Luther's understanding of ordination, Krarup highlights Henry VIII's defence of the role of bishops when writing (perhaps alone, perhaps with the support of John Fisher, Bishop of Rochester 1505–1535, or Thomas More) against Luther in the *Assertio septem sacramentorum* of 1521, the treatise for which he was granted the title *Defensor fidei*. The *Assertio* maintained the importance of the episcopate, arguing on the basis of scriptural evidence including 1 Tim 5:22 that the authorisation to priesthood lay, not in the consensus of the congregation, as Luther had implied in *De captivitate babylonica*, but in ordination by a bishop and specifically in the laying on of hands.[4] Luther's response, sent in summer 1522, argued against this position that ordination was not to be understood as a means of grace but as a call or vocation (Krarup: 2007, 31), and denied that any action by a bishop is necessary to confirm this calling or that any form of ordination was necessary for the celebration of the Lord's supper (Krarup: 2007, 65–66; 107–108). However, as the Reformation church took shape in Saxony, ordinations began to take place in the Wittenberg Faculty of Theology administered by Luther and his

---

3 In making this comment, Heal contrast the situation of bishops in England to that in Scandinavia, where, she says, "the bishops posed the major threat to the crown", and implies that in Scotland the situation was one of competition between nobles and bishops, and argument to which we shall return below.

4 Henry VIII, *Assertio septem sacramentorum* (1521); trans.: Henry VIII: 1908, 395–429. Henry's position and Luther's response are discussed by Krarup (2007, 32).

colleagues (Krarup: 2007, 120–121; Smith: 1996, 5; 87–88; 98–99; Hendrix: 2015, 254).

Did Henry remain consistently convinced of the essential role of bishops? He had written the *Assertio* (or had it written) nearly a decade before he began seriously to contemplate a break from Rome. It would be easy to conclude from the position he expressed in it, combined with the fact that new dioceses were established in England during the 1540s and that the Henrician church bequeathed an episcopal system through which reformation measures were enacted under Edward VI to conclude that the episcopal nature of England's church was never in question. However, a closer examination of the position of bishops in the 1530s suggests that the reality was more complex, and that the English bishops saw their position as less assured than it looks in hindsight. Questions of the relationship between spiritual and temporal power and the extent of the spiritual power of temporal rulers were exercising many temporal rulers at this period: were temporal rulers responsible for the spiritual well-being of their people? And if so, how was their care of their subject's souls to be executed? Henry was not the only prince to have become convinced that they were.[5] His position was buttressed by that findings of Edward Foxe, provost of King's College Cambridge, who towards the end of the 1520s had begun compiling the *collectanea satis copiosa*, a compendium of authorities suggesting that the monarch had no superior but God, and that "divinely ordained power [was] ultimately vested in the Crown" (Carleton: 2001, 11; cf. Yarnell: 2013, 132). In September 1530, the King was asserted by the Dukes of Suffolk and Norfolk to be "absolute both as emperor and pope in his own kingdom" (Yarnell: 2013, 127). This principle underlay the series of parliamentary acts through which Henry took control of the English Church: the Act for the Pardon of the Clergy (1531), the Act of Restraint of Appeals (1533) and the Act of Supremacy (1534), which together asserted that "All dominion, authority, honour, nobility and freedom, as well as the power of coercion and restraint are derived from the person of the king" (Carleton: 2001, 12–13). The king's headship over the church included, as the Act of Supremacy declared, not only "matters of jurisdiction and administration", but also doctrine and the interpretation of Scripture (Carleton: 2001, 13; cf. Act of Supremacy: 1534, 113–114). Henry's appointment in 1536 of Thomas Cromwell, a layman, to be Vicar-General and Vicegerent of the King in spirituals was, suggests Carleton, "a visible expression of the Henrician concept of the supremacy in action" (Carleton: 2001, 13). So too was the King's requirement in 1535 that the English bishops petition

---

5 Yarnell (2013, 128) claims that "from early on, Henry displayed a care for souls which went far beyond the late medieval ruler's responsibility to defend the ecclesiastically defined faith with the temporal sword". However, a similar care for the souls of their subjects had also motivated a number of German princes to introduce the Reformation. See for Philip of Hesse: Schneider-Ludorff: 306; for Duke Ulrich of Württemberg: Methuen: 1994, 841.

him to be reappointed to their sees and for the right to perform episcopal functions including ordinations, visitations and the granting of probate (Carleton: 2001, 14). Episcopal jurisdiction was now to be understood to be exercised "by virtue only of the King's supremacy and at his good pleasure"; bishops' authority to carry out diocesan visitations (through which they were to support the supremacy) was given to them "of God and the King" (Carleton: 2001, 14; 16). This was the practical outworking of principles which Henry, probably with the help of Cromwell and Christopher St. German, had formulated in 1531. The first of these asserted the King's right to assent to the election of bishops and to license them, and emphasised that even after their installation, bishops are still the King' subjects: "although he listens to their message from Christ, as soon as they cease speaking, the clergy immediately return to the status of private people" (Yarnell: 2013, 134). Henry saw himself, suggests Yarnell, as "a new shepherd-king embodying both sacerdotal and regal powers" (Yarnell: 2013, 136). Similarly, against those scholars who argue on the basis of these actions that Henry considered himself a lay bishop, Carleton proposes that "the King himself [...] considered the Crown to hold within itself all the rights and powers of both the spiritual and temporal spheres" (Carleton: 2001, 14, n. 16). Whatever Henry's understanding of his role, there can be little doubt that, as Carleton asserts, "by the end of the 1530s, the bishops had become entirely dependent on the king for the exercise of their power" (Carleton: 2001, 15). Moreover, suggests Yarnell, the bishops justifiably feared that the ordained ministry might disappear altogether: "The dissolution of the monasteries and the radical threats in Parliament called into question the need for the clergy [...] The ministry was under siege from king and laity" (Yarnell: 2013, 181).

That not all English bishops saw this situation positively is scarcely surprising. Reform was recognised to be necessary, and the revised canons proposed by the Convocation of Canterbury in conjunction with the Reform Parliament in 1529 had called for reform of the church, including the role of the bishops. Canon 1 instructed that the bishops should "diligently carry out the things which are written below as well as other things which pertain to their office" (Canons: 1529–1947, 2/3). The "things [...] written below" included the presence of bishops in their cathedral churches to celebrate mass at Christmas, Easter and Pentecost and in Holy Week, and their responsibility to be active in their dioceses, "reforming monasteries and residences, disciplining the clergy and people, eradicating heresies, and sowing the Word of Life in the Lord's field" (Canons: 1529–1947, 2/3–6/7). By the late 1530s, a number of English bishops had begun to explore the consequences of the Act of Supremacy in ways that offered a more differentiated understanding of the relationship between king and bishops. Cuthbert Tunstall, Bishop of Durham and John Stokesley, Bishop of London, writing probably in 1537, argued that the principal duty of the secular ruler is "to defend the faith of Christ and his religion, maintain true doctrine, abolish abuses, heresies, idolatries, to oversee priests and bishops in exercising their power, office and jurisdiction faithfully." They saw the King excluded from holding a preaching or sacramental function, and argued that ecclesiastical office holders should also be excluded from temporal power, except as delegated by secular ruler (Carleton: 2001, 16–17). Tunstall and Stokesley's position chimed with the terms of the Act of Supremacy, whilst trying to maintain and define the bishops' authority. Similarly, both Edward Foxe, appointed Bishop of Hereford in 1535, and Stephen Gardiner, Bishop of Winchester since 1531, considered the position of bishops in the context of the Act of Supremacy. For Foxe, the king holds "the supreme authority of spiritual and temporal things". He "makes", "ordains", and "consecrates" bishops, whose office is "to pray and preach the word of God, and to offer gifts and sacrifices for sin". Bishops cannot claim the temporal sword and must obey their prince" (Yarnell: 2013, 166–167). Gardiner argued that the king, as supreme head of the realm, must also be supreme head of the church in England, since the people concerned are "is one and the same congregation"; however, he has a God-given cure for spiritual and eternal affairs which precedes his responsibility for "corporal matters." He exercises these through the hierarchy of "the very real degrees of clergy – archbishop, bishop and curate," also divinely instituted, who "cooperate in the offices of teaching and ministry of the sacraments" (Yarnell: 2013, 167–169). Gardiner's position, as Yarnell observes, "offered a constitutional arrangement for increasing the power of prelates over the lower clergy and the laity […] [T]here is no room for power sharing with nobility, commons or lower clergy. King and bishop are united in a rigid ecclesiocracy" (Yarnell: 2013, 169). In 1537, eight bishops at the London Synod issued a "Judgement of some Bishops" which argued that "kings have a general charge but not a sacerdotal cure", and that "bishops and priests […] are to teach and determine doctrine, and loosen (sic) and bind sin." Moreover, in the view of the bishops, "Kings are subject to them in these matters. On their part, kings are to ensure that bishops and priests do their duty" (Yarnell: 2013, 181).

The theological justification for the questions raised about the need for – and meaning of – ordination could be found in Tyndale's English translation of the New Testament, which had rendered Greek PRESBYTEROS as "elder". His understanding of the New Testament church affirmed a ministerial office, but believed it to be defined by function: an elder "is nothing but an officer to teach"; he should not be understood as a mediator between God and other Christians, and he did not need episcopal ordination (Yarnell: 2013, 169–170). Tyndale's position was congruent with that of a number of evangelical theologians who held that the church did not need an ordained ministry, let alone an episcopally ordained ministry. Krarup observes, for instance, on the basis of Luther's and Melanchthon's correspondence, that ordination was not always considered necessary for the celebrant at the Lord's Supper (Krarup: 2007, 120–121). Within German evangelical territories, the consensus that an authorised ministry was necessary had been articulated in the 1530

Augsburg Confession, which asserted: "Of Ecclesiastical Order they teach that no one should publicly teach in the Church or administer the Sacraments unless he be regularly called" (Augsburg Confession, Article XIV). However, agreement over the proper liturgical form for evangelical ordination, was only beginning to emerge in the mid-1530s, and the question of who should ordain was a part of this discussion.[6] Luther had argued in 1520 that a bishop ordained on behalf of the wider church: "in the place and stead of the whole community, all of whom have like power, he [the bishop] takes a person and charges him to exercise this power on behalf of the others" (Luther, *To the Christian Nobility of the German Nation*, WA 6, 407; LW 44, 128). In 1523, when he was consulted about the possibility of establishing an evangelical (arch-)bishopric in Bohemia, Luther advised that such an (arch-)bishop should take overall responsibility for the leadership of the church leadership and should lead visitations, but, at least in Krarup's reading of the sources, Luther did not identify ordinations specifically as part of the (arch-)bishop's responsibility (Krarup: 2007, 65–66). In the visitation order for Saxony, the *Unterricht der Visitatoren*, in contrast, the Wittenberg Reformers identified the original responsibilities of a bishop as the examination and ordination of the clergy, oversight over church courts, the organisation of synods, and oversight over schools, universities and all worked in them or served the church.[7] These responsibilities must be fulfilled, and if this were not being done by the bishop then someone else must be appointed to do so. As already observed, in 1537 ordinations began to take place in the Wittenberg Faculty of Theology administered by Luther and his colleagues, on the basis of demonstration of adequate theological preparation and the living of a godly life (Krarup: 2007, 120–121; Smith: 1996, 5; 87–88; 98–99; Hendrix: 2015, 254). This was not the pattern that was envisaged in England. When in 1540 questions on the sacraments were sent to bishops and other theologians, they included the power to ordain and the source of episcopal authority in making priests, and specifically asked whether appointment sufficed, or whether consecration or ordination is necessary? In response, "most of the bishops and divines asserted that some form of consecration in addition to appointment was necessary" (Carleton: 2001, 18–19).

In England, questions about the form of ministry and the role of bishops did not arise only in the context of theological concerns. It is commonly recognised that a key result of the dissolution of the English monasteries, which had begun in the 1520s, although it reached its peak in the later 1530s and early 1540s, was to move land from spiritual ownership to secular ownership. Heal observes that in 1534 similar proposals for "the alienation of superfluous church wealth" were

---

6 Thus Smith (1996), identifies 1525–1535 as a "decade of transition" for Lutheran ordination rites and practices, and 1535–1570 – long after Luther's death – as a period of "emerging consensus" (titles of chapters 3 and 4).

7 Butt: 2014, 53; for the process of drafting the *Unterricht der Visitatoren*, see: Michel: 2014, 153–167.

also made relating to bishops; indeed, a key theme of her study is to show the more or less successful attempts to curtain the power and wealth of bishops throughout the Tudor period. The dissolution also transferred (or in some cases, returned) patronage of parishes and other ecclesiastical offices which had previously been held by monastic houses and exercised by the abbot or abbess, prior or prioress, into the hands of the secular powers. A third effect of the dissolution was to secularise those episcopal sees in which the cathedral had been an abbey church in the sense that it placed them under the authority of a dean and a bishop who were no longer members of a religious order (cf. Heal: 1980, 104–107). As these measures came into effect, it cannot have been clear that the process of secularisation would not become even more radical to the extent of transferring episcopal functions to laymen. If the layman Thomas Cromwell could be made Vice-Gerent in spiritual matters, why could this principle not extend to the appointment of bishops? There were precedents, criticised by those who called for church reform, of late-medieval bishops who had been consecrated long after they had taken up their responsibilities, or not at all.[8] Moreover, by the mid-1530s, there were also precedents in those territories which had embraced German Reformation for the transfer of episcopal power to secular rulers. In particular, the visitations initiated by the Wittenberg Reformers in 1528 were carried out under the authority of the Elector of Saxony: the *Kurfürstliche Instruktion* for the Visitation (1527) presumed that it was the prince who "who by virtue of his authority as the ruler of the state introduces and effects the visitation."[9] This affirmation was to some extent mitigated in the introduction to the *Visitation* itself, in which Luther affirmed that "although his Electoral Grace is not commanded to teach and rule spiritually, nevertheless he is responsible, as secular ruler, to maintain things so that dissension, bands, and disorder do not arise among the subjects."[10] There are clear parallels to the English debates about the relationship between the king and the Church in England after the Act of Supremacy.

However, here again the complexity of the German jurisdictions and their difference to the English situation becomes clear. In authorising the 1528 visitation of the Saxon churches, Elector Johannes Friedrich was appropriating the jurisdiction of the Bishop of Brandenburg over the Saxon churches, a transfer of authority which, as Natalie Krentz has recently demonstrated, had been taking place with

---

8 For instance, a series of three younger sons of the family of the Dukes of Savoy, grandsons of the Antipope Felix V, also Amadeus VIII of Savoy, were made bishop, Pierre in 1452 aged just 8, Jean-Louis in 1460 aged 12 and François in 1482 or 1484, in his late twenties, but holding the post simultaneously which his appointment as Archbishop of Auch (cf. McGrath: 2012, 2; Richard 1760, vol. 3, 41–42).

9 See Spitz: 1953, 131; the *Instruktion* can be found in WA 26, 195–240 (translation: LW 40, 269–320).

10 Cited according to Spitz: 1953, 132; cf. WA 26, 201 (LW 40, 273).

respect to Wittenberg since at least the turn of the sixteenth century.[11] In order to maintain order with the Saxon church, superintendents were appointed, who had regional jurisdiction which was subordinate to that of the Elector. Bishops were more properly bishops understood as "inspectors or visitors," suggested Luther in his lectures on Titus, given in 1527 (WA 25, 17; translation: LW 29, 17). Here he may have drawn on Augustine's explanation that the most appropriate Latin translation of the Greek term EPISCOPOS was superintendent (Latin superintententor).[12] Although for political reasons the areas of jurisdiction in the German lands were generally different from those of the medieval dioceses,[13] the pattern of a German prince overseeing a church by means of superintendents which emerged in most Protestant territories during the 1530s was not so very different from the pattern of the English king overseeing the church by means of bishops which by 1540, was being confirmed as the shape of the Henrician church. However, the geographical continuities in England meant that many bishops presided over dioceses which were contiguous with medieval boundaries; they were enthroned in cathedrals and presided over cathedral chapters as their medieval predecessors had done. The new dioceses that were founded after the dissolution of the monasteries, often to preserve abbey churches with royal connections and elevate them to cathedral status, mirrored the medieval structure. They too had cathedral churches with cathedral chapters, although the legal and constitutional status of the new dioceses – and indeed of all those English dioceses whose cathedral churches had until the early 1540s been monastic foundations – was not entirely clear.[14]

Heal suggests that in England the order of bishops was necessary for the preservation of traditional Catholic discipline and for the enforcement of the changes introduced by the Reformation Parliament. It was the bishops who were required to defend Henry's caesaropapism before the international community as well as to their own parochial clergy" (Heal: 1980, 106). Certainly there can be no question that bishops in the Henrician church were expected to enforce the changes ecclesiastical introduced by king and parliament. The extent to which the retention

---

11 As argued in Krentz: 2014; cf. Krentz: 2017, 30–49.

12 Augustine writes, "For thus a higher place is accorded to bishops, so that they direct and, as it were, take care of the people. For what is called *episcopos* in Greek is translated in Latin as superintendent, because he directs, because he oversees" (Commentary on Psalm 126, v. 3; in: PL 37, 1669). I am grateful to Timothy Wengert for this reference.

13 This was not always the case, as when Nikolaus Amsdorff was "ordiniert und eingeweiht" as Bishop of Naumburg in 1542. See Hendrix: 2015, 270–271; cf. Brunner: 1961.

14 The dioceses founded by Henry VIII were: Westminster (established 17 December 1540), with Westminster Abbey as its cathedral; Chester (4 August 1541); Gloucester (3 September 1541), with St Peter's Abbey church, the burial place of Edward II, which had been in Benedictine hands since the 11th century, as the cathedral.; Peterborough (4 September 1541); Bristol (4 June 1542); and Oxford (1 September 1542).

of bishops was motived by a concern for "the preservation of traditional Catholic discipline" seems harder to determine. And whilst bishops clearly were used to defend the Henrician reform of the church, others could – and indeed did – take this role. Christopher Mont or Mount, for instance, was not a bishop but was a member of every embassy sent by Henry to the Schmalkaldic League (cf. McEntegart: 2002). Moreover, it is apparent from the discussion that took place in the context of these embassies that the ordering of the church was considered a matter of adiaphora rather than what we might now call a church dividing issue is apparent from the interactions between the Wittenberg theologians and an English embassy in the winter of 1537/38 which was led by Edward Foxe, newly appointed Bishop of Hereford probably in view of precisely this role (McEntegart: 2002, 31–32). Luther's followers, the Catholic Anthony Musa commented, were concerned to observe that in the English church "monasteries, mass, indulgences, and intercessions for the dead, are pertinaciously adhered to."[15] The retention of bishops was not identified by Musa as one of the reasons why Luther and his followers were suspicious of the English developments, and it also did not emerge as a key issue in the long negotiations in the spring of 1538. There were on-going disagreements relating to Henry's divorce from Katherine of Aragon, about which the Wittenbergers continued to be unhappy. Moreover, although some agreement had been reached and articulated in what have come to be known as the Wittenberg Articles,[16] there were "no slight differences about other articles of doctrine."[17] These centred on private masses, clerical marriage, monastic vows, and the reception of communion in both kinds (McEntegart: 2002, 55–58; 60); church order was not identified as an issue. Similarly, Bucer's advice to Cranmer regarding the English Reformation took account of the episcopal structure of the English Church.[18] Bucer believed that overseers, pastors, elders and deacons were all necessary offices to fulfil the ministry of the church, and he seems to have understood England's bishops as fulfilling the role of overseer,[19] although he affirmed that "the bishop could not properly fulfil his office 'sine reliquorum presbyterorum consilio'" (Collinson: 1966, 107). What was important to the German reformers, as they emphasised when defining the

15 Antony Musa to Stephen Rothe, 16 January 1536: CR 3, col. 12–14 (no. 1389); LP 10, 38–39 (no. 112).

16 The Wittenberg Articles draw heavily on the *Confessio Augustana*. The only extant copy was discovered in Wittenberg in 1907; the text can be found in Documents: 2004, 118–161. For a in my view, rightly, cautious assessment their influence in England, see McEntegert: 2002, 58–60.

17 Melanchthon to Camerarius, 29 March 1536: MBW 2, 242–243, MBW T7, 7 (no. 1714); cf. CR 3, col. 52–53 (no. 1409); LP 10, 230 (no. 584). NB: CR and LP have 30 March 1536.

18 Van 't Spijker (1996, 387), citing Bucer's letters to Calvin and Farel, 14 August 1549 (CO 13: 356); cf. Collinson: 1966, 107; 109, referring to Martin Bucer, *De Regno Christi* II (BOL 15: 118–130).

19 Spijker: 1996, 387; 389. In Bucer's view, however, "wider oversight and government of religion [...] does not mean more ministerial power" (Spijker: 1996, 423).

church in the Augsburg confession, was that the true gospel be preached and the sacraments properly administered (*Confessio Augustana*, art. X). Increasingly, they recognised that structures needed to be defined in order that clergy could be trained to ensure that this was the case; however, they were relatively unconcerned about the particular shape of those structures.

2. Bishops in the later Tudor Reformation

2.1 The Episcopate under Edward VI

Under Henry VIII, then, the monarch became responsible for maintenance and continuation of ministry in the realm. As Carleton recognises, by the end of his reign, "ministry within the Church could only be exercised with the consent and authority of the secular ruler […] The King had effectively taken on all responsibility for the continuation and maintenance of ecclesiastical office in the English Church by virtue of his supreme headship" (Carleton: 2001, 24). This situation continued under Edward VI, or more specifically his under his Regents. That episcopal authority was to be understood as derived through the king is evident from the fact that on Edward's accession, as after the Act of Supremacy, the bishops were again required to petition for licences to exercise office (Carleton: 2001, 24; Heal: 1980, 126). Moreover, in a move against which Gardiner protested, the episcopal commissions then issued included the word "delegate", implying that bishops "could not exercise jurisdiction by virtue of their power as ordinaries but only as royal deputies," and removed several functions which had previously been regarded as episcopal, including that of visitation (Heal: 1980, 127–128). In recognition of this, ordinary episcopal jurisdiction was suspended during the general visitation of 1547, and although bishops were given authority to carry out subsequent visitations they received this in their capacity as royal commissioners (Carleton: 2001, 24–25). Moreover, from 1548, licences to preach could be issued only by the king (Carleton: 2001, 25). Somerset's government also abolished the system of *congé d'élire*, which had given the church "at least a semblance of independent election to its highest offices" (Heal: 1980, 126). The result, as Heal observes, was to emphasise the dependence of the bishops on the monarchy, and the similarity between the power of bishops and other servants of the crown (Heal: 1980, 127). This was not, however, evident from the new ordinal of 1550, which made no mention of the king except to require each ordinand to swear an oath recognising the king's supremacy, and to include in the consecration service of bishops and archbishops the reading of the king's mandate for their consecration (Carleton: 2001, 25). It also, as observed at the outset of this paper, affirmed the three-fold ministry, which Cranmer must have known was not the pattern of ministry used in other reformed territories.

Diarmaid MacCulloch suggests that Cranmer's assertion may have been a strategy to win approval for the revised ordinal from the more conservative bishops, similar to the addition of 'commonly called the Mass' to the title of the Lord's Supper in the 1549 Book of Common Prayer, which had helped it to pass the Lords.[20] It may also have been intended as reassurance to the imperial ambassador. Heal believes that the need to appease the Emperor and to keep him from interfering in England's negotiations with Scotland was a key reason why moves towards appropriating episcopal wealth and reconfiguring the bishop as "a preaching supervisor supported by an appropriate 'competent maintenance'" resulted in less radical reforms than might initially have been envisaged. Apart from the political complexities facing the regency, and the diplomatic interest in not alienating the emperor, the bishops also helped to stabilise the new religious structures and thus contributed to the maintenance of national stability (Heal: 1980, 128–130). Nonetheless, Heal shows that some sees lost substantial value between 1547 and 1549, mainly through the ceding of manors by the bishop to the king or to the nobility (Heal: 1980, 130–132), and in the second half of the reign Somerset too showed an "essentially acquisitive" attitude towards ecclesiastical property (Heal: 1980, 137–138). Heal postulates that these policies were intended to achieve "a levelling of all episcopal wealth" and a humbling of the bishops "whilst leaving them with the means to perform their new duties as Protestant supervisors" (Heal: 1980, 146). However, Edward's death at the age of fifteen, just six years after his accession, means that it is impossible to say with any certainty what the outcome of a longer-term Edwardian Reformation would have been.

2.2 The Episcopate under Mary I

Mary Tudor ascended to the English throne in 1553, after a nine-day interlude under the Protestant Lady Jane Grey, whom Edward had been persuaded to nominate as his heir in an attempt to preserve England's Protestantism. It was clear that Mary wold seek to return England to papal authority, and she did, abolishing Letters Patent and restoring the *congé d'élire* in 1553 (at least in theory: in reality she continued to exercise powers of appointment) (Loades: 1997, 181–182; Loades: 2005, 40; 55; cf. Duffy: 2009, 23–25), and March 1554 instructing bishops to cease to use the clause "*Regia auctoritate fulcitus*" in their "ecclesiastical writings in process, or other extrajudicial acts" (cited according to Carleton: 2001, 27). In November 1554, England was reconciled with the see of Rome. In consequence, Carleton observes, for much of 1554 "the authority of the Marian bishops was no longer sustained or upheld by the Queen's authority [...] [and] their authority was not

---

20 Diarmaid MacCulloch to Charlotte Methuen, private communication 20.05.2016.

derived from the pope either [...] For all practical purposes the bishops were, for that period, acting on the sole authority of episcopal order alone" (Carleton: 2001, 27). Additionally, Mary sought to return bishops to their previous status, returning episcopal lands where possible and forgiving debts; nonetheless, as under Edward VI, her bishops did not generally exercise secular functions. The bishops appointed during her reign were theologically educated, rather than being lawyers or diplomats. The expectation of both Mary and Pole was that the bishops must be the key in the task of restoring the church, although Loades suggests that initially the episcopate was burdened by too many who lacked the necessary "zeal and commitment", and that this was only corrected in the second half of Mary's reign (Loades: 2005, 55). Under Pole, diocesan seminaries were established; he sought to regulate diocesan finances and the Diocese of Durham received new statutes (Duffy: 2009, 25–28; Loades: 1997, 181–183; Mayer: 2005, 149–175). The episcopate was central to this project: at the London Synod in 1556, Pole argued that the bishops must "rectify their non-residency and preach the gospel to the flocks they should love."[21] Edwards notes the influence of Spanish Dominicans on the Marian church, particularly Bartolomé Carranza. Like Pole, the Spanish Dominicans encouraged preaching, and placed a strong emphasis on ecclesiastical – above all clerical – discipline imposed through diocesan structures of visitation by bishops and control of parishes by clergy (Edwards: 2005, 201–226). Carleton sees these developments as entirely congruent with the reformation of the episcopate being proposed across early modern Catholicism (Carleton: 2001, 30–32), and indeed the Marian church picked up on many aspects of the kinds of diocesan reform which had been popular with the *spirituali* – amongst them Pole – and other humanist influence Catholic reformers in the first third of the sixteenth century, and offered a precursor for the kind of reforms envisaged by the third phase of the Council of Trent (1561–1563). The significance of the renewal of diocesan structures and parish discipline under Mary and Pole for the shape of the Elizabethan Settlement and its long-term success should not be underestimated. In addition, Mary's reforms also demonstrated that even the most devout nobles who had gained property from the dissolution of the monasteries or the exchange of church lands would not consider returning it (Heal: 1980, 150–156). However, the re-catholicization of England and the persecution of Protestants during Mary's reign also prompted the development of a more radical approach to church order. Heal suggests that it was in 1554 that the question of the abolition of the episcopacy first began to be explored seriously in England (Heal: 1980, 144), and Yarnell notes that "among the exiles, self-government became a

---

21 Yarnell: 2013, 260. Pole believed that the bishops had a responsibility not only to reform the clergy, but also to influence and reform the papacy when needed: the pope's office, he taught, "must be carried out in the midst of the bishops, for all bishops share equally in the succession, and papal inerrancy 'inhered in the college of cardinals, not the pope'" (Yarnell: 2013, 258–269).

way of life", with some, including the future Archbishop of York, Edwin Sandys, having experienced and approved congregational self-government", and specifically "congregational election and discipline of ministers" (Yarnell: 2013, 265). By the mid sixteenth century, Calvin's reflections on the role of bishops and his advocacy of a fourfold ministry of doctors (i.e. teachers), preachers, elders and deacons had begun to emerge as an alternative way of thinking about church order. English divines began to consider whether the church might not be better off without bishops at all, and those who were exiled to the German lands and particularly to the Swiss confederation and founded or became involved in strangers' churches there found themselves having a quite different ecclesiological experience.[22] This too was a legacy bequeathed by the Marian restoration to the Elizabethan English church.

2.3 The Episcopate under Elizabeth I

It is perhaps not surprising, therefore, that it was in the reign of Elizabeth that deep conflicts about the retention of episcopacy in the English church began to surface. The differences began to emerge as the Settlement took shape. Brett Usher argues convincingly that "there must be a very strong presumption" that in the first eleven months of Elizabeth's reign William Cecil, her main adviser at this period was in favour of the type of reforms proposed by Armigail Waad and Robert Beale which would have transformed bishops from prelates who drew incomes from their own estates into "superintendents" with fixed salaries (Usher: 2003, 14–15). However, Elizabeth herself "held grimly and tenaciously" to the principle of *cuius regio, eius religio*, which resulted in a "refusal to countenance any fundamental alteration of the episcopal order" (Usher: 2003, 4; 182). The 1559 Settlement re-established the controls over the English bishops (and indeed all clergy) which had been put in place under Henry VIII, although it did not reintroduce all of the Edwardian developments: the *congé d'élire* was maintained, and thus the formality of appointment by the cathedral chapter, although in practice a royal mandate commanding the chapter to elect the candidate of the Queen's choice was sent to the chapter together with the *congé d'élire* itself (Heal: 1980, 205; for the practice, see Usher: 2003, 11). Through the Act of Exchange, moreover, the government provided "a general framework for appropriations from the bishops" which replaced the practice of seeking to acquire or exchange property from individual dioceses (Heal: 1980, 204–210; Usher: 2003, 13–14). The power base of the Elizabethan bishops,

---

22 Usher cites the example of one London congregation which ordained its own ministers without episcopal involvement. As the new Elizabethan bishop of London, Grindal validated several of these ministers' ordinations (Usher: 1997, 233–251; cf. Yarnell: 2013, 265).

although they continued to be "members of the House of Lords, possessors for life of landed estates, and prominent leaders – moral, judicial, financial and military – of provincial society" (Usher: 2003, 5), was thus significantly eroded. This left the episcopate with a problem: "the crown was expecting its senior clerics to discharge their secular duties as effectively as they had done before the Reformation, but [...] it failed to offer them the support which would have given them the authority and enthusiasm to fulfil those duties" (Heal: 1980, 236). Indeed, many of the Elizabethan bishops did not view these secular responsibilities as proper to the episcopal office. Usher recognises that, "it was possible for many who had not succumbed to Genevan advances to return home as committed Elizabethans and yet to view with various degrees of suspicion and dismay the reimposition of unfettered state control of ecclesiastical affairs" (Usher: 2003, 19). However, it was also possible for bishops appointed by this state system to understand their role in ways which stood in tension with the queen's perception of it. The conflict between Archbishop Grindal and the queen is one example of these tensions, which from the 1570s gave rise to significant differences about polity. In Cambridge, Thomas Cartwright envisaged a polity in which lay leaders or elders would be responsible with the priest to instil godliness to the church at the parish level (Yarnell: 2013, 267–268). Yarnell suggests that there was an ecclesiological difference here: whilst puritans generally wanted to localise power in the parish and believed that godly consciences should decide liturgy and other "indifferent" matters, for the upholders of the royal supremacy and episcopal jurisdiction, it was the monarch who should decide ceremonial questions or other adiaphora (Yarnell: 2013, 265). Conflict arose, since "in calling for 'an equality of ministers' and for the *classis* to oversee not just the education of but the governance of the parishes, the puritans shifted from meddling in the realm of conscience to meddling with the queen's realm" (Yarnell: 2013, 268). Elizabeth took measures to suppress these ideas, but they did not disappear (Collinson: 1967, 92–108).

Overall, however, as Yarnell suggests, "the progressive Elizabethan bishops saw their primary responsibility as reforming the ministry to that the land would be filled with preachers" (Yarnell: 2013, 264, drawing on Wenig: 2000, 147–153; 159–161; 222–223; 228), and the Settlement offered them a means of achieving this end. Wenig shows how John Jewel, Edwin Sandys and James Pilkington, as bishops of Salisbury, Worcester, and Durham, respectively, tackled opposition to reform in their dioceses: "to change the faith of the English church, the Protestant prelates used the traditional diocesan machinery of episcopal visitations and clerical appointments to uproot popery, reform the ministry, and promote the new religion" (Wenig: 2000, 184–185). He observes, however, that, "when faced with a significant degree of Catholic opposition in the dioceses, the bishops were forced to turn to the power of central government in order to make headway at the local level" (Wenig: 2000, 185).

3. Bishops and the Scottish Reformation

Thus far this discussion has proceeded, as discussions of the English Reformation so often do, as though there were only one political territory in what Diarmaid MacCulloch likes to term the Atlantic Islands (2003, xxvi). Whilst it is legitimate to consider the English and Welsh – and to some extent the Irish – churches together at this period, the course of the Reformation in Scotland, as a separate and politically distinct nation, was quite different. By 1603, when James VI of Scotland on Elizabeth's death succeeded her as James I of England, thus uniting the crowns, the Scottish church had – at least in theory – opted for a Presbyterian system of church government, and James and his successors found themselves king of two nations with entirely different churches and polities. The tensions surrounding the ordering of the Scottish church led to major political conflicts during the seventeenth century, which affected not only Scotland but also England, leading to civil war and the period of the Interregnum during which both episcopacy and the Scottish form of Presbyterian, which formed a national church, were both suppressed in favour of congregationalism.

The different approaches taken in Scotland and England towards episcopacy and church polity during the Reformation reflected the very different political theologies which underlay the Reformations of those counties. But the differences between the Scottish and English churches did not begin with the Reformation. Considering the situation of the Scottish church in the late fifteenth century shows a very different picture of the relationship between bishops, monarch and nobility than that of England. Scotland's ecclesiastical structures were much more recent than those of the English church. Until the fifteenth century, the jurisdictional authority over the Scottish church did not lie within Scotland, Scottish dioceses were nominally under the jurisdiction of the Archbishops of Trondheim or of York, both of whom were established political forces in territories with which the Scottish kings not infrequently found themselves in conflict or at the least diplomatic negotiation (Dawson: 2007, 17). By the latter half of the fifteenth century the Scottish dioceses had essentially become an independent province under the direct jurisdiction of the pope, who in 1476 elevated the bishop of St Andrews to archbishop, giving his jurisdiction over all the Scottish dioceses. This development was resisted by king, by the other Scottish bishops and by the Archbishop of York. In 1492 the diocese of Glasgow also became an archdiocese and the new archbishop was given jurisdiction over Galloway, Argyle, the Isles, Dunblane, and Dunkeld, although the Archbishop of St Andrews remained primate of Scotland. A legal battle ensued and in 1493 the two archbishops were instructed to cease action against each other or lose their revenues. As Jane Dawson has observed, "the intense rivalry between the two archbishops prevented the Scottish church from acting as a single body or speaking with a single voice" (Dawson: 2007, 17). The situation of the Scottish church was further complicated by the control exercised over the church and its wealth by the Scottish king, lairds and nobility and the financial benefit which they derived from this. By 1560, two-thirds of Scotland's religious houses were headed by "commendators", who exercised power and drew revenues but did not take religious vows. Similarly, the son of the Earl of Glencairn, William Cuningham, was elected bishop of Dunkeld in 1539; fourteen years later he still remained unconsecrated, "effectively running the bishopric as part of his family's estate" (Ryrie: 2006, 14). Their power to nominate church appointments provided James IV and James V with "a pre-paid administration" and a "substantial pool of patronage and gifts"; in addition, from the 1530s James V financed his court through the imposition of heavy taxes on income from church lands, a measure to which the pope probably agreed in the hope of keeping a foothold in the British Isles (Dawson: 2007, 19–20). This does not mean, however, as Ryrie points out, that there were no calls for reform; indeed, "the high nobility continued to provide committed and able churchmen up to and beyond 1560" (Ryrie: 2006, 16). It did mean, however, that the crown, nobles and lairds, who were already drawing a high proportion of the income from Scotland's church lands, had "a strong vested interest in the status quo" (Ryrie: 2006, 16).

Another significant factor was the power struggle between different factions of the Scottish nobles and lairds which resulted from the series of Stuart minorities through the sixteenth century. James V was seventeen months old at his accession in 1513; James V's daughter Mary just six days old at his death in 1542; her son James VI thirteen months old when his mother was forced to abdicate the Scottish throne in his favour. The result was that Scotland had fifty-one years of government by Regent between 1500 and 1600; in the same period, England had six. This was destabilising both politically and ecclesiastically, for different factions amongst the nobles favoured alliance with England or with France, which from the mid-1540s – which coincided with the period of Mary's minority – also implied favouring Protestantism or Catholicism. Mary's first Regent, was James Hamilton, Earl of Arran, who in 1543 gained Parliament's approval for a betrothal between the infant queen and the young Prince Edward in England. The same year, Arran also oversaw the legalising of the New Testament in English and allowed criticism of the Pope to be expressed; however, no Reformation was introduced and no changes made to church order. Arran soon found himself having to concede to the pro-French faction, supported by the queen's mother, Mary of Guise, and the Archbishop of St Andrews, Cardinal Beaton; vernacular Bible reading was condemned, Arran was forced to recant his "heresies" publicly. However, at about the same time, George Wishart began preaching Reformation, probably Zwinglian, ideas in central Scotland. He was arrested and tried for heresy in 1545 and burned in St Andrew's in March 1546. Just weeks afterwards, Cardinal Beaton was murdered at St Andrew's castle, a siege ensued which was broken with the help of the French navy.

It is apparent from this that the Scottish bishops functioned as one power amongst many in the maelstrom of Scottish regency politics. However, bishops could also instigate reform. If a first hesitant move towards reform had been made by Arran in 1543, a second was made by John Hamilton, Arran's illegitimate half-brother, who in 1548, after a two-year vacancy, was appointed Beaton's successor as Archbishop of St Andrews. The Scottish church had been left for most of that period without clear leadership, for the Archbishop of Glasgow had died in July 1546 and was not replaced until 1552 (Dawson: 2007, 184). Hamilton, suggests Ryrie, "was not a bishop of any great moral stature," but he did initiate a programme of "vigorous renewal" (2006, 95). In 1549, Hamilton called a Provincial Council, and further Councils met in 1552, perhaps in 1556, and in 1559. Drawing on the decrees of the first session of Trent, and the reform proposals put forward by Hermann von Wied, Archbishop of Cologne, the Councils called for improved clerical discipline, better theological education (St Mary's College in St Andrews was founded in response to this call), and more regular and frequent preaching (2006, 97–98; 103–104; Dawson: 2007, 186). The 1552 council drew up a catechism and required it to be used (Ryrie: 2006, 98–100). However, the Councils neither required visitations nor put in place any other mechanism for implementing reform (Dawson: 2007, 186), and Ryrie believes that the net result may have been to weaken rather than strengthen the church (Ryrie: 2006, 96). Neither was there much contact to the English church, although at this period it had returned to Catholicism and Pole was implementing a very similar programme of Catholic Reform with rather more success (2003, 130–131). Clare Kellar describes the religious relationships and links between England and Scotland throughout the period 1534 and 1560 as "multifaceted", but identifies a "nominal Catholic consensus between the governments during the 1550s" (Kellar: 2003, 221; 220). Dawson in contrast identifies a decision of Scottish and English churches to remain "determinedly separate" at this crucial time which she considers "a weakness that contributed to Catholicism's defeat in both British kingdoms in the following decade" (Dawson: 2007, 185–186). However, given the very different situations of the two churches and their bishops, and particularly the English's episcopate's close connection to the queen, it is hard to see how they could have worked together to introduce reform. Ryrie's analysis, that Hamilton "lacked the political support necessary to finish what he had begun" (2006, 96), seems more plausible and reflects the fragmented nature of Scottish power and authority whether political or ecclesiastical. Kellar points out that not only religious opinion, but also "varying levels of state intervention, and contrasting political circumstances" led to varying degrees of success (2003, 131).

When Reformation came in 1560 it was, suggests Ryrie, the result of a "complex three-way negotiation between reformist Catholicism, radicalising Protestantism and a non-confrontational regime [which] could have had several outcomes" (2006, 197). The actual outcome was heavily shaped by the theological interests of John

Knox, who had spent several years in Geneva, where he had become a protégé of Calvin. Knox was influenced by Calvin's vision of the Reformed ministry, and he and the other Scottish Reformers faced the challenge of extending a system designed for a comparatively small territory to the situation of a national church. But it was also shaped by French policies towards the Reformation – in 1559 Mary's husband François became King of France, making Mary Queen of not only Scotland but also France. This was a period in French engagement with the Reformation in which the Protestant church was being allowed to take shape in France. In 1559 the French National Synod in Paris drew up a confession of faith and an order of church discipline. This brief period of tolerance was reflected in Scottish policies. Also significant was the death of Mary of Guise in June 1560 at a crucial juncture, leaving Scotland with an absentee monarch just as the Reformation was being officially implemented. Mary Queen of Scots returned to Scotland in 1561, after the death of François I on 5 December 1560, five days before her 18th birthday. As the Reformation church in Scotland took shape, Mary and her court were allowed to continue to have mass celebrated at the court in Holyrood, and tensions characterised her relationship to John Knox and other Scottish Reformers (see, for instance, Dawson: 2015, 234–239).

In 1560/61, as part of the *Book of Discipline*, the Reformers proposed a new structure of ministry. As Donaldson observes, the reformers "acknowledged the need for a rank of clergy who should have the oversight of inferior ministers," and proposed to appoint ten superintendents, each responsible for around one hundred parishes, who would admit an supervise parochial clergy and undertake visitations in their "dioceses" and receive an annual salary of between 500 marks plus barley, meal and oats (Donaldson 1987, ix-x; John Knox: 1966/1985, 289). However, since the Book of Discipline did not receive parliamentary approval, this proposal received no financial support. Instead, earlier church appointees continued to draw their normal revenues, although they were expected to give up one third, of which a proportion went to fund Reformed preaching. The Reformed church was radically under-financed (Kirk: 1980, 30; 35–36). Moreover, only five superintendents were ever appointed (Donaldson: 1987, ix; see also Sykes: 1956, 45–46), and they were indeed appointed, and not elected as the Book of Discipline ultimately intended. The bishops continued in post with a guaranteed stipend for life. Although, as Donaldson (1987) has shown, three of them at least proceeded to engage in the reforming their dioceses (Alexander Gordon, Bishop of Galloway; Adam Bothwell, Bishop of Orkney; and Robert Stuart, Bishop of Caithness), this was not the way that Knox and his followers had envisaged that the church would be ordered.

In 1578, under the influence of Andrew Melville, the *Second Book of Discipline* removed "superintendents", introducing in their stead a national Presbyterian (synodical) structure of kirk sessions (i.e. parish councils), regional presbyteries and the national general assembly.[23] This represented an attempt to devise a national structure for Scotland's Kirk which would enable it to function without the need for superintendents or bishops. Adopted by the 1588 General Assembly, the Second Book of Discipline effectively did away with any possibility that the king could influence the appointment of key ecclesiastical leaders. The proposal was not formally accepted by James VI until 1592, and then only reluctantly. In 1599, James moved to reintroduce episcopacy, and in 1604, by which time he had succeeded also to the English throne, he tried to suppress the General Assembly. In 1610/1611, three Scottish bishops were consecrated by four English diocesan bishops under the Great Seal of England as part of a move to restore episcopacy in Scotland.[24] However, this was episcopacy on a different footing to the English episcopate: presbyteries and kirk sessions were to continue, with the bishops working through and with them (cf. Todd: 2004, 305–306). The General Assembly also continued to meet, although James frequently sought to suspend it as though it were parliament (Stewart, 2006, 152; 160). Having found himself, from 1603, king of two countries with very differently organised churches, James VI/I arguably sought to bring together what he understood to be the best aspects of both systems: episcopacy on the English model for Scotland, but better preaching on the Scottish model for England. Charles Prior sees this period as defined by "a ceremonial and episcopal ecclesiology" which "placed a high premium on conformity, and with it a universal concept of the church" (Prior: 2012, 35). Underpinning this approach was "the proposition that the disruption of the church entailed a disruption of the commonwealth and its fundamental laws" (Prior: 2012, 34). However, although this assumption was shared in Scotland and England, it could not disguise the very different theologies of kingship found in the two churches and nations: in Scotland James VI was a member of the Kirk, subject to the authority of Christ and the discipline of the church, and not the mediator of God's will and Supreme Governor, as James I found himself in the English Church.

In 1617, James VI required the Kirk to observe the festivals of the Christian year, to administer Episcopal confirmation, to allow private baptisms and private communion for the sick and to instruct that communion be received kneeling. These requirements were accepted by the 1618 General Assembly – the Five Articles of Perth – but there was wide-spread disobedience, especially with regard to kneeling to receive communion, and concerns that the Kirk was being expected to revert to "papist" practices (Stewart: 2006; cf. Stewart: 2007, 1013–1036). James's successor, his son Charles I, who had never lived in Scotland, did nothing to calm

---

23 John Knox: 1980, chapter 7, "Of the Elderships, and Assemblies, and Discipline".
24 See Sykes (1956, 101–106), who also offers a comparison of the ordination rites used in Scotland and England.

the Scots' fears. Charles' coronation at Holyrood Abbey in 1633 not only did not take place at the traditional Scottish coronation sites of Scone or Stirling, but also included elements that to Scottish eyes seemed suspiciously Catholic: the Abbey was reordered with a platform at east end on which the communion table had been placed in an elevated position and upon which candles had been placed; a tapestry including a depiction of the crucifixion was hung on the wall behind the table, and the coronation took place in the context of a celebration of the English Book of Common Prayer's service of Holy Communion. Of the Scottish bishops present, half were on the dais in rochets, surplices and copes, and "were seen to bow their knee and beck", whilst the other half sat in the congregation in black gowns.[25] Charles subsequently allowed (or encouraged) his Archbishop of Canterbury William Laud to propose a revised version of England's Book of Common Prayer for Scotland.[26] On its introduction in 1637, there were widespread protests, leading to the drafting and signing of the National Covenant in 1638, which emphasised the Protestant nature of the Church of Scotland, sought to define the king's relationship to the church and – in an additional statement, added later – rejected the appointment of bishops for Scotland. The conflict came to centre on the question of whether or not the church had bishops, but this debate was at a deeper level a statement about the relationship of the monarch to the church. Similar unhappiness about the Erastian intertwining of church and state in the English settlement existed in England, although in the English context there was no church- and nation-wide proposal for an alternative. When episcopacy was rejected by Oliver Cromwell and his followers during the Commonwealth, it was not (despite the frequent claims to the contrary) the presbyterian system to which they turned, but as observed above, a more loosely congregationally based structure. In return for the support of the Scots, Charles II swore an oath committing himself to restore the presbyterian polity to Scotland should he succeed in reclaiming the throne. However, when the Commonwealth collapsed and was succeeded by the restoration of the monarchy in 1660, Charles reneged on this promise, introducing episcopacy across England and Scotland, including, in England what Sykes sees as "the outstanding innovation of the Anglican restoration settlement [...] the unvarying requirement of episcopal ordination for ministry" (Sykes: 1956, 118). It was not until the 1690 ecclesiastical settlement, introduced after the accession of William and Mary to the English and Scottish thrones in 1688, that presbyterian polity was lastingly established in Scotland. It did so, as Ann Shukman has argued, as part of a move to abolish in Scotland both the 1669 Act of Supremacy, which gave the monarch "unrestricted

---

25 Harris: 2014, 363–364; cf. Shaw (2004, 481–502) explores the reasons for the choice of Holyrood over St Giles as the place of Charles' coronation.

26 For Archbishop William Laud's role in devising the 1636 Scottish Canons and the 1637 Scottish Prayer Book, see James: 2017, 506–525.

authority over the Church" and the Lords of the Articles, in whose hands much of the authority over the Scottish parliament lay, and who under James VI had often been appointed by the king.[27] Reform of ecclesiastical polity and of political structures here went hand in hand, reinforcing a very different understanding of godly kingship than that being presented in Restoration in England.[28]

Conclusions

This paper has suggested that light is can be shed on the varying polities of the Reformation churches, and particularly their respective political theologies, by considering these against the backdrop of pre-Reformation patterns of relationships between bishops and territorial rulers. The situation and status of a bishop in England and his relationship to the king of England was quite different from the situation or status of a bishop in the German lands, and his relationship to the local lords and princes. The challenges posed by implementing the reformation in a smaller territory within a diocese or one which straddled two or more diocesan boundaries was a quite different proposition from those posed by implementing the reformation into a country in which the bishops were – at least to some extent – subjects of the king. Although the example of Scotland seems to show how the Reformation might also be introduced into a nation in such a way as to redefine the relationship between church, nation and king, it is clear that the Reformation proposals, whilst strongly influenced by the principles proposed by John Calvin, could take advantage of much less well-defined relationships between bishop and monarch in the pre-Reformation era. Much more work needs to be done, but this initial consideration suggests that later mediaeval relationships between bishops and rulers are deserving of closer comparative study by Reformation historians.

Bibliography

Sources

ACT OF SUPREMACY (1534), The Act of Supremacy, 1534, in: Documents of the English Reformation, Gerald Bray (ed.), Cambridge: James Clarke, corrected edition 2004, 113–114.

---

27 For the Convention and Parliament of 1689 which proclaimed William and Mary king and queen of Scotland and the series Claim of Right and the Articles of Grievances which William and Mary recognised as part of this process, see Shukman: 2012, 27–46; for the shape of the settlement: 89–103.

28 Rose (2011) traces the different approaches to monarchy in England in this period and the relationship between these and the earlier ideals discussed above.

CANONS (1529–1947), The Anglican Canons, 1529–1947, Gerald Bray (ed.), Church of England Record Society 6, Woodbridge: Boydell 1998.

DOCUMENTS (2004), Documents of the English Reformation, Geralt Bray (ed.), Cambridge: James Clarke.

HENRY VIII (1521), Assertio septem sacramentorum.

HENRY VIII (1908), Defence of the seven sacraments, Louis O'Donovan (trans.), New York: Beziger Brothers, 395–429.

JOHN KNOX (1966/1985), First Book of Discipline, in: The Works of John Knox, D. Laing (ed.), New York: AMS Press, 1966/Edinburgh, 1985, vol. 2, 183–360.

JOHN KNOX (1980), The Second Book of Discipline, J. Kirk (ed.), Edinburgh: Saint Andrew Press.

Secondary Literature

BRANDT, HANS-JÜRGEN (1988), Furstbischof und Weihbischof im Spätmittelalter. Zur Darstellung der 'sacri ministerii summa' des reichskirchlichen Episkopats, in: W. Brandmüller e.a. (ed.), Ecclesia militans. Studien zur Konzilien- und Reformationsgeschichte. FS R. Bäumer, Paderborn: Ferdinand Schöningh, vol. 1, 1–16.

BRUNNER, PETER (1961), Nikolaus von Amsdorf als Bischof von Naumburg, Gütersloh: Gütersloher Verlagshaus.

BUTT, ARNE (2014), 'Wir sehen nicht gerne Unordnung'. Protestantische Kirchenleitungsmodelle und Ordnungsprinzipien on Konsistorialordnungen des 16. Jahrhunderts, in: Irene Dingel/Armin Kohnle (ed.), Gute Ordnung. Ordnungsmodelle und Ordnungsvorstellungen in der Reformationszeit, Leipzig: Evangelische Verlagsanstalt, 49–64.

CARLETON, KENNETH (2001), Bishops and Reform in the English Church, 1520–1559, Woodbridge: Boydell.

COLLINSON, PATRICK (1966), Episcopacy and Reform in England in the Later Sixteenth Century, Studies in Church History 3, 91–125.

COLLINSON, PATRICK (1967), Elizabethan Puritan movement, Oxford: Clarendon.

DAWSON, JANE (2007), Scotland Re-Formed, 1488–1587, Edinburgh: Edinburgh University Press.

DAWSON, JANE (2015), John Knox, New Haven: Yale University Press.

DONALDSON, GORDON (1987), Reformed by Bishops, Edinburgh: Edina Press.

DUFFY, EAMON (2009), Fires of Faith: Catholic England under Mary Tudor, New Haven: Yale University Press.

EDWARDS, JOHN (2005), Spanish Influence in Marian England, in: Eamon Duffy/David Loades (ed.), The Church of Mary Tudor, Ashgate: Aldershot, 201–226.

FLÜCHTER, ANTJE (2006), Der Zölibat zwischen Devianz und Norm: Kirchenpolitik und Gemeindealltag in den Herzogtümern Jülich und Berg im 16. und 17. Jahrhundert, Köln: Böhlau.

HARRIS, TIM (2014), Rebellion: Britain's First Stuart Kings, 1567–1642, Oxford: Oxford

University Press.

HEAL, FELICITY (1980), Of Prelates and Princes: A Study of the Economic and Social Position of the Tudor Episcopate, Cambridge: Cambridge University Press.

HENDRIX, SCOTT H. (2015), Martin Luther: Visionary Reformer, New Haven: Yale University Press.

JAMES, LEONIE (2017), 'I was no "master of this work" but a servant to it'? William Laud, Charles I and the making of Scottish ecclesiastical policy, 1634–6, Historical Research 90, 506–525.

KELLAR, CLAIRE (2003), Scotland, England, and the Reformation, 1534–61, Oxford: Clarendon Press.

KIRK, JAMES (1980), 'The Polities of the Best Reformed Kirks': Scottish Achievements and English Aspirations in Church Government after the Reformation, Scottish Historical Review 59, 22–53.

KRARUP, MARTIN (2007), Ordination in Wittenberg: die Einsetzung in das kirchliche Amt in Kursachsen zur Zeit der Reformation, Tübingen: Mohr Siebeck.

KRENTZ, NATALIE (2014), Ritualwandel und Deutungshoheit. Die frühe Reformation in der Residenzstadt Wittenberg (1500–1533), Tübingen: Mohr Siebeck.

KRENTZ, NATALIE (2017), The Making of the Reformation: The Early Urban Reformation Between Continuity and Change, Reformation and Renaissance Review 19, 30–49.

LOADES, DAVID (1997), Tudor government: structures of authority in the sixteenth century, Oxford: Blackwell.

LOADES, DAVID (2005), The Marian Episcopate, in: Eamon Duffy/David Loades (ed.), The Church of Mary Tudor, Ashgate: Aldershot, 33–56.

MACCULLOCH, DIARMAID (2003), Reformation: Europe's House Divided, London: Allen Lane.

MAYER, THOMAS F. (2005), The success of Cardinal Pole's final legation, in: Eamon Duffy/-David Loades (ed.), The Church of Mary Tudor, Ashgate: Aldershot, 149–175.

McENTEGART, RORY (2002), Henry VIII, the League of Schmalkalden, and the English Reformation, Woodbridge: Boydell.

McGRATH, ALISTER E. (2012), Reformation Thought: An Introduction, 4th edition, Oxford: Wiley-Blackwell.

METHUEN, CHARLOTTE (1994), Securing the Reformation through Education: The Duke's Scholarship System of Sixteenth Century Württemberg, Sixteenth Century Journal 25, 841–851.

METHUEN, CHARLOTTE (2017), The German Catholic Dioceses and their Bishops on the Eve of the Reformation, in: Derek R. Nelson/Paul R. Hinlicky (ed.), Oxford Research Encyclopedia on Martin Luther, Oxford: Oxford University Press, vol. 1, 521–538.

MICHEL, STEFAN, 'Der Unterricht der Visitatoren' (1528). Die erste Kirchenordnung der von Wittenberg ausgehenden Reformation?, in: Irene Dingel/Armin Kohnle (ed.), Gute Ordnung. Ordnungsmodelle und Ordnungsvorstellungen in der Reformationszeit, Leipzig: Evangelische Verlagsanstalt, 153–167.

PRIOR, CHARLES W. A. (2012), A Confusion of Tongues: Britain's Wars of Reformation, 1625–1642, Oxford: Oxford University Press.

RICHARD, CHARLES-LOUIS (1760), Dictionnaire universel, dogmatique, canonique, historique, géographique et chronologique des sciences ecclésiastiques, 3 vols., Paris.

ROSE, JACQUELINE (2011), Godly Kingship in Restoration England: the Politics of the Royal Supremacy 1660–1688, Cambridge: Cambridge University Press.

RYRIE, ALEC (2006), The Origins of the Scottish Reformation, Manchester: Manchester University Press.

SCHNEIDER-LUDORFF, GURY (2006), Philipp of Hesse as an Example of Princely Reformation: A Contribution to Reformation Studies, Reformation & Renaissance Review 8, 301–319.

SHAW, DOUGAL (2004), St. Giles' church and Charles I's coronation visit to Scotland, Historical Research 77, 481–502.

SHUKMAN, ANN (2012), Bishops and covenanters: religion and politics in Scotland 1688–1691, Edinburgh: John Donald.

SMITH, RALPH F. (1996), Luther, ministry, and ordination rites in the early reformation church, New York: Lang.

SPIJKER, WILLEM VAN 'T (1996), The Ecclesiastical Offices in the Thought of Martin Bucer, Leiden: Brill.

SPITZ, LEWIS W. (1953), Luther's Ecclesiology and his Concept of the Prince as 'Notbischof', Church History 22, 113–141.

STEWART, LAURA (2006), 'Brothers in Treuth': Propaganda, Public Opinion and the Perth Articles Debate in Scotland, in: Ralph Houlbrooke (ed.), James VI and I: Ideas, Authority, and Government, Aldershot: Ashgate, 151–168.

STEWART, LAURA (2007), The Political Repercussions of the Five Articles of Perth: A Reassessment of James VI and I's Religious Policies in Scotland, Sixteenth Century Journal 38, 1013–1036.

SYKES, NORMAN (1956), Old priest and new presbyter: Episcopacy and Presbyterianism since the Reformation with especial relation to the Churches of England and Scotland, being the Gunning lectures delivered in the University of Edinburgh 1953–54 and the Edward Cadbury lectures in the University of Birmingham, 1954–55, Cambridge: Cambridge University Press.

TODD, MARGO (2004), Bishops in the kirk: William Cowper of Galloway and the puritan episcopacy of Scotland, Scottish Journal of Theology 57, 300–312.

USHER, BRETT (1997), In time of persecution: New light on the secret Protestant congregation in Marian London, in: David Loades (ed.), John Foxe and the English Reformation, Aldershot: Scolar, 233–251.

USHER, BRETT (2003), William Cecil and episcopacy, 1559–1577, Aldershot: Ashgate.

WENIG, SCOTT A. (2000), Straightening the altars: the ecclesiastical vision and pastoral achievements of the progressive bishops under Elizabeth I, 1559–1579, New York: Lang.

YARNELL III, MALCOLM B. (2013), Royal priesthood in the English reformation, Oxford: Oxford University Press.

Florian Wöller

Corpus and *Communio*

Two Key Themes of Late Medieval Ecclesiology

The conviction that the Church is more than just a gathering of individual people loosely held together by an ecclesiastical organization is as old as the church itself.[1] Likewise, also the history of theological reflection on the Church goes back to the apostolic beginnings of Christianity. First of all, it was Paul who wrote about the universal Church in his letters to particular churches throughout the Mediterranean, conveying to them that they belong to something bigger, transcending, as it were, the local community or assembly. Paul, however, did not just reflect on the external dimensions of the ecclesiastical community but also on its religious and spiritual nature. Generally speaking, two ideas were central to his ecclesiology: first, the certainty and the desire that "Christ [is] in me" (e.g. Gal 2:20) and that all are "in Christ" (e.g. Gal 3:26); and second the vision of the Church as "body of Christ" complete with head (e.g. Eph 1:22f) and members (e.g. 1 Cor 12:27). As is well known, Paul's terminology acquired a tremendously formative influence in the history of ecclesiology, a history that, like any other, went through rises and declines both in quantity and quality.

As to the quantitative aspect, the late medieval period of this history may be characterized as a time of ecclesiological emergence. Assessing the political and religious conflicts in the fourteenth and fifteenth centuries, from the struggle between pope Boniface VIII and king Philip IV down to the Great Western Schism, I take Francis Oakley's words as a guiding principle: "Taken as a whole, [...] the writings produced by all these crises confront us with a body of thought on matters ecclesiological at once more extensive, more varied, more developed, and more systematic than anything emerging from the centuries preceding" (Oakley: 1979, 158). Thus, my contribution on late medieval ecclesiology to this volume on 'Church' in the time of the Reformation does not seem to be in need of any further justification.

Yet, Oakley also mentions the qualitative rise in late medieval ecclesiology. In this respect, the presence of my contribution in this volume deserves another remark, since at least in one of the traditional perspectives of Reformation historiography it was Martin Luther who rehabilitated ecclesiology and purged it of the medieval

---

1 Evidently, the word 'church' has many meanings. In order to distinguish those that are most important for the present chapter, I have capitalized 'Church' when referring to the idea or concept, while the lower case 'church' refers to the institution, a particular church, etc.

residues of moralism, reification, and self-seeking justification. In this perspective, any medieval ecclesiology appears as not much more than a dark chapter of and a woeful deviation from the history of Christian ecclesiology (cf. Althaus: 1929, 27–36). And while I neither subscribe to this perspective, nor wish to suggest that this is the only possible view of the relation between 'medieval' and 'Reformation' ecclesiologies, the dubious reputation of late medieval ecclesiology or, to say the least, the problem of partisan denominationalism in the face of 'Reformation' and 'medieval' ecclesiologies is a burden that any reader of ecclesiological thought from either period has to deal with.[2]

This being so, my task is a discussion of nothing other than late medieval ecclesiology. I interpret this task as a necessarily incomplete and, at the same time, a sympathetic discussion of some late medieval accounts in their own right rather than as dark or bright backgrounds for 'Reformation' ecclesiology. I have chosen the accounts of Giles of Rome, Jean Quidort, John Wyclif and John of Ragusa as the objects of this discussion. However, I neither wish to suggest that these authors represent a canonical selection, nor will I discuss their accounts to the fullness of their extents.[3] Rather, I am attempting to trace their respective use of the terms *corpus* and *communio* in ecclesiological context, seeking thus to provide a common thread through what often may seem like a complex and intricate doctrinal debate. In this chapter, therefore, *corpus* and *communio* should be understood as themes rather than clear-cut concepts. This is to say that the term *corpus* does not always designate a body (of whatever kind) and that the term *communio* not always means sacramental communion. As will be clearer below, these terms rather stand for different though not mutually exclusive claims about the nature of the Church. Finally, by employing the themes *corpus* and *communio* I also hope to render the history of late medieval ecclesiology accessible to readers with primary interests in the Reformation history of ecclesiology. For although they may have quite different meanings in either period, both terms recur again and again, even beyond the Reformation and well until the present day.

The individual sections of this chapter can be read separately, as I provide historical introductions at the beginning of each of them. Every section ends with a conclusion on the ecclesiology there discussed. The final conclusion at the end of the chapter is kept on a general level. Unless stated otherwise, all translations in this chapter are mine.

---

2 Prügl (2013, 3) makes a similar point, although his own discussion transcends these limitations.

3 For an excellent and comprehensive although at times outdated survey of late medieval ecclesiology, see the respective chapters in Congar: 1971a and 1971b.

1. Introduction: *Corpus* and *Communio* in Medieval Ecclesiology

As theological terms, *corpus* and *communio* have a long history preceding the years that this chapter is concerned with.[4] Their meaning and function in ecclesiology, however, underwent momentous change during the late Middle Ages. In order to better appreciate this change, it may be helpful to begin here with a brief and somewhat general outline of the doctrinal developments leading up to the late medieval period. For this, it is paramount to note that throughout the Middle Ages *corpus* and *communio* were neither contradictory nor contrary terms in ecclesiological contexts. They both originated in sacramental theology and retained this origin in different ways until the end of the medieval era and beyond.

An early medieval exposition of the Apostles' Creed illustrates the sacramental origin of the term *communio* by expounding the term *communio sanctorum* thus: "There is sacred sharing (*communicatio sancta*) by way of the invocation of Father, Son, and Holy Spirit, where every day of the Lord all faithful must share."[5] Accordingly, the Church as *communio sanctorum* is being realized whenever there is sacramental communion.

Likewise, also the ecclesiological meaning of the term *corpus* is rooted deeply in medieval sacramental theology. Yet, to conceive of the Church as *corpus* and as *corpus Christi* more specifically was less straight forward than to conceive of it as *communio*. Throughout the medieval period *corpus* rather remained an elusive and ambiguous term, sometimes less so, and sometimes more. In the ninth century, a debate on the eucharist between the Carolingian monks Paschasius Radbertus and Gottschalk of Orbais reflected some of these ambiguities. In a treatise on the sacrament of the altar, Paschasius Radbertus had claimed that the body of Christ may be conceived of in three ways. First, following Paul's ecclesiology, *corpus Christi* could signify the Church. Second, it could be understood as a mystical body, which Radbertus took to be the consecrated bread of the eucharist. And third, *corpus Christi* could be understood as the historical body of Christ, which died on the cross. Although these three bodies are really one, Radbertus argued, they are at the same time somehow distinct.[6]

It is this latter point that Gottschalk of Orbais took issue with. He taught against Radbertus' threefold distinction that in a natural way (*naturaliter*) there is but one body of Christ, whereas in a special way (*specialiter*) there are two, namely

---

4 On Paul's use of τὸ σῶμα τοῦ Χριστοῦ in ecclesiological contexts, see Walter: 2001, ch. 5–7. For the origins of *communio sanctorum*, see Benko: 1964.

5 Burn: 1900, 130: "Sanctorum communionem. Ibi est communicatio sancta per invocationem Patris et Filii et Spiritus Sancti ubi omnes fideles omnibus diebus dominicis communicare debent".

6 Cf. Paschasius Radbertus: 1969, 37–40 (= *De corpore et sanguine Domini* VII). For a detailed discussion, see Cortoni: 2016, 113–119.

the sacramental and ecclesiastical bodies on the one hand and the historical body on the other (cf. Gottschalk of Orbais: 1945, 333–335 [= *De corpore et sanguine Domini*]). Gottschalk thus strengthened the association of the sacramental with the ecclesiastical body by distinguishing the latter two bodies from the historical body of Christ. But at the same time, however, Gottschalk also tried to stress the unity of the body of Christ, as according to him it is only by way of a "special" mode of theological language that the distinction holds in the first place.[7] In the light of later developments, Gottschalk's "natural" and "special" ways may be interpreted as a literal or proper mode on the one hand and a metaphorical or indirect mode of theological language on the other hand. Properly speaking, 'body of Christ' denoted the one and undivided body, whereas indirectly the expression denoted first the historical body and second the mystical or sacramental body of Christ. This second, mystical meaning of *corpus Christi*, then, also signified the ecclesiastical body. The Church, therefore, derived its meaning as the *corpus Christi mysticum* from the sacrament (cf. Lubac: 2009, 39–46).

Roughly two hundred years later, in the wake of the condemnation of Berengar of Tour's tropological explanation of the eucharist in 1050, this semiotic sequence changed. Now it became mandatory to argue for a strict identity between the historical and the sacramental bodies of Christ, so much so that the sacramental body lost its qualification as 'mystical'. In turn, the attribute 'mystical' was applied almost exclusively to the ecclesiastical body, so that by the end of the twelfth century *corpus Christi mysticum* had become a common expression for the Church. The identification of the historical with the sacramental body and the concomitant dissociation of the sacramental from the ecclesiastical body paradoxically resulted in a de-mystification of the *corpus Christi mysticum*. For notwithstanding the qualification of the ecclesiastical body as mystical, the Church did not anymore derive its meaning as this mystical body of Christ from the mysteries of the sacrament. Thus, what was now known as the *corpus Christi mysticum* was ever less a sacramental and spiritual community. It rather became ever more coextensive with the visible church.[8]

The late medieval result of this remarkable transformation in ecclesiological language has become known as corporative ecclesiology both in the history of law

---

7 Cf. Cortoni: 2016, 134–138 for context. For Gottschalk, the dispute was also a matter of diverging authorities, in this case, of Ambrose and Augustine; cf. Lubac: 2009, 36–38.

8 Cf. Lubac (2009, 116–135) for an account less condensed than I can discuss here. Lubac's book remains the most concise study on the transformations of "corpus mysticum" in the Middle Ages, but see now also Cortoni: 2016. Kantorowicz (1957, 193–272) discusses these transformations in the broader history of political thought. His understanding of medieval body politics as hierarchical corporations has been critically re-examined in Nederman: 2004.

and of theology.[9] Yet, corporative ecclesiology did not only originate in sacramental theology but also in christology. More precisely, when scholastic theologians from the thirteenth century onward engaged in ecclesiological discussion, they often based their reflections on a section in the third book of Peter Lombard's *Sentences*, and that is in the context of christology.[10] While discussing Christ's possession of divinity, the Lombard had explained that whereas Christ has fullness of divinity, to human beings divinity may be given only in proportion to their human nature. Quoting from Augustine's *Epistola ad Dardanum*, the Lombard then drew an analogy between the saints' participation in Christ's fullness of divinity on the one hand and the relation between a body's members and its head on the other. In the head "'there is sight, the senses of hearing, smell, taste, and touch, whereas in the remaining [members] there is only the sense of touch'; likewise also in Christ there resides fullness of divinity, for he is the head, in which all senses dwell."[11] The saints, then, relate to Christ like a body's members to its head, because just like a bodily member has one sense alone (the sense of touch, for example) and thus only participates in the fullness of the sensitive faculties residing in the head, so do the saints possess Christ's divinity according to their human nature and thus only participate in his fullness of divinity.

These few remarks prompted later scholastics who commented on the *Sentences* to develop a proper section or treatise "On Christ as head" (*De Christo capite*) or "On the grace of head" (*De gratia capitis*). In the 1250s, Thomas Aquinas for instance asked "Whether Christ is head of the Church according to his human nature" (Thomas Aquinas: 1933, 405 [= *Sent.* III, d. 13, q. 2, a. 1]), to which he gave the standard answer in the affirmative,[12] concluding that "Christ is said to be head

---

9 Cf. Prügl (2017) on the prequels of corporative ecclesiology at the Fourth Lateran Council and in the works of Innocent III. Pennington (2004) studies the rise of corporative ecclesiology from the perspective of legal history.

10 Within the framework of the *Sentences*, the context of sacramental theology, which appeared in the fourth book, was reserved for the legal aspects of ecclesiology; for more on this, see Congar: 1971a, 101f. On the systematic place of ecclesiology in scholastic thought, see also Professor Walter's contribution to the present volume.

11 Cf. Peter Lombard: 1981, 84 (= *Sent.* III, d. 13, § 2): "Ut 'in nostro corpore inest sensus singulis membris sed non quantum in capite: ibi enim et visus est et auditus et olfactus et gustus et tactus, in ceteris autem solus est tactus'; ita et in Christo *habitat omnis plenitudo divinitatis* [cf. Col 2:9], quia ille est caput, in quo sunt omnes sensus; in sanctis vero quasi solus tactus est, quibus datus est spiritus ad mensuram, cum *de illius plenitudine* [cf. John 1:16] acceperunt".

12 Aquinas' line of reasoning goes like this: Insofar as the head excels the body in certain respects, as from the head flow forth the powers of all bodily members, and as the head directs the members in their actions, Christ is the head of the Church according to both his human and divine nature. Properly speaking, however, he is the head of the church according to his human nature, for the head "is conformed to the members with respect to their nature" (Thomas Aquinas: 1933, 407 [= *Sent.* III, d. 13, q. 2, a. 1, co.]).

of the Church by way of a likeness with a natural head"[13]. And some years later, Thomas explained that

> as the whole Church is called one mystical body from its likeness to the natural body of man, which in diverse members has diverse acts, as the Apostle teaches in Rom 12 and 1 Cor 12, so likewise Christ is called head of the Church according to a likeness with the human head.[14]

Thomas goes on to argue that there are three relations between a body and its head, namely order, perfection, and power. Order, because the head ranks higher than the body, perfection, because it encloses all senses, whereas any bodily member has only one sense, and power, because the head commands the members and their acts. These three relations also apply "in a spiritual way" to Christ as head of the body that is the Church.[15]

The difference to earlier ecclesiological thought could not be clearer, for while early medieval thinkers such as Radbertus or Gottschalk held the sacramental to signify the ecclesiastical body of Christ, in Aquinas this sequence has changed. According to him, the Church is a mystical body in analogy not to the (or any) body of Christ but to the natural human body. The same applies to the head of that body: Christ according to his human nature is head of the Church, Aquinas argues, because he relates to the Church like a natural head to its natural body and – as we may supply from the earlier tradition – not because the Church is said to be a body with head and members in analogy to the sacramental body of Christ. This now became a fundamental assumption of late medieval corporative ecclesiology, namely that the Church is being called a mystical body and Christ its head because of an analogy with the natural human body.

---

13 Thomas Aquinas: 1933, 407 (= *Sent.* III, d. 13, q. 2, a. 1, co.): " [...] Christus dicitur caput Ecclesiae per similitudinem capitis naturalis".

14 Thomas Aquinas: 1903, 126b (= *STh.* III, q. 8, a. 1, co.): "[...] quod, sicut tota Ecclesia dicitur unum corpus mysticum per similitudinem ad naturale corpus hominis, quod secundum diversa membra habet diversos actus, ut Apostolus docet, *Rom.* XII et I *Cor.* XII; ita Christus dicitur caput Ecclesiae secundum similitudinem humani capitis".

15 Cf. Thomas Aquinas: 1903, 126a–b (= *STh.* III, q. 8, a. 1, co.): "In quo tria possumus considerare: scilicet ordinem, perfectionem et virtutem. Ordinem, quia caput est prima pars hominis, incipiendo a superiori. Et inde est quod omne principium consuevit vocari caput [...] Perfectionem autem, quia in capite vigent omnes sensus et interiores et exteriores: cum in ceteris membris sit solus tactus [...] Virtutem vero, quia virtus et motus ceterorum membrorum, et gubernatio eorum in suis actibus, est a capite, propter vim sensitivam et motivam ibi dominantem. Unde et rector dicitur caput populi [...] Haec autem tria competunt Christo spiritualiter. Primo enim, secundum propinquitatem ad Deum gratia eius altior et prior est [...] Secundo vero, perfectionem habet ad plenitudinem omnium gratiarum [...] Tertio, virtutem habuit influendi gratiam in omnia membra Ecclesiae".

2. Giles of Rome and Jean Quidort: Ecclesiastical and Imperial Power at the Beginning of the Fourteenth Century

Thomas Aquinas also mentioned the early medieval analogy and, more generally, maintained a solid association between his concept of Church and its sacramental origins, because for him eucharistic *communio* still constituted the prototype of ecclesiastical unity (cf. Thomas Aquinas: 1906, 142a–b [= *STh.* III, q. 73, a. 4, co.]). Aquinas, therefore, should not be subsumed under those thinkers who already advanced an idea of the church as an autonomous body politic, but still he argued along the lines that led toward corporative ecclesiology. Roughly thirty years after Aquinas' death, in the constitution *Unam sanctam* issued by pope Boniface VIII in 1303, we now see the Church as a body politic in full flesh. This famous text claims that the unity of the Church is in fact constituted by its 'bodily' qualities: "Of the one and only Church there is but one body, one head – not two heads as if it were a monstrosity –, namely Christ and the vicar of Christ, Peter, and the successor of Peter".[16]

This legal document, directed against the French king Philip IV and known for its final conclusion that the submission under the Roman pontifex is necessary for salvation, was flanked by a series of theological works.[17] One of them, perhaps a source for the *Unam sanctam* or a memorandum for its drafting, was the *De ecclesiastica potestate* by the Augustinian Hermit Giles of Rome from 1302.[18] Giles defended the same hierocratic claims put forward by Boniface and the curia and corroborated them with a theory about the pope's "fullness of power" (*plenitudo potestatis*).[19] Giles vindicated the assumption that "the Supreme Pontiff, who has lordship of spiritual things universally within the mystical body, also has lordship of all temporal things."[20] According to this order of power, the king – and even

---

16 Boniface VIII: 1921, 889: "Igitur ecclesie unius et unice, unum corpus, unum capud, non duo capita quasi monstrum, Christus scilicet, et Christi vicarius, Petrus, Petrique successor […]".

17 Cf. Miethke (2008, 68–82) for a concise presentation of the conflict between Boniface VIII and Philip IV of France and Ullmann: 1976 for a study of the theologians gathered around the pope. Ubl (2004) discusses the legal scope of the *Unam sanctam* along with the efforts to theologically support its claims.

18 Cf. Miethke (2008, 94–96) for the genesis of Giles' treatise and Ubl (2003, 70–71) for its relation with the *Unam sanctam*.

19 Cf. Congar (1971a: 164–172) and the literature mentioned there for notes on the origin of *plenitudo potestatis*.

20 Giles of Rome: 2004, 90 (= *De ecclesiastica potestate* II, 4, trans. Dyson): "[…] Summus Pontifex, qui in corpore mystico universaliter dominatur spiritualibus, manifestum est quod eciam omnibus temporalibus dominatur".

the king of France[21] – reigning in the temporal or corporeal realm yields to the spiritual power of the pope who has fullness of power.

Giles argued that this is the natural state of affairs, because the order existing between pope and king reflects the order between the spiritual and the corporeal realms most generally. But it is "with regard to our bodies" that this order is best illustrated. To our bodies, Giles tells us, all temporal and corporeal things outside our bodies are ordered, because these things serve the necessaries of bodily life.[22] The highest instance, however, ruling even over our bodies is the soul:

> Since the soul has lordship, and since it is right and fitting that it should be lord of the body – for we may see by experience that our bodily members are moved according to the command and will of the soul: that, as the soul wills, so are the feet moved, and so are the fingers clenched and unclenched, and so are the hands and arms moved, and also the head itself – it follows that the priestly power, and especially the power of the Supreme Pontiff, who is known to have lordship over our souls, may be the ruler and lord of our bodies and of the temporal things which are ordered to bodies.[23]

From this passage it is hard if not outright impossible to understand what is being said in analogy to what. For even though Giles uses traditional ecclesiological language by picking up the word *corpus*, he does not talk about *corpus* in an analogous way but rather uses the term for a proof from experience. Consider, he tells us, what you are familiar with from your daily life, and you must agree that this is the natural order of power: the soul has power over the body and the body has power over all corporeal and temporal things. In an utterly literal move, Giles then transfers this order to the Church: "It follows that priestly power, which has lordship

---

21 Perhaps the most important subject of the *Unam sanctam* and of the controversy between Boniface and Philip more generally was the interpretation of the decretal *Per venerabilem* (1202), which stipulated that the king of France does not recognize any superior in secular matters; the *Unam sanctam* changed that, cf. Ubl: 2004, 142.

22 Cf. Giles of Rome: 2004, 90–92 (= *De ecclesiastica potestate* II, 4, trans. Dyson): "Secunda via ad hoc idem sumitur ex parte corporum nostrorum, in quorum subsidium sunt temporalia ordinata. Sumus enim [...] quodammodo finis omnium, ut omnia in nostrum obsequium ordinentur. Corporalium ergo sumus finis, inquantum ipsa corporalia famulantur corporibus nostris et subveniunt quantum ad necessitatem corporalis vite". For Giles' use of nature and natural philosophy cf. now Adamson: 2019.

23 Giles of Rome: 2004, 92 (= *De ecclesiastica potestate* II, 4, trans. Dyson): "Et quia anima dominatur et quia dignum et iustum est ut dominetur corpori, cum experimentaliter videamus quod nostra corporalia membra moventur secundum nutum et voluntatem anime, ut sicut vult anima, sic moventur pedes, sic digiti constringuntur et aperiuntur, sic moventur manus et brachia, sic et ipsum caput: consequens est quod sacerdotalis potestas, et potissime potestas Summi Pontificis, que super nostris animabus noscitur habere dominium, corporibus nostris et temporalibus rebus que ordinantur ad corpora principetur et dominetur".

over souls, may rule bodies and temporal things."[24] According to Giles, this proves the fact that the Roman pontifex has fullness of power and that accordingly the temporal realm, including secular kingship, is subordinated to the papal rule over the spiritual realm.

But what does 'fullness of power' actually mean? For his answer to that question, Giles relies on the distinction between natural and preternatural causation. He argues that whoever has fullness of power "can do without a secondary cause whatever [he] can do with a secondary cause."[25] Consider God, Giles tells us. According to natural causation, he brings forth "a horse by means of a horse, but if he wished and when he wished, he could do this without seed; and an ox by means of an ox, but he could make an ox without an ox, for he could make a calf out of a block of wood."[26] The same holds for the pope, because according to the laws given to the Church, that is to say, according to the 'natural' order of things, a prelate, for instance, is elected by the chapter of canons. Yet, the pope

> could provide a prelate for any church without this secondary cause: that is, without the choice of the electors. And what has been said of the election of a prelate is true of the other things which are done in the Church: that the Supreme Pontiff, as having fullness of power, in whom all the power of the Church is acknowledged to reside, can act without other agents.[27]

We should carefully note that Giles here talks about the pope's 'preternatural' power within the church, where by way of his fullness of power he may circumvene the

---

24 Cf. Giles of Rome: 2004, 92 (= *De ecclesiastica potestate* II, 4, trans. Dyson): "Erit ergo hic ordo: quod potestas Summi Pontificis dominatur animabus, anime dominantur vel de iure dominare debent super corpora [...] Ipse autem res temporales nostris corporibus famulantur. Consequens est quod sacerdotalis potestas, que dominatur animabus, corporibus et rebus temporalibus principetur".

25 Cf. Giles of Rome: 2004, 360–362 (= *De ecclesiastica potestate* III, 9, trans. Dyson): " [...] quod plenitudo potestatis est in aliquo agente quando illud agens potest sine causa secunda quicquid potest cum causa secunda". Giles borrows this principle from the *Liber de causis*, cf. Bertelloni: 2004, 97–108.

26 Cf. Giles of Rome: 2004, 362 (= *De ecclesiastica potestate* III, 9, trans. Dyson): "In ipso autem Deo est plenitudo potestatis, quia quicquid potest cum causa secunda potest sine causa secunda, ita quod posse omnium agencium reservatur in primo agente, scilicet in Deo. Nam in produccione mundi producit hominem sine homine precedente et equum sine equo precedente. Nunc autem producit equum mediante equo, sed si vellet et quando vellet sine semine; et bovem mediante bove, sed sine bove posset facere bovem. Posset enim facere de trunco vitulum, vel de nihilo facere vitulum, et sicut vellet, sic res ageret".

27 Giles of Rome: 2004, 364 (= *De ecclesiastica potestate* III, 9, trans. Dyson): "Posset tamen Summus Pontifex sine huiusmodi causa secunda, idest sine eleccione eligencium, providere cuicumque ecclesie de prelato. Et quod dictum est de eleccione prelati veritatem habet de aliis que fiunt in Ecclesia: quod potest Summus Pontifex sine aliis agentibus agere tamquam ille qui habet plenitudinem potestatis, in quo totum posse Ecclesie dignoscitur residere".

'natural' or legally established order of things and procedures. This makes him hold "the summit of the Church", and this is the reason why he "can be called the Church", that is, the epitome of Church.[28]

Giles says that the pope does not have all power absolutely and universally, because he acts according to the fullness of power bestowed upon him by Christ within the boundaries of the Church. In contrast to the pope's limited fullness of power, Christ has fullness of power universally and thus is the only head of the Church, that is, of his mystical body. Christ's influence upon the believers, however, "cannot come to us except through the Church. For just like the head can bring influence to bear upon a member only insofar it is joined to the body", nobody will receive grace given by Christ unless she or he is a member of the body that is the Church.[29] The pontifex, therefore, quite literally constitutes a bridge between Christ as head and the members of the body that is the Church. He is the soul of this mystical and at the same time 'visible' body and thus reigns over its members and over all temporal things, inasmuch as they are ordered to serve the body.

By conflating the mystical with the 'visible' body, Giles contributed to the tendency in late medieval ecclesiology to separate the ecclesiastical from the sacramental body – and to banalize the ecclesiological use of *corpus mysticum*. This current of thought, according to Henri de Lubac, benefitted "the most external aspect of the church in its most contingent realization: the papal power claim over temporal goods" (Lubac: 2009, 131–132). In Lubac's narrative, the excessively hierocratic ideas at the beginning of the fourteenth century mark an unprecedented low point in the history of ecclesiology. The price of this was, according to Lubac, another excess, namely a "'spiritualistic' reaction to completely dissociate the mystical body of Christ from the visible body" (Lubac: 2009, 132), and thus an excessive emphasis on the invisible, spiritual, or heavenly aspect of the church. But while this may accurately characterize later ecclesiological approaches,[30] the immediate context of Giles' and Boniface's claims presents us with a different perspective.

Perhaps the strongest oppositional voice against the pope and for the king was the Dominican Jean Quidort, also known as John of Paris, who became member of a scholarly team put together by the chancelor of Philip IV in order to rebuke the claims for hierocracy put forward by Boniface VIII and his men. In this tense context, Quidort composed his *De regia potestate et papali* in 1302, probably some

---

28 Cf. Giles of Rome: 2004, 396 (= *De ecclesiastica potestate* III, 12, trans. after Dyson): " [...] Summus Pontifex, qui tenet apicem Ecclesie et qui potest dici Ecclesia [...]".

29 Cf. Giles of Rome: 2004, 206 (= *De ecclesiastica potestate* II, 12, trans. Dyson): "Influencia enim passionis Christi non potest ad nos pervenire nisi per Ecclesiam. Sicut enim a capite non potest venire influencia ad aliquod membrum nisi prout est coniunctum corpori [...]".

30 Lubac mentions Wyclif, Hus, Luther, and Calvin.

little time before the publication of Giles of Rome's *De ecclesiastica potestate*.[31] Taking the opposite standpoint to Giles, Quidort argued for a separation of powers between church and state and for the limitation of ecclesiastical and papal power to the realm of the church.[32] His vision of the Church as a mystical body differed from Giles' accordingly:

> It is *one* Church, *one* Christian people, *one* mystical body, not however in Peter or Linus, but in Christ, who alone is properly and supremely head of the Church and from whom both distinct powers are distributed according to different degrees [...] Nevertheless, the Supreme Pontiff may be said to be head with respect to the external behavior of ministers, inasmuch as he is chief among ministers, and inasmuch as it is him, the principal vicar of Christ in spiritual matters, on whom the whole order of ministers depends like on a high priest and master builder.[33]

Therefore, as Quidort continues, the pope only exerts power within the 'visible' church and not in the secular sphere, because here the king is said to be head of his kingdom and the emperor head of the world (*caput mundi*).[34] Pope, king, emperor, and their respective 'bodies', all belong to a proper, limited, and well-defined sphere, and as such they essentially differ from the mystical body, which, according to Quidort, is the universal Church: "one Christian people, one mystical body"[35]. Therefore, it is correct to say that the Roman pontifex is the highest ranking member in the 'visible' church and hence also its head.[36] But of the universal Church there cannot be any other head but Christ. For this mystical body, the universal Church both in heaven and on earth, is in Christ (*in Christo*), and its 'being in' constitutes the relation between head and body.[37]

---

31 Cf. Ubl: 2003.

32 Cf. Miethke: 2008, 116–126 for a helpful introduction.

33 Jean Quidort: 1969, 164 (= *De regia potestate et papali* 18): "[...] una est ecclesia, unus populus Christianus, unum mysticum corpus, non quidem in Petro vel Lino, sed in Christo, qui solus est proprie et maxime caput ecclesiae et a quo distributa est utraque potestas distincta quoad diversus gradus [...] Potest nihilominus dici summus pontifex caput quantum ad exteriorem ministrorum exhibitionem, in quantum est principalis inter ministros et a quo ut a principali Christi vicario in spiritualibus totus ordo ministrorum dependet ut a hierarcha et architecto". Quidort is getting at the theory of two swords (*duo gladii*), which was introduced into the debate already by Bernard of Clairvaux. The whole passage is the rebuttal of a hierocratic counterargument in Jean Quidort: 1969, 122 (= *De regia potestate et papali* 9).

34 Cf. Jean Quidort: 1969, 83–84 (= *De regia potestate et papali* 3), where Quidort adduces the Aristotelian idea of the natural generation of kings – but not of emperors and monarchies – of single polities in order to justify the plurality of secular 'heads'. For more on his Aristotelian leanings, cf. Miethke: 2008, 123–126.

35 See the quote above, note 33.

36 Cf. Jean Quidort: 1969, 81 (= *De regia potestate et papali* 3).

37 Cf. the quotation above, note 33.

Since it is not immediately apparent what Quidort means by the body's being *in Christo*, it may be helpful to first establish what he does not intend, and that is an organological or naturalistic relation between head and mystical body in analogy to the human head and body. We had found such in Giles of Rome and Thomas Aquinas, who defined this relation as order, perfection, and power, implicating different kinds of lordship and influence of the head upon the body. Quidort acknowledges these relations, yet he applies them to the hierarchy within the visible church alone, that is to say, to the order between the pope, bishops, clerics, and the laity. Accordingly, the Roman pope is

> the universal dispenser generally of all ecclesiastical goods, both spiritual and temporal; he is not, however, the lord over them. Rather, it is the community of the universal Church (*communitas ecclesiae universalis*) that is the lord and proprietor over all goods generally, while single communities and churches have lordship over the goods appropriate to them.[38]

While the ecclesiastical hierarchy with the pope at its top administers and dispenses the goods of the church, lordship over the Church universally is held by the *communitas ecclesiae*. Quidort distinguishes this *communitas* as the community of believers (*communitas fidelium*) from the congregation of clerics (*congregatio clericorum*): the latter, again, exerts spiritual power within the church, but it does not hold lordship over the Church universally.[39]

This, then, is Quidort's concept of the universal Church: it is a community of believers, united in the one faith.[40] To be sure, this is not without precedents in the history of medieval ecclesiology,[41] but Quidort's distinction between *communitas fidelium* and *congregatio clericorum* and, going even further, the assertion that the community of believers has lordship over the Church as opposed to the clergy, marks an important step. The hierarchically organized, 'visible' church, that is, the congregation of clerics, exists to the end of administering the sacraments to the

---

38 Jean Quidort: 1969, 92 (= *De regia potestate et papali* 6): "[Papa] est universalis dispensator omnium generaliter ecclesiasticorum bonorum spiritualium et temporalium; non quidem quod sit dominus, sed sola communitas ecclesiae universalis domina est et proprietaria illorum bonorum generaliter, et singulae communitates et ecclesiae dominium habent in bonis sibi correspondentibus."

39 Cf. Jean Quidort: 1969, 153–154 (= *De regia potestate et papali* 16): "Si vero accipiatur ecclesia non solum pro congregatione clericorum sed generaliter vocetur ecclesia communitas fidelium, sic ecclesiae praesunt et ecclesiasticus iudex in spiritualibus et saecularis in temporalibus."

40 Cf. Jean Quidort: 1969, 83 (= *De regia potestate et papali* 3): " [...] omnes fideles conveniunt in una fide catholica sine qua non est salus."

41 On the history of the term *congregatio fidelium*, cf. Tierney: 1998, 121–129.

believers.[42] However, through the sacramental communion the believers receive the gift of eternal life not from the 'visible' church but rather from Christ alone, "who brought men to eternal life by making them their sons."[43] Therefore, because they are sons of God by way of the sacraments, the believers are *in Christo* and thus form one community, one people, one Church, and one mystical body of Christ.[44]

Quidort's ecclesiological thought has been described as a well-balanced position between papalist and royalist claims.[45] The moderate character of his approach also transpires from his use of the terms *corpus* and *communitas/communio*, because both have a spiritual and a 'visible' or institutional aspect. In Quidort we may, therefore, recognize a critique of corporative ecclesiologies that envisaged the church as an autonomous body politic, but at the same time we should not count him among the proponents of the diametrically opposite position, that is to say, of thoroughly spiritualistic ecclesiological thought. For this, we have to go further down into the fourteenth century and beyond the conflict between Boniface VIII and Philip IV, which provided the occasion as well as the limitation for Giles of Rome's and Jean Quidort's ecclesiologies.

3. John Wyclif: The Rise of Spiritualistic Ecclesiology

John Wyclif (*ca.* 1330–1384) published his *De ecclesia* at the beginning of the Great Western Schism in 1378–1379.[46] In this treatise, however, Wyclif did not directly react to the world-shattering events in Rome and Avignon but rather to a local conflict between church and state in England, which culminated in the excommunication of the keeper of the Tower of London by the bishop of London. Chasing down two of the Tower's fugitives, the keeper and his men had invaded Westminster Abbey and killed one of these fugitives at the steps of the altar while

---

42 Cf. Jean Quidort: 1969, 80 (= *De regia potestate et papali* 2): "Ex quibus praedictis definiri potest sacerdotium in hunc modum: sacerdotium est spiritualis potestas ministris ecclesiae a Christo collata ad dispensandum fidelibus sacramenta."

43 Cf. Jean Quidort: 1969, 78 (=*De regia potestate et papali* 2): "Ad illum igitur regem pertinet huiusmodi regimen, qui non solum est homo sed etiam Deus, scilicet Jesum Christum qui homines filios Dei faciens introducit in vitam aeternam." On the relation between Quidort's ecclesiology and his idiosyncratic theology of the eucharist cf. Briguglia: 2015.

44 Some few years later, the relation between laity and clergy and the idea of the believers' immediacy to God, as it transpires from Quidort, became a cornerstone of William of Ockham's ecclesiology; cf. Leppin: 2011.

45 Cf., for example, Congar: 1971a, 183–185.

46 In the present context, I am limiting my discussion of Wyclif's ecclesiology for the greatest part to his *De ecclesia*. For comprehensive survies cf. Schmidt: 1955, 72–90 (English and Latin works) and Shogimen: 2006 (Latin works).

mass was sung. A few months later, after the bishop had proclaimed the keeper's excommunication in retaliation for the killing in Westminster Abbey, the crown, in order to make its case against the bishop, assembled a team of jurists and theologians, among them Wyclif.[47] Wyclif found the fugitives to be guilty of the most serious of all crimes, for they had disobeyed the law of their king and, thereby, the law of the church, which, according to Wyclif, amounted to an offense to divine law.[48] But furthemore, Wyclif argued that the bishop of London, by granting the fugitives shelter, had made the church a dwelling for criminals and thus had turned against civil as well as divine law, just like the fugitives (cf. John Wyclif: 1886, 148 [= *De ecclesia* 7]).

This accusation was but one in a series of attacks launched by Wyclif against his contemporary church, whose defects were rooted, according to Wyclif, in the church's own wealth and lust for power. Therefore it was in dire need for reform.[49] However, in contrast to Jean Quidort, who argued for political and legal measures, such as a limitation of ecclesiastical power, to bring about reform, Wyclif chose a more properly theological and, as will be clearer below, a christological line of reasoning. This was Wyclif's definition of 'Church', of the true Church without qualification:

> Although Scripture talks in different ways about the Church, it is my assumption to take it for the present discussion according to the notion better known, and that is, as the congregation of all predestinate (*congregacio omnium predestinatorum*).[50]

The Church, Wyclif goes on, also is a bride according to the Song of Songs and Isa 61:10; it is the virtuous woman from Prov 31:10; it is Jerusalem, our mother, the Lord's temple, the reign of the heavens, the city of a great king, according to Augustine; and it is the "mystical body of Christ, which 1 Cor 12 [talks] about" (John Wyclif: 1886, 3 [= *De ecclesia* 1]). Yet, according to Wyclif, these are non-essential

---

47 For more on the so-called Haulay-Shakyl incident and Wyclif's involvement, cf. Dahmus: 1960, 61–63.

48 Cf. John Wyclif: 1886, 150 (= *De ecclesia* 7): "Dicti autem fugitivi iuxta nobis exposita offenderunt in legem Dei ex inobediencia suis prepositis, offenderant insuper in legem ecclesie racione multiplici, quia (ut dicunt docti in illis iuribus) inobedientes mandatis suorum principum committunt quoddam genus sacrilegii, et cum inobedientes remanserint legi Dei de obediendo legibus regis sui, que lex iusta illos protegeret?".

49 In John Wyclif 1886: 157–387 (= *De ecclesia* 8–16) he discusses the nature of ecclesiastical privileges, the privileges themselves, their legal status, and the reasons for why they need to be seriously cut back at great lengths. For more on Wyclif's call for reform, cf. Shogimen: 2006, 222–223.

50 John Wyclif: 1886, 2 (= *De ecclesia* 1): "Quamvis autem ecclesia dicatur multipliciter in scriptura, suppono quod sumatur ad propositum pro famosiori, scilicet congregacione omnium predestinatorum."

expressions, whereas the term *congregatio praedestinatorum* alone describes the Church according to its very nature.[51]

Wyclif's use of *corpus* and *corpus mysticum* reflects this difference between metaphorical and essential expressions for the Church. When he uses *corpus* metaphorically, Wyclif often advances a naturalistic notion of the term by employing analogies to the human body and its parts sometimes so drastic that they evoke disgust for the aspects of the Church thus described.[52] But whenever he employs *corpus* in a properly ecclesiological sense signifying the congregation of the predestinate, Wyclif stresses this body's spiritual character. Hence, for example, the members of the ecclesiastical body are held together not by bonds analogous to fibers or other jointings as in natural body parts but rather by the bond of the love that never ceases.[53] Accordingly, the congregation of the predestinate does not constitute a corporation in time and space but rather a spiritual aggregate, in which one predestinate is joined together with every other by way of being joined together with one common center, and that is the grace and love of Christ (cf. John Wyclif: 1886, 104–109 [= *De ecclesia* 5]). The true Church, therefore, "is being made a continuum by way of a spiritual continuity stronger [than natural continuity], which is poured out by the Spirit of God in the hearts of all members of the Church".[54]

Perhaps the thorniest issue in Wyclif's ecclesiological teachings lies in the fact that ecclesiastical membership transcends human recognition, because the grace of predestination, which is the only true touchstone for Church membership, is freely given by God alone. Only God, therefore, knows who is a member of the body of Christ, and who belongs to the opposed body of the devil.[55] Wyclif argues that in this world both these bodies are contained in what he calls "man who is mankind". In this collective sense, man is "partially foreknown and partially predestined, and thus, at [the end of] his time, he is partially saved and partially reprobate, but this

---

51 Throughout the treatise, these and further non-essential or metaphorical concepts for the Church help Wyclif to discuss different aspects of ecclesiology. In a rather traditional manner, for instance, he associates the Church as virgin with its purity in heaven, and so forth.

52 Cf., for instance, John Wyclif: 1886, 75 (= *De ecclesia* 4), where Wyclif compares those who are excluded from the spiritual congregation of the predestinate with ulcers growing within the church as a body.

53 Cf. John Wyclif: 1886, 4–5 (= *De ecclesia* 1): "Caritas autem que numquam excidit est vinculum continuans membra illius corporis".

54 John Wyclif: 1886, 109 (= *De ecclesia* 5): "[...] continuatur alia continuacione spirituali plus forti per spiritum Dei diffusum in cordibus omnium membrorum ecclesie [...]".

55 Cf. John Wyclif: 1886, 138–139 (= *De ecclesia* 6). Gordon Leff (1967, 519) identifies "men's ignorance" of church membership as the crucial disruptive feature in Wyclif's teachings on the Church, because of which "the church in its traditional form [...] lost its *raison d'être*" (emphasis Leff). For a more sympathetic account, extensively discussing the theological and philosophical underpinnings of Wyclif's ecclesiology, see Lahey: 2009, 169–198.

[man] is not the Church".[56] The true Church, Wyclif insists, encompasses the saved part of mankind exclusively, and thus it is not a mixed body (*corpus permixtum*), as Augustine, of whom Wyclif claims to be a faithful follower, had taught.[57]

This hidden character of the true Church leads Wyclif to a thoroughly skeptical attitude towards the 'visible' church. Because they simply cannot know, Wyclif argues, neither laymen nor clerics or popes can truthfully claim Church membership unless they receive a special revelation about the distribution of the grace of predestination.[58] In the absence of such revelation, any confession of faith in the 'visible' church will therefore be beset with doubt.[59] For Wyclif, however, this is not to say that among the hierarchy of the 'visible' church there are no predestinate men necessarily. He rather aims at false religious claims about the 'visible' church, as for instance the *Unam sanctam*'s assertion that the submission under the Roman pontifex is necessary for salvation.[60] According to Wyclif, the subject of any true religious claim about the Church has to be the congregation of the predestinate with Christ as its head. Thus, any "faithful layman should be held to believe that he has Christ as his priest, ruler, bishop, and pope"[61].

This demand corresponds directly with Wyclif's more general point discussed above that the relation between Christ and the individual predestinate constitutes a "spiritual continuum", which unifies the whole Church.[62] Wyclif elaborates on this

---

56 Cf. John Wyclif: 1886, 121 (= *De ecclesia* 6): "Conceditur ergo quod homo qui est humanum genus est partim prescitus et partim predestinatus, et sic tempore suo partim salvatus et partim dampnatus, sed ille non est ecclesia [...]".

57 Cf. Leff: 1967, 516–517 and Lahey: 2009, 187 for this important disagreement between Augustine and Wyclif. On Wylcif's Augustinianism more generally, cf. Evans: 2013.

58 Cf. John Wyclif: 1886, 5 (= *De ecclesia* 1): "Prima, quod nullus vicarius Christi debet presumere asserere se esse caput ecclesie sancte catholice, ymmo nisi habuerit specialem revelacionem, non assereret se esse aliquod membrum eius".

59 Cf. John Wyclif: 1886, 25 (= *De ecclesia* 2): "Et tunc [...] possunt discernere, si sit sanum vel stolidum quod asseramus absque formidine non esse membra sancte matris ecclesie, hoc est, de numero predestinatorum. Debemus autem hoc sperare et credere sed cum formidine de gracia perseverancie: ideo talis fides habet formidinem annexam quam non habet fides qua credimus nos esse in gracia secundum presentem iusticiam [...]"

60 Wyclif does not attack the *Unam sanctam* explicitly, yet the constitution clearly lurks in the background of his polemics; cf., for example, John Wyclif: 1886, 37 (= *De ecclesia* 2). Remarkably, when adressing the *Unam sanctam* directly, Wyclif pretends to be in full agreement; cf., for instance: 1886, 7 (= *De ecclesia* 1).

61 Cf. John Wyclif: 1886, 43 (= *De ecclesia* 2): "[...] quilibet laicus fidelis tenetur credere quod habet Christum sacerdotem suum, rectorem, episcopum atque papam, et sic de aliis sanctis Christi vicariis." In the following passage, Wyclif carefully points out that in order not to undermine the validity of the sacraments adminstered by the 'visible' church, laymen should "at least implicitly" believe that their priests belong to the church and act as its heads, ultimately because such implicit faith can only be directed by God who "does not bring men to believe falsehood" (cf. ibid).

62 See above, at around note 54.

fundamental ecclesiological relation, initially by arguing along rather traditional lines of *corpus* and *communio*. He thus reaches a conclusion similar to Jean Quidort's assumption that the members of the mystical body are being incorporated in Christ through eucharistic communion. At the same time, however, Wyclif goes beyond Quidort by equating "Church" and "Christ":

> [The Church] is collectively all and individually the single predestinate, and every one of all of them is united in Christ as head. But then we have to understand the person (*persona*) as head, and the base of the whole composite as well as each of its members as absored and hidden in a confused way, as it were, within Christ, such that the Church of Christ is called Christ with every believer incorporated therein.[63]

Wyclif now has to defend this equation against the objection that a strict identity of the Church and Christ would result in twisted christological claims.[64] He tries to escape this danger by arguing that on the one hand Christ and his Church are numerically one and indeed one person,[65] while on the other hand they remain somehow distinct. Therefore, Christ as head of the Church figures as the person, which is identical with the Church and into which the believers are being incorporated.

In order to make this idea of a most intimate ecclesiastical union between Christ and the predestinate concur with traditional theology and in order to "not offend the school[men]"[66], Wyclif once again invokes the authority of Augustine and of the latter's *Totus Christus*-doctrine in particular.[67] In the eucharist, Wyclif states with Augustine, Christ commited himself to his Church and thus predestined each and every member of the true Church to be his body and hence to live for eternity.[68] It "is numerically the same body that is the Church and the body in the

---

63 John Wyclif: 1886, 134 (= *De ecclesia* 6): "[…] que est collectim omnes predestinati et singillatim singuli, ac singulus eorundem omnes uniti in Christo capite, sed tunc oportet intelligere personam ut caput, basim tocius compositi et quodlibet membrum suum confuse tamquam absorptum in Christo absconditum, sic quod ecclesia Christi dicat Christum cum quocunque fideli sibi incorporatum".

64 Cf. John Wyclif: 1886, 136 (= *De ecclesia* 6): "Posset enim seductus credere quod omnis christianus foret idem personaliter cum Christo secundum corpus et animam, ita quod non forent dispares persone essencie vel nature, quod foret nimis erroneum".

65 Cf. also John Wyclif: 1886, 134 (= *De ecclesia* 6): "Tercio videtur quod sicut Christus mansit eadem persona in numero pro tempore mortis sue, tam in sepulchro mortuus quam in inferno vivus, ita videtur eandem personam ecclesie disiunctive regnantem in celo et peregrinantem in mundo, et sic Christus assumpsit ypostatice personam ecclesie peregrinantis in beata virgine".

66 Cf. John Wyclif: 1886, 136 (= *De ecclesia* 6): "Unde ne darem scandalum scole, distuli istam materiam".

67 Note that "*Totus Christus*-doctrine" is a modern expression. On Augustine's use of "totus Christus" and "Christus integer", cf. Madec: 1994, 879–882.

68 The reference Wyclif provides is a canon from Gratian's *Decretum* (d. 2, C. 36 de cons.), which in turn cites Augustine, cf. John Wyclif: 1886, 137 (= *De ecclesia* 6): "'Christus in eucaristia commendavit

sacrament and [the body that was] born of the virgin, since it is Christ himself."[69] Thus, because they are one single body, one may indeed say that Christ and his Church are numerically one. However, Christ and the believers are this body and, hence, numerically one in two different ways:

> In one way, Christ is the [ecclesiastical] body in a personal manner, and in another way a Christian [is this body] in a sacramental manner; the first way is properly, the second through participation. And thus I believe to understand Christ's prophecy in Matt 24:5: 'Many will come in my name, saying, I am Christ; and they will deceive many.' For I do not suppose that a Christian or false apostle says that he is Christ personally, but rather in a sacramental manner through the incorporation into the mystical body of Christ.[70]

Real identity, therefore, holds only between Christ and the believers but not the other way around, because to claim personal union with Christ would, for a Christian believer, result in false prophecy. Whereas Church members, thus, may only participate in this union through eucharistic communion, Christ by way of committing his body, that is, himself in his human nature, to his Church establishes numerical and real identity with the congregation of the predestinate.[71] Therefore, the predestinate are Christ "in a sacramental way" and by way of participation, while only Christ *is* the true Church, properly and personally.

All this, of course, sounds rather mysterious or, to say the least, idiosyncratic. Hence, in order to provide a greater and clearer perspective, it may be helpful to summarize the relative merits of Wyclif's ecclesiogical thought in three brief observations. First, by arguing for numerical identity between Christ and his Church, Wyclif stretches the concept of the Church as a body complete with head and members to such an extent that every member appears as a more integral part of this body than the traditional terminology would suggest. According to Wyclif, indeed, the predestinate are members of Christ rather than members of the mystical body

---

corpus suum quod eciam fecit nosmet ipsos'". Before 1930, modern scholarship has found this quotation in the *Decretum* to go back only to Bede the Venerable, but since the edition of Augustine's *sermo* 229, the reference is easily identifiable as Augustine of Hippo: 1930, 30.

69 John Wyclif 1886: 137 (= *De ecclesia* 6): "[…] idem est corpus in numero quod est ecclesia, et corpus in sacramento ac natum de virgine, cum sit ipse Christus".

70 John Wyclif: 1886, 137–138 (= *De ecclesia* 6): "Aliter tamen est Christus ipsum corpus quia personaliter, et aliter christianus quia sacramentaliter, unus proprie et alius participative; et sic credo ego propheciam Christi intelligi Matth. XXIV°, 5: *Multi venient in nomine meo, dicentes quia ego sum Christus, et multos seducent.* Non enim reor aliquem christianum vel pseudoapostolum dicere quod ipse est Christus personaliter, sed sacramentaliter per incorporacionem in corpus Christi misticum".

71 For the distinction between the participatory and the personal union between Christ and the Church, cf. also John Wyclif: 1886, 136 (= *De ecclesia* 6): "Aliquis enim est participative Christus ut quodlibet membrum eius, et aliquis personaliter ut solum ipsum caput".

of Christ, so that there is neither room nor need for any intermediary between the individual predestinate and Christ.

Second, Wyclif's insistence on the unity of the historical, the sacramental, and the ecclesiastical body of Christ implicates a return to early medieval ecclesiology as, for instance, in Gottschalk of Orbais. But while Gottschalk still allows for a "special" distinction of multiple bodies as opposed to "natural" identity of the one and undivided body of Christ (Lubac: 2009, 39–46), Wyclif emphasizes identity more emphatically. According to him, there simply is but one body of Christ, and that is "Christ himself" and the Church at the same time.[72]

Third, the concept of *persona* is central to Wyclif's ecclesiological approach. As discussed above, Wyclif describes the Church as *persona* while reflecting on the way in which Christ relates to the predestinate. While the latter are being incorporated into Christ through eucharistic communion and therefore become the body of Christ in a participatory sense, Christ relates to the Church personally, that is, in real and complete identity. In this christocentric perspective, Wyclif's ecclesiology has a christological upshot. Christ *is* the Church, because he commits his body, that is, himself according to his human nature, to his Church. Yet, by so drawing the Church, as it were, into his person, Christ not only is the Church in his human but also in his divine nature. Put another way, the whole Christ – one person in two natures – is the Church.

The reason why this christological terminology matters for Wyclif's ecclesiology more generally transpires from his discussion of the headship of the Church. On the one hand, Wyclif agrees with the medieval tradition that "Christ is head of the Church […] according to his humanity"[73]. This makes good sense, because, as we have seen, it is Christ's human nature that yields the idea of the Church as the body of Christ committed to the Church in the eucharist. The headship of the Church, however, also involves the problem of rulership, and in this respect it is not surprising to see Wyclif arguing for strict divine lordship. Therefore, on the other hand, he also assumes Christ's divinity as head of the Church:

> The universal Church, which is the whole mystical body of Christ, has two heads, namely an extrinsic head which is divinity and an intrinsic head which is Christ's humanity […] These two natures are two heads of the Church, and yet they are one according to the person (*personaliter*).[74]

---

72 Cf. above, note 69.

73 Cf. John Wyclif: 1886, 7 (= *De ecclesia* 1): "Ad quid igitur oportet contendere circa caput ecclesie? 'Ipsa' inquit Augustinus 'caro Christi est caput ecclesie', id est, humanitas secundum quam Christus predestinatus est […]".

74 John Wyclif: 1886, 22 (= *De ecclesia* 1): "Ecclesia autem universalis que est totum corpus Christi misticum habet duo capita, scilicet caput extrinsecum que est divinitas et caput intrinsecum que est

Without elaborating on the exact distinction between the Church's intrinsic and extrinsic heads, Wyclif goes on to make his actual point. For in stark contrast to Christ's twofold lordship over the universal Church, the headship of any human being extends only to a local or particular church. Relegating the function of bishops, prelates, and other clergy members to mere organizational offices in the 'visible' church,[75] Wyclif unambiguosly defends the supreme power of Christ both according to his humanity and his divinity within his Church, not least with regard to the distribution of the grace of predestination and thus to real Church membership. Once again, the christological term *persona*, therefore, allows Wyclif to combine Christ's divine and human agency in and with respect to the Church.

This rebuttal of hierocracy in favour of theocracy nicely exemplifies how thick the layer of polemics is, beneath which Wyclif's ecclesiology is to be found. And although his severe anti-papalist criticism forms an important part of Wyclif's writings on the Church, it is also worthwhile to dissect these layers, as it were, and appreciate his ecclesiology in its own right. What then comes to the forth is a spiritualistic and christocentric vision of the Church. But perhaps more importantly, Wyclif's ecclesiology emphazises the christological core of ecclesiology in contrast to the more political approaches from the beginning of the fourteenth century.

That being said, Wyclif did not stand outside the medieval tradition. He was neither the only author to argue for the Church as a spiritual body of Christ, nor the first theologian to criticize organological ecclesiology that advanced too naturalistic a notion of the term *corpus*. At the same time, however, Wyclif introduced the christological term *persona* as a centerpiece of his ecclesiology. By claiming personal union between Christ and the Church – that is, real identity surpassing participation through eucharistic communion – Wyclif emphatically argued for immediacy in the relation between the body that is the Church and Christ as its head.[76] The fact that this immediacy aimed at a serious devaluation of ecclesiastical intitutions determined Wyclif's fate in the history of ecclesiology.

Christi humanitas [...] iste duo nature sunt duo capita ecclesie, et tamen sunt personaliter unum caput".

75 Cf. John Wyclif: 1886, 23 (= *De ecclesia* 1): "Istis positis dico quod nec dominus Ardmacanus nec aliquis doctor catholicus debet asserere quod aliquis christianus sit caput universalis sed particularis ecclesie [...]" The term for these heads of particular churches is *capitaneus* (cf. John Wyclif: 1886, 19), which may be translated as "captain" or "leader".

76 Wyclif's idea of a personal union between Christ and the Church indirectly influenced the Augustinian Hermit Agostino Favaroni, who extended it by arguing for *communicatio idiomatum* between Christ and the Church. These teachings were condemned by the Council of Basel in 1435; cf. Eckermann: 1975.

4. John of Ragusa: *Corpus* and *Communio* in Conciliarism

Wyclif's teachings were indeed fraught with disapproval. Since 1381, when he was ousted from Oxford University, a series of examinations and condemnations protracted until well after his death in 1384, topping out with the condemnation of 45 articles that were gathered from his writings at the Council of Constance in 1415. From this time on, Wyclif was increasingly considered as the heresiarch *par excellence*, not only because of his own teachings but also – and chiefly – because of the popularity that his doctrines enjoyed in the Lollard and Hussite movements. As much as the council fathers strove for a reform of the church "in head and members"[77], they also distanced themselves, to put it mildly, from those dissident approaches to reform.

Despite these quarrels, however, a productive aspect of the mostly negative reception of Wyclif's thought in the conciliarist movement can hardly be ignored. After all it were his and Hus' writings, the resulting reforms, revolts, and revolutions on national levels, and the blindingly obvious ecclesiastical crisis during the Great Western Schism, which provoked new and more mainstream ecclesiologies as well.[78] In this respect, the Council of Basel (1431–1437/49) inaugurated a new era in the history of ecclesiology, which saw the publication of the first systematic treatises on the nature of the Church in the Middle Ages. Obviously, this is not to say that the ecclesiological writings we have discussed thus far were unsystematic and only provided random accounts of the Church. Yet, the firstling of these new works, the *Tractatus de ecclesia* by John Stojković of Ragusa (*ca.* 1395–1443) "widely abstained from polemics that permeated most ecclesiological literature at his time" (Prügl: 2013, 16) and presented a fresh approach to ecclesiology both from a biblical and dogmatic vantage point.[79]

This being said, the *De ecclesia* leaves little room for doubt against whom the treatise is directed. Ragusa calls his adversaries the "Church of the wicked" and the "congregation of evil, godless men, such as the unbelieving Jews, pagans, and heretics, who have fallen away from the truth of faith and the unity of the Church. In our time such are the Wycliffite and Hussite heretics."[80] Indeed, these are called

---

77 On this important formula, cf. Bellitto (2009, 304–305) and the literature mentioned there.

78 Prügl (2013) provides an excellent overview of these developments, cf. also Congar: 1971b, 5–6.

79 On the biblical foundations of Ragusa's ecclesiology, cf. Prügl: 2007, 230–234. Léger: 2013 offers a comprehensive account of Ragusa's changing ecclesiological thought. For a biographical study, cf. Krchňák: 1960.

80 John of Ragusa: 1983, 13 (= *De ecclesia* I, 2): "Et malignantium [ecclesia] quidem est congregatio malorum iniquorum hominum, ut infidelium Iudaeorum, paganorum et haereticorum, qui a veritate fidei et ab unitate Ecclesiae apostataverunt. Cuiusmodi sunt praesentis temporis haeretici wyclifitae et husitae".

'Church' only in an improper way, according to Ragusa, because properly the Church is defined as the "congregation of all believers united in faith, hope, and the revelation of Jesus Christ."[81] Stressing the unity of the Church even more, Ragusa advances the following definition:

> Properly the name 'Church' signifies only the believers who are, as it were, members at once bound together by the bond of love or faith in one body, whose head is Christ.[82]

Surprisingly now, this sounds similar to what we have read in Wyclif, because also in his ecclesiology the body that is the Church appeared as a spiritual aggregate with Christ as its head (cf. John Wyclif: 1886, 134). And as if to emphasize this point, Ragusa presents his definition in the context of a discussion of what he calls the spiritual Church made "of living and animated stone and wood, namely of human beings".[83]

These apparent similarities, however, spring from the fact that the *De ecclesia* originated in the efforts of the Council of Basel in 1432–1433 to bring about a union with the Hussites. In terms of theological debate, this effort was split up according to the famous Four Articles of Prague (Fudge: 2017). The debate on the first article on the necessity of communion in both kinds (*sub utraque specie*) fell under the responsibility of John of Ragusa and his Utraquist counterpart John Rokycana. Of these debates, it has been observed, ecclesiology was the "substrate", and the Hussite and Wycliffite concept of Church was the "grindstone" that sharpened the ecclesiologies of the council fathers (Helmrath: 1987, 365–366). John of Ragusa lifted much of his *De ecclesia*'s content from exactly these debates. Hence, the apparent similarities and the generally diplomatic atmosphere of the treatise should also be understood as parts of this attempt of a union.[84]

The other side of the same coin, however, accentuates the fundamental disagreement between Rokycana and Ragusa, as for the latter the Church as the congregation of believers forming one body unified by love and faith is compatible with the traditional analogy between the Church and a natural body. With Thomas Aquinas and along the lines of corporative ecclesiology, Ragusa unequivocally states that

---

81 John of Ragusa: 1983, 13 (= *De ecclesia* I, 2): "Ecclesia igitur fidelium est congregatio omnium in fide, spe et revelatione Iesu Christi unitorum".

82 Cf. John of Ragusa: 1983: 13 (= *De ecclesia* I, 2): "Unde proprie nomen ecclesiae signifcat solum fideles, qui sunt quasi quaedam membra vinculo caritatis vel fidei in uno corpore, cuius caput est Christus, in simul coniuncta".

83 Cf. John of Ragusa: 1983, 13 (= *De ecclesia* I, 2): "Ecclesia vero spiritualis est, quae constat ex vivis et animatis mapidibus et lignis, scilicet hominibus […]" The counterpart to this "spiritual Church" is the "material church", that is, the "place or house for blessing, praising, and glorifying God" (John of Ragusa: 1983, 12).

84 On the redaction of the *De ecclesia*, cf. Krämer: 1980, 92–95.

the present Church "is a mystical body by way of the likeness with a natural body", adding that in this mystical body lay people act like bodily members, while clerics act like the soul, because just like the soul directs the members, it is the clerics' task "to move and direct the laity by word and example toward eternal life"[85]. Furthermore, like the soul prays to God for the body and its needs, so do the clerics intercede with God on behalf of the laity. And among the clerics, representing the soul of the mystical body, "the pope, the cardinals, the primates, the patriarchs, the archbishops, the bishops and further prelates of the churches who have judicial authority are called 'Church' more properly"[86]. For although "the name 'Church' applies *most* properly and principally to the general council because of its universal authority", which excels all other authority in the church, "nevertheless any lower ecclesiastical authority is not excluded [from this eminent notion of 'Church']"[87].

Ragusa thus uses the concept of the mystical body in order to highlight ecclesiastical authority and hierarchy. As we have just seen, it is because of its universal authority that the general council takes on the pre-eminent position and hence deserves to be called 'Church' most properly. However, as Ragusa adds, the mystical body is called 'Church' not only because of its entirety and its most eminent part but also because of "the administrative head of the church", which is the pope, and the "church first among all", which is the Roman Church.[88] "Hence, the catholic and universal Church and the Roman Church are often taken to be the same and they signify the same."[89] According to Ragusa, this holds both in a material and a formal way. In material hindsight, the Roman Church consits of the basilica of Saint Peter in Rome, the pope and his cardinals, and those papal statutes and decrees that are promulgated outside of general councils. In its formal aspect, the

---

85 Cf. John of Ragusa: 1983, 15 (= *De ecclesia* I, 2): "Ulterius cum ecclesia militans sit quoddam corpus mysticum ad similitudinem corporis naturalis [...] [i]deo in hoc corpore mystico aliquid se habet per modum corporis, aliquid per modum animae moventis et dirigentis corpus. Et quidem omnes laici habent se per modum corporis. Ecclesiastici vero et in sacris constituti per modum animae, quia ecclesiasticorum est movere et dirigere laicos verbo et exemplo in finem vitae aeternae".

86 Cf. John of Ragusa: 1983, 16 (= *De ecclesia* I, 2): "Et inter hos superiores eorum, ut papa, cardinales, primates, patriarchae, archiepiscopi, episcopi et alii ecclesiarum praelati auctoritatem corrigendi habentes magis proprie Ecclesia nominatur [sic!] [...]".

87 Cf. John of Ragusa: 1983, 16 (= *De ecclesia* I, 2): "Quo in loco licet nomen ecclesiae ratione universalis auctoritatis generali concilio propriissime principaliter conveniat [...], nichilominus non excluditur quaecumque inferior ecclesiastica auctoritas [...]."

88 Cf. John of Ragusa: 1983, 17 (= *De ecclesia* I, 2): "Quia verum non solum pars nobilior et formalis alicuius totius nomine totius consuevit appellari, verum etiam et ipsum caput, idcirco cum romanus pontifex, qui est caput ministeriale Ecclesiae, et ipsa Romana ecclesia prima inter omnes, [...] aut quod facit, saepe dicitur absolute et sine determinatione Ecclesia facere [...]".

89 John of Ragusa: 1983, 17 (= *De ecclesia* I, 2): "Unde saepe catholica et universalis Ecclesia et Ecclesia romana pro eodem accipiuntur et idem significant".

Roman Church is equivalent with the universal Church by way of the entirety of the believers subjected to the Roman pontifex, by way of the council representing this entirety, and by way of the jurisdiction of the council.[90] For John, therefore, the Roman Church is the irreducible and "indefectible reality of the Church; it [is] a synonym of the Church's steadfastness in faith" (Prügl: 2013, 18), not rivalling but rather complementing the general council.

This concept of Church has justly been recognized as a systematization that accounts for "the local congregation, for the particular church led by officials, and for aspects of universal ecclesiology" (Krämer: 1980, 97). By accentuating the Roman Church and by elaborating on its ecclesiological meaning, Ragusa thus positioned himself against the denial of any equivalence between the Roman and the universal Church, as proposed in the tradition of Wyclif's ecclesiology.[91] Yet again, as though he was offering the Spiritualists a line of reasoning that they could relate to, John elaborated on the mystical body that is the Church not only in hierarchical terms but also with an emphasis on the spiritual unity holding among the members of the mystical body.

While discussing the first of the four *notae ecclesiae* taken from the Creed (i.e. *una, sancta, catholica,* and *apostolica*), Ragusa identified three ways according to which a body may be said to be one in number.[92] In a natural body, this unity is brought about by nerves and anatomical jointings, by way of animated spirits and the powers of the soul, and insofar all members are being perfected by the soul, which is numerically one in all members (cf. John of Ragusa: 1983, 60–61 [= *De ecclesia* II, 2]). These three kinds of unity are also found in the mystical body. But instead of nerves and jointings, in the mystical body it is first the content of faith, that is, the *credibilia*, that renders the members one continuum. This "unity of faith", John remarks, "is the first unity, through which anybody begins to be incoporated into the Church, and it is the fundament and root of the whole spiritual edifice".[93]

---

90 For John's disgression on the Roman Church, see the whole passage in John of Ragusa: 1983, 17–20 (= *De ecclesia* I, 2).

91 It must be noted that after 1437, when pope Eugene IV convoked the Council of Ferrara-Florence, John of Ragusa, who became a cardinal under the antipope Felix V, developed an anti-Roman ecclesiology and became a commited conciliarist in the strong sense; cf. Krämer: 1980, 198–204 and Léger: 2013, 34–37. For an account of the legal controversies concerning the term *romana ecclesia* in the Middle Ages, cf. Tierney: 1998, 36–46.

92 This discussion inaugurates the second part of the *De ecclesia*. Note that John here enumerates five notions of unity among the members of both the natural and the mystical body but dwells only on those three that constitute numerical unity as opposed to unity in kind; cf. John of Ragusa: 1983, 59–62 (= *De ecclesia* II, 2).

93 John of Ragusa: 1983, 65 (= *De ecclesia* II, 4): "[…] unitas fidei est prima unitas, per quam quis incipit Ecclesiae incorporari, et est fundamentum et radix totius aedificii spiritualis." On the image of the *aedificium spirituale*, cf. Madrigal Terrazas: 1995, 328–331.

Second, in analogy to the powers of the soul and the animated spirits in a natural body, in the mystical body love and the gratifying grace given by God in the sacrament of baptism give one unifying life to all its members. Because grace and love thus animate the ecclesiastical body constituted by faith, they are the perfection of faith (cf. John of Ragusa: 1983, 68 [= *De ecclesia* II, 5]). In this respect now, any member of a body is such only if it is actually (*in actu*) alive and actually has the vivifying spirit existing in it. In the mystical body, this actual inherence of grace and love in the soul constitutes membership of "Christ or of the Church".[94] Ragusa uses this point as a rebuttal against Wyclif's claim that only those are Church members that have received the grace of predestination (cf. John Wyclif: 1886, 2). Predestination does not have any such effect, Ragusa tells us. For although it is a consequence of God's predestination that someone will be a member of Christ in the afterlife, nonetheless he or she

> does not become [a member of] Christ through or by way of [predestination] but rather by way of the perfected grace, which will be inhering in the soul, uniting it with and incorporating it into the heavenly Church [...]".[95]

This is to say that predestination does perfect the grace given by God in the sacrament of baptism, but in and of itself it does not make any one a member of the heavenly Church, not to mention the Church in this life. Ragusa thus uses the analogy from the natural body in order to establish that the mystical body of Christ is one spiritually animated body not because of God's predestination but rather by way of love and gratifying grace given by God in the sacrament of baptism, which is the "entrance to the Church" (*ianua Ecclesiae*) (cf. John of Ragusa: 1983, 64 [= *De ecclesia* II, 4]).

Finally, the third kind of unity provided by the soul in a natural body translates to the mystical body as the unity brought about by the Holy Spirit. Just as in a natural body there is "one soul that makes the eye see, the ear hear, and likewise in the other [senses]"[96], so "does the Holy Spirit bind together the members of the

---

94 Cf. John of Ragusa: 1983, 69 (= *De ecclesia* II, 5): "Non potest esse aliquis membrum vivum alicuius corporis vivi naturalis, nisi illud actu sit et actu corpori uniatur habeatque vitam in ipso formaliter inexistentem. Ergo non potest esse aliquis membrum corporis Christi vel Ecclesiae nisi actu sit actuque uniatur et habeat vitam in se formaliter existentem."

95 Cf. John of Ragusa: 1983, 69 (= *De ecclesia* II, 5): "ergo gratia praedestinationis non est secundum se sufficiens, ut per eam aliquis efficiatur formaliter membrum corporis Christi mystici, nec in praesenti nec etiam in futuro, quod licet ad ipsam consequatur ut aliquis finaliter efficiatur membrum Christi, non tamen efficitur Christi per ipsam aut ipsa mediante, sed mediante gratia consummata, quae erit alqiuid in anima formaliter inexistens, ipsam ueniens et incorporans Ecclesiae triumphanti [...]".

96 John of Ragusa: 1983, 72 (= *De ecclesia* II, 6): "una anima faciens in oculo ut videat, in aure ut audiat, et sic in caeteris." As Ragusa points out, this is a quote from the *Glossa ordinaria* on Eph 4:4.

body of Christ, which are the Church, and it distributes the graces to the single members as it wishes, while remaining one and the same spirit."[97] According to Ragusa, therefore, the one and single Holy Spirit specifies or determines the grace inhering in the members of the mystical body, which is fundamentally unified by faith. Thus, "the Holy Spirit, one and indivisible, is the ultimate and first perfection of the whole mystical body, much like the soul in a natural body".[98]

Among the many authorities that John of Ragusa cites for his ecclesiology, that of Thomas Aquinas loomes in a particularly large way. At one point, John even asserts that his own "doctrine previously established [...] is almost entirely that of Saint Thomas".[99] By and large, all evidence from Ragusa's De ecclesia confirms this claim. And more particularly, the greatest part of Ragusa's analogies between a natural and the mystical body as discussed above are taken, sometimes even verbatim, from Aquinas. In a way, this even holds for John's 'hermeneutical principle', that is, for his application of the analogy and his generally careful transferral of select properties of a natural to the mystical body. This principle is spelled out at the end of Ragusa's discussion of the mystical body's unity:

> However, it should be noted that 'with respect to manners of speaking in metaphors and likenesses one should neither expect nor seek a similitude in regard to everything, because then it would not be a similitude but rather the factual truth.' Therefore, also in the mystical body of Christ, which we are discussing here in its likeness with the natural body (be it with regard to the whole, to the head, or to the members), we should not seek each and every similitude or property of a natural body [...], because then it would not be a mystical but rather a natural body.[100]

---

97 John of Ragusa: 1983, 72 (= *De ecclesia* II, 6): "Ita Spiritus Sanctus membra corporis Christi, quae sunt Ecclesia, continet et vegetat dividens singulis gratias prout vult, unus et idem spiritus manens [...]"

98 John of Ragusa: 1983, 61 (= *De ecclesia* II, 2): "[...] Spiritus Sanctus, unus et indivisibilis, qui est ultima perfectio et principalis totius corporis mystici quasi anima in corpore naturali."

99 Cf. John of Ragusa: 1983, 78 (= *De ecclesia* II, 8): "Praedicta doctrina de capite est quasi tota sancti Thomae ex 3° Sententiarum." Note that this accounts first and foremost for the relation between head and members of the mystical body. For more on this, cf. ibid., 73–76 (= *De ecclesia* II, 7).

100 John of Ragusa: 1983, 76 (= *De ecclesia* II, 8): "Sed notandum quod 'in metaphoricis et similitudinaribus locutionibus non oportet attendi nec expetere similitudinem quantum ad omnia; sic enim non esset similitudo, sed rerum veritas.' Ideo nec in corpore Christo mystico, de quo ad praesens loquimur, ad similitudinem corporis naturalis, sive in toto sive in capite aut in membris, expetendae sunt omnes et singulae similitudines seu proprietates corporis naturalis, aut eodem modo, quia iam non esset corpus mysticum, sed naturale."

The quote within this passage is taken again from Aquinas's *Summa theologiae*.[101] Aquinas, however employed it as a counterargument to a point contradicting his own analogy between the head of a natural body and that of the mystical. In the *Summa theologiae*, therefore, the argument strengthens the analogy, whereas in Ragusa's *De ecclesia*, on the higher level of a 'hermeneutical principle', it loosens it. Hence, while it cannot be disputed, as Ragusa himself makes clear, that Aquinas is a major source for the *De ecclesia*'s arguments, it is also clear that the *De ecclesia* uses this source in an independent and original way, stressing the mystical nature of the body of Christ that is the Church.

The same holds, I take it, for Ragusa's ecclesiology more generally. As we have seen above, employing the notion of the mystical body of Christ John of Ragusa argued for both an ecclesiastical hierarchy and a spiritual community. In his ecclesiology there simply is no contradiction between the one and the other, that is, between the material and the spiritual Church, between the mystical body as corporation and as *communio*.[102] And while he used Aquinas' analogy between the natural and the mystical body as an important source of inspiration, he factored out, as it were, what after Aquinas, for instance in Giles of Rome, had become of this analogy. In the light of the history of ecclesiology that this chapter has traversed in a few spotlights it appears that Ragusa returned to a model of late medieval ecclesiology from before the rise of corporative ecclesiology, which employed an organological notion of the Church as the mystical – but, as we have seen, in fact a de-mystified – body of Christ.

I would not go as far as to follow the suggestion that in Ragusa's *De ecclesia* "the doctrine of the eucharist was again considered in ecclesiological terms, in contrast to high scholasticism but in agreement with the older tradition",[103] that is, in agreement with early medieval accounts such as that of Gottschalk of Orbais. Rather, if we see John of Ragusa in the context of the efforts of a union with the Hussites and their fundamentally Wyclifite ecclesiology, it seems safe to say that Ragusa was at least prompted, if not inspired, by his opponents to emphasize the *communio*-character of the Church to such a large extent. He argued, at any rate, for the sacrament of baptism and for the grace thus divinely conveyed being the entrance to the Church and the touchstone for Church membership. In this perspective, the mystical body –

---

101 Cf. Thomas Aquinas: 1903, 127a (= *STh*. III, q. 8, a. 1, ad 2). The original source, however, is John of Damascus' *De fide orthodoxa*, cf. ibid.

102 J. Santiago Madrigal aptly describes the latter point as "eclesiología del *Corpus-caput* en clave de *communio*", cf. Madrigal Terrazas: 1995, 335.

103 Cf. Helmrath: 1987, 368: "Dogmengeschichtlich gesehen könnte man vielleicht sagen, daß die Eucharistielehre *wieder* ekklesiologisch gewendet wurde, im Unterschied zur Hochscholastik, aber in Übereinstimmung mit der älteren Tradition" (emphasis Helmrath). Cf. Schmidt: 1955; Shogimen: 2006 for the works of ecclesiology thus characterized.

conceived of as an emphatically *mystical* body, "bound together by the bond of love or faith" (cf. John of Ragusa: 1983: 13) – also appears as a fundamentally spiritual continuum, rooted in sacramental communion.

In view of the manifold history of late medieval ecclesiology outlined in this chapter, the view of this period's ecclesiological thought as strictly corporative and, in reaction to that, as no less strictly spiritualistic should be emended.[104] Giles of Rome's, Jean Quidort's, John Wyclif's, and John of Ragusa's ecclesiologies rather transmit the image of a history oscillating between the poles of corporative and spiritualistic accounts of the Church. The concepts of *corpus* and *communio* illustrate and exemplify this dynamic, as they were rarely employed independently from one another. Rather, in the ecclesiologies here discussed, these themes illuminate each other in different angles and intensities, such that in Giles of Rome, for instance, the ecclesiastical *communio* is but a corollary to the organological *corpus mysticum*, whereas in Wyclif it is roughly the other way around. In contrast to these extremes, however, Quidort's and Ragusa's ecclesiologies both exhibit the search for a balance. Most explicitly so, Ragusa's *De ecclesia* is an impressive attempt to emphasize the mystical character of the Church in late medieval terms.

It seems that this late medieval history of ecclesiology is not as straightforward bound for decline, as if it was all but waiting for the Reformation to revive the doctrine of the Church. But neither does this history already anticipate the new impulses that the Reformation would later bring about. Rather, if seen in its own right, late medieval ecclesiology is a complex fabric made of political, ecclesiastical, and intellectual fibres that originate in quite specific contexts, intersect at multiple points, and each follow their own course at the same time. A more comprehensive account of late medieval ecclesiology would certainly dissect these fibres more thoroughly and perhaps also clarify their continuities and discontinuities with the thought of sixteenth century Protestant reformers; not in order to diminish their achievements, of course, but rather attempting to cross the bridge between reformatory and late medieval theology. This bridge, at times, is more solid and more supporting than we may have been led to believe.

---

104 I have introduced Henri de Lubac's account (2009) as an example of this historiographical approach above.

Bibliography

Sources

THOMAS AQUINAS (1903), Tertia pars Summa theologiae a quaestione I ad quaestionem LIX (ed. Leonina 11), Rome: Typographia Polyglotta.

THOMAS AQUINAS (1906), Tertia pars Summa theologiae a quaestione LX ad quaestionem XC (ed. Leonina 12), Rome: Typographia Polyglotta.

THOMAS AQUINAS (1933), Scriptum super libro tertio Sententiarum, ed. M.F. Moos, Paris: Lethielleux.

AUGUSTINE OF HIPPO (1930), Sermo 229 (= s. Denis 6), in: Miscellanea Agostiniana. Testi e studi pubblicati a cura dell'ordine eremitano di s. Agostino nel XV centenario dalla morte del santo dottore, 1: Sancti Augustini sermones post Maurini reperti, ed. G. Morin, Rome: Typographia Polyglotta, 29–32.

[BONIFACE VIII] (1921), Les registres de Boniface VIII: recueil des bulles de ce pape, vol. 3, ed. G. Digard, Paris: E. De Boccard.

GILES OF ROME (2004), On Ecclesiastical Power: A Medieval Theory of World Government. A Critical Edition and Translation, ed. Robert W. Dyson, New York, NY: Columbia University Press.

[GOTTSCHALK OF ORBAIS] (1945), Œuvres théologiques et grammaticales de Godescalc d'Orbais. Textes en majeure partie inédits, ed. C. Lambot (SSL 20), Leuven: Spicilegium Sacrum Lovaniense.

PETER LOMBARD (1981), Sententiae in IV libris distinctae, tomus II: liber III et IV (SpicBon 5), Grottaferrata: Ad Claras Aquas.

PASCHASIUS RADBERTUS (1969), De corpore et sanguine Domini, ed. B. Paulus (CCCM 16), Turnhout: Brepols.

[JEAN QUIDORT] (1969), Johannes Quidort von Paris, Über königliche und päpstliche Gewalt (De regia potestate et papali). Textkritische Edition mit deutscher Übersetzung, ed. F. Bleienstein (Frankfurter Studien zur Wissenschaft von der Politik 4), Stuttgart: Klett.

JOHN WYCLIF (1886), Tractatus de ecclesia, ed. J. Loserth, London: Trübner.Secondary Literature

ADAMSON, PETER (2019): *Interroga virtutes naturales*: Nature in Giles of Rome's *On Ecclesiastical Power*, Vivarium 57, 22–50.

ALTHAUS, PAUL (1929): Communio Sanctorum. Die Gemeinde im lutherischen Kirchengedanken, Munich: Christian Kaiser Verlag.

BELLITTO, CHRISTOPHER M. (2009), The Reform Context of the Great Western Schism, in: Joëlle Rollo-Koster/Thomas M. Izbicki (ed.), A Companion to the Great Western Schism (1378–1417) (Brill's Companions to the Christian Tradition 17), Leiden: Brill, 303–331.

BENKO, STEPHEN (1964), The Meaning of Sanctorum Communio (SHT 3), London: SCM Press.

BERTELLONI, FRANCISO (2004), Die Anwendung von Kausalitätstheorien im politischen

Denken von Thomas von Aquin und Aegidius Romanus, in: Martin Kaufhold (ed.), Politische Reflexion in der Welt des späten Mittelalters/Political Thought in the Age of Scholasticism. Essays in Honour of Jürgen Miethke (SMRT 103), Leiden: Brill, 85–108.

BRIGUGLIA, GIANLUCA (2015), Theology, Sacramental Debates, and Political Thought in John of Paris: The Case of the Eucharist, in: Chris Jones (ed.), John of Paris: Beyond Royal and Papal Power (Disputatio 23), Turnhout: Brepols, 401–421.

BURN, ANDREW E. (1900), Neue Texte zur Geschichte des apostolischen Symbols II, ZKG 21, 128–137.

CONGAR, YVES (1971a), Die Lehre von der Kirche. Von Augustinus bis zum Abendländischen Schisma (HDG III, 3c), Freiburg: Herder.

CONGAR, YVES (1971b), Die Lehre von der Kirche. Vom Abendländischen Schisma bis zur Gegenwart (HDG III, 3d), Freiburg: Herder.

CORTONI, CLAUDIO UBALDO (2016), "Habeas Corpus". Il corpo di Cristo dalla devozione alla sua umanità al culto eucaristico (sec. VIII–XV) (StAns 170), Sankt Ottilien: EOS.

DAHMUS, JOSEPH H. (1960), John Wyclif and the English Government, Speculum 35, 51–68.

ECKERMANN, WILLIGIS (1975), Augustinus Favaroni von Rom und Johannes Wyclif. Der Ansatz ihrer Lehre über die Kirche, in: Cornelius Petrus Mayer/Willigis Eckermann (ed.), Scientia Augustiniana. Studien über Augustinus, den Augustinismus und den Augustinerorden, Festschrift Adolar Zumkeller, Würzburg: Augustinus-Verlag, 323–348.

EVANS, GILLIAN (2013), Wycliff, John, in: Karla Pollmann/Willemien Otten (ed.), The Oxford Guide to the Historical Reception of Augustine, Oxford: Oxford University Press, vol. 3, 1922–1925.

FUDGE, THOMAS A. (2017), The Hussites and the Council, in: Michiel Decaluwé/Thomas M. Izbicki/Gerald Christianson (ed.), A Companion to the Council of Basel (Brill's Companions to the Christian Tradition 74), Leiden: Brill 2017, 254–281.

HELMRATH, JOHANNES (1987), Das Basler Konzil 1431–1449. Forschungsstand und Probleme (KHAb 32), Wien: Böhlau.

KANTOROWICZ, ERNST (1957), The King's Two Bodies: A Study in Mediaeval Political Theology, Princeton, NJ: Princeton University Press.

KRÄMER, WERNER (1980), Konsens und Rezeption. Verfassungsprinzipien der Kirche im Basler Konziliarismus. Mit Edition ausgewählter Texte (BGPhMA, N.F. 19), Münster: Aschendorff.

KRCHŇÁK, ALOYSIUS (1960), De vita et operibus Ioannis de Ragusio (Lat., N.S. 26), Rome: Fac. Theol. Pontificiae Universitatis Laternanensis.

LAHEY, STPEHEN E. (2009), John Wyclif (Great Medieval Thinkers), Oxford: Oxford University Press.

LEFF, GORDON (1976), Heresy in the Later Middle Ages: The Relation of Heterodoxy to Dissent c. 1250–c. 1450, Manchester: Manchester University Press.

LÉGER, YVAN (2013), L'ecclésiologie de Jean de Raguse, Bulletin du centre d'études médiévales d'Auxerre, Hors-série 7 (= Les nouveaux horizons de l'ecclésiologie: du discours clérical à la science du social), http://cem.revues.org/12783, doi:10.4000/cem.12783.

Leppin, Volker (2011), Unmittelbar zu Gott oder unmittelbar zum Papst? Kirchliche Leitung und einzelner Glaubender bei Aegidius Romanus und Wilhelm von Ockham, in: Mariano Delgado/Voker Leppin/David Neuhold (ed.), Ringen um die Wahrheit. Gewissenskonflikte in der Christentumsgeschichte, Fribourg: Academic Press/Stuttgart: W. Kohlhammer Verlag, 145–155.

Lubac, Henri de (2009), Corpus Mysticum. L'Eucharistie et l'Église au Moyen Âge: Étude historique (Œuvres complètes 15), Paris: Éditions du Cerf.

Madec, Goulven (1994), Article "Christus", AugL 1, 845–908.

Madrigal Terrazas, J. Santiago (1995), La eclesiología de Juan de Ragusa O.P. (1390/95–1443): Estudio e interpretación de su Tractatus de Ecclesia (PUPCM.E 60), Madrid: Universidad Pontificia Comillas.

Miethke, Jürgen (2008), Politiktheorie im Mittelalter. Von Thomas von Aquin bis Wilhelm von Ockham, Third edition, Tübingen: Mohr.

Nederman, Cary J. (2004), Body Politics: The Diversification of Organic Metaphors in the Later Middle Ages, Pensiero politico medievale 2, 59–87.

Oakley, Francis (1979), The Western Church in the Later Middle Ages, Ithaca, N.Y.: Cornell University Press.

Pennington, Kenneth (2004), Representation in Medieval Canon Law, The Jurist 64, 361–383.

Prügl, Thomas (2007), Das Schriftargument zwischen Papstmonarchie und konziliarer Idee. Biblische Argumentationsmodelle im Basler Konziliarismus, in: Andreas Pečar/Kai Trampedach (ed.), Die Bibel als politisches Argument. Voraussetzungen und Folgen biblizistischer Herrschaftslegitimation in der Vormoderne (HZ.B, N.F. 43), München: Oldenbourg, 219–241.

Prügl, Thomas (2013), Dissidence and Renewal: Developments in Late Medieval Ecclesiology, Bulletin du centre d'études médiévales d'Auxerre, Hors-série 7 (= Les nouveaux horizons de l'ecclésiologie: du discours clérical à la science du social), http://cem.revues.org/12782, doi:10.4000/cem.12782.

Prügl, Thomas (2017), The Fourth Lateran Council – A Turning Point in Medieval Ecclesiology?, in: Gert Melville/Johannes Helmrath (ed.), The Fourth Lateran Council: Institutional Reform and Spiritual Renewal. Proceedings of the Conference Marking the Eight Hundredth Anniversary of the Council, Organized by the Pontificio Comitato di Scienze Storiche (Rome, 15–17 October 2015), Affalterbach: Didymos-Verlag, 79–98.

Shogimen, Takashi (2006), Wyclif's Ecclesiology and Political Thought, in: Ian Christopher Levy (ed.), A Companion to John Wyclif: Late Medieval Theologian (Brill's Companions to the Christian Tradition 4), Leiden: Brill, 199–240.

Schmidt, Martin (1955), John Wyclifs Kirchenbegriff: Der Christus humilis Augustins bei Wyclif. Zugleich ein Beitrag zu Frage: Wyclif und Luther, in: Friedrich Hübner (ed.), Gedenkschrift für D. Werner Elert. Beiträge zur historischen und systematischen Theologie, Berlin: Lutherisches Verlagshaus, 72–108.

Tierney, Brian (1998), Foundations of the Conciliar Theory: The Contribution of the

Medieval Canonists from Gratian to the Great Western Schism, New Enlarged Edition (SHCT 81), Leiden: Brill.

UBL, KARL (2003), Johannes Quidorts Weg zur Sozialphilosophie, Francia 30, 43–72.

UBL, KARL (2004), Die Genese der Bulle *Unam sanctam:* Anlass, Vorlagen, Intuition, in: Martin Kaufhold (ed.), Politische Reflexion in der Welt des späten Mittelalters/Political Thought in the Age of Scholasticism. Essays in Honour of Jürgen Miethke (SMRT 103), Leiden: Brill, 129–149.

ULLMANN, WALTER (1967), Boniface VIII and his Contemporary Scholarship, JThS n.s. 27, 58–87.

WAGNER, WILHELM (1937), Die Kirche als Corpus Christi Mysticum beim jungen Luther, ZKTh 61, 29–98.

WALTER, MATTHIAS (2001), Gemeinde als Leib Christi. Untersuchungen zum Corpus Paulinum und zu den "Apostolischen Vätern" (NTOA 40), Fribourg: Universitätsverlag/Göttingen: Vandenhoeck & Ruprecht.

Violet Soen

A Church or Churches?

The Aristocracy Divided over Ecclesiology during the Dutch Revolt

1. Introduction

Tracing ecclesiology back to the sixteenth century might initially seem like an odd task: the word itself first appeared in the seventeenth century and only came to denote the systematic study of church conceptions in the early nineteenth century. Since then, scholars have applied the term in a more metaphorical sense as a tool to analyze the ancestry of modern ecclesiologies; reformation historians have used this methodology to study the works of Luther, Zwingli, Calvin, and others, in order to better understand the organization of the Churches which implemented their teachings. Even so, ecclesiology did not exist as an all-encompassing endeavor in the sixteenth century: except for Catholic and Protestant theologians, most believers assembled, reassembled, and reconfigured their personal beliefs, as Carlo Ginzburg (English translation, 1980) carefully reminds us through the *microstoria* of Menocchio, the unfortunate miller from Friuli tried by the Inquisition in 1599 for making up his personal cosmogony.

The current task of analyzing 'the ecclesiology' of 'the aristocracy' (defined here as the upper strata of the nobility) in sixteenth-century Habsburg Netherlands thus risks creating a fragmented picture (Soen/Vanysacker/François: 2017). With a few exceptions, mighty noblemen and noblewomen justified their actions and beliefs with a mix of traditional teachings, reform impulses, family motives, and pragmatic considerations. They relied upon their court priests and theologians for advice in religious matters, but, if not predestined for an ecclesiastical career or service in the church (and even then), they usually did not possess an elaborated expertise in either theology or ecclesiology. For most modern observers, these aristocrats seemed to hopelessly contradict themselves, writing to one addressee that they were ardently defending the Catholic faith, while denying that very commitment to another (usually in an attempt to either win friends or make allies) (Goosens: 1996). Even in the well-documented correspondence of Prince William of Orange (1533–1584), who became the leader of the Revolt in the Netherlands and who first converted to Lutheranism and then Calvinism, the rarely used word *church* only referred to the infrastructure of church buildings, Antwerp's local Protestant Churches or the

Church of England. It never figured as a metaphor for Christianity.[1] Thus, this contribution focuses on the actions (rather than on the discourse or writings) of members of the most important aristocrat families from the sixteenth-century Low Countries in order to unravel how they conceived the relation between Church and State at this crucial juncture of time. As such, it will show how in 1579 shifting aristocratic coalitions helped facilitating a negotiated restoration of the Catholic faith in those parts of the Low Countries returning under Habsburg rule, and the adoption of a liberty of conscience in the other territories joining the Union of Utrecht.

2. A Divided European Nobility

Historians have written many works on the Reformation and its impact on the European nobility (a bibliography on that theme is provided by Soen: 2015a). They have concluded that the Reformation presented a far-reaching challenge to the nobility's power and possessions in Latin Europe: while some noble families converted to the newer Protestant confessions, others patronized reforms within the Catholic faith. Religious convictions often turned into a cause for revolt, not only for Protestant noblemen intent on defying the Catholic establishment, but also for their Catholic counterparts when faced with insurgent Protestant regimes. Confessional choice usually included repercussions on landed properties, the main source of wealth and privilege for the second estate within the Ancient Regime: Protestant princes often redistributed confiscated Catholic lands, while Catholic rulers acted similarly towards Protestant noblemen (Junot/Soen: 2020). The nobility's confessional division eventually prevented it from forming one united block in emergent European states (Ash: 2003). This fragmentation was particularly visible in the Holy Roman Empire, where the Peace of Augsburg accorded territorial princes the *jus reformandi*, later coined in the famous adage *cuius regio, illio est religio* (Soen: 2017b). While the very definition of nobility relied upon a nucleus of political and juridical prerogatives, land ownership and social status, virtue and faith, the Protestant and Catholic Reformations challenged all components of the traditional noble 'habitus'.

During the last decades, historians have shattered most of the blind presuppositions on social status and its link to the Reformation by disproving two popular overarching narratives (Soen: 2015a). The first long maintained that the nobility, and especially the upper aristocracy, took the lead in implementing the Reformation throughout Europe (Carroll: 2013). Indeed, Frederick III, Elector of Saxony,

---

1 Based on sample searches in different languages through William of Orange's correspondence, as edited by the ING-Huyghens Institute for History: http://resources.huygens.knaw.nl/wvo/en.

acted as Luther's protector and helped to establish the young Lutheran Church, while the Schmalkaldic League depended on both aristocratic princes and cities for its success. The aristocrat Gustav Wasa facilitated the reformation in Sweden. In France, Huguenots wisely sought noble protection from Condé and Coligny. Even so, other aristocrats from France, Spain, and Italy made it their mission to fight the Reformation by introducing Tridentine Catholicism. This included the Borgia and Farnese dynasties, but also the family of Lorraine-Guise, which boasted mighty cardinals and even a Queen of Scotland (Béguin: 1999, Carroll: 1998, Carroll: 2009; Mantini: 2003). Most of these families, inspired by Christian humanists and the Council of Trent, adopted a renewed Catholicism. Moreover, new reform-minded Catholic orders, such as Jesuits, Theatines and Carmelites, often drew largely on female noble patrons to reach their goals (François/Soen: 2018).

A second narrative argued that gentry, the lower strata within the noble estate, defended Protestantism and influenced its eventual success. This so-called *protestantisme seigneurial* has been particularly placed within the vast territories of the Kingdom of France, and accounted for the many privileges that protestant lords (*seigneurs*) received in the various pacification edicts passed during the Wars of Religion and the Edict of Nantes (Neuschel: 1989). In other European regions, the lower nobilities – though still the privileged rank of society – also mattered. In 1573, the Confederation of Warsaw, concluded by a Parliament (the *Sejm*) crowded with the noble *szlachta,* allowed the local lords to choose the religion practiced within their lordship. At least *verbatim,* the Confederation of Warsaw went beyond the famous Peace of Augsburg, allowing lords with local, instead of regional, power to accept the Reformation or even Orthodox churches. In practice, scholars acknowledge that Catholic opposition obstructed most of its practical implementation, showing the resilience of the Catholic nobility throughout Europe (Kaplan: 2007). Hence, the Reformation not only divided Europe as a continent, but also its Second Estate, making some groups within the aristocracy and the gentry chose for the Reformation, and others reject it, leading to capricious coalitions in local circumstances (Geevers/Marini: 2015).

3.   A Diverging Path of the Dutch Nobility

This historiographical and geographical overview reminds us how hard it remains to accurately determine the nobility's position within the Habsburg territories of the Low Countries, which Emperor Charles V made 'one and indivisible' between 1548 and 1549 (Duke: 2004, Soen: 2017c). Living at the commercial crossroads connecting Antwerp and Amsterdam, as well as in the buffer zone between the Holy Roman Empire and France, the nobility of these so-called 'Seventeen Provinces' did not comfortably fit within either of the aforementioned patterns. Noble status relied, as in much of Europe (with the possible exceptions of Poland-Lithuania), on land ownership and the privileges attached to it, such as participating in sessions of the provincial estates, rights of justice, coinage, or arms, and the nobles' own capacity to *vivre noblement* and their ability to demonstrate it through conspicuous consumption. Before 1595, when noble titles became subjected to the legislating activity of the King of Spain (comparatively late to both the Castilian and French lands), a noble 'status' thus depended on lands, titles, and the manner in which they displayed their social position in daily life, although there were great divergences from Frisian-speaking territories in the extreme north to French-speaking borderlands in the extreme south (Janssens: 1998, Van Steensel: 2010; Gietman: 2010, Buylaert: 2012).

To belong to the upper segment of the nobility, aristocrats needed additional sources of power and prestige to discern them amongst their noble peers: membership in the Order of the Golden Fleece, a position in the collateral councils at the Coudenberg Palace in Brussels, an appointment as provincial governor in one of the seventeen provinces, or a military commandership over Habsburg troops (Les élites: 2001; Cools: 2001; Rosenfeld: 1959). In this respect, the top five families of the Dutch aristocracy included the well-known and still-thriving (though not in direct male line) Orange-Nassau, Croÿ, and Lalaing dynasties, and the (more or less) extinct Egmond and Montmorency families (Soen: 2012). Often, these noble 'dynasties' (Geevers/Marini: 2015) are identified as 'southern-Netherlandish', as they owned lands and properties primarily in the French-speaking border provinces of Hainaut and Artois, though all of them also possessed territories in either Dutch-speaking Holland or further to the north, and in the Kingdom of France (Soen: 2017a).

It remains a puzzle why no *chef de famille* from any of the five aforementioned families championed the Protestant faith before 1567, which was already quite late from a pan-European perspective: until then, Coligny, Condé, and Wasa had no counterpart in the territories between the Rhine, the Meuse, and the Scheldt (Van Nierop: 1995, 26–68). This might be all the more surprising, because all five families had Protestant relatives living either within or across borders. Antoine 'le Calviniste', a nephew of the Croÿ family, was one of the protagonists for the Protestant cause, serving Condé in adjacent Picardy (Soen: 2015b and Soen/Junot: forthcoming). William of Orange was the only Catholic son raised in Brussels within the Lutheran Nassau branch living in German Dillenburg, and his Lutheran brother Louis frequently came to the Netherlands to raise support for the Protestant cause (Geevers: 2010). In 1561, the Prince married (in a generally unlucky marriage) Anne of Saxony, who had received special permission to continue practicing Lutheranism within the King of Spain's famously Catholic empire (Pollmann: 2015). Count Lamoral of Egmond had married Sabine of Bavary, for whom the Calvinist Elector of the Palatinate had previously acted as a guardian (Geevers: 2014). Philippe de

Montmorency, Count of Horn, married the Calvinist Walburgis of Nieuwenaer, who introduced the Reformation to the lordship of Weert, as did her brother to his seigneuries (Kloek: 2014, Groenveld: 2003). Yet, despite these Protestant relatives and mixed households, none of the aforementioned male aristocrats chose to openly patronize the Protestant faith, as they likely sought to avoid the sad fate of the Schmalkaldic League's Protestant leaders (Soen: 2017b). Most of all, they realized that Charles V's son, and their immediate overlord, Philip II, viewed himself as a staunch defender of the Catholic faith, both to the south and north of the Pyrenees, and that, also according to the stipulations laid out in the Peace of Augsburg, he was allowed to choose the religion of his subjects.

Historian Hendrik Enno van Gelder has already remarked that it were second-ranked noblemen outside the established power structures of the Brussels State Councils or the Order of the Golden Fleece, or those noblemen deprived of a provincial governorship who supported the Reformation during its earliest sixteenth-century phase and who led the opposition against the traditional power structures of State and Church. In his now classic article, Enno van Gelder sketched the fate of three noblemen: Henry of Brederode; Henry of Bailleul; and Herman of Bronkhorst; all three of whom used their own privileges and power to spread the reformation within their lordship (Enno van Gelder: 1936). Noblewomen within these same circles, especially when widowed, also became important promotors of the Reformed cause. The mother, daughter and niece of Bronkhorst, for example, welcomed the disciples of Geneva and Emden into their household, and allowed Protestants to preach within their lands, even offering to help with organizing, facilitating, or at least allowing iconoclasm (Valkeneer/Soen: 2015). These cases showed that the Reformation was not only supported by the *bourgeoisie* and *regents* who would eventually flourish in the Dutch Republic, but also by much of the region's nobility (Gietman: 2010), making the pattern similar to the French *protestantisme seigneurial*.

4. Negative Programs (1562–1566)

Even without family leaders converting to Protestantism, clear aristocratic opposition towards the reign of Philip II emerged by 1563. The Counts of Egmond and Horn, together with the Prince of Orange, formed a triumvirate and drafted letters of complaint for the king, while actively mobilizing their younger brothers and relatives to join their alliance. This resulting League compromised three leading dynasties, yet it left out the Croÿ and the Lalaing (this could have been due to the fact that the *chefs de famille* were still rather young and that long-standing strife existed between the leading dynasties). Most historians agree that these aristocratic families primarily centered their opposition around political themes (Geevers:

2008). In this respect, local elites felt there was much to complain about: their loss of influence after the king left the Low Countries for the Iberian Peninsula in 1559, the intertwined fear of a Hispanization of the government, and shaky royal finances that made it hard to pay the troops under their command. In short, they protested against the changing relationship between Madrid and Brussels within the global Spanish monarchy, and shared their discontent over the limitations placed on their ability to channel patronage (Van Nierop: 1999; Geevers: 2008; Soen: 2019).

Unsurprisingly, this first manifestation of aristocratic opposition also included religious matters, as politics and religion were never separate spheres in the sixteenth century. Here, the League reiterated two complaints, one personal and the other infrastructural. The first, and most commonly voiced grievance until 1564, concerned the new bishopric scheme introduced in 1559 and the influence of the new Archbishop of Mechelen, Antoine de Perrenot, Lord of Granvelle, and close councilor to governess-general Margaret of Parma. They denounced his increased influence through the bishopric reform, as he had become the president of the Estates of Brabant and would also receive a cardinal's hat, thus overruling them in matters of precedence and ceremony both at a provincial and a governmental level. Moreover, they complained that he took too much liberty in counselling the governess-general and that he controlled most of the channels of communication and patronage in and around Brussels (Rodríguez-Salgado: 2000). They also privately argued that Granvelle counseled the king to introduce the Spanish Inquisition, a position that had already appeared in clandestine pamphlets (Verberckmoes/Soen: 2017).

Secondly, the triumvirate shared objections concerning the infrastructure that had been set up for the persecution of Protestants: secular courts implemented the harsh 'heresy placards' and were assisted by episcopal, papal and specially entitled inquisitors (Gielis/Soen: 2005, Goosens: 1997/1998). Most governing elites felt that the repressive system had reached its limits, as the number of Protestants grew exponentially after 1559, and the many public executions (which they co-coordinated as provincial governors) seemed to cause increased societal unrest (Woltjer: 1976). Yet, the sources remain surprisingly silent when historians search for these aristocrats' systematic programs or ecclesiologies. Today, we can read in their letters that the triumvirate always reacted 'against' something, but we unfortunately cannot reconstruct the many secret meetings that took place in their castles, possibly on greater schemes and endeavors. Even though the grumbling triumvirate initially only opposed Granvelle and his 'laws' (hinting at the 'placards'), they subsequently protested against the public execution of Protestants, the alleged schemes that introduced or would introduce the Spanish Inquisition, and the resulting harsh legislation. After the Council of Trent ended in 1563, they linked their opposition against its disciplinary measures of episcopal visitation (Soen: 2018). The only positive things they formulated in official letters was the king to change his location and the convocation of a States-General, which seemed to have been the magical solution to all contemporary problems (Parker: 2002).

Within this juncture, it was the gentry which acted as the main patrons of the Reformation, with some of its members rallying for the formation of a nobility-led league and called it the 'Compromise of the Nobility' (Van Nierop: 1991). Similarly to contemporary events in France, this new league publicly protested against the religious repression. The initiative lay with the lower nobility, many of whom were either Lutherans or, especially, Calvinists, though Catholic elites and the city patriciate also joined; while the aristocracy abstained, they had their secretaries and spies keep an eye on the developments (Geevers: 2008, 165–171). Philip of Marnix, lord of Sainte-Aldegonde, who had attended the Academy in Geneva, and the younger Lutheran brother of Orange convinced peers and urban elites to join their protests. The aforementioned Henry of Brederode, aspiring to finally have a say in Brussels, eventually championed the movement. More institutionalized than the aristocratic League, the Compromise received a foundational charter and its leaders submitted two Requests in April and late July 1566. The Requests excelled in vagueness (or, rather, compromise), as it was easier to unify Lutherans, Calvinists, and Catholics against a cause than for one. The 'Compromise of the Nobility' was thus *against* religious persecution, and especially its harshness, and condemned the public burnings of 'innocent Christians'. The leaders conveniently placed all of the blame on the emerging 'Inquisition', directly pointing to their fear of the proclamation of the Council of Trent in the Low Countries. The numerous sides lacked a positive program of coalition, and the Lutherans and Calvinist members would later find themselves divided on the questions surrounding armed resistance, with the former against it and the latter endorsing it, and the question of liberty of conscience (Soen: 2018).

5. Positive Programs? (1566–1567)

The Iconoclastic Fury starting in the Summer of 1566 – though late, disparate, and capricious when compared to earlier waves of European iconoclasm – greatly altered the nobility's perspectives (for a new interpretation, see the thematic journal issue edited by Van Bruaene/Jonckheere/Suykerbuyk: 2016). While a part of the lower nobility had facilitated and even fostered iconoclasm, in both their lordship and neighboring cities (Soen/Valkeneer: 2015), the 'Fury' had traumatized a larger part of the noble elite and they became frightened by the 'popular' forces which seemed beyond their control. Most aristocrats disliked that public opinion blamed them for starting the whole iconoclastic movement. A crisis meeting at Coudenberg Palace with provincial governors and Knights of the Golden Fleece concluded that the confederated noblemen should use their arms and authority to restore order, and that they should no longer protect hedge preaching, as they often had throughout the Seventeen Provinces. Henceforth, the nobility had to act as the 'reasonable head' of the 'lower parts' of society during the Fury, as they alone could defend King and Faith according to the duties inherent to their estate. As a result, the Compromise of the Nobility disbanded at Coudenberg Palace, and its leaders (only handing in their second Request two weeks before) solemnly swore that their confederation was 'nil, broken and dissolved'.[2] The agreement formally limited the noble elites' ability to act as the religious peacemakers to which they aspired (like their German and French counterparts) and forced them into the position of defending Catholicism (Soen: 2016b; Soen: 2012).

Nonetheless, the late Juliaan Woltjer identified this agreement as the 'first victory' for the moderate party, who were seeking a *modus vivendi* between all confessions, as there was a remarkable caveat which seemed to allow some temporal rights for Protestants (Woltjer: 1976; updated in Woltjer: 1999). Initially, the Compromise obtained some kind of allowance for Protestant preaching, as the agreement allowed them to preach outside the city walls on places where this had occurred before 23 August, but governor-general Margaret of Parma seems to have vetoed this a short time later. Moreover, the caveat was more confused and complex than Woltjer realized, as it was changed in the final printed version of 25 August. It now prescribed that former advocates of the Compromise had to prevent Protestants from preaching in areas where it had not occurred before 23 August, and that preaching outside the city walls could not cause 'scandal' or unrest under any circumstance. Permission for unarmed Protestant preaching (not even worship) was thus implicit, and had to be deduced from negative formulations. Still, the governorness-general promised that the inquisition 'of which they complained' would pause, and abrogated temporarily the handful of inquisitorial titles granted by the king and the pope. She also promised to re-initiate a plan for moderating the heresy laws with the king (Soen: 2016b). It is clear that confederates refusing to drop their opposition paraphrased the agreement as 'the end of the inquisition', and spread the message in this sloganeering way (Verberckmoes/Soen: 2017). The peculiar phrasing of the 23–25 August Agreement also led to international speculation: some Lutheran princes from the Holy Roman Empire suggested during an embassy

---

2 'nul, cassé, absolu': *Serment solempnel faicte par les confederez le 25 d'aoust 1566 d'entretenir les poincts icy declairez*, 25 August 1566: Archivo General de Simancas, Secretarías Provinciales 2604 s.f. Still, despite the dissolution, the agreement took a rather mild and reconciling tone: the members of the disbanded league now obtained open letters in the form of an 'assurance' (*lettres patentes en forme d'asseurance*) of life and goods, as they had officially requested. They would be absolved in perpetuity from any incrimination for having initiated iconoclasm, and the text confirmed that they had always served the king according to their duty. In return for these concessions, they had to 'chase' all those sacking churches and to cast out all 'foreigners', 'rebels', and 'enemies of the king'.

in Brussels that governess Margaret should enlarge the agreement along the lines of the Augsburg treaty, while excluding the Calvinists from the deal (Weis: 2002).

The provincial governors were responsible for the implementation of the Agreement and for the restoration of order after iconoclasm. Most proceeded with the exemplary banishment or punishment of iconoclasts, although they did not succeed to either completely contain or counter the Protestant movement. In their local attempts to restore peace after the Iconoclastic Fury, the aforementioned triumvirate allowed Protestants to use Catholic churches within the walls of the city, which was more than conceded in the August Agreement. Orange, Egmond, and Horn experienced this respectively in Antwerp, Ghent, and Tournai. The Prince of Orange likely made the largest concessions, allowing Lutherans and Calvinists to take over churches in the Antwerp[3], with Egmond first allowing and then chasing Calvinists from Ghent (Goosens: 1996), and Horn permitting Calvinist temples temporarily within the city walls of Tournai (Groenveld: 2003). Nonetheless, the three of them remained divided on the questions of armed resistance against Philip II and continued support for the Protestant cause. When a Calvinist volunteer army neared the city, for example, Orange closed the city gates in order to prevent the destruction of the urban patrimony.

For the first time, the triumvirate experimented with a variety of practical solutions that would allow different denominations to coexist within city walls, as they sought to spare commerce and incite concord. However, when the situation calmed down in the autumn and winter of 1566–7, Habsburg authorities turned on local Protestants by declaring that the August agreements had been concluded under duress and could thus be revoked, and that Protestant preaching caused dangerous public 'scandal' under any circumstance. By May 1567, Margaret was able to finish her task in Antwerp, where she withdrew all earlier concessions to the Protestants, though she provided some symbolic mitigation of their persecution (Janssens: 2012; Soen: 2016b). Confronted with this, Orange fled to his family, converted to Lutheranism, and henceforth engaged in open resistance against the Habsburg dynasty. In 1572, he could anchor this resistant movement in Holland and Zeeland, and the insurgent regime in these two provinces would herald him als *pater patriae*.

In contrast, the Counts of Egmond and Horn stayed in the Netherlands, where officials famously arrested and later executed them on 5 June 1568, with the two men professing their Catholic faith on the scaffold. The execution of Horn, and later of his younger brother, Montigny, in the castle of Simancas, ended the Montmorency

---

3 The famous treaty of 2 September 1566 for Antwerp is edited by L.P. Gachard, Correspondance de Guillaume le Taciturne, vol. 2, 215–-218, and can be retrieved by http://www.dutchrevolt.leiden.edu/dutch/bronnen/Pages/1566_09_02_ned.aspx, cf. Marnef: 2011.

branch in the Netherlands, reducing the number of leading dynasties to four (Soen: 2012). Dutch officials allowed Egmond's widow and sons to reconcile and they received back most of the family's properties (Janssens: 2013, Junot/Soen: 2020). By 1567, the nobility in the Netherlands had become formally divided between those now protesting against Philip II with armed resistance and those trying to induce changes in the regime by engaging in loyal opposition. This last group, even though pamphlets and the subsequent historiography have depicted them as marionettes controlled by the Spanish king, retained their own power and seemed remarkably open to temporary solutions embracing the existence of Calvinists in Holland and Zeeland (within the scheme only to convert them in a later stage). They continued the loyal opposition that Egmond, Horn, and Orange had started, and continued to look for *modus vivendi* and to moderate repression, whether religious or otherwise (Janssens: 1998 and Soen: 2011a and b).

6.   The Pacification of Ghent (1576–1579)

The Pacification of Ghent, concluded on 8 November 1576, presented another milestone in the Dutch Revolt, provoking a remarkable series of shifting coalitions amongst the aristocracy. In the power vacuum that occurred after the death of governor-general Luis de Requesens, and after the rather spectacular seizure of the interim Council of State, the States-General (now including delegates from both the insurgent Holland and Zeeland and the other 'fifteen' provinces that had remained loyal) could assemble on its own initiative. They agreed upon a status quo in religious matters, but still proclaimed an end to religious persecution, while leaving the definitive religious settlement for a future States-General. In the meantime, Holland and Zeeland remained Calvinist, but Catholics could continue to worship privately as long as they did not provoke public 'scandal'; the other fifteen provinces would remain Catholic, but allowed Protestantism, likewise, as long as its practitioners did not provoke 'scandal'. Many believed that this would lead to the 'end of the inquisition' (even though modern historiography has proved this false) and Protestants now mobilized in Flanders and Brabant, while Catholics continued to struggle in Holland and Zeeland (Scheerder: 1976; Gielis/Soen: 2015).

During the three years after the 1576 'Pacification', the four remaining aristo-cratic dynasties supported a regime now led by the States-General, despite their intra-confessional divide between the Calvinist Orange and mostly Catholic Croÿ, Lalaing and Egmond families. The half-brothers of Lalaing for example, raised Walloon troops to support the regime from the southern border of the Low Countries. The sons of Egmond tried to find a middle-ground between supporting the States and not compromising the requests for recuperating their father's confiscated goods (Soen: 2012). Yet, the longer standing factional strife between the competing dynasties continued, as the antagonism between Orange and Croÿ became noticeable to foreign observers. Meanwhile, the Pacification of Ghent impressively restored Orange's honor: the agreement returned his confiscated possessions and he now officially held the governorships of Holland and Zeeland, at least according to the States-General's stipulations (Soen/Junot: forthcoming). The Croÿ family, with the Duke of Aarschot as its family leader, succeeded in securing the new Habsburg governor-general Don Juan's ratification, with all members of the clan now obtaining honorable positions in his court and household (Soen/Masschelein: 2016). The Croÿ, however, abandoned the royal camp half a year later after the Governor-General captured Namur, and they called upon Archduke Matthias to exert the governorship-general in name of the States-General. Once Matthias arrived, Orange became his primary advisor and soon arrested the Duke of Aarschot in order to continue his own strategy (Soen/Junot: forthcoming, Bussels: 2002; De Bruyne: 2010).

In this position, Orange tried to mediate between the Flemish and Brabantine cities, while slightly adjusting the conditions of the Pacification of Ghent. He initiated two attempts at establishing a religious peace with the States-General, first with a widely-circulated plan on 12 July 1578 and secondly with an 'Eternal Religious Peace' on 12 June 1579 that was specifically tested in Antwerp and Ghent.[4] With him, the States-General repeatedly insisted that the *Religioensvrede* had to be interpreted as the necessary complement to the Ghent Pacification, not as a document that violated it; for them, the Ghent Pacification ended religious persecution, not promote it. All this was done in order to prepare the now planned general peace conference in Cologne, where imperial delegates would mediate between representatives from the Spanish Crown and the States-General. The Prince of Orange feared that the Crown would never ratify the Pacification of Ghent, and knew that his projects had virtually no chance of being accepted as they went far beyond what the Peace of Augsburg permitted (Marnef: 2011, Swart: 1994). In addition, a general peace treaty would most likely result in the deterioration of his prestigious position and force him into exile. Eventually, hardline Calvinists now took over in key cities like Ghent, Bruges, and Antwerp, where they installed Calvinist regimes, despite Orange's desire for religious peace (Weis: 2010).

It was in these conditions that the two leading half-brothers of the Lalaing family, now adults, took the lead in expressing discontent on behalf of the Catholics within

---

4 Niederländischer Religionsfrieden (12. Juli 1578) – Einleitung, bearbeitet von Alexandra Schäfer, is currently in preparation, but can already be consulted in this temporary form on http://diglib. hab.de/edoc/ed000227/start.htm, in the framework of the larger work, Irene Dingel (ed.), *Religiöse Friedenswahrung und Friedensstiftung in Europa (1500–1800): Digitale Quellenedition frühneuzeitlicher Religionsfrieden*, Wolfenbüttel, ongoing. For more information, consult our current H2020-consortium (grant agreement n° 770309)www.retopea.eu on this and other peace treaties.

the States-General. The elder of the two, Philippe, Count of Lalaing and provincial governor of Hainaut, was so fed up with the moderating policies of both the Prince of Orange and Archduke Matthias that he enlisted the help of the Catholic Prince of Anjou, who, in this instance, briefly visited the southern border of the Netherlands (Duquenne 1998). The younger Lalaing, Emmanuel, the new Baron of Montigny, also opposed Orange's religious peace measures. Both brothers shared the opinion that the Pacification of Ghent called for an end to religious persecution, while reinforcing the idea that Catholicism would remain the only public religion in the fifteen provinces that had remained loyal before 1576. The two brothers adorned themselves, and their servants, with rosaries, and their troops earned the nickname the *'pater noster'*. On the first of October 1578, Montigny seized the Flemish city of Menen to dramatically show his *malcontentement* with the States-General, a small *coup* that he intended to use as a signal to stop the Ghent Calvinists. Even so, while successfully obstructing Orange and the States General gathered in Antwerp, the two malcontent brothers refused to reconcile with Philip II (Soen: 2011). Only after long negotiations with local noblemen and clerics, the *malcontent* Montigny accepted a reconciliation with the king in the abbey of Mont-Saint-Eloy on the 6th of April (Soen: 2012; Junot/Soen: 2018). The subsequent *traité de reconciliation*, concluded in Arras on 17 May 1579 between Hainaut, Artois, and Lille, focused on an honorable reconciliation and restoring Catholicism as the only religion allowed.[5] Only afterwards, Count Philippe of Lalaing accepted a similar reconciliation and permanently defected from the camp of the States-General, a move that the Egmond sons soon emulated (Soen: 2012).

At this peculiar moment, when negotiated reconciliation occurred within the southern border provinces of the Low Countries, Croÿ family members were negotiating on behalf of the States-General in and around Cologne during Rudolf II's imperial mediations. The Croÿ clan consisted of the aforementioned father Philippe, Duke of Aarschot, his son Charles, Prince of Chimay, and his half-brother, Charles-Philippe, Marquis of Havré. Aarschot and Havré, though both nominally Catholic, were still trying to find a compromise that could hold all seventeen provinces together. When it became painfully clear that they could not reach a middle ground,

---

5 The most important negotiation documents, albeit reproduced from a loyalist and royalist standpoint, are to be found in: *Receuil des lettres, actes et pieces plus signalees dv progres et besogne faict en la ville d'Arras et ailleurs, pour parvenir à une bonne paix et reconciliation avec sa Maiesté Catholicque, par les Estatz d'Arthois et deputez d'Autres Provinces*, Douai, Jean Bogard, 1579. The Treaties of Arras and Mons can be found in: *Le traicté de réconciliation faicte en la ville d'Arras le XVIIe de May (...) depuis esclaircy et mis en forme d'édict & placcart*, Douai, Jean Bogard, 1579. For the reconstruction of Catholic Print culture in early modern Douai and Cambrai, consult the database Impressa Catholica Cameracensia, https://www.arts.kuleuven.be/nieuwetijd/english/odis/ICC_search.

the Croÿ family reconciled secretly with the King of Spain, though they did not immediately return to the Netherlands. Moreover, to the despair of his father Aarschot, Chimay converted to Calvinism through his marriage with the Calvinist Marie de Brimeu. In 1584, however, the 'lost son' Chimay converted back to Catholicism and became a staunch defender of the Catholic Cause. (Soen: 2012 and Soen/Junot: forthcoming).

With the Egmond, the Croÿ, and the Lalaing reconciled, Orange reluctantly accepted the document that Jan of Nassau, his younger brother, had presented as a new reformulation of the Pacification of Ghent. The Union of Utrecht, from January 1579, again prohibited religious persecution, but simultaneously protected liberty of conscience and codified the inclination towards Calvinism as the state religion. Though the Union of Utrecht repeated the concept of ending religious persecution, Orange interpreted the document as allowing for Calvinists to set the tone in church matters, a thing he had tried to prevent during the preceding years. At first exhibiting a moderate stance, the prince had initially received much credibility over all of the Seventeen Provinces and with his Catholic peers, but he eventually ended up alone in promoting multi-confessional experiments and eventually agreed to the solutions proposed by the Union of Utrecht (Marnef: 2011).

7. Conclusion

During the sixteenth century, theology and ecclesiology became hotly debated issues throughout society, also amongst Europe's nobility. Their privileged social background, however, neither required nor prescribed a univocal or harmonious approach to religious matters. The heads of the top five aristocratic dynasties in the Habsburg Low Countries showed extreme caution when dealing with the Reformation's consequences on the relationship between Church and State in the areas between the Rhine, the Meuse, and the Scheldt. On the one hand, many of their friends, relatives, and even spouses grew up with or embraced the Protestant faith, and household priests reported on the latest developments concerning bi-confessionalism in the Holy Roman Empire and France. On the other hand, leading male aristocrats, unlike their German and French counterparts, did not convert to Protestantism or patronize the reform-minded movement until 1567, even if some of their wives and secretaries did, as well as the local gentry.

Rather, in a first phase, those aristocrats participating in the Brussels councils tried to negotiate a *modus vivendi* for the growing number of Protestants within a Catholic territory. After the Iconoclastic Fury in 1566, the three protagonists, including the Prince of Orange and the Counts of Egmond and Horn, effectively, but temporarily, succeeded in setting up local multi-confessional deals with assigned churches within city walls, while still condemning and combatting Protestant armed resistance. When confronted with the exclusive restoration of Catholicism, Orange fled, converted to Lutheranism, and engaged in armed resistance, while Egmond and Horn refused to do so. Yet, officials arrested and executed both Knights of the Golden Fleece (who died professing the Catholic Faith), which, for the Montmorency clan, resulted in the eventual extinction of branch. Thus, by 1576, the number of powerful dynasties had been reduced to four, with three of the families remaining Catholic, and the other embracing Lutheranism.

The Pacification of Ghent, signed in 1576, prescribed the end of religious persecution for anyone who did not cause 'scandal' within the public sphere and sparked a remarkable series of shifting coalitions. During the next three turbulent years, most of the aristocracy defended the States-General and temporarily overcame their interconfessional differences. While everybody seemed to have agreed to end religious persecution (both of Protestants and Catholics), no one was really sure how to best implement the treaty. William of Orange, who had now converted to Calvinism, tried to take the lead by drafting two subsequent religious peace treaties, although these also polarized society instead of pacifying it. Through a protracted series of reconciliations between many aristocrats and the king in the period between 1579 and 1581, the situation returned to its pre-1576 condition, with sharp divisions existing between the Orange-Nassau family and other local aristocrats. Now, all parties had learned from the experience and sharpened their confessional position. Confronted with Calvinist regimes, the reconciled aristocracy engaged in Tridentine Catholicism, aiming to defend its faith within a monarchical system, then headed by the King of Spain. In this isolated stance, William of Orange capitulated before his younger brother and the radical Calvinist stance as detailed in the Union of Utrecht.

Taken together, the ecclesiology of the aristocracy in the Habsburg Netherlands often came down to being against something rather than being for anything: these noble protagonists were against the bishopric reform headed by Granvelle and against religious persecution and the so-called 'inquisition', but their positive programs or visions lagged behind, especially in comparison to their European counterparts. The allowance of temporal multi-confessionalism after the Iconoclastic Fury in 1566 and the Pacification of Ghent in 1576 proved to be an experiment in the unknown, and remained outside the scheme of the Peace of Augsburg (by which Philip II could still impose Catholicism within his lands in the Low Countries), as well as the guidelines set by French *édits de pacification* (which allowed Calvinism in certain circumscriptions). William of Orange's *religionsvredes* in 1578–1579 bear witness to his effort of trying to navigate a middle-ground between an ultra-Catholic and an ultra-Calvinist position, which even he was not able to maintain when confronted with the hardening positions of those around him. As such, ecclesiology, in both its negative and carefully formulated positive variations, caused a deep rift in this social group, much as it happened across sixteenth-century Europe.

Bibliography

ASCH, RONALD G. (2003), Nobilities in Transition, 1550–1700: Courtiers and rebels in Britain and Europe, London: Hodder Education.

BÉGUIN, KATIA (1999), Les princes de Condé: rebelles, courtisans et mécènes dans la France du Grand Siècle, Seyssel: Champ Vallon.

BUSSELS, STIJN (2002), Hoe de hoogste machthebber in de Nederlanden een stroman wordt: de Brusselse intocht van aartshertog Matthias in 1578, Bijdragen tot de Geschiedenis 85, 151–168.

BUYLAERT, FREDERIK (2012), The Late Medieval 'Crisis of the Nobility' Reconsidered: The Case of Flanders, Journal of Social History 45, 1117–1134.

CARROLL, STUART (1998), Noble Power during the French Wars of Religion: The Guise Affinity and the Catholic Cause in Normandy, Cambridge: Cambridge University Press.

CARROLL, STUART (2009), Martyrs and Murderers: The Guise Family and the Making of Europe, Oxford: Oxford University Press.

CARROLL, STUART (2013), "Nager entre deux eaux": the Princes and the Ambiguities of French Protestantism, Sixteenth Century Journal 44, 985–1020.

COOLS, HANS (2011), Mannen met macht: Edellieden en de Moderne Staat in de Bourgondisch-Habsburgse landen (1475–1530), Zutphen: Walburg Pers.

DE BRUYNE, NICOLAS (2010), Een Gentse staatsgreep: De gevangenneming van de Hertog van Aarschot en andere edelen te Gent op 28 oktober 1577, Handelingen der Maatschappij voor Geschiedenis & Oudheidkunde te Gent 64, 167–212.

DUKE, ALASTAIR (2004), The Elusive Netherlands: The Question of national identity in the early modern Low Countries on the Eve of the Revolt, The Low Countries Historical Review 119, 10–38.

DUQUENNE, FRÉDÉRIC (1998), L'entreprise du duc d'Anjou aux Pays-Bas de 1580 à 1584: les responsabilités d'un échec à partager, Histoire et Civilisations, Villeneuve-d'Asq: Presses Universitaires du Septentrion.

ENNO VAN GELDER, HENDRIK (1936), Bailleul, Bronkhorst, Brederode, De Gids 100, 204–220; 348–375.

GEEVERS, LIESBETH (2008), Gevallen vazallen. De integratie van Oranje, Egmont en Horn in de Spaans-Habsburgse monarchie (1559–1567), Amsterdam: Amsterdam University Press.

GEEVERS, LIESBETH (2010), Family Matters: William of Orange and the Habsburgs after the abdication of Charles V (1555), Renaissance Quarterly 63, 459–490.

GEEVERS, LIESBETH (2014), Beieren, Sabina van, in: Digitaal Vrouwenlexicon van Nederland, [accessed 13/01/2014]: resources.huygens.knaw.nl/vrouwenlexicon/lemmata/data/SabinaVanBeieren.

GIELIS, GERT/SOEN, VIOLET (2015), The Inquisitorial Office in the Sixteenth-century Low Countries: A Dynamic Perspective, Journal of Ecclesiastical History 66, 47–66.

GIETMAN, CONRAD (2010), Republiek van adel: Eer in de Oost-Nederlandse adelscultuur

(1555–1702), Utrecht: Van Gruting.

GINZBURG, CARLO (1980), The Cheese and the Worms: The Cosmos of a Sixteenth-Century Miller, Baltimore: The Johns Hopkins University Press.

GOOSENS, ALINE (1996), Les hésitations du comte Lamoral d'Egmont concernant la politique religieuse des Pays-Bas dans les années 1560, in: A. Dierkens (ed.), Le penseur, la violence, la religion, Problèmes d'histoire des religions 7, Brussels: Éditions de l'Université de Bruxelles, 63–70.

GOOSENS, ALINE (1997/1998), Les Inquisitions dans les Pays-Bas méridionaux à la Renaissance (1519–1633), Coll. Spiritualités Libres 7, 2 vols., Brussels: Éditions de l'Université de Bruxelles.

GROENVELD, SIMON (2003), Filips van Montmorency, graaf van Horn (1524–1568): Een Habsburgs edelman tussen vorstenmacht en verzet, Limburgs Geschied- en Oudheidkundig Genootschap 139, 39–99.

JANSSENS, GUSTAAF (1998), El oficio del rey y la oposición legal en Flandes contra Felipe II, in: J. Martínez Millán (ed.), Felipe II (1527–1598): Europa y la Monarquía Católica, Tomo I: El Gobierno de la Monarquía (Corte y Reinos), Madrid: Partelluz, 401–412.

JANSSENS, GUSTAAF (2003), De graven Egmont en Horn: slachtoffers van de politieke repressie in de Spaanse Nederlanden, Brussels: Museum van de stad Brussel.

JANSSENS, GUSTAAF (2012), De ordonnantie betreffende de pacificatie van de beroerten te Antwerpen (24 mei 1567): breekpunt voor de politiek van Filips II ten overstaan van de Nederlanden, Handelingen van de Koninklijke Commissie voor de Uitgave der Oude Wetten en Verordeningen van België 50, 105–132.

JANSSENS, PAUL (1998), L'évolution de la noblesse belge depuis la fin du Moyen Âge, Brussels: Crédit Communal de Belgique.

JUNOT, YVES/SOEN, VIOLET (2018), La Révolte des Pays-Bas habsbourgeois: Reconsidérations à partir du cas des provinces francophones (Hainaut, Artois, Flandre wallonne, 1566–1579), in: G. Salinero/Á. García Garrido/R.G. Paun (ed.), Paradigmes rebelles: Pratiques et cultures de la désobéissance à l'époque moderne, Bern/Bruxelles: Peter Lang, 203–224.

JUNOT, YVES/SOEN, VIOLET (2020), User ou abuser des confiscations: les voies tortueuses de la punition, du pardon et de la récompense par les Habsbourg d'Espagne durant la Révolte (Pays-Bas espagnols, 1566–1609), in: Y. Junot/V. Soen, Confisquer, restituer, redistribuer. Punition et réconciliation matérielles dans les territoires des Habsbourg et en France (XVIᵉ et XVIIᵉ siècles), Valenciennes: Presses Universitaires de Valenciennes, 87–132.

KAPLAN, BENJAMIN (2007), Divided by Faith. Religious Conflict and the Practice of Toleration in Early Modern Europe, Cambridge: Belknap Press.

KLOEK, ELS (2014), Nieuwenaer, Anna Walburgis van, in: Digitaal Vrouwenlexicon van Nederland, [accessed 13/01/2014]: resources.huygens.knaw.nl/vrouwenlexicon/lemmata/-data/NieuwenaerWalburgis.

LES ÉLITES (2001), Les élites nobiliaires dans les Pays-Bas au seuil des temps modernes. Mobilité sociale et service du pouvoir, Brussels: Facultés universitaires Saint-Louis, Centre de Recherches en histoire du droit et des institutions.

MacHardy, Karin (2003), War, Religion and Court Patronage in Habsburg Austria: The Social and Cultural Dimensions of Political Interaction, 1521–1622, New York: Palgrave MacMillan.

Mantini, Sabine (ed.) (2003), Margherita d'Austria (1522–1586). Costruzioni politiche e diplomazia, tra corte Farnese e Monarchia spagnola, – Biblioteca del Cinquecento 109, Rome: Bulzoni.

Marnef, Guido (2011), Multiconfessionalism in a commercial metropolis. The case of 16th-century Antwerp, in: T.M. Safley (ed.), A Companion to Multiconfessionalism in the Early Modern World, Leiden/Boston: Brill, 75–97.

Neuschel, Kristin B. (1989), Word of Honor: Interpreting Noble Culture in Sixteenth-century France, Ithaca: Cornell University Press.

Parker, Geoffrey (2002), 1567: The End of the Dutch Revolt?, in: A. Crespo Solana/M. Herrero Sánchez (ed.), España y las 17 provincias de los Países Bajos. Una revisión historiográfica (XVI–XVIII), 2 vols., Córdoba: Editorial Universidad de Córdoba, vol. 1, 269–290.

Pollmann, Judith (2015), Anna van Saksen, in: Digitaal Vrouwenlexicon van Nederland, [accessed 25/04/2015]: http://resources.huygens.knaw.nl/vrouwenlexicon/lemmata/data/AnnavanSaksen.

Rodríguez-Salgado, Maria (2000), King, Bishop, Pawn? Philip II and Granvelle in the 1550s and 1560s, in: K. de Jonge/G. Janssens (ed.), Les Granvelle et les anciens Pays-Bas, Liber doctori Mauricio Van Durme dedicatus, Leuven: Leuven University Press, 105–134.

Rosenfeld, Paul (1959), The provincial governors from the minority of Charles V to the Revolt, Standen en Landen 17, Leuven: Nauwelaerts.

Scheerder, Jozef (1976), De werking van de inquisitie, in: Opstand en Pacificatie in de Lage Landen, Bijdrage tot de studie van de Pacificatie van Gent. Verslagboek van het tweedaags colloquium bij de vierhonderdste verjaring van de Pacificatie van Gent, Gent: Snoeck-Ducaju, 153–165.

Soen, Violet/Junot, Yves (ed.) (forthcoming), Noblesses transrégionales: les Croÿ et les frontières pendant les guerres de religion en France, Lorraine Pays-Bas, XVIe-XVIe siècle). Brepols: Turnhout.

Soen, Violet/Masschelein, Elisa (2016), Het Eeuwig Edict en de Intredes van Don Juan. Of de moeizame mise-en-œuvre en mise-en-scène van een vredesverdrag tijdens de Nederlandse Opstand, Tijdschrift voor Geschiedenis 129, 175–196.

Soen, Violet/Vanysacker, Dries and Wim François (ed.), Church, Censorship and Reform in the Early Modern Habsburg Netherlands, Leuven/Louvain-la-Neuve and Turnhout: Revue d'histoire ecclésiastique and Brepols Publishers, 2017.

Soen, Violet (2011a), Collaborators and Parvenus? Berlaymont and Noircarmes, Loyal Noblemen in the Dutch Revolt, Dutch Crossing: Journal for Low Countries Studies 35, 20–38.

Soen, Violet (2011b), Despairing of all means of reconciliation: The Act of Abjuration and the peace negotiations during the Dutch Revolt, in: P. Brood/R. Kubben (ed.), The Act of

Abjuration. Inspired and Inspirational, Nijmegen: Wolf Legal Publishers, 45–63.

SOEN, VIOLET (2011c), Les Malcontents au sein des États-Généraux aux Pays-Bas (1578–1581): Défense du pouvoir de la noblesse ou défense de l'orthodoxie?, in: A. Boltanski/F. Mercier (ed.), La noblesse et la défense de l'orthodoxie XIII–XVIIIme siècles, Rennes: Presses Universitaires de Rennes, 135–149.

SOEN, VIOLET (2012), Vredehandel. Adellijke en Habsburgse verzoeningspogingen tijdens de Nederlandse Opstand (1564–1581), Amsterdam Studies in the Dutch Golden Age, Amsterdam: Amsterdam University Press.

SOEN, VIOLET (2015a) Nobility, in: Margaret King (ed.), Oxford Bibliographies in Renaissance and Reformation, New York: Oxford University Press, online publication.

SOEN, VIOLET (2015b), The Chièvres Legacy, the Croÿ Family and Litigation in Paris. Dynastic Identities between the Low Countries and France (1519–1559), in: L. Geevers/M. Marini (ed.), Dynastic Identity in Early Modern Europe: Rulers, Aristocrats and the Formation of Identities, Ashgate: Farnham, 87–102.

SOEN, VIOLET (2016a), Das aufsässige Antwerpen versöhnen? Friedensstrategien der Habsburgischen Generalstatthalter während des Aufstands der Niederlande (1566–1586), in: E. Leuschner (ed.), Rekonstruktion der Gesellschaft aus Kunst. Antwerpener Malerei und Graphik in und nach den Katastrophen des späten 16. Jahrhunderts, Studien zur internationalen Architektur- und Kunstgeschichte 136, Petersberg: Michael Imhof Verlag, 24–37.

SOEN, VIOLET (2016b), The Beeldenstorm and the Spanish Habsburg Response (1566–1570), The Low Countries Historical Review 131, 99–120.

SOEN, VIOLET (2017a), La nobleza y la frontera entre los Países Bajos y Francia: las casas nobiliarias Croÿ, Lalaing y Berlaymont en la segunda mitad del siglo XVI, in: V. Favarò/M. Merluzzi/G. Sabatini (ed.), Fronteras. Procesos y prácticas de integración y conflictos entre Europa y América (siglos XVI–XX), Madrid: Fondo de Cultura Económica/Red Columnaria, 427–436.

SOEN, VIOLET (2017b), From the Interim of Augsburg until the Treaty of Augsburg (1548–1555), in: A. Melloni (ed.), Luther. A Christian between Reforms and Modernity (1517–2017), 3 vols., Berlin/New York: De Gruyter, vol. 1, 548–564.

SOEN, VIOLET (2017c), Which religious history for the (two) early modern Netherlands before 1648? Questions, trends and perspectives, Revue d'histoire ecclésiastique 112, 158–788.

SOEN, VIOLET (2018), The Council of Trent and the Preconditions of the Dutch Revolt (1563–1566), in: W. François/V. Soen (ed.), The Council of Trent: Reform and Controversy in Europe and beyond (1540–1700), 3 vols., Göttingen: Vandenhoeck & Ruprecht, vol. 2, 255–278.

SOEN, VIOLET (2019), Philippe II et les anciens Pays-Bas: Les limites d'un gouvernement à distance dans un empire global (1555–1598), Revue Histoire Économie et Société 3.2019, 11–32.

SPICER, ANDREW (2013), After Iconoclasm: Reconciliation and Resacralization in the Southern Netherlands, ca. 1566–85, Sixteenth Century Journal 44, 411–433.

SWART, KOENRAAD W. (1994), Willem van Oranje en de Nederlandse Opstand, The Hague: SDU Uitgevers.

VALKENEERS, NINA/SOEN, VIOLET (2015), Praet, Bronkhorst en Boetzelaer. Adellijke we-duwes in de bres voor het calvinisme tijdens en na de Beeldenstorm (1566–1567), Han-delingen van de Koninklijke Zuid-Nederlandse Maatschappij voor Taal-, Letterkunde en Geschiedenis 69, 265–284.

VAN BRUAENE, ANNE-LAURE/JONCKHEERE, KOEN/SUYKERBUYK, RUBEN (ed.) (2016), The-matic issue 'Beeldenstorm': Iconoclasm in the Low Countries, The Low Countries Histor-ical Review 131.

VAN NIEROP, HENK (1999), The Nobility and the Revolt of the Netherlands: Between Church and King, and Protestantism and Privileges, in: P. Benedict/G. Marnef/H.F.K. van Nierop e.a. (ed.), Reformation, Revolt and Civil War in France and the Netherlands 1555–1585, Koninklijke Nederlandse Akademie van Wetenschappen, Verhandelingen, Afd. Let-terkunde, Nieuwe Reeks 176, Amsterdam: Royal Netherlands Academy of Arts and Sciences, 83–98.

VAN NIEROP, HENK (1991), A Beggars' Banquet: The Compromise of the Nobility and the Politics of Inversion, European History Quarterly 21, 419–443.

VAN NIEROP, HENK (1995), Similar problems, different outcomes: the Revolt of the Nether-lands and the Wars of Religion in France, in: J. Lucassen/K. Davids (ed.), A Miracle Mirrored: the Dutch Republic in European Perspective, Cambridge: Cambridge Univer-sity Press, 26–68.

VAN STEENSEL, ARIE (2010), Edelen in Zeeland: macht, rijkdom en status in een laatmid-deleeuwse samenleving, Hilversum: Verloren.

VERBERCKMOES, JOHAN/SOEN, VIOLET (2017), Broadsheets Testing Moderation in the Nascent Dutch Revolt, in: A. Pettegree (ed.), Broadsheets: Single-Sheet Publishing in the First Age of Print, Boston/Leiden: Brill, 271–294.

WEIS, MONIQUE (2002), La Paix d'Augsbourg de 1555: Un modèle pour les Pays-Bas? L'am-bassade des princes luthériens allemands auprès de Marguerite de Parme en 1567, in: J.-M. Cauchies (ed.), Entre Royaume et Empire: Frontières, rivalités et modèles, Neuchâtel: Centre européen d'études bourguignonnes, 87–100.

WEIS, MONIQUE (2010), Des villes en révolte: Les 'Républiques urbaines' aux Pays-Bas et en France pendant la deuxième moitié du XVIe siècle, Studies in European Urban History 23, Turnhout: Brepols.

WOLTJER, JULIAAN (1976), De vrede-makers, Tijdschrift voor Geschiedenis 89, 229–321.

WOLTJER, JULIAAN (1999), Political Moderates and Religious Moderates in the Revolt of the Netherlands, in: P. Benedict/G. Marnef/H.F.K. van Nierop e.a. (ed.), Reformation, Revolt and Civil War in France and the Netherlands 1555–1585, Koninklijke Nederlandse Akademie van Wetenschappen, Verhandelingen, Afd. Letterkunde, Nieuwe Reeks 176, Amsterdam: Royal Netherlands Academy of Arts and Sciences, 185–200.

WOLTJER, JULIAAN (2011), Op weg naar Tachtig jaar oorlog, Amsterdam: Balans.

Church and Art

Sibylla Goegebuer

St John's Hospital in Bruges in the Sixteenth and Seventeenth Centuries

A Real and Intangible-Symbolic Interaction Between Religion & Devotion, Care and Art Forms a Holy Trinity

Introduction

The religious community of St John's Hospital in Bruges embodies a quest for spiritual perfection by perpetuating the caritas principle or the principle of charity. This immaterial and layered factor is materialised through such relics as art and architecture, which the religious community commissions. Charity inspires hospital care.

Hospital care has a dual nature. On the one hand there is the devotional care, which, in the sixteenth and seventeenth centuries, was influenced by the Catholic restoration . On the other, there is the medical care, which was subject to a process of medicalisation during this same period.

This paper discusses how hospital management, art, architecture, medical care, the changing care procedures and the extended notion of charity interact during the Reformation and the Counter-Reformation. The hospital architecture and objects may look functional but at the same time they also have aesthetic value. The art collection, hospital construction and organisational motives provide a social context for the hospital's operations (Goegebuer: 2016a, 36–39; 2016b; 2013).

I will discuss the interactive hospital rhythm based on four topics, namely the principle of charity, the clinging to a sense of tradition and the awareness of the need for innovation, the new convent for hospital sisters and finally one work of art, The Madonna with two saints and two hospital sisters with patron saints, a painting attributed to Jacob van Oost the elder, dated 1664.

1.   Caritas, a Multi-Layered Principle

The history of care in St John's Hospital is a history of continuity, which is underpinned by one constant principle, that of charity. In the sixteenth and seventeenth centuries, the notion of charity in a hospital context became layered. The meaning that Matthew attributes to caritas undisputedly continued to be the driving force for its functioning in a society which was confronted with a growing number of people who needed care and who became increasingly differentiated, along with the type of care. This is the supreme commandment in the law: the love for God. It relates to the second, equivalent commandment of charity, and also involves a sense of mercy. During the sixteenth and seventeenth centuries, charity was also incorporated in the humanist discourse about social problems. The charitable history of St John's Hospital constitutes a chapter in the European history of charity. It is written as a result of the response of those who need care and the society that make care necessary. Society increasingly wanted to centralise care. The position of those who need care and those who provide it was increasingly confirmed in a secular context. The story can be called a success story on the one hand. The desire to provide a rational motive for care already existed in the Middle Ages. The process of a policy of care for the poor, which is regulated and bureaucratised by the authorities and is fuelled by the government's sense of civic duty to provide a community service, is only accelerated by the Reformation (Dietl: 2015, 190–192). During the first half of the sixteenth century, Western Europe was engulfed by a wave of impoverishment. Emperor Charles V's attempt to organise the system of poor relief and the structure of the city's charitable institutions more efficiently by centralising the administration of said organisation (Marechal: 1976, 44), was rejected by the local authorities and the Church. The ordinances gave rise to a compromise instead of centralisation and confirmed the failure of the attempted reform, of the rationalisation of poor relief and the fight against beggars (Dehaeck/Van Hee: 2005, 16). This measure was far from successful. Linking the issuing of care ordinances – the theory – to their practical implementation and the control thereof are two aspects that are often difficult to reconcile. Hospital care can only be effective and survive if it is organised as part of a professional care industry. In 1496, the City of Bruges had issued ordinances to prevent begging and centralise the care for the poor (Marechal: 1976: 47). The fact that Juan Luis Vives moved to Bruges in 1528 is another important fact worth noting in the social and hospital context. In 1526, he published *De Subventione Pauperum* with the support of the town magistrate, in which he elaborated a system of centralised poor relief (De Bruyne: 2011, 14–19). He expanded the meaning of charity by basing his relief efforts on the input of official care providers as well as on the efforts of the poor themselves to rise above their situation. According to Vives, care had to be provided in a controlled manner and had to be combined with a reflection on the need for care for the poor (Schneider: 2015, 76). A similar tendency toward humanism was also apparent in the Council of Trent, which led to a Catholic restoration based on a human approach. Far-reaching measures had already been taken a few years before the negotiated publication of the decrees in 1565. One of these restructured the various dioceses. Bruges became the seat of the new diocese of Bruges in 1559 (Ryckaert: 1976, 20). The mediators and idealists who worked hard to achieve these reforms were the local bishops, the clergy, and local nuns and friars, such as the hospital community.

The doctoral dissertation of Lieve Vervaet shows clearly that the religious, hospital community understood very well that charity is part of a care industry. It is its driving force, its catalyst. The hospital is sensitive to cyclical economic trends. A well-thougth-out food policy in and out of the hospital is crucial (Vervaet: 2014, 31–48). The poor are a functional part of this process (Oexle: 2015, 73). The care is also characterised by devotion. The contemplative line of action, which confirms the way of life of the religious care providers in the hospital proved indispensable in the care process. Charity is undeniably subject to certain rules. It establishes a harmony between the secular and religious aspects of the hospital history, combining the tangible and immaterial hospital world into a legible essay. Devotion is part of a charitable spirituality in accordance with the hospital rules. The way in which the hospital sisters have transposed the power and significance of faith into the hospital's operation for centuries and the way in which they have also enabled the hospital's medical operation as a care institution help us identify a large number of cornerstones of the universal care story. The institution's material heritage and the hospital's architecture in particular make the history of devotional care and health care eminently recognisable. They are instruments of propaganda and memory. The hospital is a protagonist in the civil and religious care network.

2. A Sense of Tradition – the Need for Innovation

The sixteenth and seventeenth centuries were a period of change and of consolidation, marked by an awareness of the importance of tradition and the need for innovation. From the sixteenth century onwards, this was combined with the three-dimensional notion of upscaling. The hospital, a monument in the city, became a city in the city. Local care for the sick and poor had to compete with a globalising care process. Upscaling meant generating innovation. The upscaling also took place in the area of devotional care. The humanisation of care, combined with a hospital policy which was gently manipulated to become more targeted, in the sixteenth century as a result of the Reformation and in the seventeenth century as a result of the Counter-Reformation and social-political circumstances, creates a pattern of a hospital which increasingly has a medicating function. In that sense it also dictates the functioning of the convents and of the hospital pharmacy, which opened in 1645, in line with social change. An effectively operating hospital pharmacy must be able to rely on the knowledge of a pharmaceutical network, which extends beyond the walls of the hospital complex and is therefore founded on the assumption of an open operation. In Bruges the profession of pharmacist was heavily regulated. City ordinances regulated the status of the pharmacist while pharmacopoeias regulated the composition of the preparations. In 1697, the first Bruges pharmacopoeia was published. The hospital pharmacy apparently did not have to heed these regulations. There are no rules mentioning an apprenticeship, the passing of a test or adherence to pharmacopoeia. While the zeitgeist was changing, the nuns-pharmacists maintained an Apollonian independence and continual dignity (Goegebuer: 2016a, 36–39).

A number of events in the city of Bruges and in St John's Hospital point to a changing mindset and relationship between the religious and administrative powers. They reflect a changing world that is inspired by the ideas of the Renaissance and Humanism. These changes also became apparent in the hospital's policy. Three concepts manifested themselves: there was the wave of moralisation, of democratisation and finally of humanisation. The grip of religious power fluctuated between stable and firm during the sixteenth and seventeenth centuries, whereas the structure of the hospital community was both stable and fragile. Income and expenditure were influenced by the social-political circumstances. In turn, all these developments influenced the art and architecture produced by and for the hospital, and from the perspective of the hospital, the art appreciation.

An ordinance by Bishop Remigius Driutius from 1573, which was drafted in collaboration with the town magistrate, aimed to curtail the lifestyle of the nuns and friars, which was deemed too worldly. The tasks of the master and prioress, and other positions in the hospital, were regulated. Their lifestyle was carefully monitored.

The revised articles of association, which incorporated the Rule of St. Augustine of the Sisters of St Janshuus in Bruges, were published in 1598. This record, written in Flemish and issued by Bishop Mathias Lambrecht (1596–1602), clarified the roles of the nuns and the friars in the community with one sentence: "Wat verandert naer den tyt. Als datter een Vrauwe nu voort an zal overste wesen daer van te vooren den meester d'overste was" [from now on, a woman shall run the hospital whereas previously a man did] (Geldhof: 1976, 174–176).

The bishop paid great attention to convent reforms. The construction of the nuns' convent and the separation from the friars, and the subsequent disappearance of the friars – friars were no longer allowed in the hospital unless special permission was obtained from the bishop – was completely in line with the reform of the religious community, which manifested itself in the second half of the sixteenth century. Generally speaking, the efficiency and sustainability of an important objective of the convent's operations, namely to be a reflection of Celestial Jerusalem on earth, was thereby controlled. Reforming a convent means adapting the Celestial Jerusalem to suit your own renewed purposes. In this case, it also meant representing the Celestial Jerusalem in such a way that it could be understood from a reformed outlook on life. It means materialising the intangible in a different way. Following the construction of the new convent, the separation of the convents, the changes to the articles of association, the discreet elimination of the friars, the tools for this were available in St John's Hospital. The nuns of St John's continued to live by the rule of St Augustine. In that sense, they were able to continue to combine a devotional lifestyle with a worldlier mindset, which was vital for guaranteeing the hospital's operation. The Council of Trent did have a hand in these events, even controlling the cloister or clausura for nuns.

In the seventeenth century, the emphasis continued to be on protecting the hospital's own medical and religious world. One document, written by Bishop Antonius Triest (1617–1622) in 1620, shows that St John's Hospital continued to work relatively independently. The Council's influence is apparent in the level of control of the lives of the nuns – with respect for the efficient operation of the hospital, which points to a more humane and sensitive approach to the hospital as an institution. In effect, the document slightly redefines and even confirms the existing profile of a nuns' community that was also prevalent in the sixteenth century (Bruges, State Archives, TBO 123–475; Bruges, State Archives, TBO 123-475/BIS, TRIEST, ANTONIUS Bishop (1620), Official Report visitation St John's Hospital Bruges.

3. A New Convent for the Hospital Sisters

In terms of their architectural structure, style and position in the urban fabric, the Western European hospitals that were established during the Middle Ages and modern times are very similar to convents, when operated by a convent community. In the sixteenth century, neither social nor religious evolutions gave rise to a demolition of hospital sites, nor did they contribute to a complete reconstruction. Any construction that was undertaken was limited and did not undermine the identity of the hospital site.[1] Every hospital site on the whole is treated with a sense of pride, self-confidence and with an awareness of perpetual service by the care providers. The faith in the efficiency of the dual layering of the operation and the perpetuation of the continuity of the hospital's operation remain intact. This unshakeable confidence contributes to the recognisability of hospitals in the city fabric and generates stability.

In the sixteenth and seventeenth centuries, the tension between the needs for separate living quarters for the nuns and a public hospital space and the desire for

---

1 OCKELEY, JAAK (2005), Het gasthuiswezen in de Nieuwe Tijd, in: Architectuur van Belgische hospitalen (Architecture of Belgian hospitals), Brussel: Ministerie van de Vlaamse Gemeenschap-Afdeling Monumenten en Landschappen, 44–45.

THOMPSON, J./GOLDING, G. (1975), The hospital: a social and architectural history, New Haven/London.

a moderate clausura in the Bruges hospital context became intense. Architectural projects with a more pragmatic perspective and religiously-inspired achievements fulfilled both these needs. The architecture and art, which were commissioned by the religious community, played a symbolic role, displaying the community's power. They correspond to a growing need for recognition of the social significance of a female, religious community, which claims its place – individually and in the hospital context – on the social ladder. They bear witness to the changing care process, which transcends the original, religious aspect of the principle of charity.

Fig. 1 Seventeenth-century figurative tiles on the inner wall of the new convent for sisters in St John's Hospital Bruges.
Photo: Jens Compernolle/Sightways Photography.

It is therefore not unusual that a conventional nunnery – in terms of its structure – is built in the years between 1539 and 1544, which is however completely separate from the monastery for the friars, and is only connected with the southern ward through a staircase tower.

Fig. 2   The sixteenth- and seventeenth-century convent for sisters in St John's Hospital Bruges, which is completely separate from the monastery for the friars and which is only connected with the southern hospital ward through a staircase tower.
Photo: Arnout Goegebuer.

Work continued well into the 1560s and further work was carried out in the seventeenth century. Throughout the various phases of construction until the seventeenth century, the convent became larger, encompassing more than just the original living quarters for the nuns in the hospital's attic, above the wards. The convent was no longer merely a religious convent. As a result of its rather separate position in the hospital fabric and because its exterior is considered an example of the influence of civil architecture on a devotionally inspired institution, it is a rather veiled attempt at building a faux palace. The harmonious ensemble has a refined yet simple architecture, with traditional monastic quarters, which are concealed behind so-called closed walls. The care providers enter a space, which wants to compete with civilian-aristocratic residences in terms of style and allure when it comes to its external appearance.

The fact that the nuns largely come from well-off bourgeois families probably had something to do with this. The convent claims its place in a society that over time will start to approach man as an individual. The relevance of the physical clausura, the solidity and the boundaries of the site's accessibility, the church decorum, which Carolus Borromeus stressed in his *Instructiones fabricae et supellectilis ecclesiasticae*

(1577), are beautifully interpreted in reality in the Bruges hospital context. Imposing clausura on a hospital community obviously presented a great obstacle for caring for the sick. This was solved by reorganising the hospital's architecture and the community with its own hierarchy in it and by adapting the related articles of association.

The hospital and the convent managed to survive in a city marked by an urgent need for care. They engaged in the intensive care debate. Strangely enough, the first construction phase of the convent happened during a period of financial volatility (Marechal: 1976, 51). The town magistrate and the clergy struggled over who was responsible for managing the convent's resources. In 1547 the city tried to appoint a secular person as tax collector, which promptly met with protest by the hospital staff. The conflict was settled in court before the Council of Flanders, which ruled in favour of the nuns and friars because they were jointly in charge until the end of the sixteenth century. [2] The religious status of hospital personnel since 1459 and the global social and religious evolutions during the sixteenth century meant that a situation of nuns and friars operating together in one institution, in one hospital with shared but equivalent responsibilities (since medieval times, the hospital had had a mixed staff) was however no longer tenable.[3] From the sixteenth century onwards, the distinction between religious and medical care and the lives of friars and nuns as men and women and as people of the cloth, in one hospital building, became more sharply defined. This marks the commencement of the hospital's modern history.

4. The Interactive Hospital Story as Told in One Work of Art

The Madonna with two saints and two hospital sisters, attributed to Jacob van Oost the elder (1601–1671), dated 1664.

2 Brugge, Stadsarchief, Fonds Sint-Janshospitaal, Accounts 1547–1548 up to and including 1557–1558; cf. Vervaet: 2014, 30.
3 Brugge, Archief Hospitaalzusters Sint-Janshospitaal Brugge, Kloostergemeenschap van de zusters van Sint-Jan: Statuten Sint-Janshospitaal, 25 juli 1598 (sic!), f° 1r-2r; 3r-15r; 16r-30r. Brugge, Stadsarchief, Fonds Sint-Janshospitaal, Varia, Doos 12: Jesus Maria Augustinus, Regel van onsen alderheijlichsten Vader Augustinus, den XXIIII augus 1598.

Fig. 3 Jacob van Oost the elder (1601–1671), after attributed to, *The Madonna with two saints and two hospital sisters with patron saints*, 1664, oil on canvas, H 1,57 m x B 2,48 m, Musea Brugge, Sint-Janshospitaal.
Photo: Musea Brugge/Lukasweb – Art in Flanders – Dominique Provost.

The religious art and architecture, which were commissioned by the female religious community in the sixteenth and seventeenth century, are multifunctional. They are an expression of the faith of the religious care providers and the devotional aspect of charity. The nuns also seem to use the works as symbols of their independence, just like they use the construction of the new convent as a way of displaying their self-esteem. They identify themselves with the art and architecture they commission. Certain artworks are evidence that these women, who were keenly aware of the changes in society – a society in which human beings were increasingly affirming their rights as individuals – wanted to be recognised. They did not seem intimidated by the intentions of the clausura. In the margin of his inspection in 1620, Bishop Antonius Triest did not enforce the clausura on the hospital community.[4] However, the content of these works is first and foremost religious and devotional. That said, aesthetic-decorative qualities and a sense of grandeur also seem to tie in perfectly with works with a religious-devotional message. Until well into the seventeenth century, we still hear Gabriele Paleotti (1522–1597) whisper a few words on the figurative arts from his Discourse on sacred and profane images (Paleotti: 2012, 15; cf. Bianchi: 2008, 9–13). Personal

---

4 BRUGGE, Rijksarchief/State Archives, TBO 123–475/BIS, Ibid.

and collective pleasure become widely accepted. A muted sense of splendour and beauty pervades the hospital community which strikes a controlled balance between a devotional life and an active, dual care policy that takes precedence over everything else. The nuns surround themselves with precious and appealing objects that *dangerously* transcend the boundaries of monastic decorum. They create a setting that compromises the ideal of poverty as formulated in the monastic rule. They embrace the morals of poverty, but this by no means affects their sense of comfort and decoration. The hospital sisters prefer to live in a privileged zone. The medieval tradition that has produced valuable monastic art lives on. In addition to the spiritual significance, however, the aesthetic appeal and the confirmation of the authority, of female leadership within the urban care network become more manifest in the artworks they commission.

The Madonna with two saints and two hospital sisters with patron saints, attributed to Jacob van Oost the elder, dated 1664, portrays Isabelle Dailly (1630–1695) kneeling on the extreme left, her hands folded in prayer and her coat draped over her arm. Next to her is Isabelle Briellmans (1629–1680) (DeMuynck: 1998, 191), holding a prayer book in her right hand. St Elizabeth of Hungary, who is dressed as a convent nun, protects Isabelle Dailly. Isabelle Briellmans is presented to Mary by an until now unidentified saint with Christ's monogram on her chest. I'm still looking for more evidence if the saint could be St Elisabeth of Portugal. Like St Elisabeth of Hungary, she is a charitable-spiritual model of kindness as evidenced by the relief she provides to the poor and the sick. The presence of a Christ's monogram on this seventeenth-century canvas corresponds with the religious circumstances and the location of production and presentation of the work of art. Dailly took her vows in 1650 and was professed in 1653. She is listed as a sacristan (1666–1692) and worked in the hospital pharmacy (DeMuynck: 1998, 146). She died in 1695. Bri(e)llemans also took her vows in 1650. She was a hospital pharmacist (1659–1679) and died in 1680 (DeMuynck: 1998, 133). St Augustine is seen kneeling to the right. The artist has painted St John the Evangelist in the centre, who recommends the nuns with a gesture of his arm. The nuns' names and ages are inscribed on the stone pedestal. At the bottom, a cartouche on the frame bears the inscription *Mater Dei memento nostri*.

Van Oost's artwork combines the portraits of nuns and saints, of the earthly and divine world. The painting perpetuates the veneration of saints, which has taken place for centuries in the hospital. The work promotes the spiritual welfare of the nuns and confirms the identity of the hospital community. The portrait emphasises the significance of the continuity of the hospital's operation to the outside world as being blessed by God and the saints. It confirms the value of the hospital community's identity to the religious and city authorities. Much like the Council of Trent supports the visual tradition of previous centuries through its directives about the veneration of saints and relics and the portrayal of saints, the nuns also do this on a local level. They assure continuity, which is vital for self-preservation and is a guarantee that tradition will be preserved.

The saints and nuns have been portrayed in a tranquil *sacra conversazione*. This devout scene exemplifies the intimate, religious connection, to which the hospital's nuns are granted privileged access. The work was displayed in the chapter room of the new convent, where the St John's Triptych by Hans Memling was also granted pride of place after the renovation of the interior of the hospital's church in 1637 (Meulemeester: 1984, 337; Descamps: 1769, 300; Everaert: 1864, no. 13). Saints and nuns are portrayed in the immediate, almost tangible proximity of the central, divine-celestial scene. They appear as patrons and as devout women. They are led by the rules of the religious play but they also stake their place in the secular world. They appear as solo protagonists and refuse to be relegated to the side-lines, on side panels. The painting thus becomes a narrative. The colour dynamics of the celestial scene with the Virgin Mary and her Son are tempered by the simple colour palette of the presentation scene with the sisters. The painter acts in the name of the portrayed nuns, promoting a display of faith. However, he succeeds in duly dividing his attention in accordance with the rules of religion thanks to a cleverly thought out composition and the rhythm of the colours.

The narrative must bring about the nuns' salvation. However, it also has a social function. It showcases the convent's prestige and wealth, the hierarchical-social ladder on which the nuns-pharmacists find themselves (Falque: 2013, 201–303; Wilson: 1998, 41–84). The portraits veer between a muted display and disciplinary piety. The work of art is a *mise en image*, in which the religious and social ambitions of the nuns who commissioned the works are conveyed.

The devotional portrait perfectly fulfils its role. It shows how these women pray the ideal prayer. The notion of the presence of a perfect, immortal prayer raises the work to an immaterial level.

It represents a mental vision which the portrayed experience in prayer (Harbison: 1985, 87–118). They modestly gaze at the saints and hold a prayer book or have folded their hands. This alludes to the spiritual action of praying. The portrayed want to experience the sacred and feel united with God. The patron saints that present them only underscore the scene's divine nature. The natural surroundings, the stage, the position of the throne, the still-life in the foreground, the physical contact with the saints on the stage refer to a spirituality which has its foundation in the Middle Ages. This is more than a mental vision. There are no two adjacent worlds. Here the two worlds converge. The vision becomes a real encounter or in any event, a desired, imagined, mentally experienced *conversazione*, with Christ symbolising the achievement of this spiritual quest. The artwork becomes a tool for conveying in images what happens on the mental level. The nuns are literally just a step away from the spiritual ideal.

The spectator is invited to interpret the composition in a dynamic manner. All the motives visualise the spiritual process. The work shows the ultimate, durable compensation for the nuns' efforts as well as the larger part of the path to spiritual perfection which they have already covered. The spiritual unification with God above all is an encounter (Falque: 2013, 304–317). The painting is a bargaining tool.

The painting confronts the spectator with the unusual, generating a certain alienation. The confrontation between the heavenly world with the saints and reality, the earthly world, symbolised by the presence of the two nuns and patron saints who stress the devote character of the secular scene, is too direct, which in turn creates a certain distance. The seventeenth-century spectator knows his saints but at the same time he experiences a sense of alienation. And finally, he is also attracted by this divine scene, and its theatrical and rather quite atmospherical setting.

5. In Conclusion

The history of charity in St John's Hospital in the sixteenth and seventeenth centuries describes a history of cultural and social changes. It relates to power, the laws of the control bodies of the care sector, conflict management, disputes between a diverse audience of care providers, on the local level but also recognisable in care across Europe. St John's Hospital no longer acts as an isolated care factor in the city but wants to play a significant role in the history of charity. The material heritage embodies the durable nature of the hospital's identity. Tools and art objects, the monumental hospital site combine the various chapters of a history of care – borne by a continual care for the bodies and souls of patients by care providers, who are just as diverse as the collections – into one legible *Gesamtkunstwerk*.

Fig. 4 Anonymous, Southern Netherlands, *Friendship Cup*, 1664, engraved glass, faience, silver gilt
and copper, height 22,7 cm, diameter base 14,2 cm.
Photo: Musea Brugge/Lukas – Art in Flanders – Dominique Provost. The coat of arms of St
John's Hospital, with the chalice referring to St John the Evangelist and the lamb referring to St
John the Baptist.

The painting of saints and hospital sisters, attributed to Jacob Van Oost the elder serves as a source of inspiration for a devotionally inspired life, impregnated by a human dimension. It is a work of memory.

It is impossible to separate the sixteenth- and seventeenth-century, architectural interventions and art commissions from faith and devotion and from a changed outlook on life. The nuns' need to live separately, unhindered, on the hospital site no longer expresses a desire to live in seclusion for exclusively epidemiological and social motives (Coomans: 2005, 40). Instead, the community seeks to establish a compromise, a solution which strikes a balance between the ideal of physical isolation as imposed by the clausura rule and a hierarchical community, between offering perpetual devotional care and tending to the sick while satisfying the need for a personal-devotional life. At the same time, the community developed a vision on the nature of care, which transcended the original principle of charity, which was founded on religious motives.

Certain art and architectural commissions epitomise the independence and self-awareness of the women who commissioned them.

The trifecta of art, religion & devotion and care evolve to the rhythm of the society.

Bibliography

Sources

ANONYMOUS (1598), parchment. BRUGGE, Archief Hospitaalzusters Sint-Janshospitaal Brugge, Kloostergemeenschap van de zusters van Sint-Jan: Statuten Sint-Janshospitaal, 25 juli 1598 (sic!), f° 1r-2r; 3r-15r; 16r-30r. BRUGGE, Stadsarchief, Fonds Sint-Janshospitaal, Varia, Doos 12: Jesus Maria Augustinus, Regel van onsen alderheijlichsten Vader Augustinus, den XXIIII augus 1598.

ANTONIUS TRIEST (1620), Official report visitation St John's Hospital Bruges.

J.B. DESCAMPS (1769), Voyage pittoresque de la Flandre et du Brabant avec des réflexions relativement aux arts et quelques gravures, Paris.

JEAN EVERAERT (1864), Inventaris C.O.O. (Inventory Public Social Welfare Centre Bruges), Brugge.

GABRIELE PALEOTTI (2012), Discourse on sacred and profane images, The Getty Research Institute. Texts & Documents, Paolo Prodi/W. McCuaig (ed.), Los Angeles: J. Paul Getty Trust.

Secondary Literature

COOMANS, THOMAS (2005), De middeleeuwse kloosterinfirmerie: synthese van spirituele, medische en praktische beschouwingen, in: M. Buyle/S. Dehaeck (eindred.), Architectuur van Belgische Hospitalen .... Afdeling Monumenten en Landschappen, 36–43.

DE BRUYNE, HILDE (2011), Brugse zorg voor de burger in de 16de en 17de eeuw, in: Van chirurgijns tot pestheiligen. Ziek zijn in Brugge in de 16de en 17de eeuw [Care for Bruges citizens in the sixteenth and seventeenth centuries in: from surgeons to plague saints, being ill in Bruges in the sixteenth and seventeenth centuries], in: Museumbulletin Musea Brugge 2011/3:14–19.

DEHAECK, SIGRID/VAN HEE, ROBERT (2005), Van hospitaal naar virtueel ziekenhuis, M. Buyle/S. Dehaeck (eindred.), Architectuur van Belgische Hospitalen .... Afdeling Monumenten en Landschappen, 12–25.

DE MUYNCK, MIET (1998), Inventaris van het archief van de hospitaalzusters van Sint-Jan te Brugge [Inventory archives Sisters St John's Hospital Bruges], Brugge.

DIETL, ALBERT (2015), Die Kunst der praktizierten Caritas. Bilder der Werke der Barmherzigkeit, in: K., K. Petzel MA (Gesamtredaktion), Caritas. Nächstenliebe von den frühen Christen bis zur Gegenwart, Erzbischofliches Diözesanmuseum Paderborn, Petersberg: Michael Imhof Verlag, 190–192.

FALQUE, INGRID (2013), 'Mise en mots' et 'Mise en image' de la progression spirituelle. Vers une nouvelle approche du portrait dévotionnel dans la peinture flamande de la fin du Moyen Age, in: R. Deconinck/A. Guiderdoni/E. Granjon (Eds.). Fiction sacrée. Spiritualité et Esthétique durant le premier Age Moderne, Leuven, 289–317

GELDHOF, JOZEF (1976), De kloostergemeenschap van het Sint-Janshospitaal [The religious community of the St John's Hospital], 1459–1975, in: Hilde Lobelle/Marc Goetinck (ed.), Sint-Janshospitaal Brugge 1188/1976, volume 1, Brugge: Die Keure, 171–177.

GOEGEBUER, SIBYLLA (2013), The Memling in Sint-Jan – Hospital Museum re-established as Sint-Janshospitaal Museum. A history of continuity. Unpublished paper for the International Symposium Documentary and Visual sources for the historical study of hospitals, Institute for Research on Medieval Cultures - IRCVM, University Barcelona (Biblioteca de Catalunya & Hospital de la Santa Creu i Sant Pau) & l'Hospitalet de l'Infant, April 17–19, 2013.

GOEGEBUER, SIBYLLA (2016a), Passio et ratio. Het medisch en religieus erfgoed van het Sint-Janshospitaal Brugge vertelt een dubbelverhaal, in: P. Peeters/A. Montignie (ed.), Albarelli, chevrettes & Co. Le musée pharmaceutique Albert Couvreur s'invita à l'Hôpital Notre-Dame à la Rose, Lessines, 36–39.

GOEGEBUER, SIBYLLA (2016b), The function of the religious St John's Hospital community in Bruges in the sixteenth and seventeenth century history of care. How does the intangible history of care translate itself into the tangible seventeenth-century art collection commissioned by St John's Hospital? Paper to be published in proceedings Fourth RefoRC Conference Bologna, Arts, Portraits and Representation in the Reformation Era, May

15–17, 2014.

GOEGEBUER, SIBYLLA (2018), Saint John's Hospital in Bruges in the sixteenth and seventeenth centuries. Real and intangible interactions between religion, devotion, care and art are the ingredients necessary to constitute a continous hospital history, in: C. Villanueva Morte, A. Conejo da Pena, R. Villagrasa-Elias (eds.), Redes Hospitalarias: Historia, economia y sociologia de la sanidad, Colleccion Estudios Historia, Zaragoza, 2018, 161–174.

GOEGEBUER, SIBYLLA (2019), The role of St John's Hospital religious community in Bruges in the 16th- and 17th-century history of care. How did the tangible 17th-century art collection commissioned by St John's Hospital represent the intangible history of caring for people?, in: P. Foresta/F. Meloni (Eds.), Arts, Portraits and Representation in the Reformation Era, Proceedings of the Fourth Reformation Research Consortium Conference, Göttingen, 89–106.

HARBISON, CRAIG (1985), Visions and Meditations in Early Flemish painting, in: Simiolus, Netherlands quarterly for the history of art 15, 87–118.

MARECHAL, GRIET (1976), Het Sint-Janshospitaal in de eerste eeuwen van zijn bestaan [The first centuries of existence of the St John's Hospital], in: Hilde Lobelle/Marc Goetinck (ed.), Sint-Janshospitaal Brugge 1188/1976, deel 1, Brugge: Die Keure, 43–75.

MARECHAL, GRIET (1978), De Sociale en Politieke Gebondenheid van het Brugse Hospitaalwezen in de middeleeuwen (The Influence of social and political facts on the Organisation and Working of Hospitals in Bruges in the Middle Ages), Anciens Pays et Assemblées d'état LXXIII, Standen en Landen, Kortrijk-Heule: U.G.A.

MEULEMEESTER, JEAN-LUC (1984), Jacob Van Oost de Oudere en het zeventiende-eeuwse Brugge [Jacob Van Oost the elder and seventeenth-century Bruges], Brugge: West-Vlaamse Gidsenkring.

OEXLE OTTO (2015), Zwischen Armut und Arbeit. Epochen der Armenfürsorge im Europäischen Westen, in: K., K. Petzel MA (Gesamtredaktion) Caritas. Nächstenliebe von den frühen Christen bis zur Gegenwart, Erzbischofliches Diözesanmuseum Paderborn, Petersberg: Michael Imhof Verlag, 52–73.

RYCKAERT, MARC (1976), Enkele data in verband met de geschiedenis van Brugge en van het Sint-Janshospitaal [Historical data Bruges and St John's Hospital], in: Hilde Lobelle/Marc Goetinck (ed.), Sint-Janshospitaal Brugge 1188/1976, deel 1, Brugge: Die Keure, 15–21.

SCHNEIDER, BERNHARD (2015), Caritas. Begriffe und Konzepte des Helfens in der Geschichte des Christentums in Deutschland seit dem 16. Jahrhundert, in: Caritas. Nächstenliebe von den frühen Christen bis zur Gegenwart, in: K., K. Petzel MA (Gesamtredaktion), Erzbischofliches Diözesanmuseum Paderborn, Petersberg: Michael Imhof Verlag, 74–80.

VERVAET, LIEVE (2014), Goederenbeheer in een veranderende samenleving. Het Sint-Janshospitaal van Brugge ca. 1275–ca.1575 [commodity management in a changing society, St John's Hospital in Bruges, ca.1275–ca.1575]. Unpublished doctoral dissertation, University Gent, Faculteit Letteren en Wijsbegeerte.

WILSON, JEAN C. (1998), Painting in Bruges at the close of the Middle Ages: Studies in Society and Visual culture, University Park, Pa: Pennsylvania State University Press.

Geneviève Gross

Songs and Singing in a Developing Reformation

From a Scattered Community of Believers to a Visible Church (French-Speaking Switzerland, Bern-Geneva-Neuchâtel, 1530–1536)

This contribution seeks to examine three collections of songs, comprising 48 songs in total, that belong to a series of books printed between 1533 and 1535 with money from the Vallées Vaudoises by Pierre de Vingle.[1] Originally from Lyon, de Vingle moved to Neuchâtel in 1533 where he lived for three years. He was the son-in-law of Claude Nourry, the printer of François Rabelais' works. At least five songs are the work of Matthieu Malingre, a disciple of the poet Marot and a former Dominican in Blois who had become a pastor in Romandy, first in Yverdon, then in Aubonne (Vuilleumier: 1927–1933, vol. 1, 385–387; vol. 4, 628–629). Malingre signed his work with the anagram: "il me vint mal à gré". But also used poetic constructions based on a simple or double acrostic of his name or the surname Malingre de Blois. Another contributor by the name of Jacquelin operated in a similar way and signed at least one contribution in each of the collections (Honegger: 1971, vol. 1, 6). The pastor of Payerne, Antoine Saunier, can also be counted among the contributors. Before appearing in printed form, a song about the Ten Commandments that Saunier had sent to the community of Geneva in July 1532 circulated as an annex to a letter from the evangelists of Payerne (Herminjard, letter 384, 9 July, 1532, [vol. 2, 426–431]; Burdet: 1963, 63).

Due to their octavo format, these collections follow the criteria of Protestant books and religious literature of the preceding period. They could thus easily be carried around in pockets. Easy to transport and capable of being concealed if necessary, they were, in virtue of their very low price, very accessible. Printed in 1533–1534, this corpus includes a collection five polemical songs contained in a separate volume (Chansons nouvelles: 1534). With regard to the two other collections, the first contains 19 songs that lay out in a less incisive and more spiritual way the foundations of a Christ-centric faith (Belles et bonnes chansons: 1533). It nonetheless denotes a certain hybridity through the intermixing of genres, in which spiritual songs oriented towards an exposition of the faith are mixed

---

1 On Pierre de Vingle and his activites as a printer: Kemp: 2004, 146–177; Schulp: 1996, vol. 1, 259–263; Droz: 1957, 38–77. On the three collections of songs that are the subject of this article: Ullberg: 2009, 41–56.

with highly satirical songs. Incidentally, at the center of the collection we find a song composed in dialogue form, portraying the lamentations and regrets of a pope assailed by the Lutherans. In this discursive fiction, the Pope receives a fearless response from Luther, who declares himself ready to "die at your hands" and invokes rest "in Jesus", since the "the Evangel is our affair" (Belles et bonnes chansons: 1533, fol. BIIIv°-BVr). The last collection, les *Noelz nouveaulx* (1534), contains 24 carols and is concerned exclusively with themes related to Christmas. Its title and theme root it in a tradition linked to festivities of the Nativity, popular Christmases (Gennep: 1998, 3205–3268; Gastoué: 1908). It was thus able to reach a large public of Catholic believers accustomed to these songs and to this practice, and thereby attract them towards the expression of a new faith. The collection is divided into three themes mirroring three time periods: waiting for the arrival of the Messiah and his message, his birth, and, finally, the sharing of the event of his birth. It gives particular prominence to Mary, Jesus, and the witnesses, shepherds, and Magi. Beside carols about the Annunciation, we find paraphrases of psalms and free translations of Latin hymns, notably the *Conditor alme siderum* which opens the volume.[2]

These three collections connect us to a group of preachers active in French-speaking Switzerland at the beginning of the 1530s and centered around the presses of Pierre de Vingle. Gather together around editorial activities, this group also worked under the protection of Bern to evangelize bailiwicks, allied or sovereign territories of the city, which had passed to the Reform in 1528–1529. Thus Guillaume Farel, engaged between Aigle and Morat, worked alongside and socialized with the young Pierre Viret, with Antoine Marcourt, active in the region from Neuchâtel to Geneva, with Matthieu Malingre, preaching at Yverdon, but also with the scholar of Hebrew and cousin of Jean Calvin, Pierre Robert Olivétan, tasked with translating the Bible.[3]

Our corpus is situated between a pastoral theology implemented in words and actions, often offensive and practiced in the territory between Neuchâtel and Episcopal Geneva, and a version put down in writing. These preachers, in the image of Matthieu Malingre, made themselves into writers. They published around 20 works between 1533 and 1535, including notably a folio Bible, called the Olivétan Bible. They presented their claims in the form of songs, but also short treatises, placards

---

2 The poet centers his attention, in his translation of this Advent hymn, essentially on Jesus, the "very precious, Lamb of God", born to the Virgin Mary, "judge to come", and thus the only mediator men have in their quest for salvation. In 1523, Thomas Müntzer had already translated the same hymn into German, transposing it into praise of God, creator of the stars: Gott, heiliger Schöpfer aller Sterne, in: Evangelisches Gesangbuch. Ausgabe für die Evangelische Kirche in Hessen-Nassau, Leipzig, 2004, Nr. 3.

3 This group has been called the Neuchâtel group by William Kemp and Diane Desrosier in their recent work: Desrosier-Bonin: 2003, 179–189; Berthoud: 1973.

(as illustrated by the *Articles Veritables* placarded in Paris in October 1534), and plays. Their polemical attacks were essentially directed against priests, monks, and preachers. According to them, these clerical figures advocated a doctrine contrary to the precepts of Christ. By a rational occupation of communal space, by preaching and by printing works, those preachers solicited and awakened the faithful, perceived as blind and blinded by the "enchantments" of the priests. While Neuchâtel converted to Protestantism in 1530, it was not until 1535 that the Mass would be abolished in Geneva. The year 1536 marked the conquest of the Vaud by the Bernese. It was upon this imposing strip of territory that the Reformation would be established by decrees from the city of Bern after the Disput of Lausanne.

Composed of fairly free paraphrases of the Psalter, the three collections that interest us here are nonetheless situated chronologically before the progressive translation of the Psalms by Clément Marot, which would subsequently become central to the elaboration and defense of a Protestant identity.[4] The "authors" of these collections used a technique, the *contrafactum*, employed by the poets of the 13th century, the *Rhétoriqueurs*, and Clément Marot. Thus they did not compose melodies and restricted themselves to indicating the tune of a song that was already known and to "measuring" their text so that it was possible to sing it to the melody in question. They took an innovative approach, by replacing the words of fashionable profane love songs with pious verses. This way of proceeding, based on the reorientation of the content of the songs, was read as a desire to purify and moralize, which Olivier Maillard had used a century earlier to denounce from the pulpit the obscenity of certain popular songs (Gerald: 1981, 17–18). At the same time, it had the character of profanation or even degradation, when the sacred words of Latin hymns, for example, were replaced. Thus it enters into the modes of polemical writing.

It is the aim and what is at stake in the songs that we intend to examine here. The songs are not only a matter for textual analysis, they also contain a practice, the hymn, which powered the oral diffusion of the Reformation. However we will leave behind the long-term perspective and look at the period in which these three collections, which we will attempt to conceive of as a coherent corpus, were printed.[5] We will place ourselves with them at the time of an evolutionary stage of the Reformation in the Romandy, when the Reformation was coming into being

---

4 On this question, see: Higman: 1998, 449–459; Grosse: 2010, 13–31; Ferrer: 2012, 43–52.

5 Ann Ullberg has recently studied the song of the Neuchâtel group in terms of their long-term diffusion, transformation and affiliation (or lack of affiliation) with the corpus of the *Chansonnier Huguenot*: Ullberg: 2008. The three collections of Pierre de Vingle constitute the core of the *Chansonniers Huguenots* (Chansonniers: 1870), for an overview of their history, see p. VI. These *Chansonniers* contain a collection of songs going back to the first persecutions of the Evangelicals and completed before the Revocation of the Edict of Nantes. The last collection was established and printed in 1678

and a church was being created. According to Christian Grosse, in his book on the *Rituels de la cène* in Geneva, the implantation of the Reformation was the result of successive and complementary acts aiming at "overturning the altar", that is the abolition of the traditional ritual system (Grosse: 2008, 69–73). It was conceived as a collective or communitarian project through which lay-people affirmed their desire to take charge of their spiritual destiny. In the implementation of this project, singing, as a practical medium, had its place. In Geneva, between March 1533 and August 1534, the *Chansons nouvelles*, the five highly polemical songs recently published by Pierre de Vingle, accompanied, as Christian Grosse has shown, the attacks targeting the holy sacrament. The registers of the Counsel testify to this, as the hymns provoked civil disorder and even led to a prohibition on singing these songs.[6] The songs became an instrument of emancipation in the hands of the believer and of the community. They demanded that the priests justify using Scripture the dogma of transubstantiation, which grounded their spiritual power. Other songs also denounced the imprisonment of the nuns at the Sainte-Claire convent of Bourg-de-Four and were sung during acts of intimidation directed against the establishment. More generally, the formulation of critiques, sung or not, enabled, on the level of the community, the "converted" believer to warn the Catholic believer. It thus enabled raising awareness and the possibility of adhesion.

In light of this procedure nourished by a cultural and social perspective, we would like to examine the whole collection of Pierre de Vingle's songs and follow through the analyse of their content and a reflection about the practice of singing the fabric of a community, at the time of an "invisible" church in the institutional sense of the term, or of a church in gestation, fighting against a "visible" church, the Roman Catholic Church, which it rejects. From this perspective, singing is part of a mechanism of affiliation for believers that expresses their membership in a community of true Christians seeking to be recognized and to be established as only true church. We will examine the songs in light of their modalities of transmission of a religious identity and doctrinal content, a process in which common language, understood by all, play an important role (Grosse: 2006, 361–378).

Religious songs in common language did not appear spontaneously with the Reformation, but are the continuation of a practice traced back to the Middle Ages. Confraternities played an important role in the growing popularity of religious songs in common language, thanks to the movements of the "laudesi" or penitents. These devotional associations composed of laymen began from the 13th century to sing *laudes*, a sort of religious balled with a refrain, in the evening or on the

---

before being printed by Tross in Paris in 1870. For a reflection from the three collections of Pierre de Vingle's songs and the theater he published as a practice of writing: Gross: 2018, 415–450.

6 Grosse: 2008, 69–73; see also the references cited by Christian Grosse: Registres: 1900–1940, 12; 250 (30 mars 1533); Jussie: 1996, 110; 173.

holidays of a particular church. (Vauchez: 1984, 588–590; Vauchez: 1987; Vincent: 1994).

Nonetheless, here, in this context of the implementation of the Reformation, this practice served to transmit the call made to all Christians to carry out their duty, namely to be ready to defend their faith at all times and in all places, explicitly formulated in the *Petit Traité* of 1534 by Pierre de Vingle following the Paris placards ([Marcourt]: 1534, fol. D IIIv). Language and the duty required of every man who considers himself a Christian and who owns up to it, form the two central axes along which we will construct our hypothesis.

The construction of a new community or assembly of believers took place in parallel to that of the preachers, the figure of a new mediator of the Word as a counter-model to a priest vested with priesthood. These two communities, called to become the constitutive body of a new Church, understood themselves with reference to the use of sacred and religious texts and conceived themselves in terms of their respective authority to have recourse to the Word of God. This recourse was differentiated: the believers had a responsibility, namely to receive an education in agreement with Scripture; the preachers, for their part, were tasked with the teaching and instruction of the believers. In 1534, in the reprint of the *Summary and Brief Declaration (Sommaire et Brève Déclaration)*, a work that Farel published for the first time in 1529, an exhortation is directed at those listening to sermons ([Farel]: 1534). It calls upon them to verify the words of the preacher by the light of the Bible and to rise up in protest when confronted with the preaching of false doctrines ([Farel]: 1534, fol. H iiiiv–H Vv). Following this exhortation, the believer, would become a guardian of truth for himself and for his salvation, but also for that of his community.

And so in March 1534, a new edition of the New Testament by Jacques Lefèvre was published by Pierre de Vingle's Neuchâtel presses (Nouveau testament: 1534). A year later, in 1535, the Bible was published, translated by the Hebrew scholar and cousin of Calvin, Pierre Robert (La Bible: 1535). Both books contain an index of materials. Together, they offer selected passage from the Scriptures and define key concepts such as the church, abuses which have to be denounced by the preacher, Mass, baptism, minister and false prophets. In this way, the faithful had more and more tools with which to scrutinize the pastoral figure, to confirm the legitimacy of the preacher and his discourse or to reject the priest. This material thus presents, using a rhetoric impressed with religious combat, both in the proposed entries and their envisaged finality, that, according to the index of Olivétan's Bible, of helping to "confound the adversaries of the Word of God" an instruction oriented towards the defence of a faith and at the service of its affirmation.[7] This targeted

---

7 The index of Olivétan's Bible is due to Matthieu Malingre: Higman: 1998, 79; Reuss: 1867, 251.

framework to the biblical text aims at the instruction of "those who are not yet exercised and instructed in Holy Scripture" (La Bible: 1535, fol. rr r). This is why it is organized in the form of an index in alphabetical order, in order to avoid the "disorder that produces confusion" (La Bible: 1535, fol. rr r). For the reader who, "by the Spirit of God" finally arrives at a "naive and clear intelligence" of the notions and of the Scriptures, this material will have a supplementary function (La Bible: 1535, fol. rr r). It will then be put into service for the realisation of the duty of "each one (as is required)" to "be ready, equipped, and outfitted with answers to all those who demand justification of his faith" (La Bible: 1535, fol. rr r). Already, in November 1534, the *Petit Traicté*, a work dedicated to the rejection of Mass, priests, and theologians, formulated a similar injunction for all Christians ([Marcourt]: 1534, fol. D IIIv). As a polemical writing or circumstance, it provided justification for a reasoned act of occupation of communal space, the walls of Paris, covered between October 17th and 18th with an argument against the celebration of the Eucharist and its theological presuppositions.

However, the expression of such a duty and thus its realization is to be found first of all in this rejection: this new community, and especially believers and preachers, distanced itself from Catholic rituals, envisaged as contrary to the Scriptures and proclaimed by the sole authority of men. It is anchored in the imperative of marking a separation, or better of demarcating oneself by refusing communal devotional practices. This new community built itself up on rejection and manifested itself in the refusal to participate in the broader community's devotional practices. It distinguished itself by breaking fasts, and particularly Lent (Grosse: 2008, 72–82). The same goes for Mass and confession. It denounced them and justified its position. Denunciation makes it possible to distinguish oneself from the others, to escape from domination, to liberate oneself and at the same time to express oneself and define oneself as a true member of the congregation of believers in Christ, the Son of God.

The collection of *Chansons nouvelles*, put together as a demonstration in the face of the errors of the "ministers of Satan" who fill the world, carries within itself in an almost organic manner this identitary programme. This programme can be discerned from the title page and is developed through the internal organization of the five songs. The compiler frames his work with a reference to Matthew XV, in which Christ faces the Pharisees who have been offended by his words. To the disciples who point it out to him, Jesus responds: "Every plant that my father did not plant shall be uprooted". Thus, the use of attacks and offense count among the modes of expression of this community and contribute *in fine* to the formation of an identity. This passage is compulsory for the identification for the bearers of false doctrines and bad teachings. He who is offended is blind or still blind, in other words not receptive to Christ, and thus similar to the Pharisees, who were rigorous and attentive defenders of the Law and ritual. Finally, he who dares to distance himself from the Pharisees, these "leaders of the blind", shows himself to see clearly, having left the state of blindness. He becomes a partisan of Jesus and behaves as such, by putting himself at the service of his message.

It is thus, very logically, that this collection begins by laying out the origin, the authority and the power of the Evangel, the place of the revealed Word received by the first witnesses to Christ. The Evangel complains about its situation, as "human understanding" filled with arrogance and audacity torments it and has, in this way, concealed its meaning. "So many false seducers, blind leaders" "deem to be wise" "have" says the Evangel "closed the passages". Finally, in their mouth, the Evangel is called not only a new faith, but above all a wrong doctrine, showing by this judgement their disdain in the face of the "great king" and "his grace". The Word is indeed the place of "true salvation and life" (Chansons nouvelles: 1534, fol. AAiv°-Aiiir°). To serve the Evangel is to recognize and serve the glory of Christ who, by his single, effective death saved humanity from sin. This song is followed by the song of a Mass, who laments its approaching end and demands to be saved by its protectors. The Mass knows that it lacks a scriptural foundation and recognizes that there is only one way for it to survive: violence (Chansons nouvelles: 1534, fol. AAiiir°-AAiiiir°). From the Mass, the collection passes to the priests, who have usurped the name of pastor of the people. Far from teaching the believers, the priests only look to their worldly interests and cultivate their authority taken from Scripture at the expense of the faithful. The principal errors are thus identified: the change of substance of the elements of the Eucharist, bread and wine, into the body and blood of Christ and the real presence. This why, to these magicians playing "so many tricks", making "as many gods as pieces of bread", the exhortation is formulated to read "first, Saint Luke, Acts, and Saint Mark last", since "Jesus is at the right-hand of the omnipotent father". Since they make themselves even more "gods on earth" through the confession they defend, this sacrament is worthless: only Christ saves. Thus, the priests have the obligation to be conscience, in a strophe written in resonance with the evangelist Matthew, that from now on "it's no longer your season", "because everything is planted against God and reason you will be deplanted (uprooted, torn out)" (Chansons nouvelles: 1534, fol. AAiiiir°-AAVv°).

The collection exploits the arguments of the troublemakers who have been identified and who ought to be rejected in order to achieve, in the end, a rally. It appeals to the "good will" of these "poor, ignorant Papists" and works to convert them, enjoining them to return to Christ. It is a question to leading the listener or the reader to have a change of conscience, his "debonair" attitude led him to cultivate error and nourish his ignorance. From now on, he has the obligation to extract himself from it, or rather "it is time" "because Jesus is preached to you". There follows a list of gestures and devotional acts to be abandoned, leading to idolatry, to complicity with the lie and supporting idleness and the "sensuality" of the clergy

(Chansons nouvelles: 1534, fol. AAVIr°-AAVIIr°). But the collection rather tends to follow the constructive perspective and finishes with a song directed to "Christians" (Chansons nouvelles: 1534, fol. AAVIIr°). From now on, the "poor, ignorant Papists", by rejecting their former devotional habits born from human ordonnances will become true Christians and will form a community demarcated from the blind Pharisees and "obstinate and blasphemous Papists", sacrificing Christ repeatedly and selling the sacraments (Chansons nouvelles: 1534, fol. AAVv°).

The songs of the collection *Chansons nouvelles* mark the progression towards the creation of a Christian community bearing a song made in agreement with God. It is not merely a question of singing "from the mouth, but much more ardently from the heart when the Spirit of God touches me" (Chansons nouvelles: 1534, fol. AAVIIv°). In this way, the singer says, "I will praise God to the great profit and edification of my neighbour" (Chansons nouvelles: 1534, fol. AAVIIIr°). At this point, singing becomes the place in which the believing heart expresses itself, a heart touched by the Spirit of God, animating these strophes with new force. What's more, in singing this believing heart becomes an example and charged with teaching its neighbour, for, says the singer, "I will instruct him to praise God in his office" (Chansons nouvelles: 1534, fol. AAVIIIr°).

Moreover, the same advice concerning how to sing opens the collection of 19 songs entitled *Belles et bonnes Chansons*. In a rhyming poem, Matthieu Malingre, a preacher engaged in the Bernese efforts to evangelize in Romandy, places the heart at the center and exhorts his readers to follow this method. Christian readers are thus invited to sing "listening carefully to the tenor" (Belles et bonnes chansons: 1533, fol. AIv°). This tenor comes from attention to the "Holy Scriptures", of which the reader is urged not to "lose the tenor" (Belles et bonnes chansons: 1533, fol. AIv°). The heart is placed at the center and gives force to the words that without it would be empty and worthless. In this process, the use of common language is informed by a desire to convert. It guarantees the intelligence of the text, a text built on authoritative content, since it derives from the authority of Scripture. The collection as a whole, to follow the title page, was put together in the name of God and composed "as close as possible to the spirit of Jesus Christ, contained in the Holy Scriptures". But the reception of this truth required an engagement, a taking into hand on the part of the listener. The singer or the reader has the obligation to examine, on the advice and request of the poet, "what, he said, I have brought in my song, if it's well-rendered and well-received, will be holy and useful to you" (Belles et bonnes chansons: 1533, fol. AVIIr°). At this point, comprehension, which had previously been obstructed, permits the emergence of a just faith, one that recognizes the unique effectiveness of the sacrifice of Christ for the salvation of each individual. In this way, the promise inscribed on the title page of the collection was to be realized: these songs "sung with great affection of the heart" will bring relief and rest in God to Christians.

It is still this univocal message, of a salvation that can only come from Christ, which is delivered by the collection *Noels nouveaux*. Readers are led to rediscover the real importance of Christmas, which is the birth of the Saviour. Christ took on human nature in the cold and precariousness of a manger. A Christian thus has the obligation to celebrate and praise this event, while admiring the Nativity, the place where "the great humility of the Son of God, the true king" is expressed. From this gesture of love comes the submission of "Robin and you Denyse" to this lord, who alone should occupy "your ordinary conversations" "when you are at rest" (Belles et bonnes chansons: 1533, fol. AVIIr°). Not only the believer, but even more "shepherds, lords, prelates" should learn from the contemplation of the birth and life of Christ". This "in contemplating the Christ" the will be able to gauge their way of life and realize "that some are the Antichrist". Nonetheless in this devotion turned towards Christ, light of the world and prince of peace, and his teachings, we must not neglect to render homage to God, the loving Father, who gave his own son, guaranteeing the salvation of humanity once and for all. From this point on, the collection invites us to wake up and the "gentle shepherds" are called upon to recite and to get "women, children, and servants" to recite "melodiously" the paternoster, because "it is explicitly written in Saint Matthew" (Noelz nouveaulx: 1534, fol. Biiiir°). A special place is given to Mary all through the collection. Womb and receptacle of the Son of God, Mary is exalted in her dimension of respectful and submissive servant to the divine will. She becomes the figure representing Christians. Like her, the faithful should not look anywhere else for salvation but to Christ. For "Jesus was born" and "without him all is damned", thus "let us await salvation from him, because it is blasphemous to say that a woman can give rest" (Noelz nouveaulx: 1534, fol. Bv°).

Finally, this reorientation affected the celebration of Christmas, limited to a few days a year and marking for the traditional church the beginning of the liturgical year. The poet and singer asks, moreover: shouldn't it be celebrated every day of week, given its importance? (Noelz nouveaulx: 1534, fol. AVr°-v°). In this way and without explicit mention, the numerous and varied festivities practiced in the Roman Catholic Church are criticized. This underlying critique breaks the attachement to the ordering of the days, defended by the temporal and sacral calendar of the traditional church.[8] Even more important, the collection fits into a precise context of action in Geneva and probably participates in supporting the preachers, Guillaume Farel and Antoine Froment, who take the Christmas Mass as their target and attempt between 1533 and 1534 to prevent its celebration (Grosse: 2008, 54). From now on and without distinguishing between days, it is necessary

---

8 On the expression and formulation of the critiques in Romandie from the beginning of the 1530s: Grosse: 2008, 294ff.

to praise the Lord and to sing, as proposed in the *Belles et Bonnes Chansons* "a new canticle to God in all places and in all locations" (Belles et bonnes chansons: 1533, front cover). Moreover, everyone must finally be led to take part in this praise. The *Noels nouveaux* transcribe this imperative, already present in the preceding collections. In their fraternal or pastoral addresses, they seek to create the effect of a living and existing community. In fact, the singer names certain parishioners, addressing them by name, no doubt fictional, but common at the time. He refers to Robin, Margot, Marguerite, Thomin, Jacquette. This community is called to teach its neighbours, to expand the circle of adepts. This is why Roger and Thomin are requested to go look for their neighbour "because everyone has to be a teacher of truth". Christ "wants to save with great tenderness all sinners who have repented in their heart" (Noelz nouveaulx: 1534, fol. AVv).

By this defence of praising God at all times, in all places, and by all people, the social and communal space is endowed with sacrality, since it is, as a whole, suitable for praise. This sacralisation of the communal space now has its origin in the believing heart, impregnated by a lively faith that dispense truth, making the believer himself the privileged place in his relationship with God. This sacralisation is no longer polarized on the building of the church and no longer depends on this place consecrated to the sacred – the Church – which is supposed, according to the medieval conception, to irradiate the communal space with sacrality, since it would be the seat of Christ made present by the hands of the priest and on the altar of the Eucharistic consecration (Palazzo: 2008, 32ff). Through song, on the level of both its content and the practice it establishes, a community bearing a new faith is created from believer to believer, a community detached from the Church and not requiring any link with this "house of priests", this sacred place of sacrifice. By the practice of singing, but also the denunciation that it carried, a body or a new community began to emerge and dared to rise up within a space invested by or ruled by the Roman Catholic Church. It demarcated itself over and against the mass of still-blinded followers, submissive and loyal to the priests, whom it tried to warn and put on guard. Songs and the practice of singing are, here, an instrument of demarcation. It literally permitted the formation of a rampart in the face of the various errors of these "ministers of Satan".

A transmitter of denunciation, the singer was also equipped through his singing with the instruments and the education necessary to nourish and defend his position. In two volumes, the essence of the faith is formulated or reformulated with the help of the *contrafactum*. If the *Belles et Bonnes Chansons* propose a song about the Ten Commandments and articles of the faith, the *Noels nouveaux* contain a sung version of the Lord's Prayer, the *Pater Noster* (Chansons nouvelles: 1534, Biiiir°-BVv°; Belles et bonnes chansons: 1533, Aiir°-AVr°).

The putting into words of the songs and the printing of these two collections probably took place in this Genevan context and contributed to the same extent as the *Chansons Nouvelles* to the implantation of the Reformation in Geneva. They likely supported and served the evangelization drive.

At the beginning of July 1532, however, the song about the Ten Commandments, which would figure a year later in the collection *Belles et Bonnes chansons* was sent by its author Antoine Saunier, pastor in Payerne, to the small community of Evangelicals in Geneva (Herminjard, letter 384, 9 July 1532 [vol. 2, 426–431]). Less than one year later, it was printed by Pierre de Vingle. In the same year, 1533, the *Instruction des enfants* appeared ([Olivétan]:1533). This manual oriented towards the teaching of writing proposed the foundations of the catechism, including a detailed explanation of the Ten Commandments, the articles of faith, and the Lord's Prayer. The *Instruction* almost certainly supported the activity of the preacher engaged by Bern, Antoine Froment in Geneva. Having been sent by his colleague Guillaume Farel, Froment opened a school there in November 1532, where reading and writing was taught (Herminjard, letter 198, towards the end of June 1527 [vol. 1, 22–28]; letter 395, 18 November, 1532 [vol. 2, 459–461, n.14; 493] ; cf. Froment: 1854, 12–15). Set up on the model of the earlier activity of Farel at Aigle, a sovereign territory of Bern, this school taught the rudiments of a new faith between catechetic education and readings of the New Testament. In this context, the songs became a supplementary support to memorization and learning. This process was, incidentally, made easier, since the collections take up tunes from a collection of songs printed by Vivien ten years earlier in Geneva (Plusieurs belles chansons: 1520). Moreover, two songs from these collections have the exact same tune and touch on fundamental themes at the heart of this "new" faith. The song about the articles of the faith has a similar tune to that of a song about justification by faith alone (Belles et bonnes chansons: 1533, fol. AVr°; Noelz nouveaulz: 1534, fol. BIIr°). Thus, the songs accompany the appropriation of a discourse, its interiorization, and its forceful repetition. Thanks to thoughtful rewriting, they contribute to the exposition, diffusion, and defence of the fundamentals of the faith.

Written by preachers in the context of the implantation of the Reformation, the writing down and printing of these songs by Pierre de Vingle between 1533–1534 was contemporaneous with their use in Geneva between 1532 and 1533. Certain songs, as we have seen, accompanied and support the activity of Guillaume Farel and Antoine Froment in Geneva in their reasoned occupation of communal space, but also in their educational aims. In the light of this context, the three collections of songs printed by Pierre de Vingle between 1533–1534 constitute, despite their objectives oscillating between religious combat and exposition of the faith, a coherent corpus. They convey an identity inscribed in a movement of rupture and transcribed in a rhetoric of detachment. They also bear witness to a living mechanism of affiliation, built on religious content and religious claims, able to pass, thanks to use of common language, from "mouth to mouth" or "heart to heart", from the preacher to believers, but especially from believers to believers. They serve, using text and voice, to expression a sense of belonging, that of being a member apart of a congregation of believers, detached from the Roman Catholic Church, subject to Christ alone and defender of the authority of Scripture. They were tools to bring together and construct a community at the heart of the communal space of a city. It led, in the end, to the affirmation of this assembly of believers who were open partisans of the Evangel, preparing them to become a visible church, in which the Last Supper would be understood, as the singer of *Chansons nouvelles* suggests, in its commemorative dimension and would be celebrated "only once or twice a year" (Chansons nouvelles: 1534, fol. AA VIIIv°).

Bibliography

Sources

BELLES ET BONNES CHANSONS (1533), S'ensuyvent plusieurs belles et bonnes chansons que les chrestiens peuvent chanter en grande affection de coeur; pour et affin de soulager leurs esperitz et de leur donner repos en Dieu [Neuchâtel: Pierre de Vingle].

LA BIBLE (1535), La Bible qui est toute la saincte escriture. En laquelle sont contenus, le Vieil Testament et le Nouveau, translatez en Francoys. Le Vieil, de Lebrieu: et le Nouveau, du Grec. Avec deux amples tables, une pour linterpretation des propres noms : lautre en forme dindice, pour trouver plusieurs sentences et matieres, Neuchâtel: Pierre de Vingle.

CHANSONNIER (1870), Le chansonnier huguenot du XVIe siècle, 2 vols., Henri-Léonard Bordier (ed.), Paris: Libraire Tross.

CHANSONS NOUVELLES (1534), Chansons nouvelles demonstrantz plusieurs erreurs et faulsetez desquelles le povre monde est remply, par les ministres de Satan, [Neuchâtel: Pierre de Vingle].

[GUILLAUME FAREL] (1534), Summaire, et briefve declaration d'aucuns lieux fort necessaires a ung chascun Chrestien, pour mettre sa confiance en Dieu, et ayder son prochain. Item, ung traicté du Purgatoire nouvellement adjousté sur la fin, [Neuchâtel: Pierre de Vingle].

[ANTOINE MARCOURT] (1534), Petit traicté tres utile, et salutaire de la saincte eucharistie de nostre Seigneur Jesuchrist, [Neuchâtel: Pierre de Vingle].

NOELZ NOUVEAULX (1534), Noelz nouveaulx. Musiciens amateurs des Cantiques, Au nom de Dieu, chantez noelz nouveaulx, Lesquelz sont faictz sur les vieulx et antiques : Je vous supply, delaissez les lubriques : Ne chantez point brayant comme noz veaulx, Glorieux chantres, ne vault point deux naveaux Recordez vous que Dieu veult l'humble cœur En foy contrict. Note cela chanteur, [Neuchâtel : Pierre de Vingle].

NOUVEAU TESTAMENT (1534), Le nouveau testament de nostre seigneur et seul sauveur Jesus Christ, Neuchâtel: Pierre de Vingle.

[PIERRE ROBERT OLIVÉTAN], Linstruction des enfans, contenant la maniere de prononcer et escrire en françoys. Loraison de Jesu Christ. Les articles de la foy. Les dix commandemens. La salutation angelicque. Avec la declaration diceux, faicte en maniere de recueil des seulles sentences de lescripture saincte. Item les figures des chiphres, et leurs valeurs, [Genève: Pierre de Vingle].

PLUSIEURS BELLES CHANSONS (1520), Sensuyvent plusieurs belles chansons composées nouvellement lesquelles ne furent jamais imprimées et se chantent sur diver chans nouveaux pour ce qu'elles sont nouvelles et le nombre dicelles se treuve en la table qui est a la fin du present, Genève: Jacques Vivien.

REGISTRES (1900–1940), Registres du Conseil de Genève, publ. by Société d'histoire et d'archéologie de Genève, ed. Emile Rivoire, Genève: H. Kündig.

Secondary Literature

BERTHOUD, GABRIELLE (1973), Antoine Marcourt : réformateur et pamphlétaire, du "Livre des marchands" aux placards de 1534, Genève: Droz, 1973.

BURDET, JACQUES (1963), La musique dans le Pays de Vaud sous le régime bernois (1536–1798), Lausanne: Payot.

DESROSIER-BONIN, DIANE (2003), L'Epistre de Marie d'Ennetières et les écrits du groupe de Neuchâel, in: Marie-Claude Malenfant/Sabrina Vervacke (ed.), "Ecrire et conter": mélanges de rhétorique et d'histoire littéraire du XVIe siècle offerts à Jean-Claude Moisan, Laval: Presses de l'Université Laval, 179–189.

DROZ, EUGÉNIE (1957), Pierre de Vingle: imprimeur de Guillaume Farel, in: Aspects de la propagande religieuse, Genève: Droz, 1957.

FERRER, VÉRONIQUE (2012), La chanson spirituelle au temps de la Réforme (1533–1591), Studia Litteraria Universitatis Iagellonicae Cracoviensis 7, 43–52.

FROMENT, ANTOINE (1854), Les actes et gestes merveilleux de la cité de Genève: nouuellement convertie à l'évangille faicz du temps de leur Reformation et comment ils l'ont receue, redigez par escript en fourme de chroniques annales ou hystoyres commençant l'an MDXXXII par Anthoine Froment, Gustave Revilliod (ed.), Genève : J.G. Fick.

GASTOUÉ, AMÉDÉE (1908), Noël, origines et développements de la fête, Paris: Bloud.

GENNEP, ARNOLD VAN (1998), Manuel de folklore français contemporain : de Noël aux rois. 1. 8. Cycle des douze jours, Paris : A. et J. Picard.

GERALD, PAU (1981), De l'usage de la chanson spirituelle par les jésuites au temps de la contre-réforme, in: La Chanson à la Renaissance, Actes du XXe colloque d'Etudes humanistes du Centre d'Etudes supérieures de la Renaissance de l'Université de Tours, Juillet 1977, Luynes: Van De Velde.

GROSS, GENEVIEVE (2018), Théâtre et chansons dans une Réforme en devenir (Suisse, 1530–1535). Des pratiques d'écriture au service d'une communauté à construire, Revue d'Histoire des Religions 3, 415–450.

GROSSE, CHRISTIAN (2006), Que tous congnoissent et entendent ce qui se dit et se faict au Temple. Prière en français et usages liturgiques à Genève après la Réforme (1530–1570), in: La prière en latin de l'Antiquité au XVIe siècle. Formes, évolutions, significations, Turnhout: Brepols, 361–378.

Grosse, Christian (2008), Les rituels de la cène. Le culte eucharistique réformé à Genève (XVIe–XVIIIe siècle), Genève: Droz.

Grosse, Christian (2010), L'esthétique du chant dans la piété calviniste aux premiers temps de la Réforme (1536–1545), Revue de l'histoire des religions 1, 13–31.

Higman, Francis (1998), "Chantez au Seigneur nouveau cantique" : Le Psautier de Genève au XVIe siècle (1991), in: Lire et découvrir. La circulation des idées au temps de la Réforme, Genève: Droz, 449–459.

Higman, Francis (1998), The Drilhon inventory, in: Lire et découvrir. La circulation des idées au temps de la Réforme, Genève: Droz.

Honegger, Marc (1971), Les chansons spirituelles de Didier Lupi et les débuts de la musique protestante en France au XVIe siècle, Lille.

Jussie, Jeanne de (1996), Petite Chronique, intro. and ed., Helmut Feld, Mainz: P. von Zabern.

Kemp, Wiliam (2004), La redécouverte des éditions de Pierre de Vingle imprimées à Genève et à Neuchâtel (1533–1536), in: Jean-François Gilmont/William Kemp (ed.), Le livre évangélique en français avant Calvin, études originales, publications d'inédits, catalogues d'éditions anciennes, Turnhout: Brepols, 146–177.

Palazzo, Eric (2008), L'espace rituel et le sacré dans le christianisme. La liturgie de l'autel portatif dans l'Antiquité et au Moyen Âge, Turnout: Brepols.

Vuilleumier, Henri (1927–1933), Histoire de l'Eglise réformée du Pays de Vaud sous le régime bernois, 4 vols., Lausanne: Editions La Concorde.

Reuss, Eduard W.E. (1867), Fragments littéraires et critiques relatifs à l'histoire de la Bible française, Revue de théologie, Paris : J. Cherbuliez.

Schulp, Michel (1996), Pierre de Vingle, imprimeur (1495–1536), in: Biographies neuchâteloises, Hauterive: G. Attinger, vol. 1, 259–263.

Ullberg, Ann (2008), Au chemin de salvation. La chanson spirituelle réformée (1533–1678), Uppsala: Uppsala Université.

Ullberg, Ann (2009), Les premières chansons imprimées par Pierre de Vingle : la chanson populaire au service de l'Evangile, in: Cinq siècles d'histoire religieuse neuchâteloise : approches d'une tradition protestante: actes du colloque de Neuchâtel (22–24 avril 2004). Neuchâtel: Université de Neuchâtel, 41–56.

Vauchez, André (1984), La Bible dans les confréries et les mouvements de dévotion, in: Le Moyen Âge et la Bible, Paris: Beauchesne.

Vauchez, André (1987), Les laïcs au Moyen Âge. Pratiques et experiences religieuses, Paris: Cerf.

Vincent, Catherine (1994), Les confréries médiévales dans le Royaume de France, XIII–XVe siècle, Paris: Albin Michel.

Joanna Kaźmierczak

The Iconographical Motif of the Good Samaritan as a Visual Commentary on the State of the Church in the Middle of the 16th Century

The Epitaph for Nicolaus Weidner from Wrocław and Its Meaning

Introduction

In the art-historical writing, the pictorial epitaphs commisioned by Catholic, Silesian clerics in the 16th century have not gained as much attention as their Protestant
counterparts. Such artworks, designed for the supporters of Luther's teachings,
widely known and well researched, seem to outshine those connected with clergy of
the Cathedral Island (Ostrów Tumski) in Wrocław, regarding not only the incom-
parably greater number of examples that survived up to this day. The group of early
modern Silesian Lutheran epitaphs has served for years as the key examples of the
process of creating a visual confessional declaration; they also appeared to be those,
were the modern, progressive tendencies, understood as the departure from some
of the formal and functional aspects of the medieval epitaph, were especially visible.
Set on such background, the voice of the canon priests from the Cathedral Island
remained barely audible, obscured also by the research focused on artistic commissions of the bishops of Wrocław. Therefore, the aim of this article is to introduce to
a larger audience one of those almost forgotten artworks from the capital of Lower
Silesia – the painted epitaph for the canon priest of the cathedral chapter, Nicolaus
Weidner (d. 1555): a well-educated, clear-headed and acute-minded humanist.[1]
The main goal of this case study is to present the message which Weidner wanted
to pass on to his contemporaries and which had been enclosed in the iconographic
details of his own epitaph. That message contained a reflection on the state of the
Church at that time – the founder of the epitaph particularly tried to answer two
urgent questions: what is to be done with the already parted Christian Church to
prevent it from further decay and how the members of the Roman Church should
deal with the problem of heretics.

---

1 Basic bibliography on the epitaph: Lutsch: 1886, 184; Dubowy: 1922, 54; Burgemeister: 1930, 170;
  Nowack: 1932, 52; Steinborn: 1966, 18; 44, n. cat. 18; Schade: 1967, 30; Steinborn: 1967, 15; 28; 85, n.
  cat. 18, tbl. 12; Biernacka: 2003, 123. See also: Kaźmierczak: 2017.

Fig. 1 Epitaph for Nicolaus Weidner, ca. 1555–1556, Archdiocesan Museum in Wrocław.
Photo: Joanna Kaźmierczak, personal archive.

Beside those issues, immersed in the aura of the Catholic Reform, it also points at the questions concerning the differences between the Church of the Old and the New Testament, which were so frequently discussed at that time.

1. Nicolaus Weidner: a Biography

Nicolaus Weidner was born in Wrocław as the only son of an innkeeper.[2] The exact date of his birth remains unknown. As a child he attended the renowned parish school of St. Jacob's in Nysa. In 1495 Weidner had begun his studies in Cracow, where he remained for one year. Then he had moved to Rome, where he lived for five years and obtained the title *magister artium*. During that time, Weidner enroled at the service of cardinal Pietro Isvaglies, known as Rheginus,[3] the legatus *a latere* for Poland and Hungary. They had moved together to Buda and remained in Hungary for three years; Weidner served there also as the plenipotentiary (*procurator*) of the city council of Wrocław. Meanwhile, he had been named a canon priest in the cathedral chapter in Wrocław. In 1505 Weidner had been immatriculated at the university of Leipzig, where he studied law.[4] There he attended also the lectures at the faculty of the liberals arts, where he acquainted some of the eminent German humanists of that time, most notably the theologian and philologist Johannes Rhagius (Aesticampianus). His (Rhagius') commentary to the letters of St. Jerome, published in 1508 as *Septem divi Hieronymi epistole*[5] contains a number of poems written by friends of the author; among them the one composed by Nicolaus Weidner himself can be read. Then for the first time his work was published along with pieces written by some of the well-known humanists of his time, such as Hieronymus Emser, Veit Werler, Ulrich von Hutten, Valerian Seyfried and Sebastian von der Heide

---

2 Basic bibliography on Nicolaus Weidner: Pol: 1819, 12; Heyne: 1868, 227–228; Bauch: 1895, 16–17; 1896, 170–171; 1904, 328–331; 1907, 145; Sabisch: 1937, 18; Zimmermann: 1938, 565; Jujeczka: 2006, 338.

3 Pietro Isvalies (Isvaglies), d. 1511, governor of Rome in 1496, bishop of Reggio di Calabria since 1497. After being named cardinal (in 1500) known as Reginus (Rheginus). In 1510 appointed as the bishop of Messina. In the years 1500–1503 he was active as a legatus in Hungary, where he befriended Johannes Turzo, father of the future bishop of Wrocław, Johannes V, et. al.. He was a keen collector, his residence in Rome was decorated with many sculptures and paintings. Rheginus corresponded also with some of the most important figures of that time – e.g. with Erasmus of Rotterdam or Henry VIII Tudor. See: Contemporaries of Erasmus: 2003, 229–230.

4 The stay in Leipzig had been interrupted due to the outbreak of a plague in 1506 – Weidner, as well as the whole Faculty of Law, moved then for several months to Erfurt.

5 *Septem diui Hieronymi epistole ad vitam mortalium instituendam accommodatissime cum Johannis Aesticampiani Rhetoris ac poete Laureati et Epistola et Sapphico carmine aliorumque eruditissimorum virorum Epigrammatibus. Hoc libello continentur*, Leipzig 1508.

(Miricianus). In the same year 1508 Weidner had returned to Wrocław (already as *doctor decretorum*[6]), where his actual clerical career finally begun. Interestingly, in 1513 he was disinherited by his mother[7]. Wasteful, but probably never totally penniless, he obtained during his long life many important posts; most notably, he was a canon priest not only of the cathedral chapter but also a dean at the chapter by the collegiate church of the Holy Cross in Wrocław, as well as at the collegiate church in Nysa. He was also named a parish priest in Nysa, Ołtaszyn (in the nearby of Wrocław) and in Świdnica.[8] Regarding his humanistic interests, the most important fact remains his nomination in 1553 for the post of a cantor of the cathedral chapter in Wrocław. After long and interesting life, Nicolaus Weidner died by the end of 1555 and was buried in the collegiate church of the Holy Cross in Wrocław.

Although he was often sent as a representative of the cathedral chapter to the negotiations with bishops or with king Louis II Jagiellon (Pol: 1819, 12; Heyne: 1868, 227–228; 241; 304), the relationship between Weidner and this institution was far from being easy. We know about at least two situations, when his actions were definitely colliding with the official standpoint of the chapter. However, being an *enfant terrible* of an institution does not automatically mean being its implacable critic, especially when we think about the establishment of the higher kind, which stood above Weidner's chapter – that is, the Roman Church. He may had shattered some of lines of action of the chapter, but he was still a devoted defender of the Church, which he – as we will find out – had seen as one, only and united – under the papal banner. When exactly did he prove to be so troublesome for his parent institution? In 1521 he was sent by the city council of Wrocław (not by the cathedral chapter!) to Buda, in order to present to the king Louis II a controversial issue of the nomination for the post of the parish priest in St. Mary Magdalene's church in Wrocław. The question circulated from Hungary to Rome and when it finally came back to the city council, it turned out, that all went just like its members wanted it to be – the council was able to present to the bishop its own candidate for the post. However, that candidacy – of Johannes Hess, a canon priest and a preacher in the cathedral church in Wrocław – was strongly protested by the cathedral chapter, due to candidate's progressive way of thinking. When the confirmation of the nomination for the post did not come from the bishop, the city council willfully named Hess the parish priest of St. Mary Magdalene's, thus fulfilling the mission initiated by Weidner in Buda. Hess, as is commonly known, soon became a fervent protagonist of Lutheranism; Weidner, therefore, due to his connections to

---

6 It is uncertain, where he obtained that title.

7 Due to Weidner's – as his mother put it – greed and miserliness. For details from the trial see: Bauch: 1895, 16.

8 He was also a chaplain in the monastery church of sisters of St. Benedict in Legnica and an altarist in St. Barbara's Church in Wrocław.

the city council, unintentionally contributed to the introduction of the Reformation in Wrocław. The mutual bitterness between Weidner and the cathedral chapter, presumably rooted in the events of 1521, exploded years later in a conflict that had centered on the issue of Laurentius Potschel's last will (Sabisch 1937, 14–18). Potschel,[9] a fellow canon priest from the cathedral chapter, named Weidner an executor of his testament. What exactly did he resolve in that document is today unknown, however, what we do know very well is that its content caused a huge consternation in the cathedral chapter. It was decided that Potschel's last will should be kept in secrecy – only few members of the chapter, forming a special committee, were permitted to read it. No doubt, that the document was a controversial one; from the course of the matter we also know that one of the issues that made the chapter so angry was the fact that Potschel bequeathed the chapter from his presumably quite considerable property either only a small amount of money or even no money at all. Potschel definitely must had known that his testament will cause a lot of problems – the choice of Weidner (along with another fellow canon priest, Joachim Zieris) for the post of an executor is very telling. In fact, Weidner fought so bitterly for the acceptance of Potschel's last will, that at some point of the long negotiations the chapter demanded bishop's intervention and cancellation of Weidner's post as an executor.

Two other stories from Weidner's life should be told in order to shed more light on his attitude towards such questions as the Church, its institutions, methods of proceeding, and – last but not least – its attitude towards religious dissenters. Both events took place in 1531. In that year, Weidner published his most imprtrant work, *Catholicum carmen ad Philippum Melanchtonem*[10]. By then he was already a well-known person within the circle of Silesian humanists (he was a close friend of the famous poet Georg von Logau i.a.[11]), one of the re-organizers of the cathedral library in Wrocław (along with other renown humanist, Stanislaus Sauer [Fliegel: 1919, 120]), a good acquaintance with Johannes Cochlaeus (his poem opened the first edition of Chochlaeus' famous *Septiceps Lutherus*[12]). In 1531 he decided to publish a response for Melanchthons preface to the Book of Daniel, published in Speyer two years earlier.[13] Melanchthons work was a plea directed to the king

---

9 For information about Laurentius Potschel and further bibliography see: Kaźmierczak 2015; 2016; 2017.

10 *NICOLAI VVEIDNER CANONICI VVratislauien. Catholicum carmen, ad Philippum Melanchthonem* [1531].

11 About Logau see e.g.: Bauch: 1895, 5–33.

12 *Septiceps Lutherus, ubique sibi, suis scriptis, contrarius, in Visitationem Saxonicam, per D. D. Joa. Cocleum, editus*, Leipzig 1529. Since 1539 Cochlaeus was also a member of the cathedral chapter in Wrocław.

13 *Praefatio ad Regem Ferdinandum in Danielem. Autore Philippo Melanch.*, [Speyer] 1529.

Ferdinand I. Habsburg, where, as a remedy for the destruction of Christian unity (an issue so important regarding the constant threat of the Turkish invasion) such resolutions as a multi-confessional ecumenical council or – in case when the first solution was too hard to achieve – a debate between "righteous and learned men" of various denominations, had been named. Weidner answered ironically, that if there had not been such thinkers as Luther and Melachthon himself, then there would be no split in Christianity and, therefore, no need for such panic because of the Turks. What made Weidner especially angry, was the fact that – in his opinion – Luther and his colleagues from Wittenberg not only had split the Western Christianity in two, they did even worse, leading to huge inundation of the blasphemous sects. What is more (and it must had been especially painful for Weidner-the humanist) they had made all of this using the humanistic studies as a weapon against the true religion and true Church. Soon Weidner himself experienced, that indeed, the dialogue between Catholics and Lutherans was not an easy one. In the same year 1531 he was appointed a parish priest in Świdnica. Only a day later he was forced to leave the post and the town – the Protestant inhabitants had definitely not wanted a Catholic canon as a priest in their parish church (Zimmermann: 1938, 56).

Nicolaus Weidner, as well as many his contemporaries, certainly must have asked himself an urgent question: what should be done with the Church, with infidels? In the 1530s he may had criticised Melanchthon's ideas of peaceful discussion, in 1550 (if not earlier), as an older, experienced clergyman, the "righteous and learned" (using Melanchthon's words) humanist, he tried to formulate his answer. And it was his epitaph, were he decided to express it most emphatically.

2. The Epitaph of Nicolaus Weidner

The painted epitaph, preserved partially (only the middle part, without frame and inscription panels), had been executed *ca.* 1555 and hung initially in St. Martin's church in Wrocław.[14] Now it is a property of the Archdioecesan Museum in Wrocław and can be seen in the corridor in front of the entrance to the Archdioecesan Archive. For its main iconographical motif, Weidner chose the biblical parable of the Good Samaritan, which was quite popular in the pictorial arts of that time. However, its meaning in Weidner's epitaph is far from typical. In order to better accentuate its originality, some basic information regarding the motif should be reminded.

---

14 See n. 1.

2.1 The Iconographical Motif of the Good Samaritan

The Parable of the Good Samaritan appears in the tenth chapter of the Gospels of Luke (Luke 10:30–37) in the context of the Great Commandment, which is quoted few verses earlier (Luke 10:25–29). In the sixteenth century it was interpreted as a very detailed allegory of the fall and salvation of humanity (cf. Białobrzeski: 1581, 598–602; Wujek: 1582, 356–357; 1599, 1203).

Within the history of Christian art, the Parable was one of the most frequently illustrated stories told by Christ.[15] Its considerable growth of popularity dates back to the early sixteenth century and did not cease until the nineteenth. During the modern period its most popular compositional variation consisted in the division of the content of the parable into separated, simultaneously shown episodes, most often with the figure of Samaritan leaning towards the injured traveler in the foreground and the figures of the priest and the Levite in the background. Sometimes such additional scenes as the incident with robbers or the transfer of the injured to the host were also included. In the context of the interpretation of Weidner's epitaph, the most important seems to be the use of the motif in the sixteenth century graphic arts, both in signle-leaf prints and in book illustration, as well as the examples of the other epitaphs. In both cases it should be reminded that at that time the motif of the Good Samaritan was interpreted as a good illustration of the issues concerning the religious (in)tolerance, especially in its multi-confessional aspects. Despite its somewhat irenical meaning, regarding the context of the Great Commandment, the text of the parable shows also some potential for the depiction of the both intolerable and intolerant ones, who have been hidden in the figures of the priest and the Levite. They were traditionally interpreted as the personifications of the Old Testament, which laws and ceremonies in itself cannot bring the salvation for the human, as long as they are not supported by the grace and mercy of Christ. It the age of the Reformation, the old component, that needed to be cut off, was no longer interpreted only as the age of the Law, but also as the earthly Church, that is – the Roman Church and its representatives. In the pictorial arts, the new, symbolical personalities of the priest and the Levite manifested itself in very simple but telling way: by the choice of a suitable clothing. The priest was usually being depicted wearing a mortarboard (*biretta*), as a representative of the higher clergy or as a learned clergyman, presumably a scholastic – in order to criticize the then present general level of teaching (in the way how it was described in the *Epistolae obscurorum virorum* or in *The Praise of Folly* by Erasmus). The Levite usually

---

15 The oldest known example is the miniature from the so called Rossano Gospels (3d quater of the 6th century). For basic information about the history of the motif see: Poeschke: 1990; "Barmherziger Samariter" [in:] Sachs, Badstübner, Neumann: 1980, 52; Biernacka 2003, 121–122.

represented monks – he was being shown wearing a habit and a tonsure. As the examples of the polemical depiction of the parable of the Good Samaritan such illustration can be mentioned as: the woodcut of an unknown artist, from the half of the sixteenth century, now in the collection of the Herzog August Bibliothek in Wolfenbüttel,[16] the woodcut from Martin Luther's *Auslegung der Episteln und Euangelien, von Ostern bis auff das Advent* (Wittenberg 1544), or the work by Virgil Solis, published in Dietrich Veit's *Summaria uber die gantze Biblia* (Frankfurt am Main 1562). The polemical issues, so tightly associated with the prints of the Reformation era in general, in the case of the motif of the Good Samaritan appeared also within the context of pictorial epitaphs. It has been used e.g. in the epitaph for the Lutheran Georg Auersberger from about 1587 (initially St. Mary Magdalene's church, now in the National Museum in Wrocław) (Steinborn: 1967, 104, il. tbl. 23). There, the priest and the Levite can be seen wearing monk's habits.[17] Another very interesting example can be found in St. Mary's church in Gardelegen (Neumark), were a hybrid of an epitaph and a collators' lodge was erected in the 1560s as a foundation of the Biersted family. In the wooden, central panel, the episodes of the parable of the Good Samaritan have been carved – the priest can be seen wearing a bishop's garment and a headdress while reading from an open book; the Levite prays with a rosary and wanders with a dog – perhaps it is an allusion to the Dominican Order (the *domini canes*) and their activity as inquisitors.[18]

2.2 Interpretation of the Iconography of Weidner's Epitaph

Looking back at Weidner's epitaph, first of all, the elements that differentiate it from other contemporary examples should be emphasized. In Weidner's epitaph we can see neither the priest, nor the Levite; the group of robbers is presented quite differently, as well as the scene at the door of the host. Two additional figures have been included: the figure of the deceased (which is quite obvious in the case of an epitaph) and the figure of Christ. The most interesting inclusion seems to be that of

---

16 Sign. Graph. Res. D: 327.2 recto oben rechts.

17 It is also worth recalling, that another painted epitaph with the depiction of the motif of the Good Samaritan is known from the city of Wrocław. In the epitaph for Abraham Seiler (d. 1583) and his wife Anna (born Schmidt, d. 1592), now in the National Museum in Warsaw, the parable was used as an allegory of medicine, for Seiler himself had been a physician. Steinborn: 1967, 104, il. tbl. 23; 32.

18 The rich iconographical program of the Biersted's foundation consists also of the motif of the Original Sin, which directly accompanies the episodes from the parable, and two typological themes on the side panels: the Sacrifice of Isaac (left) and the Crucifixion (right, with kneeling portraits of the members of the Biersted family). The whole program is complemented by inscription panels, as well as the personifications of the virtues (Fides, Charitas, Spes, Patientia).

a burnt offering, placed on the right side of the painting. We should now consider all of those elements one by one.

The scene of the healing was composed traditionally: the Samaritan, dressed in an exotic, rich garment, is leaning toward the naked figure of a man lying on the ground; he pours oil or wine on the insured's head. The identification of the wounded traveler with a human in general and the deceased one specifically has been emphasized by the characteristic disposition of his body, bringing the associations with tomb figures – leaning on one arm, with one leg bent, neither sleeping nor awaken. It should be recalled that, as can be read in the Gospels of Luke, the robbers left the traveler "half dead" (Luke 10:30). Above the figures of the Samaritan and the traveler, an animal (an ox or a donkey) can be seen. Although it is somewhat hidden behind the men, the presence of the animal is strongly emphasized due to its central placement, even more accentuated thanks to its setting on the background of the main vertical element of the whole composition of the painting – the tree trunk. In the context of the parable, the animal had been often interpreted as a symbolical representation of the body of Christ. Regarding this fact, we can assume that also the seemingly neutral element of the landscape – the already mentioned tree trunk – can be interpreted symbolically as the Tree of the Cross, thanks to its tough compositional bond with the figure of a donkey /an ox. On the right side, closer to the frame, the group of robbers can be seen. One of them is holding a spear; its form resembles the so-called Lance of Longinus (the Holy Lance), that pierced the side of Jesus when He hung on the Cross. This element brings into mind the interpretation of the wounds of the Savior in the context of human sins which constantly pierce Him. The robbers used to symbolize sins and Satan, who attack humans on their way of life. A logical sequence of interpretations has been built here: the wounds of men are the wounds made by sin, and, at the same time, the very same sins are inflicting Christ, who suffers for all humanity.

On the left side of the painting, close to its edge, the figure of Christ pointing at the scene placed above him can be seen. Although this figure is much smaller in comparison to those of the Samaritan the traveler, its meaningful gesture indicates, that it is exactly this part of the painting that should be treated as the key for understanding of the message included in Weidner's epitaph. The scene in general shows the Samaritan and the traveler entering the host, however, in this case, the host has been depicted as a church building. The innkeepers are the apostles, shown very specifically – there are twelve of them, most of whom are holding their attributes. They are led by St. Peter (holding a key) and St. Paul (with book in his hands). As wrote Polish theologian and preacher Marcin Białobrzeski:

> Lord Jesus Christ put a sinner on the back of His animal, and took him to the stables, when He had brought him to the baptism and to the presence of the Holy Christian Church. For the stables are the host, where travelers lay down themselves and their belongings,

where they refresh their animals with rest and feed. In this way, within the Holy Church, every man lays down the burden of his sins (Białobrzeski: 1581, 601 [my translation]).

Without any doubt, in this context, the Church, as depicted in Weidner's epitaph, should definitely be interpreted as the *Roman* Church, led by St. Peter and his successors – the popes.

> The innkeeper [...], whom Lord Jesus Christ entrusted the traveler while leaving into heaven, is no other but only St. Peter himself, when our Lord commanded him: feed my sheep. The innkeepers are also the other apostles, whom he told: go and make disciples of all nations. And so the apostles' deputies are also the innkeepers: so bishops, shepherds and all those whom the very matter of the Church of the Lord is entrusted, with the words: go, feed my sheep (Białobrzeski: 1581, 601–602 [my translation]).

The New Jerusalem, depicted in the background, therefore symbolizes the one, holy, Catholic Church, whereas the road to Jericho can be interpreted as the way to heresy:

> We can remind ourselves, just like it was said in the parable, that it is wrong and harmful, to move from Jerusalem to Jericho, that is: from seeing the peace, which we absorb within the changeless faith in Lord Jesus Christ, to the otherness of the heretic faiths, which their own Jericho, that is the otherness, are, and can no longer hold the true Jerusalem in them (Białobrzeski: 1581, 602 [my translation]).

Likewise in the context of the parable of the Good Samaritan wrote Piotr Skarga:

> The apostle says: our mother, the Holy Catholic Church, the City of God [...]. He, who leaves it, who despises the obedience of its officers [...], who for a schism or heresy, or for mortal sins departs from the society of the saints, is easy to be defeated by robbers, lions of hell, for he is left alone and separated, and without any protection (Skarga: 1595, 365–366 [my translation]).

The conveyance of the wounded to the host therefore symbolizes his return to the bosom of the Church – the Catholic, Roman Church. That scene is complemented by the episode depicted in the opposite part of the painting, which somehow substitutes the traditional figures of the priest and the Levite, understood as the representatives of the Old Testament. Here, a burning pyre and two priests with offerings – sheep and a calf, can be seen. As Białobrzeski wrote:

> The Law and the Prophets show us our wounds and our sins, but they cannot heal them, for by the Law we can only get the knowledge of the sin. And it is not, and never had been such a thing, that the blood of a calf or rams could wipe off our sins (Białobrzeski 1581, 599 [my translation]).

What we deal here with is the depiction of an old-testamental episode from the history of the prophet Elijah – God's judgment over the priests of Baal (1 Kings 18:20–40). In the pictorial arts during the age of Reformation, that biblical motif have been seen as an excellent tool of manifestation of the polemical issues. Two works from Cranach's workshop can be mentioned as good examples from the Protestant side. The painting by Lucas Cranach the Younger from 1545, preserved in the Staatliche Kunstsammlungen in Dresden, depicts two altars and two pyres, and, in the background on the left side, a truly ferocious depiction of the carnage of the prophets of Baal by the river Kishon. Quite similar is the epitaph for Balthasar Hoffmann, made in Cranach's workshop probably between 1552–1557, preserved in Stadtgeschichtliches Museum in Leipzig. In both cases, the very symbolical identity of the prophets-priests of Baal remains in visual sense somewhat hidden, they are seen in general as the infidels. In the even more interesting depiction of that carnage – in Matthias Gerung's woodcut from 1548[19] – they are unequivocally identified as the highest representatives of the Catholic Church. Gerung shows a rider wearing an emperor's crown, who pierces with a lance the heart of a pope. The pope, wearing a tiara, drops a banner with two keys depicted on it. A figure of a cardinal can be seen trying to pull out the lance from pope's heart; behind him, a bishop and monks are lamenting. In the background a smaller scene has been placed – a figure with a sword, captured *HELIAS*, attacks a group of men. Anti-papal and anti-Catholic meaning of this woodcut is so obvious, that it needs no further explanation.

In the case of Weidner's epitaph, the context of the story of Elijah form the one hand emphasizes the fact, that it is his God (the God of Christians; the God, as the Catholic Church sees Him), who is the only and true one, as opposed to the false gods, idols worshiped by pagans (the heretics). From the other, however, by its placement on the side of the Old Testament (somehow resembling the protestant allegory of Law and Grace), it describes the violent practices of extermination of the infidels as no longer valid – they were compromised by the coming of the age of Grace, which was given to all humanity by the self-sacrifice of Christ. Regarding such issue in the context of the realities of Weidner's age, it can be assumed, that the interpretation reads as follows: the times of bloody persecutions of the heretics are already gone, the infidels should not be exterminated – they need to be carried back (safely!) to the one, true, Catholic Church. It is not – as was suggested many years ago by Bożena Steinborn (1967, 15; 85) – a plea for tolerance for the heretics. It is a call for conversion, which should become a cornerstone for the restoration of the lost unity of the Western Christianity.

---

19 A copy can be seen in the collection of the Herzog August Bibliothek in Wolfenbüttel: sign. MGerung WB 3.38, Inv. nr 5703; WB 53.

3. Conclusion

It can be said, that Weidner was a clear-headed pragmatic. As it was already noted, his biography contains certain moments indicating that he was not tending to accept the deepening of divisions between Christians, nor was he a friend of Protestants; in fact he had his own reasons for showing a strong aversion towards them. On the other hand, he was not a type of a papal-fanatic and probably well recognized all the symptoms of the corruption within the ranks of the Catholic clergy, including the members of the cathedral chapter in Wrocław. Similar ambiguity can be traced in the iconographical program of his epitaph. It contains both the critical, negative reflection on the state of the Church of that time (*it is* endangered by the heretics and something *has to be done* with this problem) as well as a positive program – a pointing towards a remedy. And it is this aspect of the message contained in the Weidner's epitaph – the depiction of both a problem *and* a solution – that especially makes it so unique.

Bibliography

Sources

BIAŁOBRZESKI, MARCIN (1581), Postille albo wyklady swientych Ewanyeliy, od Wielkieynocy do Adwentu, czesc wtora, Kraków.

SKARGA, PIOTR (1595), Kazania na niedziele i święta całego roku, Kraków.

WUJEK, JAKUB (1582), Postilla Catholiczna Mnieysza, Poznań 1582.

WUJEK, JAKUB (1599), Biblia To Iest Księgi Starego Y Nowego Testamentu, Według Łacińskiego przekładu starego, w kościele powszechnym przyiętego, na Polski ięzyk z pilnością przełozone, Kraków.

Secondary Literature

BAUCH, GUSTAV (1895), Der humanistische Dichter George von Logau, 73. Jahres-Bericht der Schlesischen Gesellschaft für vaterländische Cultur, vol. 3, 5–33.

BAUCH, GUSTAV (1896), Die Anfänge des Studiums der griechischen Sprache und Litteratur in Norddeutschland, Mitteilungen der Gesellschaft für deutsche Erziehungs- und Schulgeschichte, VI.2, 75-162; VI.3, 163–193.

BAUCH, GUSTAV (1904), Beiträge zur Literaturgeschichte des schlesischen Humanismus, Zeitschrift des Vereins für Geschichte Schlesiens 38, 292–342.

BAUCH, GUSTAV (1907), Schlesien und die Universität Krakau im XV. und XVI Jahrhundert, Zeitschrift des Vereins für Geschichte Schlesiens 40, 99–180.

BIERNACKA, MAŁGORZATA (2003), Ikonografia publicznej działalności Chrystusa w polskiej sztuce nowożytnej, Warszawa: Instytut Sztuki Polskiej Akademii Nauk.

Burgemeister, Ludwig (1930), Die Kunstdenkmäler der Stadt Breslau, vol. 1: Kirchlichen Denkmäler der Dominsel und der Sandinsel, Breslau: Wilhelm Gottlieb Korn Verlag.

Contemporaries of Erasmus (2003), Contemporaries of Erasmus: A Biographical Register of the Renaissance and Reformation, Peter G. Bietenholz/Thomas Brian Deutscher (ed.), vol. 1–3, Toronto/Buffalo/London: University of Toronto Press.

Dubowy, Ernst (1922), Breslauer Kirchen: Kunsthistorischer Führer, Breslau: Verlag der Schlesischen Volkszeitung.

Fliegel, Maria (1919), Die Dombibliothek zu Breslau im ausgehenden Mittelalter, Zeitschrift des Vereins für Geschichte Schlesiens 53.1, 84–133.

Harasimowicz, Jan (1990), Rola sztuki w religijnych i społecznych konfliktach wieku reformacji na Śląsku, Rocznik Historii Sztuki 18, 31–95.

Heyne, Johann (1868), Dokumentierte Geschichte des Bistums und Hochstifts Breslau, vol. 3: Denkwürdigkeiten aus der Geschichte der katholischen Kirche Schlesiens. Von der Hälfte des fünfzehnten bis in die Mitte des siebzehnten Jahrhunderts (1418–1648), Breslau: Scientia Verlag.

Jujeczka, Stanisław (2006), Duchowni średniowiecznej Legnicy. Studium prozopograficzne nad klerem diecezjalnym, Legnica: Towarzystwo Przyjaciół Nauk w Legnicy.

Kaźmierczak, Joanna (2015), The Sixteenth-Century Pictorial Epitaph in Central Europe: Between Reform' and Reformation', in: Anne Eusterschulte/Hannah Wälzholz (ed.), Anthropological Reformations – Anthropology in the Era of Reformation, Göttingen: Vandenhoeck & Ruprecht, 357–370.

Kaźmierczak, Joanna (2016), Wiping out the New, Restoring the Old: The Motif of the Cleansing of the Temple in the 16th Century Visual Arts, in: Magdaléna Nová/Marie Opatrná (ed.), Staré a nové. Staré jako východisko či překážka? Sborník příspěvků mezinárodní konference studentů doktorských studijních program, , Praha: Praha Univerzita Karlova, 153–162.

Kaźmierczak, Joanna (2017), Na ratunek Kościołowi. Epitafia wrocławskich kanoników katedralnych (1539–1556) jako wizualny postulat odnowy życia chrześcijańskiego, Wrocław: Oficyna Wydawnicza ATUT.

Lutsch, Hans (1886), Verzeichnis der Kunstdenkmäler der Provinz Schlesien, vol. 1: Die Stadt Breslau, Breslau: Korn.

Nowack, Alfons (1932), Führer durch das Erzbischöfliches Diöcesanmuseum in Breslau, Breslau: Borgmeyer.

Poeschke, Joachim (1990), Article "Samariter, barmherziger", Lexikon der Christlichen Ikonographie, vol. 2, 24–26.

Pol, Nikolaus (1819), Jahrbücher der Stadt Breslau, vol. III, Breslau: Graß und Barth.

Sabisch, Alfred (1937), Der Streit um den Nachlaß des Breslauer Domherrn Laurentius Pätschel († 1539), Schlesische Geschichtsblätter 1937.1, 14–18.

Sachs, Hannelore/Badstübner, Ernst/Neumann, Helga (1980), Christliche Ikonographie in Stichworten, Leipzig: Koehler & Amelang.

Schade, Werner (1967), Malerei in Schlesien 1520–1620. Zur Ausstellung "Malarstwo śląskie 1520–1620" im Muzeum Śląskie we Wrocławiu (Breslau), Kunstchronik 20.2, 29–32.

Steinborn, Bożena (1966), Malarstwo śląskie 1520–1620, catalogue of the exhibition, December 1966–March 1967, Wrocław: Muzeum Śląskie.

Steinborn, Bożena (1967), Malowane epitafia mieszczańskie na Śląsku w latach 1520–1620, Roczniki Sztuki Śląskiej 4, 7–125.

Zimmermann, Gerhard (1938), Das Breslauer Domkapitel im Zeitalter der Reformation und Gegenreformation (1500–1600). Verfassungsgeschichtliche Entwicklung und persönliche Zusammensetzung, Weimar: H. Böhlaus Nachfolger.

Konrad Küster

The Impact of Liturgy on Church Music

Observations in the 'Long' 16th Century

1. Introduction

Sacred music is a critical matter. Partly, it could be used outside a church, because the compositions could form a central part within private practice of piety or school life (as Johann Walter's *Geistliches Gesang Büchlein* of 1524, which explicitly was destined for the use at school). But as soon as sacred music turns out to be 'church music', liturgical matters must be taken into consideration. In effect, this is an interdisciplinary challenge: Neither could this music be understood as something absolute or autonomous, as it can appear in modern concert performances, nor was it a mere addition to an otherwise well-functioning service. 'Church music' must be understood as an integral part of (predominantly festive) services, and this affected the musical appearance to a very high degree. Thus, an approach should be open in both directions.

2. Basic Musicological and Liturgical Perspectives

Clearly, musical sources are the most important material for music historians to work with: They transmit compositions. Sources can be single sheets or small booklets, parts of bigger music collections and even single books containing a larger number of compositions. The main point of interest, however, are not the sources themselves, but rather the single pieces of music transmitted in them – and their composers. Therefore, the basic approach is roughly bio-bibliographical and philological, and this precedes all further considerations (which might be analytical, stylistic, aesthetical etc.). In effect, this can be outlined as a multi-layer model.

It is most important to know the composer's name. Pieces of music transmitted in all these sources and linked to a specific name, can be collected in an individual work-list. One single composition, however, might have been transmitted in several sources, at times with considerable differences; so, the sources must be mentioned alongside with the composition in question, at least if a work-list is made up. After that, music philologists can turn over. They can try to determine which of the sources to a single work should be regarded as the most important and reliable one: Which one comes nearest to a composer's presumably original intentions, so that a music edition (or a performance) should refer to just this source? Similarly, the result might open for detailed analytical or aesthetical considerations; certain stylistic features can be identified and compared to others which are typical for contemporaries. By this, even musical epochs have been described. Finally, it might be useful to widen the scope and to focus on the composer's context as well. It is here only, that whole source complexes might be regarded. They open for corpus research, leading to a deeper insight into a local repertoire, and the results can be compared to other sources.

At the same time, however, a completely different approach to musical sources is possible. This can be understood best, if choir-books are taken into consideration: single bound books, which form an important part in the transmission of the music from the 15th and 16th century. These books were the performing material typical of that time: single, huge books to be placed on a large music stand, and all the musicians involved were grouped around it.[1] Therefore, the music is not presented in score format; rather, the single parts were written down in standardized places on each of the double pages. The portions of music attached to a single part correspond to those of the other voices, thus allowing for a coordinated turn of pages. Clearly, the music was not composed in this kind of notation; these sources are purely performance-orientated. Music from that time has not been preserved in a composer's hand, neither as a composition manuscript nor as a fair copy. So, the knowledge about church music from the time at least until the middle of the 16th century is derived from these big books, and the performance conditions are mirrored directly in their outer design.

As this is the main transmission type of music from that time, the approach made by the posterity to most of the works by Josquin or his contemporaries depends on books of this kind. According to the multi-layer model outlined above, the results seem standardized: Compositions contained in these books have been picked out of their transmission context and assigned to the typical work-lists in question, opening for all the composer-orientated research potentials. By this, these choir-books are treated as if they were archival storages for music of their time. As far as they contain sacred music, however, any of these performance-orientated sources had direct liturgical purposes: These books were destined to be parts of a living liturgy, like missals, graduals or antiphonaries. Therefore, the inner order of these 'musical sources' is similar to all other liturgical books – with the only difference, that these choir-books contain part music. So, the approach to them should be more source-focused; they can inform about specific service customs.

---

1 For visualizations cf. the title vignette in Finck: 1556 (1971), title page, or the visually impressive realizations in the Munich choir-books containing music by Orlando di Lasso (cf. the reproductions in Leuchtmann/Schaefer: 1994, plates 4–17, 20–23, 28f).

3.   The Eisenach Choir Book From the Early 1540s

The main source to be referred to is a large choir-book from Eisenach in Central Germany, the city situated at the feet of the Wartburg castle. The book contains the first post-reformatory repertoire of the city, written during the early 1540s by the music teacher at the local Latin School, Wolfgang Zeuner.[2] With the composer-orientated approach, one would compile a bibliographic survey by grouping the works after their composers' names, then pick the groups out of their context and transfer them to the larger, individual work-lists. Apart from 21 compositions with uncertain authenticity, 12 composers are named in the book (for details cf. table 1),[3] first of all Luther's friend Johann Walter and Conrad Rein, who was active first in Erfurt and Nuremberg and later as leader of the *Kantorei* at the Danish court (Brusniak: 1999); both composers are represented with eight works. Walter is the youngest among these musicians, representing the smaller group of composers, who were still alive when the book was compiled (the same is true for the Saxon theologian and musician Anton Musa[4] and the Bavarian *Hofkapellmeister* Ludwig Senfl). All the others, however, had been dead in some time already, Obrecht since 1505, most of the others since the 1520s.

By this, the repertoire looks a bit conservative, not very promising – regarding the philological quality of the source and its importance for the transmission of the composers' works. However, it was normal for a collector not to transmit the music as reliably as possible, but to arrange it for the given local context.[5] This means: If the source appears to be less reliable than another one, it is not necessarily due to a scribe's inaccuracy, but – much more often – to a musician's targeted preparation of music for a specific performance situation.

Another general question arising around these sources is the choice of music made by the local collector. Clearly, it depended on availability, and this is discussed quite often, because this can provide arguments of philological importance. Most commonly, however, music was acquired only if it fitted the local liturgical demands – a question which is underrated, if the approach is dominantly composer- or work-orientated. If the source material doesn't consist of several single booklets stored in racks, but (as in this case) is written into a single book, the situation becomes even more 'telling': A music director should be able to use the book and cope with its

---

2 Not identical with the pastor at Schneeberg mentioned by Luther (WA Briefe 7, 122f). – The work-list given by Schröder (1931/1932) is inaccurate.

3 Misattributions are not commented; composers' names are given according to the source.

4 One of the compositions refers to him as Anton Witsch, his original name. This might be a hint to a central role he played in forming the repertoire.

5 For a survey concerning later times cf. Haenen: 2015.

Table 1   Wolfgang Zeuner (collector): Eisenach Choir Book (early 1540s). Composers and their works.

Composer (i. e. attributions)	Work(s)
Finck, Heinrich	Beatus author
Galliculus, Johannes	Dominus vobiscum
Isaac, Heinrich	Dies est laetitiae
Josquin Desprez	[Gloria] Et in terra Kyrie coronatum Sancta trinitas unus deus
La Rue, Pierre de	Kyrie coronatum
Musa, Antonius	Conscendit iubilans Kyrie fons bonitatis Sanctus – Benedictus Tecum principium Vidi aquam
Obrecht, Jacob	Passio [...] secundum Iohannem
Rein, Conrad	Alleluja. Benedictus est dominus Alleluja. Dominus dixit ad me Benedicta sit sancta trinitas Kyrie paschale Magnificat 4. toni Magnificat 8. toni Paschale Sanctus Puer natus est nobis
Rener, Adam	Gratias agimus
Senfl, Ludwig	De profundis clamavi Ecce Dominus venit Grates nunc omnes In exitu Israel Magnificat octo tonorum (= 8) Nesciens mater virgo Philippe qui vidit
Stoltzer, Thomas	Agnus redemit oves Alleluja. Resurrexi et adhuc tecum Qui coeli, qui terrae regit
Walter, Johann	Ascendo ad Patrem Dixit Dominus Domino meo Et cum introducerent/Nunc dimittis Grates nunc omnes In dulci jubilo Spiritus Domini replevit orbem Suscepimus Deus misericordiam Veni, Pater pauperum
Anonymous	(21 pieces)

contents; how, then, would he work with the acquired pieces of music and, most of all, find them again once they were written into a volume of these huge dimensions?

Thus, these codices are similar to other liturgical books both in their outer appearance and their historical use. If they were designed for the use in the Holy Mass, they should contain all the pieces to be provided as part music within the Mass Ordinary and the Proper. Normally, music belonging to these two groups might have been written down in different places of a book, far away from the other one, because the Proper was assigned to single days in the year, whilst most of the Mass Ordinary could be used much more often. Nevertheless, music of both types should interlock and, clearly, the music director should change effortlessly between both portions. So, even if choir-books are the central sources for a composer-focused approach to music from the time around 1500, they should be understood on similar terms as all the other liturgical books. They reflect the local use of specific chants – as part music, different from the solo singing of Gregorian chant.

A first question resulting from this might be, whether there was other music being performed during a service: Did two different ensembles contribute different components to it? Or did the music director use several choir-books at the same time? Any constant interchange of choir-books cannot have been very comfortable, due to their size and weight. For an answer to these questions, the Eisenach situation is perfect. Local school regulations written down during the early 1550s report that the pupils should stand as closely to the book as possible and, besides, have their hymn books with them, if they should sing German cantilenas (Rollberg: 1931/1932). Thus, this choir-book (quoted as a singular in the school regulations) was the main performing material: Every single piece the pupils should sing was contained in it – or, more precisely: This was the local source to any figural music; the only exception were German hymns contained in the smaller hymn books, and if they were part music as well, this remark might have referred to Johann Walter's famous *Geistliches Gesang Büchlein*.

Table 2 Eisenach Choir-Book (c. 1544), contents.
There are several rows of page numbers given in the source; the description refers
to them written into the right upper corner. They refer to double pages; left- and right-hand
pages belong together.

p.	com-poser (attrib.)	incipit	liturgical genre	feast	remarks
002	Rein, Conrad	Puer natus est nobis	introit	Christ-mas	
003	Rein, Conrad	Alleluja. Dominus dixit ad me	alleluia	Christ-mas	
004–5	Walter, Johann	Grates nunc omnes	sequence	Christ-mas	
006–7	–	Ecce advenit dominator	introit	Epiphany	
008–9	Walter, Johann	Suscepimus Deus misericordiam	introit	Purifica-tion	
010–12					empty
013–14	–	Loquebar de testimoniis	introit	[Sun-day]	'Dominicalis introitus'
015–17	–	Resurrexi et adhuc tecum sum	introit	Easter	
018	–	Alleluja. Pascha nostrum immolatum	alleluia	Easter	
019–22	–	Christ ist erstanden /Victimae	sequence	Easter	
023–25	–	Salve festa dies	hymn	Easter	
026	–	Surrexit Christus /Erstanden ist	hymn	Easter	
027–31	Musa Anton	Vidi aquam egredientem	antiphon	Easter etc.	
032–34	–	Viri Galilaei, quid admiramini	introit	Ascen-sion	
034	–	Omnes gentes plaudite manibus	gradual	Ascen-sion	
035	–	Alleluja. Ascendit Deus	alleluia	Ascen-sion	

p.	com-poser (attrib.)	incipit	liturgical genre	feast	remarks
036-41	Stoltzer, Thomas	Qui coeli, qui terrae regit	sequence	Ascension	
042-43	Walter, Johann	Spiritus Domini replevit orbem	introit	Pentecost	
044	–	Confirma hoc deus, quod operatus	offertory	Pentecost	
045	–	Alleluja. Reple tuorum /Veni Sancte Spiritus /Nun bitten wir	alleluia	Pentecost	
046-50	Walter, Johann	Veni, Pater pauperum	sequence	Pentecost	
051-53					empty
054-55	Rein, Conrad	Benedicta sit sancta trinitas		Trinity Sunday	
056	Rein, Conrad	Alleluja. Benedictus es Domine		Trinity Sunday	
057-59					empty
060-61	Stoltzer, Thomas	Resurrexi et adhuc tecum sum	introit	Easter	
062-63	Stoltzer, Thomas	Agnus redemit oves	sequence	Easter	
064-65					empty
066-71	Senfl, Ludwig	Grates nunc omnes	sequence	Christmas	
072-84					empty
085-87		Kyrie fons bonitatis	Kyrie		4 voices
088-90r	Musa, Anton	Kyrie fons bonitatis	Kyrie		5 voices

p.	composer (attrib.)	incipit	liturgical genre	feast	remarks
091-92	–	Gracias agimus	Gloria		alternatim
093	Isaac, Heinrich	Dies est laetitiae	carol	Christmas	
094	Walter, Johann	In dulci jubilo	carol	Christmas	
095-97	Josquin Desprez	Kyrie coronatum	Kyrie		
097-100	Josquin Desprez	Et in terra	Gloria		
101-103	La Rue, Petrus de	Kyrie coronatum	Kyrie		
104-106	Rein, Conrad	Kyrie paschale	Kyrie		
107-108					empty
109-114	–	Gracias agimus	Gloria		alternatim; p. 111–112 empty
115-116	Rener, Adam	Gratias agimus	Gloria		alternatim
117-164					empty
165-166	Musa, Anton	Sanctus – Benedictus	Sanctus		
167-169	Rein, Conrad	Paschale Sanctus	Sanctus		
170	–	Agnus Dei	Agnus Dei		
171-185					empty
186	–	Et cum spiritu tuo	liturgical answer		right-hand page only

p.	composer (attrib.)	incipit	liturgical genre	feast	remarks
187-189	–				empty
190-193	Walter, Johann	Dixit Dominus Domino meo	Psalm 110		falsobordone
194-207					empty
208-210	–	Et exultavit spiritus meus	Magnificat		
211-219	–				empty; '213' twice
220-229r	–	Facta est Judaea	Psalm 114		'Differentia peregrina'
230-237	Walter, Johann	Et cum inducerent /Nunc dimittis	Gospel	Purification	
238-252	Obrecht, Jacob	Passio [...] secundum Iohannem	Gospel	Lent	
253-257	Rein, Conrad	Magnificat octavi toni	Magnificat		
258-259					empty
260-265	Senfl, Ludwig	Magnificat octo tonorum: 1. tonus	Magnificat		
266-283	Senfl, Ludwig	2., 3. and 4. tonus	Magnificat		staves without music notation
284-289	Senfl, Ludwig	5. tonus	Magnificat		
290-295	Senfl, Ludwig	6. tonus	Magnificat		
296-301	Senfl, Ludwig	7. tonus	Magnificat		only 296r, Bassus/Tenor
302-307	Senfl, Ludwig	8. tonus	Magnificat		
308-313	Rein, Conrad	Magnificat quarti toni	Magnificat		

p.	com-poser (attrib.)	incipit	liturgical genre	feast	remarks
314	–	Benedicamus paschale	Benedicamus	Easter	
315	Musa [Wieh], Anton	Tecum principium	gradual	Christ-mas	
316	Finck, Heinrich	Beatus author	hymn	Christ-mas	[A solis ortu cardine, even-numbered verses only]
317	–	Tu tuo laetos famulos	hymn	Easter	[Vita sanctorum decus angelorum, even-numbered verses only]
318	Musa, Anton	Conscendit iubilans	hymn	Ascen-sion	[Festum nunc celebre, even-numbered verses only]
319	–	Qui paracletus dicens	hymn	Pente-cost	[Veni creator spiritus, even-numbered verses only]
320-322					empty
323-324	Walter, Johann	Ascendo ad Patrem	antiphon	Ascen-sion	
325-326	Senfl, Ludwig	Nesciens mater virgo	sequence	Christ-mas	
327-329	Senfl, Ludwig	De profundis clamavi	Psalm 130		
330-335	Senfl, Ludwig	In exitu Israel	Psalm 114		
336-339	Gallicu-lus, Johannes	Dominus vobiscum	Gospel	Easter	'Evangelium in die Pascha"
340-341	Senfl, Ludwig	Philippe qui vidit	[motet]		
342-343	Josquin Desprez	Sancta trinitas unus deus	[motet]		
344-345	Senfl, Ludwig	Ecce Dominus venit	[motet]		

A closer look to the content shows, how the book might have been used (cf. table 2). Even if no single remark can be found in the book itself, its structure and contents leave almost no doubt about its liturgical purposes. On the first 55 double pages, it contains pieces for the Mass Proper; only few pages are empty. They are followed by a smaller group of similar compositions (apparently added slightly later), flanked with several empty double pages. The next, huge part is devoted to the Mass Ordinary, in the beginning again with two smaller lacunae, but later with two large groups of empty pages in between. A single liturgical answer for four voices ('Et cum spiritu tuo') precedes the section with chants for the Divine Office, and these are followed by a group of Latin hymns and other chants of similar kind.

With the typical composer-focused approach, the pieces for the Mass Ordinary as well as the Psalms and Magnificat compositions would be named as such in the composers' work-lists; most of the other pieces would be labelled as 'other sacred' or simply 'motets'. But it would be more convenient just to use the liturgical terms: They are introits, sequences or responsories, referring to the corresponding liturgical texts and their structures; no one would have 'performed' a 'motet' during the service, but rather sung a liturgical chant as part-song instead of Gregorian monody.

Focusing upon the Mass Proper, the repertoire reveals even more details – remembering the fact that this was the only book with figural music used during the services. In the beginning, three pieces for Christmas can be found: an introit, an alleluia and a sequence. A gradual is missing; and none of the two traditional post-sermon chants is mentioned, neither an offertory nor a communio. Both might have been excluded from the local Lutheran services due to the discussions about the Lord's Supper (cf. Küster: 2016, 21; 24; 31). The gradual, however, might have been omitted in favour of the neighbouring chants, alleluia and sequence. Thus, if the music director would provide music for the Christmas service, he would open the book on the first double page, jump to the Mass Ordinary section for the Kyrie and Gloria movements, then return to the Mass Proper in order to perform the alleluia and sequence and finally (perhaps) continue with the Sanctus after the sermon.

A similar choice of pieces is offered for Easter, but neither for Epiphany nor Purification. For both feasts, only an introit is inserted into the book. The consequences of this are apparent: Only this introit would have been performed *figuraliter* on these feasts, all the other chants, however, as solo singing of the respective Gregorian chants – probably with the exception of the sequence, for which the Christmas chant was used until Purification. And on some of the ordinary Sundays, the "introitus dominicalis" might have been sung; on others, a German chant might have been used for the opening instead, following Luther's recommendation for such a replacement (Luther: 1526, fol [B iv]). And, finally, Advent is not characterized as a Feast. To which degree the parts of the Mass Ordinary were sung *figuraliter* on minor feasts or ordinary Sundays cannot be decided.

The picture is altered only slightly, if the time after Easter is taken into consideration: Part-song is provided for the Mass Proper on Ascension, Pentecost and Trinity Sunday. Therefore, most of the feasts during summer and autumn would not have any musical adornment of a similar kind. Thus, it appears that the general impression of a rich music life as a typical quality of the Lutheran service has to be revised at least for this early period: Post-reformatory culture continued not only with the traditional chants of the late medieval Holy Mass; at the same time, the rank of a feast was perceptible from the luxuriousness of the music attached, as in the late Middle Ages.

4. The Part-Books From Glashütte (Saxony)

Table 3   From the liturgical repertoire from Glashütte (Saxony): Music, Christmas to Good Friday. Cf. Steude 1974, 55

No.	Composer	Work
23	Isaac, Heinrich	Introitus in festo nativitatis Christi: Puer qui natus est nobis
24	Isaac, Heinrich	Missa (Kyrie and Gloria only)
25		Alleluia: Dies sanctificatus illuxit
26		Sequence: Grates nunc omnes
27	Crequillon, Thomas	Responsorium: Verbum caro factus est
28	La Court, Henry de	Responsorium: Iudea et Hierusalem
29		Antiphon: Tecum principium
30		Antiphon: Tecum principium
31	Resinarius, Balthasar	Responsorium: Verbum caro factus est
32	Senfl, Ludwig	Magnificat
33	Lupus, Johannes	Antiphon: Hodie Christus natus est
34		Prosa in festo Annunciationis Mariae virginis: Haec est dies quam fecit
35	Schlegel, Joseph	Passio Germanica Domini Jesu Christi

This picture becomes more differentiated, if other repertoires are taken into consideration. A similar approach (with a different result) is possible from a collection (in this case, part-books for single voices) written about 40 years later in the Saxon town of Glashütte at the Erzgebirge ("Ore Mountains"; cf. table 3; Steude: 1974, 53–61). At No. 23, the liturgy for Christmas starts, comprising all polyphonic music in liturgical order, so that the chants from the Mass Proper and the Ordinary are mingled. Pupils singing from their individual part-books could use them straightforward; no controlled jumps back and forth from Ordinary to Proper sections were necessary. By this, music designed for the Mass Ordinary was attached to a specific feast; it was used on similar terms as the chants for the Proper. And this is continued at No. 27, where the chants for the Divine Office are reached (some of them are derived from different canonical hours around Christmas, including the late Advent liturgy).

After the Christmas liturgy, a prose for Annunciation Day is inserted, followed by a passion composition – thus leaving a big liturgical gap for the time from Christmas to Lent, including Epiphany and Purification, the two feasts for which Eisenach had an introit at least. On the other hand, among the first 22 items in the Glashütte repertoire a splendid supply for the Advent liturgy is given. And, finally, the Christmas liturgy itself is not the same as in Eisenach. There, a composition by Conrad Rein was used as introit, whilst the corresponding one in Glashütte had been written by Heinrich Isaac; regarding the Alleluia section, even two different chants formed the basis for the approach to the local use of part music. It has been assumed, that people from Luther's circle, first of all the music printer Georg Rhau, had suggested a specific 'Wittenberg repertoire' for the use in early Lutheranism (Steude: 1978, 105–108); the comparison of the Eisenach and Glashütte materials reveals, that such a suggestion was not authoritative. So, the differences between the two repertoires contradict any view of a more or less uniform Lutheran figural music, even if the liturgical framework and the general musical expectations were the same. In the end, the results referred to local traditions and local demands.

5. Music and Liturgy as Inseparable Aspects

By this, it becomes clear how important these music books can be for liturgical research, even if they, at the same time, are regarded much more as the main sources to music from their time and to the composers' styles. And liturgy helps to explain basic musical characteristics. Thus, the observations can be continued in two different directions. The first one leads forward to an even more detailed understanding of single pieces, the other one back to the composer-focused approach to music and their sources.

Table 4 Eisenach Choir-Book Alternatim technique in Gloria compositions.

The text grouped almost identical on 91–92 (by Anton Musa?) and 115–116 (by Adam Rener), but slightly different on 109–114 (anonymous): 'Domine Deus I' as part music (forming a bigger section together with the two neighbouring ones); final chorus section continued with "cum sancto spiritu…"

composed as part music	not notated (plainchant resp. organ)
	Gloria in excelsis Deo. Et in terra pax hominibus bonae voluntatis. Laudamus te, benedicimus te, adoramus te, glorificamus te.
Gratias agimus tibi propter magnam gloriam tuam.	Domine Deus, Rex caelestis, Deus Pater omnipotens.
Domine Fili unigenite Jesu Christe [p. 91: "et sancte spiritus" added].	Domine Deus, Agnus Dei, Filius Patris. Qui tollis peccata mundi, miserere nobis.
Qui tollis peccata mundi, suscipe deprecationem nostram.	Qui sedes ad dexteram Patris, miserere nobis.
Quoniam tu solus sanctus, tu solus Dominus, tu solus altissimus, Jesu Christe.	Cum sancto spiritu cum gloria Dei Patris. Amen.

In the Eisenach Choir Book, some Gloria compositions start, oddly enough, with the text "Gratias agimus tibi" (see table 4). The preceding text portions are omitted, as well as some later text sections, thus pointing to an alternatim practice. One might argue that typically an organ would have played the missing parts; but equally an alternatim performance could have taken place between the priest (who, in any case, would have sung the intonation) and the choir. Again, nobody would have 'performed' this music in the service, but rather sung parts of the liturgy *figuraliter*. This case mirrors very specific liturgical demands, and the music cannot be understood without a deeper insight into them. In this case, this practice was not only characteristic for Eisenach; neither of the composers in question (Rener and perhaps Musa) had been linked to the city. Thus, this approach to the Gloria text reveals a more common Central German liturgical practice as well as a specifically local one;[6] otherwise, the inclusion of these pieces into the Eisenach performing material would have been meaningless.

The consideration of liturgical circumstances is even more crucial for younger times, when the typical music sections preceding the sermon (gradual, alleluia and sequence) were replaced with real Lutheran motets. Their texts might refer directly to a preceding section of a service, often to the Lection from the Gospel. In general, a relation of this kind might be known from Bach's cantatas, but it could be much more concrete.

---

6 For a similar instance, see Wolfgang Figulus's Gloria-insertion into a music book from his time as Thomaskantor in Leipzig, see Küster: 2017.

In 1623, the *Hofkapellmeister* at Coburg, Melchior Franck, published a collection of Gospel motets: *Gemmulae evangeliorum musicae*. A typical example is the composition for the second Sunday during Lent (Reminiscere), starting with words by Christ (Matt 15:26): "It is not meet to take the children's bread, and to cast it to dogs". The context is not made clear in the composition; the music starts abruptly. Listeners must know the story which is introduced by these words: A woman from Canaan had approached Jesus and requested him for help, but was rejected and insisted; then, Jesus answered with just the words Franck chose for the beginning of the composition. Clearly, people attending the service on that Sunday will have understood the meaning of that motet; the music would have been tied to a preceding lection from the gospel, similar to a sermon, which starts from a biblical quotation. A concert performance, however, in which the music would be heard without a preceding lection, would not be satisfactory; and this is true for the printed music collection (taken as a whole), in which this music was published. Again, a general, tight relation between liturgy and church music can be seen.

Table 5 John Dunstaple (c1395–1453): Preserved settings of Latin sacred texts.
         Apart from compositions for the Mass Ordinary

related to Marian feasts:	22
related to St Catherine:	2
related to other Saints (St Alban, St Anne, St Germanus, St John the Baptist, St Michael):	1 each
Pentecost:	2
Saturday after Trinity Sunday:	2
Magnificat setting:	1

The other facet, which is more composer-focused, dates from the 15th century and refers to one of the most influential composers of that time, John Dunstaple (or Dunstable; see table 5). His sacred music can be grouped not only by genre, but – more specifically – by their relation to specific feasts. Most of these compositions are linked to feasts of the Holy Virgin; seven more pieces refer to feasts of six other Saints (cf. Bent: 2007ff, work-list). Finally, two works have been written for Pentecost and Saturday after Trinity Sunday each.

This, however, does not necessarily characterize Dunstaple's musical œuvre; we cannot estimate, to which degree the sources mirror his real compositional output. And whilst the preserved works undoubtedly refer to English musical practices, the main sources for this music are choir-books from Northern Italy: preserved in Aosta, Trent and Modena (the last one originating from Ferrara, cf. Bent: 2007ff, section 1, Life). Seen from a liturgical viewpoint, the transmission of Dunstaple's sacred works has been filtered by the enthusiasm of contemporary North Italians:

by their demands of splendour in services held on just these feast days. Again, this music must have become available to them; but in the end, its insertion into the collections (as a result of the transmission) depended on usability and standards in North Italian communities.

6. Conclusion

For the 15th and 16th centuries, music history is not a history of great composers and their works alone, but to a similar degree the history of liturgical demands, local musical potentials and – last but not least – the interests of single collectors: Only with their eyes, the music of that time can be regarded. So, their viewpoints should be taken seriously, linked to local ecclesiastical standards – as for Wolfgang Zeuner in Eisenach and his younger, anonymous colleague in Glashütte.

By this, a hitherto scarcely practiced cooperation between church history and music history has been outlined – with a special focus on the 'long 16th century'. It is not sufficient to base the liturgical research upon church regulations and proper liturgical books only; the scope must be widened in order to include the figural music, which was performed during the services on feast days. As far as I can see, this top level of church music has never been described in typical church regulations; the reason for this might be, that musical splendour was characteristic for few bigger churches only, as an exception in several respects: compared to the hinterland as well as to smaller liturgical events. On the other hand, it will not be helpful to portray this musical epoch from a composer-focused viewpoint alone; a traditional idealistic view of music as creations of geniuses cannot be appropriate. In most cases, the distance between the composer's and the collectors' hands is too big, that the respect for the sources and their entirety might give a new perception of music and its liturgical foundation.

Bibliography

Sources

MARTIN LUTHER (1526), Deutsche Messe vnd Ordnung Gotesdiensts, zu Wittenberg, fürgenomen, Augsburg: Steiner, http://nbn-resolving.de/urn:nbn:de:bvb:12-bsb00022395-0 (retrieved 18.05.2016).

FRANCK, MELCHIOR (1623), Es ist nicht fein, dass man den Kindern ihr Brot nehme, http://www2.cpdl.org/wiki/images/3/39/FRANCK-esistnichtfein.pdf (retrieved 18.05.2016).

Secondary Literature

BENT, MARGARET (2007ff), Article "Dunstaple", Grove Music Online (retrieved 18.05.2016).

BRUSNIAK, FRIEDHELM (1999), Zur Identifikation Conrad Reins als Leiter der Hofkantorei König Christians II. von Dänemark, Neues musikwissenschaftliches Jahrbuch 8, 107–113.

FINCK, HEINRICH (1971), Practica musica (1556), Hildesheim: Olms.

HAENEN, GRETA (2015), Die Streicher in der evangelischen Kirchenmusik in Norddeutschland, in: Konrad Küster (ed.), Zwischen Schütz und Bach: Georg Österreich und Heinrich Bokemeyer als Notensammler (Gottorf /Wolfenbüttel), Stuttgart: Carus, 61–82.

KÜSTER, KONRAD (2016), Musik im Namen Luthers: Kulturentwicklungen seit der Reformation, Kassel and Stuttgart: Bärenreiter and Metzler.

KÜSTER, KONRAD (2017), Wolfgang Figulus: Gratias agimus (Gloria alternatim), Leipzig 1549, in: Hans-Peter Haase et al. (ed.), Manu propria – Mit eigener Hand: 95 Autographe der Reformationszeit, Markkleeberg: Sax, 132f.; online: https://reformation.slub-dresden.de/autograph/wolfgang-figulus-gratias-agimus-gloria-alternatim-leipzig-1549/ (retrieved 08.11.2017).

LEUCHTMANN, HORST/SCHAEFER, HARTMUT (1994), Orlando di Lasso: Prachthandschriften und Quellenüberlieferung, Aus den Beständen der Bayerischen Staatsbibliothek München, Tutzing: Hans Schneider.

ROLLBERG, FRITZ (1931/1932), Das Eisenacher Kantorenbuch, Zeitschrift für Musikwissenschaft 14, 420.

SCHRÖDER, OTTO (1931/1932), Das Eisenacher Cantorenbuch, Zeitschrift für Musikwissenschaft 14, 173–178.

STEUDE, WOLFRAM (1974), Die Musiksammelhandschriften des 16. und 17. Jahrhunderts in der Sächsischen Landesbibliothek zu Dresden, Wilhelmshaven: Heinrichshofen.

STEUDE, WOLFRAM (1978), Untersuchungen zur mitteldeutschen Musiküberlieferung und Musikpflege im 16. Jahrhundert, Leipzig: Peters.

Maria Lucia Weigel

Aspekte reformierter Ekklesiologie in Bildnissen von Zwingli und Bullinger

1. Einleitung

In Deutschland hatte sich im ersten Drittel des 16. Jahrhunderts das Reformatoren-porträt aus dem Gelehrtenbildnis humanistischer Prägung heraus entwickelt, wobei sich die Schöpfer des ersteren einer bildlichen Rhetorik bedienten, die derjenigen des Gelehrtenbildnisses vergleichbar ist.[1] Die ersten Bildnisse des Augustiner-Eremiten Martin Luther von der Hand Lucas Cranachs d. Ä. zeigen den Reformator hinter Brüstungen, die mit Inschrifttafeln versehen sind. Das Motiv ist dem antik-römischen Totenkult entlehnt. Lateinische Inschriften, in antiker Kapitalschrift verfaßt, nehmen den neuplatonischen Gedanken der Undarstellbarkeit des Geistes auf, der sich allein im Werk des Dargestellten äußere. Auch die Darstellungsweise, die Wiedergabe der Person im strengen Profil, nimmt Bezug auf die römische Vergangenheit, die in der Nachfolge italienischer Humanisten in den Blick der ultramontanen Gelehrten gerückt war. Die Profilansicht ist aus dem kaiserlichen Münzbildnis abgeleitet und stellt eine Nobilitierung des Dargestellten dar. Der Verweis auf dessen Wirken in Form von gelegentlich aufgeschlagenen Büchern mit wechselndem Inhalt zählt in diesen auch für andere Reformatoren genutzten bildlichen Strategien ebenfalls zu dem durch die Humanisten eingeführten Bil-drepertoire. Die humanistisch geprägte Bildsprache etablierte sich in der 1. Hälfte des 16. Jahrhunderts nicht nur im Kontext der Wittenberger Reformation. Sie bezeichnet die bildliche Inszenierung von Personen, die ein bestimmtes, zuvor erläutertes Motivrepertoire ebenso beinhaltet wie den Modus der Präsentation in Gestalt visueller Topoi, die als bildliche Argumente den Betrachter sowohl von der lebendigen Präsenz des Dargestellten als auch von dessen Wirken und Botschaft überzeugen wollen. Auch in die Bildnisse Schweizer Reformatoren gingen diese Bildauffassung und ein ebensolches Motivrepertoire ein, wie sich an den Werken des namhaftesten Zürcher Malers der Reformationszeit, Hans Asper, ablesen lässt (vgl. Zürcher Kunst: 1981).

Im vorliegenden Beitrag sollen je ein Bildnis von Ulrich Zwingli und Heinrich Bullinger von Hans Asper aus dem Bestand der Zürcher Zentralbibliothek auf

---

1 Noch immer grundlegend Löcher: 1995, 353–390. Zum humanistischen Gedankengut der Inschriften in Gelehrten- und Reformatorenbildnissen vgl. Ludwig: 1998, 123–161.

folgende Fragestellungen hin untersucht werden: Welche bildlichen Argumente werden vom Künstler in Dienst genommen, um dem Betrachter das reformatorische Wirken und die Bedeutung der zwei prominentesten Vertreter der Zürcher Reformation vor Augen zu führen? Inwiefern zeigt sich in den Bildnissen Zwinglis und Bullingers der Aspekt der Ekklesiologie in der jeweils spezifischen theologischen Ausprägung in den Schriften beider Reformatoren? Wie werden spezifische theologische Botschaft und *memoria* der Dargestellten inszeniert, um den Betrachter für diese einzunehmen?

2. Gestalterische Strategien im Porträtschaffen des Zürcher Stadtmalers Hans Asper

Hans Asper schuf zahlreiche repräsentative Einzelbildnisse. Diese entstanden mehrheitlich im Auftrag des Stadtstaates Zürich und dessen kirchlicher und weltlicher Mitglieder. Nicht nur diejenigen der Reformatoren der Stadt zeichnen sich zumeist durch eine Strenge der Bildkomposition ebenso aus wie durch eine Kargheit des bildrhetorischen Apparates. Einfarbige Gründe und blockhafte Körpergestaltungen heben die Dargestellten aus der Sphäre des Alltäglichen und Zufälligen heraus, monumentalisieren sie in ihrer Erscheinung und folgen dabei dem Gestaltungsprinzip der *simplicitas*, die schon im Hinblick auf das Werk Lucas Cranachs d. Ä. das Lob der reformatorisch gesinnten Zeitgenossen fand (vgl. Poulsen: 2003, 135). Einfachheit stand dabei für die Negierung augentäuschender Vorgaukelung von Realität und für den eindeutigen Zeichencharakter des Bildes, der der Bildverehrung, die vor allem im sakralen Kontext Gegenstand heftiger Kritik von Seiten der Reformierten war, einen Riegel vorschob. Andere Strategien, insbesondere diejenigen zur Verlebendigung der Darstellung und damit des Dargestellten – bedeutsam vor allem im Hinblick auf Porträts bereits Verstorbener –,[2] greifen in Form der Modellierung plastischer Volumina, wie denjenigen des Gesichtes, und der Tiefenerschließung, wie im Fall aufgeblätterter Buchseiten. Diese scheinbar gegenläufigen Gestaltungsstrategien sind in Aspers Reformatorenbildnissen miteinander verschränkt. Mit den auf bildgestalterischer Ebene angesiedelten visuellen Botschaften verbinden sich weitere, die über Texte in die Bildnisse eingebracht sind. In ihrer Gesamtheit können sie in humanistischer Tradition als bildrhetorische Topoi gelten, die sich zu bildlichen Argumentationen fügen.

---

2 Im reformierten Kontext stellen die Bildnisse von Reformatoren stets Memorialbildnisse von bereits Verstorbenen dar, vgl. Christin: 2005, 393–396. Christin stuft die zu Lebzeiten der Reformatoren entstandenen Porträts als zahlenmäßig gering und daher für die Interpretation nicht zu berücksichtigen ein.

Abb. 1   Hans Asper, Bildnis Ulrich Zwingli, 1549, Tempera und Öl auf Holz, 62,5 × 51 cm.
Quelle: Zentralbibliothek Zürich, Graphische Sammlung und Fotoarchiv.

2.1 Hans Aspers Bildnis von Ulrich Zwingli aus dem Jahr 1549

Das Bildnis Ulrich Zwinglis aus dem Jahr 1549 zeigt diesen vor blauem Grund in
Halbfigur (Abb. 1).

Das Gesicht ist, wie auch in einem Bildnis Zwinglis von der Hand Aspers aus
oder nach dem Jahr 1531, im strengen Profil wiedergegeben, nun aber, anders als
dort, nach rechts gewandt. Der Oberkörper erscheint jedoch in die Dreiviertelan-

sicht gedreht. Der Reformator trägt eine schwarze Schaube und ein Barett. Diese Kleidung war von Zwingli bereits in einem frühen Stadium der Zürcher Reformation als liturgische Gewandung eingeführt worden (vgl. Burde: 2005, 87). In den Händen hält er eine aufgeschlagene Bibel. Der für den Betrachter lesbare Text gibt Mt 11: 28–30 und Mt 12: 1–3 wieder.

Die Entstehung des Bildes steht wohl im Zusammenhang mit der Anfertigung eines Doppelbildnisses von Zwinglis Tochter Regula mit deren Tochter Anna sowie eines Porträts von Rudolph Gwalther, das heute verschollen ist. Dieser hatte die Bildnisse seiner selbst und der Familie 1549 bei Asper in Auftrag gegeben. Das Zwingli Zwingli, Ulrich-Porträt könnte jedoch auch Teil einer Serie von Reformatorenbildnissen gewesen sein (Zürcher Kunst: 1981, 62).

Lange nach Zwinglis Tod (1531) entstanden, handelt es sich bei diesem Bildnis um ein Memorialporträt des Reformators. Nicht nur die Angaben zu Lebensalter und Sterbedatum oberhalb der linken Schulter weisen darauf hin. Auch die Inschrift am oberen Bildrand positioniert den Dargestellten im Rahmen einer reformatorischen Gedächtniskultur und inszeniert ihn als Märtyrer für den rechten Glauben: „HVLDRYCHVS ZWINGLIVS./ DVM PATRIAE QVAERO PER DOG-MATA SANCTA SALVTEM/INGRATO PATRIAE CAESUS AB ENSE CADO" („Während ich das Heil des Vaterlandes durch die heiligen Lehren suche, falle ich, getötet vom undankbaren Schwert des Vaterlandes").[3] Dies spielt auf den Zweiten Kappeler Krieg an, in dem Zwingli auf Seiten der teilnehmenden neugläubigen Kantone fiel. Bullinger sollte den Gedanken der „Kirche unter dem Kreuz", auf Zürich und die eigene Lebenszeit bezogen, unter einem eschatologischen Blickwinkel in seinen Predigten über die Offenbarung später weiter entfalten (vgl. Selderhuis: 2007, 516; 520–522).

Im Hinblick auf die *persuasio* als Aspekt der bildrhetorischen Inszenierung erscheint es von Bedeutung, dass das Zwingli-Bildnis in der Ich-Form und im Präsens zum Betrachter spricht. Es wendet sich an diesen, um als Teil der Erinnerungsfigur Zwingli die wachsende zeitliche Distanz zu überbrücken. Das Bildnis ist in der Sphäre des überzeitlichen Gedenkens angesiedelt. Zugleich verleiht die Inschrift dem Bildnis Stimme, es tritt mit dem Betrachter in Dialog. Es handelt sich dabei um einen Kunstgriff, der die von der Antike inspirierte Kunsttheorie der Zeit reflektiert (vgl. Larsson: 2012, 27–34; 41–45). Nicht jede der Inschriften wendet sich direkt an den Betrachter, so sind die biographischen Daten in der dritten Person Singular gehalten. Kontinuität ist in der Sprecherperspektive ebenso wenig eingehalten wie im Einsatz anderer bildgestalterischer Mittel. Stets aber steht die Informati-

---

3 Vgl. für die Übersetzung die Dokumentation einer anderen Druckgraphik nach dem Gemälde von Asper Porträtsammlung: 2004, 425, Nr. A 24980.

onsübermittlung an den Adressaten im Vordergrund. Im Bibeltext wechselt die Sprecherperspektive erneut. Nun ist es Christus, der sich an den Leser wendet.

Mt 11: 28–30: „Venite ad me omnes qui laboratis et oneratis estis" („Kummend haer zu mir alle die arbeytend und beladen sind") ist als Zitat in lateinischer und deutscher Fassung fast allen Schriften Zwinglis vorangestellt.[4] Es kann daher als programmatisch für seine Theologie gelten und soll in seinem Gebrauch bei Zwingli im Folgenden beleuchtet werden.

Mt 11: 28 wurde zuerst von Zwingli in seinem Entwurf eines Messkanons von 1523 liturgisch eingesetzt. Der Reformator platzierte das Jesuswort unmittelbar vor der Austeilung des Brotes, die mit den Worten „Der Leib unseres Herrn Jesus Christus" erfolgte.[5] Bei Zwingli, anders als in der Rezeption in der Liturgie anderer reformierter Kirchen, liegt die Betonung dabei auf der Ruhepause für die Mühseligen und Beladenen, die mit der Errettung durch Christus verbunden ist. Etwas abweichend von der lutherischen Tradition, die die Stelle Mt 11: 28 als Heilandsruf bezeichnet, ist sie bei Zwingli vorrangig ein Trostwort, das in enger liturgischer Verbindung mit dem Abendmahl steht (vgl. Stanton: 1992, 365, s. auch Opitz: 2010, 52). Trost verheißt auch Vers 11, 29, ebenfalls im aufgeschlagenen Bibeltext aufgeführt: „Tollite iugum meum super vos [...] et invenietis requiem animabus vestris." („Nemmend auff euch mein joch [...] so werdend ir ruw finden euweren seelen.").

Zwingli widmete keine seiner Schriften ausschließlich dem Thema Ekklesiologie (vgl. Büsser: 1994, 77). Aus dem im Bildnis aufgeführten Schriftwort jedoch erschließen sich sowohl die strikte christologische Zentrierung von Zwinglis Theologie als auch die daraus gefolgerte Definition von Kirche; beide haben ihr Fundament in der Heiligen Schrift (vgl. Büsser: 1985, 95). Die sichtbare Kirche – bei Zwingli gegen die wahre, unsichtbare abgegrenzt – besteht wie diese aus fehlbaren und sündigen Menschen, die zu ihrem Heil von Christus gerufen werden, so legte Zwingli Zwingli, Ulrich in seiner 1531 verfaßten *Christianae fidei Huldrycho Zvinglio predicatae, brevis & clara expositio* dar.[6] Der Reformator hatte in seiner Antwort auf

---

4 Vielfach ergänzt um den zweiten Teil des Verses „et ego refocillabo vos" oder „et ego requiem vobis prestabo", so in Zwingli, *De canone missae epichiresis* (1523), s. Anm. 5 („und ich will euch ruw geben", deutsche Bibelzitate hier und im Folgenden nach Die gantze Bibel: 1531 (VD 16 B 2690). Die hier und im Folgenden von Asper zitierten lateinischen Bibelstellen finden sich in lateinischen Teilausgaben der Bibel von Froschauer, vgl. die in VD 16 digitalisierten Bestände).

5 Zwingli: 1523, vgl. CR 89, 23, 556–608, hier 576. Vgl. Bürki: 1983, 188. Vgl. hier und im Folgenden Stanton: 1992, 365, der von einer tatsächlich gefeierten Messe für dieses frühe Datum ausgeht. Das erste reformierte Nachtmahl wurde jedoch Gründonnerstag 1525 im Zürcher Großmünster nach einem liturgischen Formular Zwinglis von 1525 gefeiert, vgl. Bürki: 1983, 182; 189–198.

6 Zwingli: 1531, vgl. CR 93, 5, 50–163, hier 110, und die wissenschaftliche deutsche Ausgabe mit Einleitung in Zwingli: 1995, 324ff. Vgl. zum Aspekt der sichtbaren und der unsichtbaren Kirche Abraham: 2007, 449 und allgemein zur Unterscheidung der Kirchen Locher: 2004, 54–68.

Hieronymus Emser im Jahr 1524 diesen Gedanken bereits ausgeführt.[7] Das Wort des Gottessohnes an die Menschen, das im Evangelium niedergelegt ist, wird dort als konstitutiv für die Kirchenbildung hervorgehoben und in das Bild des guten Hirten gekleidet, auf dessen Stimme allein die Schafe hören sollen. Im Zentrum von Zwinglis Kirchenverständnis steht also das Wort Christi (vgl. Büsser: 1985, 81). Durch das Heilswort Christi konstituiert sich Kirche. Diejenigen, die von Christus berufen sind und ihm folgen, sind Kirche. Diese Sicht ist eingebettet in eine über das enge Kirchenverständnis hinaus wirksame gesellschaftliche Dimension, der ebenfalls das christologisch zentrierte Schriftprinzip zugrunde liegen sollte. Gemeint ist die Befreiung von Kirchengeboten und damit von Traditionen, die die Kirche als gesellschaftliche Institution betreffen. Darauf verweist das in Mt 12: 1–3 thematisierte Pflücken der Ähren am Sabbath. Die wahre Lehre, der evangelische Kern also, sollte freigelegt werden und in der Wortverkündigung gleichermaßen die als Einheit gesehene Kirche und Gesellschaft formen.[8]

Im Bildnis ist Zwingli, so lautet die hier vertretene These, vermittelt über den Bibeltext, in einem Spezifikum seiner Theologie inszeniert. Dieses hat implizit das Kirchenverständnis des Reformators zum Inhalt, das christologisch zentriert ist. Einerseits steht es über die liturgische Kontextualisierung des Matthäusverses in Verbindung mit dem Abendmahl[9] – als Gedächtnisfeier der sich an die Heilstat Christi erinnernden Gemeinde, der Kirche, die Leib Christi ist – und andererseits impliziert es gesellschaftliche Konsequenzen, wie sie in der Bildinschrift aufgerufen werden, denn die *dogmata sancta* als evangelische Lehre wenden sich an das Volk Christi, das vom Herrn berufen ist, die Kirche also (vgl. Opitz: 2014, 92). Der Reformator verkündet diese Lehren in höchster Glaubwürdigkeit, er steht bis in den Tod für sie ein, das vermittelt das Bild und fordert den Betrachter zugleich auf, das dort verbildlichte Wort Gottes selbst zu lesen und in die Nachfolge des Dargestellten einzutreten.

2.2 Hans Aspers Bildnis von Heinrich Bullinger aus dem Jahr 1550

Das Porträt Heinrich Bullingers aus dem Jahr 1550 zeigt diesen vor dunklem Grund im Dreiviertelprofil nach rechts hinter einer Brüstung (Abb. 2).

Auf dieser liegt das Buch auf, das der Nachfolger Zwinglis in der Leitung der Zürcher Kirche aufgeschlagen in den Händen hält. Auch er ist in Schaube und

---

7 Zwingli: 1524, vgl. CR 90, 38, 241–287, zum Hirtenmotiv 258f, vgl. dazu Büsser: 1985, 78f.

8 Vgl. Büsser: 1985, 81; 88 und Büsser: 1994, 238f: „Die Macht der Institutionen oder ein Versuch über die Reformation in Zürich". Opitz (2010, 46) sieht diese Gedanken auch mit Mt 11: 28 verbunden. Zum historischen Prozess der Verschmelzung von Kirche und Gesellschaft vgl. Gäbler: 1975, 94f.

9 Zur ekklesiologischen Komponente von Zwinglis Abendmahlslehre vgl. Everszumrode: 2012, 43.

Abb. 2   Hans Asper, Bildnis Heinrich Bullinger, 1550, Öl auf Holz, 62 × 49 cm.
Quelle: Zentralbibliothek Zürich, Graphische Sammlung und Fotoarchiv.

Barett gekleidet, seine Physiognomie ist durch einen langen grauen Bart charakterisiert. Oberhalb seines Kopfes sind zwei lateinische Distichen angebracht mit dem Wortlaut: „HEINRYCHVS BVLLINGERVS/VNDECIMI IAM NVNC LABVNTVR SYDERA LVSTRI,/HAEC AETAS, FORMAM PICTA TABELLA REFERT/NIL EGO VEL FORMAM VEL VITAE TEMPORA SPECTO,/SED CHRISTVM VI-TAE QVI MIHI FORMA MEAE EST" („Dies mein Alter: schon eilen des elften

Lustrums Gestirne;/meine Gestalt: sie ist auf diese Tafel gemalt./Aber sei es Gestalt oder Zeit meines Lebens: nichts acht' ich/Als meines Lebens Idee, Christ, den Erlöser und Herrn") (Übersetzung: Zürcher Kunst: 1981, 64). Das Porträt gehört zu einer Serie von Bildnissen führender Zürcher Theologen, die der Engländer Christopher Hales zur Ausschmückung seiner heimischen Bibliothek bei Asper bestellt hatte.[10] Hales hatte sich ab September 1549 bis Anfang 1550 auf Empfehlung des Reformators Heinrich Bullinger im Haus des Pfarrers der Zürcher St. Peters-Kirche, Rudolph Gwalther, aufgehalten und dort Bildnisse des Hausherrn selbst, der Gattin und des Schwiegervaters Ulrich Zwingli von der Hand Hans Aspers gesehen, möglicherweise handelte es sich dabei um das im Beitrag zuerst vorgestellte Zwingli-Bildnis. Nach seiner Rückkunft in England im März 1550 bat Hales den Gastgeber brieflich darum, bei Asper Bildnisse von Zwingli, Pelikan, Bibliander, Oekolampadius, Bullinger und Gwalther selbst zu bestellen, auf Holz gemalt und mit je vier Versen versehen, deren Inhalt er dem Briefpartner überließ. Die erhaltenen Verse auf dem Bildnis Bullingers sind jedoch zu einem späteren Zeitpunkt angebracht auf einer eigens angestückten Tafel, wohl zu dem Zeitpunkt, als Bullinger tatsächlich 11 Lustren, also 55 Jahre, zählte (vgl. Zürcher Kunst: 1981, 64). *Lustrum* bezeichnete in der Antike den Fünfjahresrhythmus, in dem die staatlichen Reinigungs- und Sühneopfer dargebracht wurden (vgl. Petersmann: 1983, 209). Hier ist dieser Rückgriff auf die Antike dem humanistisch geprägten Milieu geschuldet, in dem das Bild entstand und in dem es seine Adressaten fand.

Die gewünschten Bildnisse wurden von Hans Asper zwar angefertigt, doch zwei der Porträtierten, Bullinger und Pelikan, verweigerten die Herausgabe ihrer Konterfeis aus Furcht vor einer möglichen Bilderverehrung. Lediglich die Porträts der bereits Verstorbenen, Zwingli und Oekolampadius, wurden nach England ausgeliefert, möglicherweise auch diejenigen der zu diesem Zeitpunkt noch Lebenden, Bibliander und Gwalther. Die Bildnisse Zwinglis und Gwalthers sind verloren, die anderen vier aus der ursprünglichen Bestellung in verschiedenen öffentlichen und privaten Sammlungen erhalten.[11]

Der Text im aufgeschlagenen Buch stellt eine Kompilation aus mehreren Bibelstellen dar, eine Vorgehensweise, die bereits auf die Programmatik der ausgewählten Texte verweist. Die Stelle Mt 17: 5: „Hic est filius meus dilectus in quo placata est anima mea ipsum audite." („Das ist min lieber sun, in dem ich versoenet bin, im sind gehörig.") auf die der Reformator mit den Fingern seiner linken Hand weist,

---

10 Vgl. hier und im Folgenden Boesch (1949, 16–50) mit einer ausführlichen Analyse der Korrespondenz zwischen Hales und den Zürcher Reformatoren und dem Wiederabdruck der lateinischen Briefe. Durch den in Zürich erhaltenen und bereits 1848 in Cambridge in den Epistolae Tigurinae publizierten Briefwechsel ist dieser Fall gut belegt.

11 Vgl. Boesch: 1949, 25ff. Zu den aktuellen Standorten der Bildnisse von Pelikan, Oekolampadius und Bibliander vgl. Zürcher Kunst: 1981, 65f.

galt Bullinger als reformatorisches Erkenntnisprinzip; sie bringt die christologische Zentrierung seiner Theologie zur Geltung. Er stellte sie später sämtlichen eigenen Schriften voran.[12] Eine inhaltliche Parallele zu den im Zwingli-Bildnis integrierten Textstellen ist nicht zu übersehen. Auch jetzt wendet sich Gott in direkter Rede an den Leser. In Kol 1: 20 scheint der Gedanke der Versöhnung in Christus erneut auf. In den weiteren Stellen aus dem Kolosserbrief wird die Fülle des Heils, die Erfüllung aller Verheißung allein in Christus thematisiert. Dieser Gedanke spiegelt sich auch in Bullingers Bundestheologie (vgl. Spijker: 2007, 580). In Joh 1: 17 erscheint der Versöhnungsgedanke erneut, hier wird dem im Alten Testament sich im Gesetz manifestierenden Bund Gottes mit den Menschen Christi Heilstat im Neuen Testament gegenübergestellt, durch die der Bund erneuert wird.[13] Bullinger interpretiert bereits in frühen theologischen Schriften das Sprechen Gottes zum Menschen im Alten Testament als Versöhnungshandeln, das in Christus seinen Höhepunkt findet. Letzterer Aspekt findet in dem Johannes-Zitat seinen Niederschlag. Der Versöhnungsgedanke ist Kern des christlichen Glaubens.[14]

Die Gemeinschaft der Menschen mit Gott in Christus definiert Kirche. Die Lehre von der Kirche stellt einen zentralen Aspekt der Theologie Bullingers dar.[15] Bullinger widmete, wie Zwingli, der Kirche keine eigene Schrift, doch sind in zahlreichen seiner Schriften ekklesiologische Aspekte berücksichtigt. Die Predigten über die Offenbarung, in denen der Reformator sein christologisch fundiertes Kirchenverständnis ausführt, wurden allerdings nach der Entstehungszeit des Bildnisses gehalten. Das entscheidende Kennzeichen der Kirche ist die Verkündigung des Wortes Gottes.[16] Diese ist Gottes Wort. In diesem Wort soll die Gemeinde bleiben. Der Pastor, der Hirte, ist dabei Instrument Christi. Darin schließt sich Bullinger theologisch den Aussagen an, die in dem vorgestellten Zwingli-Bildnis bereits bildhaft formuliert sind. Diese Gewichtung des Wortes Christi spiegelt sich sowohl in der vierzeiligen Inschrift als auch in den für die Darstellung Bullingers im Bild ausgewählten biblischen Texten.

In Bullingers Theologie beinhalten diese Aussagen ebenfalls eine politische Dimension, wie sie im Zwingli-Bildnis anklingt. Das Evangelium zielt auf Gemein-

---

12 Vgl. Büsser: 1985, 95. Zu der deutschen Übersetzung vgl. Bullinger: 2005, 79, Anm. 3. Roth merkt an, dass der zweite Teil des Verses in Bullingers Interpretation nicht nur „auf ihn hört" bedeutet, sondern auch „zu ihm gehört". Hier wird sowohl der Gehorsam gegenüber Christus als auch die Zugehörigkeit zu ihm angesprochen. Zum reformatorischen Erkenntnisprinzip vgl. Staedtke: 1962, 52.

13 Campi verweist auf den christologischen Charakter des Bundes, der die vollzogene Versöhnung in Christus und die Erneuerung des Menschen beschreibt, vgl. Campi: 2005, 432.

14 Vgl. Opitz: 37f und zum Stellenwert der Versöhnungschristologie in Bezug auf Kirche 40.

15 Vgl. hier und im Folgenden Selderhuis: 2007, 516 mit einer neuen Gewichtung der Ekklesiologie innerhalb der Theologie Bullingers.

16 Vgl. hier und im Folgenden Büsser: 1985, 96.

schaft ab, es wird vor allem in Gemeinschaft erfahrbar.[17] Dadurch wird notwendigerweise die christliche Gemeinde in ihrer besonderen, „evangelischen" Gestallt konstituiert. Dies hatte in Form von kirchenstaatlichen Strukturen Auswirkungen bis in die Gestaltung der Gesellschaft hinein. Auch diese sollte sich im Blick auf Christus formieren. Die Einrichtung der „Fürträge" trägt dem Rechnung (vgl. Bächtold: 1982, 11). Spätestens seit 1532 richtete der Rat an die Zürcher Pfarrer die dringende Aufforderung, ihre Anliegen zunächst nicht auf der Kanzel zu behandeln, sondern diese zuerst dem Rat der Stadt vorzutragen. Bullinger war derjenige innerhalb der kirchlichen Führungsgruppe, der diese Aufgabe vornehmlich wahrnahm.

In dem letzten der in der aufgeschlagenen Bibel zu lesenden Texte, Joh 1: 16–17, scheint neben dem hier im Vordergrund stehenden Versöhnungsgedanken ein weiterer Aspekt der Theologie Bullingers auf.[18] Er liegt in der Verbindung von Altem mit Neuem Testament. In Bullingers Bundestheologie wird diese Verbindung zu einem zentralen Thema.[19] Sie ist dadurch charakterisiert, dass sich das Bündnis Gottes mit den Menschen über das Alte und das Neue Testament hinweg spannt und der Neue den Alten Bund nicht aufhebt, sondern fortführt. Bereits von Beginn seines theologischen Wirkens an galt Bullinger der Begriff des Gottesbundes als Schlüssel für die Auslegung der einheitlichen biblischen Botschaft des Alten und des Neuen Testaments. Im Jahr 1534 publizierte Bullinger seine Schrift *Von dem einigen unnd ewigen Testament oder Pundt Gottes* zeitgleich in Latein und Deutsch bei dem Zürcher Drucker Christoph Froschauer d. Ä.[20] Vor allem dort sind die Gedanken zur Bundestheologie systematisch dargelegt. Zu nennen ist auch die Schrift *Der alt gloub* von 1537.[21]

In dem hier aufgezeigten Kontext spielen folgende Gedanken eine signifikante Rolle. In Christus ist der Mensch mit Gott versöhnt, in ihm erfüllt sich alle Verheißung des Alten Bundes, auch die Zeremonien sind erfüllt und haben im Neuen Bund keinen Bestand (vgl. Spijker: 2007, 580) – wieder spannt sich der Bogen zu dem Zwingli-Bildnis in Gestalt des dort zitierten Gleichnisses von der Ährenlese

---

17 Vgl. Opitz: 2014, 92 zu dieser Gewichtung der theologischen Akzentuierung Bullingers und Opitz: 2004, 425f. Zusammenfassend zur politischen Dimension der Theologie Bullingers vgl. Campi: 2005, 426–429.

18 Bullingers Auseinandersetzung mit dem Johannesevangelium in unterschiedlichen Phasen seines Wirkens, vor allem in Gestalt der Vorlesung über das Johannesevangelium und des 1543 entstandenen Johanneskommentars, soll hier ohne weitere Ausführungen lediglich erwähnt werden, zu den Anfängen vgl. Gäbler: 1975, 13–27.

19 Vgl. hier und im Folgenden Opitz: 2004, 317–352 und Spijker: 2007, 575–583.

20 Vgl. die wissenschaftliche deutsche Ausgabe mit Einleitung in: Bullinger: 2004, 49–101 und den Originaltext unter VD 16 B 9728. Für die lateinische Ausgabe vgl. VD 16 B 9722.

21 Vgl. für die wissenschaftliche Ausgabe der zweiten Ausgabe von 1539 mit Einleitung Bullinger: 2004, 171–257 und den Originaltext unter VD 16 B 9600.

am Sabbath. Gleichwohl erwartet Gott im Neuen Bund neuen Gehorsam, auf den der Mensch in der Taufe verpflichtet wird. Daraus konstituiert sich Kirche. Ekklesiologie und Bundestheologie gehen dabei nicht ineinander auf, sind aber in der Zentrierung auf Christus als zwei inhaltlich nah aneinander gerückte Schwerpunkte der Theologie Bullingers zu sehen.

Bullinger ist im Bildnis somit in mehreren Aspekten seiner theologischen Ausrichtung dargestellt, die jeweils Aussagen zu seinem Kirchenverständnis beinhalten. Sie erschließen sich, wie schon im Bildnis Zwinglis, über den im Bild präsentierten Text, der nach humanistischer Bildtradition Teil der bildrhetorischen Argumentation ist.

3. Fazit

Zwingli und Bullinger sind als Verkünder des Gotteswortes inszeniert, indem sie per Geste der Hand jeweils auf den im Buch aufgeschlagenen und für den Betrachter lesbaren Text weisen. Dieser deutet pointiert auf das jeweils in eigenen Schriften ausführlicher beleuchtete und in der biblischen Ableitung individuell akzentuierte Kirchenverständnis beider Theologen hin. In beiden Fällen wird die Ableitung der jeweiligen theologischen Positionen aus der Heiligen Schrift augenfällig dargestellt. Deren Inszenierung im Bild stellt eine Legitimationsstrategie für das reformatorische Wirken dar, zugleich fügt sie sich in das humanistische Konzept von Person, indem das Äußere, Vergängliche dem sich im eigenen Werk in unvergänglicher Form manifestierenden Geist gegenübergestellt ist, ohne dass dies inschriftlich thematisiert würde. Sowohl durch die Wahl der Gewandung beider Reformatoren als auch in den Bildinschriften ist die textlich konnotierte Positionierung in weitere bildlich wirksame Topoi eingebettet. Inhaltlich-textbasierte Argumentation und motivisches Bildrepertoire ergänzen einander zu einer stringenten bildlichen Rhetorik humanistischer Prägung. In Bezug auf die Gestaltung der Physiognomie werden mimetische Aspekte des Porträtverständnisses berücksichtigt. Sie tragen zur Authentifizierung der bildlichen Erscheinung der Reformatoren bei. Diese aktualisiert sich fortwährend im Blick des Betrachters, indem die Bildnisse selbst inschriftlich zu diesem sprechen und sich in ihrer Zielsetzung ebenso erklären wie, im Fall Zwinglis, die historischen Umstände des Todes einer bestimmten heilsgeschichtlichen Deutung unterwerfen. Die Bildnisse selbst geben damit wesentliche Bestandteile der *memoria* vor. Diese hat paränetischen Charakter, indem beide Reformatoren beispielhaft für gelebte Christusnachfolge im Bild verewigt sind. Der ekklesiologischen Akzentuierung, die in den gewählten Bibelstellen zutage tritt, mag in der Konsolidierungsphase der Zürcher Reformation in ihrer von der protestantischen Kirche lutherischer Prägung in kirchenpolitischer Hinsicht abweichenden Struktur, allgemeiner vor dem Hintergrund der Abgrenzung gegen andere, altgläubige wie protestantische Strömungen als Bekräftigung des biblisch legitimierten Selbstverständnisses besondere Bedeutung zugekommen sein.[22]

Literatur

Quellen

DIE GANTZE BIBEL (1531), Die gantze Bibel / der ursprünglichen ebraischen und griechischen Waarheyt nach auffs aller treüwlichest verteütschet, Christoph Froschauer, Zürich (VD 16 B 2690).

HEINRICH BULLINGER (1534a), Von dem einigen unnd ewigen Testament oder Pundt Gottes, Christoph Froschauer, Zürich (VD 16 B 9728).

HEINRICH BULLINGER (1534b), De testamento seu foedere dei unico & aeterno Heinrychi Bullingeri brevis expositio, Christoph Froschauer, Zürich (VD 16 B 9722).

HEINRICH BULLINGER (1539), Der alt gloub, Christoph Froschauer, 2. verb. Aufl., Zürich (VD 16 B 9600).

HEINRICH BULLINGER (2004), Heinrich Bullinger, Schriften, I, Zwingliverein/Emidio Campi/Detlef Roth/Peter Stotz (ed.), Zürich: Theologischer Verlag.

HEINRICH BULLINGER (2005) Heinrich Bullinger Werke, 3. Abtlg.: Theologische Schriften, Bd.5: Pastoraltheologische Schriften, Detlef Roth (ed.), Zürich: Theologischer Verlag.

ULRICH ZWINGLI (1523), De canone missae epichiresis, Christoph Froschauer, Zürich (CR 89, 23, 556–608).

ULRICH ZWINGLI (1524), Adversus Hieronymum Emserum antibolon, Christoph Froschauer, Zürich (CR 90, 38, 241–287).

ULRICH ZWINGLI (1531), Christianae fidei Huldrycho Zvinglio pradicatae, brevis & clara expositio, Froschauer, Zürich (CR 93, 5, 50–163).

ULRICH ZWINGLI (1995), Huldrych Zwingli, Schriften, IV, Zwingliverein/Thomas Brunnschweiler/Samuel Lutz (ed.), Zürich: Theologischer Verlag.

Sekundärliteratur

ABRAHAM, MARTIN (2007), Evangelium und Kirchengestalt. Reformatorisches Kirchenverständnis heute, Berlin: De Gruyter.

---

22 Für wertvolle Hinweise im Hinblick auf die hier diskutierten theologischen Aspekte geht mein herzlicher Dank an Pierrick Hildebrand, Institut für Schweizerische Reformationsgeschichte der Universität Zürich.

BÄCHTOLD, HANS ULRICH (1982), Heinrich Bullinger vor dem Rat. Zur Gestaltung und Verwaltung des Zürcher Staatswesens in den Jahren 1531 bis 1575, Zürcher Beiträge zur Reformationsgeschichte 12, Bern/Frankfurt am Main: Peter Lang.

BOESCH, PAUL (1949), Der Zürcher Apelles. Neues zu den Reformatorenbildnissen von Hans Asper, Zwingliana 9, 16–50.

BÜRKI, BRUNO (1983), Das Abendmahl nach den Zürcher Ordnungen", in: Irmgard Pahl (ed.), Coena Domini I. Die Abendmahlsliturgie der Reformationskirchen im 16./17. Jahrhundert, Spicilegium Friburgense. Texte zur Geschichte des kirchlichen Lebens 29, Freiburg: Universitätsverlag Freiburg, 181–198.

BÜSSER, FRITZ (1985), Wurzeln der Reformation in Zürich. Zum 500. Geburtstag der Reformators Huldrych Zwingli, Studies in medieval and reformation thought 31, Leiden: Brill.

BÜSSER, FRITZ (1994), Die Prophezei. Humanismus und Reformation in Zürich. Ausgewählte Aufsätze und Vorträge, zu seinem 70. Geburtstag am 12. Februar 1993, Alfred Schindler (ed.), Bern/Berlin/Frankfurt am Main/New York: Peter Lang.

BURDE, CHRISTINA (2005), Bedeutung und Wirkung der schwarzen Bekleidungsfarbe in Deutschland zur Zeit des 16. Jahrhunderts, Bremen: Universität Bremen, http://nbn-resolving.de/urn:nbn:de:gbv:46-diss000012149, Zugriff 29.8.2016.

CAMPI, EMIDIO (2005), Heinrich Bullinger als Theologe, in: Gudrun Litz/Heidrun Munzert/Roland Liebenberg (ed.), Frömmigkeit – Theologie – Frömmigkeitstheologie. Contributions to European Church History. Festschrift für Berndt Hamm zum 60. Geburtstag, Studies in the history of Christian traditions, 124, Leiden/Boston: Brill, 423–436.

CHRISTIN, OLIVIER (2005), Mort et mémoire: Les portraits des réformateurs protestants au XVIe siècle, Schweizerische Zeitschrift für Geschichte 55, 383–400.

EVERSZUMRODE, FRANK (2012), Mysterium Christi spiritualis praesentiae. Die Abendmahlslehre des Genfer Reformators Johannes Calvin aus römisch-katholischer Perspektive, Göttingen: Vandenhoeck & Ruprecht.

GÄBLER, ULRICH (1975), Bullingers Vorlesung über das Johannesevangelium aus dem Jahre 1523, in: Ulrich Gäbler/Erland Herkenrath (ed.), Heinrich Bullinger 1504–1575. Gesammelte Aufsätze zum 400. Todestag. Erster Band: Leben und Werk, im Auftrag des Instituts für Schweizerische Reformationsgeschichte, Zürcher Beiträge zur Reformationsgeschichte 7, Zürich: Theologischer Verlag, 13–27.

GÄBLER, ULRICH (1975), Huldrych Zwingli im 20. Jahrhundert. Forschungsbericht und annotierte Bibliographie 1897–1972, Zürich: Theologischer Verlag.

KOLIND POULSEN, HANNE (2003), Fläche, Blick und Erinnerung. Cranachs 'Venus und Cupido als Honigdieb' im Licht der Bildtheologie Luthers, in: Lucas Cranach. Glaube, Mythologie und Moderne, Ausstellungskatalog Hamburg, Ostfildern-Ruit: Hatje Cantz Verlag, 130–143.

LARSSON, LARS OLOF (2012), „…Nur die Stimme fehlt!". Porträt und Rhetorik in der Frühen Neuzeit, Kiel: Ludwig.

LÖCHER, KURT (1995), Humanistenbildnisse – Reformatorenbildnisse. Unterschiede und

Gemeinsamkeiten, in: Hartmut Boockmann/Ludger Grenzmann/Bernd Moeller/Martin Staehelin (ed.), Literatur, Musik und Kunst im Übergang vom Mittelalter zur Neuzeit. Bericht über Kolloquien der Kommission zur Erforschung der Kultur des Spätmittelalters 1989 bis 1992, Abhandlungen der Akademie der Wissenschaften zu Göttingen, Philologisch-Historische Klasse, Göttingen: Vandenhoeck & Ruprecht, Folge 3, 208, 353–390.

LOCHER, GOTTFRIED WILHELM (2004), Sign of the Advent. A Study in Protestant Ecclesiology, Ökumenische Beihefte zur Freiburger Zeitschrift für Philosophie und Theologie 45, Freiburg: Institut für ökumenische Studien Freiburg Schweiz.

LUDWIG, WALTHER (1998), Das bessere Bildnis des Gelehrten, Philologus 142, 123–161.

OPITZ, PETER (2004), Heinrich Bullinger als Theologe. Eine Studie zu den 'Dekaden', Zürich: Theologischer Verlag.

OPITZ, PETER (2010), Kanzel und Gefletz – theologische und räumliche Verschiebungen zur Einführung des reformierten Abendmahls in Zürich, in: Christoph Sigrist (ed.), Kirchen Macht Raum. Beiträge zu einer kontroversen Debatte, Zürich: Theologischer Verlag, 45–58.

OPITZ, PETER (2013), Historische Zugänge zum Heidelberger Katechismus aus Schweizer Sicht, in: Martin Ernst Hirzel/Frank Mattwig/Matthias Zeindler (ed.), Der Heidelberger Katechismus – ein reformierter Schlüsseltext, Zürich: Theologischer Verlag, 21–50.

OPITZ, PETER (2014), Der spezifische Beitrag der Schweizer Reformation zur reformatorischen Bewegung, in: Petra Bosse-Huber/Serge Fornerod/Thies Gundlach/Gottfried Wilhelm Locher (ed.), 500 Jahre Reformation. Bedeutung und Herausforderungen. Internationaler Kongress der EKD und des SEK auf dem Weg zum Reformationsjubiläum 2017 vom 6. bis 10. Oktober 2013 in Zürich, Zürich: Theologischer Verlag/Leipzig: Evangelische Verlagsanstalt, 88–98.

PETERSMANN, HUBERT (1983), Lustrum. Etymologie und Volksbrauch, Würzburger Jahrbücher für die Altertumswissenschaft, N. F., 9, 209–230.

PORTRÄTSAMMLUNG (2004) Die Porträtsammlung der Herzog August Bibliothek Wolfenbüttel 1580–1850, Peter Mortzfeld (ed.), Reihe A: Die Porträtsammlung, vol. 37: Biographische und bibliographische Beschreibungen mit Künstlerregister, vol. 9, München: De Gruyter.

SELDERHUIS, HERMAN J. (2007), Kirche am Kreuz. Die Ekklesiologie Heinrich Bullingers, in: Emidio Campi/Peter Opitz (ed.), Heinrich Bullinger. Life – Thought – Influence. Zurich, Aug. 25–29, 2004. International Congress Heinrich Bullinger (1504–1575), vol 2, Zürcher Beiträge zur Reformationsgeschichte 24, Zürich: Theologischer Verlag, 515–536.

SPIJKER, WILLEM VAN'T (2007), Bullinger als Bundestheologe, in: Emidio Campi/Peter Opitz (ed.), Heinrich Bullinger. Life – Thought – Influence. Zurich, Aug. 25–29, 2004. International Congress Heinrich Bullinger (1504–1575), vol 2, Zürcher Beiträge zur Reformationsgeschichte 24, Zürich: Theologischer Verlag, 573–592.

STAEDTKE, JOACHIM (1962), Die Theologie des jungen Bullinger, Studien zur Dogmengeschichte und systematischen Theologie 16, Zürich: Theologischer Verlag.

STANTON, GRAHAM (1992), A Gospel for a New People. Studies in Matthew, Edinburgh: Westminster John Knox Press.

ZÜRCHER KUNST (1981), Zürcher Kunst nach der Reformation. Hans Asper und seine Zeit, Ausstellungskatalog Zürich, Zürich: Schweizerisches Institut für Kunstwissenschaft.

Church and Ecclesiology

Ariane Albisser, Peter Opitz

The Concept of 'Visible' Church and 'Invisible' Church in the Reformed Tradition

The Ecclesiology of the Second Helvetic Confession[1]

1. The Ecclesiology of the Second Helvetic Confession in Its Mid-Sixteenth-Century Context

The Reformation reignited the debate about the nature of the Christian church, about the criteria for the existence of that church and for how it might be identified. Earlier arguments had revolved around the authority and competencies of the church or had addressed how salvation was present within a space understood as Christian and the nature of the sacraments and sacramentals. Now, however, as competing concepts of church circulated, the question of precisely why a Christian church *was* a Christian church had become acute. Theological writings addressed the identity of the church explicitly, and with theological disputes embedded in religious and political conflicts, religious and bellicose arguments could readily converge.

The position on the church adopted by the Second Helvetic Confession is to be understood in this contemporary context. The church order introduced by Frederick III in the Electoral Palatinate, with the Heidelberg Catechism as its centrepiece, had been deemed neither Roman nor Lutheran, but simply 'Christian'. Subsequently, in the run up to the Imperial Diet to be held in Augsburg in 1566, the elector found himself under political pressure. In addition to the traditional Roman faith, the Religious Peace of Augsburg of 1555 had embraced only those who adopted the Augsburg Confession. Non-Lutheran Protestants, including those in the Swiss/south German confessional tradition (for which this article will use the term 'Reformed', the designation that gradually became standard), were explicitly excluded. Frederick III requested that Heinrich Bullinger provides a theological text that would defend the church order of the Electoral Palatinate as a legitimate and orthodox Christian church order. The task Bullinger faced was clear, particularly when it came to the doctrine of the church: the distinctive Reformed understanding of the church was to be presented such that it appeared not as the idiosyncratic teaching of a new sect but as a rigorous approach to fundamental Christian doctrine, as the Reformed believed was absolutely the case.

---

1 Translated by Rona Johnston.

The text sent by Bullinger to Heidelberg in late 1565/early 1566 and published within a matter of weeks had not been composed, however, solely for this occasion. Bullinger was able to draw on an existing confession that he had drafted in the name of the Zurich church in the early 1560s as his 'spiritual testament'.[2] Bullinger had used the composition of the original version of the text, not written for a specific occasion, as an opportunity to formulate the Zurich church's essential positions on ecclesiology. The cornerstones of the Reformed perception of church were presented in a language that was not polemical and were explained with systematic reference to Scripture, avoiding invented human teachings. In the process, Bullinger emphasised commonalities with other confessions. The ecclesiology of the Second Helvetic Confession shared with the Roman Church and with Roman theology roots in the theology of the early church as formulated by the first church councils. When it came to ecclesiology, common ground with the Lutherans was already so great that from the Reformed perspective no break with the Lutheran position would ever have been necessary. As a result, in an irenic spirit the Reformed could seek out and tacitly emphasise areas of agreement without surrendering their own theological positions and convictions.

Broadly conceived, the ecclesiology of the thirty-chapter Second Helvetic Confession is found in its final fourteen chapters. Here, along with his discussion of ecclesiastical offices, Bullinger addressed the sacraments, worship and its ceremonies, prayer, instruction, interment, administration of church property, marriage and the relationship with political authority. A more narrowly conceived discussion of the nature of the church is found in chapter seventeen. In the discussion that follows, the focus will be on this seventeenth chapter, which contains the essential central and basic elements of Bullinger's view of the church. The picture is given greater definition through comparison with the classic counter-position of Roman theology, usefully laid out in the *Enchiridion* of prominent Roman theologian Johannes Eck, a work first published in 1525 and repeatedly printed and expanded.[3] An opponent of both Luther and Zwingli, Eck had been spokesperson for the Catholic party at the disputation held at Baden in 1526 (Schindler/Schneider-Lastin/Jung/Murner: 2015). Fiercely and shrewdly critical of the Swiss Reformers, Eck knew their teachings well, and he was willing to enter the arena armed with the only weapon that the Reformed would permit, scriptural exegesis. Eck's translation of the complete

---

2 See the introduction by Emido Campi to the edition of the Second Helvetic Confession (Heinrich Bullinger: 2009, 243–267). The English citations of the Second Helvetic Confession are taken from The Second Helvetic Confession (2010), 809–881. For the Second Helvetic Confession in German, see: Zweite Helvetische Bekenntnis: 1936.

3 Eck's Enchiridion appeared 1525 and would eventually go through forty-six editions. The version used in this article is Johannes Eck: 1561; the citations in English are from Johann Eck: 1978. In his controversial theology, Bullinger made repeated reference to Eck, see Bullinger: 2004–2007, vol. 7, 85.

Bible into German, published in 1537, was intended as a direct challenge to the Bible translations of the Reformation (Bibel: 1537). Additionally, as we explore the ecclesiology adopted in the Second Helvetic Confession, we can usefully turn on occasion to Bullinger's *Decades*, which addresses the topic far more extensively (Bullinger: 2008; for a German translation, see Bullinger: 2004–2007, vol. 3–5). As a classic text with historical relevance that is hard overestimate, the Second Helvetic Confession certainly deserves our renewed attention on its 450th anniversary. Even if earlier studies do not need to be fundamentally revised, now, fifty years after its previous significant anniversary in 1966,[4] new emphases inevitably emerge when we tackle the text in light of fresh questions and debates.

Bullinger's approach to Christian doctrine was strongly influenced by the *loci* method. At the beginning of each topic he formulated a thesis, often in the form of a complex definition that encompassed all the essential points; he then explicated the elements of that thesis one after another, providing at times substantial layers of argumentation and making reference to problems and points of disagreement. This method was deployed when the Second Helvetic Confession tackled the doctrine of the church. The heading for chapter seventeen named two weighty themes: "Of the Catholic and Holy Church of God, and of the One Only Head of the Church" (*De catholica et sancta Dei Ecclesia et unico capite Ecclesiae*) (Second Helvetic Confession: 2010, 844; Bullinger: 2009, 310,l,12). The first of these topics concerned interpretation of the attributes of the church identified in earlier confessions: what did it mean that a Christian confession spoke of *one* church, what did it mean to confess the *catholicity* of that church and its *holiness*? (Second Helvetic Confession: 2010, 845; Bullinger: 2009, 310,l,12–312,l,2) The second topic concerned the confession of a single *head* of the church and noted the contrary position adopted by Roman theologians (Bullinger: 2010, 312,l,3–313,l,26). In stating that what was at stake was the church of *God*, and in asserting that the church has a *single head*, the heading gave advance warning that the doctrine of the church would be explained as entirely theocentric and Christocentric. It also indicated that the two distinct topics named in the heading were objectively intertwined. From those positions a third topic emerged, in the relationship of this theocentric and Christocentric church with the church as historically realised, in effect the issue of the relationship between the 'visible' church and the 'invisible' church (Bullinger: 2010, 313,ll,1–26).

---

4 Still significant are Koch: 1968; Van der Linde: 1966, 337–367.

2. The Confession: a Single, Catholic Church of God

We turn to the first topic. The Second Helvetic Confession's teaching on the church naturally drew in particular on the attributes of church formulated in the early church, and set out in the Apostle's Creed and Nicene Creed. The confession of the 'holy catholic church', a church understood as the 'communion of saints' could be found in the Apostles' Creed (Second Helvetic Confession: 2010, 844),[5] and a church designated 'one' and 'apostolic' in the Nicene Creed. (See: Denzinger, 30; 150).[6]

Bullinger placed a densely formulated definition of church at the start of the discussion. His statement embraced the ecclesiology of the Apostles' Creed but as embedded in the acts of the triune God in word and Spirit, making evident from the outset that for the Second Helvetic Confession ecclesiology was a matter not of describing human organisation or religious tradition, but of confessing the church of *God*. The prefixed etymological explanation of the term *ecclesia* traced the 'one', 'holy' and 'catholic' church back to God's saving grace. The 'holiness' of the church is the true knowledge and right worship of God by Word and Spirit, and it is faith through which the participation in all the benefits of Christ is reality. Church is portrayed as,

> a company of the faithful, called and gathered out of the world; that is, a company (I say) of all saints, that is, of them who do truly know, and rightly worship and serve, the true God, in Jesus Christ the Savior by the Word and the Holy Spirit, and who by faith are partakers of all those good graces which are freely offered through Christ (Second Helvetic Confession: 2010, 844).[7]

The first topic as a whole, indeed all of the Second Helvetic Confession's chapter on the church, can be understood as a multifaceted explanation and elaboration of this definition.

From this theological explanation we are led to conclude that inevitably there can be only *one* church (Bullinger: 2009, 310,l,12–311,l,22). Its oneness is guaranteed by the one God, through his singularity of being and acting:

---

5 'Credo sanctam ecclesiam catholicam, sanctorum communionem' (Bullinger: 2009, 310,ll,23f).

6 Bullinger prefaced his Decades with the Nicene Creed (Bullinger: 2008, vol. 1, 20,11,16f).

7 The first chapter of Johannes Eck's Enchiridion tackles 'the church and her authority' and immediately cites scriptural passages on the church as the 'body' and 'bride' of Christ, including Ephesians 4. The German version of 1533 states, '… seyt sorgfelltig zuo halten die ainigkeyt des gaysts im ad des fridens / Ain leyb und ain gayst / wie ir beruofft seyt in ainerlay hoffnung ewrer beruoffung. Ain Her / an glaub / ain Tauf / ain Gott und vatter unser aller / der ist über uns alle …', (Johannes Eck: 1533, 3f).

there is always but 'one God, and one mediator between God and man, Jesus Christ' (1 Tim. 2:5); also, one shepherd of the whole flock, one head of this body, and to conclude one Spirit, one salvation, one faith, one testament or covenant (Second Helvetic Confession: 2010, 845).

The church is termed 'catholic' because 'it is universal, spread abroad through all the parts and quarters of the world, and reaches into all times, and is not limited within the compass either of time or place' (Second Helvetic Confession: 2010, 845; Bullinger: 2009, 310,29–31). As a historian and as a reformer who repeatedly thought and argued with history (García Archilla: 1992; Moser: 2007, 459–492), here Bullinger highlighted the temporal: 'there always should have been, and should be at this day, and to the end of the world, a church' (Second Helvetic Confession: 2010, 844; Bullinger: 2009, 310,l,12). At the same time he had to counter all arguments grounded in the temporal catholicity of the Roman Church, a continuity that the latter invoked against the 'new Christians', the representatives of the 'new teaching'.[8] Eck could argue that the church had existed before Luther, had even predated the Bible to which Luther appealed, for the church had formed the canon and had deemed it authoritative (Eck: 1561, 16; cf. 22f, 26f). In response Bullinger argued for a highly theological interpretation of the uninterrupted temporal existence of the church. The church has always existed in the moment, for its existence is grounded in God's primordial and unrestricted declaration of salvation for humanity.

> Forasmuch as God from the beginning would have men to be saved and to come to the knowledge of truth (1 Tim. 2:4), therefore, it is necessary that there always should have been, and should be at this day, and to the end of the world, a church (Second Helvetic Confession: 2010, 844; Bullinger: 2009, 310,ll,12f).

Thus just like the confession of the oneness of the church, the confession of the church's catholicity is part of and implicit in the confession of a Christian God and of that God's unchanging salvific intent. The church's catholicity is not a product of verifiable links in a chain of historic tradition, either institutional or in office holding.

As the title of chapter seventeen suggests, the ecclesiology of the Second Helvetic Confession speaks of the church *of God*, of a church called into existence and preserved by God's addressing of humanity. That character is also evident when Bullinger, unlike Eck, has the catholic church start not with the apostles and thus

---

8 Translated here are Eck's polemical German-language terms 'Neuchristen' and 'neue Lehre'; the Latin translates as 'heretic' and 'enemies of the church': for the German, see: Eck: 1533,6 and frequently subsequently.

with the office given to Peter, but with the first human couple after the Fall. Immediately after the Fall, God had addressed Adam and Eve, giving them his promise and thereby pledging his covenant.[9] For Bullinger, the Old Testament in particular bore witness that God repeatedly selected humans and spoke to his people. Thus through the 'truth of his word', the 'catholic faith' and 'true worship', called into existence by God, have been preserved by God through all times, despite the faithlessness and disobedience of God's chosen people – and their leader (Second Helvetic Confession: 2010, 849; Zweite Helvetische Bekenntnis: 1936; Bullinger: 2009, 85; 315,ll,13–20). For the 'leaders' of the church have by no means created the church or guaranteed its existence, as the story of Elijah makes clear. The Bible does not recount a history of earthly triumph for the church or the people of God; instead it tells again and again of episodes of falling away and idol worship, during which only a small band continued to hear the Word of God and, thus, to believe. The post-biblical history of the church only repeats that pattern. Not infrequently even political and religious office-holders and representatives of the church have descended into impiety or idolatry, to the extent of persecuting and seeking to eradicate with fire and steel the truly god-fearing who sought the restoration of the church (Heinrich Bullinger: 2004–2007, vol. 5, 99; cf. 95–99). Repeatedly, however, Bullinger explains,

> God has raised up the church, for that church 'also he furnished and repaireth with true teachers whom he sendeth to the same, albeit they be not acknowledged for true ministers and teachers of God's church by those who will seem to be the true and the ordinary governors of the church, but are rather condemned as seditious disturbers of the church and execrable heretics (Bullinger: 1851, 69–70; Bullinger: 2008, vol. 2, 779,ll,25–28; Bullinger: 2004–2007, vol. 5, 95).

In accord with the definition of 'church' with which Bullinger launched the chapter, the human counterpart to God's self-disclosure and saving grace is found not in a particular office or institution but in the living out of daily existence: in knowing, in worshiping rightly, in serving, and in partaking by faith in all the good graces. All this is always mediated by the divine word and the divine spirit, and therefore by God who acts; by contrast, all church tradition is never anything but human tradition.

The accusation that the reformers had destroyed the unity of the church was also tackled in light of this understanding of the church. For Roman theologians the inner-Protestant divisions made all the clearer the schismatic spirit inherent in Protestantism. Yet, they contended, surely unity was a central aspect of the Christian church, required by Christ himself (Eck: 1561, 21). Bullinger countered that the

---

9 The reference is to the protevangelium at the end of Genesis 3:15.

history of the church to date had hardly been marked by such unity. From its very beginnings, the church had seen theological disputes and conflicts. Long before the Reformation, it had been perfectly possible for outstanding doctors of the church to be 'at variance' on 'matters of religion', producing quarrels "maintained not so much in the schools as in the holy chairs, even in the audience of the people". And yet, Bullinger wrote, "the church ceased not to be the church".[10] For Bullinger, that the church, beset by quarrelling and divided over doctrine, had never been abandoned by God was a sign of its deep theological rooting. Thus although Bullinger was certainly some way from justifying disputes within the church theologically – such conflict was to be understood as evidence of human failing and ignorance within the 'church militant' – he located such disagreements within God's providential action: in the final analysis disputes within the church would be used by God "to the glory of His name" (Second Helvetic Confession: 2010, 847; Zweite Helvetische Bekenntnis: 1936, 82) and ultimately truth would emerge. His faith judgement is christologically founded and has an eschatological outlook.

This understanding of the unity of God's church allowed differences to be acknowledges and differentiations to be made. Bullinger named in particular the traditional distinction between the 'church militant' on earth, with enemies both internal and external, and the 'church triumphant', which had left behind such earthly battles. Additionally, he distinguished between, on one hand, the church of the "old people of the covenant" – the chosen people of Israel from before Christ – which is equally 'church' in its fullest theological sense, and, on the other hand, "new people of the covenant", comprising all those who believe in Christ, be they Jews or Gentiles. He also acknowledged that a good number of local and particular churches had laid claim to the designation 'church'. In the end, however, at every time there has been only "one fellowship, one salvation in one and the same Messiah", for the idea of church is based in a single divine resolution.

3. The *Holiness* of the Church and the *Sole Head* of the Church

According to the Second Helvetic Confession, the unity and catholicity of the church were not alone in being rooted in the words and actions of the one God. Above all, the third attribute of the church, its *holiness*, grew from the same source (Zweite Helvetische Bekenntnis: 1936, 79; Bullinger: 2009, 311,ll,23f). For Bullinger, supported by the relevant biblical texts he cited, 'holy' meant participation in Christ

---

10 Second Helvetic Confession: 2010, 847. Eck had to concede this point particularly in relation to the contentious issue of synods, but ultimately he compensated by citing the papacy, which he believed scripturally substantiated, as the guarantor of truth, see Eck: 1561, 46–107.

as a result of election by God and realised through God's sanctifying spirit, and thus being drawn into the acts of the living triune God. 'Holiness' is not an immanent quality of the church but is assigned to the church (only) in as far as the church is in relationship with the triune God.[11] The christological-pneumatological foundations of the church were thus highlighted and the Second Helvetic Confession's characterisation of the 'holiness' of the church transitioned seamlessly into a combination of biblical images and metaphors used to describe the relationship of the church to Christ.

Johannes Eck began his defence of the Roman church with reference to the close relationship between Christ and his church, described in the Letter to the Ephesians, chapters 4 and 5, in particular, tied in with places in the Song of Solomon. There the church is characterised as the 'body' of Christ and as the 'bride' of Christ, subordinate to Christ in everything and yet at the same time as profoundly at one with Christ as is a wife with her husband. The church is "holy and without blemish"; it is "a glorious Church, not having spot or wrinkle", for Christ has made the church holy through his giving of himself.[12] Additionally, looking to established theological tradition reaching back to Augustine (*De Civitate* Dei, 20,9 [CCSL 47–48]), Eck identified the "kingdom of Heaven" that is spoken of in the Gospel of Matthew with the 'church militant', the historical Roman church on earth. The metaphors for the kingdom of heaven in the Gospel of Matthew were to be understood as references to the Roman church, in which God was at work; that church therefore neither could err nor had existed only since Luther (Eck: 1978, 7–9).

While the Second Helvetic Confession does not address this kingdom of God metaphor for the church, which is not given explicitly in Scripture, it does adopt the preceding two biblical metaphors for the church cited by Eck, as the body of Christ and bride of Christ. Bullinger transfers the emphasis, however, from the 'bride' to the 'bridegroom' and from the 'body' to the 'head': the church is 'a virgin', and 'the spouse of Christ' and 'his only beloved'; the church is the 'spiritual body' with Christ as the 'spiritual head' (Second Helvetic Confessio: 2010, 846). In other instances, too, when Eck has cited scriptural references for a theological definition of the church, Bullinger points to their constitutive relationship with Christ. Thus, where Eck cited 1 Tim 3:15 in defining the (Roman) church as "the church of the living God" and as the "pillar and foundation of truth" (Eck: 1978, 9), Bullinger adds as explanation that because the church is built on Christ, it is called "the pillar and foundation of the truth" (Second Helvetic Confession: 2010, 846; Bullinger: 2009, 311,ll,25–28). Drawing together images provided in 1 Tim 3:15, 1 Pet 2:4f, and 1

---

11 "… credimus sanctam esse ecclesiam, id est sanctificatam per deum patrem in sanguine filii et dono spiritus sancti", (Bullinger: 2008, vol. 1, 101,ll,20–25; 102,ll,6–9; see also vol. 2, 740,ll,16–32).

12 Eck: 1978, 7. See also Eph 4:1–16; 5:22–24; 27; Song of Solomon 6:9; 4:12. Both Eck and Bullinger usually drew their scriptural evidence from the Vulgate.

Cor 3:11, he describes the church in Trinitarian terms, as 'the house of the living God' (2 Cor 6:16), "builded of living and spiritual stones" (1 Pet 2:5) "founded upon a rock" (Matt 16:18) "that cannot be removed" (Heb 12:28) "upon a foundation, besides which none can be laid" (1 Cor 3:11)' (Second Helvetic Confession: 2010, 845–846; Zweite Helvetische Bekenntnis: 1936, 79; Bullinger: 2009, 311,ll,23–26). For Bullinger the multiple scriptural images of the church have a common thrust, for they all make clear that the church is entirely dependent on Christ as its only master, the only reason for its being and its continuing to be. Its existence as church is conditional on its exclusive relationship with Christ. The metaphor of the 'body' of Christ is thus entirely a product of the implicit relationship between 'body' and 'head':

> It is the head which has the preeminence in the body, and from whence the whole body receives life; by whose spirit it is governed in all things [...] Also there is but one head of the body which was agreement with the body; and, therefore, the church cannot have any head beside Christ. [...] Neither can it be governed by any other spirit than by the Spirit of Christ (Second Helvetic Confession: 2010, 846; Bullinger: 2009, 312,II,3–8).

That relationships brings us to the associated second ecclesiological topic addressed by the Second Helvetic Confession, and the indubitable core of that ecclesiology: Christ as "the One Only Head of the Church" – an unambiguous assertion from the start, for, as we have seen, it appears in the title to chapter seventeen (Second Helvetic Confession: 2010, 844; Bullinger: 2009, 310,l,10). For Bullinger this issue concerned the very foundations of a Christian doctrine of the church, and this theological conviction therefore not only characterises chapter seventeen as a whole, but also is explicated extensively, with critical reference to positions promoted by Eck and with scriptural corroboration, in the middle section of the chapter. The church's exclusive relationship to Christ was constitutive for the doctrine of the church, for that connection was with the 'head' that gave the church life and enabled redemption.

As a result the higher theological attributes of the church are not simply descriptive, for they form a divine promise and honour-filled invocation "in the name of Christ" to every "company of the faithful" in their particularities and contingencies.[13] That promise and invocation require an appropriate response and have a specific objective, as Bullinger makes evident in his discussion of the *inerrancy* of the (historical) church.[14] According to Eck, "The church does not err, not only because she always has Christ as her Bridegroom, but also because she is ruled by

---

13 Second Helvetic Confession: 2010, 844; for "coetum fidelium" see: Bullinger: 2009, 310,l,15.

14 The inerrancy of the church represented by the (legitimate) council tradition was well known as a central point of conflict in Eck's disputation with Luther at Leipzig. See WA 2, 404.

the teaching authority of the Holy Spirit who never forsakes her". The church can therefore truly be called the "church of the living God" and "pillar and foundation of the truth" (Eck: 1978, 9). According to Bullinger, however, inerrancy cannot be deduced from that profession of divine fidelity, and it cannot be claimed by the historical church as either tradition or organisation. The divine profession of faithfulness is always to be understood as an *address* to God's people and God's church, and thus as an invitation and summons to hear the Word of God and to trust in Christ as the sole foundation of truth, and not in anything else, including the church itself as tradition.[15] The Second Helvetic Confession interprets in this light the biblical metaphors for the church that had been deployed by Eck, and supplements them with additional metaphors that express this dialogical relationship between God and God's people, or God's church. Eck's appeal to biblical metaphors for the Roman church largely ignored that the ecclesiological designations have paraenetic intent, speaking of the *summonsing* of the church, which is viewed in terms of orientation to Christ. The church as an earthly, human community and organisation is called upon in Scripture *to be faithful* as is a 'virgin' to her bridegroom, *to be led* as is the 'body' by the 'head', *to remain sure* on the foundations on which it is constructed, and *to listen truly* to the voice of the shepherd (Second Helvetic Confession: 2010, 848). The church can do otherwise, and therefore is accountable.

Even less in accord with Bullinger's Christological explanation of the church is Eck's proposal that the church has a dual foundation, with the 'militant' church on earth held together and led by an authorised office-holder who is its representative.[16] For Bullinger Christ could have no representative, a concept that he held to be counter to the very nature of the church, for all the biblical metaphors cited testified to a living relationship with Christ, a relationship constituted and animated by Christ himself or by his Spirit. The metaphors speak of a Christ who, in becoming human, being crucified, and rising again, was truly the son of God and the son of man, justified und sanctified the church of the sinner by means of his death, such that the being of the church and its 'holiness' are to be found only in Christ.[17] The spirit of this Christ exists for all time, and therefore is extant and active in his church in the present. This Christ requires no substitute, no one to stand in

---

15 "that does not err, so long as it relies up on the rock Christ, and upon the foundation of the prophets and apostles" (Second Helvetic Confession: 2010, 846); "Non errat illa quandiu (!) innititur petrae Christo et fundamento prophetarum et Apostolorum" (Bullinger: 2009, 311,l,27).

16 "Even if Christ is the chief rock and primary foundation, yet He has vicars and substitutes, secondary rocks" (Eck: 1978, 32).

17 A point explored more extensively by Bullinger in his Decades (see Bullinger: 2008, vol. 2, 792,ll,26–36).

during his absence; Christ "is present in His church, and is the head that gives life thereunto".[18]

Essentially, Bullinger criticised Roman ecclesiology for lacking an adequate Christology, an allegation that he could also make in the case of the ecclesiology of the Anabaptists and 'Gnesio-Lutherans', although it was not formulated as explicitly as in the case of the Roman church. According to Bullinger, in separating themselves from other Christians and in proposing their own human-invented and human-tested criteria for the true church, Anabaptists were denying in effect the power, presence, and sovereignty of the living Christ. And in making a specific understanding of the sacrament into a shibboleth of true Christian faith, Gnesio-Lutheran theologians were also shifting the balance, in denigrating the centrality of the living Christ as head of the church and the significance of proclamation and faith.

But how can order in the form, for example, of unity, continuity, and identity be created and safeguarded for a historical, finite, and human gathering and community that understands itself as 'church' when the earthly authority bound to represent that 'church' not only fails to guarantee but even denies the essence of the true church of God, and therefore disavows the true unity of the 'church' itself. If the 'church' lacks a figure to represent it as an entity in the present day, is it nothing more than an idea, a 'mathematical' church very far from that which the Apostle Paul doubtlessly envisaged?[19] Or perhaps that church inevitably will disintegrate into a multiplicity of Christian sects and gatherings, each of which will claim that it stands for Christian truth, turning the confession of a 'single' church of God into nothing more than a delusion.

4. The Marks of the Church

Very aware of this potential splintering as a fundamental challenge for any talk of a Christian 'church', Bullinger made his third theme the "marks and tokens" of the (true) church (Second Helvetic Confession: 2010, 848). An essential definition in the background of this explication of the ecclesiology of the Second Helvetic Confession now moves centre stage: the distinction between the 'visible' and 'invisible' church. In upholding Roman ecclesiology Johannes Eck had stood for the inseparability of the spiritual church authored by God and the institutional papal church. He had criticised the Reformation idea of a church essentially hidden from the human eye

---

18 Second Helvetic Confession: 2010, 846. See the broad exposition and debate with Eck in the Decades (Bullinger: 2008, vol. 2, 790–793).

19 "Let Luther say whether they were hidden and only mathematically the Church, when Paul said: 'Now you are the body of Christ, and members each in his part'" (Eck: 1978, 16; Eck: 1561, 35).

as evidence of Docetism and sectarianism.[20] For Eck the 'spiritual' and true church of God was tied constitutively to the 'visible' church given concrete form in the Roman episcopal tradition. With the reverse also the case, biblical texts that use the term 'church' or 'community' were to be understood directly in relation to this Roman episcopal tradition. By contrast, Luther had already distinguished between a spiritual and inner Christendom, for which the term 'church' in its true sense is used in the Bible, and a bodily and external Christendom, to which all those whose external appearance suggests they are Christian belong, including popes, cardinals, bishops, prelates, monks and nuns ('Vom Papsttum zu Rom wider den hochberühmten Romanisten zu Leipzig', 1520, WA 6, 295ff). Zwingli had gone a step further and, surely encouraged by his reading of Augustine, had made the distinction between the 'visible' and 'invisible' church a primary ecclesiological categorisation.[21] He described the 'invisible' church as a product of God's self-presentation and formed of the community of the faithful illuminated by the spirit of God and awoken to love of God and neighbour. For Zwingli the 'visible' church was certainly formed not of the splendour-relishing representatives of an institutional church, but simply of all humans who deemed themselves Christians and confessed Christ.[22]

Bullinger drew on Zwingli's distinction between the 'visible' and 'invisible' church for the Second Helvetic Confession, although the terms themselves are used only once in chapter seventeen.[23] He ties his characterisation to the 'marks' (*notae*) of the church as found in the Confession of Augsburg of 1530, for the designation as 'church' cannot be brandished at will along with a claim to be recognised as the true

20 "Because the supreme authority, which we contemplate in councils and in the Apostolic See, is within the Church, it is fitting that we briefly affirm the primacy of the Roman Pontiff and of Peter" (Eck: 1978, 28; Eck: 1561, 57). "Item die kirch ist der leyb Christi / und die Christen seind dy gelider / nun sag mir Luther oder Rotenacker / ob die auch verborgen seind gewesen / und allain ain fantaseiische Kirch zuo denen Paulus sagt: Ir seyt der leyb Christi" (Eck: 1533, 9).

21 "Credimus et unam sanctam esse catholicam, hoc est universalem ecclesiam. Eam autem esse aut visibilem aut invisibilem. Invisibilem est iuxta Pauli verbum, quae coelo descendit hoc est quae spiritu sancto illustrante deum cognoscit et amplectitur. De ista ecclesia sunt, quotquot per universum orbem credunt. Vocatur autem invisibilis, non quas, qui credunt, sint invisibiles, sed quot humanis oculis non patet, quinam credant; sint enim fideles soli deo et sibi perspecti. Visibilis autem ecclesia est non pontifex Romanus cum reliquis cidarum gestantibus, sed quotquot per universum orbem Christo nomen dederunt" (Zwingli: 1991, 108,l,12–110,l,6).

22 "Breviter: spiritus, ubi vult, spirat, hoc est: sic flat ventus, ut fert ingenium, et vocem eius quidem audis, sed nescis, unde oriatur aut ubi sidat. Sic est omnis, qui nascitur ex spiritu [see John 3:8], hoc est: invisibiliter et insensibiliter illustratur ac trahitur [see John 6:44]", (Zwingli: 1983, 803,ll,22–26).

23 "Whereupon the church of God may be termed invisible: not that the men whereof it consists are invisible; but because, being hidden from our sight, and known only unto God, ti cannot be discerned without the judgment of man" (Second Helvetic Confession: 2010, 849; Bullinger: 2009, 315,ll,20–23).

church. A 'true' church, realised by divine election and ruled by Christ as its 'head' – here Bullinger was referring to the 'invisible' church – can be recognised, however, by certain minimal phenomena, characteristics or marks: the pure preaching of the Gospel and the correct administration of the sacraments.[24] In his interpretation of the two marks of the true church as they appeared in the Confession of Augsburg, Bullinger made very evident his 'reformed' ecclesiological credentials. While fundamentally agreeing with Melanchthon's 'Lutheran' designations, he approached them from the standpoint of his own position on the 'Word of God'. Where the Confession of Augsburg placed preaching and the sacraments on a par, as the two distinct marks of the church, Bullinger ranked these same marks, with preaching the superior mark of the true church. He immediately qualified preaching more closely in light of its substance, speaking of an address with specific foundations and clear, fixed intent. His concern here was not with the address given from the pulpit during worship per se, but rather with the proclamation of Christ such that word of Christ himself was heard:

> First and chiefly, the lawful or sincere preaching of the Word of God, as it is left unto us in the writings of the prophets and apostles, which all seem to lead us unto Christ, who in the gospel has said, 'My sheep hear My voice, and I know them, and they follow Me; and I give unto them eternal life. A stranger they do not hear, but flee from him, because they know not his voice' (John 10:5, 27–28) (Second Helvetic Confession: 2010, 848; Zweite Helvetische Bekenntnis: 1936, 82; Bullinger: 2009, 314,ll,3–9).

According to Bullinger's position, only Christ himself can be the sole subject matter for true Christian preaching and must be the objective of its scriptural exegesis. The goal of all proper biblical exegesis and preaching must be that Christ's own voice is heard, that Christ the subject who is proclaimed also speaks himself. Here then is the import of the much-cited marginal comment from the first chapter of the Second Helvetic Confession that records, *Praedicatio verbi dei est verbum dei* [the preaching of the word of God is the Word of God] (Bullinger: 2009, 273,l,28), a statement that is so much more than a neat identification of a sermon given from the pulpit with the Word of God. Later in life, Luther drew criticism from Bullinger precisely for ascribing too much to the human word in preaching. Just like the sacraments, the sermon is by no means simply a vehicle for the Holy Spirit (Zwingli: 1983, 803,10f). The congruence of the visible church, as a gathered, local community of people, and the invisible church, the church of God called into being through the work of the divine spirit, is therefore not to be taken as a matter of course, as simply endowed

---

24 "Est autem ecclesia congregatio sanctorum, in qua evangelium pure docetur et recte administrantur sacramenta" (Bekenntnisschriften: 1979, 61,ll,2–6).

on a specific historic and contingent Christian tradition.[25] That congruence is conditional. Like the division between the spirit and the flesh for the human, the distinction between the 'visible' and 'invisible' church is not to be confused with the distinction between materiality and spirituality. Bullinger, following on from Zwingli, makes clear that the church is not termed 'invisible' because the people are invisible (Second Helvetic Confession: 2010, 849), but because their being drawn to God does not grow out of their human, or even 'religious', capacity or tradition, but is granted to them only "from heaven", as a free, undeserved gift of God's own Spirit (Zwingli: 1983, 108,l,11–110,l,6). 'Invisible' church means 'true' church, a creation of the Holy Spirit.

Bullinger can certainly acknowledge the historical significance of the succession in office, raised by Eck, for the early church. But that succession by no means guarantees the uninterrupted presence of the truth, for just as false prophets can exist and have existed, so too can false bishops exist. Without the Word of God, which is the sole criterion, even the most impressive tradition is nothing more than a great array of idols (See Bullinger: 2008, vol. 2, 755,ll,13–33). For that reason, Bullinger recorded in the Second Helvetic Confession,

> we condemn all such churches as strangers from the true church of Christ, who are not such as we have heard they ought to be; howsoever, in the meantime, they brag of the succession of bishops, of unity, and of antiquity (Second Helvetic Confession: 2010, 848; Bullinger: 2009, 314,ll,20–23).

How, then, can we discern – or how is 'visible' – that the voice of Christ, and not just that of the pastor, is really present and heard in the church?, a question that points to the nerve point of Bullinger's teaching on the marks of the church. Bullinger's answer is that the church is not to be found simply anywhere Christ is spoken of or anywhere certain Christian rites and rituals are performed. 'True' church is found where a community listens to Christ's words and puts them into practice.

This response, at first glance simple, is in accord with Bullinger's definition of church given at the beginning of the chapter, where he wrote of this exclusive 'hearing' of the voice of Christ and its experiential results both for the church as the community of the faithful and for the actions of the faithful. Everything that is to be spoken of as church flows from this hearing of the voice of Christ.

---

25 See, for instance, "Die sichtbare Kirche ist vom Herrn als sakramentales Symbol der Gottesherrschaft der Geschichte eingestiftet worden [...] Daher muss sie vom Menschen als Ja zu dieser Gottesh- errschaft anerkannt und die Gliedschaft an der Kirche als Leben unter Gottes Herrschaft und im Lebensbereich seines gnädigen Heilswillens verstanden und vollzogen warden" (Semmelroth: 1972, 334).

And they that are such in the church of God [those who hear the voice of Christ the shepherd] have all but one faith and one Spirit; and, therefore, they worship but one God: and Him alone they serve in spirit and in truth, loving Him with all their hearts and with all their strength, praying unto Him alone through Jesus Christ the only mediator and intercessor; and they seek not life or justice but only in Christ, and by faith in Him: because they acknowledge Christ the only head and foundation of His church, and, being surely founded on Him, daily repair themselves by repentance and with patience bear the cross laid upon them; and besides, by unfeigned love joining themselves to all the members of Christ, they declare themselves to be the disciples of Christ, by continuing in the bond of peace and holy unity (Second Helvetic Confession: 2010, 848; Bullinger: 2009, 314,ll,7–17).

The crucial points of this packed passage should be underscored: the hearing of the voice of Christ, the only shepherd – the word 'solus' appears no fewer than nine times in this passage – leads automatically to veneration and love of the one triune God, which in turn is only possible through participation in Christ's life (in Spirit), which implies recognition of Christ as the only mediator of salvation and the only agent of righteousness and love. When in a church worship of God takes the form of hearing the voice of Christ, then that worship is founded on Christ, the sole foundation, and all the characteristics of the church recorded in this passage take shape of their own accord: from the *one* faith thus understood stems the veneration of the *one* God, from which comes a life of repentance,[26] Christian discipleship, readiness to suffer, patience, and true love for *all* fellow Christians as members of a single body.[27]

We can construe that what thus takes shape, notwithstanding all enduring differences and distinctions, is the reality and experience of the *one* church of God. That church is constituted through the life and actions of those who gather to form a visible community in the name of Christ, behaviour that is attended by invocation of the 'invisible' church and that is 'visible' and 'experiential' in relation to cult and doxology and, equally, in relation to confession, doctrine, order, organisation, and actions both internal and external. Communal worship based on the proclamation of the Word and the celebration of the sacraments is without doubt at the heart of the 'visible' church. In such a gathering the divine word is heard by those who have come together, in their listening to Scripture read, in their appeals to God in prayer, in their confessions of sin, in their communal celebration of the sacraments,

---

26 Not by chance, penance is foremost. Penance is not a religious work, but rather in turning one's existence towards God – and thus 'listening' to him – the necessary first step for a Christian life. For Bullinger, ultimately 'faith' und 'repentance' are two sides of the same coin (see chapter 14 of the Second Helvetic Confession).

27 In essence this line of thinking could already be found in Zwingli's 'Theses' of January 1523 and in their exposition, for which see Zwingli: 1908, 52–73.

and in their giving of the collection. But the life of the church is not limited to such celebration in worship, and accordingly the marks of the church are also not limited to worship. Wherever a Christian church listens in all seriousness to the voice of Christ, for whom that church is named, in its love for fellow Christians as members of the same body and its striving for peace and unity, that church, according to Bullinger, becomes concrete and visible, whatever the concomitant plurality within the one 'body' of Christ.

As laid out in the Second Helvetic Confession, the decisive marks of the true church are thus not phenomena that can be taken as simple facts. Rather, Bullinger addresses Spirit-animated faith in Christ and human behaviour fashioned by the Spirit of Christ: church happens where humans are moved from deep within by the divine Spirit and are set in motion by that Spirit such that the Spirit is essential to and manifest in their beliefs, attitudes and visible deeds. God is thus to be worshipped "in Spirit and truth" (Bullinger: 2008, vol. 2, 605,ll,19–33). For Bullinger, therefore, the marks of the 'true' church are not found simply in liturgical forms or doctrinal statements, but instead, and above all, are experienced in human behaviour, inter-actions and exchanges. In his *Decades* Bullinger explicitly differentiated between the 'internal' marks of the church, with the divine Spirit at work in and through humankind, and the 'external' marks of the church, with the word proclaimed and the sacraments celebrated. And he makes very clear that ultimately the internal marks, not the external marks, determine whether the true church – the 'invisible' church is present 'in' a 'visible' Christian congregation and community (Bullinger: 2008, vol. 2, 751,ll,22–29).

The explosive force of this ecclesiology only really became evident in the context of confessional theological polemics and of the political conflicts of the 1560s, which did not rule out a military option. According to the Second Helvetic Confession, Jesus's disciples prove that they truly are his disciples in that "by unfeigned love joining themselves to all the members of Christ, they declare themselves to be the disciples of Christ, by continuing in the bond of peace and holy unity".[28]

Only now does the Second Helvetic Confession turn to the sacraments as a mark of the church – having first dealt with the primary sign of the true church, the preaching of the Word of God that leads to the Word's being heard,[29] and

---

28 Second Helvetic Confession: 2010, 848. In the preface to the Second Helvetic Confession Bullinger had already named interconfessional peace and mutual recognition as the central concern of the confession (Bullinger: 2009, 269,ll,30–37).

29 Bullinger's understanding of office is not discussed in detail here. We should note, however that the status, dignity and limits of ecclesiastical office are in accord with this ecclesiology, including its teaching on the three-stage marks: with the hearing of the word of God alone constituting the church, the only ecclesiastical office is the office of the word, which is to be carefully defined in light of its pairing with the community as part of the community (cf. Opitz: 2004, 81–108).

having then provided a broad explication of the 'hearing' of the word as 'life in the Spirit', characterised by faith, love, and peace amongst Christians. Set within this ecclesiological reframing, the discussion of the sacraments turns not on their administration (*administratio*) as a ritual act performed by those who hold ecclesiastical office but on participation (*participatio*) in their celebration. As 'sacramental signs' proffered by God and as 'appendages' (*adiuncta*) to the divine Word, the sacraments belong in the realm of the 'visible' church, whose particular task is to take visible action in community that will lead to the invisible Spiritual community with Christ, constituted by the divine Spirit alone and made reality only through faith (Bullinger: 2009, 323,ll,14–23; 326,ll,12–14).

But what of the idea that there is no salvation outside the church (cf. Denzinger, 1351), an expression that went back to Cyprian of Carthage (Cyprianus: 1871, Epistula 73,21,2 [CSEL 3/2: 795]) and had been affirmed as official church doctrine at the Council of Florence in 1442? Eck bound that statement in with the teachings on the indissoluble bond between the 'visible' and 'invisible' church, the 'body of Christ', and Roman episcopal tradition and arrived at the exclusivity of the papal church. But are the limits of a Christian historical tradition also the limits of the divine Spirit? Amongst the reformers, Zwingli led the way in questioning this assumption and insisted that the Spirit of God– as the spirit of Christ – must be attributed a broader, and ultimately universal, sphere of action. Bullinger was in a position to defend Zwingli's controversial statements, but he did not repeat them. That the freedom of the divine spirit also extended to the relationship with the church on earth as Zwingli emphasised was also fundamental for Bullinger, as our earlier discussion has made evident. He was therefore able to agree with Cyprian's statement as long as it was understood in reference to the invisible church and not the visible church: being outside the church is then not a reference to there being no salvation outside the visible church but to there being no salvation outside Christ (Second Helvetic Confession: 2010, 848–849). If the presence of the living spirit of Christ constitutes the church of God, then the boundaries of that church are not staked out by human teachings, offices, or rites, but are established by God's unbound election and action (Bullinger: 2008, vol. 2, 769,13–18). And so, while for Bullinger deliberate distain for the sacraments, established and made holy by God (Bullinger: 2009, 323,l,17; 327,l,19; 229,ll,13–22), is incompatible with Christian faith, at the same time, participation in the sacraments is not necessary for salvation, for such participation is not possible for all Christians. And additionally, even those "in whom faith sometimes fails, though not quite decay, nor altogether die" and those "in whom some slips and errors of infirmity may be found" can certainly belong to the true church. As the Old Testament makes clear, God "had some friends in the world that were not of the commonwealth of Israel". Bullinger's references here are to the Babylonian Captivity, Peter's denial, and the lamentable circumstances in the earliest church as documented by the Pauline epistles.

Bullinger is able to adopt this position because he has grounded the church in a theology of election and in a Christological spirit. Those roots have another consequence too, for they suggest that the presence of phenomena is not sufficient to serve as evidence of the presence of the thing itself: participation in preaching and the sacraments can be for show only; confession of Christ and love can both be feigned. And as a third implication, no human can or should judge the faith of any other human, and thus rule on the latter's membership of the true church (Bullinger: 2009, 315,ll,24–38), an idea already voiced by Zwingli (Zwingli: 1983, 800, 25f), but given particular weight in the Second Helvetic Confession. The limits of the true church of Christ cannot be perceived by humans. Again, once located in the context of contemporary confessional conflict and condemnation, a simple reference to a passage in Scripture, here the parable of the separation of the chaff from the wheat found in the gospel of Matthew, gains immediacy: at the conclusion of his discussion of the characteristics of the true church, Bullinger emphasises, "we judge not rashly before the time, nor go about to exclude and cast off or cut away those whom the Lord would not have excluded not cut off, or whom, without some damage to the church, we cannot separate from it".[30]

The limited status that Bullinger allows the hallmarks of the church, in that they remain simply 'signs' (*Zeichen*) is a direct consequence of his rooting of the church in the theology of election. The true church is ultimately the work of God alone and is known only to God, and as all humans are imperfect in terms of both their faith and their capacity to judge. Faith and love demand that we conclude that if the visible marks of the church are present, the true church is present too, although the presence of the latter does not require the presence of the former.

This position raises a topic that the Second Helvetic Confession addresses twice, in chapter 17 as well as in chapter 18, which is on the servants of the church, on both occasions with reference to the passage in Matthew at 13:24–30, the parable of the Wheat and the Tares. That topic is excommunication, which is tackled in light of the evangelical understanding of the 'keys' and of the authority exercised by the "servant of the Word" (Second Helvetic Confession: 2010, 856; cf. 855–856). Bullinger's approach to excommunication is entirely in accord with his position on ecclesiology. He not only returns to the purpose of all that the church does – "all things ought to be done to edification, decently, and honestly" (Second Helvetic Confession: 2010, 858, citing 1 Cor. 14:40) – and warns of new tyrannies exercised under the banner of the "divine word", but he also challenges the exegetical legitimacy of the

---

30 Second Helvetic Confession: 2010, 850. Bullinger's great reticence on the subject of excommunication is the flipside of his irenical-ecumenical ecclesiology, which understands the church primarily as the 'body' of Christ, given life and set in motion by the Spirit of Christ, in which mutual love and acknowledgement, despite differences, are naturally integral to the fact of being governed by the head. His christological ecclesiology both underpins and buttresses that position.

combination of Matt 16:18f; 18:15–19 and 1 Cor 5 claimed e.g. by Calvin as grounds for excommunication. Instead Bullinger assigns authority over excommunication to the whole community.[31]

Accordingly, for Bullinger the evangelical preaching office only continues the Roman 'office of the keys' in the sense that its preaching *points* to reconciliation with God, who unlocks himself. The 'opening' and, in particular, the 'shutting' of the kingdom of heaven take place not through ecclesiastical office or ecclesiastical authority, but as the word is heard, in light of faith or its absence. The authority of preaching stems from its subject matter, with the preacher's own contribution in exercising the office of the keys limited to 'announcing' (*annunciare*) the gospel and calling to faith and repentance (Second Helvetic Confession: 2010, 836–837). Correct account of the theological significance of the office of the word is only possible when its responsibilities and its limits are seen in terms of the Word of God and the Spirit of God.[32] The office has function and value beyond the 'priesthood of all believers people', but ultimately it has no competency and authority in relation to the community; on the contrary, for Bullinger the authority of those who hold ecclesiastical office lies in serving, not ruling, which is why they are to be designated 'servants'. This understanding of church and office is in line with a collegial model of church leadership. Drawing on Cyprian and Jerome, Bullinger interpreted any earlier superordering of offices by the church an emergency measure rather than an ideal, for originally the apostles had "an equal fellowship with [Peter] both in honor and power" and "the churches were governed by the common advice of the elders" (Second Helvetic Confession: 2010, 857). And so too in the church reformed according to the Word of God, 'the power or function that is given to the ministers of the church is the same and alike in all'.[33] For Bullinger the highest authority within the church rests therefore with the synod, whose task it is to examine the teachings and behaviour of the servants of the church and to admonish them; if they are 'incurable' they must "be deposed, and, as wolves, be driven from the Lord's flock by the true pastors" (Second Helvetic Confession: 2010, 858–859; Bullinger: 2009, 322,l,42–323,l,1).

---

31 "Disciplina ecclesiastica, est increpatio vel castigatio ac correctio, quae ab ecclesia vel membris ecclesiae fit …", (Bullinger, 'Tractatus de excommunicatione', cited from Baker: 1975, 147). On this point see Büsser: 2004, 284–288.

32 "Cura ecclesiarum et functio docendi, increpandi, adhortandi et compellandi, adeoque conservandi ecclesiam in ordine recto, adque ducendi eam per viam veritatis in regnum coelorum" (Bullinger, 'Tractatus de excommunicatione', cited from Baker: 1975, 152).

33 "Certainly, in the beginning, the bishops or elders did, with a common consent and labor, govern the church; no man lifted himself above another" (Second Helvetic Confession: 2010, 856).

5. The Challenge and Contribution of the Second Helvetic Confession to Christian Ecclesiology

In entitling the Second Helvetic Confession's chapter on ecclesiology 'Of the Catholic and Holy Church of God, and of the One Only Head of the Church' (*De catholica et sancta Dei Ecclesia et unico capite Ecclesiae*) (Second Helvetic Confession: 2010, 844; Bullinger: 2009, 310,l,12), Bullinger adopted a radical theological perspective on the traditional attributes of the Christian church: the doctrine of the (true) church is the doctrine of the triune God who elects, sanctifies and rules over his people, who live in different ages and places, thereby unifying them invisibly with him and with each other. This, according to Bullinger, is the necessary starting point of a Christian ecclesiology, not the historical or sociological phenomenon called 'church', which is always a human tradition. Every Christian tradition, organisation and congregation must live up to its origins. It is to be measured by how seriously it takes this basic tenet of its own existence and legitimacy, or, in other words, by the extent to which, beyond creeds and confessional texts used in the liturgy, its organisation and life reflect and honour the triune God who calls the church into existence, who is its only head and who creates it as a living, spiritual 'body' of Christ.

The dependency of the 'body' on the 'head', that is the dependency of the Christian community on Christ and his spirit, is then the essential criterion for 'church'. While this exclusive constitutive reference to Christ is critical for all Christian communities and traditions, it also provides an irenic starting point for ecumenical discussions and for approaching the multiple forms of Christianity. Recognition that the church has no head other than Christ and as a result can be ruled only by the spirit of Christ (Second Helvetic Confession: 2010, 851; Bullinger: 2009, 312,ll,3–8) implies consciousness of dependence on the spirit of God. This spirit, we know, blows where it pleases (John 3:8). Acknowledging the freedom of the Holy Spirit, we must understand all human Christian organisation and tradition as relative – 'relative' in its etymological sense of not containing the thing itself (as the church must recognise in its own case, and express consistently in word and deed!) but also 'relative' in its being in relationship with the thing, a relationship constituted by God's call and humankind's response. A space for mutual recognition of historical forms of church is thus created, within which positions adopted by individual confessional traditions but in accord with Scripture can be deemed to have been prompted by the Spirit and must be respected accordingly.

At the same time, for Bullinger the church is no 'civitas platonica', a mere theological idea. Church is always a concrete tradition, congregation and organisation with offices and leaders occupying specific times and spaces; it consists of people who 'listen' to Christ's word. As a consequence, he agrees with the two minimal marks of the church mentioned in the Augsburg Confession: pure preaching of the Gospel and the celebration of the sacraments – insofar they are understood as two forms of listening to God's word. Although the proclamation of Christ and the celebration of the sacraments do not as such guarantee the confluence of the 'visible' locally realised human community and the 'invisible' church called into being by the spirit of God, they are indispensable and necessary. Preaching and sacraments can become the focus of the visible, and thus publically recognisable church, but in Bullinger's eyes the 'visible' church includes much more, as an human organisation responsible for teaching and education, exercising caring duties, and tasked with administration and financial oversight. And he does not conceal his conviction that a synodal, congregational structure of the 'visible' church is more likely to do justice to Christ, confessed as its only head.

But church as the body of Christ is to be reduced neither to the church service and its liturgical acts nor to a temporal organisation. Unlike other contemporary confessional texts, the Second Helvetic Confession takes into account the whole life of a Christian community, which is to listen to Christ as its 'head' and be animated and driven by Christ's holy spirit. Church should be experienced not just in terms of liturgy and doctrine, but also, and in particular, in light of human lives, interaction and exchange. As a consequence of the unity of the 'invisible' church of the one God, unity, which is experienced as confraternity, as 'brotherly' love, is an essential 'mark' of the church, as can be seen everywhere in the New Testament. This 'mark' is not found in the structures of the 'visible' church, but is first and foremost a matter of respect and love of others, of those who claim also to be members of the one church of God.

The Second Helvetic Confession points to what might be termed a dialectial dynamic between the 'visible' church and the 'invisible' church: confessing the one 'invisible' church leads to concrete forms of community, organisation and member behaviour which are 'visible' and can be experienced in space and time. At the same time, the principal task of all these 'visible' forms and features of church is to point to the 'invisible' church of the triune God as the church's sole grounds for existence. As a consequence, Bullinger's doctrine of the church is more than a description of either the 'invisible' church or the 'visible' church; his position has a parenetic dimension, for it is an admonition to become 'true' church – by listening to Christ alone.

Bibliography

Sources

BEKENNTNISSCHRIFTEN (1979), Die Bekenntnisschriften der evangelisch-lutherischen Kirche, 8th ed., D. Kapler (ed.), Göttingen: Vandenhoeck & Ruprecht,

Bibel (1537), Bibel. Alt vnd new Testament nach dem Text in der hailigen kirchen gebraucht / durch doctor Johann Ecken / mit fleiß/ auf hohteutsch / verdolmetscht. M.D.XXXVII. Augsburg: Alexander I. Weißenhorn, Ingolstadt: Georg Krapf, http://gateway-bayern.de/VD16+B+2702.

Heinrich Bullinger (1851), The Decades of Henry Bullinger, Minister of the Church of Zurich: The Fifth Decade, Thomas Harding (ed.), Cambridge: Cambridge University Press.

Heinrich Bullinger (2004–2007), Heinrich Bullinger Schriften, 7 vols., Emidio Campi/Detlef Roth/Peter Stotz (ed.), Zürich: Theologischer Verlag Zürich.

Heinrich Bullinger (2008), Sermonum Decades quinque, de potissimis Christianae religionis capitibus (1552), Peter Opitz (ed.), in: Heinrich Bullinger, Heinrich Bullinger Werke, vol. 3: Theologische Schriften, Emidio Campi (ed.), Zürich: Theologischer Verlag Zürich.

Heinrich Bullinger (2009), Confessio Helvetica posterior, Emidio Campi (ed.), in: Reformierte Bekenntnisschriften, im Auftrag der EKD, vol. 2/2, Andreas Mühling/Peter Opitz (ed.), Neukirchen-Vluyn: Neukirchener Verlag, 243–345.

Cyprianus (1871), Opera omnia. Pars 2: Epistulae, W. Hartel (ed.), CSEL 3/2, Vienna: Geroldi Filium Bibliopolam Academiae.

Johann Eck (1978), Enchiridion of Commonplaces of John Eck against Luther and Other Enemies of the Church, Ford Lewis Battles (trans.), Grand Rapids: Calvin Theological Seminary.

Johannes Eck (1533), Enchiridion. Handbüchlin gemainer stell unnd Artickel der jetzt schwebeden Newen leer, Augsburg/facsimile Münster 1980.

Johannes Eck (1561), Enchiridion locorum communium adversus Lutherum et alios hostes ecclesiae libellus, Coloniae: Peter Horst, http://gateway-bayern.de/VD16+E+355.

Schindler, Alfred/Schneider-Lastin, Wolfram/Jung, Martin H./Murner, Thomas (2015), Die Badener Disputation von 1526. Kommentierte Edition des Protokolls, Zürich: Theologischer Verlag Zürich.

Second Helvetic Confession (2010), The Second Helvetic Confession (1566), in: Reformed Confession of the 16th and 17th Centuries in English Translation, vol. 2: 1552–1566, James T. Dennison Jr. (ed.), Grand Rapids (Mich.): Reformation Heritage Books, 809–881.

Zweite Helvetische Bekenntnis (1936), Das Zweite Helvetische Bekenntnis. Confessio Helvetica posterior. Verfasst von Heinrich Bullinger, Walter Hildebrandt/Rudolf Zimmermann (trans.), Zürich: Zwingli Verlag.

Huldreich Zwingli (1908), Huldreich Zwinglis sämtliche Werke. Band 2: Werke 1523, Emil Egli e.a. (ed.), CR 89, Berlin: Schwetscke.

Huldreich Zwingli (1983), Huldreich Zwinglis sämtliche Werke. Band 6.3: Werke von August bis November 1530, Emil Egli e.a. (ed.), CR 93.3, Zürich: Theologischer Verlag Zürich.

Huldreich Zwingli (1991), Huldreich Zwinglis sämtliche Werke. Band 6.5: Werke von

Sommer bis Herbst 1531, Nachträge zu den Werken und Briefen, Emil Egli e.a. (ed.), CR 93.5, Zürich: Theologischer Verlag Zürich.

Secundary Liturature

GARCÍA ARCHILLA, AURELIO A. (1992), The Theology of History and Apologetic Historiography in Heinrich Bullinger: Truth in History, San Francisco: Edwin Mellen Press.

BAKER, J. WAYNE (1975), In Defense of Magisterial Discipline: Bullinger's Tractatus de excommunicatione of 1568, in: Ulrich Gäbler/Erland Herkenrath (ed.), Heinrich Bullinger: 1504–1575: gesammelte Aufsätze zum 400. Todestag, Zürich: Theologischer Verlag Zürich, 141–159.

BÜSSER, FRITZ (2004), Heinrich Bullinger (1504–1575). Band 2: Leben, Werk und Wirkung, Zürich: Theologischer Verlag Zürich.

KOCH, ERNST (1968), Die Theologie der Confessio Helvetica Posterior, Neukirchen-Vluyn: Neukirchener Verlag.

LINDE, SIMON VAN DER (1966), Die Lehre von der Kirche in der Confessio Helvetica Posterior, in: J. Staedtke (ed.), Glauben und Bekennen: 400 Jahre Confessio Helvetica Posterior: Beiträge zu ihrer Geschichte und Theologie, Zürich: Zwingli Verlag, 337–367.

CHRISTIAN MOSER (2007), Die Evidenz der Historie: zur Genese, Funktion und Bedeutung von Heinrich Bullingers Universalgeschichtsschreibung, in: Emidio Campi/Peter Opitz (ed.), Heinrich Bullinger: Life – Thought – Influence. Zurich, Aug. 25–29, 2004. International Congress Heinrich Bullinger (1504–1575), Zürich: Theologischer Verlag Zürich, 2007.

OPITZ, PETER (2004), Das Amt und die Ämter – eine Erinnerung an die Anfänge der reformierten Ämterlehre, in: Cla Reto Famos/Ingolf U. Dalferth (ed.), Das Recht der Kirche. Zur Revision der Zürcher Kirchenordnung, Zürich: Theologischer Verlag Zürich, 81–108.

SEMMELROTH O. (1972), Die Kirche als Sakrament des Heiles, in: MySal 4.1.

Frank Ewerszumrode

The Church as a Sign and Instrument of God's Grace

Sacramental Ecclesiology in Calvin and in *Lumen Gentium*

To call the Church a sacrament was not common in Roman Catholic theology for centuries. It gained popularity the middle of the 20th century. Before that notions like *societas perfecta* or *Corpus Christi mysticum* dominated ecclesiology. They seemed to be apt for rejecting what was to be believed as the Protestant invisibility of the Church. To underline the visibility of the Church was the main issue of Post-Reformation Roman Catholic ecclesiology. This focus even led to an initial rejection of the ecclesiological use of the terms sacrament/mysterium among the Council Fathers (cf. Grillmeier: 1966, 156–209; 156). The Second Vatican Council, however, went finally back to patristic traditions and described the Church as a sacrament, although some bishops at the Council felt uneasy with this term (cf. Hünerman: 2004, 263–563; 354). Despite all that, the Dogmatic Constitution of the Church *Lumen Gentium*, 1 speaks about the Church in terms of sacrament:

> Christ is the Light of nations. […] Since the Church is in Christ like a sacrament or as a sign and instrument both of a very closely knit union with God and of the unity of the whole human race, it desires now to unfold more fully to the faithful of the Church and to the whole world its own inner nature and universal mission.

Protestant theologians have great difficulties with this kind of ecclesiology. They fear the Church to be somehow a mediator between God and God's people when the Church is called a sacrament (cf. Sattler: 2013, 91). Michael Beintker summarizes Protestant hesitancy concerning the sacramentality of the church:

> When the Church puts herself on the same level with her origin or even identifies with it, faith in the Church is in danger of outstripping faith in Christ. In this case, one blurs the essential Reformation distinction between what God (and *only* God) does and what humans do.[1]

---

1 "Wenn sich die Kirche mit ihrem Grund auf eine Stufe stellt oder gar identifiziert, wird sie soteriologisch und sakramental so überhöht, dass der Glaube an die Kirche dem Glauben an Christus den Rang abzulaufen droht. Die für die reformatorische Theologie zentrale Unterscheidung, zwischen dem, was Gott (und nur Gott) tut, und dem, was Menschen tun, wird dann unscharf" (Beintker: 2010, 45–59; 55).

It seems that Catholic ecclesiology seems to ascribe too much to the Church from a Protestant point of view. The consequence would be that the Church claims to do what God alone is capable of doing.

This paper argues that the sacramentality of the Church needn't be an obstacle in ecumenical dialogue. Rather, the contrary is the case because calling the Church a sacrament safeguards the typical Reformation issues concerning ecclesiology, i.e. the difference between God and the Church. To underline this thesis, the ecclesiology of John Calvin and the meaning of 'sacrament' in LG 1:8 are analysed. At the end, both views are compared. As Calvin's ecclesiology in particular has a great ecumenical potential, his position has been chosen in this paper.

1. Calvin's sacramental view of the Church

The Church plays an important role in Calvin's theology. The classical texts about the Church can be found in the fourth book of his *Institutes of Christian Religion* which is "about the outward means or tools by which God invites us into the fellowship with Christ and preserves us in it".[2] This part of the *Institutes* deals with the church and the sacraments.

In Calvin studies, there is a debate on the understanding of 'tool', in particular in the doctrine of the sacraments. Does God act through created things or do they only designate his agency? This discussion goes back until the debate between Charles Hodge (1797–1878) and John W. Nevin (1803–1886) about the authentic Reformed understanding of Christ's real presence in the Lord's Supper (cf. Mathison: 2002, 134–156). However, 'symbol' and 'tool' are not metaphors in Calvin's theology. They all do have a realistic meaning, especially symbol.[3] Although the outward means have only a secondary role they can be used by God. The last aspect can be called the invisible and inward dimension of the outward symbols. God uses the outer means used even to confer grace[4] although this never happens by their own natural power but by the Holy Spirit. Calvin, thus, understands the sacraments not just as mere signs, but rather as symbols by which the signified thing is exhibited (cf. Ewerszumrode: 2012, 88–98; 154–180). When Calvin counts the Church among

---

2 "DE EXTERNIS MEDIIS vel adminiculis, quibus Deus in Christi societatem nos invitat, et in ea retinet" (Calvin, *Institutes*, 4 [OS 5:1]).

3 Cf. e.g. "non ideo tantum signo imponi nomen rei signatae, quoniam sit figura: sed magis quia symbolum sit, quo res exhibetur" (Calvin, *Commentary on 1 Cor 11:24* [CO 49:486]).

4 "Sed hac obiectione non evincis sacramentum non esse instrumentum gratiae conferendae" (Calvin, Praestantiss[imo] Christi viro, d[omino] Henricho Bullingero, Tigurinae ecclesiae fideliss[imo] pastori, fratri et amico observando, in: Emidio Campi/Ruedi Reich: 2009, 98–109).

the outward tools this signifies that the Church is a divine real-symbol like the sacraments.

The Church has a similar function like the sacraments.[5] God uses the Church as an outward mean to create and nourish faith until its eschatological fulfillment because of human weakness (Calvin, *Institutes*, 4.1.1 [OS 5:1]). God could lead everybody without the Church, but he chose ecclesial mediation as the way to adapt to human conditions (Calvin, *Institutes*, 4.1.4 [OS 5:7]). This is the famous *accommodatio Dei* in Calvin. "The visible church is necessary because of human weakness" (Douglas: 2009, 135–154; 138).

It is helpful to keep in mind the typically Calvinian dialectic. The origin of whatever salvific action lies in God. No created thing has power in itself because God did not bind his power to created things. But God uses created things as the ordinary way to speak to his people. E.g. he makes use of human tongues – i.e. of the ordained ministers – to be present in their voices (cf. Calvin, *Institutes*, 4,1,5 [OS 5:9]). This is made possible by the action of the Holy Spirit (Calvin, *Institutes*, 4.3.2 [OS 5:44]). The historical background for this position lies in Calvin's debates with Anabaptists and Roman Catholics (Faber: 2012, 113–127; 115).

But God did link the proclamation of the Gospel with the human ministry, especially preaching. That is why humans are instructed in a human way. So they can understand and receive the gospel. Thus, the Church's ministry feeds people with spiritual food until the elected receive their eschatological goal (cf. Calvin, *Institutes*, 4.1.1 [OS 5:1]; 4.1.5 [OS 5:5]). Calvin spells out the consequences thusly: "So great can be the participation in the Church, that it maintains us in God's fellowship".[6] Whoever partakes in the Church, its proclamation of the Gospel (cf. Calvin, *Institutes*, 4.1.5 [OS 5:8]), its celebration of the sacraments and its fraternal community[7] partakes in God and his goods (cf. Calvin, *Institutes*, 4.1.10 [OS 5:14f]). Calvin even goes so far to follow the *extra Ecclesiam nulla salus*, which many associate with Catholicism (cf. Calvin, *Institutes*, 4.1.4 [OS 5:7]).

Between these two positions Calvin keeps two things in tension: the visibility of the Church and its inner, invisible dimension (cf. Calvin, *Institutes*, 4.1.7 [OS 5:12]). The visible Church is for Calvin the mother of all believers. Everybody must be in communion with this Church (cf. Calvin, *Institutes*, 4.1.4 [OS 5:7]; 4.1.7 [OS 5:12]). It can be recognized by the two *notae Ecclesiae* (cf. Calvin, *Institutes*, 4.1.8

---

5 Even Georg Plasger, who does not share the instrumental interpretation of the sacraments asserts that in Calvin the Church is a tool by which God invites people into his fellowship. (Plasger: 2008, 317–325; 317).

6 "Tantum potest Ecclesiae participatio ut nos in Dei societatem contineat" (cf. Calvin, *Institutes*, 4.1.3 [OS 5:6]).

7 cf. Calvin, *Institutes* 4,2,5 [OS 5:36]. The aspect of fraternal community is pointed out more clearly in Calvin's commentary on the Psalms (cf. Selderhuis: 2003, 195–214; 205ff).

[OS 5:12]), the right proclamation of the gospel and the right administration of the sacraments (cf. Calvin, *Institutes*, 4.1.9 [OS 5:13]). The right piety also can be called among these notes (cf. Calvin, *Institutes*, 4.1.12 [OS 5:16]).

In the inner dimension of the sacramental signs God performs His salvific action. By preaching the gospel and celebrating the sacraments God forgives sins. In this manner, ordinarily, Christians receive God's forgiveness. Calvin even goes so far to say not to seek forgiveness at any other place than in the proclamation of the gospel and the celebration of the sacraments, i.e. in the ministry of the Church.[8] The forgiveness is proper to the Church so that it cannot be received anywhere else. The ministers of the Church who are Christ's instruments and even his deputies give it to the people. Thus, the Church employs the power of the keys that Christ entrusted to the Church through Peter and his disciples (Matt 16:18) (cf. Calvin, *Institutes*, 4.1.22 [OS 5:25]; 4.3.1 [OS 5:42]).

The outer structure and reality of the Church thus are a real-symbol. The forgiveness of sins is not only proclaimed but also truly offered and exhibited by the actions and ministries which are performed by the Church and its ministers. So the outer appearance transmits the invisible reality. The main reason for Calvin's position is God's will who arranged everything in this way.

For Calvin the Church is more than the place where just people gather to worship (cf. Faber: 1999, 325). God gathers in the Church all those having been predestined for salvation before the foundation of the world (cf. Calvin, *Institutes*, 4.1.2 [OS 5:2]). He elected the Church for this reason (cf. Plasger: 2008, 318). It is by means of the Church that God exhibits grace and love. It is the Church and its ministry where the individuals get in touch with salvation and receive it.

2. The Roman Catholic notion of Sacramentality

The first chapter of LG has as title "The mystery of Church". This word was chosen to designate the complex reality of the Church. In the time after the Reformation Catholics emphasized the visible dimension of the Church, in order to combat what it considered the Protestant overemphasis on the invisible church. The Council wants to go back to more ancient traditions, which have a broader conception of the Church. The outward institution and the spiritual reality of the Church are bound together by "mystery" and its Latin translation *sacramentum* (cf. Grillmeier: 1966, 156). The Church is something "like a sacrament". The little word *veluti* makes clear that the Church is not the 8th sacrament besides the other seven sacraments. The

---

8 In his commentary on the Psalms, Calvin expresses the same thought (cf. Calvin, *Commentary on Ps 87:5* [CO 31:803]).

Council aims to offer a notion of sacrament that works more broadly and in an analogous way (cf. Kasper: 2008, 306–327, 310; 314.).

LG, 1 understands "sacrament" "as a sign and instrument". But only through Christ is the Church like a sacrament. He is the origin of salvation. The Church is only the sacrament of salvation, and not salvation itself (cf. Kasper: 2008, 311). But in Christ, in the realm of faith, the Church is a complex reality and not only a visible institution. The Church is a "society structured with hierarchical organs", yet at the same time it has spiritual dimensions. The outer means serve this invisible dimension, just as Christ's humanity was an organ of the divine Logos. (LG, 8) Both belong together and cannot be separated (Hünermann: 2004, 366). The Church is a sacrament because grace and salvation are exhibited by its visible structures and actions (Kraus: 2012, 190).

The Church aims to mediate communion with God and communion of humans with one another. The church is a sign of this communion and its instrument. Communion with God and among humans comes by having the same confession of faith, the same sacraments and the same ministers (cf. Hünermann: 2004, 367). This is possible because the Spirit of God makes the Church the "universal sacrament of salvation" (LG, 48). *Lumen Gentium* clearly accents God's primary action. The Church as God's sacrament is capable of leading people to God because the triune God is at work in it. The Church could not be spiritually fruitful without God's agency. The power of the Gospel leads people to deeper communion with God (LG, 4). For this reason, the primary office of bishops is to proclaim the gospel (LG, 25). The importance of the Word is mentioned here, but not always fully elaborated in the Constitution.

So whoever gets in touch with the visible and concrete Church enters by its ministry into communion with God and with the whole human race (cf. Grillmeier: 1966, 158; 174). This communion and the mystery of the Church will be manifested eschatologically; in this life it only can be seen "in a shadowy way" (*sub umbris*) as LG, 8 points out (cf. Hünermann: 2004, 370). Even if it is seen only in a shadowy way, the inner spiritual reality of the Church is signified and performed by its visible ministry (cf. Kasper: 2008, 314).

3.   Calvin's instrumental view and *Lumen Gentium*'s sacramentality

What Calvin elaborates in his ecclesiology can be called a sacramental structure. "The notion of sacrament stands for the coming together of two realms of reality in the sacrament. It links visible and invisible things, earthly and divine things in a way that the invisible is accessible by the visible".[9] This is exactly what happens in Calvin's doctrine on the Church.

Calvin's concerns are safeguarded in sacramental ecclesiology. Calling the Church a sacrament underlines how God is the one working and acting through the church. Only God can procure salvation and speak God's word of mercy, love, and justification. The Church is just the instrument for all this, but not a mediator between God and humanity. This is only Jesus Christ as SC, 5 points out.

LG, 1 states very clearly that the Church is a sacrament only in Christ. Apart from him it cannot do anything. Or to say with words from Alexandre Ganoczy: „The Church means nothing outside Christ."[10] The notion of sacraments highlights this important difference because sacraments always refer to a reality outside them, i.e. Christ. The Church is only a sacrament and not the ground of salvation. It is only a mean in Christ's hands to make people get in touch with God's love (cf. Kasper: 2008, 28).

Speaking of the Church in terms of sacrament underlines God's primary role. God is the ground of salvation and the Church is only its tool. This difference and even self-relativization is expressed by the sacramentality of the Church (cf. Werbick: 2010, 832ff). The term "sacrament" was used to combat triumphalism (cf. Kasper: 2008, 315). But as God's instrument the Church has spiritual effects because Christ and the Spirit are active in it. Even if the term "sacrament" may be problematic for some Protestants, its content is in accordance with Calvin's ecclesiology. "Sacrament" rather expresses the main concerns of Reformation theology, the distinction between what God only can do and what humans do.

Bibliography

BEINTKER, MICHAEL (2010), Grund und Gestalt der Kirche im Denken Calvins und im Horizont der Barmer Theologischen Erklärung, KuD 56, 45–59.

CAMPI, EMIDIO/REICH, RUEDI (ed.) (2009), Consensus Tigurinus. Heinrich Bullinger und Johannes Calvin über das Abendmahl, Zürich: Theologischer Verlag.

DOUGLAS, JANE DEMPSEY (2009), Calvin and the Church Today: Ecclesiology as Recevied, Changed and Adapted, ThTo 66, 135–153.

EWERSZUMRODE, FRANK (2012), Mysterium Christi spiritualis praesentiae: Die Abendmahlslehre des Genfer Reformators Johannes Calvin aus römisch-katholischer Perspektive, RHT 19, Göttingen: Vandenhoeck & Ruprecht.

---

9 "Der Sakramentsbegriff steht somit für das Zueinander zweier Wirklichkeitsbereiche im Sakrament. Es verbindet Sichtbares und Unsichtbares, Irdisches und Göttliches so, dass durch das Sichtbare das Unsichtbare zugänglich wird" (Faber: 2011, 28).

10 "Außer Christus ‚bedeutet' die Kirche [...] nichts" (Ganoczy: 1968, 375).

FABER, EVA-MARIA (1999), Symphonie von Gott und Mensch: Die responsorische Struktur von Vermittlung in der Theologie Johannes Calvins, Neukirchen-Vluyn: Neukirchener.

FABER, EVA-MARIA (2011), Einführung in die katholische Sakramentenlehre, 3rd ed., Darmstadt: Wissenschaftliche Buchgesellschaft.

FABER, EVA-MARIA (2012), Das kirchliche Dienstamt bei Calvin, in: André Birmelé/Wolfgang Thönissen (ed.), Johannes Calvin ökumenisch gelesen, Paderborn/Leipzig: Bonifatius/Evangelische Verlagsanstalt, 113–127.

GANOCZY, ALEXANDRE (1968), Ecclesia ministrans: Dienende Kirche und kirchlicher Dienst bei Calvin, Freiburg im Breisgau: Herder.

GRILLMEIER, ALOYS (1966), Kommentar zur Dogmatischen Konstitution über die Kirche, in: Das Zweite Vatikanische Konzil. Konstitutionen, Dekrete und Erläuterungen, vol. 1, LThK² supplementary volume, Freiburg im Breisgau/Basel/Wien: Herder, 156–209.

HÜNERMANN, PETER (2004), Theologischer Kommentar zur dogmatischen Konstitution über die Kirche *Lumen Gentium*, in: Peter Hünermann/Bernd Jochen Hilberath (ed.), Herders Theologischer Kommentar zum Zweiten Vatikanischen Konzil, vol. 2, Freiburg im Breisgau/Basel/Wien: Herder.

KASPER, WALTER (2008), Die Kirche als universales Sakrament des Heiles, WKGS 11, Freiburg im Breisgau/Basel/Wien: Herder 2008.

KRAUS, GEORG (2012), Die Kirche als Gemeinschaft des Heils: Ekklesiologie im Geist des Zweiten Vatikanischen Konzils, Regensburg: Pustet 2012.

MATHISON, KEITH A. (2002), Given for you: Reclaiming Calvin's Doctrine of the Lord's Supper, Phillipsburg: P&R Publishing.

PLASGER, GEORG, Kirche, in: Hermann J. Selderhuis (ed.), Calvinhandbuch, Tübingen: Mohr Siebeck 2008, 317–325.

SATTLER, DOROTHEA (2013), Kirche(n), Paderborn: Schöningh.

SELDERHUIS, HERMAN (2003), Kirche im Theater: Die Dynamik der Ekklesiologie Calvins, in: Peter Opitz (ed.): Calvin im Kontext der Schweizer Reformation. Historische und theologische Beiträge zur Calvinforschung, Zürich: Theologischer Verlag, 195–214.

WERBICK, JÜRGEN (2010), Den Glauben verantworten: Eine Fundamentaltheologie, 4th ed., Freiburg im Breisgau: Herder.

Csilla Gábor

Arguments, Roles, Games in a 17th Century Hungarian Polemic on Ecclesiology[*]

1. Preliminary considerations

If we only superficially skim over the Hungarian literature of the 20th century referring to the *endless quarrels*[1] about the true faith in the age of the reformation taken in the wider sense – that is of the 16th and 17th century –, we may observe the signs of continuous interest in the topic. However, the intensity and direction of this interest has been fluctuating. The authors of some descriptions and/or analyses of polemics 'deal out justice' while denominationally identifying themselves with one or the other of the early modern age antagonists and characterize the other party as 'heretical' (Zoványi: 1925, 264; Horváth: 1918). On other occasions the interpretation is carried out from an explicitly antireligious and antiecclesiastical platform, the evaluation being made along the progressive/retrograde polarization where the Catholics are assigned the role of retrograde, narrow-minded apologists what opposes them, as it were, to the Protestants representing progress, development (cf. Pirnát: 1964, 59).[2] At times we may read early 20th century outlines on polemical literature which are conspicuous because of their balanced character (Samu: 1901). In yet other cases the witty or hardly printable, gross linguistic inventions to be found in the polemics and the purely literary approach disregarding the polemical context are dominant. Here the stylistic features are the main object of analysis (Barabás: 1978, 88–93). The character of international researches basically does not differ from this: to realize this it is enough to consider the complaints of an article reviewing the latest German literature on this topic (Bremer: 2005, 3–24).

---

* The study was completed with the support of the Ministry of Human Capacities, reference number: REB-16-1-ELOADAS-0003.

1 The expression is borrowed from Péter Pázmány, who in the dedicator letter of his work (Pázmány: 1626,):(3) addressed to Bihar County says that the irresponsible preachers submerge the believers in "the gulf of a sea of endless quarrels" raising in them thus doubts in the matters of faith.

2 The Catholic–Protestant religious debates are worthy of attention "not because of their literary value, but due to the positive political function which unintentionally became the lot of the works polemizing with the advancing Counterreformation." Furthermore, especially the Calvinists "served by these [the polemical works written by them] more or less consistently the interests of the formation of market town bourgeoisie".

The renewed interest of the last couple of decades may have formulated its questions with the intent to rise above the problems just mentioned. Instead of completely identifying themselves with one of the polemizing parties, researchers focused on the methods by which the truth was searched for, on the rhetoric of polemics. They explored thoroughly the ideological, historical, and social background and context of the debates. Apart from and instead of summing up the creative invectives, they looked at the differences or latent similarities between the argumentations, the attitudes towards tradition, and mentalities. Thus religious polemic came to be analyzed as a cultural and communicational phenomenon (Heltai/Tasi: 2005; Jürgens/Weller: 2013).

However the rhetorical-communicational approach presents further questions and difficulties, and, at the same time, new research perspectives mainly related to the fact that *polemic, controversy* practically does not exist in the terminology of classical rhetorical system. It comes up in homiletical compendia, where the authors discuss the possibilities lying in the refutation of erroneous views. These discussions however can only partially help understanding religious polemics. Partially, because they concentrate on the argumentative structure of a single text; they do not offer guidance with reference to polemics with several rounds (that is real debates). In fact there is no theoretical description for a speech type which would discuss the possibilities of debate (especially of written debate) in general and which could be used in the analysis of religious polemics, though disputes have been a constant phenomenon in the communicational culture since the beginning (Stauffer: 2003, 1403). Thus present-day research is trying to deduce the theory of polemic from the texts of religious debates themselves, and it is trying to construct such models by which the operation of controversies and the rules of textual representations can be theoretically grasped and described.

There is an approach which speaks directly about rhetorical Manichaeism in relation to the praising and censuring speech (*laudatio, vituperatio*), emphasizing that polemic is indeed an aggressive speech, although it tries to preserve its impersonal, argumentative character – and in this it differs from the quarrel which allows for and contains emotions as well (Stenzel: 1986, 3–4). The elements of Jürgen Stenzel's model are: the subject in the situation calling for a polemic (who polemicizes, or attacks), the object of the polemic (on whom the polemic is directed, who is challenged to a debate by the subject), and of course the debated topic itself. The attacker and the attacked are placed on the opposite ends of the imaginary pole of values (the allusion to Manichaeism derives from this). A change of roles is possible of course during the dispute, the attacker may become the attacked and vice versa. And if we imagine this as a court room situation, the public (listeners or readers) lands in the role of the judge: they decide "who is right". Since the objective is to win the judge over, the aim of the polemical *elocutio* is to stir up hostility against the antagonist and his views. This aim determines the instruments of the argumentation among which may figure the over-emphasizing of some extant favourable characteristics as well as the attribution of disparaging traits or deeds to the opponent (Stenzel: 1986, 5–8).

This paper analyzes a several rounds long 17th century ecclesiological polemic started by Péter Pázmány's[3] 1626 booklet, *Two Short Booklets on the Scripture and the Holy Mother Church*. On account of the choice of topic we do not discuss in detail that part of the debate which focused on the Bible, however we shall look at each text of the dispute about the Church: Pázmány's writing, the response given to it and the further replies). We shall interpret the controversy in the context of the 17th century ecclesiological views paying attention to the particular local circumstances, the strategies of argumentation, as well as the shifts in emphasis and tone occurring during the debate.

2. Pázmány on the Church: from the *Diatribe* to the *Two Short Booklets*

The topic of ecclesiology did not become an acute problem during the Age of Reformation: different ecclesiological models, reflecting also the shifting emphases of theological thought, had existed in parallel since the Antiquity, or they may have competed with one another (Bockmuehl/Thompson: 1997). They also had important role later in shaping the self-interpretation of both Catholics and Protestants. In the age of religious controversies this (too) allowed any (both the Protestant and the Catholic) community to define – and they did so – the signs of the true Church by referring to the Christian tradition. It is therefore understandable that the tradition considered to be common could serve as a suitable foundation for different opinions and parallel views.

Pázmány's début as a theologian is connected precisely to the topic of ecclesiology. His first polemic, the Latin *Diatriba theologica* (Pázmány: 1605/1975) carries already in its title one important trait of the Catholic view on the Church: emphasizing the institutional framework and the hierarchical structure it speaks about Christ's *visible* Church. By this emphasis it brings to the foreground one of the most striking differences from the spiritual approach of the Protestant view. The material encompassed in this book laid the foundations for and prefigured Pázmány's later activity as a polemicist. The topic was discussed again in the form of a systematic treatise, this time in Hungarian, in the *Kalauz* (*Guide*), books 8th and 9th (Pázmány: 1637: 649–773), in a sermon on the fourth Sunday after Epiphany (Pázmány: 1903,

---

3 Péter Pázmány (1570–1637) was a Hungarian Jesuit, from 1616 archbishop of Esztergom and a leading figure of Catholic renewal in the Hungarian Kingdom throughout his organizational activity and polemic as well as devotional writings.

360–373), as well as in the form of an independent book section in the *Two Short Booklets* (Pázmány: 1626, 294–309).

3. The "Matches" of the Ecclesiological Controversy

3.1 Two Short Booklets: Dedications, Structure, Train Of Thoughts

The author dedicated his work "To the honourable Bihar County" (Pázmány: 1626,):(2r), referring to the fact that he had originated from Várad (today: Oradea, Romania, at the time belonging to the Principality of Transylvania ruled by a Protestant prince). For forty years (since "the Lord called me graciously from my home, that is, from the inheritance of my ancestors, from the society of my acquaintances, from among my family and kin, and chose me for the ecclesiastical condition", ibid.) he would always have wished to express his gratitude to *His sweet rearing country*, but since he had not been given the chance, "in my old age, by dedicating this little work of mine to you (...) I want to make known my efforts of thanksgiving" (Pázmány: 1626,):(2v).

The emotional words are not only the expressions of love, but also symbolical attempts of expansion on a field quite untrodden from a Catholic point of view. Várad (also on account of its military importance) at this time was experiencing a Protestant renewal thanks to the activity of the Transylvanian princes, more precisely of Gábor Bethlen and even more of György Rákóczi I, of generous patrons and impressive preachers, even if this thriving was not as great as in the Principality itself (Sulyok: 1901, 430–436). At the same time, however, the signs of a Catholic revival were also discernable especially in the not so far away royal Hungary. The Archbishop of Esztergom wished to extend this to the territory of the Principality which was also regarded as a missionary field. One sentence in the dedication reveals by the way the deliberateness of this attempt. Pázmány vows that he will do everything in his power "to serve your soul and to clear a path with my writing to your salvation" (Pázmány: 1626,):(2v). In continuation he urges the readers from Bihar to weigh on the balance of reason the Protestant teachers' ideas.[4] He does not attempt to achieve the *captatio benevolentiae* on this occasion by praising the addressee directly, but by the help of *docilitas* and *insinuation*. On the one hand he takes into consideration the difference between his views and those of the targeted public, on the other hand he tries to convince the reader that the topic is worth

---

4 "But you, my Beloved Country, if you do not wish to perish, proceed with sense and reason; follow nobody immoderately; understand the matters of your soul yourself"; "Favour, my Beloved Country, favour yourself, and arrange the matter of your salvation led by reason, not only by the preference of your will." (Pázmány (1626):,):(3r;):(4v).

considering.[5] Naturally, a seemingly cursory *laudatio* mentioning the cleverness of Bihar people is also present. However this is combined with an emphatic mention of the external pressure they are under and with the promise/threat of eternal life: "I know that it is easier to acquaint you with the Truth than to induce your will to follow it against people's regard. But remember that God judges you according to the truth and not according to people's opinion" (Pázmány: 1626,):(4v–):( ):(().

The second book of the work discusses the nature of the true Church and its distinguishing marks divided into six parts and each part into paragraphs. The argumentation usually consists of the presentation of opposite opinions and their systematic refutation. The first part, in contrast with the views of the reformers, says that the Church is visible (Pázmány: 1626, 61–69), the second that it is inexhaustible and infallible (Pázmány: 1626, 69–78).

Parts III–V (Pázmány: 1626, 78–139) represent a separate unit, the parts being circularly built on one another from a thematic point of view. The topic is the characteristics of the Church (*una, sancta, catholica, apostolica*). First it presents the viewpoint of Pázmány's own Church regarding the problem, then it formulates the conclusion that the four characteristics apply to the *Roman congregation*. This is followed by the reformers' viewpoints in the same order. The conclusion is that the four signs are "not to be found in the Opposite congregation" (Pázmány: 1626, 105). Part V (Pázmány: 1626, 116–139) returns again to part III in order to emphasize that the 'Roman congregation' is the true Church, since the four marks of the Church can only be found completely in it.

Finally part VI (Pázmány: 1626, 139–153) offers responses to the current controversial topics justifying the Catholic views from quotations by Saint Augustine. This part somewhat deviates from the theme of the book, since it discusses briefly such as the veneration of saints, the purgatory, justification, the relationship between faith and good deeds, the holy tradition, the Eucharist.

As a summing up it can be said about the argumentation that it deals systematically with the Catholic teachings: it presents their own views, it describes the reformers' counterarguments, then, resorting to different sources (the Old and New Testament, prestigious textual witnesses, *true reasoning*), proves the truth of the former and the false, erroneous character of the latter.

3.2 Péter Pécsváradi's *Answer*: Response on two Fronts and Attack

Three years after the publication of the *Two Short Booklets*, an 888 pages long answer was published to Pázmány's 153 pages long book (Pécsváradi: 1629). Its author,

---

5 "If it contains untruth, you are strengthened in the condemnation of papistry, but if you experience truth in it, do not run into danger for anybody's word or sentence to villainy." (Pázmány (1626):,):(4v).

Péter Pécsváradi (end of the 16th century – 1645), according to the title page, was at this time a minister at Várad. Having studied at Pápa, Sárospatak, Marburg and Herborn, in 1621 at the University of Heidelberg he became the student of David Pareus (1548–1622), who was considered the leading figure of Irenicism which urged the unity in faith of the Protestant denominations. From 1622 with a short pause he was a minister at Várad. The city had a quite significant role in the religious controversies that took place at the turn of the 16th and 17th centuries. Although he did not attain higher functions than the deanery of Zaránd (today: Zărand, Romania), Pécsváradi also belonged to the circle of intellectuals and ministers who assumed a representational role in the institutional system of the Principality during the reign of prince Gábor Bethlen (and later of György Rákóczi I), trying to strengthen the Calvinist Church (Péter: 2002, 208–223).

Nevertheless, the author did not dedicate the book to the Prince, but to a retired meritorious (*emeritus*) official of the Prince, Benedek Fodor. The dedicatory letter offers some basic information on him: first of all, that he was a faithful follower of Gábor Bethlen, after whose "devout service he has been given a suitable reward and a peaceful leave" (Pécsváradi: 1629, a2r). He surpassed "all the other officials" by his "truthfulness, devoutness, praiseworthy gentleness, and the industrious listening and following of God's word", and has been rewarded for this by God himself (Pécsváradi: 1629, b1r). Further on the text mentions Benedek Fodor's patronage: he financially supported ministers, the reparation or building of churches. Furthermore, he was "the first to activate externally in the *reformation*" of the Church of Szalka (Pécsváradi: 1629, b1v), he supported the expenses of a student's foreign studies. The information is due to the longstanding good relationship between Pécsváradi and Fodor.[6]

The dedication offers information on the birth of the volume and the circumstances of its publication. According to this Pécsváradi at first responded to the Archbishop's books "in public in the house of God" (Pécsváradi: 1629, b1v) – that is, in the form of a sermon series. Benedek Fodor, having listened to these sermons, published them at his own expense. At the same time the dedication also anticipates the methodology used in the book: the author promises to answer to the Archbishop's every argument and at the same time he presents the views of his own denomination as well. Regarding the argumentation he says that "I made my writing useful with fine depending *summa*s and lessons" (Pécsváradi: 1629, b2r) – and indeed, these comprehensive and generalizing, often moralizing depending

---

6 ... "I remember the beautiful acquaintance that has been flourishing between us for a long time. Besides this Christian love and a friendly life are before me and some alliances and responsibilities have resulted from both" (Pécsváradi: 1629, b1r).

summas[7] appear at the end of each thematic unit –, and that "in the demonstration I used the Holy Scripture, the professions of the Fathers, the writings of the *Doctors*, the decrees of the *Councils*, the power of reasoning, everyday *proofs*, and the papists' own opinions" (Pécsváradi: 1629, b2r). The statement sums up one of the basic rules of polemic, according to which the opponent must be defeated with his own weapons. Then the author elaborates on the mode in which he applied the rules of dialectics: how he formulated into syllogisms the theses found at Pázmány and how he corrected "the *status* of the controversies, the cornerstones of the debates" (Pécsváradi: 1629, b2r).

The dedication finally mentions that because Pázmány's disputed work refers its readers to the *Kalauz* (Guide) in many places, Pécsváradi's work is intended to be a reply not only to Pázmány's *Two Booklets*, but also to the *Guide*, therefore "we, on our part, do not need to respond in detail to the *Guide* later on" (Pécsváradi: 1629, b3r).

The main part of the work – resulting from the nature of the dispute – repeats the structure of Pázmány's *Two Short Booklets* but in a much longer form. Pécsváradi gives a seven pages long comment merely on the title page of Pázmány's book.[8] The meticulous explanation and polemic point to an author well-versed in dialectics who is able to build long, systematic trains of thought on any detail, concept interpretation, or problematizing question. Because of this (and because it often raises issues which did not appear in Pázmány's discussed book) his volume meant to be a response may also be read as a kind of Calvinist handbook of religious instruction.

3.3 and *Reasons, Non-Reasons*: answers to the answers

The retaliation (314 pages long this time) that arrived to Péter Pécsváradi's book in 1630, its author being according to the title page István Sallai ([Pázmány]: 1630), shows on the one hand the acceleration of the dispute, on the other hand the slackening of weighty arguments and together with this a further coarsening of the tone. Perhaps the same holds true for Pécsváradi's reply of which no copies have survived and only some of its ideas are known from the short work concluding the dispute entitled *Okok, nem okok* (Reasons, Non-Reasons) signed again by István Sallai.

---

7 A further part of the book elucidates what exactly this term which cannot be found in logical-dialectical treatises means. At the end of a polemicizing series of arguments the author recommends: "let us emphasize a few depending summas from our response made so far for the sake of edification" (Pécsváradi: 1629, 477).

8 The title of the chapter is *Inspecting the titles of the Archbishop's books* (Pécsváradi: 1629, 8–14).

The appearance of this new actor posed a philological problem for the researchers. Who is in fact the real author: a parish priest serving in Pozsonypüspöki (today: Podunajské Biskupice, Slovakia) named István Sallai about whom hardly anything is known, and the information we have is that he often left his seat (Beke: 1994, 297)? Or is it Pázmány, who used to hide behind pseudonyms, if he considered his opponent beneath him, or if he wished to attract potential Protestant readers by entering a new name into the dispute (Bitskey: 1986, 194)? Nowadays there is a consensus regarding the authorship, however, it is expedient to sum briefly up the possible questions and arguments.

The arguments in favour of Pázmány being the author are partly stylistic. According to these an "insignificant" country priest could not have had such a forceful style and impressive erudition as the one shown by *The Cure of Várad*. Other arguments refer to the rules of polemic set by Pázmány and quoted above: in case of a significant difference in rank, the Archbishop used to hide behind a pseudonym (cf. Sík: 1939, 141–143, Bitskey: 1983, 483–487). This habit of his was known to and mentioned by Pécsváradi.[9] Accordingly, in his lost reply he polemicized with Pázmány and not Sallai. The researchers stating Sallai's authorship (not denying however Pázmány's role as a corrector in shaping the final form of the work) refer to the scarcity of data on the parish priest of Püspöki and inquire what advantage Pázmány could have gained from taking the guise of a parson known for being too often away from his place of service. In other words: what could the sense have been in acting contrary to the general practice? While others hid behind the name of important personages, would the powerful and distinguished Archbishop of Esztergom have assumed the mask of an unknown priest?

Others ask what reason would have been in keeping up Sallai's alleged authorship, if Pécsváradi knew and mentioned in his writing that the Archbishop was behind the name (Fraknói: 1868–72, II. 420–421; Varjas: 1938, 176–177). Recently an "old-new" data surfaced, using the different spellings of the episcopal parson's name as an argument. There is mention of a certain István Szal(l)ay, who was a Jesuit novice dismissed from the order in 1626, maybe through Pázmány's intercession, in order that he may continue his activity as a parish priest, and who might have been the author of *The Cure of Várad* (Fukári: 2001, 282–283).

Even this short summary can reveal that, based on the data we possess, the attribution of author in anybody's case is an act of fiction. Be the aim to prove the authorship of either Pázmány or Sallai, the external facts that can be enumer-

9 According to the *Reasons, Non-Reasons* Pécsváradi retreated from the further debate "Beacuse the Archbishop issued his book under the name of Parson István" ([Pázmány]: 1631, 3). We shall come back to the details later.

ated must be completed by uncertain suppositions. Therefore it is expedient to concentrate on the content – that is on the text – from now on.

The title of *The Gentle Cure of Good and Noble Várad* already signals the direction of the dispute: unlike in the case of the previous two works, the object, the topic of the polemic is not even mentioned. There is, however, even more rudeness in it than in Pécsváradi's work, which already often used coarse expressions. It is full of defamatory labels for his opponent, but the author promises that he will "turn a deaf ear to his adversary's vain verbosity, lies, and obscenity".[10] Then he gives an ironic explanation, disguised as discretion, why he does not mention him by name: "Although he earned and gained by his writing such names as 'Ignorant', 'Obscene', 'Liar', 'Grumbler', 'Inhuman', 'Foolish', and many more, but in order not to shame him more, I shall not reveal his name in my writing, and I shall only mention him by the name Christ gave to the false teachers, and I shall call him 'Wolf'". (([Pázmány]: 1630, A3r). Then he answers Pécsváradi's "unfounded, foolish insinuations",[11] that is, his topics, one by one, summing up and confronting the content of the *Two Short Booklets* and Pécsváradi's responses. It is an often used method of his argumentation that, by contrasting suitable passages, he proves that his adversary contradicts himself. He does not fail to announce the lesson: "Who does not walk on the path of truth hesitates: therefore the Wolf too vacillates, and as a drowning man grabs here and there. What he recommends in one passage, scorns in another" ([Pázmány]: 1630, 111). The structure of the book and of course its argumentation repeat again that of the former works, although with some variations. The space dedicated to the different topics changes. It discusses much longer the topic of the true Church than that of the Scripture. The division and the argumentation on this occasion as well follow the four characteristics of the true Church (*una, sancta, catholica, apostolica*). These are varied according to the viewpoints that appeared in the previous works as well. The conclusion can only be that these four marks apply to the *Roman congregation*, but not to the reformers. Furthermore, the four signs both separately and together prove the erroneous character of the reformers' teachings.[12]

Before going on, it is time to take a stand on the issue of authorship. The philological arguments may be more deceptive this time than the text itself: the latter's Pázmány-like verve, suggestive expressions, clear order of ideas and intellectual pre-

---

10 Word by word: "we shall turn a deaf ear to vain verbosity and elongations of the book"; "We shall ignore the Wolf's lies and cheeky obscenities" ([Pázmány]: 1630, A4r).

11 "The Wolf fills the whole writing with such unfounded, foolish insinuations, and senseless explanations" ([Pázmány]: 1630, 5).

12 A few examples from among the chapter titles discussing this topic: *The second sign reveals the falseness of the new congregations* ([Pázmány]: 1630, 191); *The fourth sign excludes the reformers from Christ's fold* (Ibid., 206).

cision reveal the obvious author, who – as the literature agrees – was the Archbishop of Esztergom.

That the debate was not over with the publication of *The Cure of Várad*, is known since 1904 when Viktor Récsey proclaimed the existence of the *Reasons, Non-Reasons* in the catalogue of the library of Benedictines of Pannonhalma (Récsey: 1904). However, it was a few decades later that Hiador Stripsky became interested in this short work surviving in a single copy and published its facsimile with an introduction (Stripsky: 1937). Stripsky in this introductory study discusses the circumstances of the debate, reconstructs the title and arguments of Pécsváradi's lost treatise, and concludes his philological analysis with the conclusion considered latter decisive that "in the two-quire long booklet presented here Pázmány quotes often and 'word by word some sentences from the *Kilencz Okok*' [Nine Reasons] and he himself 'reinforces the tradition' that Sallai in fact is Pázmány" (Stripsky: 1937, 11).

The role-play, as it is well-known, continues in the *Reasons, Non-Reasons*. The name figuring on the title page is again István Sallai's, and the narration refers back to Pécsváradi's response given to *The Gentle Cure of Good and Noble Várad* (this would be the missing link, the work of which no copy has survived), which would have summed up in nine points why the minister of Várad did not wish to continue the debate. Immediately after this reference the *Reasons, Non-Reasons* justifies the birth of this new writing and explains its title as well: "so that the Wolf should not consider himself clever because of our silence, I shall show as briefly as possible that in his writing Reasons are also Unreasonable" ([Pázmány]: 1631, 2).

One of the reasons enumerated by Pécsváradi refers to the use of a pseudonym,[13] while the *Reasons, Non-Reasons* drops the supposition of Pázmány's authorship with a concession. Then it launches a counterattack and labels Pécsváradi's argument unfounded:

> "Even if it were so, how can the conclusion derive from it that you do not need to defend your Faith, your Teaching, your Previous work? For the true Teacher must consider the case and not the person [Jas 2:1.9]. Must you defend your Religion only against the Archbishop? If you love and search for the truth, if you defend that, you must not consider who is the one who writes and with what kind of pen he writes, but you must attend to what he writes. The first excuse is therefore not Reason, but hiding" ([Pázmány]: 1631, 3).

The Archbishop is mentioned several times in the quotations taken from Pécsváradi's lost writing, but the *Reasons, Non-Reasons* never returns to the issue again.

---

13 "1st REASON. 'Because the Archbishop published his book under the name of Parson István'" ([Pázmány]: 1631, 3.).

In the short, 15 pages long text there is in fact no real discussion of the original topics. The derisive answer given to Pécsváradi's *reasons* masks in fact considerations referring to the methodology of the debate. These expose the deficiencies of the opponent's argumentation or logic, and question the legitimacy of his approach to the topic as well as his participation in and present retreat from the debate. According to the second reason for example "'the Archbishop did not name' the Wolf of Várad" ([Pázmány]: 1631, 3). The response given to this argues that based on this logic Pécsváradi should not even have written the *Answer*, since the *Two Short Booklets* did not mention his name. Therefore the minister of Várad entered the debate uninvited.[14] Pécsváradi's fourth reason finds fault with the tone of *The Cure of Várad*.[15] Pázmány as a response to this only refers back to the *Answer*:

> "I do not deny that I sometimes scared the Wolf with harsher words (...): when I wrote harsh words in my answer, I did nothing else than to send home what the Wolf vomited on us: that is, I gathered what harsh abuses he threw on us in his writing, and I sent them home to him in order to make him cry out and to learn from his pain that he ought not regurgitate on us such things which he would not gladly suffer" ([Pázmány]: 1631, 5).

Finally the eighth reason objects that the Archbishop in his writing "makes empty promises: and he delegates to others what he should answer pointing to Bellarminus, Becanus" ([Pázmány]: 1631, 11). That is, he does not give satisfactory answers to the questions raised by Pécsváradi. Pázmány's counterargument to this refers again to the logic of the text:

> "in my answer I did not want to dispute about other controversies, but only about the Scripture and the Church. Therefore when you were running into another direction, I did not want to run after you, and I wrote: that did not belong here, and the Catholics had long ago defeated that which you had got stuck on. I noted who and in what books had written about that" ([Pázmány]: 1631, 11).

The conclusion regarding Pécsváradi's reasons is more or less that they are bad, wicked, unreasonable, foolish, and faulty ([Pázmány]: 1631, 2; 4; 9; 10; 13).

---

14 "Did the Archbishop mention your name in the first writing dedicated to Bihar County? Then you were not named, but you stood forth and started trouble: now, only because you are not mentioned by name, you abandon your cause and you wash your hands of everything by silence." ([Pázmány]: 1631, 3).

15 "For the Archbishop responds with anger, abuses, and by making me a liar." ([Pázmány]: 1631, 4).

4. The Sign system(s) of the Church(es). Signs and Sign Conceptions in the Debate

As we have mentioned when describing its structure, the third part of Book II in the *Two Short Booklets* deals with the signs of the true Church.[16] The polemical context in which the topic is raised is the difference in the characteristics which function as signs. "According to the teachings of the reformers the true Church is nothing else than a congregation in which the word of God is truly preached and the Sacraments are purely administered" (Pázmány: 1626, 79).[17] The bases for the Catholic standpoint are the decrees of the Councils of Nicaea and Constantinople (which were by the way accepted by Calvin and the Helvetic Confession). These "give four main Signs of the Holy Mother Church, namely: that it is One, Holy, Universal, and Apostolic" (Pázmány: 1626, 81–82). The author of the *Two Short Booklets* (seemingly) does not offer theological arguments to explain why he considers the signs named by the Protestants and the argumentation connected to them faulty. He includes instead a short semiotic treatise. Discussing the nature of signs, he says that the sign "must be different from that which is made known by it", and that "the Sign must be more easily recognized than that which we look for through it" (Pázmány: 1626, 79). Further criteria are that signs should be recognizable by all[18] and unambiguous.[19] The signs used by the Protestants, continues the argumentation, essentially do not differ from the reality denoted by them. This is why "it follows that the true teaching cannot be the distinguishing Sign of the Church, because they are the same, and the true Church and the congregation in which the Word of God is truly preached are recognized together" (Pázmány: 1626, 79). The meaning of the *difference* mentioned by Pázmány is illustrated by the parable following the explanation:

> If you wished for a treatment and inquired after the best Medical Doctor in Vienna, I would not give you his distinguishing Signs if I said that he was the one, who healed the patient in the surest, easiest and quickest way, because, although in other words and in another way, but I would give you as signs that which you wished to know (Pázmány: 1626, 79–80).

---

16 "By what signs can the true Church be recognized" (Pázmány: 1626, 78).

17 The expression is a reference to the identical wording of the Augsburg Confession and the Helvetic Confession in the question, the key expressions are: "Evangelium recte docetur et recte administrantur Sacramenta" (*Confessio Augustana*, art VII., http://www.ccel.org/ccel/schaff/creeds3.iii.ii.html 2014. 02. 14.)

18 "The sign of the Holy Mother Church must be such as by which everyone may recognize the Church" (Pázmány: 1626, 80).

19 "That cannot be considered a distinguishing Sign which is almost as easily misinterpreted as that which is searched by it." (Pázmány: 1626, 81).

It is hazardous to judge which interpretative community (by the word used in the debate: *congregation*) preaches the word of God trustworthily, because in order to form a correct opinion, one "must be familiar with the true meaning of the entire Scripture, since, if one does not understand one of its parts, one may be mistaken in that" (Pázmány: 1626, 80). The understanding of the whole Scripture, however, requires a knowledge which is not at the disposal of the uneducated masses, nor even of the teachers in its entirety. This is why the guidance of the institution (the Church) is needed, and why one of the two interdependent things cannot be the sign of the other.[20]

Pécsváradi's answer to the argumentation presented above shows clearly the difference in the two parties' thinking, and by this the reason why real communication could not be established between them. The minister of Várad added a third sign to the two attributed by Pázmány to the Protestants: this is "the ecclesiastical punishment and its sanctity" (Pécsváradi: 1629, 493). Then he arranged them in a hierarchical order. The most important is the word of God and its pure preaching. This is a "main sign", which one line below is called an "essential sign", which is a "fundamentally necessary sign, constant and everlasting" (Pécsváradi: 1629, 493). Pécsváradi's commentary on the relationship between the sign and the signified is most illuminating: "it shows the nature and the characteristics of the true Congregation more closely and intimately" (Pécsváradi: 1629, 493), the one cannot exist without the other. He calls the administering of the Sacraments the "middle sign", "since it follows the first, but it is not always necessary" (Pécsváradi: 1629, 493). It can be suspended under certain circumstances, "but despite that the people are God's Church" (Pécsváradi: 1629, 493). Regarding the third sign, the ecclesiastical punishment, he emphasizes its changeability. However later on he refers to the fact that even Pázmány neglected to discuss the topic (Pécsváradi: 1629, 494).[21] Pécsváradi stipulates that "spiritual sense, a wise and erudite mind", as well as "*accurate cognitio*, diligent and infallible knowledge" (Pécsváradi: 1629, 493) are necessary to get to know, to understand the signs and the signified. He contrasts this requirement with the Papists' pursuit for unambiguity. They "believe that the Church must have signs based on which any unholy fool can judge which Congregation is the true Church" (Pécsváradi: 1629, 493).

After this he lays the foundations of the Protestant interpretation by means of *true reasons* in thirty-one points (Pécsváradi: 1629, 494–518). Pécsváradi in each case transforms the thesis to be proved (which formalizes some feature or detail of the two signs) into a syllogism, then dividing the *maior* and *minor propositios* into

---

20 "I do not know who from among the community, not even from among the Teachers, can be familiar with the deep secrets of the entire Scripture unless he were to know first the true Church and be instructed by it" (Pázmány: 1626, 80.)

21 "We need not prove the third sign, because the Archbishop does not discuss it here".

further elements and supporting them with arguments, he reaches the conclusion that we are right to regard the true preaching of God's words and the administering of the sacraments as the signs of the true Church; the Papists, unless they are fools, must yield to the strength of the Protestant arguments. It would take too long to survey thoroughly each part of the argumentation that raise different subtopics but follow the same structure. To get a general view on the train of thoughts it will be enough to observe more closely only a few of them selected on account of the rhetorical-dialectical remarks included in them.

Argument 10 for example builds the syllogism based on the criterion of dividing truth from falsehood. The *propositio* of this syllogism named by Pécsváradi is: "That which judges and shows both the true and the false sense, judges and shows the true and the false Church as well." Its *assumptio* (sub-thesis) is: "But God's word, the true preaching of this, and the pure administering of the *Sacramenta* judge and show both the true and the false sense." The *conclusio* can only be the joining of the two theses: "Therefore they judge and show the true and false Church as well" (Pécsváradi: 1629, 504).

The explanation offers a glimpse on a basic agreement – "I believe the Papists agree with the *propositio*" – in order to emphasize all the more the difference in views: "they will deny the *assumptio* as it is their habit. But they deny it erroneously", continues the text. Afterwards it declares that the Scripture is the measure against which the true and false things can be discerned, since it "mentions only [these] two (...): Truth so that we may follow it, Falsehood so that we may avoid it" (Pécsváradi: 1629, 504). And if the Bible presents to us both truth and falsehood, "it is a judge of both true and false meaning" (Pécsváradi: 1629, 504). The next step is the delivery of judgement: "Thus it is necessary for the Papists to accept the *Conclusio*: and if they accept it, they accept our *sententia*, which makes us contented" (Pécsváradi: 1629, 505).

The 27th argument constructs the syllogism on the basis of Pázmány's texts. Its *propositio* is: "The signs of the Church are: the believers' unity in faith and its preservation, the chaste life and pure doctrine of the Church, Christ's flock being extended to all times and places, and the preservation of the apostolic teachings." The *assumptio* also relies on Pázmány: "But all these are preached by God's true words and the Prophets' and Apostles' pure teachings", while the *conclusio* is: "Therefore God's pure words, the Prophets' and Apostles' pure teachings are the Sign of the Church" (Pécsváradi: 1629, 509).

Pécsváradi attributes the *propositio* to Pázmány referring back to Sections two and three, Chapter 3, Book II of the *Two Short Booklets*. Pécsváradi does not give the page numbers this time. However, at the referred to part of the *Two Short Booklets*, we can read the following sentence among others: "These [that the true Church is one, holy, universal, and apostolic] are signs each of which alone distinguishes the true Church from a false congregation" (Pázmány: 1626, 82). To prove the *assumptio* Pécsváradi again quotes Pázmány in agreement. He copies (with insignificant orthographical modifications) the following sentence from page 78 of the *Two Short Booklets*: "Those who honour the Holy Scripture can recognize the Church from the Signs given in the word of God" (Pécsváradi: 1629, 509). He introduces the arguments supporting the immediately following *conclusio* in this way: "now it is the time to demonstrate the foolishness of the Papists to the Reader" (Pécsváradi: 1629, 509). Then, contrasting two statements, he accuses his opponent of self-contradiction: "They say that the true signs of the Church are founded on the word of God, nevertheless, they deny that the word of God could be a certain sign, a sufficient instrument to reveal the Church" (Pécsváradi: 1629, 509). This is followed by another quote by Pázmány[22] in order to enable Pécsváradi to characterize the result: "They preach an impossible and unbelievable thing, and even the *Logicus Canon* proves them wrong: *Propter quod unum quodque tale est, illud magis tale*" (Pécsváradi: 1629, 509).[23] He gives the translation of the school maxim by applying it to the debated topic: "If the Signs reveal the Churches, the Scripture all the more does so, since the signs too are revealed by it" (Pécsváradi: 1629, 509).

The Gentle Cure of Good and Noble Várad returns to the signs of the Church in part 3 of Book II ([Pázmány]: 1630, 161–189). As a start Pázmány presents the essence of Pécsváradi's teaching by compiling a collection of quotes. Then he discusses the mode of his argumentation, of course evaluating it as well.[24] He refers back to Pécsváradi's thirty-two proofs summing them up in this way: "they all are not worth a wormy apple" ([Pázmány]: 1630, 164). He therefore does not elaborate on all the 32 arguments, repeats instead as an emphasis what he said about the nature of signs in his previous work: "the Sign must differ from that which it presents, so that we may recognize the Sign more easily than that which it signifies: so that in general those who need to know the Church may recognize her from it" ([Pázmány]: 1630, 165). From this logically derives the argument because of which the true preaching of God's word and the administering of the sacraments cannot be the signs of the Church: "For it cannot be its own distinguishing Sign" [Pázmány]: 1630, 168), and: "these things expressed in two ways being one, we cannot recognize one more quickly or easily than the other" ([Pázmány]: 1630, 169).

In what follows we shall briefly examine the crossing of swords related to the four catholic signs – one, holy, catholic, apostolic – without, however, analyzing

---

22 From page 78 of the *Two Short Booklets*: "In it (in the Church) true doctrine and the purity of the sacraments is always preserved. But nevertheless these are not signs by which we may recognize the Church." (Pécsváradi: 1629, 509).

23 In English: "If that which stands for another thing is characterized by something, the thing itself even more has those same characteristics".

24 The title of the chapter: "How does the Wolf prove his teaching?" ([Pázmány]: 1630, 164).

them one by one. Pázmány says about them in general that they fulfil the criterion of unambiguity and difference, the Church can be known through them,[25] and that they "are such Signs, that each of them alone distinguishes the true Church from a false congregation. And all the four together do not fit anything else except the True Church" ([Pázmány]: 1630, 82). Pécsváradi responds to this by his usual method: first of all he denies that the four criteria are signs, and that by them the Church can be recognized,[26] then he goes on to discuss the errors of the syllogism. Thus the main thesis (*maior propositio*) is only "true within certain limits", namely, not anyone can recognize the Church from these signs, but only those "to whom it has been given by the spirit of God to recognize her: for the signs in themselves do not show the Church to anyone salutarily" (Pécsváradi: 1629, 521). The *minor propositio* is also faulty according to Pécsváradi, as those who have received the grace from God alone or as a community can distinguish between the true and the false Church on the basis of the true preaching of God's word and the correct administering of the sacraments.[27] Furthermore, the four signs are not the suitable marks of the true Church because they are not external signs, but internal ones: they are not visible, but the objects of faith.[28] It is curious that here Pécsváradi formulates the same critiques as those raised by Pázmány related to the signs enumerated by the Protestants. The signs "in themselves are uncertain, and they are deficient without being strengthened by further signs" (Pécsváradi: 1629, 530). They do not fulfil the criteria of signs because "they do not differ from the Church, but they are all one with it. For what *One* is the Church if not that one Church? (...) If therefore the Archbishop's *rule* is true, these cannot be true signs, as they are recognized together with the Church" (Pécsváradi: 1629, 530).

Pázmány also realized that Pécsváradi tried to turn the Archbishop's weapons against him: "the Wolf turns foolishly against us the guns by which the Archbishop defeated the Signs of the Reformers" ([Pázmány]: 1630, 177). His refutations and answers essentially do not contain new elements.

---

25 Cf. [Pázmány]: 1630, 80: "The sign of the Holy Mother Church must be such as through it all may recognize the Church".

26 "Why does the Archbishop call it the *One, Holy, Universal*, and *Apostolic Church*, though neither we, nor anyone else can recognize it by these signs as the true Church?" (Pécsváradi: 1629, 520).

27 Pécsváradi: 1629, 521: "each chosen man is guided by God so that he may recognize, know, and believe in the true Church as far as it is sufficient for his salvation and eternal life".

28 Pécsváradi: 1629, 529: "we also believe and confess in the *Credo* that the true Church is *One, Holy, Universal*, and *Apostolic* because some of the reasons brought up by the Archbishop and because of some more and different ones. However, these are not true and sufficient distinguishing signs for the visible Church, neither together, nor separately (...) for they are not the external and visible, but the internal and invisible characteristics of the internal and invisible Church".

5. Something on the two Church concepts

The fact that the Catholic and Protestant side considered different characteristics of the true Church as acceptable signs first and foremost is not a logical or ecclesiological question. The basic differences in the theological thought of the two parties may be recognized in background of the problem. In what follows we shall take a short look at these discrepancies.

Discussing the signs neither Pázmány nor Pécsváradi referred to the books written on signs by Augustine in his *De doctrina Christiana*. Nevertheless, what they say about the nature of signs corresponds to the Augustinian view, though their statements are connected to different aspects of Augustine's theory. We do not intend to present in detail Augustine's semiotics;[29] it is more useful if we refer to the important definitions of the text. The first chapter of Book Two speaks about the external form that reaches our senses and about the *some other thing* recalled in us by this form.[30] That which can be grasped by our senses points beyond itself, the physical perception leads to the spiritual recognition. This definition implicitly states that through the thing (*res*) affecting our senses it will (could) be easier to understand, grasp, get to know the nature of the thing the sign (*signum*) refers to.[31] In fact this is in Pázmány's definition as well, when he (as we have quoted above) states that the sign must differ from the thing it tries to make better known, and that it must be more easily recognized than that "which we seek by it" (Pázmány: 1626, 79).

Pécsváradi refers to the signs shown by God in the Scripture and he calls the signs of the Church "the characteristics concerning us" "by which through God's spirit" (that is by some kind of pact, convention with God) we distinguish between the true and false *congregations* (cf. Pécsváradi: 1629, 492). Somewhat later he repeats, what he only suggested before, that they are efficient "not through themselves, but through the spirit of God" (Pécsváradi: 1629, 493). In some of the above mentioned 32 arguments he returns to the presentation of one or two sign characteristics. For example in the second one he states: "That which is the evidence of the Believers' unity with Christ and themselves is a true sign of the Church" (Pécsváradi: 1629, 497). He rejects Pázmány's definition (namely that the sign must differ from the

---

29 From the point of view of this analysis a good guide to the topic from among the countless interpretations is: Jackson: 1969, 9–49.

30 "Signum est enim res praeter speciem quam ingerit sensibus aliud aliquid ex se faciens in cogitationem venire". [For a sign is a thing which of itself makes some other thing come to mind, besides the impression that it presents to the senses] (Augustine: 1995, 56–57; *De doctrina Christiana*, 2.1.1; from now on the work will be referred to by indicating the number of the book and chapter.)

31 Cf. "Omnis doctrina vel rerum est vel signorum, sed res per signa discuntur". [All teaching is teaching of either things or signs, but things are learnt through signs] (*De doctrina Christiana*, 1.2.2).

signified) by referring to the source of the arguments: "the Archbishop does not oppose us on the basis of the Scripture, but by some feeble and false reasoning" (Pécsváradi: 1629, 518–519). With respect to the statement that signs must be more quickly and easily recognizable than that which they signify,[32] the counterargument mentions "complete lies" too, when it refers to the difference between cause and effect also illustrated by an example: "*Causa differt a Causato*; the causing motive differs from its effect". For example, the tree is told apart from its fruit: the spirit is distinguished from the life it causes in man. As the true preaching of God's word and the pure administering of the sacraments are the creative causes of Christ's Church, since this is gathered and collected by those regarding its members, consequently they differ from the Church" (Pécsváradi: 1629, 519).

However, he does not offer a general, theoretically founded definition on what he understands by signs, and does not discuss systematically in what differs his conception from his opponent's.

Nevertheless, they disagree most vehemently on the application of the sign definition: they both state that the general criteria, which in fact neither of them finds fault with, does not apply to the *other's* 'sign'. Moreover, they both point out the same mistake in their opponent's approach: that his signs are not unambiguous enough.[33] The first – easy but rather primitive – explanation of the contradiction could be that the signs proposed by both denominations belong to the group of conventional signs (*signa data*), where the sign and the signalled are paired not only on the basis of pure analogy or organic connection, but of some convention or cultural code.[34] If, furthermore, we wish to apply the other categories given by sign typologies, we must pay attention to the symbolic signs having a double nature, where not the strictly objective knowledge, but the cognitive and axiological aspects of the symbol and the symbiosis of these aspects are decisive, as well as the fact that the symbol hides and reveals something at the same time (Veress: 1999, 120–129). And it is caused exactly by this ambivalence that the sings that seem unambiguous for one party are completely unacceptable for the other.

Glancing behind the differences we must consider the fact that the self-interpretation of the post-tridentine Catholic Church – reshaping and continuing the medieval tradition – remained law- and hierarchy-centred at least equal to the semiotic perspective. The continuous emphasis on the visibility of the Church is related to this and to the underlining of the institutional guarantees (Wood:

---

32 "the Sign must be recognized before and more easily than that which we seek by it" (Pázmány: 1626, 79).

33 Cf. for example: "Why does the Archbishop call it the *One, Holy, Universal*, and *Apostolic Church*, though neither we, nor anyone else can recognize it by these signs as the true Church?" (Pécsváradi: 1629).

34 For a concize, systematic elaboration see: Johansen/Larsen: 2002, 43–46.

2011, 149–150). In contrast with this the Protestant image of the Ecclesia (both the Lutheran and the Calvinist) placed the spiritual dimension into the foreground and stressed the invisible elements of the concept about the true church. Here the institutional frame is an important, but maybe not the primary, and definitely not the only element. In the logical-dialectical and naturally the semiotically-based combats of arguments both Pázmány and Pécsváradi started from and returned to the standpoint of his own denomination.

6. As a summary

If we followed attentively the rounds of the analyzed polemic, the completely different answers and argumentations given to the same topic, it may have occurred to us that both polemists succeeded in creating a unified, coherent intellectual structure within their own system. These constructions, however, were not able to connect with one another: borrowing Hans-Robert Jauss' expression, this was a contest of closed horizons (1996, 386). The frontlines (those referring to the concept of the Church as well) were made impassable by the difference in such basic principles of faith as the issue of justification, the role of good deeds in salvation, the existence or non-existence of the purgatory, and the theological foundations of the veneration of saints. The variations in view became embodied in the linguistic signs of the mistrust expressed toward the other party as well. Related to this we should recall the disparaging, abusive arguments. This phenomenon, however, was more than an attack on the antagonist, an attempt to convince him that he was in the wrong: it also served to reinforce the convictions of the polemist's own side.

Bibliography

Sources

AUGUSTINE (1995), De doctrina christiana, ed./transl. R.P. H. Green, Oxford: Clarendon Press.

PÉTER PÁZMÁNY (1605/1975), Diatriba theologica. De visibili Christi in terris ecclesia, Graz, 1605. (Facsimile with an introductory study edited by Miklós Őry, Eisenstadt, Prugg Verlag).

PÉTER PÁZMÁNY (1626), Az Szentírásrul és az Anyaszentegyházrul két rövid könyvecskék [Two Short Booklets on the Scripture and the Holy Mother Church], Vienna.

[PÉTER PÁZMÁNY] (1630), Io nemes Varadnak gyenge orvoslasa. Mellyel Sallai Istvan pap, püspöki plebanos, Gyógyitgattya, Farkas-marásból esett Sebeit Bihar-Vár-megyének [The Gentle Cure of Good and Noble Várad, by Which István Sallai, Priest, Parson of Püspöki

Is Healing the Wounds of Bihar County, Caused by Wolf Bites], Pozsony.

[PÉTER PÁZMÁNY] (1631), Okok, nem okok, mellyekert iria a' varadi farkas, hogy nem meltóztatik továb az én irásom-ellen tusakodni. Irta Sallai István pap, püspöki plébános [Reasons, Non-Reasons because of which the wolf of Várad writes that he no longer deigns to fight against my writing. Written by István Sallai, priest, Parson of Püspöki], Pozsony.

PÉTER PÁZMÁNY (1637), Hodoegus. Igazsagra-vezerlö Kalauz [Hodogeus. Guide to the Truth], Pozsony/Bratislava.

PÁZMÁNY, PÉTER (1903), A Christus hajója, az igaz ecclesia, győzhetetlen [Christ's Ship, the True Church, Is Invincible], in: Pázmány Péter Összes munkái VI. [The Complete Works of Péter Pázmány, VI], ed. György Kanyurszky, Budapest, M. Kir. Tud-Egyetemi Nyomda.

PÉTER PÁZMÁNY (1994), Pázmány Péter egyházlátogatási jegyzőkönyvei: 1616–1637 [Péter Pázmány's Visitation Reports: 1616–1637], Margit Beke (ed.), Budapest, Márton Áron Kiadó.

PÉCSVÁRADI, PÉTER (1629), Feleleti Pazmany Peternek, esztergami erseknek ket könyvetskeire, mellyeket az Szent Irasrol es az Anyaszent egyhazrol irt, es Bihar vár-megyenek Dedicálván, MDCXXVI. Esztendöben kibocsatott [Answer to the Two Book-lets of Péter Pázmány, Archbishop of Esztergom, written on the Scripture and the Holy Mother Church and dedicated to Bihar County, published in the year 1626], Debrecen, 1629.

Secondary Literature

BARABÁS, MÁRIA (1978), Pázmány Péter: Öt szép levél (stilisztikai elemzés) [Péter Pázmány: Five Beautiful Letters (Stylistic Analysis)], in: István Bitskey, Mrs Szabolcs Gomba, Pál Varga (eds.), Eszmei és stilisztikai kérdések a régi magyar prózában: Egyetemközi tu-dományos diákköri vitaülés Debrecenben 1977. november 24–25 [Ideological and Stylistic Questions in the Old Hungarian Prose], Debrecen, 88–93.

BITSKEY, ISTVÁN (1983), Egy modern Pázmány-kép elé [A Foreword to a Modern Pázmány Image], Vigilia, 483–487.

BITSKEY, ISTVÁN (1986), Pázmány Péter, Budapest: Gondolat,.

BOCKMUEHL, MARKUS/THOMPSON, B. MICHAEL (ed.) (1997), A Vision for the Church. Studies in Early Christian Ecclesiology in Honour of J.P.M. Sweet, Edinburgh: T & T Clark.

BREMER, KAI (2005), Religionsstreitigkeiten: Volkssprachliche Kontroversen zwischen alt-gläubigen und evangelischen Theologen im 16. Jahrhundert, Tübingen: Max Niemeyer Verlag.

FRAKNÓI, VILMOS (1868–1872), Pázmány Péter és kora [Péter Pázmány and His Age] I–II., Budapest: Ráth.

FUKÁRI, VALÉRIA (2001), A Pázmány–Sallai kérdés nyomában (Kritikai jegyzetek a mai Sallai-képhez és egy régi-új adat) [Following the Pázmány–Sallai Question (Critical Notes on the Present-Day Sallai Image and an Old-New Data)], in: Emil Hargittay (ed.), Pázmány

Péter és kora [Péter Pázmány and His Age], Piliscsaba: PPKE BTK, 274–284.

HELTAI, JÁNOS/TASI, RÉKA (ed.) (2005), „Tenger az igaz hitrül való egyenetlenségek vitatásának eláradott özöne...” Tanulmányok XVI–XIX. századi hitvitáinkról ["There Is an Overflowing Flood of Debates on the Differences about the True Faith": Studies on the 16–19th Century Religious Polemics], Miskolc: ME BTK.

HORVÁTH, LAJOS (1918), Sámbár Mátyás élete és művei [The Life and Works of Mátyás Sámbár], Budapest, „Élet” Irodalmi Nyomda és Részvénytársaság.

JACKSON, B. DARRELL (1969), The Theory of Signs in St. Augustine's *De doctrina christiana*, Revue des études augustiniennes, 9–49.

JAUSS, HANS ROBERT (1996), Das Religionsgespräch oder: the Last Things before the Last, in: Karlheinz Stierle/Rainer Warning (ed.), Das Ende. Figuren einer Denkform, München: Wilhelm Fink Verlag, 384–414.

JOHANSEN, JØRGEN DINES/LARSEN, SVEND ERIK (2002), Signs in Use. An introduction to semiotics, London/New York: Routledge.

JÜRGENS, HENNING P./WELLER, THOMAS (2013), Streitkultur und Öffentlichkeit im konfessionellen Zeitalter, Göttingen: Vandenhoeck & Ruprecht.

PÉTER, KATALIN (2002), The Golden Age of the Principality (1606–1660), in: Béla Köpeczi–Gábor Barta (eds.), History of Transylvania, II., Toronto, Hungarian Research Institute of Canada.

PIRNÁT, ANTAL (1964), Protestáns hitvitázó-teológiai irodalom [Protestant polemical-theological literature], in: Tibor Klaniczay (ed.), A magyar irodalom története 1600-tól 1772-ig [The History of Hungarian Literature from 1600 to 1772], II., Budapest: Akadémiai Kiadó, 59–67.

RÉCSEY, VIKTOR (1904), Ősnyomtatványok és régi magyar könyvek a pannonhalmi könyvtárban [Incunabula and Old Hungarian Books in the Library of Pannonhalma], Budapest, Part II. 34, No. 123.

SAMU, JÁNOS (1901), Hitviták a XVII. század második felében: Irodalomtörténeti tanulmány [Religious Polemics in the Second Half of the 17th Century: A Literary Historical Study], Budapest: Révai és Salamon könyvnyomdája.

SÍK, SÁNDOR (1939), Pázmány az ember és az író [Pázmány the Man and the Writer], Budapest, Szent István Társulat.

STAUFFER, H. (2003), Polemik, in: Gert Ueding (ed.), Historisches Wörterbuch der Rhetorik VI, Tübingen: Max Niemeyer Verlag.

STENZEL, JÜRGEN (1986), Rhetorischer Manichäismus: Vorschläge zu einer Theorie der Polemik, in: Franz Josef Wortsbrock/Helmut Koopmann (ed.), Der Literaturstreit, Tübingen: Max Niemeyer Verlag.

STRIPSKY, HIADOR (1937), published in facsimile and presented, Pázmány Péter ismeretlen magyar könyve: Okok, nem okok, Pozsony, 1631 [Péter Pázmány's Unknown Hungarian Book: Reasons, Non-Reasons, Pozsony, 1631], Budapest, a Pázmány-Egyetem Könyvsajtója.

SULYOK, ISTVÁN (1901), Az ev. református egyház [The Evangelical Reformed Church], in: Bihar vármegye és Nagyvárad [Bihar County and Nagyvárad], ed. Samu Borovszky, Budapest.

Varjas, Béla (1938), Pázmány Péter ismeretlen magyar könyve [Péter Pázmány's Unknown Hungarian Book], Magyar Könyvszemle.

Veress, Károly (1999), Filozófiai szemiotika [Philosophical Semiotics], Kolozsvár, Studium.

Wood, Susan K. (2011), Continuity and Development in Roman Catholic Ecclesiology, Ecclesiology 7, 147–172.

Zoványi, Jenő (1925), Sámbár Mátyás és Kis Imre hitvitái s az ezekkel egyidejű hitvitázó művek [The Religious Disputes of Mátyás Sámbár and Imre Kis and the Polemical Works Contemporary with These], Theologiai Szemle.

Gábor Ittzés

Church and Community in Luther's *Sermon on Preparing to Die* (1519)

Introduction

In May 1519, Luther received a request from an adviser to Elector Frederick the Wise of Saxony. Markus Schart (d. 1529) asked for a text on how to prepare for dying.[1] The Reformer, already busy preparing for a more imminent ordeal, initially responded with a short recommendation.[2] He suggested that the counsellor should read Johann von Staupitz's book.[3] After the Leipzig debate, however, he returned to the issue in September, and in early November Luther already sent complimentary copies of his own work on the subject to Schart, thanking him for a honorarium of ten guilders, which he had immediately donated to a needy person.[4]

The resulting work, *A Sermon on Preparing to Die*[5] was an immediate and lasting success. Although the first Wittenberg edition came out relatively late in the year, it was reissued in Leipzig, Nuremberg, and Augsburg still in 1519, and within a few years it was also printed in Erfurt, Altenburg, Strasbourg, Basel, and Vienna, effectively covering the length and breadth of the Empire.[6] The number of German

---

1 The details of the sermon's genesis are widely known and are readily available in most editions and in numerous discussions of the text. Here I only summarise the most salient stages of the story.

2 Cf. WABr 1:381.17–20, No. 171 (8 May 1519) and 1:394.15, No. 175 (16 May 1519), both by Luther to Georg Spalatin. Since Schart's original request has not been preserved, we do not known whether he had asked Luther for a recommendation or an original piece.

3 *Ein buchlein von der nachfolgūg des willigē sterbēs Christi* (1515): VD16 S 8697. Cf. Endriss: 1978.

4 Cf. WABr 1:508.12–13, No. 198 (22 Sep 1519) and 1:548.3–11, No. 215 (1 Nov 1519), both by Luther to Spalatin. The copy with Luther's autograph dedication to Schart is still available in the collection of the Herzog August Library, Wolfenbüttel, Germany (M: Li 5530 Slg. Hardt [19, 222], cf. http://dbs. hab.de/luther/search.php?m1=luthernr&st1=272, last accessed 25 Sep 2016).

5 English translation by Martin H. Bertram in *LW* 42:95–115. For the German original, see WA 2:679–697. Several early editions have been digitised and are readily available on the Internet through VD16. I only provide the link to the original Wittenberg edition here: http://dfg-viewer.de/show/?set%5Bmets%5D=http%3A%2F%2Fwww.dhm.de%2Fdaten-bank%2Fdhm_volldigi%2Fmets_RA000332.xml (VD16 L 6482, last accessed on 25 Sep 2016).

6 Cf. VD16 L 6473–6498.

editions rose to over two dozen by 1525.[7] In 1522, Luther incorporated the *Sermon* in the *Betbüchlein*, adding another fourteen to the number of its reprintings by his death in 1546.[8] Stephan Roth also included the *Sermon* in the Winter Postils, where it went through scores of further editions in German and Latin by the end of the sixteenth century.[9] The first Latin translation had actually appeared as early as 1519 in Antwerp, and it was followed by a Danish, a Dutch and even a Greek version before 1600 (cf. WA 2:683 (a–b); VD16 L 6339, 6499–6501; Benzing Nos. 458–460; 456b; 459a).

Interest in the *Sermon* has not abated. It is still in print[10] and, what is more, in active use in the church by practical theologians, pastors, and counsellors (see: Lasogga: 2014, Ngien: 2007, Schwambach: 2001, Ulrich-Eschemann: 2008, Winkler: 2000, 466–467). This small treatise of spiritual counsel is a landmark in the history of pastoral theology and a major contribution to the renewal of the *ars moriendi* tradition.[11] It is also a fascinating document of Luther's evolving views during the first years of the Reformation, not least of the development of his sacramental theology (cf. Gerke: 1934; Reinis: 2007, 75–82; Schwab: 1977; Stock: 1982). The *Sermon's* structure, and its use and understanding of images are further issues extensively discussed in the literature (cf. Brunner: 1978, Buchrucker: 1993, Jørgensen: 1993, Preul: 1997, Rau: 1983). My concern in this paper will be with the ecclesiology of this work, which has received relatively little critical attention (cf. Pinomaa: 1977; Scheele: 1996; Vajta: 1993).

I.

A convenient point of entry is a widely noted contrast between the Reformer's text and its fifteenth-century antecedents. The *ars moriendi* typically had a chapter on

---

7 The exact number depends on the criteria used to define an 'edition' by different bibliographies. In addition to VD16, cited in the previous note, see WA 2:680–683 (A–W), and Benzing Nos. 435–456, 451a, 455a, and 456a.

8 WA 10.II:331/375–482/501; on the editions, see WA 10.II:341; 368–369 (V, X–d, f–g, i–n); cf. VD16 L 542, 4099–4109, 4124; ZV 10039.

9 *Winterpostille*, 1528 (WA 21:IX/1–193); on the editions, see WA 21:XXIV and 192; cf. VD16 L 5591–5666, ZV 4666, 10097, 18461, 23097. This channel of transmission is disregarded by Reinis, who otherwise gives a relatively complete account of the work's publication history (2007, 48).

10 Esp. in German and English, but a new translation has also been recently published in Hungarian (Luther: 2015).

11 On Luther and the medieval tradition, see Akerboom: 2003; Barth: 1989; Goez: 1981; Hamm: 2014, 110–153; Ittzés, Gábor (2015) Luther sermója a halálra készülődésről (1519) és a középkori *ars moriendik*: Egy ötszáz éves könyvsiker nyomában, *Keresztyén Igazság* n.s. No. 107 (2015/3) 4–17.; Reinis: 2007, 1–75; Schottroff: 2012, esp. 32–49 (the book is an unaltered printing of the author's dissertation of 1958); Wicks: 1998.

what questions those present should ask of the dying person,[12] another on how they should behave at the deathbed, and the manuals also offered prayers that could be said for and with the dying person (Ars moriendi: 2004; cf. Comper 1907). In other words, the community which accompanies the terminally ill or weak to the very end of their earthly journey is of great concern to medieval instructors on the art of dying and features prominently in their works. Luther, by contrast, takes a very different approach.

Saints make their first appearance in section ten of the *Sermon on Preparing to Die*,[13] but we first meet the community in the very short opening paragraphs of the text. The first clause of the treatise deserves attention: "First, since death marks[14] a farewell from this world and all its activities…" [1].[15] This is deceptively simple. What the text leaves out is as important as what it says. We would expect the well-known formula, 'since death is a farewell of the soul to the body…', but Luther decidedly takes a practical theological (rather than metaphysical) approach. His initial focus is on the social, interpersonal aspect of death. Hence, brief instructions follow on the physical, or external, and spiritual leave in the first two sections. Both passages are short, but the first is especially so. In the original, it is not more than a single sentence. That is not where Luther's interest lies; he directs attention elsewhere. The beginning of section three clearly marks the shift in focus: "since everyone must depart, we must turn our eyes to God" [3]. The Reformer does not downplay the importance of one's departure from the community: "it is necessary that a man regulate his temporal goods properly" [1], and "we must cheerfully and sincerely forgive […and] earnestly seek […] forgiveness" [2]. Luther's crucial point is that worldly issues must be settled *before* one's deathbed. In the last hour, such mundane concerns no longer have a legitimate place. In the *Sermon*, the human community that is being left behind quickly recedes into the background and is only implicitly present throughout the tract in and for the administration of the sacraments. What we see instead is the welcoming community of saints.

Words like 'church' (*Kirche/ecclesia*) and 'congregation' or 'parish' (*Gemeinde*) are not used by Luther in this tract. He consistently speaks of 'the saints' instead. Disregarding adjectival uses, the word *heyligen* occurs eighteen times as noun in the

---

12 This goes back to what is usually considered the earliest example of the genre and called the Anselmian questions, i.e. PL 158:685–688 (*Admonitio morienti et de peccatis suis nimium formidanti*).

13 The *Sermon* consists of twenty verbally numbered passages (roughly, paragraphs), which provide easy orientation not only within the text but also across editions and even translations. When referencing the primary text, I will provide these internal section numbers in square brackets. Verbatim quotations will be supplied with specific page references to LW.

14 Actually, "is", cf. the German original: "Zum Ersten, Die weyl der todt eyn abschid ist von dißer welt und allen yhrer hendellen…" (WA 2:685.4–5).

15 All verbatim quotations in this paragraph are taken from LW 42:99.

text of the *Sermon*. The evidence can be arranged into four broad categories, with somewhat blurry edges. The saints are, first, those who died in Christ.[16] Second, they are a community;[17] and third, they are connected to the sacraments (especially, the Eucharist).[18] Finally, they can also be an item on a list including other creatures such as angels, all Christians, all creatures, and so on.[19] It might be added that, on the one hand, some instances are rather difficult to associate with any of the above categories, and, on the other hand,[20] 'saints' in the text of the *Sermon* are at times not impossible to interpret in a conventional late medieval sense as those to be called upon (*anruffen*) for intercession.[21]

There are several conclusions to be drawn from this brief analysis. One thing to notice is that Luther's usage is somewhat equivocal. He never defines the precise meaning of the term 'saints'. He uses it extensively, but its meaning is presupposed rather than explained. If we want a definition, it must be reconstructed from his usage. In other words, a 'medieval' or 'Catholic' understanding of the term as 'outstanding dead Christians canonised by the church' cannot be ruled out from the start. In fact, there is little in the *Sermon* that would fully exclude such an interpretation. On the other hand, the term can also refer to all believers, dead and alive, exceptional and ordinary. Thus even if we admit an apparently careless 'pre-Reformation' aspect of Luther's usage (and I am not saying we should), it will be clear that his views significantly diverge from a popular religious concept of saints as intercessors and 'merit-dispensers'. When Luther directs the dying person's attention to 'the saints', he surely does not so much want to refer them to intercessors certified by the institutional church and the Roman hierarchy as to incorporate them in the reassuring fullness of God's people. Finally, the semantic associations

---

16 [10]: WA 2:689.8–10 and [11]: WA 2:689.33–34 seem quite unambiguous. Two further occurrences ([10]: WA 2:689.12 and [11]: WA 2:689.29) are likely to have the same meaning, not least because of their proximity to the clear instances. Election is the key feature of the saints in the first instance in section twelve (WA 2:690.26–27), but since the dying person can thus recognise that he or she is *already* elected ("ßo bistu schon auch erwelet"; WA 2:690.28), the word naturally acquires the meaning of saints as dead people. Again given its proximity and, hence, the shared context, the second occurrence in the section (WA 2:690.30–31) takes on the same meaning, although we might also consider it of uncertain reference.

17 Here categorisation is based on explicit reference (chiefly, the occurrence of *gemeynschafft* in the original): [15]: WA 2:692.34; [16]: WA 2:694.24; [18]: WA 2:695.17–34. The last group obviously has a similar connotation.

18 [15]: WA 2:692.33–34; [17]: WA 2:694.1–2; [18]: WA 2:695.17–34.

19 [16]: WA 2:694.24; [18]: WA 2:695.17–20 and 31–34; [19]: WA 2:696.24–25 and 697.5–6; [20]: WA 2:697.22–23.

20 E.g., [13]: WA 2:690.37–38; [18]: WA 2:695.31–34; [20]: WA 2:697.22–24. Given the image of reaching *down* with their hands and *receiving* the soul of the dying person in the last two instances, respectively, they are perhaps closest to the first group.

21 Esp. [19]: WA 2:696.24–25; 697.5–6.

which we have identified as central to the Reformer's usage of the term 'saints' give us a helpful orientation for his thought.

To draw out implications of our philological findings, community is the central aspect Luther emphasises in connection with the saints. They never appear one by one in the *Sermon*. We always see them together as a group. Sometimes they are a subgroup of an even larger circle, and they are always connected to Christ. Third, saints and the sacraments are routinely mentioned in the same context, which signals some important connection between them. After this general overview based on the semantic connotations of a key term of Luther's text, we must now explore these themes in more detail.

II.

When they first appear, we see saints as 'members of Christ's court'. We must look at death in Christ and all his saints [10]. The image of grace is nothing but the image of Christ and his saints [11]. Predestination will not frighten us if we contemplate it in Christ and the saints, whom God elected [12]. "[D]eath, sin and hell will flee [...] if [...] we [...] keep our eyes on the glowing picture of Christ and his saints" [13] (LW 42:106). Conversely, we reject God and the saints if we trust in ourselves [12]. When God looks upon us, so do the saints and the angels because God commands them to [20]. Examples could be amplified, for this is a foundational role of saints in Luther's thought: they are members of Christ's court, keep him company and are inseparable from him. Wherever Christ is, there are also his saints.[22]

It is the sacraments that connect the dying person to this community. That is one of the most important functions of the sacraments. Luther makes the point repeatedly: "through the same sacraments you are included and made one with all the saints. You thereby enter into the true communion of saints so that they die with you in Christ, bear sin, and vanquish hell" [15] (LW 42:108). The Eucharist has been given as a promise and pledge of the communion of saints.[23] It strengthens faith by providing tangible evidence, irrespective of one's own merit, that one is a member of universal Christendom. Put differently, sacraments are "signs[...] tested and tried by all the saints and found reliable" [17] (LW 42:111), that is why the dying person can also trust them. Saints are thus witnesses to the efficacy of the sacrament.

---

22 Exploring a broader textual corpus, Vilmos Vajta generalises the point: "The fellowship of Christ and his saints constitutes the condition that Christ cannot be invoked in and of himself, isolated from his saints" [Krisztus és szentjeinek közössége azt a feltételt képezi, hogy Krisztust nem lehet önmagában, szentjeitől elszigetelve segítségül hívni] (1993, 72–73).

23 Cf. "the holy body of Christ[...] is a sign and promise of the communion of all angels and saints" [17] (LW 42:111); "in the most venerable Sacrament of the Body of Christ [...] are pointed out, promised, and pledged the communion, help, love, comfort, and support of all the saints in all times of need" [18] (LW 42:112).

While the sign (sacrament) is useless without faith, Luther puts tremendous emphasis of the 'givenness', the *extra nos* character of the sacrament. He would definitely reject as *Schwärmerei* a 'subjective' understanding of the sacrament in which faith played a constitutive role. Faith does not constitute the sacrament; God's promise does. Faith appropriates it. That is why the sacrament can effectively strengthen faith, which Luther keeps reiterating. Ecclesiologically, it is not the church that creates the sacrament but the other way round. Church is where the sacraments are rightly administered – a thesis that will find its ways into Lutheran confessions.

The role of saints on behalf of the dying person is not intercession but sharing in his or her burden. The point is made time and again in the *Sermon*, primarily in the context of bearing or overcoming the dying person's death, sin, and hell.[24] The basis is provided by the famous Pauline injunction: "Likewise," writes Luther, "all the saints who suffer and die in Christ also bear your sins and suffer and labor for you, as we find it is written: 'Carry each other's burdens, and in this way you will fulfil the law of Christ' [Gal 6:2]" [11] (LW 42:105). The communion of saints, on Luther's understanding, is true fellowship – with Christ and the Trinity on the one hand, but also with one another.

The urgency of personal faith – a central concern of the *Sermon* – is in part due to the fact, about which Luther was always very clear, that nobody can die my death for me (cf. LW 51:70 [*Eight Sermons at Wittenberg*, 1522]). If never before, at the hour of death each one of us will face the living God, and whether we meet God as a loving father or as a wrathful judge will be literally all-decisive, with eternal consequences. The Reformer is dead serious (pun intended) about the sheer personal immediacy of this business. But he is equally convinced that this personal immediacy need not entail loneliness in the face death. On the contrary, the believer is surely not alone, as Luther argues in a powerful passage in which numerous central themes come together:

> Eighteenth, in the hour of his death no Christian should doubt that he is not alone. He can be certain, as the sacraments point out, that a great many eyes are upon him: first, the eyes of God and of Christ himself, for the Christian believes his words and clings to his sacraments; then also, the eyes of the dear angels, of the saints, and of all Christians. There is no doubt, as the Sacrament of the Altar indicates, that all of these in a body run to him as one of their own, help him overcome sin, death, and hell, and bear all things with him [18] (LW 42:112).

---

24 [11]: WA 2:689.33–35; [15]: WA 2:692.34–35*; [17]: WA 2:694.24–26*; [18]: WA 2:695.22–24*, 28–29, 32–33; passages marked with an asterisk (*) also referencing the shared burden of death, sin, and hell.

In the continuation of the passage Luther even speaks of the eyes of all creatures being upon the dying person. Beyond an assurance and a hyperbolic expression of the totality of the community, this is also a proleptic reference to the eschatological renewal of creation.

The motif returns in the closing section: "[God] commands his angels, all saints, all creatures to join him in watching over you, to be concerned about your soul, and to receive it" [20] (LW 42:114). This harks back to the medieval image, often visualised as in the last picture of the illustrated *ars moriendi*, of the departing soul being received by either devils or angels. But it is also an expression of Luther's conviction that the communion of saints is a stronger bond than death itself. The saints receive the departing soul (which I think is here not to be interpreted substantially, in counterdistinction to the body, but metonymically, as the carrier of the whole personality). The believer is not alone even in this ultimate crisis. Death, which rends asunder all human bonds, tears off the individual from all earthly community – yet that removal turns out to be a welcoming inclusion in the heavenly community. This also brings the sermon full circle. The reorientation that began in the opening paragraphs is brought to consummation in the last section.

Finally, this context of the communion of saints helps us understand the invocation of saints as well: the believer "must call upon the holy angels, particularly his own angel, the Mother of God, and all the apostles and saints" [19] (LW 42:113). Luther speaks of calling upon the saints, and this has been seen as a remnant of his pre-Reformation heritage that he later discarded. It is clear, however, that saints do not stand on their own. The emphasis is, again, on the fullness of the community. And the singing Whitsun congregation of the continuation of the passage suggests that what Luther has in mind is, first, the communion of saints both living and dead, and second, the saints' participation in (and not their reception of) prayer: "we should implore God and his dear saints our whole life long for true faith in the last hour, as we sing so very fittingly on the day of Pentecost, 'Now let us pray to the Holy Spirit for the true faith...' " [19] (LW 42:114). Luther' subtle shift from supplication to hymn also reminds us of the indissoluble link between prayer and worship. They belong together, and both are central to the life of the church.

Interestingly, one aspect that is absolutely crucial to Luther's understanding of the church and elsewhere takes centre stage in his ecclesiology remains entirely implicit in this tract. What in his mature work the Reformer identifies as the first mark of the church, *viz.*, the Word of God (cf. LW 41:148 [*On the Councils and the Church*, 1539]) is never explicitly mentioned in the *Sermon on Preparing to Die*. That should not deceive us, however. Although Luther never overtly suggests that the dying person should read the Scriptures or comfort themselves by reciting Bible passages, his entire approach reflects a deeply biblically oriented mind-set. Scriptural citations and paraphrases make up at least fifteen per cent of the whole text and can by no means be considered ornamental or external to the overall argument. Luther relies on Bible-based arguments and routinely encourages the reader with Bible verses. It is precisely the self-evident nature of his exclusively biblical orientation throughout the text that betrays its strength and centrality to his theological position. To put it more bluntly, while the medieval *ars moriendi*, in whose development such towering intellectuals as Jean Gerson played a crucial part, cite scores of authorities from ancient philosophers through church fathers to medieval saints, scholars, and popes, the Reformer quotes none except the Bible. In addition to the sacraments and prayer, the Word of God is the third indispensable gift that is available to the dying person in the church as a fellowship of saints.

III.

The *Sermon on Preparing to Die* is surely not an ecclesiological piece per se, but it reveals a good deal of the early Luther's understanding of the church as it focuses on a literally extreme and transforming experience of human life – a context in which the church can become highly relevant. Ecclesiology is never foregrounded in the tract; Luther is motivated by a deep pastoral theological concern throughout. He neither champions an institutional approach, nor is he writing a dogmatic treatise. Yet what he has to say in this piece of spiritual counsel has, as we have seen, significant systematic implications.

Perhaps the least important of them is that we can answer the question posed by the title of the Sixth RefoRC Conference. It is clear that the church, as understood in the *Sermon*, certainly did not mean a building or institutional hierarchy, nor even a local community (parish) for the early Luther. It was much rather an invisible yet living community centred on Christ and those who accept him in faith. But the *Sermon* allows us to outline the nature of the church in more detail, at least as Luther saw it. Founded on and by the Word of God, the church subsists in mutual support and prayer. Its function is to strengthen faith in God, and the individual is connected to this community through the sacraments. In these different ways, participation and sharing are at the heart of the life of the church. Sin, death, and hell cannot overcome the church, for it is stronger than them.

Ever present in Luther's exposition is the indelible Christ-centredness of the church. He presents its members as the members of Christ's court. The saints never appear without Christ, nor he without them. Finally, one of the most creative aspects of Luther's treatment of the church in the *Sermon on Preparing to Die* is that he does not actually speak of it at all. Instead, he exclusively uses the term 'the saints', which gives us an angle from which to explore and rethink ecclesiology with a focus on the dynamism of individual and community, on fellowship, or on sanctity as a constitutive characteristic – but that invitation to constructive work is a much larger project and will have to await another opportunity.

Bibliography

AKERBOOM, DICK (2003), "...Only the Image of Christ in Us": Continuity and Discontinuity between Late Medieval ars moriendi and Luther's *Sermon von der Bereitung zum Sterben*, in: Hein Blommestijn/Charles Caspers/Rijcklof Hofman (ed.), Spirituality Renewed: Studies on Significant Representatives of the Modern Devotion, Leuven: Peeters, 209–272.

ARS MORIENDI (2004) Ars moriendi: A meghalás művészete, trans. László Virág, Budapest: Arcticus.

BARTH, HANS-MARTIN (1989) Leben und sterben können: Brechungen der spätmittelalterlichen *ars moriendi* in der Theologie Martin Luthers, in: Harald Wagner (ed.), Ars moriendi: Erwägungen zur Kunst des Sterbens, Freiburg i.B.: Herder, 45–66.

BRUNNER, PETER (1978), Luthers *Sermon von der Bereitung zum Sterben* ausgelegt: In einer textnahen Paraphrase mit einigen Erläuterungen. In: Zeitwende 49, 214–228.

BUCHRUCKER, ARMIN-ERNST (1993), Wer so stribt, der stribt wohl: Martin Luther über die Kunst zu sterben, Luther 64, 125–136.

COMPER, FRANCES M. M. (ed.) (1907), The Book of the Craft of Dying and Other Early English Tracts Concerning Death, London/New York: Longmans Green; repr. New York: Arno, 1977.

ENDRISS, ALBRECHT (1978), Nachfolgung der willigen Sterbens Christi: Interpretation des Staupitztraktates von 1515 und Versuch einer Einordnung in den frömmigkeitsgeschichtlichen Kontext, in: Josef Nolte/Hella Tompert/Christof Windhorst (ed.), Kontinuität und Umbruch: Theologie und Frommigkeit in Flugschriften und Kleinlitaratur an der Wende vom 15. zum 16. Jahrhundert: Beiträge zum Tübinger Kolloquium des Sonderforschungsbereichs 8 "Spätmittelalter und Reformation" (31. Mai–2. Juni 1975), Stuttgart: Klett-Kotta, 93–141.

GERKE, FRIEDRICH (1934), Anfechtung und Sakrament in Martin Luthers Sermon vom Sterben, Theologische Blätter 13, 193–204.

GOEZ, WERNER (1981), Luthers *Ein Sermon von der Bereitung zum Sterben* und die spätmittelalterliche ars moriendi, Lutherjahrbuch 48, 97–114.

HAMM, BERNDT (2014), The Early Luther: Stages in a Reformation Reorientation, trans. Martin J. Lohrmann, Grand Rapids/Cambridge: Eerdmans.

ITTZÉS, GÁBOR (2015) Luther sermója a halálra készülődésről (1519) és a középkori *ars moriendik*: Egy ötszáz éves könyvsiker nyomában, *Keresztyén Igazság* n.s. No. 107 (2015/3) 4–17.

JØRGENSEN, THEODOR H. (1993), Wort und Bild bei Luther: Uberlegt an Hand seines *Sermons von der Bereitung zum Sterben* von 1519: Clemen I, S 161–173, in: Anja Ghiselli/Kari Kopperi/Rainer Vinke (ed.), Luther und Ontologie: Das Sein Christi im Glauben als strukturierendes Prinzip der Theologie Luthers, Helsinki: Luther Agricola Society/Erlangen: Martin-Luther-Verlag, 142–154.

LASOGGA, MAREILE (2014), Die rettende Macht der Bilder: Martin Luthers *Sermon von der Bereitung zum Sterben* (1519), Luther 85, 140–148.

Luther, Martin (2015), Sermo a halálra való készülődésről, trans. Károly Friedrich/Andor Muntag, in: Luther Válogatott Művei, 6 vols. to date, Budapest: Luther Kiadó, 2011–, 6:111–124.

Ngien, Dennis (2007), Picture Christ: Martin Luther's Advice on Preparing to Die, Christianity Today 51.4, 66–69.

Pinomaa, Lennart (1977), Die Heiligen bei Luther, Helsinki: Ari-paino.

Preul, Reiner (1997), Der Tod des ganzen Menschen: Luthers Sermon von der Bereitung zum Sterben, in: V. Drehsen/D. Henke/R. Schmidt-Rost/W. Steck (ed.), Der 'ganze Mensch': Perspektiven lebensgeschichtlicher Individualität: Festschrift für Dietrich Rössler zum siebzigsten Geburtstag, Berlin/New York: Walter de Gruyter, 111–130.

Rau, Gerhard (1983), Erfahrung und Offenbarung in der Bereitung zum Sterben, Pastoraltheologie 72, 386–390.

Reinis, Austra (2007), Reforming the Art of Dying: The ars moriendi in the German Reformation (1519–1528), Aldershot/Burlington: Ashgate.

Scheele, Paul-Werner (1996), "Eingeleibt und vereinigt mit allen Heiligen": Martin Luthers Zeugnis von der Gemeinschaft der Heiligen in seinem Sermon von der Bereitung zum Sterben in: Udo Hahn/Marlies Mügge (ed.) Martin Luther: Vorbild im Glauben: Die Bedeutung des Reformators im ökumenischen Gespräch, Neukirchen-Vluyn: Neukirchener Verlag, 171–184.

Schottroff, Louise (2012), Die Bereitung zum Sterben: Studien zu den frühen reformatorischen Sterbebüchern, Göttingen: Vandenhoeck & Ruprecht.

Schwab, Wolgang (1977), Entwicklung und Gestalt der Sakramententheologie bei Martin Luther, Frankfurt a.M./Bern: Lang.

Schwambach, Claus (2001), "Suche dich nur in Christus!": Luthers Ein Sermon von der Bereitung zum Sterben als Herausforderung fur die christliche Verkundigung und Seelsorge, in: Christian Hermann/Eberhard Hahn (ed.), Festhalten am Bekenntnis der Hoffnung: Festgabe fur Professor Dr. Reinhard Slenczka zum 70. Geburtstag, Erlangen: Martin-Luther-Verlag, 165–189.

Stock, Ursula (1982), Die Bedeutung der Sakramente in Luthers Sermonen von 1519, Leiden: Brill.

Ulrich-Eschemann, Karin (2008), Begleitung beim Sterben – Bereitung zum Sterben: Ein tröstliches Beispiel aus Luthers Sermon von der Bereitung zum Sterben, in: Leben, auch wenn wir sterben: Christliche Hoffnung lernen und lehren, Göttingen: Vandenhoeck & Ruprecht, 59–61.

Vajta, Vilmos (1993), Communio: Krisztus és a szentek közössége Luther teológiájában, Budapest: Magyarországi Luther Szövetség.

Wicks, Jared, S.J. (1998), Applied Theology at the Deathbed: Luther and the Late-Medieval Tradition of the Ars moriendi, Gregorianum 79, 345–368.

Winkler, Klaus (2000), Seelsorge, 2nd ed., Berlin: Walter de Gruyter.

Jeannette Kreijkes

Pastors and Teachers: Two Offices or One? [1]

Calvin's Reception of Chrysostom's Exegesis of Ephesians 4:11

Introduction

Calvin seems to prefer Chrysostom to other early Christian interpreters. The Reformer states that he considers Chrysostom to be the best ancient exegete (COR VI/I.403; Kreijkes: 2016a, 347, 350; Kreijkes: 2016b, 238).[2] Besides, Chrysostom is the church father most frequently cited in Calvin's New Testament commentaries (Walchenbach: 1974/2010, 49). Therefore, he could be regarded as an authority for Calvin's exegetical method. However, a close look at Calvin's reception of Chrysostom's exegesis reveals his reluctance to accept all of Chrysostom's interpretations. Therefore, one could ask to what extent Calvin regarded Chrysostom as his superior.

An intriguing example of Calvin's explicit disagreement with Chrysostom concerns the number of the offices mentioned in Eph 4:11:

> So Christ himself gave the apostles, the prophets, the evangelists, the pastors and teachers to equip his people for works of service, so that the body of Christ may be built up until we all reach unity in the faith and in the knowledge of the Son of God and become mature, attaining to the whole measure of the fullness of Christ (trans. *New International Version*).[3]

---

1 The ongoing Ph.D. research on which this paper is based has received funding from The Netherlands Organisation for Scientific Research (NWO, Doctoral Grant for Teachers, grant agreement number 023.004.106). This essay represents the state of research when the paper was delivered (2016). In the dissertation, some of these conclusions will be put into a broader perspective and, consequently, nuanced.
2 COR VI/I.403 (*Praef. In Chry. Hom.*): "Sunt autem homiliae, quae cum variis partibus constent, primum tamen in illis locum tenet scripturae interpretatio, in qua Chrysostomum nostrum vetustos omnes scriptores qui hodie extant antecedere nemo sani iudicii negaverit, praesertim ubi novum testamentum tractat. Nam quominus in veteri tantum praestaret, obstabat hebraicae linguae imperitia." Trans. Hazlett: 1991, 143: "Although homilies are something which consist of a variety of elements, the interpretation of Scripture is, however, their priority.

In this area no one of sound judgement would deny that our Chrysostom excels all the ancient writers currently extant. This is especially true, when he deals with the New Testament. For the lack of Hebrew prevented him from showing so much expertise in the Old Testament."
3 NA28: [11]Καὶ αὐτὸς ἔδωκεν τοὺς μὲν ἀποστόλους, τοὺς δὲ προφήτας, τοὺς δὲ εὐαγγελιστάς, τοὺς δὲ ποιμένας καὶ διδασκάλους, [12]πρὸς τὸν καταρτισμὸν τῶν ἁγίων εἰς ἔργον διακονίας, εἰς οἰκοδομὴν

Does this passage refer to five offices (Calvin's view) or four (Chrysostom's interpretation)? This essay aims to assess Calvin's disagreement with Chrysostom's exegesis of these verses.

Calvin rejects Chrysostom's explanation as follows:

> Some think that *pastors and teachers* denote one office, because there is no disjunctive particle, as in the other parts of the verse, to distinguish them. Chrysostom and Augustine are of this opinion. For what we read in the Ambrosian commentaries is too childish and unworthy of Ambrose (trans. Parker: 1965, 179).[4]

The attention Calvin pays to Ambrose's exegesis serves as an indication to determine which source or sources Calvin used for his references to the church fathers he mentions as is described in section 4. Calvin acknowledges the fact that the interpretation of Augustine and Chrysostom is supported by the grammatical construction of the Greek text.

In light of Calvin's esteem for Chrysostom's exegesis, given that Chrysostom was a native speaker,[5] it is striking that he contradicts Chrysostom here. This observation leads to the central question of this essay: Do pastors and teachers denote two offices or one? Taking Eph 4:11 and Calvin's commentary on it as starting points, this essay subsequently highlights the following aspects: (1) The significance of different offices to Calvin, (2) the *in*significance of different offices to Chrysostom, and (3) Calvin's and Chrysostom's views on *pastors* and *teachers*. Finally, (4) some tentative explanations for the differences between Calvin's and Chrysostom's findings are provided.

τοῦ σώματος τοῦ Χριστοῦ, [13]μέχρι καταντήσωμεν οἱ πάντες εἰς τὴν ἑνότητα τῆς πίστεως καὶ τῆς ἐπιγνώσεως τοῦ υἱοῦ τοῦ θεοῦ, εἰς ἄνδρα τέλειον, εἰς μέτρον ἡλικίας τοῦ πληρώματος τοῦ Χριστοῦ.

4 COR II/XVI.230 (*Comm. Eph.* 4:11): "Per Doctores et Pastores unum officium ideo designari quidam putant, quia disiunctiva particula, quemadmodum in prioribus, non habetur, quae alterum ab altero discernat. Qua in sententia sunt Chrysostomus et Augustinus. Nam quae in commentariis Ambrosianis leguntur, nimis puerilia sunt et indigna Ambrosio." In Parker's translation I have changed "doctors" to "teachers". According to Henderson (1965, 9n3, 41), who prefers the translation "doctors" to "teachers", Calvin used it as a technical term in his 1539 *Responsio ad Sadoleti Epistolam* (CO 5.386): "Doctoris primum, deinde pastoris munere in ecclesia illa functus sum." Trans. H. Beveridge (1844) in Olin: 2000, 44: "In that Church I have held the office first of Doctor, and then of Pastor." However, since I am assessing what exactly brings Calvin to his interpretation, I have chosen for the more neutral rendering of "teachers". Additionally, the translation of Chrysostom's explanation of Eph 4:11 in Mayer/Allen (2000, 63–64) has "teachers" as well.

5 CO 45.308 (*Comm. in Harm. Ev. Luc.* 7:35): "Deinde Chrysostomus, cui graeca lingua nativa erat, perinde hoc transit ac si nihil esset controversiae."; trans. W. Pringle: 1998, Luke 7:35: "Besides, Chrysostom, whose native language was Greek, passes over this matter, as if there were no room for debate."

1. The Significance of Different Offices to Calvin

The immediate context of his explanation of Eph 4:11–13 demonstrates that Calvin considers the very existence of offices significant. He attaches more importance to the very existence of offices than Chrysostom does. This distinction leads to different views on God's purpose with the offices and on the relationship between offices and gifts. According to Calvin, God wishes unity in the church. This unity arises out of variety: "as various tones in music make a sweet melody." Variety reveals itself in different gifts of the Holy Spirit. Through the dispensation of different types of grace, God governs the church. Calvin stresses that anything related to church government, for example, the availability of ministers of the Gospel, their necessary qualifications, and the execution of their office, is not invented by people but is a *gift* of Christ (COR II/XVI, 228–229; trans. Parker: 1965, 178).

Calvin replies to someone who is surprised that Paul enumerated *offices* instead of *gifts* – for he was speaking about the Holy Spirit:

> Whenever men are called by God, gifts are necessarily connected with offices. For God does not cover men with a mask in appointing them apostles or pastors, but also furnishes them with gifts without which they cannot properly discharge their office (COR II/XVI, 228; trans. Parker: 1965, 178).

Thus, for Calvin, offices and gifts belong together, and the gifts received correspond to the calling to a specific ministry.

Considering both the duties and the gifts of office-bearers, Calvin discerns five classes of offices: (1) Apostles, (2) evangelists, (3) prophets, (4) pastors, and (5) teachers. The different names of the offices point to the diversity of the members forming the complete body of Christ (COR II/XVI.228–231; trans. Parker: 1965, 178–180).[6] Just before commenting on these five offices, Calvin refers to the disagreement among interpreters on the number: "For some consider the two last make but one office." Although he announces that he will omit the views of others (COR II/XVI.229; trans. Parker: 1965, 179), Calvin does make an exception for the interpretations of Chrysostom, Augustine, and Ambrose further on (COR II/XVI.230; trans. Parker: 1965, 179), which indicates their importance to Calvin.

---

6 McKee (1988, 31–32) states that concerning the ministry of pastors in the 1536 *Institutes*, Calvin seems to have seen it as a "function" rather than as an "office;" it was more a reaction against the existing practice than a prescription. See also Speelman (2014, 108–109), who notes that in the second half of 1541 – thus before his 1548 *Commentary on Ephesians* – Calvin established four functions in the Genevan church: Pastors, teachers, elders, and deacons. The first two offices had already been generally accepted among the followers of the Reformation. The offices of elders and deacons, which were lay offices until then, became official ecclesiastical functions. In his 1543 *Institutes*, Calvin would explain how he derives these functions from Scripture.

Calvin takes the word *apostles* in its particular signification (the Twelve and Paul), instead of its general meaning ("those who are sent"). The apostles had to build the kingdom of Christ throughout the whole world without having churches of their own. They only had the mandate "to preach the Gospel wherever they went." The office of the *evangelists* was closely related to that of the apostles but was of an inferior rank ("Tantum gradu dignitatis erant dispares"), as Calvin explains. Therefore, the Lord employed the evangelists as assistants of the apostles (COR II/XVI.229; trans. Parker: 1965, 179).

Between these two offices, Paul inserted the class of the *prophets*, Calvin argues. Given that the context focuses on the subject of *doctrine*, Calvin considers their main duties to be interpreting prophecies and relating them to contemporary events "by a unique gift of revelation." However, he does not exclude the gift of predicting future events, which usually accompanies their teaching (COR II/XVI.229–230; trans. Parker: 1965, 179).[7] According to Calvin, the offices of *apostles, prophets,* and *evangelists* were temporary (COR II/XVI. 231). The different offices reveal the diversity of the members from which the completeness of Christ's body arises. Emulation, envy, and ambition corrupt this unification. Calvin states that "what each has received is not held for himself alone, but to be put in the common pool" (COR II/XVI.229; trans. Parker: 1965, 178).[8]

2. The Insignificance of Different Offices to Chrysostom

How does Chrysostom understand the purpose of the offices, as well as their relationship to the gifts and the unity of the church? Concerning God's purpose, Chrysostom states that Paul shows God's providential care in descending to people. Because of His wisdom, God "wouldn't have distributed the spiritual gifts at random" but aimed at the unity of faith giving one more, one less (PG 62.83–84, Field, 218A–219A (*In Eph. hom.* 11.2); trans. Mayer/Allen: 2000, 64; Ritter: 1972, 84–85).

Unlike Calvin, who highlights that the offices are gifts from Christ, Chrysostom focuses on the trinitarian character of these gifts. For Chrysostom, it is irrelevant whether the gifts are the work of God, Christ, or the Holy Spirit (PG 62.83, Field 218A–B; Kohlgraf: 2001, 184). Like Calvin, Chrysostom relates the distinct offices to gifts received from God. However, Chrysostom points out that someone's ministry depends on the measure of the gifts received and on human collaboration (Mihoc:

---

7 See also CO 49.517 (*Comm. I Cor.* 14:3), to which chapter Calvin refers here. COR II/XVI, 230n31 also mentions CO 49.500 (*Comm. I Cor.* 12:10) and CO 49.506f (*Comm. I Cor.* 12:28).

8 Here, Calvin refers to 1 Cor 12. COR II/XVI, 229n29 refers to CO 49.497–500 (*Comm. I Cor.* 12:4–10).

2008, 190–192), whereas Calvin argues that the skills given by God correspond to the five offices.

Chrysostom considers the common task, the edification of the church, to be more important than the different kinds of offices. This task can be performed as: (1) *apostles*, who had all the gifts; (2) *prophets*, since not everyone could be apostles; (3) *evangelists*, who preached the Gospel in their own place and did not travel; and (4) *pastors* and *teachers*, who were responsible for a whole race. Chrysostom regards the more gifted limbs of the body of Christ as more honourable because they are of greater responsibility for the entire body. Nevertheless, Chrysostom encourages people who think that they contribute less than others: It does not matter if it is only in harmony with the gifts received (PG 62.83, Field, 218B–D; cf. Mihoc: 2008, 192–193). Everyone has a common task. Regardless of position, everyone should build each other up: "Don't talk to me about the disparity among the spiritual gifts, but that they all had one task" (PG 62.83–84, Field, 218D–219A); trans. Mayer/Allen: 2000, 64–65). Despite Chrysostom's emphasis on a common task – contrary to Calvin, who focuses on different duties – he, like Calvin, warns those who have received gifts not to be jealous of someone else. Envy would harm the intended unity (PG 62.83–84, Field, 218F–219A).

3. Calvin's and Chrysostom's Views on Pastors and Teachers

How do Calvin and Chrysostom explain the *pastors* and *teachers*? As stated, Calvin believes that pastors and teachers are two offices. In contrast, Chrysostom and Augustine – contrary to Ambrose, with whom Calvin disagrees as well – suppose that they denote one single office. Calvin agrees with them in that Paul saw no difference between pastors and teachers as far as they belonged to one and the same class. Although the name of "teacher" does, to some extent, apply to all pastors, for Calvin, this broader use of the term "teacher" is no reason to mix two different offices up (COR II/XVI.230; trans. Parker: 1965, 179). Acknowledging the close relationship between them, Calvin observes two significant differences: (1) The necessary gifts to receive from Christ and (2) their working areas.

Although Calvin considers teaching to be the duty of all pastors, not all of them receive the gift of correctly interpreting the Bible. However, this gift is essential to maintaining sound doctrine, the duty of teachers. Likewise, being a teacher does not imply that one is suited to preach. Although a pastor could also become a teacher and vice versa, their abilities (*facultates*) are different (COR II/XVI.230–231; trans. Parker: 1965, 179).[9] Regarding the working areas, Calvin sees pastors as being

---

9 Parker translates *facultates* as "duties."

responsible for particular flocks. They are allowed to be called teachers as well, provided that the distinction between the teacher who is in charge of the instruction of pastors and of the whole church (teacher) and the teacher who educates the church only (pastor) is taken into account (COR II/XVI.230–231).

Despite the different gifts and working areas, Calvin discovers a similarity between these offices: Without pastors and teachers, there can be no government of the church. This prerequisite implies that these offices are intended to be permanent (COR II/XVI.231). Chrysostom, however, considers the nature and number of gifts given to pastors to be the same as those received by teachers. Therefore, he does not make a distinction between their measures of responsibility and between their ranks (cf. PG 62.83, Field, 218C).

Chrysostom also discusses the working area. Because the employment of pastors/teachers is limited to one location, he regards them as inferior to those who go into the whole world to proclaim the Gospel. Relating this passage to what Paul states in "another epistle" makes it possible to derive a hierarchy from it, according to Chrysostom (PG 62.83, Field, 218C–D; trans. Mayer/Allen: 2000, 64; cf. Ritter: 1972, 121).[10]

Thus, the overall picture is that both Chrysostom and Calvin strongly relate the offices to the gifts received from God. Calvin sees a distinction between pastors and teachers regarding their gifts, offices, and working areas, whereas Chrysostom does not. Unlike Chrysostom, Calvin emphasises the indispensability and permanence of the offices of pastor and teacher.

4. Tentative Explanations for the Differences

The question of how the differences between Calvin's and Chrysostom's interpretations can be explained is still unanswered. However, some linguistic and intertextual factors, as well as some contextual and theological ones can be identified. They are interrelated.

The linguistic argument for Chrysostom and Augustine's interpretation of one office Calvin briefly refers to concerns the missing "τοὺς δὲ" before "διδασκάλους." However, since Chrysostom, native speaker of Greek, addresses his homilies to a Greek-speaking audience, it would have been remarkable if he had explicitly mentioned the absence of "τοὺς δὲ" as an argument for his interpretation. Did Calvin derive the argument from a Latin translation of Chrysostom's homilies? The claim is not found in the Latin Chevallon edition (Chrysostom: 1536, vol. 4,

---

10 Kohlgraf: 2001, 179 refers to 1 Cor 12 and claims that Chrysostom focuses on the hierarchy of offices. Nevertheless, Kohlgraf states that Chrysostom does not provide an extensive explanation of the offices, which might be regarded as contradictory to Kohlgraf's viewpoint.

401v°), which Calvin is supposed to have used for his references to Chrysostom (cf. Ganoczy/Müller: 1981).[11] Chrysostom's Greek homily on Eph 4:11 in the Migne and the Field editions, which texts mainly correspond to this passage in the Latin Chevallon edition, does not mention this argument either. Chrysostom does not even address the question of whether *pastors* and *teachers* denote two offices or only one (PG 62.82–84, Field, 217D–219A).

Given that, for Calvin, the 'right' interpretation of scripture is in line with the exegetical tradition (McKee: 1988, 165), one would expect that the reference to Chrysostom occurs in expositions of Ephesians 4 in anthologies and commentaries in Calvin's immediate context.[12] However, the argument is not found in the *Glossa Ordinaria* (1480/1481, vol. 4, 1108v°) nor in the *Biblia sacra cum glossis Lyrani* (1545, vol. 6, 94),[13] Jacques Lefèvre d'Étaples's commentary (1512, 168r°) or Erasmus's 1516 *Annotationes* (Erasmus: 2009, 220–222), nor in Bucer's (1527, 84v°–86v°)[14] and Bullinger's (1537, 430–431) commentaries on Ephesians. Martin Luther did not write a commentary on Ephesians. Moreover, Luther only seldom referred to this letter in his writings (Schnackenburg: 1991, 311). In Catholic sources, for example, Johannes Gagnaeus's *Brevissima & facillima in omnes divi Pauli epistolas scholia* (1543, 88v–89r) and Johannes Eck's 1521 *De Primatu Petri*, Chrysostom's exegesis is considered. However, neither Gagneus nor Eck uses it to substantiate the interpretation that pastors and teachers denote one office. Nevertheless, Eck does claim that Chrysostom relates Peter's office to Eph 4:11. According to Eck, Peter's apostleship differed from that of the other apostles, since Christ had commanded Peter to take care of His sheep (Eck: 1521, I.lix v).

How about Calvin's reference to Augustine? Augustine is the church father who explicitly refers to the missing disjunctive particle as an argument for pastors and teachers as one office (PL 33.635 (*Epist.* 149.II, 11)).[15] Did Calvin confuse Chrysostom with Augustine? That could have been the case since Calvin often cites the church fathers from memory (Lane: 1999, 6). Another possibility is that,

---

11 Contra Ganoczy/Müller, see Kreijkes: 2016b.

12 The selection of sources is based on COR II/XVI.xxi–xxvi.

13 COR II/XVI.xliv, n19 refers to Ganoczy: 1969, 183, where this edition is described as appearing in the 1572 catalogue of the library of the Genevan Academy.

14 However, see also Bucer: 1562, 107–108, where Chrysostom is mentioned approvingly, but not concerning the question of how many offices "pastors" and "teachers" denote.

15 "Ideo enim non ait, Quosdam autem pastores, quosdam vero doctores; cum superiora ipso locutionis genere distingueret dicendo, *Quosdam quidem apostolos, quosdam autem prophetas, quosdam vero evangelistas*: sed hoc tanquam unum aliquid duobus nominibus amplexus est, *quosdam autem pastores et doctores*." Trans. Parsons: 1953, 248: "He [Paul, JHK] did not say 'some pastors and some doctors', but, after he had differentiated the previous terms by listing each one with its distinguishing word, 'some apostles and some prophets and other some evangelists', he joined these two nouns as if they were one term: 'and other some pastors and doctors.'"

although Calvin disagrees with Chrysostom's and Augustine's interpretations, he ascribes Augustine's argument also to Chrysostom.

If this were the case and Calvin used a secondary source, it might have been Erasmus's *Annotationes*. Calvin does not seem to know more about Ambrose's and Augustine's interpretations than the information Erasmus provides (Erasmus: 2009, 220–222).[16] Erasmus explicitly disagrees with Ambrosiaster, whom he incorrectly takes for Ambrose, as Calvin also does. Erasmus states that Ambrosiaster distinguishes pastors from teachers by regarding teachers – contrary to pastors – as exorcists (Erasmus, 2009, 222).[17] Quoting Augustine more or less literally, Erasmus gives the argument Calvin refers to (Erasmus: 2009, 220–222).[18] Regardless of whether Calvin himself relates Augustine's considerations to Chrysostom's exegesis or follows Erasmus in doing so, why did this linguistic argument not convince Calvin?

Maybe, it did. However, given that the Roman Catholics, such as Eck, used this text as proof for their primacy (McKee: 1988, 148), Calvin had no option but to argue against it. In his *Institutes*, Calvin rejects Eck's viewpoints as described in *De Primatu Petri* (*Inst.* IV.6, OS V.90–104), and he could have been familiar with the way in which Eck used Chrysostom's exegesis of Eph 4:11. In his own commentary on Ephesians, Calvin claims that "there is no passage of Scripture which more strongly overturns that tyrannical hierarchy, in which one earthly head is set up." There is only one detail: Paul himself did not say anything about the primacy. Calvin responds to this imaginary objection that, if Paul had known "a primacy with one seat," he would have exhibited one ministerial head governing all the members; but he did not ... Thus, according to Calvin, either Paul blundered in omitting "the most appropriate and powerful argument" for the primacy or the primacy deviates from "the appointment of Christ." Calvin opts for the latter: Paul rejected the primacy as being invented (COR II/XVI.231; trans. Parker: 1965, 180).

Calvin does not seem to have been aware of the context of Chrysostom's exegesis, saying that a pastor/teacher belongs to the lowest class in the hierarchy (PG 62.83, Field, 218C–D). Unlike Chrysostom, Calvin considers the ministry of the Word and Sacraments the "fundamental and chief office" in the church (cf. McKee: 1988, 123). In Calvin's context, pastors had the freedom of preaching, which makes them more independent than any other office-bearer (Speelman: 2014, 109, 120). According to Chrysostom, pastors and teachers are settled on one spot and, thus, less influential.

---

16 In his comment on Eph 4:12 (COR II/XVI.231), Calvin refers to Erasmus as well.

17 See also Ambrosius/Ambrosiaster, PL 17.409C/D (*Comm. In Eph.* 4:11); trans. Bray: 2009, 49: "The pastors may be readers, who instruct the people with readings [...]. The teachers are the exorcists because in the church they are the ones who restrain and beat the unruly. They are also the ones who used to teach children their lessons, a custom which is found among the Jews and which was inherited by us, but which has become obsolete through neglect."

18 Erasmus states that Augustine followed Jerome's interpretation.

When a pastor/teacher has supreme power, there is more need for balancing power to prevent one from forming a monarchy than when a pastor/teacher is at the bottom of the hierarchy.

In his *Institutes*, Calvin explains why there should be no monarchy in the church. The passage from book IV sheds more light on the theological factor in relation to the contextual one. Calvin allows the term "hierarchy" to be used for the ancient church government, since it was in line with Scripture. Over time, however, this church government has developed into the contemporary tyranny of the papacy (*Inst.* IV.4.1–IV.5.19, OS V.57–90). The Roman Catholics consider it to be indispensable for the constitution of the church that the pope has the same power and authority as Christ had (*Inst.* IV.6.1, OS V.90). If one office is at the top of the hierarchy, a monarch would be selected from that top. However, Calvin cannot allow that people are honoured at the expense of the glory Christ deserves. Only Christ's monarchy is lawful in the church. Ministers of the Word should be colleagues and companions (COR II/XVI.231; *Inst.* IV.6.10, OS V.97–98). The division of responsibilities between them contributes to establishing equality.

5. Conclusion

Theological and contextual factors led Calvin to his conclusion that pastors and teachers were two different offices, whereas Chrysostom thinks that pastors and teachers denote one office. The variety of offices and of the gifts matching these offices is important to Calvin. This diversity results in unity. Probably because of his use of Erasmus's *Annotationes* and his acquaintance with Eck's *De Primatu Petri*, Calvin was unaware of Chrysostom's emphasis on commonality and his understanding of pastors and teachers as being at the bottom of the hierarchy. However, Calvin regards them as maintaining the highest rank. Although he considers the interpretation of one office to be linguistically defensible, Calvin's belief that Christ is the only Monarch in the church prevented him from ascribing supreme power to individual humans. This position might have been the main reason for Calvin's distinction between pastors and teachers.

Bibliography

AUGUSTINE, Saint (1953), Letter 149, Letters, vol. 3 (131–164), trans. W. Parsons, The Fathers of the Church, vol. 20, Washington, D.C.: Catholic University of America Press.

Biblia cum glossa ordinaria Walafridi Strabonis aliorumque et interlineari Anselmi Laudunensis (1480/1481) vol. 4, Strasbourg: Adolf Rusch pro Antonio Koberger.

Biblia sacra cum glossis Lyrani (1545) vol. 6, Lyon: Antoine Vincent.

BRAY, G.L. (2009), Commentaries on Galatians – Philemon: Ambrosiaster, Downers Grove: IVP Academic, Ancient Christian Texts.

BUCER, Martin (1527), *Epistola D. Pauli ad Ephesios … commentarius …*, Strasbourg.

BUCER, Martin (1562), *Praelectiones doctiss. in Epistolam D.P. ad Ephesios*, Basel: Peter Perna.

BULLINGER, Heinrich (1537), *In omnes Apostolicas epistolas, divi videlicet Pauli XIIII. et VII. Canonicas, commentarii Heinrychi Bullingeri, …*, Zurich: Christophorus Froschouerus.

CALVIN, John (1863–1900), *Joannis Calvini Opera quae supersunt omnia (CO)*, ed. G. Baum, E. Cunitz, and E. Reuss [Corpus Reformatorum. vol. 29–87], Braunschweig: Schwetschke.

CALVIN, John (1992–), *Ioannis Calvini Opera Omnia denuo recognita et adnotatione critica instructa notisque illustrate (COR)*, ed. B.G. Armstrong et al. Geneva: Droz.

CALVIN, John (1926–1936), *Joannis Calvini Opera selecta (OS)*, ed. Peter Barth, Wilhelm Niesel, Dora Scheuner, Munich: Chr. Kaiser Verlag.

CALVIN, John (1965), The Epistles of Paul the Apostle to the Galatians, Ephesians, Philippians and Colossians, trans. Parker, T.H.L. ed. D.W./T.F. Torrance, Grand Rapids: William B. Eerdmans Publishing Company.

CALVIN, John (1998), Commentary on Matthew, Mark, Luke, vol. 2, The Comprehensive Calvin Collection, trans. W. Pringle, Albany: Ages Software.

CHRYSOSTOM, John (1536), *Divi Ioannis Chrysostomi Archiepiscopi Constantinopolitani Opera*, 5 vol., Paris: Claude Chevallon.

ECK, Johannes (1521), *De Primatu Petri adversus Ludderum Ioannis Eckii … libri tres …, liber secundus*, Paris: Conrad Resch.

ERASMUS, Desiderius (2009), *Opera Omnia Desiderii Erasmi Roterodami VI-9, recognita et adnotatione critica et instructa notisque illustrata*, ed. M.L van Poll-van de Lisdonk, Leiden: Brill.

FIELD F. (1854–1862), Joannis Chrysostomi Interpretatio Omnium Epistularum Paulinarum. I-VII, Oxford: Bibliotheca Patrum.

GAGNAEUS, Johannes (1543), *Brevissima & facillima in omnes divi Pauli epistolas scholia …*, Paris: Simon Colinaeus.

GANOCZY, A. (1969), La Bibliothèque de l'Académie de Calvin: Le catalogue de 1572 et ses enseignements, Geneva: Librairie Droz.

GANOCZY, A./MÜLLER, K. (1981), Calvins handschriftliche Annotationen zu Chrysostomus: ein Beitrag zur Hermeneutik Calvins, Wiesbaden: Steiner.

HAZLETT, W.I.P. (1991), Calvin's Latin Preface to His Proposed French Edition of Chrysostom's Homilies: Translation and Commentary, ed. James Kirk, Humanism and Reform: The Church in Europe, England and Scotland, 1400–1463, Oxford: Blackwell Publishers, 129–150.

HENDERSON, R.W. (1996), The Teaching Office in the Reformed Tradition: A History of the Doctoral Ministry, 2nd ed., Eugene: Wipf and Stock.

KOHLGRAF, P. (2001), Die Ekklesiologie des Epheserbrief in der Auslegung durch Johannes Chrysostomus: Eine Untersuchung zur Wirkungsgeschichte paulinischer Theologie, Bonn: Borengässer.

KREIJKES, J. (2016a), The *Praefatio in Chrysostomi Homilias* as an Indication that Calvin Read Chrysostom in Greek, ed. H.J. Selderhuis/A. Huijgen, Calvinus Pastor Ecclesiae. Papers of the Eleventh International Congress on Calvin Research, Göttingen: Vandenhoeck & Ruprecht, 347–354.

KREIJKES, J. (2016b), Calvin's Use of the Chevallon Edition of Chrysostom's *Opera Omnia:*Onderkant formulier

Bovenkant formulier

Onderkant formulier

The Relationship between the Marked Sections and Calvin's Writings, Church History and Religious Culture 96.3, 237–265.

LANE, A.N.S. (1999), John Calvin: Student of the Church Fathers, Edinburgh: T&T Clark Ltd.

LEFÈVRE D'ÉTAPLES, Jacques (1512), *Faber Stapulensis S. Pauli Epistolae XIV ex Vulgata adjecta intelligentia ex graeco, cum commentariis,* Stuttgart-Bad Cannstatt: Frommann-Holzboog.

MAYER, W./ALLEN, P. (2000), John Chrysostom, London/New York: Routledge.

MCKEE, E.A. (1988), Elders and the Plural Ministry: The Role of Exegetical History in Illuminating John Calvin's Theology, Geneva: Librarie Droz.

MIHOC, D. (2008), Aspects of Ecclesiology in the Letter to the Ephesians according to St. John Chrysostom, Sacra Scripta 6.2, 182–199.

OLIN, J.C. (2000), A Reformation Debate: John Calvin & Jacopo Sadoleto, New York: Fordham University Press.

PG: *Patrologia Cursus Completus, Series Graeca*, ed. J.P. Migne, Paris: 1857–1912.

PL: *Patrologia Cursus Completus, Series Latina*, ed. J.P. Migne, Paris: 1844–1864.

RITTER, A.M. (1972), Charisma im Verständnis des Johannes Chrysostomos und seiner Zeit: Ein Beitrag zur Erforschung der griechisch-orientalischen Ekklesiologie in der Frühzeit der Reichskirche, Göttingen: Vandenhoeck & Ruprecht.

SCHNACKENBURG, R. (1991), Ephesians: A Commentary, trans. H. Heron, Edinburgh: T&T Clark Ltd.

SPEELMAN, H.A. (2014), Calvin and the Independence of the Church, Gottingen: Vandenhoeck & Ruprecht.

WALCHENBACH, J.R. (2010), John Calvin as Biblical Commentator: An Investigation into Calvin's Use of John Chrysostom as an Exegetical Tutor, Eugene, Oregon: Wipf and Stock [reprint of diss. 1974].

Marta Quatrale

"Et est mirabile in oculis nostris"

Some Side Notes on Luther's Pneumatology as Augustinian Harvest: Ecclesiology and Hermeneutics in the Light of the First *Abendmahlsstreit*

Aim of this paper is to sketch some side notes to Luther's peculiar pneumatology in relation to the cristological-soteriological core plasming his whole theology. In detail, I will refer to some significant occurrences of the term *paradoxon/(ad)mirabile* in the debate with Zwingli, in the attempt to show its technical nuance of meaning, connoting the hermeneutical dimension disclosed by the pneumatology. My purpose here is so to undertake a short analysis of this underlying dialectic as *the* structural Augustinian harvest in Luther's theology.[1]

1. Metodological introduction

Luther's never systematised ecclesiological doctrine shows its deep inter-connection with his all-encompassing Pneumatology. Already in the so-called *Psalmenvorlesungen* the Church is defined as *creatura Verbi*.[2] In the *Großer Katechismus* its role is defined as follows:

---

1 The precise extent of such harvest is provided in DELIUS, 1984. The certainty of a real implication of the Antipelagian works in the development of his own theological position is provided by a letter to Spalatin (1516, WABr 1, 70, Nr. 27), in which Luther states to be into the reading of the work of Augustine, precisely the Eight volume of Amerbach's edition. "Deinde de peccato originali (quod utique admittit) non plane velit apostolum loqui cap. V ad Romanos. Qui si legerit Augustinum in eis libris, quos contra Pelagianos scripsit, praesertim de spiritu at litera, item de peccatorum meritis et remissione, item contra duas epistolas Pelagianorum, item contra Iulianum, qui omnes in parte operum octava fere habentur, [...]". That means that he was for sure aware of the whole Antipelagian production at the period, and probably of the other works too, being such edition available only as complete work, cf. DELIUS, 1984 p. 12, and being the first two mentioned works published not in the eight, but in the sixth volume (cf. PANI, 2005 p 84). A proof of a previous knowledge are furthermore the so-called *Luthers Randbemerkungen zu* Augustini opuscola (WA 9, 5–27), and the recognition of the volume *De vera et falsa poenitentia* as false (letter to Lang, October 1516, WABr 1, 65, Nr. 26), causing the initially outraged reaction of Andreas Bodenstein von Karlstadt.

2 Cf. for instance WA 2,111; WA 7,130; WA 8,419–420; WA 12, 94; WA 17,1; WA 25, 157; WA 29,365; WA 30 II, 682; WA 42,334.

Ita quoque Spiritus sanctus sanctificationis munus exequitur per sequentia, hoc est, per communionem sanctorum aut Ecclesiam Christianorum, remissionem peccatorum, carnis resurectionem et vitam aeternam. Hoc est, primum nos ducit Spiritus sanctus in sanctam communionem suam ponens in sinum Ecclesiae, per quam nos docet et Christo adducit. […] Ubi enim de Christo nihil docetur, ibi neque ullus est Spiritus sanctus, qui Christianorum communionem solet constituere, convocare ac in unum cogere, citra cuius opem et operam nemo ad Christum Dominum pervenire potest. (BSLK 654f).

So, Luther's concept of Church is first and foremost *theological* concept, due to its definition as God's Work, instead as community. The Church is a community only in the sense of the *communio sanctorum* (BSLK 655,34ff), constituited by the work of God in the Spirit.

This process – as we will see – might be described as the process of concrete historicisation of the very core of Luther's theology. If the Church is the *communio sanctorum*, it can be understood only *in fieri* – being the process of santification part of the work of the Spirit,[3] and precisely the work in which the hidden soteriological result historicises itself as historical Revelation – a "diachronical incarnation".

The Ecclesiological doctrine properly represents a Mediation allowing the disclosure of the hidden right *Ordnung* of Revelation itself, this historisation reflects the incarnation (*Menschwerdung*) of the Son, as based on the same christological figure (*Urbild Christi*). The Church is therefore strictly speaking History of the Church (*Kirchengeschichte*), intended as the process of diachronical (historical) revelation of God, veiled (*verhüllt*) through the Flesh. As long as such process is part of the work of the spirit – namely, the work of the spirit aimed at the santification of the community as *communio sanctorum*, this kind of history is 'veritable' History (*Heilsgeschichte*). Starting point of this process is not the predestination, but rather the Word itself.

This primary and constant definition of the Church seems to find its roots in the characterisation of Luther's Pneumatology as "*konkreter Geistesgedanke*" (Seeberg), stressing the actual effects of the Divine, intended not as rational or emotional grasp, but rather as the concrete movement of transformation of it in (secular) History. Luther's own concept of the Church develops *against* the theological-political structure of the Roman Church, as a first and foremost *theological* concept, consisting of a reduction to the Word and the Sacrament.[4] The reduction of it to

---

3 "Der Heilige Geist macht uns heilig […]; Die angefangene Heiligkeit wird durch den Heiligen Geist einst vollendet".

4 For a programmatic approach to the topic of the 'reduction', cf. WA 6, 448ff. This work has been written as a reply to some polemic works against Luther's position concerning the Eucharist *sub utraque specie*, namely Isidoro Isolani's *Revocatio Martini Lutheri ad Sanctam Sedem* and Augustine of Alveldt's *Tractatus de comunione sub utraque specie, quaternus ad laicos*. As the title itself makes clear, such treatise denounces the usurpation of the Word in the Church, in which the sacraments

the pure Word becomes the figure of his own characterisation, as an *effect* of the Word and the Sacrament.

The Church is the Church of Christ, whose work is revealed to us through the *caritas*, enlightening the Word and leading to Christ through *in* the Church, disclosing the mystery of the Incarnation (BSLK 654–657). This assumptions seems to summarise the deep implication between Trinity, Word, Faith and Sacrament. The Spirit reveals as Saviour (BSLK 653f) on a double level: it is the one who saved and who saves, the Relation between the Father (*Creator, Deus absconditus*) and the Son (*Deus incarnatus*, revealed *pro nobis*), and the engine historicising this process. On the other hand, the Spirit is the hermeneutical key – *per gratia* – revealing the dialectical movement hidden beyond the Word, enlighting the Word as *Verbum*, rather than mere *littera*. In the flowing of the Spirit as Faith this *hermeneutical* and *historical* process of Revelation of the Hiddeness of God is made clear.

As theological core of Luther's theological position here I am assuming the christological-soteriological structure of the *communicatio idiomatum* as systematically shown in his later *Disputationes* (1539–1540). In his debate agaist the papacy and in the one against the schwärmer, gradually arises the picture of a *Deus patiens* (papacy) and a *Deus incarnatus* (*Schwärmer*).[5] Luther's claim to place himself in the

---

are intended as one of the several domain tools. In this sense, such work is intended as the "prelude" (*praeludium*, as clearly stated in the title) to the reaction to the bull of excommunication, which is now almost a fact, and the subsequent imposition of a retraction of his own Doctrine, to which the so-called *Anticatharinus* (*Ad librum eximii Magistri Nostri, Magistri Ambrosii Catharini* [...] *responsio*, 1521, WA 7,705ff) is to be intended as a "postlude" (*postludium*) – and all in all as the perfect opposite of the retraction required: a way to legitimate his own position, assuming such historical contingencies as an eschatologically relevant event, signs of the omnipresence of the Divine in History, through which his own theological Identity is revealed and formalised, overturning (as a sign of the revelation *sub contrario*) the position of his opponents (cf. Miegge, 1964, 356). A first sign of Luther's standpoint in this respect has been given shortly before in the work entitled *An den christlichen Adel deutscher Nation von des christlichen Standes Besserung* (1520, WA 6, 405–415) nonetheless not yet so extreme in its content.

5 Cf. particularly *Disputatio de sententia:Verbum caro factum est* (11.01.1539, WA 39.II, 1ff) and *Disputatiode divinitate et humanitate Christi* (28.02.1540, WA 39.II, 92ff): "2. In theologia verum est, verbum esse carnem factum, in philosophia simpliciter impossibile et absurdum. [...] 11. Sed quia christianis sobrie, et (ut Augustinus docet) secundum praescriptum est loquendum, tales consequentiae sunt simpliciter negandae. 12. Nec utendum nec fruendum est subtilibus istis inventis, de suppositione mediata et immediata, in rebus fidei. [...] 20. Non quidem vitio formae syllogisticae, sed virtute et maiestate materiae, quae in angustias rationis seu syllogismorum includi non potest. [...] 27. Eundum ergo est ad aliam dialecticam et philosophiam in articulis fidei, quae vocatur verbum Dei et fides. [...] 39. Quanto minus potest idem esse verum in philosophia et theologia, quarum distinctio in infinitum maior est, quam artium et operum. [...] 42. Affectus fidei exercendus est in articulis fidei, non intellectus philosophiae. Tum vere scietur, quid sit: Verbum caro factum est." (*Disputatio de divinitate et humanitate Christi*); "1. Fides catholica haec est, ut unum dominum Christum confiteamur verum Deum et hominem. 2. Ex hac veritate geminae substantiae et unitate personae sequitur illa, quae

Catholic church acconding to its dogmas seems in this sense to be legitimate, and looking back from the systematical presentation in the *Disputationes* provides an overview of the theologically relevant results of its several debates. My assumption is so that the result of his theological-political debates does not essentially differs from his theological starting point.[6]

Luther's stress on the distinctive Pneumatological core in relation to the other elements pertaining his theology at this stage seems in this sense to be a consequence of the Augustinian harvest, *filtered* by the consequences of the *Abendmahlsstreit*. The stress provided to the pneumatology offers a hermeneutical key to deal with the historical opposition against the Church of Rome and the results of the *Abendmahlsstreit*: the hermeneutical enlightment of the paradoxical consequences of the exchange of properties is itself a work of the Spirit *per gratia*.

My theoretical outline might be summarised as follows:

Luther's christology contains the prolegomena of its whole theology, and subsequently, of his philosophy of history too. His own peculiar christological movement is a combination of soteriology (the doctrine of the justification as 'turning point') and the *modus* of the dialectical (christological) movement.

---

dicitur, communicatio idiomatum. [...] 14. Et Ioannis 1. dicit: Verbum caro factum est, cum diceretur aptius nostro iudicio: Verbum est incarnatum seu carneum factum. [...] 20. Certum est tamen, omnia vocabula in Christo novam significationem accipere in eadem re significata. [...] 27. Qui enim dicunt, Christum esse creaturam, veteris linguae usu, id est, separatam, nulli unquam fuerunt christiani. 28. Quin omnes hoc modo acerrime impugnant, Christum esse creaturam, quod Ariani docuerunt. [...] 30. Et homo sui immemor concedit, Deum esse carnem factum, cum carnem esse creaturam nondum audeat negare. 44. Neque illam ferre liceret, quam Athanasius ponit: Sicut anima rationalis et caro unus est homo, ita Deus et homo unus est Christus. 45. Omnes enim negant, Christum esse compositum, etsi constitutum affirmant. 46. Nulli vero insulsius loquuntur, quam Moderni, quos vocant, qui omnium volunt subtilissime et propriissime loqui videri. [...] 61. Tanta est simplicitas et bonitas Spiritus sancti, ut homines sui, dum falsa loquuntur grammatice, vera loquuntur sensu. [...] 64. Hoc est, quod dicitur haereticum esse, qui scripturas aliter intelligit, quam flagitat Spiritus sanctus." (*Disputatio de divinitate et humanitate Christi*).

6 The *communicatio idiomatum* has been presented in relation to the role of the Lord Supper already in the *Babylonica* (1520): "Sicut ergo in Christo res se habet, ita et in sacramento. Non enim ad corporalem inhabitationem divinitatis necesse est transsubstanciari humanam naturam, ut divinitas sub accidentibus humanae naturae teneatur. Sed integra utraque natura vere dicitur 'Hic homo est deus, hic deus est. Quod et si philosophia non capit, fides tamen capit. Et maior est verbi dei autoritas quam nostri ingenii capacitas. Ita in sacramento ut verum corpus verusque sanguis sit, non est necesse, panem et vinum transsubstantiari, [...]. Sic interim sapiam pro honore sanctorum verborum dei, quibus per humanas ratiunculas non patiar vim fieri et ea in alienas significationes torqueri: [...]." (WA 6, 511,34ff). And then in *Antilatomus* (1521) even more "Quod facit, quia quid gratia et peccatum, quid lex et Euangelium, quid Christus et homo sit, cum suis sophistis nunquam cognovit. [...] Ubi cautissime observandum, ut utramque naturam de tota persona enunciet cum omnibus suis propriis, et tamen caveat, ne quod simpliciter deo aut simpliciter homini convenit, ei tribuat. Aliud enim est, de deo incarnato vel homine deificato loqui, et aliud de deo vel homine simpliciter" (WA 8, 126).

The *simul* as base-form – the cristological structure of the doctrine of justifica-tion[7] – shows the movement of the commutation of properties (fröhlicher Wechsel) and its kenotical (pre-)conditions as well. Is precisely the soteriological character of the christological doctrine – the *simul* base form of the christologically ori-ented doctrine of justification – of the *communicatio idiomatum* to legitimate the dichotomical theological-historical insight and make ist a principle.

The negative, kenotical pole of such dialectic is to be understood as a "word from the cross" (cf. in this sense the concept of *theologia crucis*). The dogmatic christological-soteriological combination of *communicatio idiomatum* as *modus* of the God's Revelation *pro nobis* (Incarnation) shapes history, and in this sense offers a picture (*Urbild*) fot the interpretation of history as history of the real church (*Heils-* or *Kirchengeschichte*).

Luther's reception of the ancient Christology and Doctrine of the Trinity can be understood in ist whole weight, as negative, kenotical opposition to each willingness to compromise with the given *Religionspolitik* – with the antichristical pole of the apocalyptically-shaped history.

The particular interpretation of the revelation of the Antichrist – first and fore-most in religious-political terms, as opposition to the Roman Church[8] – as part of the process of his own theological self-legitimation discloses a *theologumenon* which already in the first decade of the Reformation reactivates a comforting func-tion of the apocalyptic interpretation of history. In this perspective, as long as the use of antichristical legends and patterns shapes the interpretation of the tradi-tional historical pattern of the duopoly as eschatological projection in which the santification of the *Heils-* and *Kirchengeschichte* enters in its true nature, and the Doomsday assumes the positive connotation of historisation of the real Church as opposed to the theological-political matter of facts, it should be considered an essential part of his theology.

The process of *reduction* of the Church to the Word and the Sacrament is the main legacy of his clash against the papacy, leading to the picture of a *Deus patiens*

---

7 As stated by Luther in 1545 while looking back to the origins of his theological turn (WA 54, 185f).
8 It is well known that Luther's position against the existent, visible Church expresses much more as an opposition of pure *theological* paradigms, grounded than as a sharp criticism as is, for example, the position of Ockham or of the so-called Conciliarists. Against the Church of Rome (cf. WA 1, 571; WA 2, 183ff), as unavoidable historical recognition and eschatological over-interpretation of the role and the primacy of the Papacy as Church of the Antichrist in the realm of the outward appearance itself (cf. for example WA 2, 186ff, 236ff; WA 3, 651) is made clear in his struggle against Eck, already the *Leipziger Disputation* (1519). The theologically-grounding revelation of the Antichrist (cf. WA 6, 597; 601; 604; WA 7, 708; 713; 722; WA 10.II, 138; WA 44, 711ff, WA 54, 224; 284; 289) – strongly denoting the supposed decaying features of the Church of Rome – in its connection with the 'reduction' of the Sacraments and the topic of the signs of the real Church appears (in a positive, non-conjectural form) in the treatise *De captivitate babylonica ecclesiae, praeludium Martini Lutheri* (1520, WA 6, 484–573).

revealing his presence over time – as *Heils-* or *Kirchengeschichte*,[9] whose signs are programmatically interpreted as christological (martyrised, persecuted, etc.) signs:[10] it lives hidden in Spirit, whereas the false Church is outwardly active and powerful, as false Doctrine and false Flesh (Cf. WA 18, 625ff; 710; 782; WA 42, 154f; 187f; 276; 310; 377; 383; 405; 412f; 479; 524ff; 527; 536; WA 43, 3; 38; 42f). Viceversa, in the context of an interpretation of concrete persons and facts as *testia veritatis*, the historical defeat represents the outstanding sign of God's presence, claiming to recognise the proper *communio sanctorum inside* the Institution itself and making the suffering Church programmatically the real Church.

This historical conception of the revelation – the revelation as the history of the real Church *in fieri* (WA 23, 261–263; WA 24, 35f; WA 26, 436; WA 27, 234) – is made concretely possible through the results of the *Abendmahlsstreit*. The reduction of the signs of God's presence is here clarified as impossibility for the Church as *communio sanctorum* to exist *without* the Word and the Sacrament.[11] Specifically, God's

---

9 For the topic *Kirchen-* and *Heilsgeschichte*, cf. Pohlig: 2007.

10 "Deum corporeum wil die welt nicht haben noch leyden, id est, qui nascitur, praedicat, arguit mundum, crucifigitur, sed schlegt in tod. Econtra incorporeum quaerit, honorat magno labore et impensis, quem tamen comprehendere non potest, cum Deus 1. Cor. 1." (WATR 1, Nr. 925). This kind of elements in the definition of the Church and referred to its Historical development pave the way to the gnesiolutheran historiographical production. For a characterisation of the customary signs of the End within the Lutherans in a period before the gnesiolutheran programmatic production in this sense, see for example Erasmus Alber's Von den zeychen des jüngsten tags, n.a., 1548, Adreas Musculus, Vom jüngsten Tag, Franckfort an der Oder, 1557, and in a broader sense the whole polemical work of the so-called Magdeburger Herrgotts Kanzley. Cf. for instance Leppin: 1999; Kaufmann 2003; 2006).

11 "Das ist nu auch nicht zu leiden, es ist Ketzerey, fur der vernunfft scheinet es, als wer es nicht war, [...], so stimmet es nicht mit seiner Vernunfft, ein Tuercke oder Papist gleubet es nicht [...]. Also predigen auch unsere Schwermer, Zwinglius und andere, man muesse die Menscheit in Christo auschliessen, die Gottheit gebe das ewige leben und die menscheit nicht. [...] sonderen [...] sprechen denn: Christus sagt hie selber: 'das fleisch ist kein nuetz', so gehet auch die Schrifft dahin und sagt, man solle auff menschen nicht trawen, sondern allein Gott vertrawen, darumb mus es diese deutung haben, das, wer an mich gleubt, der hab das ewige leben, das ist: die Gottheit, und lesst die menscheit faren. Also klug sind wir nicht, sondern wir muessen gleuben, [...] wie wir denn in unserem Symbolo bekennen: [...] Das der Son Gottes eingewickelt sey in die Menscheit und eine person sey, das ichs nicht von einander solle trennen und sagen, die Menscheit sey kein nuetze, sondern allein die Gottheit. Viel Lerer haben also geleret, und ich bin vorzeiten auch ein solcher Doctor gewesen, das ich hab die menscheit ausgeschlossen und es dafur gehalten habe, ich thete wol, wenn ich Christi Gottheit und menscheit von einander scheidete. Das haben vorzeiten die hoehesten Theologi gethan, das sie von der menscheit Christi geflogen sind zu der Gottheit und sich allein an dieselbige gehenget und gedachten, man mueste die Menscheit Christi nicht kennen. [...] Kanst du dich nu demuetigen und hengen mit dem hertzen an dem worte und bleiben bey der menscheit Christi, so wird sich die Gottheit wol finden und der Vater und h. Geist und die gantze Gottheit dich ergreiffen. [...] Das ist des h. Geistes lere, davon sonst fleisch und blut und die vernunfft nichts weis oder kan. Aber hoere du Gott zu, Gott mus hie dich leren, er mus beide, predigen und eingeben, es ist sonst unmoeglich,

presence is here clarified as free use of the local mode *through* the *communicatio idiomatum*, as wideaspread (*allenthalben*) real presence of God's flesh, humanity in history.[12] In this sense, to stress the unity between Divine and human nature of God in Christ, Luther re-activates a Cyrillian standpoint in defining the Personal Unity of the two natures in Chirst agaist Zwingli's Nestorian position.[13] The Pneumatology in so to be intended as the consistent counterpart of the Sacramental Doctrine (*crede et manducasti*), referring to which such Spiritualism a mere shadow.[14]

Focusing on the results of the first decade of Luther's 'reformed' production after the break-up with Rome – so on a period of certain theological consolidation (1521–1529 ca.) corresponding with the long absence of Charles V. from the Holy Roman Empire – my aim is to sketch some remarks pertaining the *communicatio idiomatum* as cristological-soteriological core of Luther's theology, in relation to the role of the Spirit as hermeneutical engine allowing an understanding of the *concrete* sings of revelation of the paradoxical Divine presence in history.

At this stage, immediately before the canonisation the *Confessio Augustana*, the Lutheranism grew as re-formatio against the Roman church, and developed its very

---

das ein Tuercke, Bapst oder ein ander diese Lere gleube und wisse, Gott mus es allein leren durch sein Wort." (WA 33, 153–157).

12 Cf. WA 26, 340ff; for example: "hier sey on menscheit / und dort sey mit der menscheit", "mus Christus auch da mensch sein / wo er Gott ist".

13 WA 26,439; 445. Some years later, this conception of the Dogma and the historicisation of the Dogma is systematically formalised in the work Von den Konziliis und Kirchen.

14 God as Spirit hides in the letter too, and in this sense, the mediation of the kerygma within the Sacrament itself seems to be unavoidable: without the concrete action of the Word, both the confession of God as Creator and of Christ as Saviour lose their value, as long as God and Christ are not even pronounceable words. In this sense, the spiritualist axiom of the uselessness of the Flesh produces no other than a subjective form of spiritualism, avoiding the outward objective mediation of the Word. Removing the real presence in the Einsetzungsworte, they remove the whole process of Incarnation, affecting both the Word and the Creature (cf. for instance WA 26; 431; 433; 441; 443; cf. WA 23, 157). An eloquent presentation of Luther's arguments in this context is provided by Kaspar Hedio, in his report of the Marburger Religionsgespräch: "[…] Lutherus promisit se sepositurum omnes affectus in gratiam dei et principis. Waß hin, ist hin. Utinam in posterum. Quodsi omnino concordari non possunt, ut agendum, quod pro fratribus habeantur, in fine de hoc loquemur. – Ad argumentum Helvidii: ex scriptura potest probari, quod filius pro amico assumitur. Sed hic tropus non probatur: hoc est corpus meum. Manducare dicitis vos, quod velit omnem manducationem tollere, Fleisch, Fleisch. Finge sententiam vestram veram, hoc non est ad rem, faul äpffel, hutzel, si proponeret. Ubicunque est verbum dei, ibi est manducatio spiritualis, quando nobiscum loquitur deus, ibi requiritur fides, h. e. manducare. Quodsi adicit corporalem manducationem, oportet, ut paremus. Comedimus fide hoc corpus, quod pro nobis traditur. Os accipit corpus Christi, anima credit verbis, quia edit corpus; si accipio corpus Christi in ulnas, hoc amplecti. Ihr habt Glosen, meinens gutt, an dem ists nit gelegen. Item quod dicitis deum nihil proponere incomprehensibile vobis. […] Si vias eius sciremus, non esset incomprehensibilis, qui admirabilis. […]" (*Das Marburger Gespräch nach Hedio*, WA 30.III, 118A–119A).

crucial core before being involved in the several religious-political interconfessional councils of the subsequent years. A certain attempt of canonisation and a first positive formalisation of the criteria constituting the Church as community *in fieri* – in 1529 the so-called *Großer Katechismus* came to light – combines with a sharp, polemic lexicon and attitude in the process of acheivement of a certain theological legitimation. The Church is presented in its role of visible, historical – but not really carnal – mediation, laying the basis for a formalisation of the Church as Revelation of the History of the *real* Church – *Kirchengeschichte* or *Heilsgeschichte*. My purpose is so to provide a quick glance on this not yet clearly formalised concretion of concepts.

2. Luther's concept of paradox and the Augustinian harvest: the double role of the Spirit

My hypothesis here is to sketch a derivation of the Doctrine of the forensic Justification from the already Augustinian doctrine of the predestined Grace, and to show how the soteriological role of the *communicatio idiomatum* might be intended already in Augustine's work as its necessary counterpart. A grip to such short remarks is provided by the fact that in Zwingli's production the occurrences of the term "*paradoxon/(ad)mirabile*", significantly used very scarcely, are always polemical, and always used as direct attack agaist Luther's supposed captious arguments.

If on the one hand Luther's theological position is anything but systematic, on the other hand – as already sketched – some sticking points may be identified. The core issue is from the very beginning of his production to identify in the soteriological implication of the christological movement of the *communicatio idiomatum*, the debate with Zwigli – or rather, with the 'Schwärmer' *tout court* – lead to a certain radicalisation of this position.

Building a positive theological position *on the basis of* those oppositions is a fundamental reason to explain the paradoxical form of Luther's positive claims, as long as – assuming the incarnation of the Son as the sign of the revelation and the presence of God for us (*pro nobis*) – the Doctrine of the Justification and the correlative theorisation of the revelation *per gratia* of the hiddeness of God is supposedly taking place within the framework of this theorisation of the paradox.

In 1545 Luther himself designated the Augustinian hermeneutical treatise *De-Spir.etLitt.* as an explanation of the Doctrine of Justification presented in Rom 1:17 as the preeminent source for his conversion, surely to be located before the *Römerbriefvorlesung* (1516), in which this dependence is made of explicitly clear.[15]

---

15 For example, WA 57, 36. For this topic, cf. for instance LETTIERI: 2001; LOHSE: 1990; OBERMAN: 1969;

In 1533 it has been established as fundamental doctrinal treatise at the University of Wittenberg. In this text, recalling the juridical *topos* of the relation between author's *intentio* and law's *scriptum,* over-interpreted by Augustine understanding the *intentio* no more as hidden under the *littera* (so understandable by a capable interpreter), but effectively working as *Spiritus,* living trace of the Spirit, hiding or revealing in the letter Its own predestined *intentio.* Disclosing the whole hermeneutics of the grace developed in *DeDivv.qq.adSimpl.* I, 2 – a declaration of irreducible distinction between *natura* (*doctrina*) and *gratia, littera* and *Spiritus,* it makes the bound between hermeneutics and theology of the grace clear. As long as *Littera* must be intended as relation between Creator and creature according the *lex* – not only a historical framework, but rather a kind of metaphysical knowledge, a *doctrina* (Rom 1–2; 1 Cor 1–2) – lacking of the spirit and depending from an idolatrical *intentio* (Rom 1:18–23), converting the human perverted will is a Divine work of the *Spiritus* becoming *praesentia* in it (Rom:10,3–4). *Lex Dei est Caritas* – the revelation is hermeneutical act of grace, overrunning the logical paradox of the coexistence of opposites.

This derivation[16] might be recognised in the systematic occurrence of the term *paradoxon-mirum-(ad)mirabile* in Luther's work to present his own position *in contrast to* his opponents.

Significantly the thesis against the Scholasticism contained in the *Heidelberger Disputation* are defined "*paradoxa*",[17] and against Erasmus, in *De servo arbitrio,*

PANI: 1983; 1986; 2005. In the *Römerbriefvorlesung,* the *communicatio idiomatum* is systematically presented as base form of the forensic Justification *in the light of* the Augustinian hermenetical treatise *De Spiritu et Littera,* particularly in Chapters 1 and 3.

16 Clearly stated in respect of the "Paradox" in WA 1, 353.

17 "[…] Has sententias, quas vocant Positiones, mitto ad te, et per te Patri Magistro Venceslao, et si qui alii sunt, quos huius generis deliciae delectant. Sunt (nisi fallor) haec iam non Ciceronis Paradoxa, sed Carolstadii nostri, imo Sancti Augustini, Ciceronianis tanto mirabiliora et digniora, quanto Augustinus, imo Christus, Cicerone dignior est. Arguent autem ista Paradoxa omnium eorum vel negligentiam vel ignorantiam, quibuscunque fuerint visa magis paradoxa quam orthodoxa, ne dicam de iis, qui ea potius cacodoxa impudenti temeritate iudicabunt, quia nec Aug[ustinum], nec Paulum legunt, aut ita legunt, ut non intelligant, seque et alios secum negligant. Sunt igitur paradoxa modestis, et qui non ea cognoverunt, sed eudoxa et calodoxa scientibus, mihi vero aristodoxa. […]" (WABr 1,94, Nr. 38, Luther to Scheurl); "[…] Misi ad te per M. Ottonem positiones nostras et praecepta ex me exposita, nec fuit mihi tunc tantum temporis, ut et scriberem, quia repentinus mihi abscessus eius nuntiatus fuit. Caeterum expecto valde, nimis, granditer, anxieque, quidnam vos de istis paradoxis nostris statuatis. Vere enim illis vestris haec paradoxa, imo cacodoxa videri suspicor, quae nobis non nisi orthodoxa esse possunt. […]" (WABr 1,103, Nr. 45, Luther to Lang); "[…] At ecce interim mihi in mentem venit, quod mihi opuscula Reverendi P[atris] Vicarii per Udalricum istum Pindarum ferme pro 2 aureis misisti, quae ego sane partim vendidi, partim bonis amicis Reverendi Patris gratis dedi; de venditis vero pecuniam, quam conflavi, pauperibus (uti iussisti), id est, mihi ipsi et Fratribus, impendi; pauperiorem enim me ipso nondum satis cognovi. Caeterum rogo, si potest fieri, eodem

tuo iussu mihi iidem libelli mittantur pro floreno, quem illis venditis tibi rependam fideliter. Sunt enim, qui expetant et expectent eosdem libellos. Mitto insuper Positiones nostras prorsus paradoxas, et prout multis videtur kacistodoxas, quas poteris Eccio nostro, eruditissimo et ingeniosissimo viro, exhibere, ut audiam et videam, quid vocet illas. [...]" (WABr 1,106, Nr. 46, Luther to Scheurl); "[...] Ecce alia denuo Paradoxa mitto, Reverendissime Pater mi in Christo. Quod si etiam in his tui theologi offendentur et dixerint (sicut passim de me omnes loquuntur) me nimis temere superbeque praecipitare iudicium damnareque alienas sententias, respondeo per te et has literas: primum mihi vehementer placere maturam eorum modestiam cunctantemque diu gravitatem, si eam in opere exhiberent, sicut in me reprehendunt levitatem et praecipitem temeritatem. Facile enim in me, ut video, notant vitium eiusmodi. [...]" (WABr 1,121, Nr. 52, Luther to Lang); "[...] Ad literas tuas, quas ex Lochensi arce ad me dederas, certe respondi, optime Spalatine, et per officium conductoris seu publicae fidei ministrum ad te pervenisse credidi. In quibus te oravi, ut Illustrissimo Principi pro panno gratias ageres pro me, deinde paradoxum meum de ignorantia invincibili, quoad potui, tibi declaravi. [...]" (WABr 1, 129, Nr. 55, Luther to Spalatin); "[...] Diffidentes nobis ipsis prorsus iuxta illud spiritus consilium 'ne innitaris prudentiae tuae', humiliter offerimus onmium, qui adesse voluerint, iuditio haec Theologica paradoxa, ut vel sic appareat, bene an male elicita sint ex divo Paulo, vase et organo Christi electissimo, deinde et ex S. Augustino, interprete eiusdem fidelissimo. [...]" (*Disputatio Heidelbergae habita*, WA 1, 353); "[...] Sed ecce vides plura scribendi non esse locum. Mitto per eum disputata Paradoxa iuxta et eorum explicationes, quantum inter disputandum excipere potui aut postea ab ipso fui edoctus. [...]" (Martin Bucer's report to Beatus Rhenanus on the *Heidelberger Disputation*, WA 9, 162); "[...] Senuit Isaac.1. Primum. In hoc capite est cernere horrendum dei iudicium, quia aliquandiu connivens, postea punit, ita ut veniae spem adimat. [...] Beatus, qui in omnibus timet deum. [...] Non est enim usquam securitas ponenda in ulla re nisi ἐν τῇ misericordia dei. Omnis vita nostra iudicio dei obnoxia est. Iudicii metus impellat ad misericordiam. 2. Horrendum est iudicium, quia deus non respicit opus, quantumvis splendidum. [...] 3. Timor. [...] Opera dei adeo saepe sunt occulta et mirabilia, ut plane iudicari a ratione non possint. Sic eciam cum nobiscum agit deus, ut in morte: ibi quis rationis usus? sed simpliciter ignorans dicit 'pater in manus tuas commendo spiritum meum'. [...] Sensit spiritu, quod oportuit firmam in eo benedictionem esse, qui benedictus erat. Certa quedam spiritus sensio est, quam sequentes πνευματικοὶ non errant, ut sciunt, se vere non errare. [...]" (*Geneseos historiam prosequutus*, WA 9, 487–488); "[...] Cum autem ante triennium paradoxa quaedam disputanda proposuisset Vuittenbergae, urbe Saxonum, D. Martinus adversus tyrannidem Romani Episcopi, quae lacerata sunt interim et exusta a multis, a nullo tamen aut scripturis aut rationibus convicta, coepit res ad tumultum spectare, vulgo caussam Euangelii adversus clericos tuente. [...] (*Acta comparitionis Lutheri in Diaeta Wormatiensi*, WA 7, 826 A) [...] Is enim est verbi dei cursus, casus et eventus, sicut dicit: 'Non veni pacem mittere, sed gladium: veni enim separare hominem adversus patrem suum &c'. Proinde cogitandum nobis est, quam deus noster sit mirabilis et terribilis in consiliis suis, ne forte id quod pro sedandis studiis tentatur, si a damnato verbo dei exordiamur, vergat potius in intollerabilium malorum diluvium, et curandum sit, ne adolescentis huius optimi Principis Caroli (in quo post deum multa spes est) infelix, inauspicatum fiat imperium. [...]" (*Acta comparitionis Lutheri in Diaeta Wormatiensi*, WA 7, 835 A); "[...] Cogor ego solus fere mortalium disputationibus meis aut nullum interserere paradoxum aut mox simul effundere totum secretum. Adeo caeteri omnes, cum ambulent in mirabilibus super se et non modo paradoxota sed et pseudodoxota proposuerint, hanc habent gratiam, ut longe distinguatur inter ea quae sic ostentant et ea quae plane in populo docent aut domi fabulantur. Unus est Lutherus, qui et provocatur et vi rapitur ad pugnam, disputationem, et simul exigitur dicere et rationem ante tempus reddere, aut ita dicere disputaturus, ut a cerdonibus quoque intelligi possit:

"paradoxon" is the human incapability to understand the divine voluntarism.[18] The

quod si non fecero, mox haereticus, blasphemus, scandalosus sum. […]" (*Vorwort zur Resolutio super propositione XIII. de potestate papae*, WA 2, 184 A); […] Quicunque enim ex operibus legis sunt, sub maledicto sunt. Scriptum est enim: Maledictus omnis, qui non permanserit in omnibus, quae scripta sunt in libro legis, ut faciat ea. Dixerat, benedictos esse eos, qui ex fide sunt. Iam alio argumento et a contrariis assumpto maledictos dicit, qui ex operibus sunt. Vide autem mirabilem syllogismum Apostoli. Adducit ex Deutro. c. xxvij. esse maledictos, qui non faciunt ea, quae scripta sunt in libro legis. Ex qua negativa colligit affirmativam hanc: Maledicti, qui operantur opera legis. Nonne hoc affirmat, quod Moses negat? Et quo maior sit absurditas, suam affirmativam per Mosi negativam probat. […] (*In Epistolam Pauli ad Galatas M. Lutheri Commentarius*, WA 2, 513) […] Haec autem sibi invicem adversantur, ut non quaecunque vultis illa faciatis. Vide audacem Apostolum: nihil timet ignem, negat liberum arbitrium quod est mirabile in auribus nostris: dicit, non posse fieri quae volumus cum nos voluntatem constituerimus (autore vel Aristotele) reginam et dominam omnium virium et actuum. Atque hic error et haeresis maxima erat tolerabilis, si hoc dixisset de iis, qui sunt extra gratiam. Nunc, ut nulla sit ei excusatio, quin comburatur, affirmat id de iis, qui spiritu gratiae vivunt. Idem Rho. vij. dicit: Ego autem carnalis sum, venundatus sub peccato: quod volo bonum, non facio, quod nolo malum, hoc facio. Si iustus et sanctus sic queritur de peccato, ubi peccator et impius apparebunt cum operibus suis de genere bonorum et moraliter bonis? Gratia dei nondum perfecit liberum arbitrium, et ipsummet seipsum liberum faciet? quid insanimus? […] (*In Epistolam Pauli ad Galatas M. Lutheri Commentarius*, WA 2, 586); "[…] Sic mirabiliter deus regit mundum. Er schickt die qui puniant. […]" (*Dominica Francisci Mat. 22. de doctore legis Christum interrogante*, WA 11, 188); "[…] Mirabiliter deus gubernat mundum, ita ut nos putemus humano consilio fieri etc. […] (*In Iohelem D. Martinus Lutherus*, WA 13,71) […] Deus mirabiliter pro suo more in administrando mundo semper egit et hodie adhuc idem praestat, ut putemus humano consilio omnia geri et administrari. Sed voluntas divina est, quidquid fit. […]" (*In Iohelem D. Martinus Lutherus*, WA 13, 94); "[…] Et hic observandae sunt contrariae prophetiae, quae impios prorsus excaecabant, ne possent prophetis credere. Quomodo enim crederent repugnantia nunciantibus? Sic mirabiliter agit divina maiestas." […] (*In Micheam*, WA 13, 317);"Omnia opera Dei abscondita sunt mundo, estque mirabilis Deus, qui ea abscondit mundo." (WATR 1, 491, Nr. 974); "Mirabilis est christianorum caro. Expositi omnibus Sathanae insidiis tanquam folium arboris pendulum vehementissimis ventis obiectum, qui rupes et turres impugnant, ita nos sumus in hac miserrima vita. Considerate Adam et Euam, wie es die elendesten eltern auff erden sein gewest, sicut tragicae circumstantiae indicant. Fratricidium fuit illis maximus terror." (WATi 5, 626, Nr. 6368); "Quid enim est admirabilius quam nosse illam? Admirabile et inenarrabile opus Filium Dei inducere humanam naturam et sic se demittere, ut habitu inveniatur ut homo!" (WATR 5, 90, Nr. 5360).

18 "[…] Summa, si de verbo Dei sic sentis, impie sentis, si de aliis, nihil ad nos verbosa disputatio consilii tui. Nos de verbo Dei disputamus. Ultima parte praefationis, serio nos deterrens ab isto genere doctrinae, arbitraris pene victoriam tibi partam. Quid (inquis) inutilius, quam hoc paradoxon evulgari mundo, Quicquid fit a nobis, non libero arbitrio, sed mera necessitate fieri? Et illud Augustini, Deum operari bona et mala in nobis, sua bona opera remunerare in nobis, et sua mala opera punire in nobis. […] Mi Erasme, Iterum et ego dico, si haec paradoxa ducis hominum esse inventa, quid contendis? quid aestuas? contra quem dicis? an est ullus in orbe hodie, qui vehementius hominum dogmata sit insectatus quam Lutherus? Igitur nihil ad nos ista monitio. Si autem Dei verba esse credis ea paradoxa, ubi est frons tua? ubi pudor? ubi, non dico iam modestia illa Erasmi, sed timor et reverentia Deo vero debita? quid dicis, nihil inutilius dici posse hoc verbo Dei? Scilicet, Creator tuus a te creatura sua discet, quid utile et inutile sit praedicatu, ac stultus ille vel imprudens Deus

concept of paradox comes then in Zwingli's arguments against Luther's position concerning the real presence (*Realpräsenz*) in the Eucharist.[19]

hactenus nescierit, quid doceri oporteat, donec tu magister eius modum illi praescriberes sapiendi et mandandi, quasi ipse ignorasset, nisi tu docuisses, sequi ad hoc paradoxon, quae tu infers. [...] (*De servo arbitrio*, WA 18, 630–631) [...] Hoc modo rectius disputantibus in istis paradoxis consulitur, quam tuo consilio, quo per silentium et abstinentiam vis illorum impietati consulere, Quo tamen nihil proficis. Nam si vel credas vel suspiceris esse vera (cum sint non parvi momenti paradoxa), quae est mortalium insaturabilis cupido, scrutandarum secretarum rerum, tum maxime, cum maxime occultatas volumus, facies hac monitione tua evulgata, ut multo magis nunc velint omnes scire, an vera sint ea paradoxa, scilicet, tua contentione accensi, ut nullus nostrum hactenus tantam ansam praestiterit ea vulgandi, quantum tu hac religiosa et vehementi monitione. Prudentius multo fecisses, si prorsus tacuisses de his paradoxis cavendis, si votum tuum ratum voluisses. Actum est, postquam non prorsus negas esse vera; occultari non poterunt, sed suspitione veritatis omnes ad sese investiganda allicient. Vel ergo nega illa esse vera, vel tu prior tace, si alios tacere voles. Alterum paradoxon, quicquid fit a nobis, non arbitrio libero, sed mera necessitate fieri, breviter videamus, ne perniciosissimum dici patiamur. [...] (*De servo arbitrio*, WA 18, 634) [...] Quod cum Lutherus diceret, nihil absurdius auditum erat, nihil inutilius hoc paradoxo invulgari potuit, ut etiam Diatribas in eum scribi oporteret. Sed forte mihi nemo credet, ista ab Erasmo dici. Legatur hoc loco Diatribe et mirabitur. Ego tamen non valde miror. [...] Si haec non sunt paradoxa vel potius monstra, quid tum sunt monstra? [...]" (*De servo arbitrio*, WA 18, 668–669).

19 Cf. for example WA 3, 124; WA 14, 384–387, 392–393, 458–459, 792; WA 15,785; WA 16, 39–40, 105; WA 20, 472–473; WA 24, 597; WA 31, 1; WABr 5, 591 (Nr. 1707). As examples of a latter (1540–1545) formalisation of the co-implication between Christology and Penumatology in this direction, cf. for instance *Disputatio Reverendi patris Domini D. Martini Lutheri de divinitate et humanitate Christi*, WA 39 II, 104–105 A; *Contra XXXII articulos Lovaniensium theologistarum*, WA 54, 419.
"[...] sind die paradoxa Stoicorum, die verborgnen reden Pythagoreorum, die zwyfelhafften antwurten der abgötten und ander beschlossen reden gezogen und von den menschen nit [...]" (*Auslegen und Gründe der Schlußreden* [14.06.1523], p. 110); "[...] propter verbum dominicum, et non solum hoc, sed etiam nihil prodesse. Exempla non quadrant. Ex virgine nasci fidelibus non est admirabile mentibus, sed carni. Est enim sacris dissertum carminibus. [...]" (*Vorarbeiten zur Antwort auf Luthers Schrift "Sermon wider die Schwarmgeister"*, p. 289); "[...] «Dicite igitur mihi quandoquidem sola fides iustificat, Christo ipso nihil opus esse». Id est: En tibi παραλογισμόν. Nos de cibo carnis loquimur, en de toto Christo carnem dicimus nihil prodesse, sed fidem in eum qui carne mortuus est. Tu ἀμφοτερίζεις, vide! Dic isthic de iustitia ac misericordia dei euangelii fonte. Perpetuo inculcat paradoxum nobis videri quodque ratione metiamur omnia, qum iam dictum sit nos non ratione, sed expensione verbi dominici huc adductos. Nam si ratione speraremus aliquid obtineri posse, iam olim erat huic viɇ locus, cum liber domini sermonis esset clausus. [...]" (*Vorarbeiten zur Antwort auf Luthers Schrift "Sermon wider die Schwarmgeister"*, p. 291); "[...] Erras igitur, et in quo vos maxime peccatis, in eo nos adcusas callidus patronus, dum occupas iaculando, ut bene nobiscum esse actum putemus, si spicula depulerimus, contra non iaciamus. Quomodo enim similitudinibus utimur, cum rem te iudice minime paradoxam adseveremus? [...]" (*Amica Exegesis, id est: expositio eucharistiae negoci ad Martinum Lutherum*, p. 598); "[...] si obtineri aliquid similibus posset. Sed absit, ut prɇstigiatorum more miracula isthic tradamus, ubi nihil fit miraculi, ubi is, qui mirabilis est in operibus suis, nihil quod miremur promisit, nihil monuit, priusquam faceret; quum faceret, nemo admiratus est, [...]" (*Amica Exegesis, id est: expositio eucharistiae negocii ad Martinum Lutherum*, p. 675); [...] Quid corpus Christi naturaliter manducatum? Sed inaudita erat apud vulgum igniti

My working hypothesis here is to assume such all-encompassing Hermeneutical-Pneumatological dimension as primary key to deal with a lucid theorisation of the concept of Paradox as proper way for Luther to present *polemically and nonetheless affirmatively* his position in regard of process of Revelation *within* the outward appearance as the greatest harvest of his Augustinian background.

3. Intermezzo. Augustine's concept of paradox: hermeneutical *key per gratia*

The systematic linguistic use of the oxymoron evoking a logical contradiction in the description of the Divine reality is used in Augustine's production as sign, heuristic pattern to confess *simul* the divine omnipotence transcending material and intellectual faculties of the creature. Assuming the ciceronian[20] connotation of *paradoxon/(ad)mirabile/mirum* as technical term, describing a synthesis of *repugnantia*[21] – moral fallacies and infractions to the truth – the transcendence of the Dogma (*C.Iul.* III,3,8) in regard of the human limited intellectual faculties treating is positively connoted as the grasp of the revelation *per gratia*.[22]

In this sense, the concept of paradox makes possible to deal with the 'stoic'

---

ferri comparatio, et mirabilis stupor ad omnia, quę nobis lenocinabantur, huiusmodi non penitus perspectis similibus apud eum non nihil effici posse, quum verbo dominico [...] (*Amica Exegesis, id est: expositio eucharistiae negocii ad Martinum Lutherum*, p. 683); "[...] Hic, hic tu unus fidelis David, ad hoc unctus a domino, induis quidem arma. Primum, quum iuxta illorum ritum pergis cum eis disputare ac paradoxa nodosque Gordios obiicere; mox tamen reiectis his impedimentis e coelesti flumine lapides eligis ac libras, expeditaque et rotata funda tam [...]" (*Amica Exegesis, id est: expositio eucharistiae negocii ad Martinum Lutherum*, p. 722).

20 Cicero translates in *Paradoxa stoicorum* 1,4 the Greek term *paradoxa* with *admirabilia*, translation which immediately becomes in *De Finibus* a technical term (*De Finibus* IV, 19, 55; IV,20,561; IV,27, 74), basing such (rhetorical) rejection as contradiction and moral sophisms to the Platonic and Aristotelian dialectic.

21 Augustine's excellent rhetorical background is a matter of fact. This kind of rhetorical fallacy is explicitly assumed in positive terms. Cf. *Confess.*VII,20,26: since his former production (*C.Acad., DeOrd., DeBeataV.*) Augustine follows a kind of christianised platonical dialectic, referring to the logical-ontological hermeneutical pattern presented in *Sophist* and *Parmenides*, and allowing us to understand the distinction *Creator/creatura*. *Sapientia* is namely dialectical science of *contraria*, related each other as *repugnantia vel disiunctio* (*C.Acad.* III,17,37), and referring to which the *sapientia* represents a *connexio* at a broader level. Cf. Lettieri, 2001.

22 *Epistula* 104,4,15; *Epistula* 162; In *Quaest.inHept.* I (*InGen.*),161, *mirum* is defined *quasi absurdum*, as long as the criterion is represented by the *hominum consuetudo*. Cf. *Ench.* 26,102 too.

pelagian position and to stress the logical and rhetorical contradiction in which this dialectic consists as well.[23]

To the Pelagian accusation to intend the Will (the *potestas*, that is the ability to direct the own will, *voluntas*) as Stoic Fate (*DeCiv.Dei, C.duasEpp.Pel.*), Augustine replies properly in Stoic terms, defining "*potestas*" the restricted ability to exercise the own Will, as predestined by God.

In the dialectic between creation (*natura*) and redemption (*gratia*), the notion of "Free will" shows therefore a certain ambivalence. The misperception is dispelled however subordinating the secondary cause (the human perspective of a free will) to the absolute cause (the *gratia efficax*). The eventual possibility to serve for the Good – independent from the human autonomy of the Will, and weakened by Fall and Sinn – does therefore not match with an effective power.

But this perceptive mismatch regarding the Justification is structurally express-ible only in ambiguous terms: each assumption related to the Justification is true, being each possible semi-pelagian assumption only *relatively* true from a human standpoint, and becoming unavoidably false as long as it is overrun (*aufgehoben*) in the perspective Divine Will of Election. Accepting the contribution of two order of voluntary causes is so only possible if the involvement is intended as asymmetrical. This soteriological ambivalence shows a certain discrepancy between a platoni-cally oriented ontological base structure and a voluntaristic Divine freedom. In the gap between creation and election *littera* and *spiritus, doctrina* and *gratia* – in the possibility of a non-universal election – the revelation manifests a kind of intra-divine transcendence, not rejecting the creation *tout court*, but rather intending it as *retractata* (*aufgehoben*).

The *veritas*, human *doctrina* (*lex*), remains *simul* affirmed and denied, as long as the conversion of the Will is the fundamental Divine work of the Spirit as Grace. This structural dependence on a divine act, as well as the manner in which it makes clear represent in my opinion the very core of the augustinian harvest in Luther's theology. The predestined Grace transforms the *voided* possibility to will, embodied in Christ. But in the hiddeness of the humiliation, of the *kenosis* and of the sacrifice in which the Saviour properly becomes human, the radicalism of the Sin becomes

---

23 For a theological explanation, of the analogy between the threefold rhetorical *paideia* and the natural theology intended as static *littera* merely describing the human nature itself (*quid*), and the threefold classification of the rhetorical styles (*quo modo*), corresponding to the charismatic, dynamic dimension of the Spirit (*DeCiv.Dei* XI, 25; VII, 31; *DeDoctr.Chr.* IV,7,21; 21,23), based on Augustinian rhetorical background, affected by the turning point in which A *DeDivv.qq.adSimpl.* I,2 consists, and made systematically clear in *DeDoctr.Chr.* IV, as *Aufhebung* of the Ciceronian Rhetoric and the aim of such *modus proferendi* thorugh the Holy Writ itself, LETTIERI, 2001. Referring to Pelagius, it is possible to sketch a dependence of his own theology on his rhetorical background too (cf. CIPRIANI, 1991), aiming at describing the *doctrina* governing the human nature *tout court* and its (ethical) application (*usus*).

clear, grounding a new opposition: the one between the first Adam, created by God, and the misery of the last Adam, in desperate need of the redemption of Christ.[24]

This contradiction – this composition of opposite perceptions – is thereby affirmed, and a certain stress on the soteriological outcome of the Incarnation (cf. *DeTrin.* IV, XIII; *DeCiv.Dei* VIII-X; *InIo.Ev.tr.*) might be intended as a precendent of Luther's interpretation of the *communicatio idiomatum* as hermeneutical key. *Communicatione idiomatum* – so subverting the human logic – ontological opposites are referred to Christ as a *unio hypostatica, Verbum incarnatum, Idem ipse.* Chirst is *medium* and Savior – is *medium* as much as is Savior. The *medietas Christi* (1Tim:2,5) is realised through the soteriological process of assumption of the negativity. The embodied God becomes a suffering/grieving God: in Chirst's flesh the passion and the relation to the contingency become part of the absoluteness of the

---

24 Against the Pelagian arguments (*C.duasEpp.Pel.*), Augustine stresses how the Original Sin has not killed (*perisse*) the Free will (*liberum arbitrium*), but rather has perverted it in such a way that it is *structurally* no more capable to want and do well.The Dialectic between Adam and Christ seems to summarise perfectly this ontological and hermeneutical polarisation between *natura/littera* (creation) and *Gratia/Spiritus* (redemption) as a whole, in its eschatological, pneumatological and ecclesiological sense. The criterion to distinguish Adam and the men Jesus is nothing else as the Divine predestination, in the sense of the distinction between *adiutorium sine quo non* (potentially perfect free Will, but limited in the sense of the Sin to the gift of the creative Grace) and *adiutorium quo* (effectively perfect free Will, acted by the redentive Grace). If God reveals Himself as source of Grace to the rejected too, it seems clear that such creative Grace cannot correspond to the undue redentive Grace, being it the *caritas* in which the *Spiritus* properly consists. A clearer formalisation of this dialectical movement *adiutorium sine quo non /adiutorium quo* can be found in the Jansenist production referring to *DeCorr.etGr.* 10,26–12,38. Cf. in this sense the distinction between *sensus divisum*, understanding two apparently contrary dialectical poles as asymmetrical, diachronic, so non-contradictory, and *sensus compositum*, erroneously assuming the poles as homogeneous and synchronic, so contradictory (Cornelius Jansen, *Augustinus*, II, cap. 17, exp. 165–170).

The so-called pseudo-celestinian *Indiculus* paves the way for the Modern problem of the right (Pelagian or not?) interpretation of Augustine. In this paper I assume as correct the esegetic path which, starting with O. ROTTMANNER 1892. In this perspective, cf. BOUBLÍK, 1961; ZEOLI, 1963; FLASCH, 1990 too. For a reconstruction of such *vexata quaestio*: LETTIERI, 2001 pp. 544ff. Implicit premise of my standpoint – according to the Jansenists, as well as with Simon, von Harnack, de Labriolle, Janssen, Bonner, Masai, Brown, Flasch, Ferrari, Rigby, Fredriksen, Wetzel – is the that this theological revolution in *DeDivv.qq.adSimpl.* I,2 – the interpretation of Rom:9,10–29 as doctrine of the undeserved and predestined grace – can be properly described as a conversion for Augustine, implying a crisis and re-foundation of his own theology (Cf. *Retr.* II,1,1; *DePraed.Sanct.* 3,7–4,8; *DeD.Persev.* 20,52; 21,55). Following Gaetano Lettieri, with Courcelle and Madec, I read the previous phase as an effective conversion to Christianism, believing – with Lorenz, Körner, Mayer, Drecoll, Manfredini – that the religious experience described in Cassiciacum as a platonising form of Christianism close to the position of Marius Victorinus has been successively re-semanticised through the pauline categories of the theology of the grace, in a meta-platonic system which nonetheless preserves the influence of the previous platonic categories in the construction of a *Stufenontologie*. For the whole topic, cf. LETTIERI, 1999.

divine Unity itself. Personally, as an *Alius* assuming an *Aliud* in Himself – identified with the *Idipsum*.

The theory of the Paradox provides so the key to deal with the hermeneutical results of Augustine's mature pneumatology as presented in *DeSp.Litt.* and borrowed by Luther.

In this perspective, the *veritas* does not essentially differ from the revelation, but it remains nonetheless *doctrina*, if the *Spiritus* does not convert it. The mystery of Incarnation and crucifixion is the pauline symbol of an overturning of the given order, a revelation whose acme consists in an intra-divine dialectic. Reveling himself as a Man, the God-Man transcends himself, being *absconditus* and *simul* historically revealed. He is *Caritas* transcending his own universal creating *Veritas*. In the intra-theological dialectic *littera/spiritus*, *doctrina/gratia* there is no contradiction, but a differentiation of levels. God-Man, *Idipsum* is paradoxically – as Trinity and Revelation – non-unitary, tolerating *in se* the difference pertaining the election, the *permixtio* between elected and rejected.[25]

4. Conclusion

What I am trying to point out here is the role that a different interpretation of notion of Spirit plays in such theological divergences. Erasmus, Karlstadt, Zwingli and the other so-called *Schwärmer*, intending Augustine's position only through a platonic *Stufenontologie* present a tendential minimisation of the role of the Pneumatology *tout court*, as an individualisation of his Theology of the Predestined Grace as spontaneous Free Will responding only to anthropological criteria, and interpreting the existence and the verification itself of the Presence of the *Spiritus in nobis* as *bona qualitas mentis* (cf. Rom:5,5). Its necessary counterpart is a voiding Sacramental

---

25 In trinitarian terms (*DeTrin.* and *DeCiv.Dei*), Augustine recalls the the trinitarian over-interpretation of the platonic doctrine of the *praedominantia- circumincessio* (cf. Marius Vittorinus, Ilarius, Cappadocians): understanding each trinitarian Person as a unification of all the personal perfections and *simul* unique and totally simple substance – but, differently from the Cappadocian interpretation, which understands the Spirit as proceeding from the Father through the Son, he understands the third hypostasis as proceeding *simul* from the Father and the Son, as *donum commune* (*DeTrin.* XV,17,29) or *communis caritas* (*DeTrin.* XV,17,27). The Trinity is *simul simplex et multiplex* (*DeTrin.* VI,6,8), – forcing the human reason to admit the identification of *contraria*, being God both *Unum*, *Idipsum* and *tria, alii* – being nonetheless not *aliud* (another substance), but *Alius* in the *Idipsum*. So the *Spiritus* describes the relationality between the Father and the *Verbum*. The Incarnation as process causes a distinction and a temporalisation among the Trinity itself: the Son, as *Verbum homo* (*DeTrin.* II,6,11), embodies for the eternity a hypostasis corresponding to a mortal body becoming *caro omnipotentis*. In this mediation the contingency may participate to the Eternal, as the *civitas Dei peregrina*, the mystical body of Christ.

pattern removing the Hidden Grace in the letter itself, and consequently removing the connection between the immediacy of the Divine Word and the Church and the Sacrament.

Assumed the preeminence of the Doctrine of the Justification, in Luther's standpoint its relation to an ontological dialectic gives way to an obsessive emphasis on the role of the *communicatio idiomatum*. But, as for Augustine, the problem is how to give logical consistence to the mystery of the Incarnation – how to communicate it. And the result is the same: it is not properly communicable, a nod *must* be enough, otherwise *all* is nothing. Following a perfect hermeneutic circle, the *caritas*, undue gift of the Spirit itself, is made the proper, real Object of the Writ, *as long as* it represents the Subject of the Writ too, the real Interpreter. The right interpretation – of the Word, of the Writ, of the signs – is a work of the Spirit, transferrable and understandable *per gratia*. Understanding is a matter of grace, and of the concept of Paradox as technical term seems to give a certain consistence to this point: the Word is no more death *littera*, but rather *Verbum* only if an act of grace – a divine Work – comes to enliven it. Then all is mad clear: the omnipresence[26] in the Presence of

---

26 On the possibility of the interpretation of the co-implication between *communicatio idiomatum* and Real presence as Ubiquity, cf. Martin Luther, *Daß diese Wort Christi „Das ist mein Leib" noch fest stehen, wider die Schwärmgeister*: WA 23,64–283; *De captivitate Babylonica ecclesiae praeludium*: WA 6,497–573; *De servo arbitrio*: WA 18,600–787; *Disputatio de divinitate et humanitate Christi* [28. 2. 1540]: WA 39/2,92–121; *Disputatio de sententia. Verbum caro factum est* (Joh 1,14) [11. 1. 1539]: WA 39/2,3–33; *Kurzes Bekenntnis vom hl. Sakrament*: WA 54,141–167; *Rationis* Latominianae *confutatio*: WA 8,43–128; *Sermon v. dem Sacrament des leibs u. bluts Christi, widder die Schwarmgeister*: WA 19,482–523; *Vom Abendmahl Christi. Bekenntnis*: WA 26,261–509; *Von den Konziliis u. Kirchen*: WA 50,509–653; *Von den letzten Worten Davids*: WA 54,28–100; *Wider die himm lischen Propheten, v. den Bildern u. Sakrament*: WA 18,62–214. Philipp Melanchthon, *Examen Ordinandorum*: CR 23,XXXV–CX; *Responsio Philippi Melanchthonis de controversiis Stancari*, 1553: VI, 261–277 = CR 23,87–100; *Loci praecipui theologici* ..., Wittenberg 1559 = CR 21,601–1106 = StA II/1,165–II/2,780. But Melanchthon has been the first to use explicitly the word "Ubiquity", precisely in the attempt to criticise Luther's standpoint, and then Brenz's radicalisation: "Verum Corpus et verus sanguis exhibetur in pane et poculo, Questio jam oritur, Quomodo Christus potest esse corporaliter in Sacramento, cum Corpus non possit esse simul in pluribus Locis? Respondeo, Christus dixit se adfuturum, Ergo vere adest in Sacramento et corporaliter. Nec est querenda alia ratio, Verbum ita sonat, Ergo necesse est ita fieri. Quod ad Corpus attinet, Christus quando vult potest esse vbicunq vult, Quare alia jam est ratio sui Corporis et nostri. De Vbiquitate non est disputandum. In hac controuersia est longa alia res, Nec Scholastici quicquam dicunt de Vbiquitate, Sed retinent simplicem sententiam de Corporali praefencia Christi." (WA 48,236.) Already in 1521 Melanchthon presented a christological thesis based on the *beneficia Christi*, against Luther's soteriological accentuation within the *communicatio idiomatum*: "[...] hoc est Christum cognoscere beneficia eius cognoscere, non quod isti docent, eius naturas, modos incarnationis contueri." (Melanchthon, Philipp, *Loci Communes 1521*, StA II/1, 7;cf. *Enarratio Symboli Nicaeni* (1550); CR 23,344f. Cf. BAUR, *Ubiquität* in TRE, 34.

Christ represents not a theoretical construction to the rescue of an unconvincing Sacramental Doctrine, it the basis of the Holy Writ and the revelation itself.

In the attempt of his opponents to present an immediate and rational Spirituality (*Geistigkeit*), the Trinity loses its own dialectical and dynamising role, now getting a psycologisation interpreted by Luther as *perversio* of the right order of the Revelation, subverting the inner dimension in outward appearance, the grace in human work, so missing the unity between *gratia* and *Spiritus*. So the *Abendmahlslehre*, often considered as the weak spot within Luther's theology, connects and clarifies the co-implication between christology and hermeneutics, Word and Spirit, stressing the role of the literal sense and of the "Grammar".[27] This is made possible by the strong affirmation of the Presence of the historical (essential and personal) Christ in the Sacrament. In this sense, the Word grounds (*extra nos*) and mediates what properly connects the human with the sacred, reciprocally allowing a recognition of it (*extra nos*) in us. On the other hand undestanding this paradoxical, real Presence of Christ, not a memorial act – a human work – , but rather a concrete Divine presence, 'dressed' with the Flesh – Word, bread, wine – is already an effect of the work of the Spirit,[28] redoubling, enliving the christological topic in the sacrament too, and so grounding the mystery of the real presence in the omnipotence of God, confessed as *mirum* in the eyes of the creature. How could the Flesh be spiritual? How could the bread be the Flesh of Christ? How could the man Christ be God? The double relation moving from the Word and the Faith gives consistency to this carnal-spiritual reality, the opposed poles determine nonetheless each other. The Revelation *in re*, as well *in fide* is therefore perverted by the Spiritualism, as long as The hermeneutical key must be found in the right interpretation of the mediation of the Word. In this sense, the Sacramental presence of Christ does not represent a peculiar topic within the theology, but rather determines the reception of the Revelation of God in a broader sense.

---

27 *Wider die himmlischen Propheten* (1524–1525); *Daß diese Worte Christi* (1527); *Vom Abendmahl Christi. Bekenntnis* (1528). Meaningfully, Luther's report of Oecolampad's position is summarised through the keywords: *mysterium, sacramentum, invisibile, intelligibile* (WA 23, 209 ss., *Das Diese wort Christi: Das Ist mein leib etc.*)

28 The classical *locus* for such topic is of course John:6 read on the basis of John:1,14. Cf. 1Cor:14,35ff., Isa:55,11 and Rom:11,16 too. For a biblical interpretation of such prophetic-christological dialectical movement, grounding Luther's understanding of the Holy Writ as a whole, cf. for instance Asendorf, 1988, 1998, 2004. In this sense, Luther's hermeneutical key for his dialectical interpretation of the Old Testament – as well as of the Writ in a broader sense – is to be recognised in the so-called *Protevangelium* (Gen:3,15). Asendorf recognises such hermeneutical path, acknowledging a dynamising Christological core to the Old Testament and *then* to the New Testament too – topic extensively recalled in the *Genesisvorlesung* –, even in Luther's earlier production (namely, in his *Predigten* of the year 1519).

This hermeneutics *per gratia* – explicitly pointed out *DeSpir.etLitt.*, made a fundamental doctrinal treatise at the University of Wittenberg – is the harvest of Luther's interpretation of Augustine's theology.

Bibliography

ALTHAUS, P. (1962), Die Theologie Martin Luthers, Gütersloh: Gütersloher Verlagshaus Gerd Mohn.

ASENDORF, U. (1964), Der jüngste Tag: Weltende und Gegenwart, Furche-Verlag.

ASENDORF, U. (1967), Eschatologie bei Luther, Göttingen: Vandenhoeck & Ruprecht,.

ASENDORF, U. (1971), Gekreuzigt und auferstanden: Luthers Herausforderung an die moderne Christologie, Bielefeld: Luthers Verlag Haus.

ASENDORF, U. (1982), Luther und Hegel: Untersuchungen zur Grundlegung eineren systematischen Theologie, Stuttgart: Steiner.

ASENDORF, U. (1988) Die Theologie Martin Luthers nach seinen Predigten, Göttingen: Vandenhoeck & Ruprecht.

ASENDORF, U. (1998) Lectura in Biblia, Göttingen: Vandenhoeck & Ruprecht.

ASENDORF, U. (2004) Heiliger Geist und Rechtfertigung, Göttingen: Vandenhoeck & Ruprecht.

BAUER, K. (1926), Die Abendmahls Zwinglis bis zum Beginn der Auseinandersetzung mit Luther, Theologische Blätter 5, 217–226.

BAUER, K. (1927), Symbolik un Realpräsenz in der Abendmahl Zwinglis bis 1525, Zeitschrift für Kirchengeschichte 46, 97–105.

BAUER, K. (1928), Die wittenberger Universitätstheologie und die Anfänge der deutschen Reformation, Tübingen: Mohr Siebeck.

BAUR, JÖRG (2002), Article "Ubiquität", TRE 34, 224–241.

BAYER, O. (1969), Die reformatorische Wende in Luthers Theologie, ZThK 66, 115–150.

BIZER, E. (1958), Luther und der Papst, München: Chr. Kaiser.

BORNKAMM, H. (1942), Iustitia dei in der Scholastik und bei Luther, Archiv für Reformationsgeschichte 39, 1–46;

BORNKAMM, H. (1961), Zur Frage der Iustitia Dei beim jungen Luther, Archiv für Reformationsgeschichte 52, 16–29.

BOUBLÌK, V. (1961), La predestinazione. S. Paolo e S. Agostino, Corona Lateranensis 3, Rome: Lateran University Press.

CIPRIANI, N. (1991), La morale pelagiana e la retorica, Augustinianum 31, 309–327.

DELIUS, H.-U. (1984), Augustin als Quelle Luthers, Leizpig: Evangelische Verlagsanstalt.

DEMMER, D. (1968), Lutherus interpres. Der theologische Neuansatz in seiner Römerbriefexegese unter besonderer Berücksichtigung Augustins, Untersuchungen zur Kirchengeschichte 4, Witten: Luther-Verlag.

DE NEGRI, E. (1967), La teologia di Lutero, Firenze: La Nuova Italia.

DENIFLE, H. (1906), Luther und Luthertum in der ersten Entwickelung: quellenmässig dargestellt, vol. 1, Mainz: F. Kirchheim.

EBELING, E. (1951), Die Anfänge von Luthers Hermeneutik, ZThK, 172–230.

GRANE, L. (1962), Contra Gabrielem. Luthers Auseinandersetzung mit Gabriel Biel in der Disputatio Contra Scholasticam Theologiam 1517, Copenhagen: Gyldendal.

GRANE, L. (1973), Divus Paulus et S. Augustinus, interpres eius fidelissimus: über Luthers Verhältniss zu Augustin, Tübingen: JCB Mohr (Paul Siebeck).

GRANE, L. (1975a), Modus loquendi theologicus. Luthers Kampf um die Erneuerung der Theologie (1515–1518), Leiden: Brill.

GRANE, L. (1975b), Luthers Auslegung von Rom 2, 12–15 in der Römerbriefvorlesung, Neue Zeitschrift für Systematische Theologieund Religionsphilosophie 17.1, 22–32.

GRANE, L. (1994), Martinus Noster. Luther in the German Reform Movement 1518–1521, Darmstadt: Verlag Philipp von Zabern.

FLASCH, K. (1990), Logik des Schreckens. Augustins von Hippo De diversis quaestionibus ad Simplicianum 1,2, Mainz: Dieterich'sche Verlagsbuchhandlung.

HAGEN, K. (1990), Augustin, the Harvest, and Theology (1300–1650). FS H. A. Oberman, Leiden: Brill.

HAMEL, A. (1934), Der junge Luther und Augustin. Ihre Beziehungen in der Rechtfertigungslehre nach Luthers ersten Vorlesungen, 1509–1518, Gütersloh: C. Bertelsmann.

HERMANN, R. (1930), Luthers These "Gerecht und Sünder zugleich", Gütersloh: C. Bertelsmann.

HIRSCH, E. (1954), Initium theologiae Lutheri, in: Lutherstudien, vol. 2. Gütersloh: Spenner, 9–35.

HIRSCH, E. (1963), Das Wesen des reformatorischen Christentums, Berlin: De Gruyter.

JOEST, W. (1967), Ontologie der Person bei Luther, Göttingen: Vandenhoeck & Ruprecht.

KAUFMANN, T. (2003), Das Ende der Reformation. Magdeburgs 'Herrgotts Kanzlei' (1548–1551/2). Tübingen: Mohr Siebeck.

KAUFMANN, T. (2006), Konfession und Kultur. Lutherischer Protestantismus in der zweiten Hälfte des Reformationsjahrhunderts, Tübingen: Mohr Siebeck.

KÖHLER, W. (1900), Luther und die Kirchengeschichte, Hildesheim: Georg Olms Verlag.

KÖHLER, W. (1926), Zu Zwinglis älterster Abendmahlsfassung, Zeitschrift für Kirchengeschichte 45, 399–408.

KÖHLER, W. (1928), Zur Abendmahlskontroverse in der Refomationszeit insbesonere zur Entwicklung der Abendmahlslehre Zwinglis, Zeitschrift für Kirchengeschichte 47, 47–56.

KRODEL, G. (1955), Die Abendmahlslehre des Erasmus von Rotterdam und seine Stellung am Anfang des Abendmahlsstreites der Reformatoren, Erlangen: Universität.

LEONI, S. (1991), Fides creatrix divinitatis, Archivio di Filosofia 59, 13–35.

LEONI, S. (1996), Nicht Nachwort, sondern Machtwort, in: P.C. Bori (ed.), In Spirito e Verità. Letture di Giovanni 4, 23–24, Bologna: Edizioni Dehoniane, 131–148.

LEPPIN, V. (1999), Antichrist Und Jüngster Tag: Das Profil Apokalyptischer Flugschriftenpublizistik im Deutschen Luthertum 1548–1618, Gütersloh: Gütersloher Verlagshaus.

LETTIERI, G. (1999), Il metodo della Grazia. Pascal e l'ermeneutica giansenista di Agostino, Bologna: Edizioni Dehoniane.

LETTIERI, G. (2001), L'altro Agostino. Ermeneutica e retorica della grazia dalla crisi alla metamorfosi del De doctrina christiana, Brescia: Morcelliana.

LIENHARD, M. (1980), Martin Luthers christologisches Zeugnis: Entwicklung und Grundzüge seiner Christologie, Göttingen: Vandenhoeck & Ruprecht.

LOEWENICH, W. von (1933), Luthers theologia crucis, München: Chr. Kaiser.

LOHSE, B. (1965a), Die Bedeutung Augustin für den jungen Luther, in: L. Grane/B. Moeller/O.H. Pesch (ed.), Evangenlium in der Geschichte. Studien zu Luther und der Reformation, Göttingen: Vandenhoeck & Ruprecht, 11–30.

LOHSE, B. (1965b), Luther und Huß, in: Luther. Zeitschrift der Luthergesellschaft 36, 108–122.

LOHSE, B. (1988), Der Durchbruch der reformatorischen Erkenntnis bei Luther: neuere Untersuchungen, Stuttgart: F. Steiner Verlag.

LOHSE, B. (1990), Zum wittenberger Augustinismus. Augustins Schrift De Spiritu et Littera in der Auslegung bei Staupitz, Luther und Karlstadt, in: K. Hagen (ed.), Augustine, the Harvest, and Theology (1330–1650). FS H. A. Oberman, Leiden: Brill, 89–109.

MIEGGE, G. (1964), Lutero giovane, Milan: Feltrinelli.

MÜHLEN, K.-H. ZUR (1999), Der Begriff "Signum" in der Sakramentslehre des 16. Jahrhunderts, in: Signum. Florence: Leo S. Olschki.

MÜLLER, A.V. (1920), Luthers Werdegang bis zum Turmerlebnis, Gotha: Verlag Friedrich Andreas Perthes.

Neebe, G. (1997), Apostolische Kirche, Berlin: De Gruyter.

OTTO, R. (1898), Die Anschauung vom heiligen Geste bei Luther, Göttingen: Vandenhoeck & Ruprecht.

PANI, G. (1983), Martin Lutero, lezioni sulla Lettera ai Romani (Römerbriefvorlesung 1515–1516): i riferimenti ad Agostino, la giustificazione, Roma: Pubblicazioni Agostiniane.

PANI, G. (1986), Il De spiritu et littera nella Römerbriefvorlesung di Lutero, in: Annali di Storia dell'Esegesi 3, 109–138.

PANI, G. (2005), Paolo, Agostino, Lutero: alle origini del mondo moderno, Soveria Mannelli: Rubbettino.

POHLIG, M. (2007), Zwischen Gelehrsamkeit Und Konfessioneller Identitätsstiftung: Lutherische Kirchen- Und Universalgeschichtsschreibung 1546–1617, Tübingen: Mohr Siebeck.

ROTTMANNER, O. (1892), Der Augustinismus. Eine dogmengeschichtliche Studie, München: J.J. Lentner.

SEEBERG, E. (1940), Grundzüge der Theologie Luthers, Stuttgart: Kohlhammer.

STANGE, C. (1957), Die Anfänge der Theologie Luthers, Giessen: A. Töpelmann.

STRACKE E. (1926), Luthers grosses selbstzeugnis 1545 über seine entwicklung zum reformator historisch-kritisch untersucht, Bremen: M. Heinsius Nachfolger/Eger & Sievers, 1926.

VERCRUYSSE, J. (1976), Luther's Theology of the Cross at the Time of the Heidelberg Disputation, Gregorianum, 523–548.

VERCRUYSSE, J. (1981), Gesetz und Liebe. Die Struktur der Heidelberger Disputation Luthers (1518), Luther Jahrbuch Hamburg 48, 7–43.

VOGELSANG, E. (1929), Die Anfänge von Luthers Christologie, Berlin: De Gruyter.

ZEOLI, A (1963), La teologia agostiniana della grazia fino alle "Quaestiones ad Simplicianum" (396) Napoli: Liguori.

Herman A. Speelman

From Assembly of Believers to an Official Institute

Morély versus Chandieu on Ecclesiology in the 1560s

Introduction

The search for a diplomatic solution

Towards the end of the 1550s, the growing Calvinist movement in France longed very much for the end of the persecutions and chose to unite itself in a structured organization in order to survive these times of heavy persecution. The implicit assumption behind this organization was that the federated local evangelical communities constituted a lawful church alongside the Roman Catholic Church, in spite of the absence of government recognition. In the tense month of May 1559, the synod had no realistic prospect whatsoever for better days, and yet the Huguenots were convinced that they could no longer simply stand by and watch. The leading Calvinistic nobles and ministers in France no longer avoided the confrontation. They had a specific goal in mind, and also in the following years they stayed the course, namely, to obtain from the Roman Catholic government recognition for two denominations and confessions within a single state.

After the political climate had undergone certain changes in light of the death of Henry II in July 1559, leading figures like the noblemen Coligny and Chandieu, on behalf of the reformed believers, made a request to the new king in March 1560 to grant them some religious freedom and to organize a religious dialogue. They longed for a limited degree of freedom of religion and sought to introduce some order into the great Kingdom of France, so heartily loved by all. But the concept of a gathered church of true Christians as the secret and spiritual body of Christ and as visible sacral community within that same Kingdom, without the cooperation of the civil governments, would run counter to the ideal of civic unity and of the unity of the visible church.

At the French court the question regarding a policy of reconciliation gradually grew in importance. The former policy of persecution had passed, and under the leadership of the new Chancellor, Michel de l'Hôpital, a new policy was introduced. L'Hôpital soon showed himself to be the leading spokesman at the court for the *moyenneur*-party. Like the Huguenots, the more moderate or *moyenneurs* were ready to meet with the different parties; both parties favored a peaceful solution to the conflict. Contrary to the Huguenots, however, the *moyenneurs* were intent on keeping the different groups within the one established church, at all costs.

Calvin did not support a situation in which the government was to allow a second church to exist beside the existing church. On this point, however, his followers in France struck out on a course of their own. Calvin disagreed altogether with the course of events. In Calvin's way of thinking it was dangerous for the Reformed to gain a reputation as rebels (CO 17, 526), but above all, it was simply unthinkable for two churches to exist side by side in one state. He insisted on the unity of the Church and on the unity of church and state, which for centuries had been founded on a religious unity. To Calvin it was of primal importance for the churches in France to retain their clandestine character until the tides turned. For that reason, Calvin, from late 1559 on, did not cease to demand attention for his view on the developments in the Reformed church in France and on the status of the Reformed confession there, and to warn his coreligionists that they should be wary of holding such wily discussions with the opponents of "the true religion", both moderates and radicals (CO 18, 616; 619; 620). This disagreement revealed two conflicting views on church and confession.[1] The solution desired by the Reformed in France, however, would prove highly influential in large parts of Western Europe. The new edict of Saint-Germain on 17 January 1562, the so-called January edict, a decree of tolerance, which followed soon after, would be an important step on the way to this religious pluralism. This would show itself to be an important first step worldwide on the road to confessional and ecclesiastical plurality – and, as a result, to the separation of church and state.[2]

In Protestantism, being a Christian had become a matter of personal faith and a protestant lifestyle. Thereby became for the Huguenots, the presbyteral-synodical system a practical solution for the search for identity in the French churches. Speaking in ecclesiastical terms, the consistory was the driving force in the Calvinist way of life, rather than a repressive aspect of communal living. Although the ideals of people like Chandieu and Morély were similar, they followed a different path to achieve them (Chandieu: 1566, 68). They had very different views on church and church life, and, subsequently, they also disagreed on the question of how to forge the widespread and scattered ecclesiastical communities in France into a unity.

---

1 CO 9, 731f; CO 17, no. 3122, 652–653. See further Herman A. Speelman: 2014a; 2014b. For Calvin's objection to the presentation of the French confession to the King, see Speelman: 2014a, 167–179. See also Speelman: 2016a.

2 However, religious plurality first took shape on a large scale in 1562 in the Western world (cf. Speelman 2014a, 200–207), two small Swiss cantons form an exception. After the defeat of the reformed Confederates in the Battle of Kappel of 1531, Appenzell and St. Gallen/Toggenburg had already remained territories with two confessions equal in status and with equal rights (Bryner: 2016, 250, 253, 262).

While the beginning of the 1560s brought better times for the French evangelical movement, there was still great uncertainty in those days of turmoil and tribulations, also within the church. After great persecution and suffering, a church developed with a synodical structure, relatively independent of the government. What alternatives did they have for an underground church or Church under the Cross?

In this paper on Morély's and Chandieu's ecclesiology, I want to examine in what respect their views differ in four paragraphs, about the church as a community of saints (1), discipline as an independent characteristic of the church (2), church as a clerical or more democratic institution (3), and the function of the Eucharist in forming a church (4).

1. Church as a group of faithful people forming a holy communion

1.1 Church as a communion of believers

When referring to the process of church formation in France, with people gathering spontaneously as they had done in the 1540s, and with a more formal church structure in the late 1550s, the status of these groups, worshipping by reading the Bible, praying and singing together in secret meetings, can best be captured, as Sara Barker rightly suggested, by the term *assemblée des fidèles* (Barker: 2009, 57).

When Antoine de la Roche-Chandieu, minister of the Reformed church in Paris, stayed in Poitiers in the autumn of the year 1558, he was commissioned (possibly by the provincial synod of Poitou) to examine the possibility of convoking a first national synod. It was a year after the brutal disruption of an illegal assembly held in the rue Saint Jacques on the evening of 4 September 1557. Towards the end of this meeting, shortly after the Lord's Supper had been celebrated, hundreds of participants, men and women, had been crudely attacked, captured and even killed in a raid led by monks and students. It was deeply felt that this action could not remain without response, but what the appropriate response should be, was under discussion among the churches.

After years of persecution, the continuously harassed fugitive believers had grown accustomed to their clandestine life in small underground churches and they considered themselves principally *communions des fidèles*. Hundreds of smaller and larger of such churches had arisen throughout the country, bringing together millions of supporters and members. In the 1560s, a new generation of reformed church leaders, like Beza, Chandieu and Morély, took up the baton in France, building upon the innovative thoughts of the previous generation and trying to transform the reformed ideas of church polity – especially those of Geneva – to a national level in the Kingdom of France and to consolidate these for the future, in an attempt to establish a reformed orthodoxy.

While the protestant believers were scattered all over the country and had diffi-culty convening, they experienced being a member of a local church as belonging to the invisible spiritual body of Christ (*Corpus Christi*), the sacral communion of saints, as being "united as citizens of one community," because we "all share in the privileges of Jesus Christ," as Theodore de Bèze explained in 1559 (de Bèze: 1559, art. 5.4).[3] With regard to 'church', Beza confessed that the church consists of "all believers," spread out among many places, united and connected with each other like citizens of a city-state (*comme les bourgeois d'une communauté*), in so far as all partake in the privileges of Jesus Christ (cf. De Brès: 1561, art. 27 [= CB]).

This participation in the privileges of Christ, Beza went on to say, we call that the "communion of saints" (*communauté des saincts*) (De Bèze: 1559, art. 5.4). And in his *Confession de foy*, Beza zoomed in on the individual believer (de Bèze: 1559, art. 5.8; cf. CB, art. 29). In that same year 1559, the French confession described 'church' in a similar way, as "the company of the faithful" (*compagnie des fidèles*) (CG, art. 27).[4] In the protestant way of thinking, one was no longer a Christian solely because of birth or infant baptism, but being a Christian had become a matter of conscious choice. No longer was the institution of the church to control life through its system of sacraments, but believers themselves were to make free use of the instruments of grace offered to them by the Gospel. The churches in France were to become "a uniformly godly community" through "disciplining of people's daily lives," Karen Spierling concludes (Spierling: 2008, 100). The church members became personally responsible for seeking and maintaining the union of the church by submitting "to the public teaching, and to the yoke of Jesus Christ," so the French protestant church confessed in 1559.[5]

The French Reformed (i.e., the Huguenots) saw no other way than to enter into a mild, diplomatic, yet 'radical', confrontation with the government. The preparations were made in the greatest secrecy, since the plan for a synod amounted to a conscious transgression of the government policy and would elicit a sharp response were it to become known. It soon did come into the open that the Huguenots were intent on establishing an ecclesiastical organization of their own, a national synodical alliance,

---

3 "coinoincts comme les bourgeois d'une communauté, estans tous participans des privileges d'icelle, c'est à scavoir de Jesus Christ". For Calvin the sacral community (*corpus Christi*) is very different from the civic commune (*corpus politicum*) (CO 49, 501; 1 Cor. 12:12).

4 Cf. De Brès spoke about "the assembly of true Christian believers" (CB, art. 27).

5 CG, art. 26. From the start of Protestantism the churches in Germany and in the Swiss Cantons were supported by the government and often also openly by charismatic preachers. In France there was at first an active persecution policy so that it was not without danger for evangelical believers to openly come out for their faith.

without the approval of the state. The decision taken by the first national synod of Paris in late May 1559 to establish a national confession without approval from the state formed a turning point. Was this new church structure to be aristocratic or democratic? The debate on this question revealed two conflicting views on church.

1.2 Jean de Morély's attack on the Reformed church order

With his *Traicté de la discipline et police chrestienne*, Morély, Sire de Villiers, an active Calvinist layman, became in 1562 the leader of the first formidable internal attack on the structure of the French Reformed Church.[6] He did not come from the highest ranks of nobility, but was from a family accustomed to serving at the royal courts and belonged to that group of noble converts which made Calvinism into a potent force in sixteenth-century European politics.[7] He became a Protestant somewhere around 1547, and moved to Geneva somewhere in the 1550s, when many other French Protestants were crowding into that city.[8]

While Morély had endured a relatively negative image for quite a period of time, in the previous century Henri Naef had reinstated his importance by describing him as one of the first defenders of 'equality and Christian freedom', and a short while later Emile Léonard described him as a Congregationalist, the victor of "Congregationalism in the French Reformation", the movement which had emerged from "meetings relating to the Bible" (Léonard: 1961, vol. 2, 115–117).

Morély wished to reinstate the churches' freedom and independence, and it was his opinion that the churchgoers should have discretion over church affairs such as doctrine, excommunication, the election of the preachers and vigilance over the unity across the churches (Morély: 1562, 75). His more democratically inspired church structure design, however, did not coincide with the more clerical

---

6 Morély's *Treatise on Christian Discipline* is divided into four books. The first book argues for the necessity of ecclesiastical discipline, book two discusses at more length how proper discipline should be applied to prevent the spread of dangerous doctrine and to control the behavior of individual Christians, the third book discusses the different orders of the clergy and outlines what he feels to be the appropriate way to select them and in the last book he discusses the general organization of the Church.

7 Both his father and his father-in-law had apparently served the court of Francis I, King of France, as physicians and Morély himself was to serve the court of Jeanne d'Albret, Queen of Navarre, as a tutor.

8 Twice Morély got into trouble with the city's leading pastors. The first incident was an aftermath of the Conspiracy of Amboise in 1560 and the second time was over his critique of Calvinist ecclesiastical institutions. In their marvelous study on Morély, Denis and Rott convincingly argue that during the 1560s Morély was repeatedly treated unjustly, and that probably several personal elements and elements of church politics played a role in this. It is also remarkable that no one notices the similarities between the proposals put forward by Viret and by Morély in the same year 1561 (Denis/Rott: 1993; cf. Kingdon: 1967, 44–45).

presbyteral-synodical plan outlined in the *Discipline des Eglises réformées de France* in 1559. As a result, the unity of this young and unexampled French protestant church was at stake.

1.3 A simultaneously visible and invisible church

Morély did not support an open church of which everyone, without distinction, could be a member. Does a church distinguish itself, not only through a pure administration of word and sacraments, but also through the purity of its members? Regarding this last issue, his views remain unclear. Other than the Anabaptists, who favored a holy community, Morély remained undecided on this matter (Denis/Rott: 1993, 162f).

Like Bucer and Calvin before him, Morély described the church as 'the body of Christ'. The different factions within the young French Reformed church favored the image of 'the body of Christ' to signify their view on what 'church' is. This metaphor refers to Christ and to the communion in Him, and with each other. The local and universal church is sometimes hidden and totally invisible to the eye, but at the same time its catholicity is tangible, "spread and dispersed over the whole world; and yet joined and united with heart and will, by the power of faith, in one and the same spirit."[9]

Although reformers such as Bucer and Calvin also aspired to a holy community, they maintained a strict distinction between the visible and the invisible church. They carefully separated the two, thus creating a dialectical tension in their ecclesiology, which means that the visible church as a confessional church is a mixed church, comprising believers as well as hypocrites. This broad people's church has room for the flock, although it should not be confused with the church of the chosen.[10] Paradoxically speaking, the visible church can also be invisible, either because it is not tolerated above the surface and therefore hidden, or because it cannot be located due to its dispersion. It is only joined and united with heart and will, by the power of faith. In the same spirit, Morély called this church "the mystical body of Christ." For him each local church is, at the same time, a visible and invisible communion, and every believer has his or her own responsibility.[11]

---

9 CB, art 27: "[A]ins elle est espanduë et dispersée par tout le monde, estant toutesfois joincte et unie de coeur, et de volonté en un mesme Esprit par la vertu de la Foy."

10 About Bucer's crusade for the sacral city against the late medieval commune: Oberman: 2009, 181ff; Maruyama: 1978, 23–25; Wendel: 1950, 22; Courvoirsier: 1964.

11 Morély speaks about "l'excellente beauté du corps mystique et spiritual de l'Eglise du Seigneur, et de l'union qui est en lui" (Morély: 1562, 75; cf. Calvin, *Institutio*, 4.1.2).

1.4 The church as mystical body of Christ: catholic, scattered, yet one

Morély's ecclesiology contained a mystical as well as an institutional aspect. On the one hand he described the church as "mystical body," showing less restraint in his words than others, while on the other hand he stated that God comes to us through the course of his ecclesiastical ordonnances. In this respect, he deviated from the path taken by the young French church, which was characterized by a flexible church order that adjusted itself to the circumstances of the oppressed minority churches.

According to Morély, the believers are connected to Christ through the church. They are connected through the Spirit to "the mystical and true body of Christ," while the church is connected to God through Christ, its Head. Thus, for him, the Trinitarian communion is the ground for the ecclesiastical communion. It is led by the Holy Spirit, and therefore Morély calls it spiritual, as the church also consists of a "gathering (*rassemblement*) of spiritual people" (Morély: 1589, vol. 1, 70/71; 81/82). The Kingdom of God and the visible church were for him one and the same.

1.5 Chandieu answered Morély

A few years later, at the request of the national synod, the protestant minister Antoine de la Roche, Baron of Chandieu, gave Morély an official rejoinder. In February 1565, the provincial synod in Paris decided that a written refutation of Morély's ideas was necessary, in order to inform people of the true nature of the *Traicté de la discipline*. Chandieu was entrusted by both the French Churches and Geneva to set the record straight. By the time the fifth national synod, held in Paris in December 1565, condemned Morély's tractate for the second time, Chandieu was already well under way in composing his defense of the legitimation of the reformed vision on discipline. He simply called it: *La Confirmation de la Discipline ecclesiastique*, a book in which Chandieu tried to confirm the self-image of the Protestants in France in a scholastic, comprehensive tractate, comprising 248 pages, in which he focused more on the ecclesiastical institute than on the people. The book especially confirmed the need for discipline in the church (Chandieu: 1566, 4).

Although Chandieu did not mention Morély by name in his *Confirmation*, it was clear to whom his argument referred (Chandieu: 1566, 69). He rejected Morély's ideas as not merely false and dangerous, but in fact impossible (Chandieu: 1566, 239–240). At the same time, he cherished the many good things brought, through the grace of God, by the French evangelical movement in the 1550s and early 1560s and he wished to reassure the members of the church that they had followed the right course. Our times give us an opportunity to see the church return to its former glory, Chandieu argued (Chandieu: 1566, 4). But familiar concepts of 'church' as an 'assembly of faithful people' or a 'community of saints' are missing in his manual. Chandieu's conclusion was that Morély's view endangered the Church. What Morély proposed in his *Traicté de la discipline* ran contrary to the provisions made in the *Discipline* by the French churches in 1559. If a greater voice had been given to the congregation as a whole, in all kinds of affairs, there would have been a danger of fragmentation which, in the precarious political climate of the 1560s, might have crippled the churches for God.[12]

2. The dominant place of discipline

Chandieu agreed with Morély and his followers that the church order (*discipline de l'Eglise*) "is as necessary as a hedge (*haye*) to protect and conserve the purity of the doctrine", but in their opinion it was impossible to have an order that differed from "what they see before them", said Chandieu (Chandieu: 1566, 69). He did not, however, apply this principle to his own idea of a church order, so that he dialectically ascertained that the whole earth has "only one church of God, one true religion, one faith, one doctrine and one church order, which does not depend on the opinion of people" (Chandieu: 1566, 124). For both Chandieu and Morély, the order of the church was essential for the unity of the church. According to Chandieu, the church order (*ordre ecclesiastique*) formed an external "wall against all sects and deviations surrounding us" and he warned the members of the church not to violate this order. The order functioned like nerves in a body "through which God wishes to conserve the church as a whole." A breach could counteract the unity.

They also viewed the independent ecclesiastical discipline as one of its necessary elements and as a characteristic of the church (Chandieu: 1566, 43; 53; 64; see also n.37). In this respect, they differ from Calvin, among others. For Calvin, 'church' was "without any doubt" wherever "the word of God is preached and received purely and where the sacraments are administrated according to Christ's institution" (*Institutio* 4.1.9). The ecclesiastical discipline was to be mainly viewed as a human institution that was necessary due to human weakness.

For someone like Bucer, however, the church was rather "a communion of confessors" (cf. Courvoisier: 1933, 79; Maruyama: 1978, 20ff). The administration of word and sacrament does not suffice, in his opinion. An additional, necessary feature of the church was its discipline, so that its members could make progress in

---

12 The final chapter 5 of the *Confirmation* demonstrate how far-reaching Chandieu feared Morély's system, challenging internally by division and externally by opposing forces who might exploit these divisions.

their spiritual lives. Morély also predicted that there would be freedom and unity as there was in the days of the apostles, should Christ's order be followed faithfully. The flock would share one heart and soul. This unity of the church was a matter of faith: "For as the church is the communion of saints, because there is a unification of all in the mystical body of Jesus Christ, likewise this being-one must become visible in all gatherings so that unity can be attained during collective issues and, more specifically, those matters that need it the most. The salvation of each member should be the aim and care of all other members" (Morély: 1562, 302).

Morély also emphasized the sanctity, perfection and timelessness of the ecclesiastical discipline. This is why Morély equated the church with the kingdom of God, to a constitution which transcended "in wisdom all affairs devised by humans to make a republic peaceful, virtuous and happy" (Morély: 1562, Préface, A2 r). Therefore, it is wrong to adapt this fixed church order to circumstances, he writes. The manner in which the church is to be governed is of high importance and "this should not be adapted continuously according to the people and the changing circumstances of place and time" (Morély: 1562, Préface, A2v). This opinion ran counter to that of the French synod that rather stated that the articles of the church order could be changed "if the church's interest should so require".[13]

2.1 Flexible church ordonnances[14]

Chandieu, who presided over several synods, reproached Morély for confusing the disciplinary order with "the form that can and should be adapted to circumstances" (Chandieu: 1566, 233). With reference to Tertullian and Cyprian, Chandieu stated that affairs concerning the ecclesiastical discipline were "subject to change". Surely, we should not blindly copy the early church's regulations! The external form of the church order "can and should be adapted to time, place and other circumstances." This did not implicate that the content was to change in any way. Because Morély did not distinguish between form and content, he overlooked the fact that all external regulations should "be adapted to time, place and other circumstances" (Chandieu: 1566, 223; 234f; cf. Beza: 1559, V, art. 18f).

Chandieu strove for a more sovereign position of the church (*sa proper vie*) and emphasized the importance of an independent church order for a good cooperation with the government. The Roman church had also its own jurisdiction for centuries. Our church order, however, is merely spiritual, said Chandieu, and "only concerns the consciences and has no other sword (*glaive*) than the admonitions coming

---

13 "[Q]ue si l'utilité de l'Eglise le requiert" (Actes du Synode reformée de France 1 [1559], art. 40; cf. Niesel: 1939, 79).

14 See *Speelman*: 2014c, 187–192. Erik de Boer spoke in his inaugural address on 19 February 2016 about "the lightness (*lichtvoetigheid*) of the Reformed denomination" (De Boer: 2016, 26).

from God's word and the improvements that they cause". This 'spiritual regulation' (*reiglement spiritual*) does not decrease the government's civil authority at all. On the contrary, it in fact stimulates obedience to the government, as well as "a good and holy life" and "obedience to God and government," so he claimed.[15]

At the heart of Chandieu's argument lay the idea that church leadership cannot be taken up by the church people as a whole (*tout le people de l'Eglise*) or through a majority of votes, because "the larger part of the church people is generally highly sinful", as we have repeatedly stated, he says.[16]

> In each church we have a consistory that consists of preachers, elders and deacons, who share the collective task to guard over the church and to manage it [...] and to purify it of all sins and scandals (Chandieu: 1566, 71).

Although both Chandieu and Morély viewed the church order as an institution of God, changing the perfect church order of our Lord was, in Morély's view, a lack of faith and an insult to its Creator. "When Jesus Christ establishes his church and ordained His laws, He did not institute an aristocratic form of government", but He hands "eternal laws to his eternal kingdom". But He does not install a kind of aristocratic government.[17] And this is why Morély fiercely opposed a clerical form of government, because it endangered the unity of the church.

In the heat of his argument, Chandieu noted that Morély and his followers acted as if the ecclesiastical discipline "should be implemented by means of armies and battles", but this is impossible, he said, because the weapons that the church has at its disposal are merely spiritual.[18] This is a politically correct, but hardly credible, statement for an active man such as Chandieu, who was intensely involved in the battle for more religious freedom and ecclesiastical independence in France, increasingly using radical methods and brute violence to implement this, like the conspiracy of Amboise (1560), iconoclastic activities (1561), and even military weapons in a religious war (1562).

---

15 Chandieu: 1566, 53; 11–12. The government was suspicious of the developments and had made an inventory of the power of the more than 800 Reformed churches in 1562 (Mentzer/Van Ruymbeke: 2016, 17).

16 Chandieu: 1566, 74; 215–216. Chandieu accuses Morély of using the phrase "church as a whole" to indicate only a part of the church, as he excludes women and children from the ecclesiastical gathering (Chandieu 1566, 176; cf. De Bèze: 1560, art. 35, 210f.)

17 Morély: 1562, 63. An aristocratic trait of the synodical system was, among others, that the majority of the ministers at the synods prove to be of nobility, with titles like Baron and Lord.

18 Chandieu: 1566, 128; cf. Chandieu on discipline as an inner spiritual church event, (1566, 195; 202; 238). The first war of religion ended on March 19, 1563, the second war started in September 1567.

2.2 Man's salvation and the ecclesiastical discipline

In his Preface, Morély, fully in the spirit of Calvin,[19] immediately emphasized the importance of church discipline, for as each society is to be governed in a certain manner in order to preserve internal peace (*repos domestique*) and to ward off external enemies, the church, too, cannot exist without its own regulations and constitution (*propre constitution*) (Morély: 1562, Préface f.A2r).

Morély was not a spiritualist. To him, 'church' was not a mere invisible work of the Spirit, along the lines of Gaspard Schwenckfeld or Sebastian Franck. Christ endowed his church with a visible discipline. It is the Spirit that is to transform a person, but this is more than a mere personal affair. Spiritual conversion is also a shared process, taking place in the communion of the church, and the Holy Spirit works through the discipline of the church. Either the church is disciplined, or it isn't, according to Morély, and at the same time the church and its discipline are spiritual. To Morély, discipline was much more than a matter of survival for ecclesiastical life in a hostile environment. The believers' salvation partly depended on it. To achieve salvation, it was important that a person was a member of the church, and to attain this membership a person was to conform to the church order. After all, the church is not merely internal, just as a person is not merely external.

> I know very well, Morély said, that the church is the spiritual kingdom of Christ [...] and that it is governed by the Spirit. But every one of us partly consists of a spiritual man, in other words, the inner man, reborn by the Spirit of Christ, and partly also consists of an external being that is called to rebirth and justification [...]. However, with regard to the external man that is in us, we also need an external discipline, which Paul calls education [...]. Therefore, we must abide by this order accurately, so that sin within us is controlled. And the same Spirit of Christ, which acts internally with a view to salvation, also acts externally through word and ministry (Morély: 1589, vol. 1, 80; Denis/Rott: 1993, 122).

It this context, it was important to emphasize the absolute necessity of the right church order. There was no salvation without conversion and no conversion without the support of the external discipline of the spiritual church, because man was and remains a sinner. Morély's intention was to reinstate within the church the one, true and pure disciplinary order of Christ. He did not deny that Christ's salvation is a gift of grace, but he did connect it to a life in accordance with the discipline of the church (Morély: 1589, vol. 1, 72; Denis/Rott: 1993, 122).

---

19 "Our first consideration is this: if we see that every company of people needs some polity in order to keep peace and harmony among them; if in all things there must be some order so as to preserve public decency and even humanity among people; then these ought to be principally observed in the church. First, these things are maintained by good order, and they are torn completely to pieces by discord" (*Institutio* 1541, 4.10.27).

3. Church as a more or less hierarchically and clerical institution

3.1 The problem of leadership in the French Calvinistic movement

To what extent were the noble leaders of the Huguenots willing to submit themselves to the judgement of the consistory or the synod? The tradition of bi-level consistories would become an ongoing issue in the early years of the French Reformed churches. The *Articles polytiques* of Poitiers (1557) and the early structure of the church at Le Mans (1561) shared this point. Both included two consistories, one charged with discipline, a *consistoire des censures*, the other with administration, a *consistoire de police*.[20] In 1561 the second national synod of Poitiers specifically rejected multiple consistories or church councils in an attempt to eliminate a potential distinction that may arise when there are a number of councils in a church.[21] The idea was that in a second local church council could include members of the church who were neither elders nor deacons, but the *hommes de biens*, *notables*, or even *nobles* of the community. Thereby, concerning the leadership of the churches, arose an increasing struggle between the ministers and the secular leaders, the political and military leaders. Unfortunately, the growing militarization and politicization of Protestantism in France increased tensions and division in the church.

3.2 A clerical or a more democratic church structure

In Morély's opinion, the church should not be governed from the top down, but from the bottom up. This guarantees the unity in the church. He advocated people living and deciding together, according to the order of Christ, without a specific chair or city, person or church exerting supremacy over the others. The latter was also prohibited in the more hierarchically designed presbyteral-synodical church structure of the Reformed church, one principle being utterly clear in the synod's formulation of the first French church order – in Quick's later English version of the *Discipline des Eglises réformées de France*: "No Church, nor Church-Officer, be he Minister, Elder, or Deacon, shall Claim or Exercise any Jurisdiction, or Au-

---

20 Sunshine: 2003, 127f. The French Church Order of 1559 can, according to Sunshine (2003, 133), be interpreted in the same way.

21 "Item: it is resolved and recommended that there is to be but one consistory in each church, composed of ministers, elders and deacons exercising their charges, which when necessary can call whomever they think good for counsel and advice" (Actes du Synode reformée de France 2, Poitiers [1561], *faits particuliers*, 4).

thority over another".[22] But this principle was not consistently applied in the end; representatives of certain churches took decisions for others without consulting them.

This was unacceptable for Morély. Church councils and different gatherings only have an advisory function, he claimed, and "no power at all to determine or decide anything" (Morély: 1562, 289) that should be decided over by a local church on the basis of consensus. This was a basic principle for him. Just as Morély sanctified his 'democratic' church structure, a person like Beza did the same with his aristocratic model, in which Christ is not represented by the gathering of believers, but by the consistory.[23]

The position of the church council is somewhat different in the vision of Bucer and Viret, as it only has an administrative function. They distinguish between the judicial and administrative power of the church, or, in other words, between those who have the 'power' and those who execute 'functions'. They place the actual power in the hands of the gathering believers (Denis/Rott: 1993, 150).

3.3 A key Bible passage

In a solid Calvinistic mindset, Morély stated that that new church needed a discipline to call sinners to repentance and conversion and to maintain the purity of the church (Morély: 1562, 124; *Institutio*, 4.12.5). But who is to exercise this discipline? Who should execute ecclesiastical administration of justice? In answering this question, Matt 18:15–17 provided one of the most important key texts; to be more precise, the answer lies in the interpretation of the words "*dic ecclesiae*" ("tell the church") as the third step towards discipline. Chandieu, who elaborately discussed the exegesis of this text, pointed out that 'church' is sometimes used to designate a certain group of administrators. For this he referred to Chrysostomos.[24]

Here, Chandieu was actually completely in line with Calvin, who revised his interpretation of this text in 1555, explaining 'church' as 'consistory', because Jesus was understood to have used 'church' for the 'Sanhedrin' in this context. The same explanation reappeared in the definite edition of Calvin's *Institutes of the Christian*

---

22 Quick: 1692, vol. 1, 2, ch. 2. For comparison the first article of the French version of 1559: "Premiè-rement que nulle Eglise ne pourra prétendre principauté ou domination sur l'autre" (Niesel: 1939, 75; cf. Mentzer/Van Ruymbeke: 2016, 20).

23 According to Beza three elements determine the government of the Church: Christ, the consistory and the magistrate who represents the "universal multitude". The congregation does not have any power (Maruyama: 1978, 117; 121–122).

24 Chandieu: 1566, 188. Chrysostum describes 'church' as "those who are in charge" (John Chrysostum, Homélie 40, Matthew 18:15f, in PG 58, 586; cf. McKee: 1988, 34).

Religion. Beza, too, adopted this explanation in his Comment on the New Testament in 1557.[25]

3.4 The right to represent

Against this background, Morély published his *Traicté de la discipline*, in which he stated that the church is essentially one, on the condition that it is founded on Christ's church order, as we mentioned above. Christ's church is one "in Him" (Morély: 1562, 75). He has granted his powers to the church as a whole. The unity of the church is violated when a minority speaks and acts in the name of the whole church. This is why Morély rejected the idea of representation. The church as a whole exerts its power directly and not through a representative person, church council or synod.

Inspired by the developments in refugee churches abroad, in which the churchgoers were sometimes allowed to voice their opinion in, e.g., disciplinary cases, Morély wanted to take the common people in the church more seriously, for instance by involving them more in the vigilance over a virtuous lifestyle.[26] The church's leadership is in the hands of the whole and not in the hands of a part of it, a small group of people. No one has the right to represent the church, Morély stated.[27] With respect to the unity between the churches and of the believers mutually as a characteristic of the church, discipline is of major importance. But on what grounds do the people have the right to voice their opinion concerning the doctrine or to take decisions together concerning the church?

Morély distinguished between, on the one hand, divine prescriptions, such as the church order, church services and sacraments, and, on the other, human traditions. Divine "prescriptions (*préceptes*) were to be followed, for this was a commandment (*mandement*) of God or rather its content was. Because the commandment of God was never ineffective (*inactif*), it was effective (*efficace*) through the power of the Holy Spirit" (Morély: 1589, vol. 1, 92). The punishment of sinners and the evaluation of the doctrine and the prophecies were part of the content of the commandment

---

25 Calvin: 1555, 514; *Institutio*, 4.11.1; 4.12.2. In the Latin edition describes Calvin 'Eglise' with '*Seniors consensus*', but in the French edition of 1560 'Eglise' stayed untranslated (Maruyama: 1978, 101; McKee: 1988, 36).

26 Laski: 1556, f.169v -170r. In London Morély became acquainted with the Prophecy (*Prophezei*), and he wants to turn it into a place for free speech (Denis/Rott: 1993, 180f; 190).

27 Unlike Chandieu would have us to believe, Morély was not for the principle of a majority of votes. He opposes it vigorously (Chandieu: 1566, 32; 73–74; 183; cf. 68; 75; 77; Morély: 1562, 41). On representation and such: Denis/Rott: 1993, 124; 132; 141f; 169–174; 202. The unity between the members of the church is a geometric unit, equality in portion, and no arithmetic unit, equality in number, "that is to say that the portion and the value of each is weighed" (Morély: 1562, 278; 298).

of God. These matters were to take place during collective gatherings, according to Morély, and this course of affairs provided the best guarantee for unity in the church.[28]

3.5 Membership of the church

The general opinion was that, in order for someone to belong to the church, this person should confess and should voluntarily submit to the ecclesiastical discipline. Above all, this discipline was a matter of survival and the only way to maintain the union of the church. The church, in which Christ gathers his own, is the body of Christ, and it is a spiritual body. Members of the church are they "who have been born again and sanctified by the Spirit." The unity of the church, which is central to Morély, is that "of all blessed spirits and souls and the gathering of all believers in Jesus Christ, who for all times are chosen and predestined for eternal life in Jesus Christ, they who precede us as well as they who are to follow us" (Morély, *Traicté*, 55–63). According to him, an adult member of the ecclesiastical community has a responsibility in the church, the spiritual kingdom of Christ.

For Morély, the administrative board of the church was the "communion of believers". Men could take part in this gathering if they had "publicly confessed their faith and were admitted to the communion of the body of the Lord" (Morély, *Traicté*, 119–120.). According to Morély, the visible church has all the aspects of the church of the chosen, in so far as the order of Christ is functioning. In *De ecclesia* he idealistically writes that the church is "the gathering of the sanctified and the justified" (Morély: 1589, vol. 2, 3; Denis/Rott: 1993, 115; 135).

According to Chandieu, the established church finds itself in a state of total destruction. The apostolic order (*discipline Apostolique*) needs to be restored, and this is what happens in the Reformed churches (Chandieu: 1566, 39–40). These are "God's churches" and God recognizes its members "as members of his universal church". Its characteristics, i.e., the proclamation of the true doctrine, the pure administration of the sacraments and the use of the ecclesiastical discipline instituted by Christ, are the signs that it is "God's church" concerned here, which is also confirmed by the testimonies of its members, more specifically, their "works of mercy", "the perseverance of its martyrs" and the "renewal of their lives" (Chandieu: 1566, 16–17).

---

28 Prophecy completes the preaching and is, according to Morély, a short, simple and clear explanation of the Scriptures, "adapted to the doctrine and the admonition," and this should to take place on a weekly base in public. All members of the church are invited (Morély: 1562, 83–88). The Genevan Congrégation was intended primarily for the forming of the ministers and to promote the unity of the preaching, like Calvin says: "It's the best way to preserve the unity of doctrine" (Calvin to Musculus, 7 Dec. 1549, CO 13, 491).

3.6 The flock is inexpert

Morély was not the only one to cherish these innovative church order ideas. Reformers such as Bucer, Vermigli and Viret endowed the church with the characteristics of the *politeia*. They all viewed 'church' primarily as a 'community of believers'. Morély, who adopted this view on church structure and church government, placed himself in an existing tradition (cf. Denis/Rott: 1993, 125–151). It is simultaneously innovative and traditional.

Compared to other reformers, Beza was more innovative – or, should we say, with respect to the Roman Catholic Church, more traditional – in withholding any form of sovereignty from the gathering of churchgoers. In 1559 he still subscribed to the necessity of an "approval of the body of the church" during elections. But in the following editions of his *Confession de foy* he revised this view, with the same type of argumentation we saw with Chandieu, "because usually the flock is inexpert and difficult to align and almost always the best part is in the minority" (Beza: 1559, 162–163; 1560, art. 35, 210f; 1561, art. 35, 203f).

3.7 Election as an example

In 1561, Pierre Viret wrote the following, concerning the election of ministers:

> Although the power and authority is given to the community of believers as a whole," and, like in a free city, "lies in the hands of the people and the people's state, as it was formerly called a democracy, this does not detract from the fact that the church elects certain people from the body of this holy community, these are persons who have the special task to execute and administer public services, services that have been installed in the church by God, as in a free city, in which the election of the public services happens by the citizens and inhabitants of the city, who are all of the same community (Viret: 1561, 360–361; 1564, vol. 1, 86).[29]

In the government of the Genevan church, the believers played a minimal part. When preachers were elected, the churchgoers were not consulted. The people were only tacitly involved, after a city council and the council of preachers had ruled on a candidate: "to produce finally to the people when he preaches, in order that he be received by the common consent of the company of the faithful" (OS 2, 329).[30] The possibility of filing a complaint with the *Compagnie des Pasteurs* was, in fact, no

---

29 See for Viret's contributions for the Provincial Synods of Languedoc and Dauphiné also Sunshine: 2003, 77f.

30 In the *Discipline des Eglises réformées de France* of 1559 the candidate will be introduced to the congregation, after the election in the consistory, and "if there is opposition, it will be up to the consistory to decide" (art. 6). In 1571 is added, that the silence of the church is considered as an

more than a theoretical option (Denis/Rott: 1993, 155; 191). The annual multistage election of the less specific ecclesiastical functions of elder and deacon in the three city councils followed a more democratic procedure.

The election of pastors in France was a highly sensitive issue. Externally the preacher's status was still unclear, and did not have the broad public support that the priest had. Internally, Morély and his followers opted for letting the church as a whole decide on which preacher they wished to choose. The French church, however, did not opt for the use of a referendum when ministers had to be elected, except when a new community was established. In that case, the elders and deacons were chosen "by the general voice of the people and their preacher."[31] The churchgoers were "merely" expected to attend church to pray and to be administered to with word and sacrament and furthermore, they were to lead a virtuous life, but they were not expected to participate in governance and to voice their opinion on doctrine and life. Morély wanted to change this.

Morély and his followers were convinced that unity could only be reached by giving the church members full sovereign discretion over all matters, including the elections of preachers. A minority should not govern the majority. In their view, the assembly of the chosen was the foundation of the unity of the church (Denis/Rott: 1993, 127). The ecclesiastical regulations were there to maintain and guarantee mutual unity and peace.

Morély's idea was very different from the church order of the Paris synod in 1559. His proposal, therefore, was immediately rejected by the synod of Orléans in April 1562. One could hardly expect a synod to agree to a curtailing of its own power because of the decision making authority and decisiveness. Chandieu stated that this idea created confusion and that it was practically unfeasible to take the opinions of the people into account during decision making at a local or supra-local level.[32]

3.8 An independent church ruled by clergy and laity

The edict of January 1562 seemed an adequate solution to the problem of the protestant nobles raising armies. The edict forbade the Huguenots to worship in towns, to assemble at night, or to meet under arms, but they were free to assemble

---

approval (Actes du Synode reformée de France 8, Nîmes [1572], art. 19; in: Aymon: 1710, vol. 1, 116).

31 Actes du Synode reformée de France 1, Paris, (1559), art. 27, in: Aymon: 1710, 5: les Diacres que les Anciens seront élûs "par la voix commune du people avec leur Pasteur: mais dans ceux où la discipline seroit déja dressée, de sera au Senat de l'Eglise, avec leur minister de les élire".

32 Chandieu: 1566, 239–240; 284. Morély thoughts go out to a big church with the size of a bailiwick (*bailliage*), something like a small diocese in England, and with a mother church.

peacefully in the countryside. The nobility was free to organize and protect churches on their rural estates.[33] The national synod of Orléans asked the nobles to create a consistory made up of the minister and the "best approved" *gens de biens* of the household to deal with scandals and vices. If there was already a local church, the nobles were asked "to eliminate all division."[34]

The Wars of Religion made the nobility for a serious part the effective leaders within Protestantism instead of the pastors. Pastors, too, became involved in military activities, much to the chagrin of Calvin, stated Emile Léonard (1961, vol. 2, 112). The general disregard for synodical government among the Protestant nobility was reflected in the ideas which the nobleman, Jean Morély, brought forward. He advocated holding synods as necessary to discuss problems which arose in the churches, but he argued that these synods had no right to issue "canons" or decrees. Their decisions were strictly advisory.

Fearing the consequences, Chandieu decided not to react to Morély's ideas on the synodical system because of the political situation faced by the French Reformed Church. Synods had been illegal since de Peace of Amboise in March 1563. Half a year later, the national synod of Lyon would consider that consistories ought to decide all of the affairs of the church.[35]

Morélys approach to synods matched the indifference of the nobility toward the collective synodical government of the Reformed Church. In essence, the nobility continued to be Congregationalists. Synods were irrelevant. The disinterest with which the nobility usually treated the synods was not far removed from reducing them to bodies that could advise but not legislate, as advocated by Morély. Overall policy was set by the Princes, the Party, and the nobility themselves (Sunshine: 2003, 144–148). In the 1570s this position was taken over by the Reformed civil authorities in the Netherlands.

---

33 This left most of the Protestant population without any right to worship, because Protestantism was still primarily an urban religion. The third national synod in Orléans in 1562 added a rather lengthy article to the Discipline which asked the princes and other seigneurs at court who wished to establish churches in their houses to choose legitimately called pastors who would sign the Discipline and the Confession.

34 Actes du Synode reformée de France 3, Orléans (1562), 3; cf. Actes du Synode reformée de France 5, Paris (1565), 14.

35 Actes du Synode reformée de France 4, Lyon (1563), 26. Quick: 1692, vol. 1, 38, ch. 16, art. 6: It is the duty of consistories to determine all church affaires and another "Standing Council besides those who are officers in it" is needless.

4. A dominant church-shaping use of the Eucharist

The familiar, age-old notion of a European Christendom guided by the church, whose pastoral care and rituals structured and disciplined peoples' whole life, as well as the notion of the *corpus christianum* – all of this more or less changed in the time of the Reformation. People were interested in a reformation and especially in a Christian life for all citizens – in fact, in a godly life for all of society. From this perspective, one could consider Calvin's efforts in Geneva to be a prolongation and intensification of the rules of the Fourth Lateran Council in 1215 (Speelman: 2016b, 29–64). However, on numerous occasions Calvin heavily criticized the existing penitential law of 1215 as well as the practice of penance yet in the course of time he would, nevertheless, attempt to recast external as well as internal aspects of it in his own system – both the social, pastoral and educational side, as the more specifically spiritual side of comforting the troubled conscience and the related process of the sinner's restoration through a movement from sorrow, to repentance, to forgiveness, and finally to reconciliation. But for him, the innermost circle of church life and worship centered around the administration of God's Word and the sacraments. This 'secret' operation of God's Spirit sets forth the presence of Christ and makes us His table-companions.[36] His thinking was dominated by the strong connection between the most holy mystery of the Lord's Supper and what he called "Christian confession," which he saw to be connected in the same way that the foci of an ellipse are inextricably bound together.

At a local level, the church takes shape wherever people gather together and "keep and maintain the union of the Church, and submit to the public teaching, and to the yoke of Jesus Christ", the French church confessed. The central importance of the Lord's Supper was made clear by the notice that only through the celebration of the sacraments a new congregation could be formed. We preach, baptize and bury; now we think about celebrating the Lord's Supper "in order to testify that we are now fully Christ's church" (*pour declairer que nous sommes une eglise de Christ*

---

36 About the existing penitential law Calvin wrote: "I shall sum up what sort of law this is. First, it is simply impossible; therefore it can only destroy, condemn, confound, and cast into ruin and despair. Then, depriving sinners of a true awareness of their sins, it makes them hypocrites, ignorant of God and of themselves. Indeed, while wholly occupied with the cataloguing of sins, they in the meantime forget that hidden slough of vices, their own secret transgressions and inner filth, the knowledge of which ought particularly to have brought home to them their own misery" (*Institutio* 1536, 3.4.18). Calvin further described the papal confessional as a "tyrannical law", (*Institutio* 3.4.24) and he considered auricular confession an altogether erroneous, impracticable rule, which turned people into hypocrites.

entierement), someone wrote to Calvin, in complete agreement with him, because to Calvin, the Lord's Supper was the heart of the ecclesiastical community.[37]

In the Calvinistic churches in France of the 1560s, however, discipline became a more independent third mark of the church[38] and the celebration of the Lord's Supper became, in the first place, "a moment to heal the fissures within the community and confirm solidarity", as Raymond Mentzer (2008, 26; 41f) rightly states.[39] In this line, the Holy Supper was necessary for the believers, because "those who trust Christ, must walk as he walked" and in celebrating Communion, the congregation obliged itself time and again to act as a redeemed church community.[40] The church vision and the discipline of the French church became less Eucharistic, as it was in Calvin's view.

In comparison with Geneva, the church view of the Reformed Church of France had changed. The emphasis was laid more on membership of a congregation and, in this sense participation at the Lord's Table was, in the first place, of community-shaping significance. The effect was a more horizontal social-ethical, Zwinglian perception of the Holy Communion, whereby the purpose of the Holy Supper became particularly to define the uniformity and godliness of the community. For Calvin, however, the Eucharist was in the first place a mystical, spiritual meal, in the Augustinian sense and the church was in the first place a Eucharistic community under a Eucharistic Church Order (Speelman: 2016b, ch. 9; ch. 11, 2; 3).

---

37 "Furthermore, this holy Church is not confined, bound, or limited to a certain place or to certain persons, but is spread and dispersed over the whole world; and yet is joined and united with heart and will, by the power of faith, in one and the same spirit." CB, art. 27; cf. CG, art. 26: "se soubmettans … au ioug de Iesus Christ". About the readiness to submit voluntarily to live "under the yoke of Christ" ("*se renger entierement sous le ioug de Christ*"), (CO 19, 22).

38 For discipline as a third mark of the church, see Chandieu: 1566, 21; 27; 36; Beza: 1559, V, art.7; *Confessio Scotica*, art. 18 and CB, art. 29.

39 Mentzer concludes in his beautiful case-study of the congregation of Archiac: "Screening participants, composing lists of the eligible, inviting sinners to ask forgiveness, and barring the obstinate accentuate the Lord's Supper as the centrepiece of a civic and religious experience". Each time every congregant is confirmed to live in good standing. The sacral meal, celebrated by quarter, continually bolstered and reified the supreme value of membership in a true church. Inclusion in the Eucharist or, conversely, denial of access offered an immediate, perceptible indication of a person's relationship to fellow believers. Composing lists of the eligible and barring the obstinate accentuate the Lord's Supper as the centrepiece of a common social and religious experience. Each time the sacral meal is used, every participant had to be confirmed as living in good standing, and the supreme value of membership in a true church is confirmed and concretized.

40 "Qui ergo eo [sc. Christo] fidunt, debent ambulare, sicut et ipse ambulavit." (ZW 2, 807). In Zwingli's view of the Supper, the emphasis rests on the ethical consequences for the congregation celebrating the Supper. The subject of the celebration, in Zwingli's view, is the congregation as the body of Christ. See for the community-shaping effect of the Lord's Supper also: Speelman: 2016b, 296f.

Conclusion

Both parties in the 1560s in the French Reformed church, represented respectively by Morély and Chandieu, essentially opposed a dominant, hierarchical church structure. However, soon after their official recognition, the French churches made an inward movement regarding their church polity, in an attempt to survive as an independent church and to hold the churches together.

Four centuries after Morély and Chandieu, the eminent scholar Robert Kingdon wrote an elaborate study concerning the Morély issue, under the title *Geneva and the Consolidation of the French Protestant Movement, 1564–1572*. In it, he came to the conclusion that Morély and his followers "sought substantial autonomy for local congregations in church polity, a greater role for the laity in church government, and less clerical control over the morals and ideas of ordinary church members. In short they developed a platform which we might label *Congregational*". And to describe a primary characteristic of the Calvinist movement in this particular period, Kingdon used the term *consolidation*, bearing in mind also the title of Chandieu's book: "consolidating a church already established, of maintaining discipline within it, and of protecting it from the increasingly formidable challenges of a revived Roman Catholic Church and a suspicious government" (Kingdon: 1967, 14–15; 44–45).

Morély was headed towards a more mystical understanding of the church, a visible church which, at the same time, transcended the visible. In this regard, he was inspired by the ecclesiastical regulations emerging in the refugee churches. Throughout the course of the years, the evangelical movement in France followed an increasingly independent path from Geneva. They wished no longer to be an underground church, a Church under the Cross or even as a persecuted heretical sect. For decades, their missionary operations did have taken place underground. In the early sixties of the sixteenth century, the enthusiastic Calvinist movement in France had grown rapidly and was at its peak. They first used all their diplomatic skills and political means to reach their goal but, in the end, also reverted to armed resistance.

We conclude that the French protestant church did not strive for an ecclesiology of the diaspora in this period. Rather the opposite. The French people yearned for a form of religious freedom and unity in the church of France. However, neither the model of the Reformation of the Princes, such as in Germany and England, nor the Swiss City Reformation offered a solution. In the meantime, in Geneva, a new model of a church of foreigners or refugees was developed. From the end of the 1550s Calvin constantly warned his fellow believers in France, continuously calling them to patience and prayer.

Calvin looked after the interests of the French Huguenots seeking refuge (*salus*) within the walls of Geneva. According to Heiko Oberman, Calvin modified the model of urban reformation and "called upon all inhabitants of Geneva, including those who enjoyed the privileges of citizenship, to regard themselves as refugees, and to live accordingly" (Oberman: 2009, 188). That was really new. Salvation was no longer located in a monastery or a city, but "in exile between heaven and earth, so that under the 'yoke of Christ' ordinary believers could live rightly with God." Paradoxically speaking one could confess to believe in a church of persecuted martyrs spread around the world, like before in the time of the edict of Theodosius I in 380, instead of a church with worldly power, while at the same time confessing to believe in one church, like a year later the council of Constantinople coins this expression in the famous Creed.

So, in Geneva arose the ideal of an exile or refugee church that had initially functioned as a model for churches in the diaspora of France, which in turn had, in 1559, chosen to form a national denomination and were recognized as church by the government only a few years later, so that, from that moment on, one could speak of a more or less established Reformed church in France. That was no longer a "church of the diaspora, stripped of all protection and lacking the security of the city walls, discovers its safe place in the eternal city firmly established before all time" (Oberman: 2009, 40; 46). But in fact, the religious and political leaders of the Calvinistic movement in France thought otherwise and worked towards a form of public recognition.

The greatest differences between the ideal of the French Calvinist and Calvin's view on the organization of church and worship was that the unity of church and nation was effectively undone and the vision of the church and the church order became less Eucharistic. Let's hope that in future spirituality the Holy Supper will function again as the very symbol of peace and reconciliation, a place where we can meet each other in Christ Jesus, and, specifically, a place of religious unity. All the more reason to view the church as a Eucharistic community, as, for example, Calvin did (Speelman: 2014a; 2016b, ch. 7 and 8).

In the 1560s, both parties within the Reformed Church of France agreed on many key issues. In retrospect, we can say that the unity of the church does not so much depend on its church structure, whether it is governed bottom-up or top-down, congregationally or more clerically. The true church is gathered and led by God and the foundation of its spiritual unity lies in the community with and in Him and includes the multifaceted accents of the missions that arise from the holy Gospel. It was clear for both parties, that the church is fundamentally a communion and not merely the sum of individual believers, and that the bottom line is that this holy and secret communion through word and sacrament is a communion in which Christians gratefully participate in the church as the body of Christ time and again with a view to eternity as living members of this mysterious unity of God through the true faith in Christ as the source of all real communion.[41]

---

41 Much of the biblical expressions are used both in Catholic and Protestant ecclesiology's and its interpretation influence each other over the centuries. Take for example the body-talk as an expression of the *communitas fidelium*. Pius XII invigorated in 1943 the notion of the church as a body, the mystical

The disagreement between Chandieu and Morély did not concern the church as a communion through Christ in God, but regarded the question whether the church should primarily been seen as an aristocratic and clerical institution of ministers who served the flock, i.e., only their own sheep's, or more as a small church of faithful people, a community of "saints" or an assembly of "believers". In our times, both these models of church could probably be beneficial to greater ecclesiastical unity, if they are worldwide, flexible, without a one-sided attention to their own organization, and open, undenominational, that is, without a tightly bound obligation of membership and without national or group borders. That one and holy universal church is united in the Triune God through Jesus Christ our Lord, although it might not always be visibly identifiable.

Bibliography

Sources

Jean Aymon (1710), Tous les synods nationaux des Eglises Réformées de France, 2 vols., La Haye: Charles Delo.

Théodore de Bèze (1559), Confession de la foy chrestienne contenant la confirmation d'icelle, [Genève]: Conrad Badius.

Théodore de Bèze (1560), Confessio christianae fidei et eiusdem collatio cum papisticis haeresibus, [Genève]: Iohannes Bonae Fidei.

Théodore de Bèze (1561), Confession de la foy chrestienne contenant la confirmation d'icelle et la réfutation des superstitions contraires, [Genève]: Jean Crespin.

Guy de Brès (1561), Confession de Foy, faicte d'vn commun accord par les fidèles qui conuersent és pays bas, lesquels desirent viure selon la pureté de l'Euangile de nostre Seigneur Iesus Christ, s.l.

Jean Calvin (1555), Harmonia ex tribus evangelistis composita, Genève: Robert Estienne, in: CO 45.

Antoine de la Roche Chandieu (1566), La Confirmation de la discipline écclesiastique, observée és eglises réformées du royaume de France, [Genève: Henri Estienne].

body of Christ, in the encyclica *Mystici corporis*. In 1964, this notion was reaffirmed in *Lumen gentium*, the ecclesiological centerpiece of the Second Vatican Council, and gave it a sacramental twist. According to the council fathers, Christ, by sending his spirit, "made his brothers ... mystically the components, as it were, of his body" (LG 1.7, Denzinger 4112). Though this sacramental union with Christ the church is a communion held together by faith, hope and love (LG 1.8, Denzinger, 4118). See the article of Florian Wöller, 'Between corpus and communio. Varieties of late medieval ecclesiology' in this volume. See also the World Council of Churches-document *The Church* (2007), vii, par. 23; 27; 31.

JOHN LASKI (1556), Toute la forme et manière du ministère ecclésiastique en l'Eglise des estrangers, [Emden]: Gilles Ctematius.

JEAN MORÉLY (1562), Traicté de la discipline et police chrestienne, Lyon: Ian de Tournes [Reprinted Genève: Slatkine, 1968].

JEAN MORÉLY (1589), De Ecclesia ab Antichristo per ejus excidium liberanda, eaque ex Dei promissis beatissime reparanda Tractatur ..., London: George Bischop.

JOHN QUICK (1692), Synodicon in Gallia Reformata: or, The acts, decisions, decrees, and canons of those famous national councils of the Reformed Churches in France, 2 vols., London: T. Parkhurst and J. Robinson.

PIERRE VIRET (1561), Exposition familière des principaux poincts du Catéchisme faite en forme de dialogue, [Genève]: Jean Rivery.

PIERRE VIRET (1564), Instruction chrestienne en la doctrine de la Loy et de l'Evangile, Genève: Jean Rivery.

Secondary Literature

BARKER, SARAH K. (2009), Protestantism, Poetry and Protest: The Vernacular Writings of Antoine de Chandieu (c. 1534–1591), Cornwall: Ashgate.

BRYNER, ERICH (2016), The Reformation in St. Gallen and Appenzell, in: Christopher M. Bellitto (ed.), A Companion to the Swiss Reformation, Leiden/Boston: Brill, 238–263.

COURVOISIER, JAQUES (1933), La notion d'Eglise chez Bucer dans son développement historique, Paris: Libraire Félix Alcan.

COURVOIRSIER, JAQUES (1964), La dialectique dans l'ecclésiologie de Calvin, Revue d'histoire et de philosophie religieuses 44, 86–101.

DE BOER, ERIK A. (2016), 'Verbreid en verstrooid': Ecclesiologie van de diaspora en de reformatie van de Lage Landen, Kampen: Theologische Universiteit Kampen.

DENIS, PHILIPPE/ROTT, JEAN (1993), Jean Morély (ca 1524–ca 1594) et l'utopie d'une démocratie dans l'église, Genève: Droz.

KINGDON, ROBERT M. (1967), Geneva and the consolidation of the French Protestant movement, 1564–1572: A Contribution to the History of Congregationalism, Presbyterianism, and Calvinist resistance theory, Geneva: Droz.

LÉONARD, EMILE G. (1961), Histoire générale du protestantisme, 3 vols., Paris: Presses Universitaires de France.

MARUYAMA, TADATAKA (1978), The Ecclesiology of Theodore Beza: The Reform of the True Church, Geneva: Droz.

McKEE, ELSIE ANNE (1988), Elders and the Plural Ministry. The Role of the Exegetical History in Illuminating John Calvin's Theology, Genève: Droz.

RAYMOND A. MENTZER (2008), Communities of Worship and the Reformed Churches of France, in: Michael J. Halvorson/Karen E. Spierling (ed.), Defining community in Early Modern Europe, Cornwall: Ahsgate, 25–42.

Mentzer, Raymond A./Van Ruymbeke, Bertrand (2016), A Companion to the Huguenots, Leiden/Boston: Brill.

Niesel, Wilhelm (1939), Bekenntnisschriften und Kirchenordnungen der nach Gottes Wort reformierten Kirche, Zürich: Zollikon.

Oberman, Heiko A. (2009), John Calvin and The Reformation of the Refugees, Geneva: Droz.

Speelman Herman A. (2014a), Calvin and the Independence of the French Calvinist Church from 1559 to early 1562, in: idem, Calvin and the Independence of the Church, Göttingen: Vandenhoeck & Ruprecht, 143–207.

Speelman Herman A. (2014b), 'We were right to follow the Genevans': Calvin and the Church in the Netherlands 1572–1578, in: idem, Calvin and the Independence of the Church, Göttingen: Vandenhoeck & Ruprecht, 209–246.

Speelman Herman A. (2014c), Distinctly Flexible: A key feature of the Protestant Church Polity, in: Leo J. Koffeman/Johannes Smit (ed.), Protestant Church Polity in Changing Contexts II: Proceedings of the International Conference, Utrecht, The Netherlands, 7–10 November 2011, Berlin/Münster/Wien/Zürich/London: LIT Verlag, 187–192.

Speelman, Herman A. (2016a), Calvinism, the Changing Relationship between Church and State, and the Origins of Religious Plurality, in: Gijsbert van den Brink/Gerard den Hertog (ed.), Protestant Traditions and the Soul of Europe, Beihefte zur Ökumenischen Rundschau 110, Leipzig: Evangelische Verlagsanstalt, 41–54.

Speelman, Herman A. (2016b), Melanchthon and Calvin on Confession and Communion: Early Modern Protestant Penitential and Eucharistic Piety, Göttingen: Vandenhoeck & Ruprecht.

Spierling, Karen E. (2008), The Complexity of Community in Reformation Geneva: The Case of the Lullin Family, in: Michael J. Halvorson/Karen E. Spierling (ed.), Defining Community in Early Modern Europe, Ashgate: Aldershot and Burlington, 81–101.

Sunshine, Glenn S. (2003), Reforming French Protestantism. The Development of Huguenot Ecclesastical Institutions, 1557–1572, Kirksville: Truman State University Press.

Wendel, François (1950), Calvin. Sources et évolution de sa pensée religieuse, Paris: Presses Universitaires de France.

Maciej Szumowski

Visible Signs of Virtues

External Profession of Faith and Robert Bellarmine's Sacramental Ecclesiology

1. Introduction: (In)communicability of the invisible within the visible

The heat of the historical debate over the visibility of the Church from the Reformation period has long since passed, but the conceptual framework in which it was situated certainly endures. The basic problem which has been communicated to contemporary thought is precisely the seeming (in)communicability of the invisible within the visible. The visible rituals, linguistic expressions, gestures and artifacts – namely practices governed by their inner logic – have been in an act of self-limitation taken as the proper field of postmodern social sciences. A wide array of thinkers from Nietzsche to pragmatists such as Foucault and Searle have labored to render the concepts that may presuppose some kind of 'metaphysics' like 'essence', 'consciousness' or 'personality' the blind spots of their thinking. I would also like to think of the problem of the visible Church in terms of an unsurpassable difference between practice and consciousness. The incommensurability of the two and the apparent superiority of the realm of soul over the realm of body was the bone of contention among the early modern thinkers proposing a duality of Churches – the coexistence of an institutional, imperfect, and even false Church and an invisible, spiritual *Ecclesia*.

Robert Bellarmine's decision to determine his ecclesiology solely in terms of visible and recognizable bonds that are able to precisely define the boundaries of the society of the Church seems in this respect to be a kind of Catholic exaggeration. My primary aim is to apply a modern, pragmatic scheme of speech acts to his doctrine, in order to reconstruct a certain problem regarding the precise membership of the Church and to reveal the apparent materialism of Bellarmine's ecclesiology. My secondary objective and, moreover, one of wider scope, is to show how Bellarmine consciously refrains from acknowledging the compelling opposition of internal and external or spiritual and bodily, and how in an act of self-limitation he grounds the Church on the basis of external practices. This is because he seems to identify a vicious circle of representation of the invisible in the visible and attempts to leave it by means of a "materialistic" and objectified view of the Church. Yet this view should be grounded in his (yet insufficiently examined) sacramental ecclesiology and the doctrine of a hypostatic union of Christ and the Church.

2. Bellarmine's definition of the Church

Robert Bellarmine (d. 1621) is regarded as one of the most influential theologians of the Counter-Reformation. His life was abundant in theological polemic and political struggles both inside the Roman Curia and with European powers. Politically he was engaged most notably in the clashes between the papacy and King James I over the Oath of Allegiance and in the 1606 controversy over the Venetian Interdict. As a theologian he held the office of rector of the Gregorian University in Rome. However, he was most well known as the author of *The Controversies* – a large and celebrated work of polemical theology. Bellarmine prepared drafts for this during his assignment at the faculty of polemical theology in Leiden. His work was first published between 1581 and 1593, becoming a staple of Catholic doctrine, despite its non-systematic character (Brodrick: 1928).

Bellarmine's *Disputationes de Ecclesia militante* is the fourth Controversy in order. It is preceded by tractates dedicated to The Word of God, to Christology, and to the authority of the Roman Pontiff, which close the first volume. The controversy over the earthly Church militant opens the second and is followed by considerations on purgatory and on the Church as a community of saints triumphant in heaven. Subsequent controversies are dedicated to the problems of grace, the sacraments and predestination. Each controversy is divided into several books and their arguments are based primarily on quotations from various non-Catholic writers, most notably Calvin himself and different Lutheran theologians of the late 16th century.

In the second book of *On the Church Militant* we find a well-known, commonly-cited and unambiguous definition of the Church which presents three criteria (bonds) of its membership: "Our statement is that Church is only one [...] and that the one and true Church is an assembly bound by profession of the same Christian faith and communion in the same sacraments under the rule of legitimate pastors, and especially Christ's only vicar on earth, the Roman Pontiff" (Bellarminus: 1857, 75, 5.3.2; my translation)

Such an ecclesiology seems to agree with the common understanding of Bellarmine as a key figure in the post-Tridentine 'politicization' of the government of the Church (Höpfl: 2004, 339–365; Prodi: 1982; Tutino: 2010). In support of this argument another well-known statement can also be cited:

> everybody else requires internal virtues in order to place somebody inside the Church and therefore they render the real Church invisible. We also confess that in the Church all virtues, faith, hope, love etc. are encountered. But we do not consider it necessary to require any internal virtue in order to call someone somehow a part of the true Church, concerning which it is written in the Scriptures, but only external profession of faith and communion in the sacraments, which can be perceived by the senses only. For the Church is an assembly visible and tangible, as is an assembly of the Roman people, or the Kingdom of France, or the Republic of Venice. (Bellarminus: 1857, 75, 5.3.2; my translation)

So the Church militant consists of living body, composed of external, visible flesh and an internal, invisible soul. The former is the 'visible and tangible' community of believers. The latter consists of the "internal gifts of the Holy Spirit: faith, hope and love etc." (Bellarminus: 1857, 75, 5.3.2; my translation). Both are united internally and externally by Christ as the body's head. This allows Bellarmine to introduce different degrees and aspects of union with Christ, and therefore different degrees of membership of the Church. The principal distinction cuts between dead and living (albeit with various degrees of life) parts of the body. The dead parts are those deprived of internal virtues and grace, although connected to the external community by the three bonds (*vincula*).

In the course of my argument I will develop this short overview of Bellarmine's ecclesiology. For now, on the basis of the above outline, the traditional reading seems appropriate: that for Bellarmine one's access to the Church rests on his compliance with definite religious practices which are not necessarily connected with other, either internal or external, acts of faith. According to a functionalist reasoning, this theory might in turn be considered as authorizing the institutional powers of the Roman Church as a political entity in the long wake of Counter-Reformation reinforcement. My present question is to what extent this materialistic interpretation can hold on the basis of Bellarmine's account of the visibility of the Church. It should be found whether or not his insistence on the visible nature of the Church leads to a disintegration of practice from faith and superficial indifference to internal recognition of the spiritual content of Christ's Gospel.

My method will be to establish whether Bellarmine's exposition of the nature of the Church tends to disconnect these actions definite for a Catholic from other spheres of activity and to fragment one's life into several fields – partaking in the community of the Church being only one of them – or rather whether she considers it necessary to construe a set of obligations aiming to form a united and integrated Christian form of life. Of course, the scope of this investigation will be limited to the ecclesiological doctrine of Bellarmine. Regardless of its influence, too many discontinuities would need to be taken into account in order to determine its relation with the whole realm of early modern Catholic Reform. For my purpose I would like to concentrate on the first of the three bonds, the profession of the same faith, and the case of those who profess, but do not acknowledge: the secret unbelievers.

3. Disconnection of the internal from the external

It is important to note that all three elements constituting the visibility of the Church according to Bellarmine are considered primarily in their external aspect. In the discussion found in *On the Church Militant*, book III, this especially pertains to the role of faith in establishing the Church visible. Bellarmine distinguishes between internal and external faith – faith as an internal, infused virtue, and faith as an external act. Bellarmine quotes authors who explicitly disconnect linguistic activity and internal recognition of truth, such as Thomas Netter, Pedro de Soto, Stanislaus Hosius (Bellarminus: 1857, 89, 5.3.10), but also the councils of Toledo which phrase their confessions of faith in such a way, that the word *profiteor* seems to need further qualification.[1] On its own 'profession' is primarily an external speech act, to which other psychic or epistemic aspects are accidental. Bellarmine takes care to use the term *profession fidei* in the sense of an outward "enunciation" or "utterance of faith".

It can be rightly claimed that the act of profession consists in outward manifestation of the connection between the speaking subject and the content of words he utters – i.e. that it consists in their affirmation and confirmation. It will be fruitful to apply a pragmatic interpretative scheme to Bellarmine's usage of the 'profession of faith' in order to grasp the function of this performative, linguistic manifestation. So how does the act of profession bind and determine the subject who speaks, the believer?

This connection can be understood in a nexus of pragmatic obligations that the speaker enters when he says something. Using Foucaldian terms we may call this nexus a regime of truth or truth-telling. However, beneath this notion typical of post-structuralist vocabulary we find an useful intuition. A regime of truth works in a similar manner to a political regime. It is a complex of procedures and institutions which function as a framework within which individuals submit themselves to certain obligations – in this case obligations to make certain acts of truth.[2] These acts – and among them speech acts in particular – are not reduced to the logical form of a statement in which something is spoken. In a regime of truth – Foucault writes – as long as it is a regime, what is essential is the compulsion of affirming the truth, or admitting the truth as a truth (Foucault: 2014). Adding – one would say – a sign of assertion to a form of sentence in which a connection is made between the subject and the words he has spoken.

We should develop this thought further. Assertion is a force which joins the form of a sentence (such as A is B; I believe in X) and fixes it to the speaking individual.

---

1 See especially the preface to the confession of faith of Sixth Council of Toledo (638): "Quamobrem ex abundantia nostri cordis sit confessio vocis, ut fidem quam omnium mens intrinsecus gestat, in confessione interpres lingua foras effundat" (http://www.benedictus.mgh.de/quellen/chga/chga_049t. htm [4.01.2016]).

2 In the terminology of Foucault „acts of truth" are nothing else than acts that intend to state or reveal something about oneself. These acts have usually the form of serious speech acts (Dreyfus/Rabinow: 1983, 44–50), such as confessions, medical investigation etc., but not only, as in the case of the act of penance in the early Christianity.

This connection (or subjectivization) will last longer than the passing of one's utterance if it entails some kind of commitment. Referring to the more contemporary pragmatist view of Robert Brandom we can say that it is a commitment to take the content of your declaration as a ground for future statements and deeds (Brandom: 2001, 141–198). Assertion of faith would entail then a twofold commitment: discursive, consisting in accordance of one's speech with the basic dogmatic truths, and practical, consisting in abiding by the religious commandments. Thus breaking these commitments would provide a visible sign of a lack of connection between the subject and the truth he utters. These pragmatic criteria can also be treated as an indecisive sign of an individual's internal, psychic or intellectual sphere. This pragmatic reference to something other than the external we may call an instance of the principle of representation. To put it straightforwardly: if you say something and are not lying, I have a right to imply that you both think so and act in accordance with your words. Otherwise I have grounds to think that you do not really know what you are saying.

The problem lies in the fact that for Bellarmine – contrary to any reasonable pragmatic approach – the profession of faith does not have to be combined with an internalization of its content, morally consistent deeds or any other kind of connection between the subject and what he speaks. If this were true, it would give strong arguments for the proponents of the substantially political and institutional function of Bellarmine's ecclesiology and that of the sixteenth-century Catholic Reformation in general. The faithful are supposed to perform faith, not to live by it, because their faith does not entail any commitments that would link different spheres of activity in order to compose a single form of life. Yet, for Bellarmine the profession of faith retains its fundamental function as constitutive of the visible community of the Church and seems to be grounded in a more profound ecclesiological perspective. First, let us look into this apparent disconnection both between being and practice and between being and speech which is discussed in detail by Bellarmine under the question of sinners and secret unbelievers. He asks: "Do sinners and great sinners belong to the Church?" and "Do secret unbelievers – those, who have no faith or do not have the Catholic faith; all those, who speak and do, but only superficially – do they belong to the Church?"

4. Do sinners and secret unbelievers belong to the Church?

Bellarmine answers the first question: yes, they do. His point of departure is the aforementioned Christocentric, corporal ecclesiology: that the visible body of the Church is also mystically the body of Christ. This incorporation is still valid even without having a full degree of life or without the actualization of internal virtues. So the first argument is that neither of the external bonds – neither profession of faith nor participation in the sacraments – are substantially restricted to the good. According to the second argument we can speak of the members of the body not only with respect either to their essence, but also with respect to their instrumental function. And as long as partakers of the body of Christ act legitimately on His behalf as doctors, pastors, prophets etc., they are truly a part of the Church. Such instruments may be sinners and have no 'life', that is internal virtues, even though they remain connected with the mystical body as its organs (Bellarminus: 1857, 75, 4.3.2). In either case, Bellarmine argues that one's fulfillment of the minimal criteria of membership to the visible Church is independent of his moral conduct.

Bellarmine dedicates the longest chapter to the problem of secret unbelievers (*infideles occulti*). By secret unbelievers Bellarmine understands those, who "are deprived either of the internal faith, and any Christian virtue, but profess the Catholic faith and through the participation in the sacraments mix with the real believers for the sake of some earthly good" (Bellarminus: 1857, 89, 4.3.10; my translation). He considers the problem of their status as the pivotal point of the whole issue of the visibility of the Church. "If only those", writes Bellarmine, "who lack in internal faith, were not nor could not possibly be in the Church, the question of the visibility of the Church between us and the heretics would be no more. And all such refined disputes which carry on to this day would be vain" (Bellarminus: 1857, 91, 4.3.10; my translation). In other words, if the Church was constituted only by those, who possess true faith, the problem would vanish and along with it the criterion of recognizing who is and who is not her member.

This is a point where Bellarmine makes an important distinction, between the formal rule of faith and its profession. In the course of the first *Controversy* concerning the Word of God he has already established the former (Bellarminus: 1856, 110, 1.3.9). It is defined by the authoritative judgment of the Pope or the Council. Catholic faith is composed materially by the doctrine of the Church being Revelation and formally by the specific, defined rule of faith. Bellarmine writes – "the form of the Church is not the internal faith, but the external, that is the confession of faith" (Bellarminus: 1857, 92, 4.3.10; my translation).

An authoritative, outward rule of faith makes the visibility of the Church possible. It provides an external standard making it possible to determine the orthodoxy of one's own faith – for personal certitude – or of one's teaching – for social, i.e. disciplinary and pastoral aims. But this can be checked only if the faith is professed. And only if the faith is professed does the Church become a community of men. That is because a community or a society begins where there is recognition between its members as its members, Bellarmine writes: "The Church is a sort of community, but not of angels nor souls but of men. One cannot, however, speak of a human community which is not built on external and visible signs. It is not a community, where members cannot recognize themselves as members, and men cannot recognize themselves without external and visible bonds" (Bellarminus:

1857, 95, 4.3.1; my translation 2). The visibility of the Church and its being as a community of humans is granted not only by mere existence of the formula of faith, but also by its usage, in which activity its members are able to recognize themselves. And this is provided by a particular application of the rule through its linguistic, articulate use in the profession of faith: "oral profession of faith" (Bellarminus: 1857, 92, 4.3.10; my translation). Bellarmine insists on this use of language in order to define a minimal condition of visibility. And since he considers the Church a visible community of men, he argues for the inclusion of anyone who professes the Catholic faith – i.e. also the secret unbelievers.

The result of Bellarmine's discussion on the visibility of the Church may seem surprising. It would seem obvious that the profession of faith makes sense only if it is a manifestation of something else: of the connection between the subject and the expressed truth. Such a bond could be tested, because one would expect a discursive and practical accordance – an accordance of works and words which would stand as a sign of an internalization of this connection. But Bellarmine does not consider one nor the other a sufficient condition in order to establish a human society, i.e. a visible society.

Bellarmine rejects any internal criteria of its membership and extends the boundaries of the real Church to external bonds: profession of faith, communion in the same sacraments and subordination in doing so to the legitimate pastors. As we have seen, he pushes these limits even further and defines society (of which the Church is a kind) in pragmatic terms by the possibility of mutual recognition in the same usage of language. But in doing so, Bellarmine cuts away the reference to one's works, as well as one's conscience. It is not the principle of representation that serves as a criterion of membership to the Church. His quest for establishing the Church as a visible society with firm and certain boundaries is completed, but at great cost. He has to neglect that what one is, does and thinks should be necessarily coherent and interconnected. But can this connection between practice and faith be restored?

5.   Embracing the vicious circle of representation

Bellarmine seems to leave two ways to address this disintegration. The first concerns Church's jurisdiction and belongs to the history of discipline; the second – somewhat more promising – concerns the Christocentric nature of the sacraments in the Church's community and pertains to the history of ecclesiology.

The first possibility is that Bellarmine admits the materialism of his doctrine with all the consequences. He seems to deliberately strengthen the Church's empire over souls by the means of her earthly rule. In the controversy titled *On the Highest Pontiff* Bellarmine confronts Calvin in an argument on the impenetrability of conscience and its exemption from any jurisdiction. He admits that in one sense only God is able to see through one's conscience and to judge over the internal acts which have no outward effect and hence no witnesses. But the internal forum does not need to be seen, nor "heart and kidneys scrutinized" in order to be regulated. "It is sufficient, to legitimately command one to perform an external act, so that if this external act is not performed, one can surely know, that an evil is done" (Bellarminus: 1856, 518, 3.4.20; my translation). Bellarmine identifies the problem of implication from the external to the internal forum, but his argument seems devious and problematic: he admits there is no human jurisdiction over conscience, nevertheless he wants to regulate it through the *speculum* of external acts.

On the other hand it may be, that Bellarmine only attempts here to protect the legitimate jurisdiction over the external from the 'conscience clause'. That is, he reaffirms the disjunction of the external from the internal forum and states that the former is the proper field of jurisdiction. The latter cannot answer to the juridical apparatus of the Church (*de occulta ecclesia non judicat*), because one cannot 'surely know' if an evil is done there, but this knowledge is not necessary to judge over the external. Bellarmine does not have to circumvent the inaccessibility of the conscience, but he may simply decline its relevance to effective jurisdiction.

His reasons may be twofold. The first one is related to the aforementioned problem of uncertainty. Clear knowledge about the membership of the governed society is required for jurisdiction to operate. Rejection of any internal dispositions as a mark of the community of the Church may grant such certitude. Using a biblical (and somewhat Cartesian) example, Bellarmine writes that:

> When we see a human figure we cannot acknowledge with infallible certitude, that he, whom we see, is a man. It may be that when we believe we are seeing a man, we are actually seeing an angel or a demon in a human form. Certainly Abraham, Lot, Tobias and others in the Old Testament not infrequently have considered men those, who in reality were angels? On the contrary, we want to have an infallible certitude of the Church not as we have of a man himself, but as of his figure and external colors and outlines of body about which our sight cannot deceive us (Bellarminus: 1857, 92, 4.3.10; my translation).

Bellarmine's ecclesiology defined in terms of external conduct serves this purpose and addresses a big, contemporary question of certitude in social and religious matters (Schreiner: 2010) and gives the grounds for effective jurisdiction, although all the counterarguments pointing to her rigid materialism remain in force.

Another reason relates to the problem of representation and the disciplinary authority of the Church and early modern states. This interpretation may seem more intricate, but let us ask what is at stake when Bellarmine writes that "while the effects of life are natural and necessary, the effects of faith are free and voluntary, and therefore much less certain and only conjectural" (Bellarminus: 1857, 92, 4.3.10; my translation). This somewhat enigmatic maxim may be explained in the following way: that faith or any other internal disposition cannot be deduced from one's action. Two otherwise identical activities are indistinguishable, regardless if one of them is an effect of free will informed by faith, because one's conduct points only to the nature, but not to the content of one's free will. It is not possible to call for showdown and verify the representation of the soul in its actions. The representing object is wholly visible and disciplinable, whereas the object represented is an empty grid to be filled with values and moral ideals; a variable open for arbitrary institution of its content.

Now the abovementioned distinction becomes essential: between disciplining through jurisdiction over the external which Bellarmine advocates, and disciplining through jurisdiction over the external *as a representation* of the internal, where proper (and invisible) criteria of the membership to Church would lie. In the second instance jurisdiction is at face value subordinated to a paradigm of moral perfection. However, if so the ability to produce ideology or moral representations becomes an instrument of power. The Church as only one among many powers executing discipline over spirits may be taken over by heterogeneous, areligious, secular ethics, substituting their own ideals and sources of moral life and deeming ecclesiastical law irrelevant to instruction and the formation of a good life. The popular idea of "Christians without Christ" as depicted in Thomas More's *Utopia* and Erasmian humanist ethics is a valuable example.[3] On the other hand, her instruments of discipline may be considered insufficient and superseded with the juridical apparatus of the early modern state. The latter would retain the spiritual legitimization of the discipline it forces while gaining independence from the ecclesiastical order.

6. Breaking out of the vicious circle: Christocentric ecclesiology

Let us leave the attempts to accept the apparent materialism of Bellarmine's concept of the Church with all the struggles to rationalize the consequent disintegration of practice and faith. I would like to suggest that Bellarmine does not discuss the ensuing problems, because they are addressed precisely at the core of his ecclesiology. Its full context is certainly not exhausted in the aforementioned doctrine of the three bonds, in spite of its enormous popularity (Dietrich: 1999, 469). As a

---

3 The argument is: the core of the Christ's teaching consists in ethical precepts and moral example that he gave for people to imitate Him and live a good life. Hence, those who are truly virtuous and contribute to a just and peaceful society are the actual adherents of the Christ's doctrine. So the Utopians receive Christianity happily once they discover that the rule lived by Christ and his followers was similar to their own. (More: 2012, 167; Erasmus: 1963, B 438).

definition of the Church this doctrine has been preserved until and through the Second Vatican Council, although not without amendments and critique of its quantitative, materialistic interpretation from intellectuals such as Henri de Lubac and Walter Kasper (Kasper: 2004). In fact, the concept of the three bonds should not be easily reduced to its institutional consequences, but put back into the context of Bellarmine's scholastic, Christocentric ecclesiology.

This is a very complex and intricate matter, because a relatively recent study of Thomas Dietrich has shown that Bellarmine's ecclesiology should not be viewed through the lenses of a materialistic merging of the concepts *corpus mysticum* and *corpus sociale* (1999, 191–239). On the contrary, in *Controversies* he was not leaning towards reducing the *mystical body* to the institutionally structured society, but attempts to conceive the Church in terms of the principle of Incarnation. The Church is a reality that begs a wholly different conceptualization. Bellarmine tends to underline the difference between the concepts of natural bodies and of the body of the Church (Bellarminus: 1857, 71, 4.2.19), diverging in that aspect from the tradition of Aquinas and from the late medieval tradition described by de Lubac (de Lubac: 2007).[4]

Bellarmine sees the Church to be in a hypostatic union with Christ:[5]

> When we call the Church the body of Christ, the word 'of Christ' can refer not to Christ as a head, but to Christ as a hypostasis of this body [...] In this sense Christ is not head of the Church but he himself is as if a great body which consists of many and different members (Bellarminus: 1856, 329, 3.1.9; my translation).

Bellarmine's use of the concept of *hypostasis* is here univocal with 'individual substance' and *suppositum* or 'person', since he speaks only about rational natures. 'Christ' and 'the Church' as his body are here spoken of as when we point to the body of the Christ on the Cross and refer not to the body but to the individual substance to which the visible accidents we see are attributed. In case of the Church,

---

4 St. Thomas Aquinas is conscious of the analogical sense of speaking of the Church and Christ as is the body to its head, but makes it the base of his argument and does not elaborate on the differences (*Summa Theologiæ* 3.A, q. 8, a. 1). He relates the concept of *suppositum* to purely Christological matters. But it is precisely the notion of *suppositum* that serves to indicate a beings *esse*, the principle of its being, regardless of its component parts, such as being animate, being bodily, having a head, arms, feet etc. in case of living creatures. (Cross: 2005, 52)

5 During my research I have not yet found predecessors to Bellarmine's idea. The union of the Christ to the Church was of course explored in the medieval neoplatonic tradition, but this type of union was clearly distinguished from both hypostatic union in Christ and 'absolute' or simple unity in God (e.g. Nicholas of Cusa, *On Learned Ignorance*, 3.12). Pseudo-Dionysius the Areopagite was also apparently highly admired by Bellarmine himself (Höpfl: 2004, 43).

the individual substance or *hypostasis* which underlies (*suppositum*) and sustains the accidents is Christ.

The concept of the *suppositum* embraced by the highly influential Thomist Christology served to address issues regarding the agency and actions in Christ. The full preservation of the two distinct natures in Christ according to the formula of the Council of Chalcedon lead to disputes whether the Incarnation has produced two different principles of agency in one being. The Thomist scholastics argued that in Christ there are two distinct species of actions of the two different natures, each having its proper potencies, but only one agency or first principle in which all operations originate and all passions terminate: the *suppositum* or *hypostasis* (cf. Thomas Aquinas, *De unione Verbi*, a.5). Analogically, due to the hypostatic union of the Christ in the *Ecclesia*, the person of Christ joins two natures by one *suppositum*.

> The principal agent in each body is always its *suppositum*. But the *suppositum* of the body of the Church is Christ […] We can say that Christ is the head of the Church, because Christ as he flows in all members can be called the head, and as he sustains and moves, can be called *suppositum* (Bellarminus: 1857, 71–72, 4.2.19; my translation).

The function of the *suppositum* is twofold: as it sustains, it is the principle of unity, and hence of being as an individual substance; as it moves and operates, it is the principle of agency. Thus, accordingly to the scholastic formula *actiones sunt suppositorum*, also the actions of the Church are attributed to Christ Himself as their first principle.

The precise relation between the two is a question that needs further consideration. The case of the mutual relations of the human and divine actions in the Church is problematic, primarily due to the imperfect subordination of the human nature to the divine. Nevertheless, Bellarmine seems to acknowledge the primary agency of Christ in His members hardly with any reservations: "Christ as the hypostasis of this body sustains all members and operates in them, sees through eyes, hears through ears – he teaches through doctors, baptizes through ministers, and does everything through all." (Bellarminus: 1856, 329, III,I,9; my translation) He, who operates through these instruments is Christ Himself as the *suppositum* which grants unity to the Church and determines the beginning and the end of all Her actions. The visible body of the Church in this interpretation is really the body of Christ, but their mutual relation is far more metaphysical than materialistic. The Church is not wholly defined by Christ due to the imperfect subordination of the rebellious, human nature. On the other hand, Christ is not reduced to the Church, but governs her as her *hypostasis* and, hence, her proper agent. To say on this basis that Christ subsists in the Church, as was done in the 20th-century encyclical *Mystici Corporis Christi* (referencing Bellarmine) is a hasty leap, but also a promising association to investigate.

7. A "sacramental" ecclesiology?

How does it relate to the problem of the material visibility of the Church in Bellarmine's ecclesiology and her apparent spiritual indifference? The dual interpretation of Christ as the head of the Church which operates on the ambiguity of Christ as both *principium* and *princeps*, *suppositum* and sovereign, has a twofold implication of legitimizing the form and tradition of the practices of the institutional Church in the past of Christ's Incarnation, and furthermore establishing Christ as the real agent of those visible practices. And among a myriad of examples, one type of ritual stands as a normative example: that is the sacraments.

The sacraments seem to lay at the junction of the various aspects of Bellarmine's ecclesiology reconstructed from his non-systematic exposition in the *Controversies*. The Church in this understanding gains a significant "eventive" or discrete character. The three bonds that unify the Church coincide *par excellence* at the event of the sacrament, where the profession (1st bond) and administration (2nd bond) under legitimate rule (3rd bond) intersect. She manifests herself by the expressions that enable its members to be recognized: and the most important events connecting being with speaking, essence with practice, are the sacraments administered in Church by Christ in the words of the faithful.

Hence, the problem of the materialistic superficiality inherent in the doctrine of the visibility of the Church would be solved at the heart of a "sacramental" ecclesiology based on the foundation of her hypostatic union with Christ. Because He is the true agent in the rituals of the sacraments, the material execution of their form grants participation in His grace. What is invisible acts and really is in the visible, and what is only visible and superficial, i.e. the profession of faith, under certain conditions grants communion in an invisible reality. The Church becomes truly visible during the administration of the sacraments involving the profession of faith, and because of this Bellarmine can say that the true and only Church is only the visible Church.

Bellarmine in his basic premises did acknowledge the incommunicability of the internal in the external, and realized that it could not be free of an arbitrary, subjective constitution of the object (Foucault: 1972). At the same time he certainly did lack the means to escape the dualism of the internal and the external, or even to formulate the heart of the problem. He did, nevertheless, acknowledge difficulties emerging should he admit this framework and put forth a doctrine that attempted to circumvent the ensuing problems: the hypostatic union of the Church in Christ. The invisible would become communicable in a very particular practice which strays from the opposition internal-external, because the act annuls the difference between its participants and its divine agent. Notwithstanding this, it is certain that Bellarmine in his *Controversies* was mainly occupied with defending the very efficacy of the sacrament, resting upon the legitimacy of the tradition and rule of the Catholic Church, hence my work was one of reconstruction, rather than description. And secondly, the many questions regarding Bellarmine's ecclesiology, taking into account the broad development of the issue of *suppositum* in medieval scholastics and in the recent history of logic, still need further examination.

Bibliography

ROBERTUS BELLARMINUS (1856), Opera Omnia, vol. 1: Disputationum Roberti Bellarmini. De Controversiis Christianae Fidei. Tomus Primus, Napels: Giuliano.

ROBERTUS BELLARMINUS (1857), Opera Omnia, vol. 2: Disputationum Roberti Bellarmini. De Controversiis Christianae Fidei. Tomus Secundus, Napels: Giuliano.

BRANDOM, ROBERT (2001), Making it Explicit: Reasoning, Representing, and Discursive Commitment, 4th ed., Cambridge/London: Harvard University Press.

BRODRICK, JAMES (1928), The Life and Work of Blessed Robert Francis Cardinal Bellarmine S.J., 1542–1621, London: Burns Oates and Washbourne.

CROSS, RICHARD (2002), The Metaphysics of the Incarnation. Thomas Aquinas to Duns Scotus, Oxford: Oxford University Press.

DIETRICH, THOMAS (1999), Die Theologie der Kirche bei Robert Bellarmin, Paderborn: Bonifatius 1999.

DREYFUS, HUBERT L./RABINOW, PAUL (1982), Michel Foucault. Beyond Structuralism and Hermeneutics, Brighton: Harvester.

DESIDERIUS ERASMUS (1963), The Education of a Christian Prince, Lester K. Born (trans.), New York: Octagon Books.

FOUCAULT, MICHEL (1972), The Archeology of Knowledge, New York: Pantheon Books.

FOUCAULT, MICHEL (2014), On The Government of the Living: Lectures at the Collège de France, 1979–1980, London: Palgrave Macmillan.

HÖPFL, HARRO (2004), Jesuit Political Thought: The Society of Jesus and the State, c. 1540–1630, Cambridge: Cambridge University Press.

KASPER, WALTER (2004), The Decree on Ecumenism. Read Anew After Forty Years, http://www.vatican.va/roman_curia/pontifical_councils/chrstuni/card-kasper-docs/rc_pc_chrstuni_doc_20041111_kasper-ecumenism_en.html [20.05.2016].

LUBAC, HENRI DE (2007), Corpus Mysticum: The Eucharist and the Church in the Middle Ages, Notre Dame, Indiana: University of Notre Dame Press.

MORE, THOMAS (2012), Utopia, ed. by St. Duncombe, Minor Compositions, theopenutopia.org [29.09.2016].

PRODI, PAOLO (1982), Il Sovrano Pontefice. Un Corpo e Due Anime: La Monarchia Papale nella Prima Età Moderna, Bologna: Il Mulino.

SCHREINER, SUSAN (2010), Are You Alone Wise? The Search for Certainty in the Early Modern Era, Oxford: Oxford University Press.

TUTINO, STEFANIA (2010), Empire of Souls: Robert Bellarmine and the Christian Commonwealth, Oxford: Oxford University Press.

Church and Unity

Linda Stuckrath Gottschalk

Caspar Coolhaes

Diversity in the Visible and Invisible Church

Caspar Janszoon Coolhaes (1534/6–1615) was a controversial Reformed preacher in Leiden in the late sixteenth century. Coolhaes identified as Reformed, but pleaded for a great amount of diversity and tolerance towards all other confessions, as well as within each confession. He believed that the invisible church was characterized by a God-ordained diversity, and that a similar diversity should be encouraged in the visible church. This article will introduce Coolhaes and his distinctive views, and then turn to a discussion of this fervent desire of the eclectic preacher and writer for a diverse, inclusive, and tolerant church.

A description of the eclectic Coolhaes immediately shows his broadness. First, one must point to Coolhaes' Erastian support of secular government and its power, exemplified in the case of elder and preacher selection in Leiden in 1579. This was the so-called "Coolhaes affair," which was the conflict between the Calvinist consistory, and Coolhaes' stricter fellow-preacher Pieter Cornelisz, with the broader city magistracy. This local conflict is significant because it encapsulated, in several personalities and in one city, the vital contemporary question of who had the authority over the public church – the secular powers or the ecclesiastical ones. As Christine Kooi (2000, 57) wrote, Coolhaes became the focus and also the scapegoat for this dispute over power, especially since he was "the most vociferous polemicist and partisan for an open, non-confessional Reformed Church subject to the supervision of a Christian magistracy."

Second, one must note that Coolhaes' views about predestination and free will were recognized early on to prefigure those of Arminius. After his death in 1615, he was labelled "the forerunner of Arminius and the Remonstrants." This title was first given to him by a Calvinist detractor – the Contra-Remonstrant Jacobus Trigland (1650, 188–90; 1617, 36–37; cf. Haar: 1891, 159; 166–167). Coolhaes was also listed in the foreword of the *Acta* of the National Synod of Dordrecht (1618–19) with two others with whom the Contra-Remonstrants differed: Herman Herbertsz of Dordrecht and Gouda, and Cornelis Wiggers of Hoorn.[1] Much later, nineteenth-

---

1 This list is reproduced in the "Acta of handelingen der nationale synode Dordrecht 1618–1619," *Kerkrecht*, www.kerkrecht.nl/node/1857 (accessed 26 jan. 2016). For more background on those mentioned and on the Synod as a whole, see also the following recent works relating to it: Acta: 2015; Goudriaan/Lieburg: 2011.

century Remonstrant H. C. Rogge, Coolhaes' first biographer, used the same phrase in a positive sense to describe Coolhaes, who certainly foreshadows Arminius and the Remonstrants on the question of free will and on dislike of narrow Calvinist discipline.[2]

Third, one must mention that Coolhaes has been recognized as a defender of religious freedom and tolerance.[3] Coolhaes was also connected with the writings of Spiritualists such as Sebastian Franck. Coolhaes defended the late Franck and translated and expanded part of one of his works for the Dutch audience.[4] Also, Coolhaes was known to have befriended and helped the future Socinian, Erasmus Johannes (Erasmus Janssens, c. 1540–96), as the latter passed through Leiden.[5] In addition, he defended the freedom of Mennonites against the "Severe Edict" of Groningen (1601) (Zijlstra: 1989, 65–78). He demonstrated by his own writings and friendships the diversity and acceptance which he advocated.

Coolhaes' exact confessional and theological identification is a fascinating question. He discloses it himself in twenty-some written works (the authorship of two or three is in dispute). Most scholars – including his first biographer, nineteenth-century Remonstrant H. C. Rogge – had read only some of his writings, and thus have been unable to produce a truly nuanced identification of Coolhaes or of the answers to the questions which he thought were most important. Since that time, more of Coolhaes' works have been rediscovered and reread.[6] A fuller and more nuanced definition of his views can now be made.

What, then, did this diversity mean to Coolhaes?

Caspar Coolhaes pleaded for religious diversity. First, on the societal level. Second, as the right of individuals, within any confession or congregation, to hold diverse views and lifestyles.

His own broader thinking was first noticed when, in Leiden, he drew the fire of his stricter Calvinist colleagues for his nonconformity on various issues. For example, he defended couples who married at City Hall instead of in the Reformed Church buildings, which had been Roman Catholic before the city became Protestant in 1572 and the Reformed church became the "public" church.[7] He allowed Catholic

---

2 For more information, please see my book: Gottschalk: 2017.

3 For example, by the Global Anabaptist Mennonite Encyclopedia Online. http://gameo.org/index. php?title=Kotte,_Johann_Clausen_(1563/64-1623/24).

4 Coolhaes: 1598a. This is the final section of: Franck: 1539.

5 Moes/Burger: 1915, 44–46. About Johannes, see also: Knijff/Visser/Visser: 2004, 26; 48–49; Schmeisser: 2012, 40; Janssens, Erasmus: 1880.

6 For more information on these points, see: Gottschalk: 2017.

7 Coolhaes: 1598a, folio 21Fv.; Coolhaes: 1602, B. From 1580, those who did not want to marry in the Reformed Church could marry before magistrates in Holland. See: Woltjer/Mout: 1995, 407.

practices to continue in the city, such as graveside sermons after funerals, and holidays on days other than Sunday (Coolhaes: 1580a, folio 73Tv; 1610a, 99–100). He baptized infants, but in cases of families of former Anabaptists did not always insist on it (Coolhaes: 1580b, folio 2r). He preached about hell not as flames of fire but as a place of primarily spiritual punishment. This caused his opponents to question his belief in the doctrine (Coolhaes: 1580a, 90Zija–90Zijb). He questioned Calvinist views, particularly predestination and election, and especially the correctness and usefulness of the emphasis on it in the churches (Coolhaes: 1609, Aiijb/4). Perhaps worst of all in the eyes of his strict colleagues and consistory, he backed the right of the city magistrates to lead in elder selection, as we have mentioned.[8] He was clear in his message that he did not see the Reformed Church as the "true church," despite his membership and ministry in it.

This desire for diversity can also be seen in one of his most characteristic behaviors: criticism. Coolhaes was a critic and spent many pages criticizing stricter Calvinist discipline and attitudes. Anyone who reads him will immediately see his scathing denunciations of preachers he considers to be "hypocrites." However, he did not reserve his critique for the Reformed only. He criticized all denominations and found all confessions wanting in one way or another. This can be seen most clearly in his books *Seeckere pointen* and *Toutzsteen*, both published in 1584 (1584a; 1584b). These books are written in a disputational style and take on each major confession at the level of what each considers to be its distinctive. Is the Roman Catholic Church truly "apostolic," he asked? Is the Lutheran Church really "evangelical"? Can the Reformed Church be said to be really "reformed"? Are the Anabaptists and Mennonites actually "pure"? The answer, he said, is no. His conclusion, then, is that *none* can be said to be the "true church."

Because the "true church" cannot be identified as just one confession, therefore, Coolhaes believed that tolerance and diversity were absolutely essential for Christendom at large – for the "visible church." In this he was countering a strict, Genevan-style attitude to discipline, which involved close examinations of church members by clergy or elders, with deviances punishable by temporary banning from the Lord's Table, or even excommunication. Removing such discipline seemed crazy to his opponents. He wrote in his first book *Apologia*, in 1580, that his opponents insisted that a diverse congregation such as this, existing without clerical discipline, would produce a chaotic "pigpen" of a church, full of sinners and compromise. But Coolhaes believed that the Spirit would not permit that. He believed that a free atmosphere would actually promote sanctification and spiritual insight (Coolhaes: 1580a, folio Cv).

---

8 The story of the "Coolhaes affair" fills much of Coolhaes' first two books, *Apologia* (1580a) and *Breeder bericht* (1580b).

For these and other reasons, he was mistrusted, eventually defrocked as a Reformed preacher at the Synod of Middelburg (1581), and soon after excommunicated ([Cornelisz: 1582; Coolhaes: 1582, Giiir). To support his wife and large family, he took the surprising step of learning the trade of distilling. He ran a shop between Leiden's Rapenburg and Papengracht, close to the University's Academy building, and later in Amsterdam in St. Olof's Gate near the Old Church. In these shops he sold medicinal potions, *genever*, and books, many his own writings on theological topics (Moes/Burger: 1915, 66; 365–367). These writings were often a thorn in the side of the stricter Calvinist clergy of his day. But Coolhaes' most distinguishing feature was his belief in the value of religious diversity – diversity in both the visible church and the invisible church, and we will look at his ideas about both in more detail now.

Coolhaes, like many others, defined the visible church as made up of all those who called themselves Christians in all confessions, and who build on the common foundation of the Bible and the Apostles' Creed (the so-called "Twelve Articles") (Coolhaes: 1584, folio Er). Using Paul's parable from 1 Corinthians 3:10–15, it is this foundation on which each preacher, each confession starts. Then, different churches build in diverse ways. Each preacher, each confession, is building a "house" with stronger or weaker materials, which will be tested by fire on the Last Day.[9] So we see that Coolhaes believed that some ways of building are more right, or stronger, than others. Still, he maintained that each must build as he sees fit, according to what he knows from God.

In various lists Coolhaes made of the groups of the visible church, he included the Reformed, the Lutherans, the Anabaptists/Mennonites, and Roman Catholics. Also, surprisingly, he sometimes included Arians (Coolhaes: 1582/1585, folios Bijv–Bijr). Coolhaes found it important that all confessions be included, because he was convinced that a certain skepticism is necessary around some dogmatic questions. Coolhaes was inspired by Spiritualist Sebastian Franck, and perhaps by the skeptic philosophy of Sextus Empiricus, to doubt that some theological questions could be answered conclusively.

Here we must remember that the conflict which would lead to the division between Remonstrants and Contra-Remonstrants at the National Synod of Dordrecht, mentioned above, was heating up in Coolhaes' lifetime. The party of the "stricter" Reformed Church was becoming ever more dogmatic and certain, even as Coolhaes and others were questioning that dogmatic attitude and seeking a broader definition. Soon, the Dutch Republic would be split politically and religiously by deep division.

---

9 There are many places where Coolhaes discusses this. See: Coolhaes: 1580a, folio 85Yv.; Coolhaes: 1584, folio Er.

So, he believed that no one can be certain that they have the whole truth of God in their confessional interpretation of Scripture. He deeply distrusted confessional preachers, who forced compliance by discipline. However, he was confident that the Spirit will lead searchers into truth. But, even if the full doctrinal truth is not known, love and tolerance should characterize true followers of Christ more than a doctrinal "purity" expressed with lack of love. One could say that Coolhaes was "ahead" of his time, as this attitude could be said to foreshadow the religious diversity of much later periods.

This, then, must be the reason that Coolhaes helped Socinian Erasmus Johannes. It was not because he questioned the Trinity, but because his idea of the visible church was diverse enough to consider Johannes a brother who should be tolerated and even helped. It is also why he defended Mennonites in Friesland against the Severe Edict (*Scherpe Plakkaat*), which was enacted by the magistracy of Groningen in 1601 against the free assembly and worship of Mennonites and other non-Reformed groups, including Roman Catholics (Zijlstra: 1989, 65–78). This preoccupation with the rights of Mennonites has led some to suspect that he may have moved from a Reformed self-identification after his excommunication and defrocking to doctrinal sympathy with Mennonites. But there is no evidence of his becoming a Mennonite, while there is evidence to show that he stayed within the Reformed camp throughout his life.[10] Nevertheless, Coolhaes authored and co-authored several books relating to his protest against what he saw in Groningen as a terrible injustice to Mennonites and others. One was a compilation of earlier Friesian Anabaptist writings (Coolhaes: 1603), while another was the fictional dialogue *Tsamensprekinge*. Coolhaes has one character in the latter book reason,

> What does it hinder us, if around us live Turks, Tartars and Moscovites, not to mention Catholics, Lutherans, Anabaptists, and so forth, if they do not molest us, and everyone can keep their own view? If we want to bring them from unbelief to true faith, let us do it not with name-calling, slandering, gossiping and persecution, but in friendliness and modesty speak to them out of the Lord's Word.[11]

If Amsterdam continues to tolerate this diversity, he says, God will continue to bless them with prosperity (Coolhaes/Claussen Kotte: 1601/1602, Gij).

---

10 . For instance, Reformed preacher Petrus Plancius' pastoral visits to Coolhaes: Rogge: 1856, vol. 2, 120; Pater: 1946, 118; Evenhuis: 1965, 172–175.

11 "Wat hindert ons dat neffens ons, by, ende om ons woon, Turcken, Tartaren, Moscoviters, Ich verswighe dan papistens, Martinisten, Doopsghesinden, ende haers ghelijcken, als sy ons niet en molesteren, ende elcken een van ons zijn ghevoelen laten houden? Willen wy haerluyden van het ongheloove totten rechten gheloove brenghen, laet ons sulcks niet met schelden, lasteren, achterklappen ende vervolginghe doen: Maer met aller vriendtlickheyt ende bescheydenheyt, spreeckende met hun uyt des Heeren woordt:" (Coolhaes/Claussen Kotte: 1601/1602, Gij).

Coolhaes found this diversity both inevitable and good. In his theological book *Sendbrief*, he described the visible church as a house for all, a ship at sea which must be steered by all working together, and an army in which all soldiers should fight on the same side.[12] It should be noted that not everyone in it is equally spiritual; there are hypocrites in the visible church; the visible church is not the "true church" as Calvin had maintained (Kärkkäinen: 2002, 51–58; Stackhouse Jr.: 2003, 179–80; 190). Despite the impurities in this *corpus Christi mixtum*, to use Augustine's phrase, God has ordained it and so it will remain in existence. Also, unlike Sebastian Franck and some other Spiritualists, many of whom saw no use for visible church, sacraments or clergy, Coolhaes believed the visible church had an important role to play in society. Its very diversity has a stabilizing influence, and possesses a sort of "political righteousness" – the creation of peaceful and honest citizens (Coolhaes: 1610b, folios Biiijr–Cijv).

Coolhaes not only advocated a surprising diversity of religious confessions in society, he also maintained that each individual in each part of the visible church should have the right to hold his or her own opinions about doctrinal matters and make his or her own lifestyle choices, regardless of the individual confession's rules or scruples. There would thus be no need of secret "Nicodemism;" personal diversity in a congregation would not be unusual and would not be punished. Coolhaes called this "Christian freedom." Such an individualistic standpoint was unknown in his age; some would say it was an enlightened and forward-looking view. It is also a link to other Spiritualists, who united in holding that the Spirit was free and would blow where He wished (Coolhaes: 1580a, folio 84 Xiiijv; Biiijv–r. R; McLaughlin: 1993, 77).

Thus, the visible church was not the "true church." For Coolhaes, the true church was the invisible church, the Creed's "communion of saints" – purified, blessed and eternal. Like many before him, he also included in the invisible church true believers who are alive in the present. For living believers, he said, this church is a pure refuge from outside sin (Coolhaes: 1606, 16), a mystical idea of an invisible bond. For both the living and the departed, it is the "true heavenly Jerusalem, the mother of us all, the true Bride of the Lamb, the one, holy universal Christian church."[13] In this he differed with Calvin in calling not the visible but the invisible church the "mother of believers." This is a significant difference. The Reformed Church saw their visible church as the "true" church and so it is logical that their desire to keep that church pure led them to introduce the third "mark" of the true church: discipline. For those who agreed, the visible church could thus be called the true church because it is pure. The invisible church could be called the true church

---

12 Coolhaes unpacks these metaphors in Coolhaes: 1582, folio Aiiijv.
13 Coolhaes: 1584c, folio Aijr; "Heavenly Jerusalem" is a reference to Galatians 4:26.

also, because it is composed of the elect (Kärkkäinen: 2002, 51–58; Stackhouse: 2003, 179–180; 190). But this was not Coolhaes' view.

For Coolhaes, it is the invisible church which is *corpus Christi merum* (the body of Christ elect). The membership of the invisible church is diverse and cannot be fully seen or judged by humans – it is known only to God (Coolhaes: 1584a, Biiijr; Cr; Coolhaes' own phrase; cf. Mark 8:34). It was normal for preachers in Coolhaes' circles to despair of so-called "notorious sinners," who lived a lifestyle seemingly far from God. Coolhaes strongly opposed condemning such people. In this Coolhaes was opposing the view, of many Calvinist clergy, that the visible evidence of a person's Christian walk was sufficient to judge a person's election. But in Coolhaes' view, one could never know whether such a person was actually a member of the invisible church. It is not necessary to belong to the visible church in one of its forms to belong to the invisible, true church. Invisible church members may be outside of any visible church (Coolhaes: 1584a, Biiijr).

On the other hand, members of the invisible church may also be members of the visible church. These are often godly, observant people. In fact, they may find themselves to be a small, spiritual minority in the visible church. This should not necessarily cause them to leave it. As we have said, each visible church confession is flawed – falls short of its ideal and self-definition (Roman Catholic as "apostolic," Lutheran as "evangelical," Zwinglians and Calvinists as "Reformed," and Anabaptists and Mennonites as "pure.") There is no need to separate from or leave any church because of its flaws.

But continued membership of living members of the invisible church is not assured. Coolhaes does not appear to believe in assurance. One can be "spat out" of the true church and not saved, if one does not continue in truth. Those outside of the true church – the invisible church – are lost, he wrote, just as those outside of the Ark were lost in the waters of the Flood (Coolhaes: 1580a, folio 81 Xr–folio 82 Xiiv). Satan is also active in this, and tempts true believers to forget about their "sure shelter" (Coolhaes: 1584c, folio Aijv–Aijr). In short, anyone who is outside of the invisible church is not a true believer – he or she is a member of the "Devil's church" (Coolhaes: 1571, vol. 3, folio 1–34, HEG/SAE, 5r). In this, Coolhaes sees membership in the invisible church to be a matter of assent and intention, not performance.

What is particularly notable about Coolhaes' view of the invisible church? It is the way he includes such diverse members, even including members who seem to originate in non-Christian religions. This caused the most controversy in his day. Coolhaes produced works in many varied genres, and one was the writing of texts to accompany woodcut prints on spiritual themes. One of his non-extant woodcut prints, "Afbeeldinghe vande waerachtige kercke Godts" ("Illustration of the true church of God") (Coolhaes: n.d.) is described by Coolhaes' opponents, Reformed preachers Arendt Cornelisz and Hendrik van der Corput, as well as by Coolhaes himself. It is said to have illustrated a haloed Christ, standing on a branch, while at his feet are men and women with white clothes holding palms. Under that are Roman Catholics celebrating mass and holding processions. Some older people are being baptized – perhaps a reference to Anabaptists. Turks, Tartars, Jews, Greeks, and Muscovites are labelled – a seeming reference to followers of Islam, Asian religions, Judaism, and Greek and Russian Orthodoxy. Lines connect each group to the group in white clothes, and then to Christ. Small, naked figures, with crosses around their necks, fly from each group to the group in white clothes and to Christ (Cornelisz/Van der Corput: 1600, 62). Coolhaes explained that the small figures who are naked but have the cross on their necks are those who come through Christ to God, representing those in every people and even religion, who are (eventually) saved through Christ.[14]

In "Afbeeldinghe vande waerachtighe kercke, hoe sy is in deser werelt" ("Illustration of the true church and how it is in this world"), also non-extant, the true church was drawn as a lily among thorns.[15] It was also represented as a person surrounded by venomous scorpions, with the caption: "They will serve God with pure hearts, and will unite with God in their inner selves."[16] These are the godly people who endure various difficulties. They are not holy in and of themselves, he says, but through Christ's grace and everlasting, sacrificial, sanctifying love (Coolhaes: 1580a, folios 91Ziijr–92Ziiijv). This seems to show that though Coolhaes said that the visible church *should* be diverse and tolerant of non-conformity, he knew full was that it was not.

The last example is in a book which was missing and was recently "rediscovered" in Rotterdam. It speaks to an important question – did Coolhaes believe that non-Christians could also be members of the true church? Coolhaes has been called "confessionally indifferent." Was Coolhaes so non-confessional that he believed that

---

14 His words are: "Maer daerom en verdoem ick niet, houde oock voor zeecker, dat Godt almachtich niet en verdoemt alle menschen wt een onverstandt noch levende, onder een van sondanige religien. Die valsche religien ende Godsdiensten zijn alle verdoempt ende vervloeckt van Godt, maer alle menschen wt onverstandt stekende in soodanighen valschen religien ende afgodendienst, en zijn niet verdoemt [sic]: want van herten Godt soeckende, sullen tot haerder tijt daer wt verlost worden" (Coolhaes: 1600, 109). Burger also gives an abbreviated quote of this (Moes/Burger: 1915, 64).

15 Coornhert had earlier used this simile (cf. Roobol: 2010, 34). Coolhaes had already used it also, in Coolhaes: 1580a, folios 91Ziijr–92Ziiijv.

16 Coolhaes: 1598b, point 119, 72. Also described by Moes/Burger: 1915, 14–15. It was also mentioned in Coolhaes: 1610c, 112. The original of the quote in the text above is: "Met herten reyn wil sy Godt dienen, ende inwendigh met Godt vereenen." It is also quoted in Cornelisz/Van der Corput: 1600, 65.

non-Christians could also please God?[17] In this book, his *Grontlicke waerheyt*,[18] a book which was not known to Rogge and apparently also not to many other scholars, Coolhaes states clearly that this diversity in the invisible church does not mean that all beliefs are equal. God condemns all false religion, he says: that of the Turks, the Tartars, the Indians, the Muscovites, the papists, and the Jesuits. But he is sure that God does not condemn people who through misunderstanding find themselves in these false religions, because those who are seeking God with their whole hearts will be at a certain time saved out of them.[19]

So we see that these (non-extant) prints, as well as *Grontlicke waerheyt,* show an invisible, true church of great diversity (Coolhaes: 1584b, folio Cr). Perhaps this view enraged Coolhaes' opponents so much because it was portrayed as woodcut prints reproduced in great number for a popular audience. Perhaps this is why no copies survived. However, this view was not unique. Luther also wrote that Christians can be found "under the Pope, Turks, Persians, Tartars, and everywhere." This is in his *Confession Concerning Christ's Supper* (1528; LW 37, 161–372). He says this, despite invective by Luther in other places against the papacy and the Turks. So, it is not unlikely that Coolhaes was inspired by Luther in this idea.

Therefore, members of the invisible church will be saved out of all confessions and even non-Christian faiths. To illustrate this, Coolhaes translated Sebastian Franck's use of and interpretation of Jesus' parable of the workers in the vineyard, who came at various times in the day, but received the same salary, to mean that some outside Christianity would repent and embrace Christ even at a very late date – even in the "evening."[20] So, no one should be judged by human standards, since

---

17 This question was brought up at the Middelburg Synod, as the fifth of the "doctrinal theses" which Coolhaes had to answer. See: original Latin verison as reproduced by Fatio, *Nihil pulchrius ordine*, 113–114. The manuscript version is in Inventarisnr. 672, AD.

18 Coolhaes: 1610c. Dr. A. H. van der Laan, curator at the Erasmus Center for Early Modern Studies, Bibliotheek Rotterdam, wrote, "Inderdaad hebben wij dit boek in beheer als bruikleen van de Remonstrantse Gemeenschap Rotterdam. Omdat het niet ons eigen bezit is, hebben we dit boek nog niet beschreven in onze online catalogus. Het boek is het zevende onderdeel van een convoluut (signatuur Erasmuszaal 29 E 2) dat ooit deel uitmaakte van de bibliotheek van Johannes Vvtenbogaert, die overigens geen sporen in het boek heeft nagelaten." E-mail to author, 14 August 2015.

19 His words are: "Maer daerom en verdoem ick niet, houde oock voor zeecker, dat Godt almachtich niet en verdoemt alle menschen wt een onverstandt noch levende, onder een van sondanige religien. Die valsche religien ende Godsdiensten zijn alle verdoempt ende vervloeckt van Godt, maer alle menschen wt onverstandt stekende in soodanighen valschen religien ende afgodendienst, en zijn niet verdoemt [sic]: want van herten Godt soeckende, sullen tot haerder tijt daer wt verlost worden." (Coolhaes: 1610c, 109). Burger also gives an abbreviated quote of this (Moes/Burger: 1915, 64).

20 Matt. 20:1–9, NIV: "For the kingdom of heaven is like a master of a house who went out early in the morning to hire laborers for his vineyard. 2 After agreeing with the laborers for a denarius[a] a day, he sent them into his vineyard. 3 And going out about the third hour he saw others standing idle in the marketplace, 4 and to them he said, 'You go into the vineyard too, and whatever is right I

only God knows the heart (Franck: 1539, CCCCXXVII; Coolhaes: 1598a, CVIIa). Even those whose lives do not show any evidence of true belief may still take the opportunity to repent and follow Christ truly.

In conclusion, then, Caspar Coolhaes was a controversial Reformed figure who pleaded for a diversity which was unusual in his time and place. While many in the Dutch Republic, and indeed across Europe, would increase the process of confessionalization into the seventeenth century, Coolhaes encouraged the opposite – a disregard for strong confessional borders. First, he encouraged this in regard to the visible church. His picture of a diverse visible church was not a "pig pen," as he said in his *Apologia*, but a free and inclusive space filled with the Spirit. This is mirrored, secondly, by his belief in a diverse, true, abiding, heavenly, invisible church, full of people from every tribe and nation, and redeemed out of every other religion, singing praise to the Lamb forever. Perhaps we in our present time might be inspired by this vision – the beautiful picture which Coolhaes paints of diversity in both the visible and the invisible church.

Bibliography

Sources

ACTA (2015), Acta of the Synod of Dordt, Donald Sinnema/Christian Moser/Herman J. Selderhuis (ed.), Göttingen: Vandenhoeck & Ruprecht,

CASPAR COOLHAES (n.d.), Afbeeldinghe vande waerachtige Kercke Godts, mitgaders de sichtbaerlijcke Kercken, ende der ghenen die niet voor Gods Kercke ghehouden werden, ende nochtans niet al te samen God mishagen.

CASPAR COOLHAES (1571), Glaubensbekenntniss von Caspar Coelhas, Rep. 100, inventarisnr. 2231.

CASPAR COOLHAES (1580a), Apologia: een christelijcke ende billijcke verantwoordinge Caspari Coolhaessen, dienaer des goddelijcken woorts tot Leyden, daer in hy hem nootsakelijk sonder eenighe blamatie, met der waerheyt ontschuldicht, teghen eenighe quadtwillighe ende onverstandighe, die hem van valscher leer, ende onchristelijcken leven beschuldighen, ghestelt in forme eens dialogi van twee personen. Met een corte voorreden, ghestelt in forme eens dialogi van twee personen. Met een corte voorreden aen

will give you.' 5 So they went. Going out again about the sixth hour and the ninth hour, he did the same. 6 And about the eleventh hour he went out and found others standing. And he said to them, 'Why do you stand here idle all day?' 7 They said to him, 'Because no one has hired us.' He said to them, 'You go into the vineyard too.' 8 And when evening came, the owner of the vineyard said to his foreman, 'Call the laborers and pay them their wages, beginning with the last, up to the first.' 9 And when those hired about the eleventh hour came, each of them received a denarius."

die edele erntseste, hochgheleerde ende wijze heeren, burgemeesters ende regeerders der loffelijcker vrije hanzestadt Deventer, Leiden: J. Paets Jacobszoon and/or J. Bouwensz?.

Caspar Coolhaes (1580b), Breeder bericht van die scheuringe der kercken Christi tot Leyden, ende den negen questien die rechte voort heen ende wederom ghedraghen, ende na eens yegelijcken goetduncken werden geinterpreteert, welcke deselve zijn, en tot wat eynde die ghestelt, en door wien sy in yeder mans handen zijn ghecomen, oock by wien het staet dat deze scheure tot deser tijt toe niet is gheheelt worden, etc., Leiden: J. Paets Jacobszoon and/or J. Bouwensz?.

Caspar Coolhaes (1582), Sendtbrief Caspars Coolhaes, dienaer des godlicken woorts, residerende tot Leyden. Aan de dienaren des goddelicken woordts in Suyt- ende Noort-Hollant, te samen ende eenen yeghelicken besonder. Om niet ontijdelick voort te gaen, int oordeel ghegheuen by de versamelinge binnen Middelburch in iunio anno 81. ghehouden, die buyten recht voor een nationael synodus wt gaet. Waer wt oock yederman sal verstaen mogen, met wat onrecht de selue Coolhaes verleden sondach, wesende den 4. nu loopende martij, tot Delft (een weet niet of aen ander plaetsen meer) der gemeynte opentlick van den predictoel, als onboetueerdiche erghenis met zijn schrijven aenghericht te hebben, met name voorghedraghen is, om met der scherpheyd van af-snijdighe teghens hem te proceduren. Waer van de summa breeder te vinden is int volghende blat, N.p.

Caspar Coolhaes (1582/1585), Van de christelijcke discipline ende excommunicatie vanden kercken raedt ende ouerlinghen [sic], aen dien plaetsen daer een christelijcke magistraet is, het ghevoelen der kercken Christi tot Zurich, tot Bern, ende anderen dierghelijcken vermaerden steden ende plaetsen in Zwitzerlandt, door den eerweerdighen welgeleerden Rodolphum Gwalterum, in verscheyden zijnen sermonen int latijn beschriven, uit het latijn ouergheset door C.C.V.M.I.D.H.G, Gouda.

Caspar Coolhaes (1584a), Seeckere pointen met die heylighe godtlicke schriftuur, ende vervolch vandien ghenomen: aenwisende het ghene, dat allen gheloovighen, bysonder doch den predicanten ende leeraren van allerhande partien, soorten, ofte exertitie van religien, wel aen te mercken, ende tachtervolgen van nooden is: ende grootelijcks, soo wel tot gherustheyt van eens yeghelicken menschen conscientie, als tot tijdtlijcken vrede, soude mogen dienen. N.p., 1584.

Caspar Coolhaes (1584b), Toutzsteen tot een seecker proeve welcx in der waerheydt die apostolische, catholijcke, evangelische, gereformeerde reyne kercke sy. Allen leergieri-gen menschen, ten besten voor ooghen ghestelt, ende in handen ghegheven, door C.V.M.I.D.H.G, N.p.

Caspar Coolhaes (1584c), Een christelijcke vermaninghe, aen alle onpartydighe predican-ten: om te waecken, ende by tijts te voorsien, dat die Sathan gheen nieu pausdom, aen des ouden benaest veruallen plaets wederom oprechte, N. p.

Caspar Coolhaes (1598a), Apologia Sebastiani Vranck; De welcke hy zelfs in synen leven gheschreven: ende achter syn boec van den seven zegelen: tot defensie van syn persoon ende schrijften, heeft doen drucken. Nu eerst in Nederduytsch over gheset door Caspar Coolhaes, N. p.

CASPAR COOLHAES (1598b), Wederantwoort Caspari Coolhaes op een faemroovende boexken sonder naem des autheurs onder eenen gedichten ende versierden naem van een verantwoordinghe des dienaers. oulingen [sic] ende diaconen der kercken tot Leyden, voor seventhien jaren tegen die Justificatie van Leyden geschreven, ende nu eerst tot Rotterdam gedruckt by Jan van Waesbergen int jaer 1598, Rotterdam: Jan van Waesbergen.

CASPAR COOLHAES (1600), Grontlicke waerheyt op het min dan waerachtich schrijven van eenen, schuylende onder t'decksel van die gereformeerde kercke, sonder ontdeckinghe zijns naems teghens die Wederantwoort Caspari Coolhasen, [Amsterdam]: Peeter Gevaertsz.

CASPAR COOLHAES/JOHANN CLAUSSEN KOTTE (1601/1602), Tsamenspreeckinghe van drie persoonen, over het regireus placcaet van Groninghen, ghekondicht den 7. September, oude stijl. Anno sestien-honderd ende een. Hollander, Embder, Gherefoormeerde. Door welcke tsamensprekinghe naecktelijk vertoont wort, dat die van Groninghen doort self de soecken nieuwe conscientijs d'wangh inte voeren, tot berovinghe des dueren gecochten landts, vryheden, ende beroovinghe des landts middelen, N.p.

CASPAR COOLHAES (1602), Een noodtwendighe broederlijcke vermaninge aen zijnen voor zeeckere jaren bekenden Vriendt, ende nu ter tijt door zijn eyghen in druck wt ghegeven schriften bevonden zijnde onwetenden broeder, genaempt Wijnant Kras, woonende buyten Jan Rooden Poort, opt Lijnbaens Pat, Peeter Ghevaerts.

CASPAR COOLHAES (ed.) (1603) Summa, ende bekentenisse christelijcker leer der predicanten, die in Oost-Vrieslandt omtrent tachtentich iaren voorleden, opentlijck ghepredickt ende gheleert hebbe: met een supplication der selven, aen den welgheboren en edelen heere, Heer Enno, te dier tijt zijnde grave en heer van Oost-Vrieslandt, van woorde tot woorde gevolght het exemplaer, tot Embden ghedruckt Anno 1565. Met noch een schoone bekentenisse, schriftuerlijk inventeert, ende rethorijlijck ghecomponeert, by Johan Baptista Houvvart, consilier ende meester ordinaris van die reeckeninghen des hertichdoms van Brabandt, beschreven in zijn boek van de vier wtersten des meschen, ende anno 83 t'Antwerpen ghedruckt by Christoffel Plantijn, Antwerp: Christoffel Plantijn.

CASPAR COOLHAES (1606), Comptoir Almanach: oft journal, op het jaer nae de geboorte onses Heeren ende salijcmakers Jesu Christi, M.DC.VI. Warin achter aen plaetse van duslange gebruyckten ende mit de warachtighe prognosticatien, ofte practijcken, tot onderwijsinge ende stichtinge des lesers, het recht gebruyck eens yeghelijcken voornaemsten feestdaghs angewesen ende het misbruyck derselver, als oock de verscheyden Bachus feesten: vastelavont: vasteldaghen: bededaghen ende vierdaghen uyt des Heeren woort bestraft worden, seer profijtelijck ende stichtelijck te lessen. door C. Crambi-Lagon, t'Amstelredam: Jan Thennisz.

CASPAR COOLHAES (1609), Naedencken of de disputatien vande Godtlijcke predestinatie, ende derghelijcken meer, des natuerlijcken menschen verstant verre te boven gaende, oorbaerlijck ende stichtelijck ghetracteert, ofte verhandelt konnen worden: Ende of Christus onse salichmaker: sijne h. apostelen ende propheten, op eene sodanighe manier van doen, de kercke des Heeren (dewelcke sy tot haren tijden geheel vervallen te zijn ghevonden) ghereformeert hebben, so men huyden-daechs, ende omtrent in de hondert jaren herwaerts te doen, onderstaen heeft. Den eerwaerdighen ende welgheleerden heeren Francisco Gomaro, ende Jacobo Arminio, beyde doctores ende professores theologiae, in de universiteyt tot Leyden in Hollandt: mitsgaders oock der gantscher kercken des Heeren Christi Iesu, ter proeve voorgestelt, Gouda: Jasper Tournay.

CASPAR COOLHAES (1610a), Een cort, waerachtich verhael van tsorgelicke vyer, der hatelicker, ende van God vervloecter oneenicheyt in religions saken, ontsteecken zijnde in Hollandt anno 1574: door wien het selve ontsteecken ende smoockende gheleghen heeft tot int jaer 1579: door wien, ende wat plaetsen in Hollandt, tselve op gheblasen, dattet brandende gheworden is: Des welcken vlam een weynich gedaelt zijnde, door wien tselve opt nieuwe weder op gheblasen, stercker ende grooter gheworden is, dan het te voren was: des welcken vlam oock metter tijt minerende, nu wederom met veel ende verscheyden, so grooten, als cleynen blaesbalghen, teffens op gheblasen wort om stercker te branden, ten eynde, dat het gheheele landt, door het selve vernielt, ende inden gront soude moghen bedorven worden: door wat mannen tselve vyer by tijts uytgebluscht, ende soo gheheel tot niet soude connen ghedaen worden, dat van tselve gheen coolken meer over blijven, van t'welcke men te besorghen mocht hebben, dat t'eenigher tijt, aen tselve, een nieu vyer soude moghen ontsteecken worden. Tot ghetrouwer waerschouwinghe, ende opwecken van den ghenen, der welcken ampt is, om tselve by tijts te remedieren, Leiden: N.p.

CASPAR COOLHAES (1610b), De basuyne ofte trompette Godes. De welcke sijn goddelijcke majesteyt, den propheet Esaia, ende allen sijnen h. profeten, apostelen, getrouwen herders ende leereren, sonder ophouden te blasen bevolen heft, om sijn volck voor haren erfvyandt, den duyvel, te verwaerschouwen, ten eynde dat sy van hem niet verrascht, ende met den eewighen doot geslaghen mogen worden, tot hunlieden eewich verderffenisse ende onderganck, Gouda: Jasper Tournay.

CASPAR COOLHAES (1610c), Grondlicke waerheydt, op het min dan waerachtigh schrijven van eenen schuylende onder 't decksel van die gereformeerde kerck, sonder ontdeckinge syns naems, teghens die Wederantwoort Caspari Coolhasen, N.p.: Pieter Gevaerts.

[ARENT CORNELISZ (CRUSIUS)?] (1582), Cort eenvoudich ende waerachtich verhael, waaromme Caspar Coolhaes predikant gheweest zijnde binnen Leyden: eyntelick (na langhe handelinghe diemen met hem vander ghemeyner kercken weghen gehadt heeft) den 25 martij anno 1582 by den synode provinciael van Hollandt van der kercke Christi is gheexcommuniceert. Ghestelt van weghen der predicanten ende ouderlinghen in den voorsc. Synode vergadert, tot noodwendighe verantwoordinghe der waerheyt, ende onderwijs der ghene, die vander saken qualick oft onrecht bericht moghen zijn. Waerinne verhaelt wort het beghin des twists binnen Leyden, ende wat neersticheyt ghedaen is, om dien neder te legghen, ende den voorsc. Casparen tot afstant zijns onrechts ende dwalingen te brenghen, Dordrecht: Jan Canin.

ARENT CORNELISZ (CRUSIUS)/HENDRIK VAN DER CORPUT (1600), Corte antwoordt op de valsche beschuldiginghen end' blameringen van Casper Coolhaes teghen de ghemeene kercken, begrepen in syn boecxken ghenaemt Wederantwoort: waer inne ooc vervatet is een corte aenwijsinge end' wederlegginge van dwalinghen, stekende inde boecxkens end' afbeeldinghen hier voren van Coolhaes uytghegheven, door Adr. Cornelisz van der Linden, N. p.

SEBASTIAN FRANCK (1539), Das verbüthschiert mit siben Sigeln Verschlossen Büch, das recht niemandt auffthun, verstehen, oder laesen kan dann das lamb, und die mit dem Thaw bezeichne, das lamb angehören, sampt einer Vorred von den siben Sigeln, was sie seyen, und wie die auffthan werden. Zu letst ein klain einlaiting und anweysung in die Heylige Schrifft, wie man sich in Mosen richten, die Propheten laesen, und Christum das Buch dess lebens verstehen soll, allen schuleren Christi, zur Christlichen vbung, vnd Götlichen räterschafft, von Sebastian Francken fürgestellet. Facsimile reprinted Frankfurt/Main, 1975.

JACOBUS TRIGLAND (1617), Klaer ende grondich teghen-vertoogh, van eenighe kercken-dienaren van Hollandt ende West-Vrieslandt, gestelt tegen seker vertoogh der Remon-stranten, Amsterdam: F. M. J. Brandt.

JACOBUS TRIGLAND (1650), Kerckelycke geschiedenissen. begrypende de swaere en bekommerlijcke geschillen, in de Vereenigde Nederlanden voorgevallen, met derselver beslissinge, ende aenmerekingen op de kerchelycke historie van Johannes Vvtenbogaert, Leiden: A. Wijngaerden,1650), 188–90.

Secondary Literature

EVENHUIS, R.B. (1965), Ook dat was Amsterdam, vol. 1, Amsterdam: W. Ten Have.

GOTTSCHALK, LINDA STUCKRATH (2017), Pleading for Diversity: The Church Caspar Cool-haes Wanted, Göttingen: Vandenhoeck & Ruprecht.

GOUDRIAAN, AZA/LIEBURG, FRED VAN (ed.), Revisiting the Synod of Dordt (1618–1619), Leiden: Brill, 2011.

HAAR, H. W. TER (1891), Jacobus Trigland, The Hague: Nijhoff.

JANSSENS, ERASMUS (1880) Janssens, Erasmus (Lat. Erasmus Johannes), in: McClintock and Strong Biblical Cyclopedia, http://www.biblicalcyclopedia.com/J/janssens-erasmus-(lat-erasmus-johannes).html

KÄRKKÄINEN, VELI-MATTI (2002), An Introduction to Ecclesiology: Ecumenical, Historical and Global Perspectives. Downer's Grove: InterVarsity Press.

KOOI, CHRISTINE (2000), Liberty and Religion: Church and State in Leiden's Reformation, 1572–1620, Leiden/Boston/Cologne: Brill.

KNIJFF, PHILIP/VISSER, SIBBE JAN/VISSER, PIET (ed.) (2004), Bibliographia Sociniana: A Bibliographic Reference Tool for the Study of Dutch Socinianism and Antitrinitarianism, Hilversum: Verloren.

McLAUGHLIN, EMMET (1993), Sebastian Franck and Caspar Schwenckfeld: two Spiritualist 'Viae', in: Jan-Dirk Müller (ed.), Sebastian Franck (1499–1542), Wiesbaden: Harrassowitz Verlag, 39–112.

MOES, E.W./BURGER JR., C.P. (1915), De Amsterdamsche boekdrukkers en uitgevers in de zestiende eeuw. Begonnen door E.W. Moes en voortgezet door C.P. Burger Jr, Amsterdam: C.L. van Langenhuysen.

PATER, J.C.H. DE (1946), Jan van Hout, 1542–1609, een levensbeeld uit de 16e eeuw, The Hague: D.A. Daamen's Uitgeversmaatschappij.

ROGGE, HENDRIK CORNELIS (1856), Caspar Janszoon Coolhaes, voorlooper van Arminius en de Remonstranten, Amsterdam: H. W. Mooij.

ROOBOL, MARIANNE (2010), Disputation by Decree: the Public Disputations between Reformed Ministers and Dirck Volckertszoon Coornhert as Instruments of Religious Policy during the Dutch Revolt (1577–1583), Leiden/Boston: Brill.

SCHMEISSER, MARTIN (2012), Sozinianische Bekenntnisschriften: Der Rakower Katechismus des Valentin Schmalz (1608) und der sogenannte Soner-Katechismus, Munich: Oldenbourg Akademieverlag.

STACKHOUSE JR, JOHN G. (ed.) (2003), Evangelical Ecclesiology: Reality or Illusion?, Grand Rapids: Baker Academic.

WOLTJER, J.J./MOUT, M.E.H.N. (1995), Settlements: The Netherlands, in: Thomas A. Brady Jr./Heiko A. Oberman/James D. Tracy (ed.), Handbook of European History 1400–1600, vol. 2, Leiden/New York: Brill, 1995.

ZIJLSTRA, S. (1989), Het 'scherpe plakkaat' van Groningen uit 1601, Doopsgezinde bijdragen 15, 65–78.

Tabita Landová

Ekklesiologie der Böhmischen Brüder

Ökumenischer Kirchenbegriff von Johannes Augusta[1]

Die Ekklesiologie der Böhmischen Brüder zog bis heute die Aufmerksamkeit der Forscher vor allem durch ihr außergewöhnliches ökumenisches Potenzial heran.[2] Das Maß der religiösen Toleranz, die die Brüderunität – sich selbst nur als einen Teil der Kirche Christi begreifend – zu anderen Kirchen hatte, war ungewöhnlich groß. Der Grund für das besondere Wachstum der Ideen der Toleranz auf dem Boden der Brüderunität kann aus der historischen Perspektive in ihrer Minderheitsstellung gesehen werden, denn sie war dem fortwährenden Druck sowohl seitens der römisch-katholischen als auch der utraquistischen Kirche ausgesetzt. Als eine bedrohte Minorität suchte sie verwandte religiöse Gruppen und zeigte ihnen Solidarität (Macek: 2001, 409).

Aus der theologischen Perspektive ist für die religiöse Toleranz der Brüder ihr spezifischer Kirchenbegriff entscheidend, der zwischen der Wirklichkeit der einen, heiligen und apostolischen Kirche Christi und den einzelnen institutionellen Kirchen differenzierte (vgl. Molnár: 1982, 15). Dieser Aspekt kann als einer der wichtigsten Identitätszeichen der Brüderunität betrachtet werden, durch das sie sich von den damaligen ekklesiologischen Konzepte sowohl der römisch-katholischen als auch der utraquistischen Kirche in Böhmen und Mähren deutlich unterschied,

---

1 Diese Studie entstand im Rahmen des Projektes "The Preaching and Homiletic Theory of Jan Augusta within the Context of the Czech Brethren's Homiletics" (Nu. 16-09001S) mit der finanziellen Unterstützung der "Czech Science Foundation".

2 Ausführliche Studien über die Ekklesiologie der Brüderunität schrieb Erhard Peschke, der den Kirchenbegriff des Begründers der Unität Gregor Schneiders (d. 1474) und des brüderischen Bischofs und Theologen Lukas von Prag (1460–1528) erforschte (1955/1956; 1957; 1981). Die Ekklesiologie des Lukas von Prag sowie die Frage nach der dreifachen Kirchenmitgliedschaft in der Unität und das ökumenische Anliegen der böhmischen Reformation behandelte Amedeo Molnár (1948: 72–80; 1956a: 149–165; 1956b: 12–25; 1982: 9–18). Weitere Studien über die Ekklesiologie der Brüderunität wurden von Josef Bohuslav Jeschke (1959: 12–23), František Mrázek Dobiáš (1959: 45–47) und Josef Smolík (1967; 2008) verfasst. Jüngst behandelten den Kirchenbegriff von Johann Amos Comenius Daniel Neval im Buch über Comenius' Bibelverständnis (2006: 30–33) und Atwood Craig im Rahmen seiner Monographie über die Theologie der Böhmischen Brüder (2009: 177, 224–227; 284–286; 391–394).

deren Auffassung der Kirche Christi mit der geschichtlich ununterbrochenen apostolischen Sukzession untrennbar verbunden blieb.[3]

Für die Ekklesiologie der Brüderunität gilt ganz offensichtlich, was Amedeo
Molnár über die böhmische Reformation als solche behauptete, nämlich, dass sie
von ihren Anfängen bis zu den Zeiten von Johann Amos Comenius durch "eine
doppelte Bewegung" charakterisiert werden kann: "die Bewegung zu einer äußeren
Trennung [..] um der Wahrheit und der wahren Einheit willen einerseits, und
die Bewegung zur äußeren Einigung auf Grund erkannter und bekannter wahrer
Einheit anderseits" (1982: 10). Beide angedeutete Bewegungen finden wir ebenso
im Leben und Werk von einem der bedeutendsten Bischöfe der Brüderunität,
Johannes Augusta (1500–1572). Nach seiner Trennung von der utraquistischen
Kirche wurde er zum Mitglied der Brüderunität, um wieder nach der Findung
der gemeinsamen Rede mit den Utraquisten zu trachten. Als partielle Erfüllung
seiner Idee der Annäherung zwischen den beiden Kirchen kann man das Verfassen
der gemeinsamen Böhmischen Konfession (*Česká konfese*) von den böhmischen
Lutheranern und den Vertrettern der Brüderunität im Jahre 1575 betrachten und
ihre Unterstützung seitens der Utraquisten vor dem König Maxmilian II. (vgl. David:
2012, 291–335; Hrejsa: 1912). Den Gipfelpunkt der brüderischen Tendenz zur
Einigung kann man schliesslich in Comenius Vision eines ökumenischen Konzils
der unabhängigen Glaubensgemeinschaften sehen, die viele Verbindungspunkte
mit dem Selbstverständnis des heutigen Weltkirchenrates hat (Molnár: 1982, 16f).

Augusta beschäftigte sich mit den ekklesiologischen Fragen vor allem im Zusammenhang seiner kritischen Auseinandersetzung mit der Theologie der Utraquisten[4]
und unter dem Einfluss der Theologie Luthers. Sein theologischer Begriff der Kirche, wie er ihn nach dem Tode seines theologischen Lehrers Lukas von Prag in
seinen Schriften entwickelte, wurde bisher eigenständig nicht erforscht. Im Bereich
der Ekklesiologie waren es vor allem seine langfristigen Bemühungen um die Annäherung der Brüderunität und der utraquistischen Kirche, die die Aufmerksamkeit
der Forscher angezogen haben. Mit dem ökumenischen Aspekt von Augustas Leben und Werk beschäftigte sich langfristig Josef Smolík (1973; 1984; 2000a; 2000b;

---

3 Die Utraquisten erkannten den Papst als den Garanten der apostolischen Sukzession in der Priester-
  weihe an, aber sie lehnten seine Verwaltungs- und Gerichtskompetenz ab (David: 2012, 95).

4 Für die Utraquisten im 16. Jahrhundert wird manchmal die Bezeichnung Neu-Utraquisten benutzt.
  Mit diesem Begriff wurde eine "entschieden evangelische" Strömung in der tschechischen utraquistischen Kirche bezeichnet, die seit dem 1517 mit der lutherischen Reformation als auch mit den
  heimischen radikalen Strömungen, den Taboriten und der Brüderunität, sympathisierte (Hrejsa:
  1948, 37). Die neueste Forschung dagegen zeigt, "that Neo-Utraquism did not really exist but was
  invented for its extraordinary (almost magic) effectiveness" (David: 2005, 329). In Wirklichkeit gingen
  also die Utraquisten eher den Mittelweg zwischen Wittenberg und Rom. Von den Utraquisten muss
  man deutlich die böhmischen Lutheraner unterscheiden. Über ihre Existenz und Geschichte vgl.
  Just/Nešpor/Matějka: 2009.

2008), der sich gegenüber der "einseitigen politischen Interpretation von Augustas Gestalt" abgrenzte und eine theologische Deutungsperspektive einnahm (2008: 324). Aus der historischen Perspektive behandelte Augustas Leben und Werk Josef Theodor Müller (1915).

In letzten Jahren hat die Forschung über Johannes Augusta dank seiner neulich entdeckten Schriften einen neuen Impuls bekommen. Im Jahre 2011 wurde sein Perikopenbuch, das von Johannes Černý überarbeitet und etwa 1558 herausgegeben wurde, in einem anonymen alten Druck der tschechischen Nationalbibliothek identifiziert (Augusta/Černý: 1558).[5] Ein Jahr später wurde seine umfangreiche Postille, die während seiner Internation auf der Burg Pürglitz im Jahre 1557 beendet und 1570 gedruckt wurde, ebenso in einer anonymen Schrift, die in mehreren, teils unvollständigen Exemplaren und Bruchstücken erhalten ist, entdeckt (Augusta: 1570).[6] Weitere Überraschung kam, als ich während der Arbeit an diesem Beitrag eine anonym gedruckte Schrift aus dem Jahre 1543 erforschte, die bisher einem anderen Verfasser, Adam Šturm, zugeschrieben wurde. Ich bin zur Hypothese gekommen, dass diese Schrift ebenso ein Werk von Johannes Augusta sein könnte, wofür ich unten einige Argumente vorlegen möchte.

Das Wesen dieses Artikels besteht in der theologischen Darstellung von Augustas Kirchenbegriff im Kontext seiner Auseinandersetzung mit den Utraquisten. Ich gehe in fünf Schritten vor. Den Ausgangspunkt bildet eine kurze Behandlung über die soteriologische Relevanz der Frage nach der Kirche im Kontext der Brüderunität. Im zweiten Schritt werden die Hauptzüge des Kirchenbegriffs von Augustas Vorgängern behandelt, nämlich von Gregor Schneider und Lukas von Prag. Drittens lege ich die chronologische Übersicht Augustas ekklesiologischer Texte und Übersetzungen dar, die während seiner Auseinandersetzung mit den utraquistischen Priestern in den dreißiger und vierziger Jahren des 16. Jahrhunderts veröffentlicht wurden. Im vierten Schritt werden die Hauptzüge von Augustas Kirchenbegriff aufgrund seiner Texte systematisch dargestellt. Im letzten Punkt versuche ich die Erträge zusammenzufassen und das Spezifische von Augustas Kirchenbegriff im Vergleich mit den Positionen der Utraquisten zu identifizieren.

1. Ohne Christus und ohne die Kirche gibt es kein Heil: die soteriologische Relevanz der Frage nach der Kirche

Die Frage nach der Kirche Christi wurde bei den Böhmischen Brüdern eng mit der Frage nach dem Heil verbunden. Schon im Jahre 1470 drückten sie die Annahme

---

5 Näher vgl. Landová: 2012; Landová: 2014, 133–142; Baťová: 2012; Baťová: 2013.
6 Näher vgl. Landová: 2014, 124–133; Baťová: 2015.

aus, dass "es kein Heil als in der Einheit der heiligen Kirche Jesu Christi gibt" (Bidlo [ed.]: 1915, 272). Die Annahme, dass der Kirche eine soteriologische Funktion zukommt, erinnert an die berühmte Sentenz von Cyprianus *extra ecclesiam nulla salus*. Man braucht die Kirche als eine Mittelinstanz zwischen Gott und Mensch, denn ohne ihre Hilfe – ohne ihre Verkündigung des Evangeliums und ihre Sakramentsverwaltung – würde man nie zum Glauben kommen können. Diese Überzeugung finden wir bei Lukas von Prag und ebenso in den Schriften von Johannes Augusta: "Ohne Christus und ohne die heilige Kirche gibt es kein Heil." (Augusta: 1543b, f. A3v).[7] Christus und Kirche gelten hier als zwei notwendige Voraussetzungen für jeden, der sich nach der Erlösung seines sündhaften und unvollkommenen Lebens sehnt.[8]

Doch Augusta ist sich gleichzeitig dessen bewusst, dass die Bedeutung dieser Aussage davon abhängt, was mit der Kirche tatsächlich gemeint wird und welche Wirklichkeit mit diesem Begriff als sein Denotat verbunden wird. Diese Fragestellung drückt er in seiner Vorrede zur tschechischen Übersetzung Luthers Schrift *Von den Schlüsseln*:

> Welches Volk kann als die heilige Kirche in Wahrheit genannt werden in der jetzigen Zerrissenheit und Zusammenrottung der Christenheit? Und wo kann sie mit Sicherheit in einer kleineren oder größeren Versammlung gefunden werden und ebenso wonach kann sie deutlich erkannt werden, [die Kirche,] der sich jeder heilssüchtiger Mensch (wenn er sie erkennt) anschließen kann als der Braut Christi und seiner Schafherde und mit ihr eine heilige Gemeinschaft haben? (Luther: 1540, f. A 3v–4r).

Nicht nur für Theologen, sondern ebenso für geläufige Laien stellt diese Frage nach der Kirche ein ernstes Problem. Ihre Dringlichkeit besteht darin, dass der Mensch sich seines Heils verfehlen könnte, wenn er die wahre heilige Kirche, die die Teilhabe am Hören des Wortes Gottes und an den Sakramenten vermittelt, nicht erkennt. In gleicher Weise erklingt diese Fragestellung im *Dialog*:

> Und nun gibt es eine nicht kleine Schwierigkeit, welches Volk die heilige Kirche ist und welches nicht. Und es ist in Wahrheit notwendig danach zu fragen, damit sich der Mensch nicht täuscht und das Heil verfehlt. (Augusta: 1543b, f. A3v).

Hinter der geschärften Frage nach der wahren Kirche, die man in mehreren Augustas Schriften findet, steht seine kritische Wahrnehmung der konkreten geschichtlichen Situation der Kirchen in böhmischen Ländern in dreißiger und

---

7 Zur Verfasserschaft dieser Schrift siehe unten.

8 Ähnlich vgl.: „Ebenso diejenigen [Heiligen Schriften] sind wahr, dass ohne Christus und ohne die Kirche gibt es kein Heil […]" (Augusta/Řezník: 1542, f. C1v).

vierziger Jahren des 16. Jahrhunderts.[9] Die Realität der mehreren selbständigen kirchlichen Gemeinschaften rief mit besonderer Schärfe die Frage hervor, welche Kirche die wahre ist. Allerdings die Frage nach der wahren Kirche war in der Brüderunität so alt wie sie selbst, denn sie stand gleich bei ihrer Entstehung.[10]

2. Kirche als Versammlung der Erwählten: Gregor Schneider und Lukas von Prag

Augustas Kirchenbegriff knüpft ganz unmittelbar an die Schriften seiner theologischen Vorgänger in der Brüderunität, Gregor Schneider und Lukas von Prag, in deren Ekklesiologie Spuren vom Kirchenbegriff Johannes Hus ersichtlich sind.

In seiner Schrift *De Ecclesia* (1413) verlässt Hus die institutionelle Auffassung der heiligen Kirche als der Gemeinschaft mit dem römischen Papst und seinen Kardinalen (Hus: 1965, 61.115–116) und in Anknüpfung an die Prädestinationslehre Augustins und Wyclifs versteht er die Kirche als *numerus omnium praedestinatorum,* das heißt als die Zahl der gegenwärtigen, vergangenen und zukünftigen Auserwählten (Hus: 1965, 23–24; Hus: 1956, 2–3).[11] Die bestehenden kirchlichen Strukturen und das Kirchenamt wurden von Hus nicht aufgehoben, aber sie wurden der sie übergreifenden Wahrheit untergeordnet. Infolgedessen trat Hus mit einer revolutionären These heraus, dass der Priester in der Todsünde sein Amt verliert. Mit dieser These wurde ebenso das Primat des römischen Papstes weitreichend relativiert. Der Rezeption dieses Verständnisses begegnen wir später ebenso bei den Brüdern: die Struktur des Kirchenamtes wird behalten, doch ihre Bedeutung wird neu konzipiert (Smolík: 1967, 53–54).

Der Begründer der Brüderunität, Gregor der Schneider (d. 1474), entwickelte seinen Kirchenbegriff in mehreren Traktaten im Anschluss an die Prädestinationsanschauungen Augustins, Wyclifs und Hus. In *Tractat bratří starých o církvi svaté* ("Traktat der alten Brüder über die heilige Kirche", 1470) versteht er die Kirche als Gemeinschaft gotterwählter Gläubiger aus verschiedenen Ländern und Zeiten, die dazu vorherbestimmt werden, damit Christus sie rechtfertigt und zu seiner Braut macht (Bidlo [ed.]: 1915, 267–268). Von Wyclif und Hus übernimmt er ebenso den Brautgedanken. Die Kirche als Braut Christi soll ihrem Bräutigam in ihrem Leben in der Kraft seines Geistes nachfolgen. Der Grund und die Haupt der Kirche ist

---

9 Zur Geschichte der Brüderunität in dieser Zeit vgl. Říčan: 1957, 143–179; Říčan: 1961; Müller: 1931, 1–198; Gindely: 1857.

10 Über die Entstehung der Brüderunität vgl. Říčan: 1957, 35–50; Říčan: 1961; Müller: 1922.

11 Näher über seinen Kirchenbegriff vgl. Vogel: 2015; Soukup: 2014, 159–174; Šmahel: 2013, 89–98; Neval: 2006, 65–69; Spinka: 1966; Peschke: 1981, 15–42.

eindeutig Christus. Er ist der "Felsen", auf dem die Kirche steht (Bidlo [ed.]: 1915, 268).

Gregor hält fest an der Einzigartigkeit der Kirche, aber ihre Einheit versteht er nicht im institutionellen Sinn, sondern im geistlichen: "Und so auch die heilige Kirche, die den Geist der Wahrheit befolgt, ist durch ihn [Christus – T.L.] das Eine mit ihm. " (Bidlo [ed.]: 1915, 301). Die Einheit der Kirche wird durch das Wirken des heiligen Geistes und durch seine gehorsame Annahme seitens der Gläubigen geschaffen, also von innen, nicht durch die äußere Identifizierung mit einer kirchlichen Institution. Zur Betonung dieses geistlichen Wesens der Kirche benutzt Gregor die Bezeichnungen der Kirche als „Haus Gottes im Heiligen Geiste" (Bidlo [ed.]: 1915, 301), oder biblisch gesagt: "Tempel des Heiligen Geistes". Peschke sieht bei Gregor sogar „unverkennbar mystische, durch Chelčický vermittelte Elemente", die Kirche wird bei ihm "weniger als einheitliches Ganzes, als vielmehr als Vereinigung der einzelnen Seelen gedacht" (Peschke: 1981, 85). Das Band, durch das die Erwählten mit Christus und miteinander verbunden sind, bilden die "wesentlichen Dinge", Glaube, Liebe und Hoffnung.

Schon bei Gregor kann man Umrisse der Idee des allgemeinen Priestertums der Gläubigen sehen. In seinem Traktat *Spis o dobrých a zlých kněžiech* ("Schrift von den guten und bösen Priestern", 1470) betont er, dass alle Christen, die dem Herrn in Glaube, Liebe und Hoffnung nachfolgen, sind lebendige Steine am geistlichen Tempel der Kirche, sie sind geistliche Priester dieses Tempels. Diese geistliche Priesterschaft gilt als eine notwendige Voraussetzung für das Priesteramt in der Kirche. Wer Priester sein will, muss zuerst als geistlicher Priester zur Gemeinschaft der Auserwählten gehören (Bidlo [ed.]: 1915, 132).

Die Lehre der alten Brüder über die Kirche wurde anfangs des 16. Jahrhunderts von einem der bedeutendsten Bischöfen der Brüderunität weiter entwickelt, Lukas von Prag († 1528). Seine Kirchenlehre hat er systematisch in den Schriften *Apologia sacrae scripturae* (1511)[12] oder *O puovodu cierkve svaté* ("Vom Ursprung der heiligen Kirche", 1522) dargestellt.[13] In dieser Schrift geht Lukas vom Begriff der Kirche heraus, den er als "Zusammenrottung oder Gemeinde, Haufen, Versammlung oder Zusammenrufen der Leute" deutet (Lukas: 1522, f. A3). Den theologischen Ursprung der Kirche sieht er im Werk des dreieinigen Gottes begründet, in der Schöpfung, Erlösung und Heiligung (Lukas: 1762, f. A3v–4r).

Die heilige allgemeine Kirche definiert er dann in deutlicher Anknüpfung an Hus als "die Zahl von allen Erwählten Gottes, die in ihrer Zeit zur Welt kommen sollten von Anfang an bis Ende der Welt" (Lukas: 1762, f. A6r). Aus der zeitlichen

---

12 Tschechisch 1518 unter dem Titel *Spis dosti činiecí z viery.*
13 Die Schrift wurde 1762 vom Exulanten Jan Šlerka in Kaliningrad neu herausgegeben.

Perspektive wird sie, wie bei Hus, in drei Teile geteilt: "die vergangene oder trium-
fierende, die gegenwärtige oder kämpfende und die zukünftige" (Lukas: 1762, C9r).
Dieser Kirchenbegriff wurde manchmal mit der Kategorie der unsichtbaren Kirche
in Einklang gebracht. Doch schon Molnár wies zum Recht darauf hin, dass es in
der Lukasschen Ekklesiologie eigentlich nicht um die Unsichtbarkeit der Kirche
geht, sondern eher um die Verborgenheit ihrer Grenzen dem menschlichen Blick
(Molnár: 1948, 73). Wer unter die Auserwählte gehört, das weiß nur ihr Schöpfer,
Erlöser und Heiland (Lukas: 1522, f. D 2a). Die Grenzen der Kirche werden nur
aus der Sicht Gottes klar zu bestimmen, sie kann nicht mit keiner empirischen
Kirchengestalt identifiziert werden (Lukas: 1762, f. C9v). Auf der Seite des Men-
schen wird diese heilige allgemeine Kirche in ihrem Wesen nur dem Blick des
Glaubens ersichtlich: "Und alle diese heilige allgemeine Kirche wird nur durch den
Glauben in seiner Allgemeinheit angeschaut. " (Lukas: 1522, f. D 2a; 1762, f. C9r).

Lukas beschäftigte sich in diesem Zusammenhang ebenso intensiv mit der Frage
nach der überdauernden Gegenwart des Bösen in der Welt und der heuchlerischen
Christen in der Kirche sowie mit der Frage nach der Beziehung zwischen dem
göttlichen und menschlichen Handeln in der Kirche. Die Betrachtungen dieser
Fragen führten ihn zur gründlichen Differenzierung des Kirchenbegriffs. Einerseits
unterschied er zwischen der Kirche Gottes und der Kirche des Teufels, andererseits unterschied er in beiden Teilen "die Kirche seitens des Wesens" und "die
Kirche seitens des Dienstes" in Bezug auf das Heil.[14] Folglich spricht Lukas von
der wesentlichen und dienlichen Kirche Gottes und von der wesentlichen und
dienlichen Kirche des Teufels (Lukas: 1762).[15]

Die wesentliche Kirche Gottes ist die Gesamtheit aller, die eine wirkliche Teilnahme an den wesentlichen Dingen des christlichen Glaubens haben, also die
Gesamtschaft aller zur Erlösung Erwählten. Ihr einziges Haupt, ihr Priester, Bischof
und Hirte, ihr Grund ist Christus. Außerhalb der wesentlichen Kirche gibt es kein
Heil (Lukas: 1522, f. D 3a; 1762, C10r–C10v). Die dienliche Kirche Gottes fasst
dagegen konkrete kirchliche Gestalten in allen Nationen um, die Unitäten, in denen sich die wesentliche Kirche empirisch realisierte, realisiert und realisieren
wird. Sie wird mithilfe des Gleichnisses Jesu von einem ins Meer geworfenen Netz
geschildert, das sowohl gute als auch schlechte Fische einschließt (Lukas: 1762,
C11v). Die dienliche Kirche wird also durch die Vermischung der Erwählten mit
den toten Christen und Heuchlern kennzeichnend.

Ähnlich ist es dann mit der Kirche des Teufels, nur statt der "Erwählung" zum
Verdammnis spricht Lukas in abgeschwächter Form der Prädestinationslehre vom

---

14 Als das Gliederungsprinzip dient hier das Schema der Unterscheidung zwischen den wesentlichen
und dienlichen Dingen in Bezug auf das Heil des Menschen, dessen Ursprung in der taboritischen
Theologie liegt.

15 Vgl. näher Molnár: 1948, 72–76; Peschke: 1981, 150f.

Vorherwissen (*Präszienz*) Gottes. Die wesentliche Kirche des Teufels sind "alle Vorhergewussten zur Verwerfung vom Anfang der der Welt bis zum Ende, die ewiglich der göttlichen Teilnahme und Gnade und des Verdienstes Christi entkleidet werden [...]" (Lukas: 1762, f. D6r). Die dienliche Kirche des Teufels wird als konkrete Versammlungen der Bösen und Heuchler verstanden. In beiden werden wieder chronologisch drei Teile unterschieden: die vergangene, gegenwärtige und zukünftige wesentliche oder dienliche Kirche des Teufels (Lukas: 1762, f. D6v, D8r).

Die Auffassung der Kirche bei den theologischen Vorläufern Augustas wird vor allem durch ihren nicht-institutionellen Kirchenbegriff gekennzeichnet, der dem Kirchenamt überordnet wird. In ihren Definitionen wird die Realität der Kirche Christi als eschatologische Wirklichkeit von ihrer geschichtlichen Erscheinungen unterschieden und die Zugehörigkeit dieser Wirklichkeit der menschlichen Entscheidungsmacht entnommen. Der Kirchenbegriff wird breiter gefasst im Sinne der Versammlung von allen Erwählten und mithilfe der biblischen Metaphern der Kirche als Braut Christi und sein mystischer Körper wird die grundlegende Autorität dem Christus selbst als dem Bräutigam und dem Haupt vorbehalten.

3. Augustas ekklesiologische Schriften am Hintergrund seiner Auseinandersetzung mit den Utraquisten

Johannes Augusta entwickelt seinen Kirchenbegriff nicht isoliert, sondern im Dialog. In seinen Erwägungen über die Kirche knüpft er einerseits an die heimische theologische Tradition, wie sie oben skizziert wurde.[16] Seine ekklesiologischen Erwägungen sind aber nicht nur die Reproduktion der älteren Ansichten, sondern werden gleichzeitig stark durch die aktuellen theologischen Diskussionen geprägt: einerseits durch seine Polemiken mit der utraquistischen Priesterschaft,[17] andererseits durch den Verkehr mit den europäischen Reformatoren. Er verkehrte sowohl schriftlich als auch persönlich mit Luther in Wittenberg[18] und stand im Briefwechsel mit den Schweitzer Reformatoren, wie einige erhaltene Brief aus dem Jahre 1540 zwischen Augusta und Martin Buzer, Wolfgang Capito und Johannes Calvin belegen.[19]

Augusta selbst ist in einer utraquistischen Familie in Prag geboren und wurde in der utraquistischen Kirche erzogen. Er hatte keine Universitätsausbildung, sondern erlernte das Handwerk seines Vaters und wurde zum Hutmacher, was seine Gegner gerne verspotteten. Seine Enttäuschung vom Stand der utraquistischen Kirche und

---

16 Er beruft sich ausdrücklich auf Lukassche Schrift über die Kirche (vgl. Augusta: 1543a, f. N2r).
17 Dazu näher vgl. Müller: 1931, 125–160.
18 Zum Briefwechsel und Kontakte Augustas mit Luther vgl. Rohde: 2007; Smolík: 1984, 53–59.
19 Zur Korrespondenz Augustas mit den Reformatoren in Straßburg vgl. Molnár [ed.]: 1972.

seine Suche nach einer religiös sowie sittlich reinen Glaubensgemeinschaft führten ihn 1524 in die Brüderunität.[20] Seine Karriere in der Unität war außergewöhnlich rasch. Zuerst wohnte er einige Zeit bei Lukas von Prag in Jungbunzlau und bei ihm gewann er eine theologische Ausbildung. Im Jahre 1529 wurde er zum Diakon, 1531 zum Priester geweiht. Ein Jahr später wurde er zum Mitglied des Engen Rates gewählt, seit 1537 bekleidete er das Bischofsamt. Er verwaltete zuerst kurz die brüderische Gemeinde in Benátky nad Jizerou, 1532–1548 wirkte er in Leitomischl.[21]

Gerade diese Zeit gilt bei ihm – was die literarische Tätigkeit betrifft – zu den bedeutendsten. Während seiner Wirksamkeit in Leitomischl wurden mindestens neun seine Schriften gedruckt (Augusta: 1532; 1534; 1540a; 1540b; 1544a; 1544b; 1541; 1543a; 1543b), daneben gab er zwei ältere Texte mit den die aktuellen Auseinandersetzungen betreffenden Vorreden heraus (Augusta [ed.]: 1542; Augusta/Řezník: 1542) und zwei Übersetzungen (Luther: 1540; 1542); andere seiner Schriften wurden in Handschriften erhalten (1535; 1537). Was den Charakter der Texte betrifft, es handelt sich um theologische und polemische Texte, die primär den Utraquisten bestimmt wurden, konstruktive Schriften, die den Bedürfnissen der Unität dienen sollten, Predigten und Korrespondenz.[22]

In dieser Zeit entwickelte Augusta ebenso seine Ideen der Zusammenarbeit und Vereinigung zwischen der Brüderunität und der utraquistischen Kirche. Nach Smolík war er überzeugt, dass unter den Utraquisten viele von denen sind, die nach der Erneuerung ihrer Kirche trachten. Gleichzeitig war er der Meinung, dass diese Kirche sich erneuern lässt. Für ein taugliches Mittel hielt er "eine öffentliche Diskussion über die grundlegenden Glaubensartikel und die Erneuerung der Kirche" (Smolík: 198, 41). Diese Diskussion versuchte er durch Schriften anzuregen: *Rozmlouvanie jednoho muže učeného* ("Gespräch eines Gelehrten", 1532) und *Knížka tato bez titule* ("Dieses Büchlein ohne Titel", 1534). Beide Schriften wurden den „lieben Brüdern in Christus, besonders denen unter beiderlei Gestalten", das heißt den Lesern aus der utraquistischen Kirche gewidmet. Das Ziel seiner Bemühungen war, „einen Schafstall" zu schaffen, also zur Einheit der beiden Kirchen beizutragen (Augusta: 1534, f. 33f).

Für theologische Plattform, auf der diese Erneuerung und gegenseitige Annäherung von beiden Kirchen geschehen sollte, hielt Augusta wahrscheinlich die lutherische Reformation (Just: 2015, 36), die in den dreißiger und vierziger Jahren in Böhmen einen wachsenden Widerhall erfuhr, sowohl unter den Brüdern als auch

---

20 Näher über seine Konversion Smolík: 1984, 16ff; Nodl: 2001; Molnár: 1952, 119.
21 Näher über sein Leben Smolík: 1984.
22 Zum Verzeichnis von Augustas Werken vgl. Smolík 1984: 123–125; Opelík/Forst/Merhaut: 1985, 90.

unter den Utraquisten. Die Rezeption Luthers seitens der utraquistischen Priesterschaft war aber sehr differenziert und nicht eindeutig (vgl. David: 2012, 103–154).
Obwohl Luther bei manchen Utraquisten die Sympathien vor allem durch seine
kritische Stellungnahme zum Papst oder durch seine Bejahung der Einstellungen
von Hus erregte, in anderen grundlegenden Punkten – wie das Abschaffen der
apostolischen Sukzession oder die Ablehnung des Gedankens des Messopfers – war
er ihnen zu radikal und sie vertraten konservative Ansichten. Augusta stützte sich
dagegen auf diejenigen Meinungen Luthers, die für die Utraquisten unakzeptabel
waren.

Das gegenseitige Gespräch verwandelte sich bald in eine scharfe Polemik. Der
Gegenstand des Streites wurde zuerst die Frage nach den Gelöbnissen beim Eintritt
in die Unität. Die Priester der Brüderunität wurden beschuldigt, dass sie von den
neu gekommenen gewichtige Versprechen fordern, von denen sie profitieren. Augusta versuchte sich gegen diese Verleumdungen zu wehren. In einer Kontroverse
mit dem utraquistischen Priester Wenzel Řezník in Leitomischl, die durch die Konversion vom Tuchmacher Kašpar zur Brüderunität im Jahre 1532 hervorgerufen
wurde, half er dem Leitomischler Bürger, die Brüderunität vor der Beschuldigung
zu verteidigen. In einer Antwort an Řezník stellt er den Sinn der Gelöbnisse in
einen engen Zusammenhang mit dem liturgischen Akt der Erneuerung des Taufver-
trages.[23] Der Briefwechsel wurde mit großer Wahrscheinlichkeit von Augusta selbst
1542 herausgegeben, in der Zeit einer anderen Auseinandersetzung mit Řezník
(vgl. Müller: 1931, 148–149).

Allerdings zur Verteidigung der Verpflichtungen beim Eintritt in die Unität
schrieb Augusta eine selbständige Schrift *O závazcích křesťanských zákona Kristova*
("Von den christlichen Gelöbnissen des Gesetzes Christi"), die 1940 gedruckt wurde.
Es handelte sich um eine Schrift, die für die inneren Bedürfnisse der brüderischen
Gemeinden bestimmt wurde. Doch erregte sie eine kritische Reaktion von einem
utraquistischen Priester in der Schrift *Odpověď Petra ze Zásadí* ("Die Antwort
von Petr aus Zásadí", 1541), deren Vorwort den Anschein erweckt, „als sei die
Schrift im Auftrag, vielleicht auch unter Mitwirkung der gesamten utraquistischen
Priesterschaft herausgegeben worden" (Müller: 1931, 135).

Noch desselben Jahres erschien in Leitomischl Augustas Antwort *Ohlašenie a
ozvánie Jana Augusty proti té knížce kněžské* ("Erklärung und Entgegnung Johann
Augustas gegen das Buch der Priester", 1541). Ebenso Wenzel Řezník, der damalige
Kuttenberger Dechant, äußerte sich kritisch gegen Augustas Schrift von den Gelöbnissen mit eigenem Werk über den schlechten und falschen Gebrauch der Heiligen

---

23 Das Motiv des neuen Bundes gehört zu den Schlüsselmotiven der Theologie von Lukas von Prag,
das ebenso die liturgische Gestalt der Sakramente wesentlich prägte (vgl. Landová: 2011).

Schrift (Řezník: 1542a). Der Streit ging weiter, als Petr aus Zásadí wieder auf Augustas *Ohlašenie* mit einer weiteren Schrift *Velmi povlovná, pokojná a upřímná odpověd* ("Sehr gelinde, friedfertige und aufrichtige Antwort") 1542 reagierte und außer anderem die Gültigkeit des brüderischen Priestertums bezweifelte.

So kommen wir zum weiteren strittigen Thema zwischen Augusta und den Utraquisten. Die Bezweiflung der Gültigkeit des Priestertums der Brüderunität hatte weitgreifende Folgen, denn damit wurde ebenso die Wirksamkeit ihrer priesterlichen Handlungen – der Sakramente oder der Trauungen – in Frage gestellt (Smolík: 1984, 44). Die brüderische Auffassung des Priestertums behandelte Augusta in der Ordinationspredigt, die an der Synode der Brüderunität in Jungbunzlau bei der öffentlichen Ordination der neuen Diakonen und Priester am 20.6.1540 vorgetragen wurde. Aufgrund des Textes im Apg 1:15–16 versuchte er zu erweisen, dass die Brüder auf die apostolische Sukzession mit Recht völlig verzichteten und ihr Priestertum nur auf den Ordnungen und im Geiste der ersten Kirche gründeten (Augusta: 1540b).[24] Dieses Augustas verwegenes Vorgehen bei der Ordination erregte eine Empörung nicht nur im utraquistischen Konsistorium, sondern sogar beim König (Smolík: 1984, 44f).

Augustas Auseinandersetzungen mit den Utraquisten mündeten zuletzt in einen Streit über den Kirchenbegriff ein. Nach der Hypothese von Rudolf Říčan ist Augusta mit großer Wahrscheinlichkeit der Übersetzer von zwei Auszügen aus den Schriften Luthers über die Kirche ins Tschechische und Autor der umfangreichen Vorreden und des Anhangs (Říčan: 1967a, 291; 1967b, 142). Die Texte wurden unter den Titeln *O pravém užívaní klíčuov pravých* ("Von der wahren Benutzung der wahren Schlüssel") und *O cierkvi svaté a o jistých znameních* ("Von der Kirche und von den sicheren Zeichen") gedruckt. Genauer gesagt, es handelt sich um Teile aus Luthers Schriften *Von den Schlüsseln* (1530, WA 30,II,435–507, 497–507) und *Von den Konziliis und Kirchen* (1539, WA 50,509–653). Sie wurden – möglicherweise separat – ungefähr 1540 in Leitomischl gedruckt.[25] In zwei Vorreden (Luther: 1542, f. A2r–A4v; D5r–E5v) und im abschließenden Anhang (f. H8v–I6r) stellt der Herausgeber seine eigene ekklesiologischen Anschauungen vor. Mit diesen Schriften Luthers wollte Augusta die positive Stellungnahme der Brüderunität zur Macht der Schlüssel unterstützen und ebenso ihre Auffassung des Kirchenbegriffs, denn Luthers Definition der Kirche in diesen Schriften betont die Heiligkeit der Kirche und setzt sich mit den Antinomeronen auseinander. Die Kirche ist nach der

---

24 Die Betonung der absoluten Verzicht auf die Sukzession als eines „Vorzugs des brüderischen kirchlichen Amtes" stellt dabei ein Novum im Vergleich mit den früheren Darstellungen der ersten Wahl und Weihe der brüderischen Prieste (Müller: 1931, 129f).

25 Zur Datierung und dem Druckort vgl. Bancroft: 1955, 231; Claus/Pegg: 1982, 142; Bohatcová: 1982, 152.

hier vorgelegten Definition Luthers „das Volk, das christlich und heilig ist, oder, wie man allgemein sagt: die heilige Christenheit" (Luther: 1540, f. E 7r).

Die ekklesiologische Debatte mit den Utraquisten wurde dann vor allem durch die Übersetzung von einem Teil Luthers scharfer Schrift *Wider Hans Worst* in Gang gebracht, die seit 1521 im Reichsbann war. Augusta gab sie heraus unter dem Titel *Zrcadlo kněžské pro ty, kteříž jiné za odřezance církve svaté býti lehce ukazují* ("Priesterspiegel für diejenigen, die allzu leicht von andern beweisen, sie seien Apostaten der heiligen Kirche") im Jahre 1542.[26] Die Ausgangsfrage ist die Frage nach der wahren heiligen Kirche und nach der Möglichkeit der Trennung von Rom, die als dringend ebenso in der Brüderunität schon lange empfunden wurde.

Die unmittelbare Nähe dieser einleitenden Fragestellung den Betrachtungen der brüderischen Theologen bewirkte, dass Wenzel Řezník die Schrift sogar für ein ursprünglich Augustas Werk hielt, dass betrügerisch unter dem Namen Luthers herausgegeben wurde (vgl. Řezník: 1542b, Titel und Vorrede). Die Herausgabe der Schrift rief dann aufgeregte polemische Schriften seitens der Utraquisten hervor (vgl. Řezník: 1542b; Křížek: 1542), denn sie sich mit der als Kirche des Antichrists enthüllten Kirche identifizierten, obwohl die polemische Spitze der Schrift ursprünglich auf die römisch-katholische Kirche zielte. Sogar der König wurde so empört, dass er einen königlichen Haftbefehl herausgab, und Augusta musste zeitweilig eine Zuflucht in Wittenberg suchen (Smolík: 1984, 45f).

Systematisch behandelte Augusta die Frage nach der Auffassung der Kirche vor allem in seiner umfassenden polemischen Schrift *Pře Jana Augusty a kněžstva kališného* ("Die Streitsache Johann Augustas und der kalixtinischen Priesterschaft") aus dem Jahre 1543, die in Form einer Gerichtsverhandlung geschrieben ist. In sechs Artikeln behandelt er hier die Hauptthemen seines Streites mit den Utraquisten: (1) über den Glauben und ihre Gerechtigkeit, (2) über die heilige Kirche, (3) über die christliche Trennung, (4) über das Priestertum, (5) über christliche Gelöbnisse und (6) über kirchliche Ordnungen und Zeremonien. In jedem Teil verfährt er so, dass er die Anschauungen der beiden Seiten den Lesern zur Beurteilung vorlegt und schließlich eine Bewertung der vorgelegten Thesen und Argumente macht. Das letzte Urteil wird dem höchsten Richter, dem Christus, überlassen.

Im Teil über die Kirche skizziert er zuerst zwei zentrale Positionen, mit denen er sich auseinandersetzt: (1) Manche utraquistischen Priester sind der konservativen Meinung, dass die allgemeine heilige Kirche nur die ist, die unter der Verwaltung des römischen Bischofs ist; den von Rom getrennten Kirchen droht ihrer Meinung nach die Verwerfung (Augusta: 1543a, f. L3r). (2) Die anderen Theologen meinen, dass die allgemeine heilige Kirche unsichtbar und irgendwo verborgen ist; und obwohl sie diese verborgene Kirche mit keiner konkreten Ortskirche ausdrücklich

---

26 Näher über diese Schrift vgl. Říčan: 1956a, 291–292; Müller: 1915,144f.

identifizieren, ist es offenbar, dass sie implizit die römische und utraquistische Kirche meinen (Augusta: 1543a, f. L3r).

Die Lehre der Utraquisten über die heilige Kirche wird dann in sechs Punkten zusammengefasst aufgrund der Schriften von zwei utraquistischen Priestern und Augustas Kontrahenten: Wenzel Řezník und Petr aus Zásadí. Die Utraquisten lehren, (1) dass die Kirche nicht in diesem oder jenem Volke sei, sondern überall, (2) dass die heilige Kirche die ganze Gesamtschaft der Christenheit sei, (3) dass das ganze tschechische Volk die heilige Kirche sei, (4) dass die heilige Kirche nicht von den falschen Propheten und offenbarem Sündern rein sein solle, sondern sie einschließen könne, (5) dass in der heiligen Kirche der Antichrist wirke, nämlich die Leute, die sich dem Papst und seinen Bestimmungen widersetzen, (6) dass die heilige Kirche von Gott in den inneren Angelegenheiten erneuert werden solle, aber nicht in den äußeren (Augusta: 1543a, f. L3r–L3v). Augustas Vorwürfe betreffen vor allem die universalistische, liberale und nationale Auffassung der Kirche, die den Utraquisten eigen war.[27] Die eigenen Stellungnahmen Augustas werde ich im nächsten Teil vorstellen. Hier sei nur bemerkt, dass auf die Schrift Augustas der Administrator der utraquistischen Kirche Martin Klatovský mit eigenen Schrift reagierte (1544; vgl. Müller: 1915, 156–159).

Bei der Suche nach weiteren relevanten Quellen zur Augustas Ekklesiologie habe ich ebenso eine populäre Schrift über die Lehre des Kuttenberger Dechanten Wenzel Řezník erforscht, die bisher einem anderen Verfasser zugeschrieben wurde. Die Schrift *Dialog, to jest, dvou formanuo rozmlouvaní, Peterky a Valoucha, přepotřebné* ("Dialog oder sehr nützliches Gespräch zweier Fuhrleute Peterka und Walouch") wurde wahrscheinlich in Prossnitz von Johannes Olivetský im Jahre 1543 gedruckt.[28] Auf dem Titelblatt steht eine Angabe, dass sie "jetzt aufs neue von einem Lehrer der Brüderunität zum Nutzen der Gläubigen herausgegeben" wird. Nach Johannes Černý gab sie Martin Michalec heraus (Černý: 1543–1546; zit. nach Müller: 1931, 151). Blahoslav dagegen gewährt eine andere Auskunft, wenn er in seiner *Grammatika česká* ("Tschechische Grammatik") schreibt:

> Bruder Adam Šturm aus Hranitz, ein Bakkalaureus, […] viele Lieder komponierte sowie einige Bücher schrieb: er schrieb den Dialog des Peterka mit Walouch. Bruder Martin Michalec korrigierte nur. (Čejka/Šlosar/Nechutová: 1991, 298, f. 282b).

---

27 Augustas Charakteristik der utraquistischen Ekklesiologie konvergiert so mit den Begriffen, mit denen sie in der neusten Forschung charakterisiert wird (vgl. David: 2007; 2010).

28 Dieselbe große Initiale „P" über sechs Zeilen mit den Pflanzen- und Tiermotiven (Augusta: 1543b, f. A2v) befindet sich ebenso in der Schrift *Listove a psaní kněze Vaclava* (Augusta/Řezník: 1542, f. A2r). Beide Schriften wurden wahrscheinlich von demselben Drucker gedruckt.

Diese Behauptung Blahoslavs wurde von den bisherigen Forschern allgemein über-
nommen und die Verfasserschaft des *Dialogs* wurde gewöhnlich dem brüderischen
Lehrer Adam Šturm zugeschrieben (vgl. Smolík: 1984, 47; Říčan: 1957, 165; Müller:
1931, 151; Hrejsa: 1948, 111; Jireček: 1876, 272). Während meiner Forschung habe
ich aber konkrete Indizien für die Hypothese gefunden, dass die Schrift eher von
Johannes Augusta verfasst und vom "Lehrer der Brüderunität" Adam Šturm nur
herausgegeben wurde, was allerdings der Angabe am Titelblatt besser entsprechen
würde. Ebenso aus den Worten des Herausgebers in der Vorrede ist es deutlich,
dass er eine Schrift von einem anderen Verfasser, nicht seine eigene herausgab: "In
der Zeit, als mir dieser Dialog in die Hände kam, las ich ihn mit einer größeren
Begierde als alle vorherige [...]" (Augusta: 1543b, f. A2r).

Das Hauptindiz für Augustas Verfasserschaft entdeckt man bei der Überprüfung
der Behauptung Blahoslavs aus seiner *Grammatika česká*. Dabei finden wir einen
Widerspruch, denn an der oben zitierten Stelle schreibt Blahoslav den *Dialog* dem
Adam Šturm zu, aber an einer anderen Stelle nennt er diese Schrift ausdrücklich
unter den Schriften von Johannes Augusta, wenn er schreibt:

> Item mehrerlei Bücher vom Bruder Johannes Augusta überhaupt herausgegeben:
> Sein Streit mit den Priestern. Über die Verpflichtungen. Dialog des Peterkas. Ent-
> gegnung item Über die Ausschließung. Item Das Zeugnis über die Frau Justina etc.
> (Čejka/Šlosar/Nechutová: 1991, 287, f. 274b).

Aus diesem Widerspruch, auf den schon Jaroslav Kolár (1984, 20) aufmerksam
machte, sind Konsequenzen zu ziehen und die bisherige Attribution der Schrift
dem Adam Šturm ist in Frage zu stellen.

Das andere Indiz für Augustas Verfasserschaft ist die große inhaltliche Verwandt-
schaft des Werkes mit Augustas Texten. Am Anfang des *Dialogs* wird der Verlauf
der Auseinandersetzung zwischen Augusta und den utraquistischen Priestern de-
tailliert rekapituliert. Von Augusta wird in der dritten Person geschrieben. Ähnliche
Rekapitulation des Streites finden wir ebenso in Augustas Schriften. In denen, die
von ihm nur herausgegeben wurden, spricht er von sich selbst ebenso in der dritten Person (vgl. Augusta [ed.]: 1542; Augusta/Řezník: 1542). Weiter, im *Dialog*
werden auf Grund der Polemik mit der Schrift von Wenzel Řezník und Wenzel
Křížek dieselben ekklesiologischen Fragen und Themen ausführlich erläutert, die
Augusta in einer knapperen Form in *Pře Jana Augusty* (1543) im Kapitel über die
Kirche behandelt.[29] In beiden Schriften findet man denselben polemischen Stil und

---

29 Zum Beispiel die spezifische Polemik mit der Lehre von der sichtbaren und unsichtbaren Kirche im
    Dialog (f. E1v) korrespondiert mit Augustas kritischer Betrachtung dieser Lehre in *Pře* (1543a: L3r).

viele ähnliche Sprachwendungen.[30] Die Form eines Dialogs wurde dem brüderischen Bischof ebenso nicht fremd, denn er schrieb schon früher eine Schrift in der dialogischen Form (vgl. Augusta: 1532). Sogar in seiner Schrift *Pře Jana Augusty* (1543) werden einige Passagen in Form des Dialogs des Verfassers mit dem Leser geschrieben.

Weitere Schriften, die man bei der Erforschung von Augustas Kirchenbegriff berücksichtigen muss, sind die brüderische Konfessionen aus den dreißiger Jahren des 16. Jahrhunderts, an deren Texte Augusta einen bedeutenden Anteil hat.[31] Eine kurze Skizze über die Deutung des neunten Artikels des Apostolikums über den Glauben an der heiligen Kirche befindet sich in der einleitenden Predigt *Kázaní o víře* der neuerdings entdeckten Postille Augustas, die unter dem Titel *Summovník* bekannt ist (Augusta: 1570, f. D2r–D3v).

4. Grundzüge Augustas Ekklesiologie

4.1 Kirche als sichtbare Gemeinschaft der im Namen Christi Versammelten

Was ist die Kirche in der Sicht von Johannes Augusta? Seine Definition der Kirche ist stark christologisch fokussiert. Die heilige Kirche

> ist dort, wie es geschrieben ist, wo sich zwei oder drei im Namen des Herrn Jesu Christi versammeln und in sich den Geist Christi, sein reines und gesundes Wort, reine Sakramente, reine Ordnungen und irgendwelche Dienlichkeit untereinander haben, ebenso die wahre, reine Gottes Ehre und den Dienst. (Augusta: 1543a, f. L4r; ähnlich vgl. Augusta: 1570, f. D2v).

Die Kirche ist für Augusta – unter Bezugnahme auf den biblischen Text Mt 18:20 – die Versammlung der Menschen im Namen Christi. Christus gilt hier als der Verbindungsglied, der Grund und das Haupt der Kirche. Dies betont Augusta ebenso in seiner Vorrede zu Luthers Schrift *O cierkvi svaté*: "Hier ist ebenso ihr Kopf, Christus, wie er sagt, wo sich zwei oder drei in meinem Name versammeln, dort bin ich inmitten ihnen." (Luther: 1540, f. E2r). Ein weiteres Kennzeichen der Kirche ist, dass die im Namen Christi Versammelten in sich den Geist Christi

---

30 Im *Dialog* befinden sich oft die Wendungen: „sein Königtum, das die Kirche ist" (f. E1v), „das Reich Gottes, das ist die heilige Kirche" (f. B1r), die man ebenso in Augustas Schriften sehr oft findet (vgl. Augusta: 1543a, f. M1r).

31 *Rechenschaft des Glaubens* (1533); *Počet z viery a z učenie křesťanského* (1536); *Apologia verae doctrinae* (1538). Über Augustas Veränderung des letztgenannten Textes im Geiste der Lutherschen Lehre behandelt Rohde: 2006, 130–133.

haben. Die Kirche ist eine Gemeinschaft, in der sich ein geistliches Geschehen ereignet – die Erfüllung durch den Heiligen Geist. Das Wesen der Kirche ist der geistlichen Natur. Weitere Kennzeichen der Kirche beziehen sich schon auf ein äußeres Geschehen. Sie betreffen die gegenseitige Kommunikation, die von dem Heiligen Geist angeregt wird und die gegenseitige Beziehungen stiftet. Die im Namen Christi versammelten Menschen pflegen das gesunde Wort Christi und seine reine Sakramente, reine Ordnungen und verschiedenartige Dienstbereitschaft untereinander und sie erweisen dem Gott entsprechende Ehre und den Dienst. Weil solche Versammlung sich auf die Verheißung der Gegenwart Christi verlassen kann, kann man sie als den Ort der geistlichen Gegenwart Christi in seinen Nachfolgern bezeichnen.

Es ist auffallend, dass Augusta in dieser Definition, die sehr ähnlich ebenso in anderen seiner Schriften vorkommt, ein bisschen anderen Akzent als Lukas von Prag setzt. Die gewöhnliche Lukassche Definition klingt: die Kirche sei „die Versammlung der von Gott Erwählten" und sie kommt ebenso in der deutschen Ausgabe der brüderischen Konfession mit Vorrede Luthers *Rechenschaft des Glaubens* (1533) vor: Die Kirche ist "die Zahl der Auserwählten Gottes im Namen Christi durchs Euangelion versammelt, sie sei gleich groß oder klein" (Rechenschaft: 1533, f. B4v).[32] Selbstverständlich weiß Augusta von der Erwählung als einer wesentlichen Voraussetzung dafür, dass der Mensch zum Nachfolger Christi wird und zum Glied seiner Kirche. In seiner *Kázání o víeře* („Predigt über den Glauben") in *Summovník* strukturiert er die Auslegung des Artikels über den Glauben an der heiligen Kirche nach dem Schema, das schon Lukas von Prag in seinen ekklesiologischen Texten benutzt. Am Anfang stehen die „Wahrheiten", die den wesentlichen Grund der Kirche beschreiben, nämlich die Personen und das Werk des dreifaltigen Gottes: (1) Die Erwählung und Berufung vom Gott, dem Vater, (2) Christus als Grund und Haupt der Kirche und das Band ihrer Einheit und (3) der Heilige Geist, der die Söhne und Töchter Gottes wiedergebiert und regiert (Augusta: 1570, f. D2r). Erst dann kommen die "dienlichen Wahrheiten" an die Reihe, nämlich, (4) dass die Kirche die "Versammlung des Volkes im Namen Jesu Christi, die heilige Gemeinschaft und seine Gesellschaft" ist, (5) "die von Christus gegebene Diener der Kirche", (6) "die Gabe Christi seines Wortes, seiner Gebote, seiner Ordnungen wie der Zucht, der Taufe, der Handauflegung, der Absolution, seines Tisches", (7) "die Gehorsamkeit der heiligen Kirche, des Gottes Vaters in Christus und des Herrn Christus in den Dienern Christi", (8) „das Gesetz Gottes, die der Kirche gegebenen und von ihr angenommenen heiligen Schriften, der Glaube im Herz und im Bekenntnis, die Liebe, die Hoffnung" (Augusta: 1570, f. D2v–D3r).

---

32 Näher über diese Schrift vgl. Schweitzer: 2013.

Jedoch in seinen ekklesiologischen Texten, die aus der Zeit seiner Polemik mit den utraquistischen Priestern stammen, beschäftigt sich Augusta eher damit, was man im Rahmen der brüderischen Theologie als die "dienliche Seite" der Kirche nennt. Es ruft die Frage heraus, womit diese Akzentverschiebung verursacht wurde. Waren es konkrete Probleme der Beziehungen unter den Kirchen, die Augustas Aufmerksamkeit eher auf die Ebene der Dienlichkeiten führten? Oder kann man die Ursache in Augustas Bemühung erblicken, das Wesen der Kirche konkreter als Lukas zu bestimmen und statt der abstrakten "Gemeinschaft der Vorerwählten" die Kirche als personale Gemeinschaft der konkreten Menschen am bestimmten Ort zu erfassen? Ich neige, wie ich im Folgenden zeigen werde, eher zur zweiten Möglichkeit.

Augusta legt den Wert auf Kirche als die wirkliche, konkrete und sichtbare Gemeinschaft der Glaubenden im Sinne einer neutestamentlichen *Ecclesia*, einer personalen Gemeinschaft Christi mit seinen Jüngern. Die Kirche ist keine nur abstrakte und beziehungslose Summe von allen Erwählten, sondern eine wirkliche Gemeinschaft der Christen mit dem auferstandenen Christus und miteinander. In der Vorrede zur tschechischen Übersetzung der Schrift Luthers *Von den Konziliis und Kirchen* schreibt er:

> Wenn die Kirche eine Kirche Christi sein soll, muss ein Volk in seinem Namen beieinander sein, denn die Kirche ist nichts anderes als eine Versammlung, sie ist weder eine Zerstreuung noch eine Auseinanderwerfung des einen hin des anderen her. Obwohl hier und da auf der ganzen Welt die von Gott Auserwählten und Berufenen sind, kein von ihnen allein ist und kann sein die Kirche, denn er ist nicht mehr als ein Glied der Kirche. Aber wo sich solche Menschen in einer kleineren oder größeren Menge versammeln, obwohl es ihnen manche listig beimischen (Daniel in xi), dort ist erst die Kirche, nämlich die Versammlung oder, wie man es erklärt, die Gemeinschaft der Heiligen, die die gegenseitige Gemeinschaft der dem Gott Glaubenden und der Geheiligten und die personale Verweilung ist. Worüber der Glaubensartikel klingt und erzählt. (Luther: 1540, f. E1v–E2r).

In der Schrift *Dialog dvou formanů* (1543) drückt sich Augusta dann ausdrücklich kritisch zum Konzept der Unterscheidung zwischen der sichtbaren und unsichtbaren Kirche, die Řezník in seiner Schrift gegen *Zrcadlo kněžské* ("Priesterspiegel") machte:

> Er teilt die Kirche in zwei. Die eine sei sichtbar und die andere unsichtbar, geistlich. Der Grund und Fundament der unsichtbaren sei Christus und wer auch immer in ihr sei, erlöst werde. Dann sagt er, dass sie in der unsichtbaren Kirche seien. (Augusta: 1543b, f. E1v).

Ironisch fragt er, welche Entität mit der unsichtbaren Kirche bei Řezník überhaupt gemeint wird: ob die mit Christus triumphierende Kirche im Himmel oder die sog. schlafende Kirche, die im Fegefeuer ist? Denn diese beide sind wirklich unsichtbar. Doch, es ist offenbar, dass bei Řezník mit der unsichtbaren Kirche noch eine andere Entität gemeint wird als *ecclesia triumfans* oder *ecclesia dormiens*, nämlich die Kirche im Sinne einer rein geistlichen Wirklichkeit, die etwa wie eine platonische Idee die wahre Realität darstellt. Ebenso hier erblickt Augusta jedoch einen Widerspruch. Obwohl die utraquistische Kirche selbst eine "sichtbare Rotte" ist, ihre Theologen "formen und vergeistigen irgendwelche gedachte Kirche, von der sie nicht einmal wissen, was und wo sie ist" (Augusta: 1543b, f. E2r).

Augusta lehnt das Konzept der sichtbaren und unsichtbaren Kirche als eine Erfindung ab, die nur in einen unüberwindbaren Widerspruch einmündet, denn es bewirkt die Trennung der Kirche in zwei separate Wirklichkeiten. Dagegen weist er auf eine eindeutig sichtbare Gestalt der Kirche hin, die im Neuen Testament von den Aposteln bezeugt wird:

> Die Apostel haben sich zu den sichtbaren Kirchen bekannt, wie der heilige Paulus [...] und schreibend an sichtbare, gegenwärtige, leibliche Christen, schrieb er der Kirche Gottes, die in Korinth, der Kirche Gottes, die in Galatien, der Kirche der Thessalonicher [...] Und Glaubende strömten dieser sichtbaren apostolischen Kirche zu [...] (Augusta: 1543b, f. E2r).

Augusta übernimmt also die neutestamentliche Auffassung der Kirche, wonach die Kirche primär im Sinne einer konkreten Ortsgemeinde verstanden wird, die durch die personale Beziehung der Einzelnen mit Christus und durch die personale Beziehungen untereinander konstituiert wird.

Nachdem wir die "sichtbare Versammlung der Glaubenden" als das wesentliche Moment Augustas Kirchenbegriffs behandelten, müssen wir ebenso seine abgekehrte Seite – die Trennung – betrachten. Denn wo die heilige Kirche Christi entsteht, dort tritt gleichzeitig die Trennung der Glaubenden von den Ungläubenden ein. Die im Namen Christi versammelten Christen müssen sich, wie Augusta bemerkt, "von denen absondern oder trennen, die sich an dem Glauben nicht halten oder ihm nicht befolgen und untertan sind" (Luther: 1540, f. D5v). Durch dieses Argument verteidigt er die Entscheidung der Böhmischen Brüder, sich von Rom zu trennen, gegen die Beschuldigungen, die Brüderunität trennte sich als eine Sekte von der einen heiligen und allgemeinen Kirche. In der Perspektive der Brüder trennten sie sich nicht von der Kirche Christi, sondern nur von einer unvollkommenen Gestalt dieser Kirche, damit sie als wahre *ecclesia Christi* im gehorsam des Gesetzes Christi leben konnten (vgl. Augusta: 1543a, f. O1v–R1v; Augusta: 1543b, f. K1r–K3v).

Gleichzeitig gewann die Auffassung der Kirche als einer Schar der Bußfertigen und nach der besseren Gerechtigkeit trachtenden, die sich von den Gottlosen trennen, ein Gegengewicht in der Betonung der Gemeinschaftlichkeit des Glaubens. Augusta hält daran fest, dass die Christen das Heil nur in der Gemeinschaft von anderen Gleichgesinnten erlangen können; das Leben in der Gemeinde versteht er als einen notwendigen Teil im Prozess der Heilsvermittlung und Heilszueignung. In der Vorrede zu Luthers Schrift schreibt er:

> Denn ohne die Gemeinschaft und bewusste Verknüpfung der Kirchenmitglieder, die einander kennen, können diese Dinge nicht geschehen, stattfinden und vorkommen, die zur heiligen Kirche wesentlich gehören [...] Und wo dies nicht gibt, dort gibt es gewiss keine Kirche und keine wahre Glieder Christi. (Luther: 1540, f. E3r).

4.2 Kirche Gottes *versus* Kirche des Teufels als offenbare und verborgene Wirklichkeiten

Im Anschluss an Lukas von Prag finden wir bei Augusta die Ansicht, dass die gesamte Christenheit ein *corpus permixtum* ist, deshalb schließt sie zwei Teile ein: die Kirche Gottes und die Kirche des Teufels. Die Kirche Gottes enthält – wie Augusta mithilfe der Bilder der Gleichnisse Jesu sagt – die Söhne Gottes, Weizen, gute Fische, vorsichtige Jungfrauen etc. In der Kirche des Teufels befinden sich dagegen die Söhne des Teufels, Unkraut, böse Fische, verwirrte Jungfrauen etc. (Augusta: 1543a, f. L4v).[33] Von Lukas übernimmt er ebenso die Vorstellung, dass die Geschichte durch einen Kampf zwischen den beiden Kirchen wesentlich geprägt sei. Die Gegenwart wird als die Zeit einer verstärkten Wirksamkeit des Antichrists betrachtet, der in die Kirche unter dem Schein der Wahrheit eindringt. Auf diesen bezieht Augusta viele Texte der kritischen alttestamentlichen Prophetie und fordert zu seiner Vernichtung, aber nicht durch Gewaltmittel, sondern durch den Geist Christi (ein wesentliches Ding) und durch das reine Verwaltung des Wortes und der Sakramente (dienliche Dinge) (Augusta: 1543a, f. N1v–N2r). Die Erneuerung der Kirche wird also sowohl als das Werk Gottes als auch die Aufgabe der Christen aufgefasst. Den Maßstab für die Erneuerung erblickt er – wie schon die alten Brüder – in der Schrift und im Vorbild der ursprünglichen apostolischen Kirche.

Die weitere Differenzierung der beiden Kirchen nach dem Schema wesentlich – dienlich, wie sie bei Lukas von Prag vorkommt, finden wir bei Augusta nicht mehr, sowie die zeitliche Differenzierung der vergangenen, gegenwärtigen und der zukünftigen Kirche. Stattdessen – wahrscheinlich unter dem Einfluss von Luther – führt er eine andere Einteilung ein, und zwar zwischen dem Verborgenen und dem Offenbaren. Die Kirche Gottes hat zwei Teile: der eine Teil is "geheim und verborgen" ("tejný a skrytý"), der zweite Teil "offenbar und deutlich" ("zjevný a

---

33 Vgl. ähnlich: Augusta: 1543b, f. B1v; *Počet z viery* (1536), VIII/3.

zřetedlný"). Ebenso im Rahmen der Behandlung über die Kirche des Teufels unterscheidet Augusta zwischen den geheimen Sündern und den offenbar bösen und die Empörung erregenden Christen (Augusta: 1543a, f. M3r). Daneben arbeitet er hier noch mit einer dritten Kategorie, die des Antikrists, in die alle gehören, die sich dem Christus widersetzen.

Augustas Unterscheidung zwischen dem verborgenen und offenbaren Teil der Kirche ruft die Frage hervor, in welchem Sinne diese Unterscheidung gemeint wird. Weist er vielleicht auf ein verborgenes geistliches Wesen der Kirche hin, das unsichtbar und sinnlich nicht wahrnehmbar ist? Diese Unterscheidung lehnte er jedoch ab, wie wir oben gesehen haben. In seiner Auffassung ist die irdische Kirche immer sichtbar, weil sie die Versammlung der Menschen ist, die leibliche Wesen sind. Oder kann man diese Unterscheidung als eine Analogie zur Lukasschen Unterscheidung zwischen der wesentlichen und dienlichen Kirche verstehen? Falls ja, dann könnte die "verborgene Kirche" als Bezeichnung für die wesentliche Kirche dienen, die – wie Lukas betont – nur dem Schau des Glaubens offenbar ist, und die "offenbare Kirche" mit der dienlichen Kirche korrespondieren, die die konkrete geschichtliche Kirchengemeinschaften bezeichnet. Doch, bei der näheren Analyse von Augustas Texten sehen wir, dass Augusta die Begriffe – vielleicht unter dem Einfluss von Luther – nicht gerade in diesem Sinne benutzt. Es geht ihm nicht darum, die Problematik der universalen und den partikulären Kirchen auszudrücken, sondern eher um einen Versuch, die Problematik der wahren und falschen Kirche zu erfassen.

Im Kontext der Debatte darüber, welche Kirche als wahre Kirche Christi bezeichnet werden kann, stellt die Unterscheidung des verborgenen und offenbaren Teils der Kirche ein Begriffsmittel zur Beschreibung der Komplexität dieser Problematik dar. Mit der Rede von einem verborgenen Teil der Kirche Gottes versucht er – wie ich vermute – die Tatsache auszudrücken, dass es ebenso in der Kirche, die nach außen keine Zeichen der wahren Kirche trägt, die Christen sein können, an denen Gott selbst seine Verheißung der Ausgießung des Geistes (Jo 3:1) und der Gabe des Herzen aus dem Fleisch (Hes 36:26) erfüllte. Es handelt sich also um die Menschen, an denen Gott sein Werk der inneren Verwandlung und Erneuerung tut, obwohl diese Erneuerung durch das Maß von ihrer bewussten Erkenntnis der Wahrheit begrenzt wird. Für diese innere Verwandlung vergibt ihnen Gott ihr verirrtes und sündiges Handeln, das sie aus Unkenntnis begehen (Augusta: 1543a, M1r).

Dieser Teil der Kirche Gottes ist im strengen Sinne nicht "unsichtbar", denn lebendige Menschen sind immer sichtbar, sondern er ist nur dem menschlichen Blick verborgen, denn von diesen verborgenen Christen weiß nur Gott selbst. In diesem Zusammenhang weist Augusta auf 1Kö 19:18 hin, wo der Herr von sieben Tausend denen redet, die der Götzerei nicht erlagen, aber der Prophet Elia wusste von ihnen nicht, "denn sie sind geheim und waren verborgen, dem Gott allein bekannt und bewusst" (Augusta: 1543b, f. M1r). Die Vorstellung der verborgenen

Christen im Rahmen der verdorbenen Kirche kann allerdings ein Widerhall von Luthers Gedanken sein, denn geradezu in der tschechischen Übersetzung seiner Schrift *Zrcadlo kněžské* dasselbe Beispiel zur Illustration desselben Gedankens vorkommt (Luther: 1542, f. D6r).

Neben den verborgenen Christen gibt es die, die offenbar als Teil der Kirche Gottes erkannt werden können, weil sie die äußeren Merkmale dieser Zugehörigkeit ausweisen. Den offenbaren Teil der Kirche charakterisiert Augusta als die Christenheit, die sich nicht nur innerlich, sondern auch äußerlich von den erkannten Irrtümern distanziert. Ihr Leben zeichnet sich durch einen "reineren Dienst" ("čistší přisluhování") aus, das heißt durch die bessere Verwaltung (*regiment*) der Kirche im Bereich dessen, was zum Heil dient. Das wird durch eine bessere Erkenntnis ermöglicht. Konkret nennt Augusta vier Aspekte, die für die offenbare Kirche Gottes kennzeichnend sind:

(1) Die reine und gesunde Lehre und Predigt des Wortes Gottes in dem Sinne, wie es vom Heiligen Geist gemeint wird. (2) Die reine, ordnungsgemäße und fromme Verwendung der Sakramente im Geiste Christi und mit Zweck, zu dem sie von Christus eingesetzt und von der ersten Kirche gebraucht wurden. (3) Das reine, fromme, und ordnungsgemäße Licht, das die Diener und Verwalter der Kirche Gottes sind (vgl. Mt 5,14). (4) Der reine, klare und vor Wahrheit Gottes strahlende geistliche Körper Christi, der die Gemeinschaft des Volkes mit den Verwaltern ist, die zum Kopf, Christus, in heiliger Gehorsamkeit angeschlossen ist. Das Leben der kirchlichen Gemeinschaft samt der Priesterschaft wird dann noch weiter ausführlich beschrieben. Die Christen in der offenbaren Kirche Gottes leben alle in Frieden miteinander, gleichzeitig dulden sie aber keine offenkundigen Sünder, sondern führen sie zur Busse und Besserung. Sie üben die Zucht durch die Verweisung von Sakramenten oder aus der Gemeinde, sie machen alles nach dem Wille Christi und Gottes, sie pflegen die reinen, guten und heiligen Ordnungen und einen wahren, reinen, durch keine Abgötterei geschändeten Gottesdienst (Augusta: 1543a, f. M1r–M2r).

Diese vier "Dinge", bzw. Aspekte, die Augusta als offenbare Zeichen der Kirche Gottes anführt, versteht er als von Christus selbst eingesetzt. Überall, wo sie vorkommen, ist die offensichtliche und wahrnehmbare wahre und reine Kirche Christi, wie sie in der Apostelzeit war. Die wahre Kirche Christi lässt sich danach erkennen, dass in ihr – im Unterschied zur traditionellen Definition Bellarmins – nicht die Regierung des Kirchenamts, sondern die reine "Regierung Christi" herrscht, der reine Dienst des Wortes und der Sakramente und die gegenseitige Gemeinsamkeit. Solche Kirche kann sich sicher sein, dass sie keine "Sekte der Verwerfung" ist, sondern eine "dem Gott und Christus liebe Kirche des Heils" (Augusta: 1543a, f. M2r).

In seinem Verständnis der Verborgenheit der Kirche scheint Augusta der Auffassung Luthers nahe zu sein. Für Luther ist die Kirche in erster Linie ein Bund des

Glaubens und des Heiligen Geistes in den Herzen. Gleichzeitig hat sie aber auch äußere Kennzeichen, um erkannt zu werden (vgl. Apol. VII,5.20; zit. nach Wenz: 2005, 66). Ebenso für Augusta ist das Wesen der Kirche der geistlichen Natur. Die Kirche schließt diejenigen ein, die sich im Namen Christi versammeln und seinen Geist in sich haben. Doch dieses Geschehen wird immer an leiblichen Menschen gebunden, deswegen verweigert er, die Kirche als eine unsichtbare Wirklichkeit zu bezeichnen. Es gibt keine nur geistliche Kirche irgendwo im Himmel, sondern es gibt nur eine Kirche, und zwar die Kirche, die von den Menschen hier auf Erden geschaffen wird. In ihrem Rahmen kann man diejenigen unterscheiden, die durch den Geist Christi wirklich verwandelt werden, und die, die ihr nur äußerlich, aber nicht innerlich angehören.

Über die Zeichen der wahren Kirche Gottes behandelt Augusta ebenso in seiner Vorrede zur tschechischen Übersetzung von Luthers Schrift *Von den Konziliis und Kirchen*. Seiner Meinung nach, jeder Mensch sollte wissen, "wonach solche Kirche oder solches Volk erkannt werden kann und wo es gefunden werden könnte" (Luther: 1540, f. E5r). Zu diesem Zweck soll ebenso Luthers Schrift dienen. Nach Luther sind die Zeichen der heiligen Kirche sieben – das rein gepredigte Wort Gottes, die Taufe, das Altarsakrament, die Schlüssel Christi, die Berufung der Kirchendiener, Gebete, Lob und Danksagung, das Kreuz (das Leiden). Der Übersetzer hat doch einen Bedarf empfunden, diese Aufzählung noch zu ergänzen, deshalb fügte er der Schrift einen ziemlich umfangreichen Anhang mit weiteren Kennzeichen der heiligen Kirche zu, und zwar "nicht weil die ersten nicht genügend wären, sondern damit jeder [...] eine reichere Hilfe zu seinem Bedarf hätte" (Luther: 1540, f. H8v).

Als erstes Zeichen wird angeführt: die häufige Verwendung des Wortes Gottes, der Sakramente und Ordnungen im Dienst des Glaubens, der Liebe und der Hoffnung, und die Unterscheidung seiner dienlichen Funktion für das Heil. Das zweite Zeichen ist die Einmütigkeit der verschiedenen Glieder in einem Leib Christi und die freiwillige Unterwerfung der Ordnung. Das dritte Zeichen ist die ordnungsmäßige Zucht des Herrn: das Volk tut Busse, verbessert sich und gibt keinen Raum dem Bösen.

4.3 Einzelne Unitäten – die eine heilige Kirche Christi

Augusta hält die Suche nach der wahren Kirche Christi für die Aufgabe aller Christen. Jeder, der nach dem Heil verlangt, hat die Pflicht in der Kirche zu sein, die er als reiner erkennt (vgl. Počet z viery: 1536, VIII/5). Deshalb empfiehlt der brüderische Bischof den Übergang aus einer Kirche in die andere, wenn diese als reiner gefunden wird. Das bewusste Leben in einer verirrten und sündigen Kirche schiebt die Schuld vom Menschen nicht. Er selbst erinnert sich an seinen eigenen Weg aus der utraquistischen Kirche in die Brüderunität, der durch eine tiefere Erkenntnis geleitet wurde (Augusta: 1543b, f. M2v). Diese Forderung ist nicht nur eine Folge des Gedankens von der vollen Religionsfreiheit des Menschen, sondern ebenso der Ausdruck eines Vertrauens in die Fähigkeit des Menschen, die Verantwortung für eigenes Handeln zu übernehmen und sein Leben nach eigenem Gewissen selbst zu steuern.

Wie begreift die Brüderunität sich selbst und die anderen Kirchen im Verhältnis zur wahren Kirche Gottes? Der Kirchenbegriff Augustas knüpft hier an die Ansichten, die schon bei den älteren Theologen der Brüderunität vorkamen und die sich durch Demut und außerordentliche Toleranz zu anderen Kirchen auszeichnen. Alle christliche Kirchen – "Sekten", "Teile" oder "Unitäten" – aus irgendwelchen Nationen und an irgendwelchen Orten bilden eine christliche Gemeinschaft zusammen. Erst die Gesamtheit aller Christen wird als die eine Kirche Christi genannt (Augusta: 1543a, f. L4r–L4v). Deshalb hatte die Brüderunität öfters nicht einmal die Bezeichnung „Kirche" für sich selbst beansprucht, weil sie diese als den Gesamtbegriff verwendet hat und sich selbst als einen Teil der Kirche Christi bezeichnet. Diese Sicht hatte konkrete Folgen für die Auffassung der Mitgliedschaft in der Unität[34] und für das Verhältnis zu den Konvertiten. Nach der brüderischen Konfession sollte das Christsein eines Konvertiten nicht bezweifelt werden. Wenn ein Glied der einen Kirche in eine andere übertritt, dann hört er nicht auf, ein Christ zu sein, und verliert nichts von den Gaben und Verheißungen Christi (vgl. Počet z viery: 1536, VIII/7).

Die Einheit der wahren Kirche Christi suchte Augusta nicht in den äußerlichen Ordnungen und der gemeinsamen institutionellen Verwaltung, sondern im Bereich der geistlichen Werte: "in einer Wahrheit Christi, in einem Geist des Glaubens, der Liebe und der Hoffnung; dies Ding macht die eine Kirche Christi aus vielen Gliedern und Kirchen oder Gemeinden". (Augusta: "Vorrede" in Luther: 1540, f. E4v.) Augustas ekklesiologische Model der Einheit kann man mit Recht als die Einheit in der Verschiedenheit bezeichnen. Dieses Modell, das durch seine nichtinstitutionelle Auffassung der Kirche ermöglicht wird, öffnet einen Raum für die gegenseitige Anerkennung der Kirchen als Teile der einen Kirche Christi und ihre ökumenische Gemeinschaft. Gleichzeitig bringt die Betonung der sichtbaren Zeichen der wahren Kirche Impulse für die Erneuerung der Kirchen und dafür, damit sie das Sonderrecht, die Kirche Christi zu sein, ernst nehmen würden.

---

34 Drei Stufen der Mitgliedschaft in der Brüderunität und ihre Wurzel in der mittelalterlichen Mystik sowie bei Chelčický behandelt Molnár: 1956a; 1956b, 12–25.

5. Religiöse Freiheit und Toleranz im Augustas Kirchenbegriff

Die Brüderunität lebte die ganze Zeit ihrer Existenz als eine Minderheitskirche und dieser Realität musste sie ihre Ekklesiologie anzupassen. Diese Erfahrung beeinflusste zweifellos ebenso den Augustas Kirchenbegriff, der sich von der Ekklesiologie seiner Zeitgenossen in der utraquistischen Kirche deutlich unterscheidet.

Für Augustas Kirchenbegriff ist eine selektive und personalistische Auffassung der Kirche kennzeichnend, die sich gegen die universalistische und institutionelle Auffassung der Utraquisten stellt. Die heilige Kirche Christi ist nicht überall, wo das Kirchenamt in der apostolischen Sukzession verrichtet wird. Augusta plädiert für die Kirche als Gemeinschaft der Erwählten, die ihre Erwählung ernst nehmen, sich im Namen Jesu Christi freiwillig versammeln und seinen Weg ganz bewusst begehen wollen. Die Kirche Christi ist eine Gemeinschaft, die durch die gegenseitige Beziehung mit Christus und mit anderen Christen geschaffen wird. Es ist die Gemeinschaft der bewussten Christen, die die befreiende Botschaft annehmen und ihre Dankbarkeit dafür in alle Bereiche ihres Lebens umwandeln. Diese Auffassung entspricht allerdings der faktischen Gestalt der Brüderunität, die aus den einzelnen zerstreuten Gemeinden der bewussten Mitglieder der Unität bestand, während die Organisation der utraquistischen Kirche die vorreformatorische territoriale Struktur der Pfarrbezirke übernahm (vgl. Kurka: 2014, 283).

Während im Utraquismus sowie im Luthertum man der Bemühung um die Bildung einer einheitlichen Kirchenorganisation nach dem Prinzip *cuius regio, eius religio* begegnet (vgl. Kurka: 2014, 282), lehnte die Brüderunität die Verbindung der Religion mit der weltlichen Macht eindeutig ab und strebte nach der vollen religiösen Freiheit des Menschen. Infolgedessen wurde die institutionelle Kirche von den Brüdern nicht als territoriale Kirche, sondern als freiwillige Gemeinschaft (*voluntary church*) verstanden und gestaltet (Craig: 2009, 404). Die Kirchenmitgliedschaft wurde bei den Brüdern zur Sache einer persönlichen Wahl nach dem eigenen Gewissen. Niemand durfte zur Kirchenmitgliedschaft gezwungen werden.

Die Betonung der persönlichen Verantwortung der einzelnen Christen ist ebenso für Augusta bezeichnend. In seinen Schriften wendet er sich häufig nicht nur an Priester, sondern ebenso an Laien mit der Aufforderung, damit sie die Gestalt der eigenen Kirche nach den von ihm vorgelegten Zeichen der wahren Kirche überprüfen und die Entscheidung für die Mitgliedschaft in dieser oder jener Kirche nach ihrem eigenen Gewissen selbst treffen. Es ist offenbar, dass Augusta in seiner Ekklesiologie ein individuelles Bewusstsein der religiösen Freiheit implizit voraussetzt. Jeder Mensch hat das Recht sich frei zu entscheiden für die Mitgliedschaft in derjenigen Kirche, wo er die Wahrheit Gottes erkennt (vgl. Augusta/Řezník: 1542, f. B4r). Die Entscheidung steht in der Kompetenz jedes Einzelnen und hängt von seinem Gewissen ab. Gleichzeitig ist sich Augusta dessen bewusst, dass dieses Vorgehen ihre Grenzen in den kognitiven Fähigkeiten der Menschen sowie im provisorischen Charakter der Kirchen hat. Deshalb spricht er nicht von der Suche nach einer vollkommenen Kirche, sondern realistisch von der Suche nach "einem reineren Teil der heiligen Kirche" (Počet z viery: 1536, VIII/5).

Der Kirchenbegriff von Johannes Augusta ist höchst ökumenisch und das Ausmaß seiner Offenheit ungewöhnlich groß. Er beanspruchte den Begriff der Kirche Christi niemals ausschließlich für die Brüderunität, sondern er verstand sie immer nur als einen Teil der wahren Kirche Gottes. Dieses Bewusstsein bewirkte seine tolerante Sicht auf andere Kirchengestalten, denen er die Teilnahme an der einen heiligen apostolischen Kirche Christi nicht vorenthielt. Ebenso die Trennung von der einen kirchlichen Institution setzte er nicht mit der Trennung von Christus gleich.

In der Gesamtheit kann man in dem ekklesiologischen Konzept der Brüderunität eine gewisse Spannung spüren. Auf der einen Seite begegnen wir einer tiefen Bescheidenheit, was das Selbstverständnis und die Selbsteinschätzung der Brüderunität betrifft, auf der anderen Seite kann man den Eindruck bekommen, dass die Brüderunität durch die Betonung der bewussten und verantwortlichen Mitgliedschaft einen Elitencharakter erwarb. Die Neugekommenen mussten beim Eintritt in die Gemeinde ihr Christsein erweisen, indem sie sich zu ihrer Taufe bekannten. An die Mitglieder wurden hohe ethische als auch spirituelle Anforderung gelegen (vgl. Halama: 2003), was von der utraquistischen Seite öfters verspottet wurde.

Diese Spannung versuchte Augusta mithilfe des Gedankens lösen, dass der Raum der wahren Kirche breiter ist, als er dem menschlichen Blick erscheint. Er lässt zu, dass Christus sein Werk ebenso dort tun kann und tut, wo die Kirchendiener Heuchler und tote Christen sind. Das ist ein "verborgener Teil" der Kirche Gottes, von dem nur Gott selbst weiß. Genaue Grenzen der wahren Kirche werden der menschlichen Sicht verborgen. Damit wird gleichzeitig die kriteriale Natur der äußeren Zeichen der wahren Kirche relativiert, denn die Kirche Gottes im Sinne einer personalen Gemeinschaft mit Christus kann ebenso dort sein, wo die äußere Zeichen der wahren Kirche fehlen.

Bibliographie

Quellen

Apologia verae doctrinae eorum qui vulgo apellantur Valdenses vel Picardi [...] (1538), Wittenberg: Georg Rhau. (Prag, Nationalbibliothek: 46 B 000152.)

AUGUSTA, JAN (1532), Rozmlouvanie jednoho muže učeného, čest a rozkoš světa viece nežli Boha milujícího, druhého neučeného ačkoli sedlského však Boha a spasenie znajicího člověka, [Mladá Boleslav]: Carmelita [=Jindřich Šturm?]. (*Knihopis* Nu. 852. Göttingen,

Univesitätsbibliothek: H. E. Eccl. 98 a; Prag, Nationalbibliothek: f Zc 26.)

AUGUSTA, JAN (1534), Kniežka tato bez titule jest o tomto: jestli to pravda by to člověk jistotně věděti mohl, že spasen bude, [Leitomischl: Alexander Oujezdecký]. (*Knihopis* Nu. 846. Stockholm, Königliche Bibliothek: Theol. Reform. Luther 173 Dd.)

AUGUSTA, JAN (1535), Kázaní o stavu manželském, kteréž se jest stalo v zboru litomyšlském od Jana Augusty zprávce téhož zboru [...], Manuskript. (Prag, Bibliothek der königlichen Kanonie der Premonstraten, Strahov: DG VI 21.)

AUGUSTA, JAN (1537), Pravidlo těch, jenž sbory Páně navštěvují a k nim dohlídají, Manuskript. (Prag, Bibliothek des Nationalmuseums: I H 37.)

AUGUSTA, JAN (1540a), [O Závazcích křesťanských Zákona Kristova, Leitomischl: Alexander Oujezdecký (?).] (*Knihopis* Nu. 857. Unerhalten.)

AUGUSTA, JAN (1540b), Kázanie o ustavenie na biskupstvie svatého Matěje miesto Jidáše, Leitomischl. (*Knihopis* Nu. 845. Prag, Nationalbibliothek: 54 S 194 přív. 2.)

AUGUSTA, JAN (1541), Ohlašenie a ozvánie Jana Augusty proti té knížce kněžské pod titulem kněze Petra Faráře v Zásadí v Litoměřic[ích] vydané, Leitomischl: Alexander Oujezdecký. (*Knihopis* Nu. 848. Brünn, Mährische Landesbibliothek: ST 50646 přív.)

AUGUSTA, JAN (ed.) (1542), List neb Spiesek starých bratří davno udělaný. S předmluvou obšírnou však potřebnou. Kteryž se nynie znovu z p[ři]čin nynějších proti bratřím kněžskych psaní vydava, [Leitomischl: Alexander Oujezdecký]. (*Knihopis* Nu. 5023. Prag, Nationalbibliothek: 54 B 127 přív.)

AUGUSTA, JAN/ŘEZNÍK, WENZEL (1542), Listove a psaní kněze Vaclava [Řezníka] Pana Děkana nyní na Horach Kutnach. A Kašpara Soukeníka Měštěnina litomyšlského, kteraž to tehdy [= 1532] se mezi nimi zběhla, když byl farařem v Lithomyšli, [Olomouc: Jan Olivetský z Olivetu starší]. (*Knihopis* Nu. 15187. Prag, Nationalbibliothek: 54 B 94 přív.)

AUGUSTA, JAN (1543a), Pře Jana Augusty a kněžstva kališného od něho saméhо věrně a pravě sepsaná všem vuobec k soudu podaná, s.l.: s.n. (*Knihopis* Nu. 850. Prag, Nationalbibliothek: 54 G 9526 přív.)

AUGUSTA, JAN (1543b), Dialog, to jest, dvou formanuo rozmlouvaní, Peterky a Valoucha, přepotřebné: o učení a víře kněze Vaclawa [Řezníka], děkana na Horach Gutnach, nyní vnově od jednoho učitele Jednoty bratrske k potřebě věrnejch vydany, Prostějov: Jan Olivetský z Olivetu starší. (*Knihopis* Nu. 16003. Prag, Nationalbibliothek: 54 B 94 přív. 3.)

AUGUSTA, JAN (1544a), Svědectvie pobožné o urozené paní, paní Justině z Kunštátu, paní manželce urozeného pána, pana Bohuše Kostky z Postupic a na Litomyšli, učiněné v zboru litomyšlském od bratra Johannesa Augusty, Leitomischl. (*Knihopis* Nu. 854. Prag, Bibliothek des Nationalmuseums: 37 B 21 přív. 3.)

AUGUSTA, JAN (1544b), O vyobcování dvou osob hřiešných ze zboru litomyšlského stalém skrze Jana Augustu. [...] Leitomischl. (*Knihopis* Nu. 856. Prag, Bibliothek des Nationalmuseums: 37 B 21.)

AUGUSTA, JAN /ČERNÝ, JAN (cca 1558), [Registrum aneb Zpráva, co se kdy a o čem čísti má z Písem svatých.] s.l.: s.n. (*Knihopis* Nu. 14 768. Prag, Nationalbibliothek: 54 B 81 unvollständig.)

AUGUSTA, JAN (1560), Umění práce díla Páně služebného dary a milostmi od Krista Pána služebníkuom od něho poslaným danými a svěřenými [...] [Prostějov: Kašpar Aorg (?)]. Prag, Nationalbibliothek: 54 F 1122 unvollständig.)

AUGUSTA, JAN (1570), První díl knih služby Slova Božího, [Prag: Jiří starší Melantrich z Aventýna]. (*Knihopis* Nu. 4055. Prag, Nationalbibliothek: 54 B 5.) [= sog. Summovník]

BEDNÁŘ, FRANTIŠEK (ed.) (1941), Jan Augusta: Umění práce díla Páně služebného, Prag: Královská česká společnost nauk.

BUCER, MARTIN (1545), Kníha o opravdové péči o duše [...], übersetzt wahrscheinlich von Jan Roh, Leitomischl: Alexander Oujezdecký. (*Knihopis* Nu. 1386. Brünn, Mährische Landesbibliothek: ST 1–24.972)

BYDŽOVSKÝ, PAVEL (1543), Tento spis ukazuje, že biskupové biskupa a biskup kněží a kněží od řádných biskupuo svěceni těla a krve Boží posvěcovati mají, s.l.: s.n. (*Knihopis* Nu. 1396. Prag, Nationalbibliothek: 54 I 12498.)

ČEJKA, MIREK/ŠLOSAR, DUŠAN/NECHUTOVÁ, JANA (ed.) (1991), Gramatika česká Jana Blahoslava, Brno: Masarykova univerzita.

ČERNÝ, JAN (1543–1546), Poznamenání některých skutků Božích obzvláštních, Manuskript. (Herrnhut, Unitätsarchiv.).

HALAMA, OTA (ed.) (2006), Edice zlomku postily Lukáše Pražského, in Miscellanea: Oddělení rukopisů a starých tisků, 19, Prag: NK ČR, 92–132.

HALAMA, OTA/MAREK, JINDŘICH (ed.) (2009), Pohřební kázání Jana Augusty o Justině z Kunštátu (1544), in Martin Wernisch (ed.), Unitas Fratrum 1457–2007: Jednota bratrská jako kulturní a duchovní fenomén, SAT ETF 15/2, 146–164.

KLATOVSKÝ, MARTIN (1544), *Rozsuzování upřimne arkykuluov(!) niekterych z Pře Jana Augusty | kterouž pod jmenem Kniežstva proti všemu křesťanstvu vuobec krom sekty vaľdenské vydaľ (...)* Prag: Ondřej Kubeš. (Knihopis Nu. 3937. Prag, Nationalbibliothek: foto f Zb 18.

KŘÍŽEK, WENZEL (1542), Čech valdenský, unbekannt.

LUTHER, MARTIN (1540), [O pravém užívání klíčův pravých. O církvi svaté a o jistých znameních]. Übersetzt und mit den Vorworten versehen von Jan Augusta, Leitomischl: Alexander Oujezdecký. (*Knihopis* Nu. 5114. London: The British Library: C 107.bb.19, unvollständig; Prag, Nationalbibliothek: foto 84 f.)

LUTHER, MARTIN (1542), Zrcadlo knězske Doktora Martina Lutera, v němž se spatřuje, kdo jso starou cierkví Kristovou a kdo novou antikristovou, übersetzt von Jan Augusta, Leitomischl: Alexander Oujezdecký. (*Knihopis* Nu. 5128. Brünn, Mährische Landesbibliothek: ST 1–50.646 přív. 4, unvollständig.)

MOLNÁR, AMEDEO (ed.) (1972), Čeští bratří a Martin Bucer: Listy kritického přátelství, Prag: Ústřední církevní nakladatelství.

MOLNÁR, AMEDEO (ed.) (1979), Bekenntnisse der Böhmischen Brüder, Hildesheim: Georg Olms.

Počet z viery a z učenie křesťanského králi jeho milosti v Vídni podaný od pánuov a rytieřstva Kralovstvija českého, kteříž jsú z Jednoty bratřie zákona Kristova. Léta 1.5.3.5. [...] (1536),

[Mladá Boleslav]. (*Knihopis* Nu. 1599. Prag, Bibliothek des Nationalmuseums: 37 B 21 přív.)

PRAŽSKÝ, LUKÁŠ (1522), O puovodu cierkvie svaté, v pravdě svatosti jejie [...], [Mladá Boleslav: Jiří Štyrsa]. (*Knihopis* Nu. 5030. Prag, Bibliothek des Nationalmuseums: sign. 25 D 17 přív.)

PRAŽSKÝ, LUKÁŠ (1762), O puovodu cierkvie svaté, v pravdě svatosti jejie [...], Kaliningrad: Jan Fridrich Driste, 1762. (*Knihopis* Nu. 5031. Prag, Nationalbibliothek: 54 E 439.)

RECHENSCHAFT (1533), Rechenschaft des Glaubens, der Dienst und Ceremonien, der Brüder in Behemen und Mehrern, welche von ettlichen Pickarten unnd von etlichen Waldenser genannt werden. Sampt ainer nützlichen Vorrhede Doct. Mar. Luther (1533), [Augsburg: Philipp Ulhart]. (Brünn, Mährische Landesbibliothek: ST1–0029.038.)

ŘEZNÍK, VÁCLAV (1542a), Zpráva a ukázaní proti zlému a falešnému požívaní Písem Svatých v tom spisu, kterýž smyslil, složil i vydal jakýs Bratr Jan Augusta, starší zboru Lithomyšlského o závazcích (tak jakož sám píše) křesťanských Zákona Kristova, Prag: Bartoloměj Netolický z Netolic. (*Knihopis* Nu. 15189. Prag, Nationalbibliothek: foto 3 f.)

ŘEZNÍK, VÁCLAV (1542b), Tato knížka proti tomu Zrcadlu kněžskemu, kteréž Jan Augusta, starší zboru litomyslského lstivou a podvodnou předmluvou přivodíl a vokřtaltoval a pod jménem Doktora Martina Lutera hrozným rouháním a všech stavuov nepravým potupováním naplniv v království tomto Českém za nové Léto vydal (...), Prag: [Jan Severýn]. (*Knihopis* Nu. 15186. Prag, Nationalbibliothek: f Za 31.)

ŘEZNÍK, VÁCLAV (1545), Ozvaní s odpovědí kněze Vaclava [Řezníka] děkana Hor Gutten proti zprávě nepravé a nářku falešnému Jana Augusty zprávce nejvyšího synagogy litomyslský[!], kterýž položil v spisu, v němž činí zmínku, co jest mluvil nad tělem mrtvým urozene paní, pani Justýny [z Kunstatu], s.l.: s.n. (*Knihopis* Nu. 15188. Osek: Klášter cisterciáků: NN 7/15 r přív.)

ZE ZÁSADÍ, PETR (1541), Odpověd kněze Petra faráře u S. Vojtěcha v Líthoměřic v Zasadí na spis Jana Kloboučníka (kterýž se jmenuje Joannesem Aukustou) biskupa Boleslavské sekty, jejž udělal vo závazcích kresťanských ač falešně [...], Prag: Bartoloměj Netolický z Netolic. (*Knihopis* Nu. 7047. Västerås, Stadsbibliotek-Stiftsavdelningen: B5 461; Prag, Nationalbibliothek: Mikrofilm 3 m.)

ze ZÁSADÍ, PETR (1542), Velmi povlovná, pokojná a upřímná odpověd kněze Petra faráře v Lithoměřicz v Zásadí na dosti prudké, bouřlivé a velmi zchytralé Bratra Jana staršího správce zboru l[i]thomyšlského ozvání a ohlášení. A přitom List kněze Jakuba Volýnského, děkan, a lítoměřického všem vuobec bratřím náboženství boleslavského svědčící, Prag: s.n.. (*Knihopis* Nu. 7046. Prag Nationalbibliothek: 54 H 1991 unvollständig.)

z ZÁTVOŘÍ, LAURYN (1542), Odpovied na list Doktora Vaclava Mitmanka ode mne Lauryna z Zatvoři, ouřadu jahenskeho v Jednoťe bratrske, [Olomouc? Jan Oliwetský z Oliwethu?]. (Knihopis Nu. 4734. Prag, Bibliothek des Nationalmuseums: 36 G 26 přív. neúpl.)

Forschungsliteratur

ATWOOD, CRAIG D. (2009), The theology of the Czech Brethren from Hus to Comenius. University Park: Pennsylvania State University Press.

BANCROFT, RICHARD (1955), An Imperfectly Recorded Early Czech Translation of Luther? *Slavonic and East European Review* 34, no. 82, 230–31.

BAŤOVÁ, ELIŠKA (2012), Koncepce liturgického roku v hymnologické činnosti Jana Augusty, Hudební věda 49, Nu. 1–2, 33–44.

BAŤOVÁ, ELIŠKA (2013). Augustovo Registrum aneb Zpráva, co se kdy a o čem čísti má a jeho kontext: nové pohledy. In: P. Hlaváček (ed.). O Felix Bohemia! Studie k dějinám české reformace. Prag: FF UK, 195–213.

BAŤOVÁ, ELIŠKA (2015). Prolegomena k interpretaci a dataci nově objeveného Augustova Summovníku. Clavibus Unitis 4.

BEDNÁŘ, FRANTIŠEK (1952). Zwei Versuche der alten Brüderunität um einen Aufbau der praktischen Theologie im 16. Jahrhundert (Lukášovy Zprávy kněžské a Augustovo Umění práce). Theologische Zeitschrift (Basel) 8, 357–385.

BEDNÁŘ, FRANTIŠEK (ed.) (1942), Jakub Bílek: Jan Augusta v letech samoty, 1548–1564, Prag: Laichter.

BIDLO, JAROSLAV (ed.) (1915), Akty Jednoty bratrské, Bd. 1. Brno: Historická komise při Matici moravské.

BIDLO, JAROSLAV (ed.) (1923), Akty Jednoty bratrské, Bd. 2. Brno: Historická komise při Matici moravské.

BOHATCOVÁ, MIRIAM (1982), Knihtiskařská linie Olivetských, Časopis Národního muzea, řada historická 151/3–4, 129–160.

ČAPEK, JAN BLAHOSLAV (1972–1973), Rozpornost osobnosti Jana Augusty: k 400. výročí Augustova úmrtí v roce 1972. Z kralické tvrze 6, 10–18.

CLAUS, HELMUT /PEGG, MICHAEL A. (1982), Ergänzungen zur Bibliographie der zeitgenössischen Lutherdrucke, Gotha: Forschungsbibliothek Gotha.

COUFAL, DUŠAN (2012), Polemika o kalich mezi teologií a politikou 1414–1431: předpoklady basilejské disputace o prvním z pražských artikulů. Prag: Kalich.

DAVID, ZDENĚK V. (2005), The Integrity of the Utraquist Church and the Problem of Neo-Utraquism, The Bohemian Reformation and Religious Practice 5, Prag: Academy of Sciences of the Czech Republic, 329–351.

DAVID, ZDENĚK V. (2007), Utraquism's Liberal Ecclesiology, in The Bohemian Reformation and Religious Practice, Vol. 6, Prag : Academy of Sciences of the Czech Republic, 165–188,

DAVID, ZDENĚK V. (2010), Nationalism and Universalism in Ecclesiology: Utraquists and Anglicans in the Later Sixteenth Century, The Bohemian Reformation and Religious Practice 9, Prag: Academy of Sciences of the Czech Republic, 198–220.

DAVID, ZDENĚK V. (2012), Nalezení střední cesty: liberální výzva utrakvistů Římu a Lutherovi, Prag: Filosofia.

DOBIÁŠ, FRANTIŠEK MRÁZEK (1959), Die ökumenische Weite in der Theologie der Böhmischen Brüder, In: Unitas fratrum. Zwei Beiträge aus der tschechischen Brüderunität, Berlin: Evangelische Verlagsanstalt, 40–54.

Eberhard, Winfried (1986), Entstehungsbedingungen für öffentliche Toleranz am Beispiel des Kuttenberger Religionsfriedens von 1485, Communio viatorum 19, 129–133.

Filipi, Pavel (1982), Tendence bratrské homiletiky, in: ders. /A. MOLNÁR (ed.), Do posledních končin. Sborník prací Josefu Smolíkovi k 60. narozeninám. (SAT KEBF 4), Prag 1982, 77–100.

Gindely, Antonín (1857), Geschichte der Bőhmischen Brüder, 1. Band, 1450–1564, Prag: Bellmann.

Halama, Jindřich ml. (2003), Sociální učení Českých bratří 1464–1618, Brno: CDK.

Halama, Ota (2015), Svatý Jan Hus: stručný přehled projevů domácí úcty k českému mučedníku v letech 1415–1620. Prag: Kalich.

Hrejsa, Ferdinand (1912), Česká konfesse, její vznik, podstata a dějiny, Prag: Česká akademie císaře Františka Josefa pro vědy, slovesnost a umění.

Hrejsa, Ferdinand (1948), Dějiny křesťanství v Československu: 5., Za Ferdinanda I. (1526–1564), Prag: Husova československá evangelická fakulta bohoslovecká.

Jeschke, Josef Bohuslav (1959), Der Hirtendienst in der alten Brüderunität. In: Unitas fratrum: zwei Beiträge aus der tschechischen Brüderunität. Berlin: Evangelische Verlagsanstalt, 7–39.

Jireček, Josef (1876), Rukověť k dějinám literatury české do konce XVIII. věku: Ve spůsobě slovníka životopisného a knihoslovného, Sv. 2. M–Ž, Prag: Bedřich Tempský.

Just, Jiří (2009), 9.7. 1609 – Rudolfův Majestát: světla a stíny náboženské svobody, Prag: Havran.

Just, Jiří (2015), Internace Jana Augusty na Křivoklátu jako příklad konfesního násilí a problém její interpretace, Folia historica Bohemica 30, 33–46.

Just, Jiří /Nešpor, Zdeněk R. /Matějka, Ondřej (2009), Luteráni v českých zemích v proměnách staletí. Prag: Lutherova společnost.

Kašpar, Ludvík Bohumil (ed.) (1880), Život Jana Augusty čili vypravování o zajetí a uvěznění Jana Augusty a Jakuba Bílka v l. p. 1548–1564, Prag: Spolek Komenského.

Kolár, Jaroslav (1984), Dosud nepovědomý souběžec českých národních humanistů? *Listy filologické /Folia philologica* 107/1, 19–28

Landová, Tabita (2011), Ein fröhliches Mahl. Die Abendmahlsliturgie der Brüderunität in der Zeit von Lukas von Prag und ihr theologisches Profil, Communio viatorum 53, Nu. 2, 6–29.

Landová, Tabita (2011), Křest jako smlouva. Křestní liturgie Jednoty bratrské za Lukáše Pražského, Teologická reflexe 17/1, 49–65.

Landová, Tabita (2012), Lekcionář Jana Augusty a jeho role v bratrském sporu o perikopy, Listy filologické 135, 333–365.

Landová, Tabita (2014), Liturgie Jednoty bratrské (1457–1620), Červený Kostelec: Pavel Mervart.

Larangé, Daniel S. (2009), Kazatelské umění jako literární odkaz Jednoty bratrské. Jan

Augusta – Jan Blahoslav – Jan Amos Komenský, in Martin Wernisch (ed.), Unitas Fratrum 1457–2007. Jednota bratrská jako kulturní a duchovní fenomén, SAT ETF 15(2), 101–121.

MACEK, JOSEF (2001), Víra a zbožnost jagellonského věku, Prag: Argo.

MOLNÁR, AMEDEO (1948), Bratr Lukáš: bohoslovec Jednoty, Prag: Husova československá evangelická fakulta bohoslovecká.

MOLNÁR, AMEDEO (1952), Boleslavští bratří, Prag: Komenského evangelická fakulta bohoslovecká.

MOLNÁR, AMEDEO (1956a), Počínající, pokračující, dokonalí, in Rudolf Říčan/Amedeo Molnár et al. (ed.), Jednota bratrská 1457–1957: sborník k pětistému výročí založení, Prag: Kalich, 149–165.

MOLNÁR, AMEDEO (1956b), Českobratrská výchova před Komenským, Prag: Státní pedagogické nakladatelství.

MOLNÁR, AMEDEO (1959), Die eschatologische Hoffnung der böhmischen Reformation, in Josef L. Hromádka (ed.), Von der Reformation zum Morgen, Leipzig: Koehler & Amelang, 59–187.

MOLNÁR, AMEDEO (1982), Das ökumenische Anliegen der böhmischen Reformation, in: Ökumene: Möglichkeiten u. Grenzen heute; [Oscar Cullmann gewidmet, dem ökumenischen Theologen, zum achtzigsten Geburtstag am 25. Februar 1982]. Tübingen: Mohr, 9–18.

MÜLLER, JOSEF THEODOR (1922), Geschichte der Böhmischen Brüder, 1. Band, 1400–1528, Herrnhut: Missionsbuchhandlung.

MÜLLER, JOSEF THEODOR (1931), Geschichte der Böhmischen Brüder: 2. Bd., 1528–1576, Herrnhut: Missionsbuchhandlung.

MÜLLER, JOSEPH THEODOR (ed.) (1895), Die Gefangenschaft des Johann Augusta, Bischofs der böhmischen Brüder 1548 bis 1564 und seines Diakonen Jakob Bilek von Bilek selbst beschrieben, Leipzig.

NEVAL, DANIEL (2006), Die Macht Gottes zum Heil: das Bibelverständnis von Johann Amos Comenius in einer Zeit der Krise und des Umbruchs, Zürich: Theologischer Verlag.

OPELÍK, JIŘÍ /FORST, VLADIMÍR /MERHAUT LUBOŠ (1985), Lexikon české literatury, Díl 1. A–G, Prag: Academia.

PESCHKE, ERHARD (1955/56), Der Kirchenbegriff des Bruders Lukas von Prag, in: Wissenschaftliche Zeitschrift der Universität Rostock: Gesellschafts- und sprachwissenschaftliche Reihe 5, Heft 2, 18–288.

PESCHKE, ERHARD (1957/58), Bruder Gregors Lehre von der Kirche: Wissenschaftliche Zeitschrift der Universität Rostock: Gesellschafts- und Sprachwissenschaftliche reihe 7, Heft 1.

PESCHKE, ERHARD (1964), Die Böhmischen Brüder im Urteil ihrer Zeit: Zieglers, Dungersheims und Luthers Kritik an der Brüderunitât, Stuttgart: Calwer.

PESCHKE, ERHARD (1981), Kirche und Welt in der Theologie der Böhmischen Brüder: vom Mittelalter zur Reformation, Berlin: Evangelische Verlagsanstalt.

ŘÍČAN, RUDOLF (1957), Dějiny Jednoty bratrské, Prag: Kalich.

Říčan, Rudolf (1961), Die Böhmischen Brüder: Ihr Ursprung und ihre Geschichte, Berlin: Union Verlag.

Říčan, Rudolf (1967a), Tschechische Übersetzungen von Luthers Schriften bis zum Schmalkaldischen Krieg, in: Vierhundertfünfzig Jahre lutherische Reformation 1517–1967: Festschrift für Franz Lau zum 60. Geburtstag, Berlin.

Říčan, Rudolf (1976b), Lutherovy spisy „O klíčích Kristových" a „O cierkvi svaté" v bratrském vydání (1539), in: Bratrský sborník: soubor prací přednesených při symposiu konaném 26. a 27. září 1967 k pětistému výročí ustavení Jednoty bratrské, Prag: Ústřední církevní nakladatelství, 136–144.

Rohde, Michael (2006), Luther und die Böhmischen Brüder nach den Quellen, Brünn: L. Marek.

Schweitzer, Franz-Josef (2013), Die Böhmischen Brüder und die „Rechenschaft des Glaubens" von Jan Augusta (1533): der Wittenberger Druck zwischen Böhmischer und Lutherischer Reform, Hamburg: Kovač.

Smolík, Josef (1967), Pojetí církve a úřadu starých Bratří, in: Rudolf Říčan/Amedeo Molnár/Michal Flegl, Bratrský sborník: soubor prací přednesených při symposiu konaném 26. a 27. září 1967 k pětistému výročí ustavení Jednoty bratrské, Prag: Ústřední církevní nakladatelství, 52–59.

Smolík, Josef (1973). Jan Augusta na Křivoklátě. Středočeský sborník historický 8, 167–180.

Smolík, Josef (1984), Bratr Jan Augusta, Prag: Kalich.

Smolík, Josef (2000a). Bratr Jan Augusta. In: Sborník slavnosti k 500. výročí narození Jana Augusty, biskupa Jednoty bratrské: 10. září 2000 Litomyšl. Litomyšl: Sbor Českobratrské církve evangelické v Litomyšli, 4–10.

Smolík, Josef (2000b). Jan Augusta na pomezí víry a politiky. Křesťanská revue 67/10, 264–269.

Smolík, Josef (2008), Ekumenický přínos Jana Augusty, in: Angelus Pacis: Sborník prací k poctě Noemi Rejchrtové, Prag: Historický ústav, 323–339.

Smolík, Josef/Somolík, Zdeněk/Hrejsa, Bohuš (ed.) (1979), Evangelický zpěvník, Karlsruhe: Synodní rada Českobratrské církve evangelické.

Tobolka, Zdeněk/Horák, František (1925–1967), Knihopis českých a slovenských tisků od doby nejstarší až do konce XVIII. století, Prag: Státní tiskárna.

Vogel, Michael (2015), Husova fundamentální eklesiologie v perspektivě biblického personalismu, Theologická revue 86/2, 158–171.

Wenz, Gunther (2005), Kirche: perspektiven reformatorischer Ekklesiologie in ökumenischer Absicht, Göttingen: Vandenhoeck & Ruprecht.

Jan Červenka

One Church or Two Churches?

Role of the Compacts in Reunification Efforts between Catholics and Utraquists until the Reformation

1. Introduction

Important, but sometimes neglected part of reformation movement is Bohemian (pre)reformation which emerged after execution of Jan Hus, during the Hussite wars. The long and bloody Hussite wars ended by peace negotiations which took place at the Basel council, where an agreement between council fathers and Bohemians called the Basel Compacts was reached. The Basel Compacts are one of the most important documents in Czech reformation history because they led to the establishment of Utraquist church, a direct descendant of the mainstream Hussite reform thinking. In a way, the Compacts can be considered as one of the earliest documents legalizing the existence of two legally equal confessions in one political body. On the other hand, the Compacts were a basis for union with the Catholic church. The roots of this paradoxical views are in fact that Basel Compacts were based on a compromise which was intentionally vaguely formulated, so both Utraquists and Catholics could be satisfied.

The council have granted full approval of the Holy Communion of both species but had somehow restricted other three articles – the secular power of priests, punishing of public sins and free preaching of the word of God (Lancinger: 1962, 53–55). This agreement made a solid basis for peace, both internal and international. Moreover, the Compacts have formally incorporated Hussites back to the Catholic Church – accusation of heresy was officially removed as well as various repressions such as economic embargo and diplomatic isolation which had been put on lands of Czech crown during the Hussite wars. However, several new problems have immediately arisen, which meant that the story of the reunion between Bohemia and Rome has just begun. Despite immense endeavour put into the fight for recognition of the Compacts, it was far from the end of reunification efforts between Bohemians and the Catholic Church. Because the Compacts were basic document for the establishment and formation of the Utraquist church, every try for full union between Catholics and Utraquists had to deal with the question of the Compacts first.

The paper is trying to deal with the role of the Compacts in these negotiations with the special focus on the question whether it is possible to consider the Compacts as beneficial or impediment to the unification efforts. It is a long and complicated story and it is impossible to cover it in its entirety in one article, therefore I am going to present only a few main themes, which played an important role during the whole period between the pronouncing the Compacts and spread of Lutheran reformation in Bohemian lands.

At first, it is important to distinguish between the different view on relationship between Utraquist and the Catholic Church, because Utraquists believed that they had never really departed from the union with the true Catholic Church. Moreover, some of the more radical Utraquists even withhold a stance, that they are the only true church because they are the only ones strictly following the law of God in their entirety (Fudge: 1994). The Catholics stance was quite different. The Utraquists departed from the church and proudly rejected the authority of the church. Since then they have not been part of the Catholic Church until the church authority, namely the Basel Council, allowed the chalice for the laics and other articles of Utraquist faith in the Compacts.

Formally, both sides agreed that by accepting the Compacts, Bohemians were incorporated back into the Roman church. However, there were still many practical issues left and some of them would prevent real reunion for the whole period.

It is also important to note that there were two different notions of reunification. Most of the Catholics thought of reunion as an abandonment of the Compacts, rejection of all Bohemian differences in liturgy, possibly with the single exception of the communion under both species. Whereas moderate parties from both Catholics and Utraquists considered reunion as the definitive acceptance of the Basel Compacts by the Catholic church (Hrejsa: 1948, 101). This was one of the main reason why all reunification efforts were vain in the end, even though both parties in Bohemia sincerely wanted reunion (Kalous: 2010, 180). However, all wanted a different kind of reunion. There is no wonder that both types of reunion failed in the end because differences between those two concepts were wide and neither side was able to communicate it to the other, not to mention to step back and accommodate itself with the other notion of reunion.

2. Emperor Sigismund and the first conflict

Emperor Sigismund had a large influence on the decision of the Basel council to accept the Compacts. His interest in these matters was purely pragmatic because his kingship in Bohemia was at stake. After the successful negotiations with Hussites, he was finally accepted by Bohemian estates as the rightful Bohemian king. Still, he had to be coronated in Prague for the second time, because even after the reconciliation, Bohemians were unwilling to recognize his first coronation during the siege of Prague at the beginning of the Hussite wars as valid (Čornej: 2000, 638).

In order to be recognized, he had to accept some other demands from various Hussite parties, which had not been acknowledged by the Council in the Basel Compacts. For example, he had to acknowledge the independence of Taborite church for radicals (Čornej: 2000, 642–642) and he had to confirm some privileges concerning secularization of the church property, along with the Basel Compacts. These additional privileges are usually called Emperor's Compacts.

However, most of the contemporaries did not differentiate between these two agreements which led to various misunderstandings during negotiations. It also complicated reunion negotiations between Bohemians and the Roman church, because some Utraquist parties wanted a reunion based on the Emperors Compacts, whereas Catholics have never been willing to even to consider going beyond the Basel Compacts.

On the other hand, both Catholic and Hussite nobles benefitted from the emperor´s confirmation of confiscation of the secular property of the church which had occurred during the Hussite wars (Čornej: 2000, 628). In order to accomplish this Sigismund has used the passage of the Compacts saying that church will not get back the property that is held unjustly:

> quod que ecclessiastici viri bona ecclesiae, quorum sunt administratores, debent fideliter administrare, juxta sanctorum patrum salubria instituta, ipsaque bona ecclesiae ab aliis non debent injuste detineri vel occupari (Palacký: 1844, 403).

This was one of the most important achievements of the whole Hussite revolution, besides the Compacts (Kalivoda: 1997, 294).

First problems concerning the union proclaimed by the Compacts emerged soon after Sigismund's coronation because of a recatholization effort exercised by Sigismund soon after the pacification of the country, which was strongly supported by the council legate and designated archbishop for Bohemian lands Philibert of Coustances. He was replacing Utraquist friars in Prague with Catholic ones, which caused much discontent amongst the leading figures of the Utraquist party, namely John of Rokycany (Zilynská: 1992; Horníčková: 2011). After he conducted preaching against the recatholization efforts and legate Philibert, Rokycana has been forced to leave the Prague and hide in Eastern Bohemia, a region which was traditionally the base for the Utraquist faction (Šmahel: 2001, 123).

Ultimately these actions aroused an aggressive response from the Utraquist party. Some riots have broken out, especially in Prague and in the end, even Emperor Sigismund himself had to leave Bohemia in haste. It might lead to another round of devastating wars but this quarrel was very quickly solved by the death of the emperor in Znojmo on his way to Hungary. But the issue was only put aside for a short time by another one – question of the new ruler of Bohemia and his attitude to the Compacts. Also this was a heavy blow for the international acceptance of the Compacts because Sigismund was their main proponent. After his death, the only institution supporting the legitimacy of the Compacts on the international level was Basel council which was about to end soon, due to its conflict with the papal power.

3. Compacts and kings

After long negotiations, Albrecht Habsburg was elected Bohemian king, as Emperor Sigismund had originally wished. However, he had to promise to withhold the Compacts in the same manner as his predecessor did – which meant not only the Basel Compacts but also all privileges from the Emperor's Compacts. Even after his dead, during the times of the long interregnum, Compacts were guaranteed by *list mírný* (Palacký: 1840, 246–247) accepted by both Catholics and Utraquists (Šmahel: 2001, 123).

Since then the Compacts have been a regular part of the electoral capitulation of every king far into the 16th century. Even Ferdinand Habsburgn had to promise that he would follow the Compacts after his ascension on the throne in 1526 (Kavka/Skýbová: 2014, 157).

The best way to secure the Compacts was to have an Utraquist king, but this option also had its difficulties. Foreign kings and lords were unwilling even to accept dubious honor of election as a king of the 'heretical' country, such as Albrecht of Bavaria, so the possibility of converting someone directly to Utraquism seemed simply preposterous. It was an expression of the high confidence of the Bohemian estates and Utraquist party, as well as functionality and importance of the Compacts in Bohemia, that leader of the Utraquist estates, George of Poděbrady could have been considered as a possible candidate, not to mention his actual later alleviation to the rank of the king.

But even this solution had its problems – international position of the 'king of heretics' was far more difficult than the position of the Catholic kings. For example, he had to deal with disobedient Catholic city of Wroclaw unwilling to pay homage to heretic (Drabina: 1984) and he had to face a strong Catholic opposition, so called Zelenohorská Jednota (Beran: 2004; Boubín: 1990) or aggressive antiheretical preaching of John Capistrano (Heymann: 2015, 70–78).

Also he had to find a way to be coronated because coronation by the unconfirmed and unconsecrated archbishop elect John of Rokycany would be hardly seen as proper and its validity could be easily doubted. In the end, he was able to be coronated only after he swore secret promise that he will obey Pope and exterminate heresy to Archbishop of Esztergom (Čornej/Bartlová: 2004, 161–162). George was willing to do so, but his notion of heresy was vastly different from the view of Rome.

George was willing to get rid of the remnants of the most radical wing – Taborites, but he has never meant to abandon Compacts:

> We are accused by the Pope of not fulfilling the oath we have sworn at our coronation. We shall read to you this very oath … You hear that we have sworn to destroy and extinguish heresy in our realm. Truly I want you to know that we do not love heretics but that we despise them and are their enemy. But that the Pope could call a heresy or make appear as heresy the Communion in the two kinds, and our Compacts, this has never been our understanding. For these are grounded in the Holy Gospel, in the acts of Christ and of the primitive Church. (…) we will also hold it and defend it and with it live and die. (cf. Heymann: 2015, 283–284).

This coronation oath was a great burden of Podebrad´s rule and it ultimately led to the abolishment of the Compacts by Pius II (Urbánek: 1962, 531).

4.   Popes and Compacts – from tacit acceptance to abolition

Arguably the most important obstacle in full reunion with the Catholic Church and was the fact that the pope has never recognized the Compacts and without it, it was impossible to reach full incorporation of Utraquists to the Catholic Church. The situation was especially dangerous for acknowledgement of the Compacts when a fight broke out between the Basel council and Pope Eugene. After the Basel Council lost its power, the Compacts, lost much of its former legitimacy. After the brief attempt to form a union with the Greek Church, which was doomed from its very beginning; the only way remaining for securing the Compacts was to get definitive approval by the Holy See.

Even though both Bohemians and Popes send numerous embassies and legations, they can hardly get any common ground. Cardinal-legate Juan Carvajal even tried to solve the question of the Compacts in the very unusual way – he tried to smuggle the Compacts out of the country (Šmahel: 2001, 123).

However, as the foremost success of the Council fathers, the Compacts were the steady remnant of the conciliarism, which put the head of the Catholic Church in an ambiguous position. In a way, Compacts might be seen as a sign of weakness of the Pope and viability of the conciliar thoughts. Indeed, conciliar ideas have never been forgotten in Czech lands, as we can see on example of the rule of George of Poděbrady. He employed one of the most vigorous proponents of the conciliarism, Gregor of Heimburg (Šmahel: 2014. 82–83) and used legacy of conciliarism in his famous Peace organization.

On the other hand, Pope might grant Compacts to the Bohemians by his own authority and thus finalize the incorporation of Bohemians into the Roman church. This might strengthen his position as the person who ends schisms. This strategy was successfully employed by Eugen in his struggle with the Basel council when he reunited Catholics with Greek Church (Geanakoplos: 1989; Gill: 2011).

However, Bohemian representatives were aware of the fragility of the international position of the Compacts and tried to get papal approval as soon as possible. The Pope Eugen even commended Compacts as a tool for the peace in one of his letters and Bohemians immediately took their chance and sent an embassy to Rome. The Pope Eugen had died before the embassy arrived and his successor only promised that he will send a legate to scrutinize the question of the Compacts. Even though Bohemian representatives have taken the Compacts as approved by Eugen, none of his bulls explicitly acknowledged the Compacts (Kalous: 2014, 180).

Another issue was vague and ambivalent formulations of the Compacts, which allowed both sides to interpret them in their own way. This was used by Popes and other church representatives to claim that Compacts were meant as a temporary solution, an exception meant for only one generation. They thought that during that time, Utraquists would abandon their agenda and fully accommodate themselves with the Catholic Church. The more favorable situation was at the beginning of the rule of Pope Pius II. After the death of John of Capistrano, Compacts lost one of their biggest enemies (Heymann: 2015, 166) and Pius II wanted to quickly solve the Bohemian question and use Bohemians in the wars with Ottoman Turks (Smolucha: 2008). After the absence of George of Poděbrady in the Council of Mantua, Pius increased pressure on George of Poděbrady, which ultimately led to abolishing of the Compacts during a hearing of Bohemian obedience delegation in 1462. These were the main arguments used by Pope Pius II in order to definitely revoke Compacts, according the Bohemian delegation to Rome (Patera: 1888, 322–354):

1) A danger of arousing heretical thoughts, especially that in Eucharist sub una is not the whole Jesus Christ
2) Spilling the sacred blood
3) The Compacts serve as a reason for conflicts in Bohemia and between Bohemia and its neighbors
4) Trespassing against rules of the Compacts
5) Pride of Bohemian nation – Pope did not want to stir unjust pride amongst Bohemians because they could boast that they were able to force the whole Catholic Church to accept their doctrine
6) Expiration of their validity – Pius claimed, that Compacts were meant only for people living in the time when they had been concluded and since most of them were dead, there was no reason for exemption for Bohemians

The abolition of the Compacts was heavy blow for the Utraquist conservative party which was hoping to fully reunite with the Roman church. But it was also a great problem for George of Poděbrady, whose position was closely tied with Compacts

– both politically and emotionally, as we can see from his speech at the land diet following the abolition of the Compacts:

> Now believe, I was born in this communion, I have been doing so as a lord, a gubernator a and do as a king and will continue to do so (...), indeed for holy truth we are ready to forfeit not just the crown, but also our life along with my wife and children of ours.[1] (cf. Urbánek: 1962, 562)

The Utraquist estates were not intimidated by the Pope's attitude and they were still willing to fight for their king and articles of faith in another round of wars. And indeed, a new war has broken out soon enough, but not until Pius II was succeeded by Paul II. The Matthias Corvinus, king of Hungary led a new crusade against Bohemian kings, firstly George of Bohemia and later Vladislav Jagiello from Poland, who was elected as his successor. In order to preserve the Compacts, George resigned on establishing his own dynasty (Odložilík: 1941, 219ff).

The war did not fulfil the hopes of the Holy See, even though Matthias was at least partly successful and get the title of the Czech king. However, his rule did not extend beyond Moravia, Silesia and Lusitania. Heart of the Bohemian Crown was staunchly Utraquist and remained loyal to George and later Vladislav.

For Matthias Corvinus this war was not so much a holy war for the reunification of the church or extermination of the heresy. He was far more interested in securing his own power and wealth and he used religious rhetoric mainly to get papal support. When he realized that conquering of the Bohemia is above his powers, he accepted a peace treaty with the king of heretics and even give a promise to hold on to the Compacts in Moravia in his electoral capitulation (Kalous: 2009). The Pope soon realized that Matthias politics goes against his own, which resulted in his confirmation of the Vladislav's kingship in 1487.

5. Internal conflicts and securing of Compacts on the national level

The internal situation was also not without problems. As every compromise, the Compacts left many radicals on both sides unsatisfied – radical Hussite took Compacts as a starting point for their church reform program, not its fulfillment, because according them 'divine law' was superior to the positive law and their program would not be finished until temporal world will fully accomodate the divine law (Kalivoda: 1997, 39), they considered Compacts only as a first step in this endeavor

---

1 "Než vězte, že v tomto přijímání jsme se narodili, tak jsme přijímali jako pán, tak jako gubernátor a tak činíme i jako král a tak činiti chceme napříště (...), ba pro svatou pravdu jsme hotovi položiti nejen korunu, nýbrž i životy s chotí svou i dětmi svými" (All translations from Czech are my own).

(Macek: 2001, 48). Catholics wanted full reunion with the Roman church without any exemptions and conservative Utraquist did not want to go beyond the permission of the chalice for the laity.

The usual place of internal clashes was Prague as the capital city of the kingdom and one of the greatest strongholds of Utraquist estates.

The fact that all kings (with the single exception of the George of Poděbrady) were Catholics did not help to decrease tension because they were more or less obviously preferring the Catholics and almost all of them did try to recatholicize Bohemia at some point during their rule. However, these attempts were all unsuccessful because of the staunch resistance of the Utraquist estates, especially the cities. So they have to find another way how to deal with the Utraquist religious controversy.

I will mention only one example, arguably the most important one. Revolts, putsches and fights for the representation in the Prague cities[2] were common events in the 15th and 16th century. Most of them were, at least partially, confessionally motivated, usually between Catholics and Utraquists, occasionally between different wings of Utraquist party.

One of the greatest and most important of these revolts took place in 1482, when members of Utraquist city council heard of preparation of violent putsch made by Catholic dissenters unsatisfied with the situation in the city. This revolt should end by the execution of the main Utraquist citizens of Prague. Utraquists quickly roused their supporters and led a surprising and violent counterattack, which disrupted preparations for the putsch. After that Utraquists completely occupied Prague city council without king's Vladislav Jagiello knowledge or permission (Šmahel: 1978).

This led to the great arousal of emotions on both confessional sides and land diets were held to deal with the situation. Finally, negotiations found their conclusion in 1485 in Kutná Hora peace agreement (Palacký: 1862, 418–427) which confirmed Compacts and incorporated them into the land law. Kutná Hora peace treaty was mainly concerned with specification and practical applications of Compacts in the church life.

In order to secure the validity and necessity of the Compacts for Bohemian lands, they were inserted into the Bohemian land law by Kutná Hora peace treaty. In Moravia freedom of communion was part of the most used law book by Ctibor Tovačovský of Cimburk (Válka: 2005, 146).

One of the most remarkable statements of this agreement is that everyone can choose between communion under the one or both kinds: "they can seek their sal-

---

2 Prague was, at least for the greater part of our period, divided into independent cities: Old town, New town and Malá Strana.

vation according to their faith and custom without any vituperation or oppression".[3] (Palacký: 1862, 419).

This was true for all social classes, nobles, burghers and common peasant alike (Šmahel: 1994, 677; Fudge: 1996, 68–71). Every priest was obliged to serve all the sacraments for both Catholics and Utraquists, with the exception of serving the Eucharist. In exchange believers of both churches had to pay church taxes to their friar, even if he was of a different denomination (Tovačovský: 1868, 120f). There was nothing in the way of principle *cuius regio, eius religio* in Kutná Hora peace treaty (Válka: 2014).

This was a clear sign of the shift in the strategy of securing the Compacts in the Bohemian kingdom, because Utraquists resigned on their effort to get the papal approval of the Compacts, at least for a time. Instead, they were focused on securing them in the law of the kingdom and by the secular power. The first sign of this shift was maintaining John of Rokycany as the archbishop of Prague even though he was lacking proper canonical investiture.

This clearly put secular land law above canonical law (Válka: 2005, 233). This attitude was also reflected by the fact, that the Lower (Utraquist) and Upper (Catholic) consistory, which served as an administrative body of both churches, took place as the head of the church after deceased archbishop elect Jan Rokycana (Fudge: 1998, 67–96). At that time there was only one possibility for Utraquists to make an appeal against decisions of the Lower Consistory, the diet of Utraquist estates. (Hrejsa: 1948). This is a clear sign of the above-mentioned move to the more 'secular' Utraquist church and its dependence on the Utraquist estates (Fudge: 1998, 70; Eberhard: 1991, 35). But it also reflects great care which was devoted to the matters of the church amongst estates. However, it would be wrong to think of the Consistory as a mere tool in the hands of king or estates, because Lower Consistory was able to make its own independent policy (David: 2012, 101).

6. Jagellonian dynasty and the Compacts – Catholic kings and heretical country

This strategy worked for some time even after the death of George of Poděbrady, who was followed by Vladislav Jagiello of Poland, but soon the reunification efforts have been renewed. This time reunification effort was greatly supported by the Catholics, because interdict which had been cast on the Bohemia was complicating their church life too (Hrejsa: 1948, 48).

---

3 *"swého spasenie hledati mohl podle wiery swé a zwyklosti bez haněnie a útiskow"*

In time these efforts were supported also by the Utraquist estates because there were great problems with the consecration of priests – Utraquists insisted stubbornly on the apostolic tradition of consecration. Therefore it was difficult for them to get consecration for the new priests and the old ones were slowly dying out. Utraquist were forced to seek their consecration in foreign countries from the hands of corrupt bishops or by means of deceiving. In two instances, Bohemians were able to convince Italian bishops – Augustin Sancturiensis and Filip de Villanova to move into Bohemia in order to consecrate new priests (Macek: 2001, 118–133). But in both cases, their activity in Bohemian lands were full of controversies with consistory about competencies (Hrejsa: 1948, 166–168) or in the question of the immodest and immoral life of bishops.

Another step in pursuing the reunion was persecution of the radicals, especially Bohemian Brethren by St. Jacob's Mandate in 1508 (Fudge: 1996, 73–73). The papal Curia was well aware of this effort and rewarded it by alleviating the interdict.

The positive attitude of the Pope was strengthened by another factor – increasing danger of Turkish military power. The Jagellonian dynasty was the key element in the *antemurale christianitas*, especially after Jagellonian joined Poland, Hungary and Bohemian lands under one rule. The Pope knew this very well and acted accordingly it in times of Turkish threat.

There is no wonder that Utraquist estates felt the need for printing the Compacts in 1500, after the king pronounced a new law called *Vladislavské zřízení zemské*, which did not mention the Compacts at all. It was a way how to remind the king and Catholics, that Utraquist faith was still vivid (Šmahel: 2001, 129).

A second printed edition of the Compacts is from 1513 and it was printed as a part of the textual corpus which should serve in negotiations between the Utraquist party and Roman Church in 1512–1513, which was dealing with the question of renewal of archbishopric of Prague (Halama: 2015, 374–375).

Another interesting print which relates to these reunification efforts is so-called Utraquist confession of 1513. It is a basic summary of the doctrine of the Utraquist Church created. The Confession defended Utraquist specifics in Scriptural authority and church liturgy, especially communion under both kinds by all the baptized and Utraquist relationship to the adoration of the images. The text expresses Utraquists' willingness not to give up their doctrine and liturgy even on the eve of Reformation. The last text was a polemical tract against Brethren, which should prove Utraquist orthodoxy (Halama: 2015, 376–379).

7. Reformation and Reunification

This led to the whole series of embassies and negotiations in the 16th century, when papal curia intensified negotiations because of fear of joining Utraquists with newly emerged Protestant Reformation, which liberated Bohemians from their international isolation. Lutherans and Utraquists were natural political allies, but they differ greatly in theological questions.

The emergence of the Reformation also aroused the interest of the papal curia in reunification, because Pope was afraid that Utraquist will follow the new churches and separated themselves completely from the Catholic Church. Also, radical Utraquist were encouraged in pressing their demands and for some time they get the main voice in the diet and council of capital city Prague.

Luther's thought was spreading into the Bohemian lands and even though it mainly inspired German population of the Bohemian lands, it also influenced Czech Utraquists, especially radicals. The main impact was the breaking of the international isolation of the kingdom because Bohemians saw natural allies in the followers of Luther.

Important revolt in Prague took place in the 1520s. This time situation was even more complicated because a controversy emerged between radical and conservative Utraquists and Reformation played a great role in its story. It encouraged radicals to spread their ideas more loudly and to go beyond Compacts in their doctrinal deviance from the Catholic doctrine. It also encouraged them to be more politically active, which resulted in the majority of the radical Utraquist in the Prague city council and later, after Zdeněk Lev of Rožmitál fall out of the king Ladislav Jagiello grace, even into acquiring most of the important land offices by the party led by Jan of Vartemberk. Even the Consistory was led by one of Luther's pupils Havel Cahera in 1523. Luther himself send Cahera a short treatise *De instituendis ministris Ecclesiae*. Luther encouraged Cahera to entirely cut off all ties with the Catholic Church and to establish a standalone church in Bohemia (Kavka/Skýbová: 2014, 153).

But soon the whole situation was turned back. After violent conservative putsch in Prague, Jan Pašek z Vratu got back the post of head of the city council and established harsh, dictatorship regime in Prague and started persecution of his opponents. Also, Zdeněk Lev of Rožmital found a way back to the grace of Ladislav and once again took the main role in the Bohemian diet. When Havel Cahera realized that situation did not favor radicals he also turned his coat and joined conservative Utraquists. Later, he was even personally engaged in negotiations of reunion with the Catholic Church (Kalous: 201, 186f).

The internal situation in Bohemia after conservative putsch in Prague seemed to favor reunion, however all efforts were vain in the end. The negotiations took place at diet in 1525 and even unconfirmed draft of the reunion charter was prepared, nevertheless it was never confirmed neither by the king nor the pope. The main reason was fact, that legate Campeggi refused to confirm the Compacts due to lack of his authority and Utraquist estates cannot entirely abandon Compacts (Kalous: 2011, 188).

Ferdinand of Habsburg, who was elected to the throne after the tragic death of Ludvik Jagiello at Mohacs, had to promise in his electoral capitulation to withhold the Compacts and to lobby for a convocation of a council. Utraquist Estates were hoping that this council might get final confirmation of the Compacts when Pope is not willing to do so (Kavka/Skýbová: 2014, 157). The circle closed and the story of reunion and the Compacts turned back to the beginning.

Different scholars provide different opinions on the question of the greatest possibility of the reunion. The opinions vary from the early reign of the Pope Pius II (Fudge: 1998), negotiations in 1513 (Halama: 2015) or late attempt to reconcile in 1526 (Kalous: 2010). However, this question is somehow meaningless because reunion simply faced too many difficulties and even the most promising attempts for reconciliation were miles away from reaching it.

When we consider the role of the Compacts in these negotiations, we must admit that it has turned upside down. Right after their pronouncement, the Compacts were the main bond which connected Utraquists to the Roman Catholic Church. But without papal approval and emergence of conflict between the Pope and the Basel Council, the Compacts slowly began to change from binding tie to the obstacle for the reunion with Rome. This process was finished by the abolition of the Compacts by Pius II. Since then, the Compacts have been a permanent obstacle for the reunion between Bohemians and Rome. Partly it was because of their importance inside the Bohemian kingdom – the Compacts were the main document guaranteeing the possibility of peaceful coexistence. On the other side, Compacts were unacceptable for the papacy, because by approving them, the papacy would have lost authority which had been hardly fought in the struggles with conciliarism and church nationalism. Paradoxically the same document, which had successfully ended Hussite wars and incorporated Bohemians to the church, became the greatest obstacle for the definitive union of the Utraquist and the Roman Catholic church. However that does not diminish the importance of the Compacts for more or less peaceful coexistence which lasted until the Compacts were formally removed from the land law in 1575 and replaced by a new document – Bohemian Confession, which was concerned not only with Utraquists but also with Lutherans in Bohemian lands.

Bibliography

BERAN, ZDENĚK (2014), Katolické Panstvo na Dvoře Jiřího z Poděbrad. Procesy Vzájemné Konvergence a Divergence, Mediaevalia Historica Bohemica 17, 37–75.

BOUBÍN, JAROSLAV (1990), Nižší šlechta a vznik zelenohorské jednoty. Český Časopis Historický 88, 351–355.

ČORNEJ, PETR (2000), Velké Dějiny Zemí Koruny České, vol. 5: 1402–1437, Praha: Paseka.

ČORNEJ, PETR/MILADA BARTLOVÁ (2007), Velké dějiny zemí Koruny české, vol 6: 1437–1526, Praha: Paseka.

ČORNEJ, PETR (2011), Světla a stíny husitství. (Události, osobnosti, texty, tradice). Výbor z úvah a studií, Praha: Nakladatelství Lidové noviny.

DAVID, ZDENĚK V. (2012), Nalezení Střední Cesty: Liberální Výzva Utrakvistů Římu a Lutherovi, Praha: Filosofia.

DRABINA, JAN (1984), Rola Argumentacji Religijnej w Walce Politycznej w Późnośredniowiecznym Wrocławiu, Krakow: Nakładem Uniw. Jagiellońskiego.

EBERHARD, WINFRIED (1991), The Political System and the Intellectual Traditions of the Bohemian Ständestaat from the Thirteenth to the Sixteenth Century, in: Robert J. W. Evans/Trevor V. Thomas (ed.), Crown, Church and Estates Central European Politics in the Sixteenth and Seventeenth Centuries, London: Palgrave Macmillan, 23–47.

FUDGE, THOMAS A. (1994), The 'Law of God': Reform and Religious Practice in Late Medieval Bohemia, The Bohemian Reformation and Religious Practice 1, 49–72.

FUDGE, THOMAS A. (1996), The Problem of Religious Liberty in Early Modern Bohemia, A theological journal 38, 64–87.

FUDGE, THOMAS A. (1998), Reform and the Lower Consistory in Praha, 1467–1497, The Bohemian Reformation and Religious Practice 2, 67–96.

GEANAKOPLOS, DENO J. (1989), Constantinople and the West: Essays on the Late Byzantine (Palaeologan) and Italian Renaissances and the Byzantine and Roman Churches, Madison: University of Wisconsin Press.

GILL, JOSEPH (2011), The council of Florence, Cambridge: Cambridge University Press.

HALAMA, OTA (2015). Utrakvistická Konfese z Roku 1513. Studia Historica Brunensia 62, 373–387.

HEYMANN, FREDERICK G. (2015), George of Bohemia: King of Heretics, Princeton: Princeton University Press.

HORNÍČKOVÁ, KATEŘINA (2011), Memory, Politics and Holy Relics: Catholic Tactics amidst the Bohemian Reformation, The Bohemian Reformation and Religious Practice 3, 133–142.

HREJSA, FERDINAND (1948), Dějiny Křesťanství v Československu IV. za Krále Vladislava a Ludvíka. před Světovou Reformací a za Reformace, Praha: Husova čs. Evangelická fakulta bohoslovecká v Praze.

KALIVODA, ROBERT (1997), Husitské myšlení, Praha: Filosofia.

KALOUS, ANTONÍN (2009), Matyáš Korvín (1443–1490): Uherský a Český Král, České Budějovice: Veduta.

KALOUS, ANTONÍN (2010), The Politics of the Church Unification: Efforts to Reunify Utraquists and Rome in 1520's, in: Jaroslav Miller/László Kontler (ed.), Friars, Nobles and Burghers – Sermons, Images, and Prints: Studies of Culture and Society in Early-Modern Europe, in memoriam István György Tóth, Budapest: Central European University Press, 179–197.

KALOUS, ANTONÍN (2011), Jednání o Unii Katolíků a Utrakvistů ve Dvacátých Letech 16.

Století, in: Robert Novotný/Petr Šámal (ed.), Zrození mýtu. Dva životy husitské epochy, Praha: Paseka, 183–189.

KAVKA, FRANTIŠEK/SKÝBOVÁ, ANNA (2014), The 'Bohemian Question' in the Sixteenth Century, in: James R. Palmitess/Barbara Ch. Hopkinson (ed.), Between Lipany and White Mountain: Essays in Late Medieval and Early Modern Bohemian History in Modern Czech Scholarship, Leiden: Brill, 149–165.

LANCINGER, LUBOŠ (1962), Čtyři Artikuly Pražské A Podíl Universitních Mistrů Na Jejich Vývoji, Acta Universitatis Carolinae: Historia Universitatis Carolinae Pragensis, Sborník příspěvků k dějinám University Karlovy 3, 3–61.

MACEK, JOSEF (2001), Víra a Zbožnost Jagellonského Věku, Praha: Argo, 2001.

ODLOŽILÍK, OTAKAR (1941), Problems of the Reign of George of Poděbrady. Slavonic Year-Book. American Series 1, 206–222.

PALACKÝ, FRANTIŠEK (1840), Archiv český čili staré písemné památky české i moravské. Z archivův domácích i cizích sebral a vydal František Palacký, vol. 1, Praha: Kromber a Řivnáč.

PALACKÝ, FRANTIŠEK (1844), Archiv český čili staré písemné památky české i moravské. Z archivův domácích i cizích sebral a vydal František Palacký, vol. 3, Praha: Kromber a Řivnáč.

PALACKÝ, FRANTIŠEK (1862), Archiv český čili staré písemné památky české i moravské. Z archivův domácích i cizích sebral a vydal František Palacký, vol. 5, Praha: Fridrich Tempský.

PATERA, ADOLF (1888), Archiv český čili staré písemné památky české i moravské, sebrané z archivů domácích i cizích. Nákladem domestikálního fondu Království českého vydává Kommisse k tomu zřízená při Královské české společnosti nauk, vol. 7, Praha: Bursík a Kohout.

PAULOVÁ, MILADA (1953), L'Empire Byzantin et les Tchèques avant la Chute de Constantino-ple (L'Union Florentine et les Tchèques), Byzantinoslavica 14, 158–225.

SMOŁUCHA, JANUSZ (2008), Polityka Kurii Rzymskiej za Pontyfikatu Piusa II (1458–1464) wobec Czech i Krajów Sąsiednich. Z Dziejów Dyplomacji Papieskiej w XV Wieku, Kraków: Księgarnia Akademicka.

ŠMAHEL, FRANTIŠEK (1978), Epilog Husitské Revoluce. Pražské Povstání 1483, in: Amedeo Molnár (ed.), Acta reformationem Bohemicam illustrantia. Příspěvky k dějinám utrakvismu, Praha: Kalich, 45–127.

ŠMAHEL, FRANTIŠEK (1994), Svoboda Slova, Svatá Válka a Tolerance z Nutnosti v Husitském Období, Český Časopis Historický 92, 644–679.

ŠMAHEL, FRANTIŠEK (2001), Epilog Jedné Kauzy. Osudy Basilejských Kompaktát, in: Robert, Novotný/Petr Šámal (ed.), Zrození mýtu. Dva životy husitské epochy. K poctě Petra Čorneje, Praha: Paseka, 121–139.

ŠMAHEL, FRANTIŠEK (2011), Basilejská Kompaktáta: Příběh Deseti Listin, Praha: Naklada-telství Lidové noviny.

ŠMAHEL, FRANTIŠEK (2014), The Divided Nation, in: James R. Palmitessa/Barbara Ch. Hopkinson (ed.), Between Lipany and White Mountain: Essays in Late Medieval and Early Modern Bohemian history in Modern Czech scholarship, Leiden: Brill, 63–93.

Tovačovský, Ctibor Z Cimburka (1868), Kniha Tovačovská: aneb Pana Ctibora z Cimburka a z Tovačova Paměť Obyčejů a Řádů a Zvyklostí Starodávných a Řízení Práva v Mar. Mor. Kritické Vydání, Vincenc Brandl (ed.), Brno: self published.

Urbánek, Rudolf (1962), Věk poděbradský. Čechy za kralování Jiříka z Poděbrad. Léta 1460–1464. Díl 4. Urbánek, Rudolf. Praha: Nakladatelství Československé akademie věd.

Válka, Josef (2005), Husitství na Moravě-Náboženská Snášenlivost-Jan Amos Komenský. Brno: Matice moravská.

Válka, Josef (2014), Tolerance or Co-Existence? Relations between Religious Groups from the Fifteenth to Seventeenth Centuries, in: James R. Palmitessa/Barbara Ch. Hopkinson (ed.), Between Lipany and White Mountain: Essays in Late Medieval and Early Modern Bohemian History in Modern Czech Scholarship, Leiden: Brill, 182–196.

Zilynská, Blanka (1992), Biskup Filibert a České země, in: Jihlava a Basilejská kompaktáta: 26.-28. červen 1991 : sborník příspěvků z mezinárodního sympozia k 555. výročí přijetí Basilejských kompaktát, Jihlava : Muzeum Vysočiny ve spolupráci s Okresním archivem, 56–94.

Pierrick Hildebrand

One Church, One Covenant, One Faith

Covenantal Aspects in Zwingli's Ecclesiology

1. Introduction

Past research on Huldreich Zwingli's (1484–1531) ecclesiology has recognized the distinct contribution of the Swiss Reformer to the development of the doctrine of the church in evangelical theology, especially in the Reformed tradition. However, research has focused mainly on the church-state relation, or on the differentiated use of the very term "church" (i.e., visible/invisible, local/universal).[1] Virtually absent in these studies – at least explicitly – is an evaluation of the ecclesiological implications of the biblical leitmotif of 'covenant' in Zwingli's theological thought, which he himself does not hesitate to use as an appositive of 'church', as we will later observe. As far as I can see, there is but one exception, namely, Courvoisier's "Warfield Lectures" at Princeton Theological Seminary in 1961, where he briefly mentioned how for Zwingli "The Jewish People" relate to the "Church," referring to Zwingli's theology of the covenant (Courvoisier: 1963, 50f.).[2] This research gap can be partly explained by limited interest so far in Zwingli's covenant theology, but probably also because of its comparatively "late" development in Zwingli's short life. My paper seeks to (re-)consider Zwingli's theology of the covenant as it pertains to his doctrine of the church. (It is here assumed that the latter is derived or at least influenced by the former and not the other way round.) I will especially highlight

---

1 See, for example, Eduard Zeller: 1853, 150–165; Schulthess-Rechberg: 1909; Farner: 1930; Pollet: 1988, 114–161; Stephens: 1986, 260–281. In Walton's work *Zwingli's Theocracy*, which actually only covers the years up to 1523, a significant role is indeed given to the (Old) covenant in Zwingli's so-called theocratic view of the church. But, as the source evidences do not point to any sort of 'covenant theology' in the narrow sense of the term before the second half of 1525, I do not count his work as an exception to my assessment. See Walton: 1967, 79; 105; 106; 109; 119. and Cottrell's rebuttal in Cottrell: 1971: 27–29.

2 Courvoisier goes so far as to include indiscriminately all the Jewish people in stating that they will eventually be revealed as being part of the church. It seems to me that this bold statement is more indebted to 20th-century systematic theology (cf. Karl Barth) than to the historical sources. Zwingli can in light of Romans 11 consider an eschatological conversion of the Jews, but it is more than doubtful whether Zwingli could have considered the Jews (especially of his time) explicitly rejecting Christ to be a hidden part of Christ's body. I prefer to remain cautious and speak therefore of the *Old Testament believers* instead of the Jewish people, meaning thereby the believing Jews before and in expectation of Christ's coming.

Zwingli's stress on ecclesial unity between Old Testament and New Testament believers and add in that light a reflection on the sacraments.

2. Zwingli's covenantal turn[3]

As I mentioned above, there has not been much research done on Zwingli's covenantal theology up to now. Even the recognition of Zwingli's foundational contribution was overlooked in modern historical theology until the beginning of the twentieth century. There has been but one extensive dissertation on Zwingli's view of covenant, from Cottrell in the 1970s titled *Covenant and Baptism in the Theology of Huldreich Zwingli* (Cottrell: 1971).[4] It is in my view the best and still unsurpassed survey on the notion of covenant in Zwingli's theology, as Cottrell undertakes a historical-chronological account of its development starting from the primary sources. My own research has come to the same conclusion as his, namely, that the sources do not attest to any sort of covenant theology before the second half of 1525. The Reformation in Zurich was at that time de facto established,[5] and because of Zwingli's early death in the second war of Cappel in 1531, we are already concerned here with Zwingli's 'late' developments.

Zwingli's covenantal turn, that is, the paradigm shift from a basic discontinuity (the predominant view among humanists)[6] to a basic continuity between the Old and the New Testament in his theological hermeneutics, goes back to his exegetical lectures at the 'Prophezei'. The so-called Prophezei was a sort of theological seminary for the pastorate, which arose out of the dissolution of the Chorherrenstift (canon) at the Minster. Already planned in September 1523 the Prophezei began its teaching activities on the 19th of June 1525 (cf. Egli: 1879, 169; Locher: 1979, 151). As Zwingli started to preach in Zürich the whole Scriptures after the lectio-continua method in 1519, beginning thereby with the New Testament, the books of the Old Testament were methodically taught by the different scholars involved in the new institution. After the text was read from the Latin Vulgate and the Hebrew original, Zwingli was then in charge of the Greek reading out of the Septuagint, to which he used to add linguistic and homiletic comments in Latin. Sometimes he might also translate into

---

3 .See Hildebrand: 2017, 23–35.

4 For the sake of completeness I must mention Gillies' M. A. thesis, *Huldrych and the origins of the covenant: 1524–1527*. It was published after Cottrell's work but does surpass it and does not cover Zwingli's later years. Cf. Gillies: 1996.

5 Zwingli's program of reforming liturgy (i.e., Eucharist), social order (i.e., Ehegericht or marriage court), and academics (i.e., Prophezei) came to a point of no return in 1525, although that is not to say there was no more opposition.

6 For Erasmus' hermeneutics, see Aldridge: 1966, 44–56.

Latin what he had previously said in Early Modern German for the laymen who, by the way, were also welcome in the Prophezei.[7] Although Zwingli had learned Hebrew from Ceporin (1500–1525) in 1522, who was now responsible for the Hebrew lectures, he had become much more acquainted with Greek during his earlier humanistic studies. The first series of lectures were on the book of Genesis which lasted up to November 1525.[8] In 1527 notes on the book of Genesis "ex ore Huldrychi Zuinglii" – that is to say, "out of the master's mouth" – were published with Zwingli's approbation, and he also wrote the preface. It might be reasonably inferred that the basic content of the edition, even though published in 1527 by listeners as a de facto 'commentary', goes back to Zwingli's teaching activities in 1525. Why do I mention this? Because this commentary gives us the earliest evidence of Zwingli's covenantal turn, with the ecclesiological implications we are about to discuss.[9]

3. Church as covenant

The argumentative strength on which Reformed covenant theology stands or falls has drawn, from the earliest development on, upon the exegesis of the Abraham-narrative in the book of Genesis in light of the Pauline epistles. YHWH's covenanting with the patriarch in Genesis 17 builds the hermeneutical key or the pivotal point from which one moves back to Adam and forth to Jesus Christ reading the whole biblical narrative (postlapsarian)[10] as the historical unfolding of a gracious covenant culminating in Christ's redemption.

In his notes on the book of Genesis, Zwingli has the beginning of the Abraham-narrative in chapter 12 preceded by a preamble, which functions as a hermeneutic prolegomenon. There he writes: "Una ergo fides, una ecclesia dei fuit omnibus temporibus,"[11] that is: "There has been therefore one faith and one church of God through all times." There is no explicit mention of the word 'covenant', but the presupposition of this statement is that the same "*pledge* of divine goodness and grace" (emphasis added) has been manifested – albeit not as plainly – in the Old

---

7 Cf. Bullinger: 1838, 289ff.; Locher: 1979, 161f.

8 Cf. Bolliger: 2013, 528; Künzli: 1959, 872, against Farner: 1963, 290, who includes not only the Genesis lections but all of the lections on the Pentateuch in this period of 20 weeks.

9 For determining an indisputable terminus a quo for the earliest evidences for covenant theology in Zwingli, we must refer to the Subsidium, which was published in August 1525, that is, two months after the opening of the Prophezei. See Hildebrand: 2017, 23–35.

10 Zwingli starts his survey of redemptive history or the covenant of grace technically speaking with the proto-evangelion in Gen 3:15.

11 Zwingli: 1963, 67.

Testament as it has been in the New.[12] The word "pledge" has obvious covenantal connotations. What is this pledge, or, better, who is this pledge? Zwingli adds: "However many believers [in the Old Testament] there are, they came to God through Christ alone, the *pledge* of salvation and grace"[13] (emphasis added). Never before had Zwingli proposed with such a pointed emphasis that Christ's redemptive work projects backwards into the Old Testament. This is the result of what we call Zwingli's covenantal turn, the move from a basic discontinuity to a basic continuity between the Old and the New Testaments. This continuity is here qualified by *one faith, one church, and one covenant* across the testamental distinction. These aspects of continuity do not consist of a bare enumeration but are appositives pointing to and unified in Christ. That is, Christ has always been the same 'object' or content of faith, church, and covenant. Zwingli thinks in a promise-fulfilment pattern, as becomes evident in the comments of the following chapters. Depending on one's position on the timeline Christ is either promised, that is, he is yet to come, or Christ's coming has already been fulfilled. In Zwingli's view, divine goodness and grace are not primarily timeless or ahistorical attributes, but a concrete event in history, to which all of redemptive history must refer and be measured by. In the Old Testament church, salvation is anticipated in *prospective-cataphoric* expectation, whereas the New Testament church participates in it in *retrospective-anaphoric* remembrance. But the one *ecclesia dei* remains the same church of Christ. To speak of 'church' in respect to the Old Testament might sound anachronistic to modern ears at first hearing. But so-called pre-critical exegetes were not that naïve. Septuagint scholar Zwingli knew of course that the covenantal assembly of Israel – קָהָל in Hebrew – could be rendered by the Septuagint translators as συναγωγή or ἐκκλησία,[14] the latter being used by the New Testament authors for the assembly of Christians.

The unity of the church or covenant is again stressed in Genesis 15, but this time in a more vivid or plastic manner. The Abraham-narrative tells us that God ratifies the covenant with Abraham according to the ancient custom of passing between animals that had been cut in two pieces. Zwingli interprets quite allegorically the covenanting rite of cutting animals in two equal parts as pointing to Christ's saving

---

12 Zwingli: 1963, 67: "Euangelium enim nihil est aliud quam *divinae beneficentiae et gratiae manifestatio ac pignus*, quae et patribus (tametsi non usque adeo clare et late) facta est. In novo vero testamento per Christum manifeste exhibita et in orbem diffusa est" (emphasis added).

13 Zwingli: 1963, 67f.: "Quotquot fideles sunt, per solum Christum, salutis ac gratiae pignus ad deum iverunt".

14 Cf. Deut 5:22 and Deut 9:10.

work on the cross.[15] The two parts stand for the two natures of Christ, who spiritually unites the divided Jews and heathens through his death. Zwingli adds: "We see therefore that since the beginning the faith of the fathers and ours have been one and the same. Because all are saved by this testament and covenant, which God made with the faithful Abraham and his descendants".[16] It is remarkably evident how church, covenant, and faith function here as synonyms in Christ. Although the term 'church' does not appear, Zwingli is referring to the gathering of Jews and heathen in the crucified body of Christ. And when we turn to the paradigmatic passage for Reformed covenant theology, that is, Genesis 17 where God renews this covenant, Zwingli says explicitly: "For there is one and the same church, which is made out of Heathen and Jews".[17] And he soon adds: "One is therefore Abraham's faith and ours; because the former believed God equally through the descendant, which was promised to him, and to us, as it is now fulfilled, this promise they just believed".[18] The promise-fulfilment pattern we just talked about is here referred to by Zwingli.

4. Church sacraments as covenant signs

We cannot talk about covenant theology without talking about the sacraments of the church, because it is precisely through controversies around these that Reformed covenant theology has been shaped and refined.[19] Covenantal or ecclesial unity is repeatedly stressed in Zwingli's polemical writings on the sacraments after his covenantal turn.[20] How do the sacraments relate to the one church or covenant

---

15 Zwingli's allegoresis was probably rooted in his intuition that this sacrificial rite had some judicial-penal relevance, which has been basically confirmed by modern research on covenants in the ancient Near East. Cf. Kline: 1964/1965, 118–119. See further Jer 34:18.

16 Zwingli: 1963, 89: "Videmus ergo iam ab initio patrum fidem et nostram eandemque fuisse. Omnes enim hoc testamento et foedere salvantur, quod cum fideli Abraham et semine eius pepigit Deus".

17 Zwingli: 1963, 105f.: "Una enim atque eadem est ecclesia, quae ex gentibus Iudaeisque compingitur".

18 Zwingli: 1963, 106: "Una ergo fides est Abrahae et nostra; perinde enim ille fidebat deo per semen, quod ei promissum erat, atque nos, quam quod nunc praestitus est, cui isti promisso tantum fidebant".

19 Though not exclusively through the Anabaptist controversy as has been long asserted. See Hildebrand: 2017, 23–35.

20 See the following statements: Zwingli, 1927, 588: "[...]merck in einer summ, das der Christen kinder glych im testament, kilchen oder pundt sind wie der som Abrahams. Sind sy nun in der kilchen Christi, warumb wöllend ir inen das testamentzeichen abschlahen?" (emphasis added); 634–635: "Es ist offenbar by allen glöubigen, *das der christenlich pundt oder nüw testament eben der alt pundt Abrahams ist*, usgenommen, das wir Christum, der yenen nun verheissen was, bar habend" (emphasis added); Zwingli: 1935, 385: "Si ergo *una est fides Abrahae et nostra* – perinde enim ille fidebat deo per semen, quod ei promissum erat, atque nos, quam quod nunc praestitus est, cui isti promisso tantum fidebant; unde clarum fit, quod *una est amborum ecclesia* –, erit ergo ecclesiae huius eadem

in Zwingli's ecclesiology? Crucial here is their definition as 'Pundtszeichen' or 'signum foederis', that is, *covenant signs*. If unity between the testaments is to be sustained, this unity must be traced first of all back to the sacraments. And this is precisely what Zwingli did. For him there is a basic continuity between the Jewish Passover and its festive remembrance on the one side, and Christ's atonement and the Eucharist on the other. This is true not just by way of analogy, but in a univocal way. The same can be said of baptism, which is equated with circumcision. Before Zwingli's covenantal turn, he had already pointed to formal parallels and analogies between Genesis 17 or Exodus 12 and the New Testament institutional texts of the sacraments. But after his covenantal turn, Zwingli began to reason that the Old Testament and New Testament sacraments are ultimately signs of the one and same covenant, Christ himself. Why did the signs or sacraments change? Zwingli argues in reference to redemptive history from the promise-fulfilment pattern mentioned above. The bloody circumcision or the Passover lamb were anticipations of Christ's shed blood in his ultimate sacrifice, through which he put an end once and for all to every bloody rite.[21] The external transformation of circumcision into baptism, the Passover lamb into the Eucharist point only to a different stage of the covenantal assembly in redemptive history. This is because the internal value of what the covenant signs stand for have always been the same, namely, Christ as the epitome of the one church, of the one covenant, and of the one faith.

Defining sacraments as covenant signs implies that the sacraments can only be considered as such within a concrete assembly of believers in a specific time and place as the expression of a more abstract but no less real universal and diachronic assembly reaching from Adam to the present. In Zwingli's view the sacraments do not create the reality they signify, but already assume the reality that believers

---

quoque sors et condition" (emphasis added); 394: "*Eadem enim est fides, ac idem testamentum sive foedus*, quantum ad interiorem hominem attinet" (emphasis added); Zwingli: 1935, 649: "Apud eum autem locum cum esses, quur, quęso, non vidisti, primum *unam eandemque esse ecclesiam, unum idemque esse testamentum, unam eandemque fidem* tam eorum, qui ante Christum matutina, tertia, sexta nonaque hora venerunt quam nostram, qui undecima tandem vineam ingressi ęque tamen liberaliter atque primi isti accepti sumus, imo mercede ante donati quam isti [Matth. 20:1f], quo excidium Iudaeorum ex oliva nostraque insitio pateret [cf. Rom 11:17f]?" (emphasis added); 733: "*Una est enim ecclesia, una fides*; neque iratior est nobis liberisque nostris deus, quam fuerit Iudęis, quorum liberi *aeque in foedere perindeque in ecclesia* erant atque parentes" (emphasis added); Zwingli: 1961, 163: "Idem ergo foedus, quod olim cum populo Israëlitico, in novissimis temporibus nobiscum pepigit, ut *unus essemus cum eis populus, una ecclesia, et unum foedus quoque haberemus*" (emphasis added); Zwingli: 1990, 52: "Nam alias qui essemus filii Abrahae, si Abraham non haberet eandem quam nos fidem? Testamenta quoque non sunt diversa, quantum ad praecipua fidei ac religionis pertinet".

21 See Zwingli: 1927, 638: "Sich, was ist hie unglychs, usgenommen das pundtszeychen? wiewol dasselb der kraft halb nit unglych ist; dann yetweders ist ein usserlich sigel des pundts. Aber die bschnydung ist darumb in touf verwandlet, das alles bluot Christi gstellt ist, wie im 'Toufbuoch' gnuog gesagt ist".

need to be reminded of, that is, Christ's redemptive work as building a covenantal assembly (Christ's *body*). The *ecclesia dei* becomes visible to itself as such not so much in the administration as in the *reception* of the sacraments as assembly (of the covenant). Accordingly, an individualistic view of the sacraments in exclusively vertical or existential terms (i.e., me here and now and God) would make absolutely no sense to Zwingli and – I would suggest – most Reformed theologians.[22]

5. Conclusion

We come now to a brief conclusion. It seems that Zwingli's theology of the covenant after 1525 played a greater role in his ecclesiology than has been generally noticed by scholars up to now. That Old Testament and New Testament believers are united in one covenantal assembly is a tenet unique to the Reformed tradition within the Protestant spectrum, which can be traced back to the foundational figure of Zwingli.[23] I would here also suggest that other aspects of the church promulgated by Zwingli, such as the question of visibility, universality, and the church's relation to the state, could be re-read in light of Zwingli's covenantal turn.

Bibliography

Sources

BULLINGER, HEINRICH (1838), Reformationsgeschichte, J. J. Hottinger/H. H. Vögeli (ed.), vol. 1, Frauenfeld: Ch. Beyel.

EGLI, EMIL (ed.) (1879), Actensammlung zur Geschichte der Zürcher Reformation in den Jahren 1519–1533, Zürich: J. Schabelitz.

---

22 It is the reason why Zwingli (and Bullinger) was opposed to emergency baptism or the private celebration of the Eucharist.

23 It has been argued by Hagen that the young Luther presented even before the rise of Reformed covenant theology a biblical hermeneutic of the testaments similar to the one Zwingli developed after what we call his covenantal turn in mid-1525. Cf. Hagen: 1972, 22: "For Luther and for Zwingli after 1525, there is no hermeneutical hassle about the two Testaments". Hagen fails, however, to see that Luther's understanding of the *testamentum dei* borrowed from Augustine, which pervades the two testaments, is in no way comparable to Zwingli's univocal way of reading the Old as the promised New Testament or Old Israel as the church, which includes some sort of soteriological identification. For Luther the 'Old' Testament, however much it is or is not identified with the Old Testament canon (whether understood soteriologically or hermeneutically), is always loaded negatively. This is not the case for Zwingli after 1525. For Luther's view, see further: Hagen: 1974, 31–70.

Zwingi, Huldreich (1927), Antwort über Balthasar Hubmaiers Taufbüchlein, in: Huldreich Zwinglis sämtliche Werke, Emil Egli e.a. (ed.), vol. 4, CR 91, Leipzig: Verlag von M. Heinsius Nachfolger, 585–642.

Zwingli, Huldreich (1935), De peccato originali declaratio ad Urbanum Rhegium, in: Huldreich Zwinglis sämtliche Werke, Emil Egli e.a. (ed.), vol. 5, CR 92, Leipzig: Verlag von M. Heinsius Nachfolger, 369–396.

Zwingli, Huldreich (1935), Amica exegesis, in: Huldreich Zwinglis sämtliche Werke, Emil Egli e.a. (ed.), vol. 5, CR 92, Leipzig: Verlag von M. Heinsius Nachfolger, 562–758.

Zwingli, Huldreich (1961), In catabaptistarum strophas elenchus, in: Huldreich Zwinglis sämtliche Werke, Emil Egli e.a. (ed.), vol. 6.1, CR 93, Zürich: Verlag Berichthaus, 21–196.

Zwingli, Huldreich (1963), Farrago annotationum in Genesim: ex ore Hulryci Zuinglii per Leonem Iudae et Casparem Megandrum exceptarum, in: Huldreich Zwinglis sämtliche Werke, Emil Egli e.a. (ed.), vol. 13, CR 100, Zürich: Verlag Berichthaus, 5–288.

Zwingli, Huldreich (1990), Ad Leohardum Fontanum contra Suenckfefeldium, in: Huldreich Zwinglis sämtliche Werke, Emil Egli e.a. (ed.), vol. 6.4, CR 93.4, Zürich: Verlag Berichthaus, 26–74.

Secondary Literature

Aldridge, John W. (1966), The Hermeneutic of Erasmus, Richmond, VA: John Knox Press.

Bolliger, Daniel (2013), Nachwort, in: Huldreich Zwinglis sämtliche Werke, Max Lienhard/Daniel Bolliger (ed.), vol. 21, CR 108, Zürich: TVZ, 503–566.

Büsser, Fritz (1984), Zwingli und die Kirche: Überlegungen zur Aktualität von Zwinglis Ekklesiologie, Zwingliana 16/3, 186–200.

Cottrell, Jack Warren (1971), Covenant and Baptism in the Theology of Huldreich Zwingli, Princeton Theological Seminary: PhD diss.

Courvoisier, Jacques (1963), Zwingli: A Reformed Theologian, Richmond, VA: John Knox Press.

Farner, Alfred (1930), Die Lehre von Kirche und Staat bei Zwingli, Tübingen: Laupp.

Farner, Oskar (1963), Nachwort zu den Erläuterungen zur Genesis, in: Huldreich Zwinglis sämtliche Werke, Emil Egli e.a. (ed.), vol. 13, CR 100, Zürich: Verlag Berichthaus, 289–290.

Gillies, Scott A. (1996), Huldrych and the origins of the covenant: 1524–1527, Queen's University, Kingston, Ontario Canada: M. A. thesis.

Hagen, Kenneth (1972), From Testament to Covenant in the Early Sixteenth Century, in: The Sixteenth Century Journal 3.1, 1–24.

Hagen, Kenneth (1974), A Theology of Testament in the Young Luther: The Lectures on Hebrews, Leiden: Brill.

Hildebrand, Pierrick (2017), Zwingli's Covenantal Turn, in: From Zwingli to Amyraut: Exploring the Growth of European Reformed Traditions, Jon Balserak and Jim West (eds.), Göttingen: Vandenhoeck & Ruprecht, 23–35.

Kline, Meredith (1964/1965), Oath and Ordeal Signs, Westminster Theological Journal

27, 115–139.

KÜNZLI, EDWIN (1959), Zwingli als Ausleger des Alten Testamentes, in: Huldreich Zwinglis sämtliche Werke, Emil Egli e.a. (ed.), vol. 14, CR 101, Zürich: Verlag Berichthaus, 869–899.

LOCHER, GOTTFRIED W. (1979), Die Zwinglische Reformation im Rahmen der europäischen Kirchengeschichte, Göttingen: Vandenhoeck & Ruprecht.

POLLET, JACQUES V. (1988), Huldrych Zwingli et le zwinglianisme: Essai de synthèse historique et théologique mis à jour d'après les recherches récentes, Paris: Libraire philosophique J. Vrin.

SCHULTHESS-RECHBERG, GUSTAV V. (1909), Luther, Zwingli u. Calvin in ihren Ansichten über das Verhältnis von Staat u. Kirche, Zürich: Gebr. Leemann & Cie.

STEPHENS, WILLAM P. (1986), The Theology of Huldrych Zwingli, Oxford: Clarendon Press.

WALTON, ROBERT (1967), Zwingli's Theocracy, Toronto: University of Toronto Press.

ZELLER, EDUARD (1853), Das theologische System Zwinglis, Tübingen: L. Fr. Fues.

Michelle C. Sanchez

Does Calvin's Church Have a History?

Toward the Methodological Use of Theology in Service of Historiography

1. Introduction

The question of 'Church' at the time of the Reformation – invisible community, visible parish, confession, building, or something else – immediately suggests a set of further questions. Of course, it invites historians to continue recovering and contextualizing the range of arguments about the nature of the 'church' that were floated, forwarded, and fought over during the sixteenth century in Europe. It also invites descriptive accounts of how actual churches operated: their institutional organization, their practices, their modes of self-identification and boundary policing, and their relationships to other institutions. In a subtler way, however, the question of 'Church' at the time of the Reformation also unleashes a range of methodological questions about how we, as scholars, study such phenomena now – not only five hundred years later, but also in the wake of debates over how religious phenomena in general are most responsibly treated within the contemporary academic disciplines.

These debates have already been waged across many fault lines: theology vs. religious studies; church history vs. academic history; phenomenology vs. historicism; theoretical vs. data-driven approaches to historiography. One thing that haunts all of these oppositions is the strangeness of religiousness itself as an object of study; one that, at least in the West, has often been linked to ephemeral things like particular experience, personal belief, a revealed faith, or a communal witness– all things that challenge both the perceived stability of the object being studied and the objectivity of the person doing the studying. At stake is often two things: the need to maintain the unbiased credibility of the scholar, on the one hand; and the extent to which the religious subject of the past is to be believed, on the other.[1] I want to reposition this set of desiderata slightly, and ask instead: to what extent should certain paradigmatic claims of the past affect or amend the paradigms of modern scholarship, or the modes through which we organize the data we study?

---

1 In addition to Orsi's work on this subject which I will presently discuss at length, cf. Hollywood: 2016; particularly the introduction and chapter three; Furey: 2008; Rein: 2008.

By asking, 'Does Calvin's Church Have a History?', I do two things. First, I consider the broader question of why it might be theoretically important to perform a historical study of [a] 'church' that assumes an 'indigenous', theological definition for the church – not out of sectarian allegiance to any one definition, but for the ultimate aim of enriching the analysis of the data in question. Second, I use John Calvin's ecclesiology as a case study for what this might look like, methodologically. In other words, when I ask about 'Calvin's church', I do not primarily mean the structure and operation of the church in sixteenth-century Geneva over which Calvin assumed figurative ownership. Rather, I am interested in the church that Calvin theorizes in book four of his 1559 *Institutio Christianae Religionis*, and in the particular kind of presence that this church, the 'true church' in Calvin's view, would possess.

What I mean by 'history', in asking whether Calvin's church has one or not, has to do with *presence*. What kinds of presences, or existences, are thought to attain some form of continuity in space and time, and therefore be capable of having a history? The "time of the Reformation" supplies an ideal context in which to ask this question, in that it produced an array of competing theories of and definitions for church that would have been unprecedented – although not altogether unforeseen –in Europe's collective recollection. So, one way of getting at the question of presence and history in the context of the church is to wonder what possible experiences of presence gave way to such an abundance of theories. By pressing this question, I am interested in pressing the tactics through which historical scholarship can perceive and acknowledge the modes of human life that might have given rise to such contestations of 'church'. Ultimately, I anticipate that following this line of inquiry has the potential to deepen our understanding of modes of life both in and beyond the church in the time of the Reformation: in times and places disjointed from institutional, confessional, or other more recognizable forms of historical continuity, yet still as recognizable iterations of 'rhyming' historical phenomena.[2]

After all, to claim that something 'has' a history – that a person, institution, nation, tradition, people, or idea *has* a history or *is* historical – is to grant certain conditions concerning that thing's existence. It assumes, for example, that the object in question is real, and is real in a certain way across time. This means that any positive claim about presence will also always be a political claim, or a claim over who and what have a rightful place in a certain kind of society governed by shared intellectual norms. In asserting or denying whether something has a presence worth studying, scholarship regulates the degree of public responsibility owed to the object

---

2 Mark Twain famously quipped that history rhymes rather than repeats. However, this also provides an apt summary for the insight of so-called genealogical or archaeological approaches to history that look for structural repetitions and repeated signatures rather than other quasi-idealistic or organic forms of continuity. For foundational works on genealogy and archeology as and in relation to historical method, cf. Agamben: 2009 and Foucault: 1977.

in question. Put simply, things that have presence also have power. To deny presence is to deny power. Historians wield an important form of power inasmuch as they make implicit claims about presences. I am also interested, then, in exploring the political implications – then and now – of acknowledging or denying a presence, and as such, a history.

This paper will proceed as follows. I will begin with the theoretical discussion, saying more about 'history' and particularly what I mean by 'presence' and the nature of its linkage to 'power'. To do so, I will engage Robert Orsi's recent intervention in the field of American religious history, and then critically assess the strengths and limitations of Orsi's contribution when considered within the domain of Reformation-era ecclesiology. Then I will shift attention to Calvin's argument over the marks of the church in the 1559 *Institutio*, and examine the kind of presence and power that Calvin articulates when he defines the church. I find Calvin to offer a particularly salient point of departure for this kind of study not only because of his relatively wide scope of influence as a reformer, but also because his definition of the "true church" challenges many familiar assumptions about what constitutes historical presence. According to Calvin, the true church is not linked to things that are easily measured: a physical lineage, a particular institutional organization, or even adherence to a written charter per se. It is marked, rather, by a set of *practices* that involve the performative engagement with a set of given scriptural signs.

Over the last century, the accumulated scholarship on Calvin's ecclesiology has tended to fall between researchers who are interested in the denominational continuity of Reformed churches and, as such, aim to clarify and promote Calvin's ideas in the service of the tradition that follows his influence; or, more commonly today, scholars who more fit the mold of an early modern historian, whose research aims at what 'really happened' either in the context of Calvin's study, church, city, or socio-political legacy. Loosely speaking, the former set of scholars will explore the intellectual content of Calvin's ideas as claims that have retained assent over time, and study the nature and implications of those claims. The latter set will emphasize the otherness of historical context, and work to reconstruct that context as a kind of controlled space, checking the temptations of anachronism. But what happens if we allow Calvin'swriting itself to cut across conceptions of linear temporal periods and stable contexts, and as such to theoretically guide the location and parameters of particular kinds of non-sectarian historical inquiry? – to furnish, in other words, a method for studying a certain particular kind of religious phenomena? This would not strictly be a matter of believing or disregarding the claims of a historical source, but rather of letting a historical account of presence trouble contemporary notions of presence, and in so doing, direct a modern scholar to relate concrete evidence that might otherwise be overlooked. By reading Calvin as a theorist in his own right, it might be possible to draw out dimensions of the presence of 'church' that would be otherwise overlooked.

2. To Have a History: Thinking About Presence

I borrow the term 'presence' from historian of American Catholicism Robert Orsi's argument in his recent book, *History and Presence* (2016). Orsi's theoretical concerns are similar to the ones I have articulated above. While he has no interest in simply acting as a transparent narrator of the accounts given by his Roman Catholic subjects, he nevertheless finds the methodological constraints of historical reductionism to be lacking when put to giving an account of Catholic life. For many historians writing, for example, on Marian shrines, "men's and women's relationships with the Virgin Mary… are representations of social or psychological facts, symbols of something else, but nothing in themselves" (Orsi: 2016, 58). The troubling underlying assumption, dominant in religious historiography, is that academic writing attaches itself legitimately to social phenomena in a way that it cannot attach to the suggestion of presences that are posited beyond the pale of what is normatively deemed 'real'. According to Orsi,

In theories of the world as always already mediated, discourse is prior to and constitutive of experience. Not surprisingly, therefore, the discursive is what needs to be studied when one sets out to describe the study of religious experience. Discursive formations of power create religious experiences, emotions, and perceptions. Religions are social constructions, in modern intellectual orthodoxy (Orsi: 2016, 58).

While Orsi rightly ties this methodological orthodoxy to a philosophical position that the world is "always already mediated," and that what scholars therefore tend to study is the mediation itself, it is also the case that the relative concreteness of discourse promises an alluring stability. By attaching scholarly claims about religion to more widely accepted social scientific theories, these claims would seem to be both translatable as acceptable objects of academic study and, as such, falsifiable. It may be possible, for example, to contextualize the role of a pilgrimage site in mediating relationships between women and men, while constructing a larger argument around accounts of an apparition of the Virgin seems, on its face, to be a more fraught task.

Orsi wants to call into question both the integrity and facility of what he calls this metaphysical "postulate of absence". To do so, he traces this postulate back to the time of the Reformation, when some Protestants began to promote an alternate account of the Eucharist. Against the Roman Catholic teaching of the time, a range of figures (many following Huldrych Zwingli) denied the 'real presence' of Christ in the Host in favor of a symbolic account in which the normative presence of the physically-present community was reinforced through remembering Christ's actual absence (cf. Zwingli: 1953).[3] According to Orsi, this logic of divine absence

---

3 It should be noted at the outset that Orsi's critique of Protestant Eucharistic theory seems directed specifically to the Zwinglian tradition, as I will make clearer later on. See Zwingli: 1953.

assumed a kind of elective affinity with emerging, quasi-scientific conceptions of nature, medicine, society, and colonial race theory. The purely symbolic Eucharist would thus present a conception of religion that reified the broader metaphysics of modernity, one that would methodologically preclude the presence of "the gods" at work in the world. According to Orsi,

> The theological destiny of the doctrine of the real presence in the sixteenth century and afterward was forged in technical language and bound up with people's changing knowledge of the world and their new experiences of themselves as bodies, minds, and souls. The presence /absence divide was also implicated in and inflected by Christian encounters with men and women of other races and religions in the successive ages of European colonialism and imperialism… Decades of struggle among competing and irreconcilable camps of theologians 'straining for ever closer definition' of what Jesus was saying to his disciples hardened divergent conceptualizations into doctrine, ecclesiology, and politics (Orsi: 2016, 18).

As this technical language mutually reinforced emerging notions of reality and rationality, assertions concerning divine presences were increasingly linked not only to irrationality, but also connected to the notion of a temporal past in which such irrationalities were mistaken for realities. Religious claims that privileged the medium of the symbolic could be more easily rationalized, and accordingly granted the status of "modern religion", while Catholicism (along with the full range of other non-Protestant traditions) were "not included in this future" (Orsi: 2016, 38–39).

Part of Orsi's intervention entails pressing the way that academic historiography tends to tacitly link a latent conception of temporality to a latent conception of rationality, and in so doing displace other accounts of presence as both irrational and as temporally "past" or "other." Kathleen Davis's *Periodization and Sovereignty* (2008) draws out this kind of argument with more explicit consideration of its political ramifications, giving an account of how the postulate of state sovereignty functioned similarly to erase or temporally-displace other more complex notions of economic governance. Following her argument will help to better frame how assumptions about presence can adversely affect the integrity of historical research. Davis's archival research looks for the origins of the concept of feudalism, and discovers that the concept was first conceived and temporalized no earlier than early modernity –by, for example, English jurists and historians such as Henry Spelman and John Selden who retrospectively theorized the "feudal past" in the aim of shoring up legal justifications for the emerging paradigm of sovereign nation-states (cf. Davis: 2008, 9). Because the concept of a homogeneous "feudalism" was automatically linked to a dated past – specifically, with the temporal period of "the Middle Ages" – the synthetic concept of a "feudal Middle Ages" would have two discernible political effects. First, in Europe, it would subtly reify the superiority of the "sovereign present" over the past, and link the state with reality and rationality. Second, it would have the effect of legitimizing colonial aggression against geographic "others" in the name of drawing those nations "out of the past".

This argument might seem to be unrelated to Orsi's. After all, Davis is largely uninterested in the role played by religion, and much less by claims of religious experience. However, what Davis and Orsi share is a similar interest in how latent metaphysical assumptions undergirding the social, economic and political structures of modern life have the effect of predetermining both (a) the legitimacy of modern methods of study and, as such, (b) the shape and order of temporality itself. For Davis, the historiographical legacy that involved modern periodization was bad historiography because it homogenizes both the medieval past and the political paradigm of feudalism *when the data itself is actually much more complex*:

> While, as Michel de Certeau has shown, historiography 'forgets' infinite possibilities for selecting and arranging detail as it carves out an apprehensible concept... the resulting concept [can thus be located] in the past, as the forgotten object toward which historiography must strive. With such confirmation of 'modern' historiography's trajectory, periodization becomes self-evident, and time runs smooth (Davis: 2008, 10).

In performing a periodizing cut that effectively focalizes the perceived essence of the past, historiography that assumes the contrasting norms of the present will inevitably also reinforce the homogenization *of* the present. This methodology is flawed on two fronts: it fails to fully attend to operative differences in data that cut across both the past and the present; and it is unable to effectively relate the distant past *to* the present with nuance. Orsi, who also cites de Certeau, makes a similar point to Davis in a different way:

> Modern historiography, French Jesuit historian Michel de Certeau writes, 'endlessly presupposes homogeneous unities (century, country, class, economic or social strata, etc.) and cannot give way to the vertigo that critical examination of these fragile boundaries might bring about'. Scholarship serves to contain ontological "vertigo." In an intellectual culture premised on absence, the experience of presences is the phenomenon that is most disorienting, most inexplicable... Constraints on the scholar's imagination become, by means of his or her scholarship, constraints on the imaginations of others, specifically those whose lives the scholar aims to represent and understand (Orsi: 2016, 64).

Orsi and Davis thus share an interest in developing historiographical methods that attend to archival and ethnographic data that is either methodologically dismissed, or simply left unrelated to other data because of paradigmatic metaphysical assumptions about conceptual difference.

Reading the two authors side by side – in spite of and moreover because of their differences – underscores two things: (a) the way that contemporary norms of historiography presume certain discourses to offer more legitimate accounts of material conditions and privileges them as more appropriate to objective, scholarly analysis; and (b) the degree to which this obscures and minimizes facets of material conditions that suggest the visible effects of complex kinds of relationships (i.e., with divine beings, ideas, or modes of life) that do not fit these perceived norms. For Orsi, historiographical attention to relationships with "the gods" challenges the postulate of absence. For Davis, historiographical attention to the conceptual origins of "feudalism" and "the Middle Ages" challenges the assumption that history is shaped in successive epochs. Both are interested in devising better ways for giving an account of the complexity of human experience both in relation to and in contrast to social order.

My interest is in whether and how the role of historical theology, when approached as historical theory rather than as timeless, propositional claims about metaphysics, can play a role in reshaping some of these patterns of research, thus attuning historians (and readers) to diverse and challenging relationships with presence that might cut unexpectedly across time and location. Here, I take both of these questions and explore them in a third domain: that of the church, an institution that is related to both religious experience and to politics, but one that is more explicitly predicated on the nature of intersubjective relationships between persons in an institutional context. What do accounts about the nature of these intersubjective relationships – between a person and the divine, those in authority and those in submission, or among a collection of persons and the divine – do to the way we conceive of a church as a historical 'thing'? I am interested in how the question of 'Church at the time of Reformation' can be enriched by strategically 'believing' historical, theological claims about the nature of the relationships that structure 'the church', rather than reducing the church to an institution consummate with ordinary empirical methods, and in how this might shape and shift both the gathering and the rendering of data precisely by encouraging a multiplicity of presences at the theoretical level.

Orsi's charge, like that of Davis, is that a more responsible historiography will look for ways to challenge the reader's historical imagination by self-consciously challenging the scholar's *theoretical* imagination. This means finding ways to read the archive precisely for those places that trouble yet-unexamined conceptions of temporality or reality. For Davis, a historian must *resist* the tendency to "retrospectively collapse the difference between history and a theory of history, and thus to reify the basis of what is always a particular sovereign claim upon 'the now'" (Davis: 2008, 20). For Orsi, "The alternative to a historiography without gods is one that allows another reality to break into history and theory, not to destroy them but to enlarge them… What is necessary is not writing, certainly not overwriting, but a kind of un-writing, to allow what is denied to break through" (Orsi: 2016, 65). As I turn to Calvin, I am interested in what close attention to an influential piece of theological writing – and particularly writing on the notion of 'church' – can contribute to the questions and aims I have laid out.

3. Calvin's Church

With a clearer sense of what I mean by presence and its relationship to whether and how a history is told or excluded, let me begin this section by looking more specifically at how the concept of 'Church' presses on competing notions of presence in different ways. Like Orsi's 'gods', conceptions of 'Church' have the potential to trouble the ordinary boundaries of historical study by asserting a kind of relationship that troubles the ordinary norms of empiricism – a relationship between an ordinary person and a divine being, but also collective and intersubjective relationships between persons and mediated by divine beings or sacred objects. Terms traditionally used to refer to the presence of the church – the 'invisible church', the 'spiritual' or 'mystical body', the 'mother of believers' – all refer, in a general sense, to a form of presence that may be claimed to encounter an individual relationally, but that is other than more ordinary presences such as a 'building', 'denominational infrastructure', 'apostolic succession', 'disciplinary procedures', a 'friendship', or even 'society' or 'discursive community'. So long as these two kinds of presence (special/divine and ordinary/empirical) are kept apart from one another in binary opposition, they map quite neatly onto the aforementioned disciplinary boundaries of academic religious studies and the study of the Reformation more specifically. To the extent that the former, heterogeneous set of definitions are privileged, so are theological-philosophical methods. The latter set yields more proper receptors for a historical study that centers on the social, political, or intellectual character of a particular ecclesial institution or denomination. However, simply accepting the integrity of this existential binary and the methods designed to study each side in isolation means performing the move that Davis warns against: mistaking a philosophy of history for history itself (or, in turn, a history of philosophy for philosophy itself).

As a strategy for questioning the integrity of this binary itself, I turn now to a canonical text of theology that also boasts clear historical significance stemming from the sixteenth century – a time that both Orsi and Davis pinpoint as pivotal for the emergence of modern conceptual methodologies. By looking at a theological text with these theoretical questions in mind, I follow the lead of Brenda Deen Schildgen who has engaged questions of historical method with a particular focus on the relationship between history and writing (cf. Schildgen: 2012). On the one hand, Schildgen notes that theorists like Hayden White have emphasized historiography's fundamental indebtedness to literary form. Historiography, as narrative writing, is necessarily organized by means of the same devices as fictional literature. These devices inevitably distance historiography from the object being described, a thing which cannot help but be cropped and organized through the use of crafted emplotment, metaphors, tropes, irony, and synecdoche.[4] Reading history also requires reading in and through these devices: reading for what appears, but also for what is left out or implied. On the other hand, Schildgen notes how scholars, following a more Foucauldian trend, have grown increasingly concerned over the extent to which dominant historiography works by reifying the very conceptual "realities" of which it purports to be giving an historical account. This anxiety has led to an increasing interest in narrating so-called hidden histories: "micro-histories, the histories of colonized and exploited, histories of minorities and exiles, or the historical lives of peasants rather than kings and rulers [as] the subjects of inquiry" (Schildgen: 2012, 7).

Like Orsi and Davis, Schildgen sees shortcomings in attempts to simply use traditional historical methods to tell excluded stories when those methods themselves are implicated in metaphysical assumptions over things like rationality, presence, and temporal periodization. As Orsi and Davis suggested, a different kind of writing is necessary to call attention to the disjunction between an objective history and a philosophy of history. For Schildgen, however, one of the ways to perform this writing (or "un-writing") is by reading canonical texts themselves, but reading them with particular attention to the forms of life they will inevitably, but tacitly, reference. According to Schildgen, Canonical works themselves might represent an "insurrection of subjugated knowledge." A canonical work today may have been sidelined when it was composed or even in its reception history. Thus, important as discovering long-ignored facts of human history, and therefore filling in important gaps in our historical understanding has been, we have simultaneously tended to ignore how writers who have been received as canonical or authoritative may themselves have confronted historical lapses or grand presuppositions (Schildgen: 2012, 7).

A text like Calvin's 1559 *Institutio* presents a compelling case for such an approach. For one, it emerged in a time and context of unparalleled institutional fragmentation and growing sectarianism, a time when the idea that a common, collective experience of life in a world ordered by familiar institutions and patterns was being openly and violently contested. Obviously, the *Institutio* has long been read for its theological-philosophical content. Abundant examples exist of scholarship that mines that content with skill and intellectual erudition. It has also been read for its intellectual history, an endeavor that usually emphasizes the strict confines

---

4 Cf. White: 1973. Also, for a fuller treatment of White's impact (and lack thereof) on historical method, cf. Paul: 2011.

of context for good reasons.[5] My aim, however, is to re-approach the *Institutio* as an example of a text that might function as a cipher for conceiving a different kind of historical method – that theorizes a different historiographical approach to 'church history' a presence generated by intersubjective *practices*. In doing so, I do not mean to suggest that reading Calvin as theory should unseat other theories or be treated as the new normative approach to the history of church. I rather focus on this text as an example of a way that theological texts might be relevant to non-theological historiography, precisely for upsetting unchecked assumptions that obtain between philosophy and history.

As I turn attention specifically to Calvin, I am not interested in what the text merely claims about the church. A number of recent studies have treated this with precision and clarity. I'm more interested in taking another look at what Calvin's claims reveal, implicitly, about a form of ecclesial presence that he takes to be central to the experience of his readership. The *Institutio* is an example of a record – and, as such, an organic theory – of Calvin's own presumed entanglement with a kind of presence that is reducible neither to the normative ecclesiastical accounts of his own historical context nor to that presumed by contemporary historiography. Ultimately, I am interested in how the presence of Calvin's church might lead historians to think of and study the impact of a 'church' in a way that is distinct from more familiar studies of either Calvin's Genevan church or Calvinist denominations more generally – in other words, from studies that presume familiar empirical-contextual methods.

When Calvin approaches the topic of the 'Church', he does so against a particular historical backdrop and with interests and assumptions that attach to his own living context. Although I want to argue that the implications of Calvin's theorizing extend beyond that narrow context, it is nevertheless important to consider some contextual features as a contrasting backdrop to the kind of presence he is theorizing. 'Church' had of course been a contested category in the Latin West since the origin of Christianity itself – from Augustine's skirmish with the Donatists to the Great Schism that divided Eastern and Western Christianity. Even as Western Christianity achieved some institutional stability under the Roman See, debates over the nature of church had arguably grown in intensity during the three centuries prior to the Reformation. Critical writings on the nature of church emerged from prominent figures like John Wycliffe, John of Paris, and Jan Hus, putting words to material tensions that were constantly exacerbated by events such as: the rise of the Franciscan order with related mendicant and lay religious movements; Pope

---

5 For methodological examples ranging more toward philosophical theology, see a work like Billings: 2007; for a methodological example ranging more toward reading Calvin as intellectual history, see a work like Muller: 2001. Note that I have only given two examples because my aim is not an exhaustive bibliography but a simple representation of the kinds of methods I have in mind.

John XXII's denunciation of the Franciscan ideal of poverty in 1323; the Avignon Papacy from 1309–1377; the subsequent Western Papal Schism from 1378–1417; and constant tension connected to simmering nationalist movements in England, German principalities, and Bohemia. However one wants to chart the intensity of debates over church prior to the Reformation, it is difficult to deny that the practical effects of these debates were felt with a kind of novelty in the wake of the sixteenth-century reform movements to the extent that competing ecclesial institutions began to emerge materially, with unprecedented political protection allowing unprecedented stability.

At the same time, the countervailing ideal of 'the Church' as a unified corporate body under Christ – and moreover as bride of Christ and quasi-physical 'mother' of believers – had been a more-or-less consistently held teaching in the Latin West, carefully theorized since Cyprian and especially Augustine. In Augustine's *De Doctrina Christiana* (397–426 CE), for example, one's presence and participation in the church is a necessary requisite for learning to interpret scripture and ultimately to advance in the Christian faith, in part because the Church provides the material sphere for habituation according to the "rule of love". According to Augustine, "The church is his body, as the teaching of the apostle shows; it is also called his bride. So he ties together his own body, with its many members performing different tasks, in a bond of unity and love like a healing bandage" (*De Doctrina Christiana* 1.33).[6] Without the habituation brought about through repeated, embodied and contextualized acts of love, the pursuit of faith becomes aimless and groundless, and the signs that constitute the scriptural text become unmoored and without meaning. This line of thinking presumes the importance of an organizational infrastructure for the church, necessary to facilitate its continuity of presence on the earth; but it also emphasizes the robustly spiritual function of this body as its primary *raison d'être*.

Against the backdrop of ongoing organizational contestation and theologically-necessary appeals to unity, Calvin's writing on the church must navigate a specific kind of dilemma. On the one hand, he stands in the tradition of those, like Hus and Wycliffe, who have actively worked to re-theorize the true nature of the church in such a way that the established church – or what many would assume as the default structure – can be resisted and reformed. Yet, Calvin also wants to support and maintain the recognizable and unified structure of the visible church as a fundamental part of what allows it to perform its most important function, that of the collective training of believers in faith. He wants to position himself as assuming the "office of doctor in the church" [*officiú doctoris in Ecclesia*] who has taken up the task of writing a manual for the benefit of "God's church" [*Ecclesiae dei*] (Calvin: 1960, 4; 3).

---

6 Citations of *De Doctrina Christiana* abbreviate the book title and cite the quote according to standardized book and section numbers.

To the extent that Calvin wants to write a distinct kind of ecclesial presence, then, it must be one that fundamentally assumes continuous presence of the nascent Reformed church *with* the "one, true, holy, and apostolic" church as the proper material site for the habituation of believers in faith. For example, when Calvin introduces his discussion of the church, he writes: "I start with the church, into whose bosom God is pleased to gather his children, not only that they may be nourished by her help and ministry as long as they are infants and children, but also that they may be guided by her motherly care until they mature and at least reach the goal of faith" (*Institutio* 4.1.1). This statement signals the extent to which Calvin is deeply invested in affirming what is fundamentally an Augustinian defense of the church as a requisite site of participation for the worldly life of the believer.[7]

But if Calvin wants to maintain the traditional conception of the church as the proper material site of Christian formation – the proper domain in which Christians learn to apply the rule of faith alongside the rule of love – then certain complexities emerge. The primary one related to the topic under consideration is this: from what standpoint can the fulcrum of his resistance to Rome be exercised? On what ground can Calvin stand in order to critique the church in which he, strictly speaking, ought to be a full and submissive participant in order for his critique itself to achieve legitimacy? This paradox is striking because it structurally echoes the concerns over historiography that I examined in part one. When a theory of history becomes inseparable from history itself, one important thing that is foreclosed is critical methodological distance. This kind of critical distance – opening a space for another kind of existence – is what scholars like Orsi and Davis are trying to recover. As both of them made abundantly clear, however, what is at stake is not simply their ability to offer criticisms, but more importantly the historian's responsibility to the complex conditions of human life and experience. Something cannot have a history if its presence is unacknowledged; and presence cannot be ascertained if it is methodologically excluded from the outset.

This similarity points to why reading someone like Calvin's ecclesiology is germane to more recent debates over religious historiography, or historiography in general. For Calvin, to critique the church while maintaining orthodox ecclesiology means pinpointing a different sense of presence than the one most likely to be inculcated in his sixteenth-century readers.[8] It is not enough to simply offer a different set of claims about the church. He must also inhabit a different sense of ecclesial

---

7 See *Institutio* 4.1.3 and discussions in Kim: 2014, especially chapter four.

8 On the one hand, a close reading of the teaching and generic structure of the *Institutio* suggests that Calvin's doctrine of divine providence is designed, at least in part, to construct the "frame of the universe" as the proper school of piety. Sanchez, Michelle C. "Ritualized Doctrine: Protestant Ritual, Genre, and the Case of Calvin's Institutes." Journal of the American Academy of Religion 85 (3) (2017): 746–774.

existence that is nevertheless tangible enough to be persuasive to his readers in a living way, and thus authorize the legitimacy of Calvin's critical alternative as a fundamental continuity with the necessary function of the church in the lives of believers. Reading for this alternate kind of presence means reading for the kind of presence – the kind of grounded experience – evoked between the lines of Calvin's writing on the church. To this end, I will proceed by outlining three distinctive moves that Calvin makes to define 'church', moves that reveal, if implicitly, certain engagements with a form of presence that is distinct from (though not mutually exclusive from) other competing approaches to 'church'.[9]

(1) First, Calvin claims that the true, invisible church exists under one head, which is Christ alone; as such, the church is truly composed of members of the elect who are in Christ by faith and through grace (*Institutio* 4.1.1–2).[10] In spite of the anti-Papal implications discernible in the context around this claim, the argument itself is uncontroversial and has a long history within biblical and theological literature. Yet, perhaps because of its relative agreeability, this claim is important to refocusing what is at stake for Calvin in the question of church *historicity*. The claim that the true church is headed by Christ is, after all, a claim that the church is founded on a relationship with divine presence, and one that moreover acts on both the worldly participant in the church and troubles the ordinary existence and temporality of the institution. By emphasizing this kind of relationship at the very root of the definition of church, Calvin is able to negotiate a starting point from which to re-negotiate a series of subsequent theoretical claims that might re-establish precisely *how* Christ's singular form of presence is mediated alongside ordinary presences. In other words, Calvin sets up the argument as one over what precisely this "presence of the gods" (to use Orsi's, and definitely *not* Calvin's term) *does* within and alongside the created world.

This is precisely where debates over sacramental presence begin, and why they are ultimately so important for questions of history, presence, and power in a (post-) Reformation Christian context. Recall that, for Orsi, the Reformers' "symbolic turn" foregrounds the contemporary historian's "postulate of absence", or tendency to interpret claims about the presence of the gods in symbolic, discursive terms. This

---

9   Risking oversimplification, I will suggest that those competing approaches might link the presence of the church to the presence of Christ in and through the apostolic line (Roman Catholics), the realization of the authentic prophetic experience of the Spirit (some Anabaptists and Spiritualists), the purity of the community (some Anabaptists), or the community called by God in submission to the preached Word (Lutherans). Each of these approaches could be conceived of giving way to its own mode of historiography, one that would either be more or less linked to empirically-visible continuities, notions of periodization, or more individualized disruptive experiences.

10   This and all subsequent citations from the body of the *Institutio* are cited according to book, chapter, and section number.

is a theoretical and methodological foreclosure that exists to the detriment of both Catholics and the fuller variety of non-Protestant religious traditions around the colonial and postcolonial world. Yet, Orsi himself admits that early Protestant interpretations of the Eucharist were both more diverse and more complex than his stricter etiology of "the postulate of absence" acknowledges (Orsi: 2016, 19; 32). Calvin's Eucharistic theology is a prime example of how, for some Protestants, the heterogeneous presence of the gods is not simply rendered absent by the domesticated function of the sign, but is rather necessary for a certain kind of relational (and potentially disruptive) engagement with the sign.

In articulating his Eucharistic theology, Calvin resists the two potential responses to the question of how Christ's special presence is mediated. On the one hand, he denies the Roman Catholic claim that the local body of Christ is made really present in the Eucharist. On the other hand, however, he also denies that Christ is only symbolically invoked in order to homogenize the ordinary presence of the church, or community of believers, in the world. Calvin instead relies on a sophisticated theory of signification, derived again from Augustine, to theorize a *sui generis* form of presence that emerges in the church itself (cf. Evans: 1989). The theory goes something like this: (a) the local body of Christ assumes a peculiar presence in which both Eternal Word and Flesh coincide, thus anchoring Sign and Signified; (b) that body is thus both heterogeneous to ordinary bodies, but assumes a relationship to them by virtue of the ritualized use of signs in the context of the church; (c) this use of signs animates, through the work of the Holy Spirit (another distinct divine presence), a special form of intersubjective presence generated by the collective relationship to Christ (cf. *Institutio* 4.14; 17).[11] This special, intersubjective relationship not construed reductively, as something supernatural translated into normative discursive terms. Rather, the special body of Christ anchors and makes possible a *particular set of practices* through which the ordinary use of signs is disrupted and the unique presence of the Church is performed, potentially with transformative consequences (cf. Locher: 2004, 72–76).

(2) The central importance Calvin attaches to this operation of signification is clear in Calvin's second move, which is to align the performative use of the Word with the marks of the true, visible church. Calvin names two *activities* as the definitive, authenticating marks of the visible church: first, the "pure preaching of the Word"; and second, the "administration of the Sacraments according to Christ's institution" (*Institutio* 4.1.9). To define the 'true church' by a list of markers is not in any way novel on Calvin's part; a number of his contemporaries, such as Menno Simons, did similarly (cf. Girolimon: 1995). What does stand out, however, is that

---

11 Particularly relevant passages supporting these three points are found in: *Institutio* 4.14.2–3; 6; 9; 11; 16; 4.17.8; 10–11.

Calvin's two marks are, properly speaking, activities that operate according to a performative logic. They are not stable marks linked to static beliefs, the condition of moral lives, evidence of structural continuity (apostolic or otherwise), or any other empirical marks. Rather, the two activities generate the kind of presence that Calvin acknowledges in the Eucharist: they enable the re-signification of relationships through a particular mode of collective engagement with the heterogeneous presence of Christ.[12]

More generally, what makes the visible church a 'true church' – what lends it its peculiar, authentic form of presence – is a set of exercises that involve relating a privileged set of Christologically-anchored signs to *any* material circumstances, across places and times, where those signs are engaged through preaching and sacramental observance. On the one hand, this alleviates the need to link the visible church to something more stable that would at the same time be more contingent, such as a building, a special hierarchical structure, a certain historical lineage, or a certain set of rules. On the other hand, it opens up a wider set of questions about the differences that might obtain as the two marks are performed in and across a variety of contexts. If the marks function according to a kind of ritual logic, then the true church is constantly involving relationships across lines of difference that are precisely not fenced by these other possible kinds of empirical markers. This not only involves human and material relational involvement with the Christological signs of Word and Sacrament, it also raises the perpetual question of *how* different voices, ears, mode of digestion, postures of the body, habits of mind, and material contexts are engaging those signs at different times (cf. Ralston: 2011).

(3) If the true visible church *is what it is* by virtue of its performative activities around a given set of revealed signs, then what distinct kind of continuity or temporality would such a church possess? This leads to the third and last of Calvin's points: the emphasis that he places on disciplines in establishing the sense in which the church assumes something like temporal continuity. On the one hand, discipline refers to the set of regulating practices that mark the true church; but on the other hand, it also refers to the emphasis on church discipline for which Calvin is so well known (cf. *Institutio* 4.12). When one considers the central importance of practices of signification, the reason why discipline is so important for Calvin can be contextualized differently: the revealed signs do not operate properly in community without the operative, visible and activated faith of participants. For example, Calvin writes that when "a sacrament that is separated from its truth by the unworthiness of the recipient... nothing remains but a vain and useless figure" (*Institutio* 4.14.15). Disciplining therefore represents, among other things, a crucial

---

12 For more on precisely how Calvin understands preaching and the Eucharist *as* activities, cf. *Institutio* 1.7–9 and 4.17.

exercise for cultivating the precision of the practices that combine to render the visible church a true one (cf. Locher: 2004, 76–79)

The role given to discipline underscores the extent to which Calvin is relying on a ritualizing logic to theorize a form of presence – one that relies on discipline. It also gives an account of how such a church might assume some form of continuity across time: namely, by passing down a set of disciplines through which the repetition of the revealed signs may occur. In a stricter sense, however, the disciplines themselves are not aligned with the presence of the true church. The presence is located in the performed, Spirit-led coincidence of Christ with the participants in preaching, baptism and communion. Discipline, in both senses of the word, is akin to the pilgrimage that elicits the encounter between a pilgrim and the Virgin; they are the ordinary markers that point to, protect, and cultivate a heterogeneous presence and anticipate something of its effects.

4. Summary

With these three moves in view, let me highlight the two common moves that Calvin does *not* make in defining the peculiar presence of the church. For one thing, he does not foreclose the role of heterogeneous presences or their ability to assume a genuine relationship with an ordinary person and, as such, to act on society in a way that is irreducible to social forces. Christ's heterogeneous presence is, in fact, theorized to be operative within the church in a way that is irreducible to all other conventional forms of recognizable presence: it is irreducible to the presence of the minister, the Host, or any genetic account of succession, whether institutional or apostolic. Christ's presence is also irreducible to the personal purity of leaders and congregants. Calvin explicitly writes that while faith is necessary for the full operation of signs, the true church may well include reprobate (cf. *Institutio* 4.1.2). What constitutes the heterogeneous "real spiritual presence" is therefore fundamentally a set of relationships obtaining between Christ and the gathered church that are performatively enacted with (purported, expected, and presumably experienced) heterogeneous intersubjective results.

Finally, Calvin also shows little interest in defending the Reformed church by making cuts in the structure of time. He does not, in other words, polemically reify opposing ecclesiologies as indebted to a past order that is no longer valid; nor does he describe his own ecclesiology in an improvement over the past. Certainly, more robust theorizations of history were available to him.[13] Yet, although Calvin

---

13 For some accounts of theories of time and history prior to Calvin, cf. the following works: Jaritz: 2003; Reeves: 1999; Strohl: 2014.

does refer to distinct covenants with God, his covenant theology actually resists the temptation to periodization by emphasizing the continuity of Christ's heterogeneous presence in and among *diverse contexts*. The differences between covenants thus stems not from cuts in time, but from the immanent diversity of figures and communities as they engage relationally with the presence of Christ.[14]

What Calvin's ecclesiology does do – and why it is relevant to the questions I am posing about history – is assert a form of presence that is irreducible to either ordinary life (by means of discursive/symbolic translation) or to the direct action of the divine breaking into time (strictly through personal revelatory encounters). What would happen, then, if a historian were to follow Calvin's intersubjective, performative theory of ecclesial presence as a guide for collecting, relating, interpreting historical data? In some ways, the enterprise of telling a history of Calvin's church might look very different from the mode of historiography that dominated most of the twentieth century. If historians sought to narrate the kind of presence that Calvin reports, this might entail finding ways to write a history of the diverse effects of a choreography of practices, perhaps through a kind of thick description of particular collections of people gathered around the performance of Word and Sacrament. Such a study could not properly be limited by any one historical, temporal or geographic context, nor even by outward markers like denominational allegiance or explicit embracing of the 'Calvinist' or 'Reformed' name. For the presence Calvin describes is one that exceeds his own context and his own impact – one that, in theory, should follow the path of scriptural signs and erupt across temporal and spatial difference, and certainly across conventional ways of dividing time (e.g., medieval vs. modern, modern vs. postmodern) or institutions (e.g., Dutch Reformed vs. Scottish Presbyterian, or even Catholic vs. Protestant). The history told would be the history of the materialization of the sign wherever it is engaged as such (cf. Ralston: 2011, 126).

5. Conclusion

In the first part of the paper, I looked at theorists who are critical of the ideal that history should, or even *can*, present historical-empirical circumstances exhaustively by circumscribing a temporal and discursive context. The scholars thus call for 'un-writing', or for a method that looks for archival details to constantly challenge and even overturn larger conceptual truisms. I then proceeded to offer my own reading of a canonical work of sixteenth-century theology with an eye to the form

---

14 For places in Calvin's 1559 *Institutio* where he most clearly discusses the relationships between the covenant, see 2.7–11; 3.17; 4.16. Also, cf. Lillback: 2002.

of presence both advocated and presumed by that canonical text. I ultimately asked what such a reading might *do* to the historical method of studying 'church', if the source were taken seriously and given credence concerning its account of presence. I want to conclude by offering some thoughts on why it might be prudent, in a general sense, to continue to challenge the binary between theology and history and to rethink theology as *theory*. At the outset, I wrote that historians of religion often experience a tension between the need to operate within accepted methodological norms and the call to believe a religious subject's account of her own experience. Should a religious subject be given credence by a historian when making claims about presence not reducible to a social-scientific model or discursive analysis? I will give some reasons why believing such sources is not only a responsible thing to do, but one that is necessary to achieve a fuller historical fluency.

My reading of Calvin's ecclesiology sought to approach his arguments as believable accounts of a certain historical experience; not a *momentary* experience (although these can be important, too); not a *phenomenological* (and thus resolutely ahistorical) experience; rather, an account of complex living conditions inflected with the peculiarities of immediate context yet causally irreducible to them. To lend theological writing this kind of credence would allow such works to theoretically guide a historian's procedure, functioning much like any ethnographic subject interview, with the potential to lend insight into the larger data under consideration. As much as theological arguments might seem designed to merely make abstract claims about metaphysical things, they are also the record of a human author's struggle to make sense of things received from the world around the author. Texts thus record one's struggles with other texts, traditions, ideas, enemies, friends, living conditions, violence, suffering, admiration, love, or many combinations thereof. As such, maintaining a strict disciplinary division between the study of the argumentative content of theology and the study of fuller historical contexts would effectively amount to a wholesale and arbitrary decision, on the part of the scholar, to "disbelieve" a certain kind of historical source. In a structural sense, this is exactly the kind of methodologically-reinforced disbelief that Orsi wants to challenge as inadequate to his American Catholic sources.

To be clear, I am not suggesting that historians simply ought to proceed uncritically as if all theological claims were metaphysically true. At the same time, there are times they should proceed as if a theological claim is experientially true. The crucial difference, I think, has to do with the historian's self-consciousness about when and how to enact this "as if" counterfactual. Let me give an example of where this ambiguity is visible. Recently, American historian of religion Amanda Porterfield has discussed the pros and cons of sectarian historiography that did, in fact, employ theological paradigms uncritically. In a brief retrospective for the journal *Church History*, she shows how Protestant historians were indeed once guilty of methodologically fusing the presence "of the gods" with the ordinary presence of empirical life. Looking at the articles that appeared in the inaugural 1932 edition of *Church History*, Porterfield notes that a bracing faith in the providential course of history characterized the three essays in that first issue and the authors conveyed that faith with erudition, narrative flair, and sweeping knowledge of Christian history. Few authors today exert such broad command of events in the larger history of Christianity, or display such facility with a wide range of primary documents, and few write with such ebullience. Such may be the price of leaving behind a world where providence is clearly in sight (Porterfield: 2011, 366).

This observation is interesting for several reasons. On the one hand, it reminds readers of the extent to which historians have often unknowingly triangulated the historical imagination around a particular paradigm of homogeneous presence. By uncritically assuming the theological teaching of a divine providence rationalizing the sequence of events in a particular way, each historian demonstrably organized his respective data set by correlating his findings with this assumption. The 1932 essays assumed the legitimacy of providence in much the same way that a more recent historian might assume the legitimacy of class struggle, gender politics, self-interested game theory, or struggles for political agency as a key determinant shaping historical events.

On the other hand, however, there is a latent positivity to Porterfield's reading. She acknowledges that even the providential-historical paradigm led to certain insights about historical relationships between things that remain striking and even instructive. While the modern historiography that "leav[es] providence behind has enabled many advances, opening windows, removing blinders, and abetting understanding of the forces Christianity has exerted within historical events," she argues that readers should not forget the many insights that did in fact emerge from the use of the earlier, overtly theological paradigm" (Porterfield: 2011, 368). The results of this earlier, embarrassingly-antiquated form of historiography are responsible for much of the complexity of understanding that present scholars take for granted and in fact build on. Even the most sectarian paradigms had a way of achieving something very much valued by the historical task: the recognition of compelling relationships between things, past and present (Porterfield: 2011, 368). What is crucial is that historians become aware of both the multiplicity of possible interpretive and methodological paradigms and their limitations.

These are relevant insights to bring back to the study of the sixteenth century, a tumultuous and important century which has been both illumined and marred by the methodological *aporiae* I have been discussing. One might think of the now-dated yet deeply-formative disciplinary debates over whether the Reformation was more of a "medieval" or a "modern" event; or whether the ecclesiological shifts that marked the various Protestant movements are best described in terms of social, political, economic, or purely theological motivations.[15] It is interesting, in light of these challenges, that both Orsi's and Davis's critical interventions treat the time of the Reformation as the historical time when a sovereign "postulate of absence" would emerge. To me, this only underscores the importance of returning to sixteenth-century material in order to better understand the tensions of our present ways of thinking and how it might be possible to think, again, with presence – to take seriously not only underexplored historical data, but also fuller range of theological-theoretical material that might help us understand and explore what was at stake in those intellectual arguments *for life*.

Along these lines, it is interesting that Orsi admits the extent to which his own characterization of 'Protestantism' brushes over many of the complexities of Protestantism itself (Orsi: 2016, 19; 32). Putting aside the obvious critique that Orsi is failing to abide by his own rules, what I take to be instructive about Orsi's reading of Protestantism is this: it is not that Protestants have always monolithically failed to acknowledge or experience "the presence of the gods"; rather, it is that a contingent historical affinity emerged between Protestant Eucharistic rationalism and hegemonic social, economic, and political rational regimes, and continues to act powerfully on the historical imagination of scholars. But what happens if one *does* re-approach the complex origins of Protestantism with Orsi's criticisms in mind? Protestantism might re-emerge as a particularly fruitful archive for recovering not only more information about the past, but more complex approaches to religious conditions at different times and locations.

This is the kind of trend that I have tried to exemplify in this paper. I have tried to show that one way to avoid eliding a philosophy of history with history itself is to take on an ever-fuller variety of philosophies of history at their word, treating them as believable testaments to experience, and to see where they lead. If Calvin's church does have a history – that is, if it has the kind of presence that yields a history – I suspect that telling that history would not only lead to new insights concerning "church at the time of the Reformation", it would also suggest ways in which the "time of the Reformation" is not the kind of thing that can ever be entirely past.

---

15 Heiko Oberman's admirable body of work is a testament to the longstanding effect of these older debates, in working both to undermine them while also tacitly reinscribing certain assumptions over modern/medieval periodization (cf. Oberman: 1992; 2001). For more on the debate over the irreducible role of religion in the time of the Reformation, see also the following two aforementioned articles: Furey: 2008; Rein: 2008.

Bibliography

Sources

AUGUSTINE, *De Doctrina Christiana*, in PL 34, 16–122.

JEAN CALVIN (1960), The Institutes of the Christian Religion, McNeill (ed.), Battles (trans.), Louisville, KY: Westminster John Knox Press, 1960.

HULDRYCH ZWINGLI (1953), On the Lord's Supper, in: G.W. Bromiley (trans.), Zwingli and Bullinger, Philadelphia: The Westminster Press.

Secondary Literature

AGAMBEN, GIORGIO (2009), The Signature of All Things, Brooklyn: Zone Books.

BILLINGS, J. TODD (2007), Calvin, Participation, and the Gift, New York: Oxford University Press.

DAVIS, KATHLEEN (2008), Periodization and Sovereignty, Philadelphia: University of Pennsylvania Press.

EVANS, G.R (1989), Calvin on Signs: An Augustinian Dilemma, in: Renaissance Studies 31, 35–45.

FOUCAULT, MICHEL (1977), Nietzsche, Genealogy, History, in: Donald F. Bouchard (ed.), Language, Counter-Memory, Practice, Ithaca: Cornell University Press.

FUREY, CONSTANCE (2008), Utopian History, in: Method and Theory in the Study of Religion 30, 385–398.

GIROLIMON, MICHAEL (1995), John Calvin and Menno Simons on Religious Discipline: A Difference in Degree and Kind, Fides et Historia 27/1, 5–29.

HOLLYWOOD, MY (2016), Acute Melancholia, New York: Columbia University Press.

JARITZ, GERHARD/GERSON MORENO-RIANO (ed.) (2003), Time and Eternity: The Medieval Discourse, Turnhout, Belgium: Brepols Publishers.

LILLBACK, PETER P. (2002), The Binding of God: Calvin's Role in the Development of Covenant Theology, Grand Rapids: Baker Academic.

LOCHER, GOTTFRIED WILHELM (2004), Sign of the Advent: A Study in Protestant Ecclesiology, Fribourg: Academic Press Fribourg.

MULLER, RICHARD (2001), The Unaccommodated Calvin: Studies in the Foundation of a Theological Tradition, New York: Oxford University Press.

OBERMAN, HEIKO (1992), The Dawn of the Reformation, Grand Rapids: Eerdmans.

OBERMAN, HEIKO (2001), The Harvest of Medieval Theology: Gabriel Biel and Late Medieval Nominalism, Grand Rapids: Baker Academic.

ORSI, ROBERT (2016), History and Presence, Cambridge: Harvard University Press.

PAUL, HERMAN (2011), Hayden White, London, Great Britain: Polity Press.

PORTERFIELD, AMANDA (2011), Leaving Providence Behind, Church History 80/2, 366–368.

RALSTON, JOSHUA (2011), Preaching Makes the Church: Recovering a Missing Ecclesial Mark, in Eddy van der Borght/Gerard Mannion (ed.), John Calvin's Ecclesiology: Ecumenical Perspectives, New York: T&T Clark.

REEVES, MARJORIE (1999), The Prophetic Sense of History in Medieval and Renaissance Europe, Brookfield: Ashgate.

REIN, NATHAN (2008), History and Vulnerability: A Response to Levine and Furey, Method and Theory in the Study of Religion 20, 399–406.

SCHILDGEN, BRENDA DEEN (2012), Divine Providence: A History: The Bible, Virgil, Osorius, Augustine, and Dante, New York: Bloomsbury Academic.

STROHL, JANE E. (2014), Luther's Eschatology, in: Irene Dingel/Lubomir Batka (ed.), The Oxford Handbook of Martin Luther's Theology, Oxford: Oxford University Press.

WHITE, HAYDEN (1973), Metahistory, Baltimore: Johns Hopkins University Press.

YOSEP, KIM (2014), The Identity and Life of the Church: John Calvin's Ecclesiology in the Perspective of His Anthropology, Eugene: Wipf & Stock.

Ulrich Andreas Wien

Reconciliation in a Village Community in the Reformation Period in Transylvania

Preliminary Remark

According to the current state of knowledge, we have a singular source: an original handwritten book of sermons of the Reformation period. The author is Damasus Dürr, born 1535 in Bod, later minister in a small village in Transylvania – Apoldu de Jos. Passed-down sermons from villages of the 16th century are unknown in historical research and as material in archives. An edition of this corpus from the last third of the 16th century could remedy the much-lamented lack of sources. It would allow a revitalisation of studies and open a new field of research (Wien: 2017b).

1. Accepting the Reformed Movements in the Pioneer Region of Religious Freedom – Transylvania Between 1520 and 1570

The church structures and institutions of Transylvania within the Latin Western Church were fundamental in shaping the different ways in which the Reformation thought and its influences were received. During the 16th century they initiated a transformation process of varying intensity, which was nevertheless character- ized by profound discontinuities (Bernhard: 2015; Fata: 2000; Fata/Schindling: 2010; Leppin/Wien: 2005; Müller: 2000a; 2000b; Reinerth: 1979; Roth: 1962/1964; Teutsch: 1921; Volkmer: 2015; Wetter: 2008). All above-mentioned phenomena took place in an economically flourishing region at the beginning of the 16th cen- tury. As part of the internationally interwoven kingdom of St. István (Hungary), cities shaped the intellectual, cultural and economic life. Central Europe extended to the Carpathian Mountains – and beyond. As the intellectual elite had no uni- versity on home soil, they participated in the development of central European universities through the *peregrinatio academica* (intellectual travelling) (Tonk: 1996, 113–124). Due to the attractive salaries – also in the pre-Reformation period – the Transylvanian-Saxon priests were academics unusually often and were even awarded academic titles and laureateships (Schullerus: 1923, 5–160; here: 135, an- notation 2; see also: 139–141). Since the reign of King Matthias Corvinus, Hungary belonged to the domain of humanistic erudition (Wien/Zach: 2004).

The humanistically minded bourgeoisie of the Transylvanian-Saxon cities was the base of the Reformation, which was incipiently orientated to Wittenberg (Teutsch: 1921, 14–35). The Hungarian king and the Hungarian diet repeatedly enacted bans and severe measures against the 'new believers' between 1523 and 1525 (Teutsch: 1921, 197–200).

Following the defeat in 1541 in Buda – definitively according to the Treaty of Adrianopel in 1568 – Hungary was split into three zones/states: the Hapsburg domain in Western Hungary and Central Hungary belonged to the Ottoman Empire (as Vilayet). The northeastern part of Hungary (called Partes) together with the Voivodship of Transylvania became a principality that had to pay an annual tribute to the Sublime Port. This princedom was given extensive internal autonomy for its three estates which were supportive of the state: firstly, the Hungarian gentry, secondly the quasi-noble group of Szekels and, last but not least, the Transylvanian Saxons. Around one million people lived in this realm.[1]

The executive authorities of the Transylvanian-Saxon cities took the first opportunity after the loss of Hapsburg predominance (1541) to establish the Reformation within a few years – beginning in the city of Brașov. In 1550 the administrative collectivity of the Saxons (the universitas nationis saxonicae) enacted the authoritative importance of the 1547 Church Order with respect to the entire field of law (Reinerth: 1979, 190). The Saxons thus founded a new, discrete institution that was independent of medieval canon law.

The political and church representatives within the Transylvanian-Saxon field of law officially represented the conservative Wittenberg line (Keul: 2009, 81).

Since 1571 the 'old believers', the reformed, the Unitarians and the followers of the Wittenberg way had attained religious freedom and obtained the status of approved denominations (*religiones*), which were definitely and explicitly listed in the resolution of the Diet in 1595 (Kirchenordnungen: 2012, 24; 98; cf. Wien: 2018, 64, cf.57–74). The Romanian-orthodox believers, who were not politically represented, were more or less tolerated. Therefore, they occupied the lowest rank of religious und also political 'tolerance'. The succeeding princes of Transylvania had to accept this constellation before their inauguration (as *conditiones Principum*).[2] These conditions were reapproved within the collection of law 1653 and had to be

---

1 The realm of the Principality comprised eight counties of Eastern Hungary, so-called „Partes adnexae" (Máramaros, Közep-Szolnok, Kraszna, Bihar, Zaránd, Arad, Temes und Krassó) including 350.000 residents, 80.000 Saxons in eleven districts (*Stühle*), 150.000 Szekels in nine districts und around 450.000 persons in seven transylvanian counties (Hunyad, Fehér, Torda, Küküllő, Kolózs, Doboka und Belső-Szolnok) (Murdock: 2000, 13).

2 The *Conditiones Principum* – a kind of capitulation terms before the election of a prince (since 1576), always included a binding agreement of chartered religious freedom (cf. Zach: 2004, 59; 96; 119).

respected by the Hapsburg emperors – in spite of de-facto constraints – until the 19th century.

At the periphery of the western church domain, Transylvania had evolved into a pioneer region of religious freedom under the protection of the Ottoman Empire. These external requirements of poly-denominational guarantees to the four denominations by political measures endured steadily. This constellation, in which pluriconfessionality and the coexistence of four denominations were politically protected, endured steadily (Wien: 2019, 24, cf.19–41).

2. Damasus Dürr – Notes on his Biography

The protestant minister and dean of Apoldu de Jos/Transylvania, Damasus Dürr, was born in Bod around 1535 (cf. Wien: 2006, 57–69). The first evidence of his existence dates back to the year 1553 with his entry in the school register of Braşov college: Damasius Dürr Brenndorfensis (Archiv der Honterusgemeinde/Schwarze Kirche, Kronstadt).

According to his statement, he went to university at Wittenberg, where he started his studies around 1556. Half of the new acquisitions of his own library were printed in Wittenberg (Gündisch: 1987, 344; cf. 340–350). This confirms his statement that he had "listened directly to the venerable Philipp Melanchthon" ("selbs aus dem mund des ehrwirdigenn hernn Philippi Melanthonis Witebergae gehört") and acquired his erudition at the Leucorea (Dürr: 1939–1941, 15). His principal subject was theology, but he gained knowledge in physics and also attended lectures of the prominent medic Vitus Winshemius in 1559 (Dürr, Predigten-Manuskript, 311).

At Wittenberg he was ordained as minister ("gen Newenstadt in Transilvania") (Keresztényfalva) on 3rd September 1559 (Duldner: 1905, 7–11). However, in 1560, his first spiritual office was as a city sermoniser (Diaconus) at Sibiu (Hermannstadt) – working alongside Matthias Hebler (1556–1571), the parish pastor of Sibiu and Lutheran superintendent for the Saxon community and church district (Jekeli/Binder: 1933, 11–22). Finally, he was elected and appointed to the pastorhood of the village Apoldu de Jos (Teutsch: 1918, 34), a parish in the deanery of Sebeş (ultrasilvanense), on 19th January 1568. Dürr was widowed twice and married three times. His daughter Anna died in 1569, his spouse Elisabeth in 1570. Also his second spouse, Sophia, died early – during the pestilence in 1573. He already remarried Margret Klein from Sibiu (Margaris, Filia Pauli Klein, *honesti civis Cibiniensis*) in 1574 (Amlacher: 1883, 8–14; Dürr, Predigten-Manuskript, 647). The ministers of the deanery elected him dean and he was a capable and vigorous administrator of the capitular interests. In 1585 he died in office at Apoldu de Jos (Amlacher: 1883, 8; cf. Dogaru: 2006, 24–26).

3. Edition of Sermons as a Desideratum

The edition of the German sermons of Damasus Dürr is an exigent desideratum of research. According to the current state of knowledge, there are no other sources comparable to them (the printed tracts of the Flacian denomination within the district of Burgenland were derived presumably from sermons, but no longer correspond to sermons as a genre). Damasus Dürr, academic Transylvanian-Saxon pastor of the second half of the 16th century passed down two handwritten volumes of his sermons. Probably the second one was already lost at the end of the 18th century. Dr. Albert Amlacher, the sermoniser at Sebeş, discovered the first volume in the capitular library. He wrote a first cursory description of this outstanding source (1883). On the verge of the Second World War, Ludwig Klaster (1897–1973) – pastor in Gârbova and dean of Sebeş – started an attempt to produce a first printed version, but it failed rapidly due to the prevailing circumstances. The leather hardback and large-sized folio volume is currently located in the central archives of the Lutheran church in Romania (catalogue number: ZAEKR 209-DA 175). The autograph of Damasus Dürr contains 47 sermons from 1569 to 1583 (44 was datetd in 1567): Its contents last from advent and Christmas to Passiontide. Amongst other things, they mirror the time after the Council of Trent and contemporary church history related to the Formula of Concord.

In the European context these sermons are also very rare: They are sermons to a rural population. In view of the lack of sources, the implementation, exercise and practice of Reformation in the villages constitute a clearly articulated research desideratum (Wolgast: 2015, 16). In the German-language area, printed sermons and manuscripts from urban and courtly contexts were passed on. Sermons by reformers such as Luther or Matesius have been printed and scientifically investigated. However, there is a broad lack of sources on the topic of the Reformation in the countryside. Therefore, the available corpus is a singular source. The broadly adopted Melanchthonian theology shaped the Transylvanian-Saxon context and also Damasus Dürr. From a temporal perspective, it dates back to the transition to the confessional age, which is mirrored partly by polemically controversial theology: in particular against the Helvetic reformed confession, but also against local antitrinitarian-unitarian theology. The sermoniser distanced himself from Islam and repeated anti-Semitic stereotypes.

The sermons are not only significant with regard to the history of theology but also concerning literature or linguistic and ethnological aspects. They are also worth researching with regard to the history of mindsets and social life. Issues such as carnival customs, handling senility or occasional references to anti-Semitic attitudes occur.

Various aspects have already been investigated, for example social discipline (witches or luxury) (Wien: 2006), sociology of space (endowment of churches or negligibilities/Adiaphora) (Wien: 2010, 441–452; cf. Wien: 2017, 123–137). Ethic impulses, notions of status or order by the sermoniser have also been explored.

At this point, his notion of church shall be presented, based on the example of reconciliation (Wien: 2014, 37–66):

It concerns the understanding and appreciation of the confession of sins, as specifically shaped by the Reformation. This is combined with the implementation of paraliturgical set phrases (rite of reconciliation: Versöhnungsfeier).

The neighbourhood(s) made up the basic structure of local social life in the countryside of Transylvania. All households (around ten to fifteen) belonged equally to a neighbourhood. The social and religious life within the Transylvanian-Saxon (religious) community was shaped by economic and socio-cultural standardisation. Uniform social behaviour or discipline and its social control were expected (Wien: 2020, forthcoming). The neighbourhood formed the lowest level of jurisdiction and conciliation. The pastor only allowed individuals who had confessed their sins and reconciled with each other publicly (within the neighbourhood) to participate in the Holy Supper (cf. Schenk: 1992, 155–157).

In the modern age of the 16th to the 20th century, the paraliturgies were an important, virtually indispensable element of social behaviour and speech in the community of neighbours. They enabled individuals and the community to use traditional and churchly set phrases in order to be voluble and eloquent in socially challenging situations.

In the year 1578, Damasus Dürr preached the gospel on Holy Thursday. This sermon provides evidence of the provenance of these set phrases and of the influence of the minister. The traditionally spiritual level of preparing to confess one's sins and preparing for the Holy Supper was interwoven with the mutual practice of solving conflicts. Dürr did not adopt the catholic understanding of confession as a basis of forgiving sins, in which the minister listened to the confession, awarded the sinner absolution and, at the same time, imposed expiation on him or her in order to reduce the churchly penal record. From now on, the minister advised his parishioners to endeavour to clarify situations personally and to reconcile with each other in a reformed sense – as *mutua consolatio fratrum*. Dürr prompted the person responsible for a domestic disturbance, quarrel or perfidy to repent and beg his or her counterpart's pardon. Therefore, he effectively gave the answer to them on how to express themselves. However, he pointed out at the same time that those receiving the confession should keep in mind how to act and prove themselves to other Christians, both in general to other sinners and to Christian brothers and sisters. The minister Damasus Dürr supported them by helping them to find the right words by providing them with formulations for reacting suppliantly to the confession of sins or for forgiving their counterparts for erratic/false behaviour.

Dürr preached on Holy Thursday:

Da ifts denn zeit, das du dein lebenn befserft, das du deine Sünd erkenneft, klageft fie dem allmechtigenn gott, vnd biteft ynn vmb gnad vnd vmb vergebung der fundenn.

Wenn du alfo dem himlifchenn vater gebeichtet haft, foltu dich darnach auch mit dem beleidigtenn neheftenn verftehenn : Du folt ym zuhaufe gehenn, du follt dich fur ym demütigenn, denn zornn abbiten vnd fprechenn : Lieber bruder, aber liebe fchwefter, Mir find ein zeit vber zu zornn gegeneinander gewefenn, da vnd da hab ich dich bechwert, ich hab dir fchadenn thann, gefchmeht vnd etwas zugeredt : Jch erkennen mein fchwacheit, vnd dieweil ich des finnes binn, das ich des hernn Abendmal empfahenn wollt : So bit ich dich vmb gottes willenn, du wolleft mir meine fünd verzeyhenn, was ich wider dich gehandelt hab, es ift mir alls leid, vnd ich will durch beyftand gottes deiner hinnfurt ymmerdar zu ehren gedenckenn.

Wenn fich aber nu der arm neheft alfo erkennet, kompt ym vertrawenn zu dir vnd bitet vmb vergebung : So foltu nicht ftoppelgrädicht feynn, wie mancher hornochs, der auß anderleut demut, ftoltzer, mütiger vnd truziger wirdt, fpricht bald : Noch hat er mirs mufsenn abbitenn, noch ift er mir mufsenn zu haufe gehenn, ich mein, ich habs ym faur gemacht, er wird einandermal drann gedenckenn. Nein, lieber freund, nicht alfo, Sondernn, du folt dich auch demütigenn, du follt ein gutes wort ein gutt ftat lafsenn findenn, vnd ym auff feine bitt alfo antwortenn :

Lieber bruder, aber liebe fchwefter : Es ift war, mir fein zufamen gewachfenn vnd miteynander gezürnet, du haft mich gefchmeht, eins vnd diefes zugeredt : Aber weil mir allzumal fünder fein, ich, gleich fo woll, wie du, vnd niemand volkommen ift, fo mög ich villeucht auch gevbriget habenn. Drumb bitt ich, du wolleft mir desgleichenn auch meine mifsethat vergebenn, meinethalbenn foll alles vergefsenn vnd vergebenn fein.

Sehet, folchs heift ein recht ynnwendige pruffung des menfchens, wie mann fich geiftlicher weyfe nach, wirdig fchickt zur genieffung des Abendmals.[3]

Thereby the people received clear suggestions on how to openly regulate disagreements in a protestant manner and solve their conflicts. Thus the theological understanding of church as priesthood of all faithful was embraced in the community. In the long run these paraliturgies strengthened and promoted the community as a place of reconciliation and peace. Not only churchly and religious peace was preserved. But also, if we consider that an ethnic minority is always vulnerable and endangered – the cohesion of the community was protected. Therefore, in the Reformation period, the Transylvanian-Saxon ministers cared for the people, making them responsible for the gospel, willing to reconcile and capable of consolation. In this way, the ministers educated their parishioners to apply uniform common standards and ways of life. Afterwards they demanded social discipline from them (Wien: 2020).

If someone was unworthy of receiving the sacrament – the sacred (heilthumb) – in the Holy Supper, Dürr – in compliance with the contemporary customs –

---

3 Zaekr 209-DA 175: Damasus Dürr, Manuscript (In Die Coena Domini. Ex prima Epistola ad Corinthios II, 592–647), 616.

threatened him or her with punishment/church discipline (Kirchenzucht) in order to protect the community.

Conclusion

The collection of sermons by Damasus Dürr should have been edited completely and introduced into scholarly debate a long time ago. Dürr's sermonising followed the example of Martin Luther. He adopted Luther's concept of sermonizing, according to which God speaks directly, thus making the sermon equal to words of the bible, or even superior (*Deus dixit*). This verbal address inspires the audience to answer directly to this encouragement. He largely avoids moral summons, using language that encourages Christian responsibility (paraliturgy), grants the faithful with Christian eloquence, which he trains as orator in the pulpit.

Damasus Dürr used the sermon of Holy Thursday in the context of the differentiated diversity of denominations in the midst of the 16th century to familiarize the community with paraliturgical set phrases. These presuppose that (the) church is the community of the justified and the sinners, and that one lives from redemption by Christ. On this basis, the set phrases popularised the model of priesthood of all faithful and offered formulations for reconciliation between the faithful. They allowed the restoration of the communion with God and also especially aimed at establishing a pacified community of Christians. In addition, they allowed the social community of the ethnic minority to be consolidated. For this reason, the paraliturgies had an eminent political function of encouraging the minority to adopt a similar/uniform behaviour and of unifying them both inwards and outwards.

Bibliography

Sources

Damasus Dürr, Predigten-Manuskript.

Damasus Dürr (1939–1941), Predigten 1554–1578, Ludwig Klaster (ed.), Mühlbach: Unterwälder Kapitel.

Kirchenordnungen (2012), Die evangelischen Kirchenordnungen des XVI. Jahrhunderts. vol. 24: Siebenbürgen, Martin Armgart/Karin Meese (ed.), Tübingen: Mohr Siebeck.

Secondary Literature

Amlacher, Albert (1883), Damasus Dürr. Ein evangelischer Pfarrer und Dechant des Unterwälder Kapitels aus dem Jahrhundert der Reformation. Aus seinen Predigten und handschriftlichen Aufzeichnungen geschildert, Hermannstadt: Drotleff.

BERNHARD, JAN ANDREA (2015), Konsolidierung des reformierten Bekenntnisses im Reich der Stephanskrone: ein Beitrag zur Kommunikationsgeschichte zwischen Ungarn und der Schweiz in der Frühen Neuzeit (1500–1700), R5AS, Göttingen: Vandenhoeck & Ruprecht.

DOGARU, DANA J. (2006), Rezipientenbezug und -wirksamkeit in der Syntax der Predigten des siebenbürgisch-sächsischen Pfarrers Damasus Dürr (ca. 1535–1585), Documenta Linguistica 7, Hildesheim/Zürich/New York: Georg Olms Verlag.

DULDNER, JOHANN (1905), Sächsische Geistliche unter den Wittenberger Ordinierten, Korrespondenzblatt des Vereins für siebenbürgische Landeskunde 28, 7–11.

FATA, MÁRTA (2000), Ungarn, das Reich der Stephanskrone, im Zeitalter der Reformation und Konfessionalisierung. Multiethnizität, Land und Konfession 1500 bis 1700 (=KLK 60). Münster: Aschendorff.

FATA, MÁRTA/SCHINDLING, ANTON (ed.) (2010), Calvin und Reformiertentum in Ungarn und Siebenbürgen. Helvetisches Bekenntnis, Ethnie und Politik vom 16. Jahrhundert bis 1918, Reformationsgeschichtliche Studien und Texte 155, Münster: Aschendorff.

GÜNDISCH, GUSTAV (1987), Die Bibliothek des Damasus Dürr, in: Gustav Gündisch, Aus Geschichte und Kultur der Siebenbürger Sachsen. Ausgewählte Aufsätze und Berichte, Schriften zur Landeskunde Siebenbürgens 14, Köln/Wien: Böhlau.

JEKELI, HERMANN/BINDER, LUDWIG (1933), Die Bischöfe der Evangelische Kirche A.B. in Siebenbürgen. Vol. 1: Die Bischöfe der Jahre 1553–1867, Hermannstadt: Schiller; reprint: Köln: Böhlau, 1978

KEUL, ISTVÁN (2009), Early Modern Religious Communities in East-Central Europe. Ethnic Diversity, Denominational Plurality, and Corporative Politics in the Principality of Transylvania (1526–1691) SMART 143; Leiden/Bosten: Brill.

LEPPIN, VOLKER/WIEN, ULRICH A. (ed.) (2005), Konfessionsbildung und Konfessionskultur in Siebenbürgen in der Frühen Neuzeit, QstGöE 66, Stuttgart: Steiner.

MÜLLER, ANDREAS (2000a), Reformation zwischen Ost und West. Valentin Wagners griechischer Katechismus (Kronstadt 1550), Schriften zur Landeskunde Siebenbürgens 23, Köln: Böhlau.

MÜLLER, ANDREAS (2000b), Humanistisch geprägte Reformation an der Grenze von östlichem und westlichem Christentum. Valentin Wagners griechischer Katechismus von 1550, TSHTh 5, Mandelbachtal/Cambridge: Cicero.

MURDOCK, GRAEME (2000), Calvinism on the Frontier 1600–1660. International Calvinism and the Reformed Church in Hungary and Transylvania, Oxford: Oxford University Press.

REINERTH, KARL (1979), Die Gründung der evangelischen Kirchen in Siebenbürgen, Stud. Trans. 5, Köln: Böhlau.

ROTH, ERICH (1962/1964), Die Reformation in Siebenbürgen. Ihr Verhältnis zu Wittenberg und der Schweiz, 2 vols., Köln: Böhlau.

SCHENK, ANNEMIE (1992), Deutsche in Siebenbürgen. Ihre Geschichte und Kultur. München: Beck.

SCHULLERUS, ADOLF (1923), Luthers Sprache in Siebenbürgen. Forschungen zur siebenbürgischen Geistes- und Sprachgeschichte im Zeitalter der Reformation, Hermannstadt: Krafft.

TEUTSCH, FRIEDRICH (1918), Zur Lebensgeschichte des Damasus Dürr, Kbl 41, 33–35.

TEUTSCH, FRIEDRICH (1921), Geschichte der evangelischen Kirche in Siebenbürgen, vol. 1: 1150–1699, Hermannstadt: W. Krafft.

TONK, SÁNDOR (1996), Siebenbürgische Studenten an den ausländischen Universitäten, in: Walter König (ed.), Beiträge zur siebenbürgischen Schulgeschichte, Siebenbürgisches Archiv 32, Köln: Böhlau, 113–124.

VOLKMER, GERALD (2015), Siebenbürgen zwischen Habsburgermonarchie und Osmanischem Reich. Völkerrechtliche Stellung und Völkerrechtspraxis eines ostmitteleuropäischen Fürstentums 1541–1699, Schriften des Bundesinstituts für Kultur und Geschichte der Deutschen im Östlichen Europa 56, Berlin: De Gruyter.

WETTER, EVELIN (ed.) (2008), Formierungen des Konfessionellen Raumes in Ostmitteleuropa, FGKöME 33, Stuttgart: Steiner.

WIEN, ULRICH A./ZACH, KRISTA (ed.) (2004), Humanismus in Ungarn und Siebenbürgen. Politik, Religion und Kunst im 16. Jahrhundert, Siebenbürgisches Archiv 37, Köln: Böhlau.

WIEN, ULRICH A. (2006), Sozialdisziplinierung in der Predigt, Spiegelungen 1, 57–69.

WIEN, ULRICH A. (2010), Formierung des konfessionellen Raums in Siebenbürgen. Zur Wahrnehmung der Reformierten durch die siebenbürgisch-sächsischen Evangelischen im 16. und 17. Jahrhundert, in: Márta Fata/Anton Schindling (ed.), Calvin und Reformiertentum in Ungarn und Siebenbürgen. Helvetisches Bekenntnis, Ethnie und Politik vom 16. Jh. bis 1918, RST 155, Münster: Aschendorff, 441–452. New reprint in: WIEN, ULRICH A. (2017), Siebenbürgen – Pionierregion der Religionsfreiheit. Luther, Honterus und die Wirkungen der Reformation, Academia 15, Bonn/Hermannstadt: Schiller, 123–137.

WIEN, ULRICH A. (2014), Reformation in Siebenbürgen. Aktuelle Forschungen und Desiderate am Beispiel der Predigten Damasus Dürrs und der Synodalprotokolle der Evangelischen Superintendentur Birthälm, Jahrbuch des Bundesinstituts für Kultur und Geschichte der Deutschen im Östlichen Europa 22, 37–66.

WIEN, ULRICH A. (2017b), Luther's Relation with Peasants and Princes, in: Alberto Melloni (ed.), Martin Luther: a Christian between Reforms and Modernity (1517–2017), Berlin/New York: de Gruyter, 327–346.

WIEN, ULRICH A. (2018), New Perspective on the Establishing of Confession in Early Modern Transylvania. Context and Theological Profile of the Formula Pii Consensus 1572 as Heterodox Reception of the Wittenberg Theology. In: JEMC 5–1, 57–74.

WIEN, ULRICH A. (2019), Flucht hinter den „Osmanischen Vorhang". Glaubensflüchtlinge in Siebenbürgen. JEMC 6–1, 19–41.

WIEN, ULRICH A. (2020), Supervision of „Authority" and „Community" by the Church as a warden of order – the Positioning of Damasus Dürr between demand and reality, in: Ulrich A. Wien, (ed.), Common Man, Society and Religion in the 16th century/Gemeiner Mann, Gesellschaft und Religion im 16. Jahrhundert, R5AS, 67 Göttingen: Vandenhoeck und Ruprecht (forthcoming).

WOLGAST, EIKE (2015), Die Einführung der Reformation im internationalen Vergleich, in: Volker Leppin/Ulrich A. (ed.), Wien Kirche und Politik am Oberrhein im 16. Jahrhundert. Reformation und Macht im Südwesten des Reiches, SMHR 89, Tübingen: Mohr Siebeck.

ZACH, KRISTA (2004), Konfessionelle Pluralität, Stände und Nation. Ausgewählte Abhandlungen zur südosteuropäischen Religions- und Gesellschaftsgeschichte, Joachim Bahlcke/Konrad Gündisch (ed.), RKOSE 6, Münster: LIT.

Image Credits

Sibylla Goegebuer
St John's Hospital in Bruges in the Sixteenth and Seventeenth Centuries.
A Real and Intangible-Symbolic Interaction Between Religion and Devotion, Care and Art Forms a Holy Trinity

Fig. 1: Seventeenth-century figurative tiles on the inner wall of the new convent for sisters in St John's Hospital Bruges.
Photo: Jens Compernolle/Sightways Photography.

Fig. 2: The sixteenth- and seventeenth-century convent for sisters in St John's Hospital Bruges, which is completely separate from the monastery for the friars and which is only connected with the southern hospital ward through a staircase tower.
Photo: Arnout Goegebuer.

Fig. 3: Jacob van Oost the elder (1601–1671), after attributed to, The Madonna with two saints and two hospital sisters with patron saints, 1664, oil on canvas, H 1,57 m x B 2,48 m, Musea Brugge, Sint-Janshospitaal.
Photo: Musea Brugge/Lukasweb-Art in Flanders – Dominique Provost

Fig. 4: Anonymous, Southern Netherlands, Friendship Cup, 1664, engraved glass, faience, silver gilt and copper, height 22,7 cm, diameter base 14,2 cm.
Photo: Musea Brugge/Lukas – Art in Flanders – Dominique Provost. The coat of arms of St John's Hospital, with the chalice referring to St John the Evangelist and the lamb referring to St John the Baptist.

Joanna Kaźmierczak
The Iconographical Motif of the Good Samaritan as a Visual Commentary on the State of the Church in the Middle of the 16th Century. the Epitaph for Nicolaus Weidner from Wrocław and Its Meaning.

Fig. 1: Epitaph for Nicolaus Weidner, ca. 1555–1556, Archdiocesan Museum in Wrocław.
Photo: Joanna Kaźmierczak, personal archive.

Maria Lucia Weigel
Aspekte reformierter Ekklesiologie in Bildnissen von Zwingli und Bullinger

Abb. 1: Hans Asper, Bildnis Ulrich Zwingli, 1549, Tempera und Öl auf Holz, 62,5 × 51 cm.
Quelle: Zentralbibliothek Zürich, Graphische Sammlung und Fotoarchiv.

Abb. 2: Hans Asper, Bildnis Heinrich Bullinger, 1550, Öl auf Holz, 62 × 49 cm.
Quelle: Zentralbibliothek Zürich, Graphische Sammlung und Fotoarchiv.

Index of Names

Hamilton, John, archbishop of St Andrews 83

Hatzer, Ludwig 52

Heal, Felicity 67, 68, 72, 74, 76–78

Hebler, Matthias 463

Heide, Sebastian van der 178

Heimburg, Gregor of 417

Henry of Bailleul 127

Henry of Brederode 127

Herbertsz, Herman 365

Herman of Bronkhorst 127

Hermann von Wied 83

Hess, Johannes 178

Hodge, Charles 250

Hoffmann, Balthasar 185

Hôpital, Michel de l' 323

Hosius, Stanislaus 352

Hugh of Amiens 55, 57

Hus, Jan s. a. Hus, Johannes 56, 60, 111, 385, 386, 390, 413, 448, 449

Hutten, Ulrich von 177

I

Irenaeus of Lyon 53

Isaac, Heinrich 192, 196, 200

J

Jan of Nassau 135

Janssens, Erasmus s. a. Johannes, Erasmus 366, 369

Jauss, Hans-Robert 275

Jerome 177, 243

Jewel, John 80

John of Capistrano s. a. Capistrano, John 416, 418

John of Paris s. Quidort, Jean

John of Ragusa 92, 111, 112, 116–118

John of Rokycany 415, 416, 421

John the Evangelist 154, 157, 471

Josquin des Prez 192, 196

Juan de Torquemada 15

Jud, Leo 52, 57, 60

K

Karlstadt, Andreas 316

Kasper, Walter 358

Katherine of Aragon 75

Kellar, Clare 83

King Charles I 85

King Charles II 86

King Charles V 125, 127, 146, 307

King Edward VI 66, 69, 76, 78

King Ferdinand I. Habsburg 180

King François I 84

King Henry II 323

King Henry VIII 68, 69

King James I 85, 350

King James IV 82, 85

King James V 82

King James VI 85, 87

King James VI/I 85

King Louis II Jagiellon, s. a. King Ladislav Jagiello, King Ludvik Jagiello 178, 423, 424

King Matthias Corvinus 419, 461

King Philip II 127, 131, 132, 134

King Philip IV 91, 97, 100, 103

King Rudolf II 134

King Vladislav Jagiello 419–421

King William III, of England, s. a. William II, of Scotland 86

Kingdon, Robert 343

Klaster, Ludwig 464

Klatovský, Martin 393

Klein, Margret 463

Knox, John 84

Kolár, Jaroslav 394

König Maxmilian II. 382

Kooi, Christine 365

Krarup, Martin 68, 71, 72

List of Contributors

Ariane Albisser, MTh, University of Zurich.

Jon Balserak, Senior Lecturer Dr., University of Bristol.

Jan Červenka, doctoral student, Palacky University Olomouc, Lecturer, University of Hradec Králové.

Frank Ewerszumrode, Prof. Dr., Johannes Gutenberg-Universität Mainz.

Csilla Gábor, Prof. Dr., Babeş- Bolyai University Cluj, Faculty of Letters.

Sibylla Goegebuer, doctoral student Ass. Curator, Musea Brugge/St.-Janshospitaal & Onze-Lieve-Vrouw ter Potterie.

Linda S. Gottschalk, Assoc. Prof. Dr., Tyndale Theological Seminary, Badhoevedorp.

Geneviève Gross, Dr.

Pierrick Hildebrand, Assoc. Researcher Dr., University of Zurich.

Gábor Ittzés, Assoc. Prof. Dr., Debrecen Reformed Theological University.

Joanna Kaźmierczak, PhD Candidate and affiliated to the University of Wroclaw, Faculty of Historical and Pedagogical Sciences.

Jeannette Kreijkes, doctoral student, University of Groningen and KU Leuven.

Konrad Küster, Prof. Dr., Albert-Ludwigs-Universität Freiburg i. Br.

Tabita Landová, Assoc. Prof. Dr., Charles University in Prague.

Charlotte Methuen, Prof. Dr., University of Glasgow.

Peter Opitz, Prof. Dr., Universität Zürich.

Marta Quatrale, doctoral student, Freie Universität Berlin.

Michelle C. Sanchez, Assoc. Prof. Dr., Harvard Divinity School.

Violet Soen, Assoc.Prof. Dr., KU Leuven.

Herman A. Speelman, Dr., Theological University Kampen.

Maciej Szumowski, MA, University of Warsaw.

Peter Walter, Prof. Dr., Albert-Ludwigs-Universität Freiburg in Br.

Maria Lucia Weigel, Dr., Director of the Erkenbert-Museum at Frankenthal (Palatinate).

Dorothea Wendebourg, Prof. Dr., Humboldt-Universität Berlin.

Ulrich Andreas Wien, Assoc. Prof. Dr., Universitatea Lucian Blaga Sibiu, Akademischer Direktor am Institut für Evangelische Theologie am Campus Landau der Universität Koblenz-Landau.

Florian Wöller, Assoc. Prof. Dr., University of Copenhagen.